Accounting and Revenue Decisions in Hospitality

Ioannis Passas
https://orcid.org/0000-0002-1261-2878
Hellenic Mediterranean University, Greece

Markos Kourgiantakis
https://orcid.org/0000-0002-2392-6952
Hellenic Mediterranean University, Greece

Panagiotis Kyriakogkonas
University of Western Macedonia, Greece

Alexandros Garefalakis
https://orcid.org/0000-0001-7980-3743
Hellenic Mediterranean University, Greece

IGI Global
Scientific Publishing
Publishing Tomorrow's Research Today

VP of Publishing Ethics & Research Integrity Melissa Wagner
Director of Acquisitions Mikaela Felty
Director of Book Development Jocelynn Hessler
Production Manager Mike Brehm
Cover Design Jose Rosado

Published in the United States of America by
IGI Global Scientific Publishing
701 East Chocolate Avenue
Hershey, PA, 17033, USA
Tel: 717-533-8845 | Fax: 717-533-7115
Website: https://www.igi-global.com E-mail: cust@igi-global.com

Library of Congress Cataloging-in-Publication Data

Names: Passas, Ioannis editor
Title: Accounting and revenue decisions in hospitality / edited by Ioannis Passas, Markos Kourgiantakis, Panagiotis Kyriakogkonas, Alexandros Garefalakis.
Description: Hershey, PA : IGI Global Scientific Publishing, [2027] | Includes bibliographical references and index. | Summary: "This book provides a coherent and integrated understanding of accounting and revenue management in the hotel industry. This book develops conceptual clarity around how accounting structures, cost behavior, performance indicators, and revenue management decisions interact in practice"-- Provided by publisher.
Identifiers: LCCN 2026013762 (print) | LCCN 2026013763 (ebook) | ISBN 9798337394794 hardcover | ISBN 9798337394800 paperback | ISBN 9798337394817 ebook
Subjects: LCSH: Hospitality industry--Accounting
Classification: LCC HF5686.H75 A2356 2027 (print) | LCC HF5686.H75 (ebook) | DDC 657/.837--dc23/eng/20260710
LC record available at https://lccn.loc.gov/2026013762
LC ebook record available at https://lccn.loc.gov/2026013763

British Cataloguing in Publication Data
A Cataloguing in Publication record for this book is available from the British Library.

Table of Contents

Detailed Table of Contents

even calculations, and sensitivity modeling. Real-world case studies, from menu engineering for restaurant profitability to food waste reduction and dynamic pricing, all demonstrate 10-20% margin improvements. By evolving from scorekeepers to strategic advisors, professionals can navigate volatile demand and fixed costs for sustainable competitive advantage.

This chapter elucidates that modern hotel profitability relies not solely on revenue augmentation but also on a "earnings logic" that facilitates the transformation of dynamic revenues into earnings, given the constraints of perishable capacity, elevated fixed-cost intensity, and asymmetric cost adjustment. It incorporates three interrelated systems: (1) cost and financial architecture (operating leverage and cost stickiness), (2) revenue architecture (pricing, segmentation, and multi-channel distribution economics), and (3) measurement coherence (USALI-oriented internal reporting aligned with IFRS 15 judgments regarding bundles and principal-agent considerations). The chapter offers a decision-useful managerial guide that focuses on break-even analysis, flexible budgeting, net-contribution governance by channel and segment, and a reconciliation framework to avoid conflicting performance indicators in bundled and intermediated transactions.

Key Performance Indicators (KPIs) are central to hotel Revenue Management (RM) because they translate complex demand, pricing, and inventory-control decisions into measurable outcomes for managerial learning, accountability and benchmarking. For decades, the hotel sector relied heavily on a small canon of room-centric metrics. Yet contemporary hospitality markets challenge the sufficiency of traditional KPIs. Distribution costs and digital intermediaries make gross revenue measures less

The accessibility of island destinations is subject to the cost, time and uncertainty involved in reaching them. Transportation is part of the hospitality economy, since it contributes to what island tourism offers to guests before a reservation is made. This chapter focuses on coastal shipping and air transportation as components of the hotel revenue chain and examines the impact of transport access on demand, accommodation prices, revenue forecasts and operations. Room rates do not only depend on the product or competition, but also on total travel cost, route reliability and perceived uncertainty. We underscore how accounting and financial information act as a bridge between external changes and internal management decisions. When access improves, pricing flexibility increases, whereas limited access puts accommodation, cash flow and operational organisation under pressure. Through the embedded case study, we identify how transport disruption is connected with booking signals, managerial diagnosis, price formation, operational action and revenue resilience.

This chapter develops a theoretically grounded and integrative analysis of corporate governance and internal control systems in the context of hotel revenue management. Within this architecture, internal control systems are examined as process-based mechanisms that operationalize governance objectives through risk assessment, control activities, monitoring, and reporting structures. The chapter argues that hotel revenue presents a distinctive empirical setting for governance and control analysis due to its perishability, simultaneity of production and consumption, decentralization across operational departments, and dependence on technology-mediated distribution channels. These characteristics intensify information asymmetries, increase exposure to opportunistic behavior, and amplify the need for robust control environments. Drawing on internationally recognized control frameworks and risk-based approaches, the chapter positions internal controls not merely as accounting safeguards but as embedded organizational processes shaped by cultural, technological, and governance determinants

This chapter redefines revenue management in hospitality from a purely growth-oriented function to a comprehensive "revenue integrity" framework. Modern hotels face a critical "Revenue-Governance Gap" between aggressive revenue generation and inadequate revenue protection. The chapter identifies key vulnerabilities across the fragmented digital distribution ecosystem, including price parity failures, OTA commission leakage, and PMS-RMS synchronization errors. It presents a governance framework featuring compensating controls for consolidated duties, human-in-the-loop algorithmic pricing, and the Revenue Control Matrix as a practical implementation tool. The chapter further addresses ethical dimensions of revenue management, including prohibitive dynamic pricing during emergencies and algorithmic bias risks.

The global business environment is being called upon to adapt to constantly changing conditions influenced by market globalization, rapid technological advancement, economic crises, and geopolitical tensions, financial scandals, the COVID-19 pandemic, and climate change. The hotel industry is also affected by these conditions, facing challenges related to fluctuating demand, strong seasonality, environmental crises, and the increasing level of digitization and technological innovation. The hotel industry operates in a new environment where the values of information quality, transparency, and adaptation to modern consumer expectations are paramount. The purpose of this chapter is to examine revenue management in hotel businesses, based on ESG practices and internal audit. The chapter contributes to the literature by proposing a holistic governance framework that demonstrates how corporate integrity, ESG criteria, and internal audit can support effective revenue management, strengthen organizational resilience, and promote sustainable value creation in hotel businesses.

Preface

INTRODUCTION

The hospitality industry has entered a period in which financial performance can no longer be understood through traditional accounting measures or conventional revenue-management practices alone. Hotels and tourism enterprises operate within increasingly complex environments characterized by volatile demand, rising operating costs, technological disruption, changing distribution structures, intensified competition, sustainability pressures, and growing expectations regarding transparency, accountability, and responsible corporate conduct. Under these conditions, managerial decision-making requires a more integrated understanding of how revenues are created, priced, measured, recognized, protected, and ultimately transformed into sustainable economic value.

This volume is positioned at the intersection of hospitality accounting, revenue management, financial decision-making, corporate governance, internal control, sustainability, and strategic management. Its central premise is that these areas should no longer be treated as independent managerial domains. Accounting information influences pricing decisions; pricing decisions affect profitability and customer behaviour; revenue-management systems shape financial outcomes; cost structures determine the economic implications of occupancy and pricing choices; internal controls protect the integrity of revenue processes; and governance mechanisms ensure that managerial discretion is exercised consistently with organizational objectives, ethical principles, and long-term stakeholder interests.

The contemporary hotel is therefore not simply a provider of accommodation. It is a complex economic organization in which financial, commercial, technological, and operational systems interact continuously. Decisions concerning room rates, distribution channels, customer segments, capacity utilization, discounts, packages, ancillary services, and promotional strategies have direct consequences for both revenue and profitability. At the same time, these decisions are influenced by accounting classifications, cost allocation, budgeting, forecasting, internal reporting, performance measurement, and managerial judgment. Understanding hotel performance consequently requires a framework capable of connecting these different dimensions.

Historically, hospitality accounting and revenue management developed along relatively distinct professional and academic trajectories. Accounting concentrated primarily on the recording, classification, control, and reporting of financial transactions, while revenue management focused on forecasting demand, allocating capacity, segmenting customers, and optimizing prices. The expansion of digital technologies, sophisticated reservation platforms, online travel agencies, artificial intelligence, automated pricing systems, and integrated hotel-management platforms has progressively reduced the practical distance between these functions. Financial and operational information is now generated continuously, creating significant opportunities for more informed decision-making while simultaneously increasing the need for data quality, managerial interpretation, effective controls, and organizational coordination.

Revenue management itself has also evolved substantially. What was once primarily associated with maximizing room revenue through occupancy management and differentiated pricing has developed into a broader strategic discipline. Contemporary revenue decisions concern not only how much a customer is willing to pay but also how much value a transaction creates after considering acquisition costs, channel commissions, variable costs, capacity constraints, service requirements, customer lifetime value, and strategic positioning. The distinction between maximizing revenue and maximizing economically meaningful value has therefore become increasingly important.

The financial characteristics of hospitality organizations further reinforce the need for such an integrated perspective. Hotels commonly operate with substantial fixed costs, significant investment requirements, relatively perishable capacity, seasonal demand patterns, and considerable exposure to economic and external shocks. A hotel room that remains unsold on a particular night cannot be stored and sold in a later period. At the same time, the marginal cost associated with selling an additional room may be considerably lower than the total average cost of maintaining hotel capacity. These characteristics make pricing, occupancy, cost control, and demand forecasting particularly important, but they also make simplistic performance interpretations potentially misleading.

A high occupancy rate does not necessarily indicate strong profitability. Similarly, an increase in average room rates does not automatically imply an improvement in overall financial performance. Revenue may increase while distribution costs, commissions, energy expenses, labour costs, and customer-acquisition expenses rise even faster. Conversely, a lower rate may sometimes contribute positively to profitability when unused capacity exists and incremental costs are limited. Such realities demonstrate why hospitality revenue management requires an accounting perspective and why accounting information must increasingly incorporate operational and market-oriented variables.

The transformation of distribution channels has added another layer of complexity. Hotels increasingly operate through a combination of direct bookings, global distribution systems, online travel agencies, corporate contracts, tour operators, loyalty programmes, and digital platforms. Each channel creates different revenue opportunities but also different costs, commissions, contractual conditions, payment structures, cancellation patterns, and customer relationships. The apparent value of a booking therefore cannot be assessed solely through its nominal selling price. Managers require a broader understanding of the net financial contribution associated with different customer and distribution segments.

Technology has intensified these developments. Dynamic pricing systems can alter room rates rapidly in response to demand conditions, competitor prices, historical booking patterns, events, seasonality, and other signals. Artificial intelligence and predictive analytics can process quantities of information far beyond the capacity of traditional manual forecasting. These technologies can improve responsiveness and analytical sophistication, yet they do not eliminate the need for professional judgment. Algorithms operate according to objectives, parameters, and data selected by organizations. Poor-quality information, inappropriate performance targets, insufficient controls, or excessive reliance on automated recommendations can therefore generate undesirable financial, strategic, ethical, or reputational consequences.

At the same time, questions of corporate governance, revenue integrity, internal control, and internal audit have become increasingly significant within hospitality organizations. Revenue systems involve numerous points of managerial discretion and operational interaction. Rate overrides, discounts, cancellations, refunds, complimentary services, commissions, packages, loyalty benefits, cash and digital transactions, and third-party intermediaries all create potential sources of error, inconsistency, leakage, or misuse. Consequently, the quality of a hotel's revenue performance depends not only on commercial success but also on the reliability and integrity of the systems through which revenues are generated and recorded.

Environmental, social, and governance considerations further broaden the meaning of performance in hospitality. Hotels operate at the intersection of local communities, labour markets, natural resources, tourism flows, infrastructure systems, and destination economies. Questions of environmental responsibility, workforce practices, ethical governance, transparency, and sustainable development are therefore increasingly connected to financial and strategic choices. ESG considerations are relevant not only to reporting and reputation but also to investment, risk, access to capital, internal controls, stakeholder relations, and long-term organizational resilience.

This volume responds to these developments by bringing together complementary perspectives on accounting, revenue management, cost structures, performance indicators, pricing, managerial decision-making, governance, integrity, sustainability, and tourism value creation. Rather than approaching these subjects as isolated specializations, the chapters collectively demonstrate the value of an integrated analytical framework. The organization of the book follows a deliberate progression. It begins with the foundations of revenue creation, accounting recognition, financial and managerial accounting, and hotel cost structures. It then develops toward performance measurement, strategic financial thinking, revenue management, dynamic pricing, and profit-oriented pricing. The later chapters extend the analysis toward transportation and destination-level uncertainty, corporate governance, revenue integrity, ESG, internal audit, entrepreneurship, and sustainable tourism innovation.

The intended audience of this book is correspondingly broad. Scholars and researchers in hospitality management, tourism, accounting, finance, managerial accounting, revenue management, corporate governance, internal auditing, sustainability, entrepreneurship, and strategic management will find a framework that connects fields often examined independently. The interdisciplinary nature of the volume can support future empirical research by identifying relationships among accounting information, pricing decisions, profitability, governance, organizational integrity, and tourism value creation.

The book is also intended for undergraduate, postgraduate, and doctoral students studying hospitality management, tourism economics, accounting, finance, hotel management, revenue management, and business administration. Students frequently encounter accounting, pricing, strategy, and governance as separate subjects. The present volume provides a means of understanding how these areas interact within actual managerial settings and how apparently technical decisions can influence broader organizational outcomes.

Hospitality professionals represent another important audience. Hotel managers, financial controllers, accountants, revenue managers, internal auditors, risk professionals, owners, consultants, and executives must increasingly collaborate across traditional functional boundaries. Revenue managers require an understanding of costs and profitability; accountants must understand the operational drivers behind financial results; hotel managers must interpret both financial and market data; and governance professionals must understand how pricing and revenue systems create control and ethical risks. The book therefore provides a common conceptual platform through which these professional groups can better understand one another's roles.

The volume may also be useful to policymakers, destination-management organizations, tourism entrepreneurs, investors, and regional-development stakeholders.

Hospitality businesses do not operate in isolation. They form part of broader systems incorporating transportation, digital platforms, suppliers, startups, financial institutions, public authorities, local communities, and tourism infrastructure. Several chapters therefore extend the discussion beyond the boundaries of the individual hotel to examine hospitality within destination-level and regional systems of value creation.

Each chapter makes a distinct contribution to this broader inquiry.

CHAPTER OVERVIEW

The opening chapter, "Revenue Creation, Recognition, and Reporting in Hotels: A Conceptual and Systematic Review of Accounting Practices, Managerial Judgment and Governance," establishes the accounting foundation of the volume by connecting revenue generation with recognition, reporting, professional judgment, and governance in hospitality settings.

The second chapter, "Bridging the Gap: Integrating Financial and Managerial Accounting for Decision-Making in Hospitality," explores the complementary roles of financial and managerial accounting and highlights their combined contribution to informed hospitality decision-making.

The third chapter, "From Fixed Costs to Dynamic Revenues: Financial Structure and Earnings Logic in Contemporary Hotel Operations," examines the distinctive financial structure of hotels, particularly the relationship among fixed costs, dynamic revenues, capacity utilization, and profitability.

The fourth chapter, "Key Performance Indicators (KPIs) in Hotel Revenue Management: A Critical and Educational Literature Review," reviews the principal performance measures used in hotel revenue management and emphasizes the importance of interpreting KPIs within their broader financial and strategic context.

The fifth chapter, "Integrating Accounting Information and Revenue Management for Strategic Decision Making in Hospitality," considers how accounting and revenue-management information can be combined to strengthen pricing, planning, profitability analysis, and strategic decision-making.

The sixth chapter, "Revenue Management Concepts and Pricing Logic in Hotels: From Algorithmic Optimization to Strategic Value-Based Pricing," examines the evolution of hotel pricing from traditional revenue-management techniques and algorithmic optimization toward more strategic and value-oriented approaches.

The seventh chapter, "Revenue Optimization and the Role of Dynamic Pricing in Hospitality Accounting," explores dynamic pricing as a core revenue-management mechanism and considers the importance of accounting information in evaluating its financial consequences.

The eighth chapter, "Profit-Driven Pricing: Bridging Accounting and Revenue Strategy," shifts attention from revenue maximization toward profitability by linking pricing strategy with costs, margins, and the economic contribution of different transactions and customer segments.

The ninth chapter, "Transport as Part of the Hospitality Revenue Chain in Island Destinations: Accounting Information, Pricing, and Managerial Decision-Making under Uncertainty," extends the discussion beyond the hotel by examining how transportation, accessibility, pricing, and uncertainty influence hospitality revenues in island destinations.

The tenth chapter, "Corporate Governance and Internal Control Systems in Hotel Revenue Management," examines the governance and control mechanisms required to support reliable, accountable, and strategically aligned revenue-management processes.

The eleventh chapter, "Revenue Integrity: Mitigating Risks, Preventing Leakage, and Navigating Ethical Dilemmas," addresses revenue leakage, operational risks, control weaknesses, and the ethical dimensions associated with revenue generation and management.

The twelfth chapter, "Corporate Integrity and ESG in Hotel Revenue Management: The Role of Internal Audit," connects internal audit, corporate integrity, ESG considerations, and revenue management within a broader framework of assurance, accountability, and responsible governance.

CONCLUSION

Taken together, these twelve chapters establish a multidimensional framework for interpreting contemporary hospitality performance. The volume begins with the fundamental question of how revenue is created, recognized, and reported and progressively develops toward the ways in which financial and managerial accounting support internal decision-making. It then examines the financial structure of hotels, the performance indicators used to evaluate outcomes, and the integration of accounting information with revenue-management systems. From this foundation, the discussion progresses toward managerial financial thinking, pricing logic, dynamic pricing, profitability, and the wider hospitality revenue chain. The final sections examine the governance mechanisms required to protect these processes and position hospitality within broader ESG, auditing, innovation, and tourism-development frameworks.

One of the principal contributions of the book is therefore its integrative character. Hospitality research and professional practice have frequently examined accounting, revenue management, governance, internal audit, and sustainability through separate disciplinary lenses. Yet managers experience these areas simultaneously. A pricing decision affects revenue, profitability, customer behaviour, market positioning, and potentially brand reputation. A weakness in accounting information may influence forecasts and pricing decisions. A poorly designed incentive structure may encourage revenue growth while undermining profitability or control. An internal control weakness can transform an otherwise successful commercial strategy into a source of financial loss. Similarly, sustainability and governance considerations can influence costs, investment decisions, stakeholder trust, and access to markets and capital.

The book also seeks to contribute to the transition from revenue-centred toward value-centred hospitality management. Revenue is essential, but revenue alone does not provide a sufficient basis for assessing organizational success. The quality of revenue matters. Its cost matters. Its reliability matters. The risks associated with generating it matter. Its consistency with corporate strategy and ethical standards matters. Ultimately, what matters is the extent to which revenue contributes to durable profitability and sustainable organizational value.

This perspective becomes particularly important as technology assumes a greater role in hospitality decision-making. Automated systems are increasingly capable of identifying patterns, forecasting demand, recommending prices, managing inventory, and evaluating customer behaviour. Such capabilities can significantly enhance managerial efficiency. However, technological sophistication does not remove the need for accounting judgment, governance, internal control, strategic reasoning, or ethical oversight. The opposite may increasingly be true. As systems become more complex and autonomous, organizations may require stronger mechanisms for understanding the assumptions embedded within them, validating the quality of information, monitoring outcomes, and ensuring appropriate human accountability.

A further contribution of the volume lies in its emphasis on interdisciplinary professional competence. Hospitality professionals increasingly need to understand concepts beyond their traditional functional specialization. Revenue managers benefit from knowledge of managerial accounting and profitability analysis. Accountants require a deeper understanding of revenue-management processes and distribution structures. Internal auditors must understand the operational and technological characteristics of hotel revenue systems. Senior managers must be capable of interpreting information originating from all of these domains. This book therefore encourages the development of a shared analytical language across hospitality functions.

For researchers, the volume highlights numerous opportunities for future inquiry. The integration of accounting and revenue-management data creates possibilities for developing more comprehensive performance models. Dynamic pricing raises questions concerning profitability, customer perceptions, organizational controls, and ethical boundaries. Revenue integrity creates opportunities for examining fraud risks, leakage, governance, and auditing mechanisms. ESG considerations can be investigated in relation to revenue strategy, stakeholder behaviour, financial outcomes, and internal assurance. The relationship between hospitality businesses and broader transportation, entrepreneurial, and regional ecosystems similarly creates opportunities for interdisciplinary research extending beyond firm-level analysis.

For educators, the volume offers an opportunity to rethink how accounting and revenue management are taught within hospitality programmes. Students should not merely learn to calculate financial ratios or individual performance indicators. They should also understand how information is generated, how measures interact, how managerial decisions influence financial results, and how financial objectives relate to governance and sustainability. By connecting theory with the institutional and operational realities of hospitality organizations, the book can support the development of professionals capable of navigating increasingly complex decision environments.

For practitioners, the book reinforces a fundamental managerial principle: no major hospitality decision is exclusively financial, operational, commercial, or strategic. These dimensions interact. Pricing influences occupancy; occupancy affects operational requirements; operating structures affect cost; costs influence profitability; profitability affects investment capacity; investment influences service quality and market position; governance determines how these processes are monitored; and integrity determines whether the resulting performance is credible and sustainable.

The significance of this integrated perspective extends beyond individual hotels. Hospitality businesses are embedded within tourism destinations whose competitiveness depends on transportation, entrepreneurship, infrastructure, environmental resources, human capital, digital connectivity, public institutions, and local communities. Sustainable hospitality therefore requires value creation at both organizational and ecosystem levels. The final chapters of this book intentionally widen the analytical lens to recognize these relationships.

Ultimately, this volume seeks to contribute to a more mature understanding of hospitality financial management—one that moves beyond narrow distinctions between accounting and revenue management and recognizes their shared contribution to strategic decision-making. It advocates an approach in which revenues are not merely generated but understood; not merely optimized but evaluated in relation to profitability; not merely recorded but protected through effective controls; and not merely maximized but aligned with integrity, governance, sustainability, and long-term value creation.

The future of hospitality will increasingly depend on the ability of organizations to combine financial discipline with commercial agility. Markets will continue to change, technological tools will become more sophisticated, consumer behaviour will evolve, and new sources of uncertainty will emerge. Organizations capable of integrating reliable accounting information, intelligent pricing, strategic leadership, robust internal control, ethical governance, and sustainable innovation will be better positioned to navigate these changes.

We are deeply grateful to the contributing authors whose scholarship, professional perspectives, and intellectual commitment have made this volume possible. The diversity of the chapters reflects the interdisciplinary character of contemporary hospitality management and the need to connect accounting, finance, revenue strategy, governance, auditing, sustainability, transportation, and innovation. We are equally grateful to the reviewers whose constructive evaluations and careful observations contributed to strengthening the quality and coherence of the individual contributions.

As editors, we offer this book as both a scholarly reference and a platform for further inquiry. We hope that it will encourage researchers to explore the intersections among hospitality accounting, revenue management, governance, and sustainable value creation; assist educators in developing more integrated approaches to hospitality finance and management; and support practitioners in making decisions that are not only commercially effective but also financially sound, transparent, strategically coherent, and responsible.

In doing so, this volume aims to contribute to a hospitality sector in which accounting information and revenue intelligence are no longer regarded as parallel systems but as interconnected components of strategic management. Such integration is essential for organizations seeking not merely to generate revenue in an uncertain world, but to understand, protect, and transform that revenue into sustainable economic and organizational value.

Ioannis Passas
Hellenic Mediterranean University, Greece

Markos Kourgiantakis
Hellenic Mediterranean University, Greece

Panagiotis Kyriakogkonas
University of Western Macedonia, Greece

Alexandros Garefalakis
Hellenic Mediterranean University, Greece

Acknowledgment

We would like to express our sincere appreciation to all the authors who contributed their expertise, research, and perspectives to this volume. Their commitment and scholarly contributions were essential to the development of the book.

We are also grateful to the reviewers for their careful evaluation, constructive comments, and valuable suggestions, which helped strengthen the quality of the individual chapters and the volume as a whole.

Our thanks are extended to the editorial and production teams at IGI Global for their guidance, support, and assistance throughout the preparation and publication process.

Finally, we would like to acknowledge our colleagues and academic collaborators whose discussions, encouragement, and professional support contributed to the successful completion of this project.

Chapter 1
Revenue Creation, Recognition, and Reporting in Hotels:
A Conceptual and Systematic Review of Accounting Practices, Managerial Judgment, and Governance

Lokeshwari D. V.
http://orcid.org/0000-0002-6112-3173
Dayanand Sagar College of Arts, Science, and Commerce, India

Reynal Lavita Fernandes
http://orcid.org/0000-0002-6502-0876
Christ University, India

ABSTRACT

The chapter provides the conceptual review and systematic review of the relationship between the hotel revenue creation and revenue management practices and accounting-based revenue recognition and financial accounting, specifically the role of managerial judgment, the risk of earnings management, and the varying mechanism of governance in the hospitality industry. Based on interdisciplinary research in hospitality management, accounting, finance, and corporate governance, there is a synthesis of the findings and concept of empirical and theoretical work of study based in various settings. The results indicated that there was limited empirical consolidation between the revenue management and accounting recognition and the managerial discretion played a major role in determining the earnings outcomes

DOI: 10.4018/979-8-3373-9479-4.ch001

as well as indicated that the governance mechanisms moderated the opportunistic behavior in context-dependent manner. The chapter goes through to develop a hospitality-specific framework that will increase the integrity and transparency in financial reporting.

INTRODUCTION

The problem of how hotel revenue creation is involved in revenue management (RM) practices and accounting-based revenue recognition and financial reporting has become more and more scholarly and practical over the years, due to its effects on the performance of firms and investor confidence and regulatory supervision in hotel management (Goncalves et al., 2024; Taliani, 2015). The hospitality industry is intense in the level of its services and has perishable capacity and volatile demand which makes the measurement and reporting of revenues more complex than the manufacturing and retailing industries. As a result managerial decisions critical in terms of pricing, capacity utilization and revenue maximization are highly intersected with accounting judgments which define when, how and how to disclose reported revenues.

In the past few decades, advanced RM strategies, including dynamic pricing, yield management, and demand forecasting, have been extremely popular among hotels in order to maximize average daily rate and revenue per available room (Li & Ma, 2015; Zaki, 2025). These business strategies have direct impacts in terms of their business revenue trends as they are reported in the financial documents, and they affect the perceptions of the stakeholders about the financial performance. Meanwhile, accounting standards that regulate the relationship between revenue recognition and more complicated contractual and bundled arrangements prevalent in the hospitality context have developed, including reflecting the adoption of new standards like demonstrate IFRS 15 and ASC 606 (Myers et al., 2022; Lu and Wang, 2018). Though these advances have been made, convergence between RM practice and accounting-based recognition of revenue has not been yet conceptually developed and fragmented in its empirical elements.

The financial reporting relies on the asset-light business model along with the lease contracts and management contracts complicated the financial reporting in the hospitality industry and increased the agency conflicts between the owners and the operators (Jang et al., 2023; Arimany et al., 2015). Such features increase the discretion of managers concerning revenues recognition and expenses allocation, which raises the risks of earnings management and probable premature recognition of revenue. As the sector is economically important and susceptible to macroeconomic shocks, as well as financial crises and the COVID-19 pandemic, clear and credible financial reporting is needed to keep it competitive and retain the confidence of its stakeholders (Campos et al., 2022; Matviienko, 2019).

Although the previous literature addressed the management of earnings in hospitality companies and the effectiveness of RM practices in improving the performance of operations, these lines of studies have grown mostly independently. The prevalence of earnings management within the hotel types and institutional context is documented in studies (Gim and Jang, 2023; Esteban and Devesa, 2011; Syahputri et al., 2023), but these studies do not provide much information regarding the interaction between the RM strategies and the accounting-based revenue recognition in order to influence the quality of financial reporting (Myers et al., 2022; Burnett et al., 2021; Caylor, 2008). In the same way, the literature of the influence of corporate governance on turning a binding earnings manipulation is still controversial, and the results differ depending on the governance systems, form of ownership, and the regulations (Al-Okaily et al., 2019; Suhaemi and Hidayah, 2025).

There are significant implications of this disjointed knowledge. The poor combination of RM and accounting views can contribute to the inadequacy of the financial performance representation, decreased transparency of the investor, and even a decline in the efficiency over the market (Jiao and Lu, 2019; Hu, 2010). In addition, the peculiarities of work and contracts in the hospitality industry mean that the use of generic theoretical expertise on accounting and governance should not be simple, which highlights the necessity of the sector-specific conceptual framework.

Based on these gaps, this chapter takes an integrative approach that integrates literature in hotel revenue creation, revenue management, accounting-based revenue recognition, earnings management and corporate governance. The chapter attempts to define how managerial judgement mediates the effect that exists between revenue management practices and financial reporting effects as well as how governance practices control managerial incentives in numerous types of hotel ownership and contractual arrangements. In this way, the chapter should promote a more holistic collection of finance reporting dynamics within the hospitality market and give a basis upon which future theoretical formulation, research, and policy should be promoted.

PURPOSE AND SCOPE OF THE REVIEW

This chapter aims at synthesizing and critically assessing the available literature concerning interaction between hotel revenue creation and revenue management practices and accounting-based revenue recognition and financial reporting with specific consideration to managerial decision-making, risk of earnings management, and other governance mechanisms in the hospitality industry. Due to the features of the industry (service-based, complicated, and bundling revenue streams) and popularity of management contracts and asset-light business models, the intersection of operational revenue strategies and accounting practices will aid in improving the level of financial transparency and the quality of reporting.

In particular, the chapter aims at synthesising the research strands that have fragmented in the past to analyse the concept of revenue management, earnings management, and corporate governance separately. Through the use of conceptual and systematic review method, the chapter is expected to offer an overall insight into the roles of revenue management choices in relation to user reactions in reported revenues via accounting recognition procedures, the role of managerial discretion in relation to earnings management practices, and the role of the governance structure in limiting or facilitating managerial discretion. Through this, the review would fill a serious gap in the study of hospitality where less attention has been given to the synergies between operational revenue strategies and accounting-grounded reporting options.

The area of the review is interdisciplinary and global as it includes peer-reviewed empirical, qualitative, and review studies based on the hospitality management, accounting, financial and corporate governance literature. The analysis does not confine itself to a particular geographic area or segment of the hotel, instead covering evidence generated by diverse institutional, regulatory, and ownership environments to make the hospitality industry be more heterogeneous. Although the hotel industry is the main target, it involves insights related to other closely related areas of the hospitality industry where they will add to the knowledge of how revenue recognition and reporting practices.

To facilitate the synthesis, the chapter is organized based on six analytical lenses that are interrelated namely: (i) hotel revenue creation models, (ii) revenue recognition standards and challenges, (iii) financial reporting and disclosure practices, (iv) role of managerial judgment and discretion, (v) earnings management risks and governance, audit, and regulatory oversight mechanisms. The combination of these lenses to the study of the conversion of revenue management practice into the financial reporting results, and governance structures that moderate the level of managerial incentives, can be known.

With this respect, the aims and objectives of this review are to:

Assess the level to which the hotel revenue management practices are combined with accounting based revenue recognition frameworks.

Earnings management risks arising as a result of managerial discretion in recognition of revenues and reporting these revenues.

Comparison of corporate governance and audit frameworks which affect discretion and reporting quality by hospitality firms.

Experiment with different revenue management strategies and how they affect the quality of financial reporting and disclosure.

Test how ownership structures and management contracts affect the earnings management behavior and results of reporting.

These objectives aim to add a logical basis of conceptual literature that enhances the development of the theory, informs the governance and the regulation practice, and future research on financial reporting integrity and operational decision making in the hospitality industry.

METHODOLOGY OF LITERATURE SELECTION

To achieve transparent, replicable and comprehensive synthesis method of the existing research on the interaction between hotel revenue creation, revenue management practices, accounting based revenue recognition, financial reporting, managerial judgment, earnings management and governance mechanism in the hospitality industry this chapter follows a systematic literature review approach. The systematic connection will be very suitable due to the interdisciplinary character of the subject and the disaggregate development of the corresponding literature on the field of hospitality management, accounting, finance, and corporate governance.

DATABASES AND SOURCES

To acquire a wide and a diverse range of scholarly publications, various academic databases were searched to ensure the identity of literature search. The main sources were Scopus, Web of Science and Google Scholar that were combined to refer to the main journals and high-impact publications used in the studied fields. The review also used scholarly books, book chapters, and authoritative working papers besides peer-reviewed journal articles in cases where they contained theoretical or methodological information pertinent in the area of hospitality revenue recognition and reporting. In order to deepen the conceptual base as well as make the material practical, professional and regulatory materials, including accounting standards, interpretative guidance, and practitioner reports provided by standard-setting bodies and professional firms, were also used.

SEARCH STRATEGY AND QUERY TRANSFORMATION

The search strategy was informed based on the key research topic of the coexistence of hotel revenue management with accounting-based revenue recognition and reporting. A general research question was converted into specific search queries to focus narrower search questions in a systematic way in order to cover the main thematic dimensions in revenue creating, revenue managing, managerial judgment, earnings managing and governance mechanisms in the hospitality industry as well. Basic search terms were combinations of hotel, hospitality, revenue management, revenue creation, recognition, financial reporting, managerial discretion, earnings management, and corporate governance as well as the mention of the applicable accounting standards, including the IFRS 15 and the ASC 606. In order to obtain changes between terminologies across disciplines, the use of Boolean operators and truncation was realized.

INCLUSION AND EXCLUSION CRITERIA

Explicit inclusion and exclusion criteria were used in the process of screening to make the selection relevant and qualitative. Studies were to be considered in case they: (i) covered the context of hospitality or hotels sector, (ii) focused on the subject of revenue management, revenue recognition, financial reporting, earnings management, or other matters pertaining to governance. To indicate an integrative orientation of the chapter both conceptual and empirical studies were taken into consideration. Articles that do not contain sufficient information on transferability of insights on non-hospitality industries, those approaches that are not scholarly, as well as those articles that do not provide enough information to revenue/reporting challenges were not used.

PROCESSES OF SCREENING, SELECTION AND CITATION CHAINING

The preliminary search of databases produced 92 potential studies and this figure had been obtained after filtering out the duplicates. The screening of these studies was conducted through the title and abstract screening basing on the inclusion criteria and the full-text screening that was conducted to determine their thematic relevance. Both backward and forward chaining of citation were used to ensure that the influential works were covered and the risk of not covering the most important works was eliminated. Backward citation analysis was in looking at the reference lists of core studies to determine the background studies and forward citation analysis was done in determining more recent studies that referred to the selected articles. The process led to the establishment of 125 more or so relevant studies making the total number of candidate papers 217.

ASSESSMENT OF RELEVANCE AND FINAL SAMPLE

The obtained set of the studies was further filtered into the relevancy score depending on their contribution to the comprehension of the topic of revenue management, accounting-oriented recognition of revenues, managerial judgment, earnings management, and governance in hospitality. They had to be based on thematic concentration, methodological soundness, and relevance to lenses of analysis of the chapter. With the help of this, 50 articles were selected as the most relevant ones and constituted the main literature foundation of the review. These studies were organized to a consistent classification and analysis based on the six analytical lenses that helped in the chapter and facilitated a systematic synthesis of the results based on various research traditions.

All in all, such a methodological perspective guarantees that the review is thorough, balanced, and analytically sound, which gives the latter a good basis to further analytical synthesis of concepts and important themes in the chapter.

FUNDAMENTAL THEMATIC LITERATURE REVIEW

The extant literature is synthesized in this section under six inter-relational analytical lenses and will serve to explain the manner in which the hotel revenue creation and revenue management practices interlink with the accounting-based recognition of revenue, managerial measurements, earnings management and the mechanism of governance. Regardless of considering these areas separately, the review accentuates the dependencies of these areas in the hospitality context.

CONCEPTUAL FRAMEWORK LINKING REVENUE MANAGEMENT AND FINANCIAL REPORTING

The reviewed literature in the previous sections shows that the hotel revenue creation, accounting-based revenue recognition, managerial judgment, and governance mechanisms are all the closely connected processes that simultaneously affect the quality of financial reporting in the hospitality industry. Nevertheless, these themes have been studied individually in past research, therefore the fragmented knowledge of the manner in which operational revenue strategies are converted into accounting results.

To fill this gap, this chapter suggests a conceptual model that combines the revenue management practices with the accounting-based revenue recognition and financial reporting performance using the mediating variable of managerial judgment and the moderating variable of the corporate governance mechanism.

Dynamic pricing, demand forecasting, the over booking strategies, and channel management are all practices in revenue management that have a direct impact on the nature, timing, and variability of hotel revenue streams. Such operational choices further influence revenue recognition under accounting principles like the IFRS 15 and ASC 606 that expects managers to recognize performance obligation, transaction prices and the suitable time of the revenue recognition.

Managerial judgment thus is an important mediating factor in the translation of operational revenue decisions into the accounting results. In cases where the nature of uncertainty and complex service bundling involves, managers need to interpret contractual arrangements with the aim of estimating variable consideration and revising when to recognize revenue.

Nevertheless, there is also the risk of earnings management that is presented by the exercise of managerial discretion. The moderating factors that limit opportunistic reporting behavior and increase the transparency of financial reporting are corporate governance mechanisms such as board oversight, audit committees, institutional ownership and external auditing.

Financial reporting quality in the hospitality business therefore emerges out of the relationship between the revenue management strategies, managerial discretion and the regulation of governance. These relationships may also be affected by external contextual forces including regulatory environment, technological innovation and economic shocks.

Figure 1. Showing Conceptual Framework Linking Revenue Management and Financial Reporting

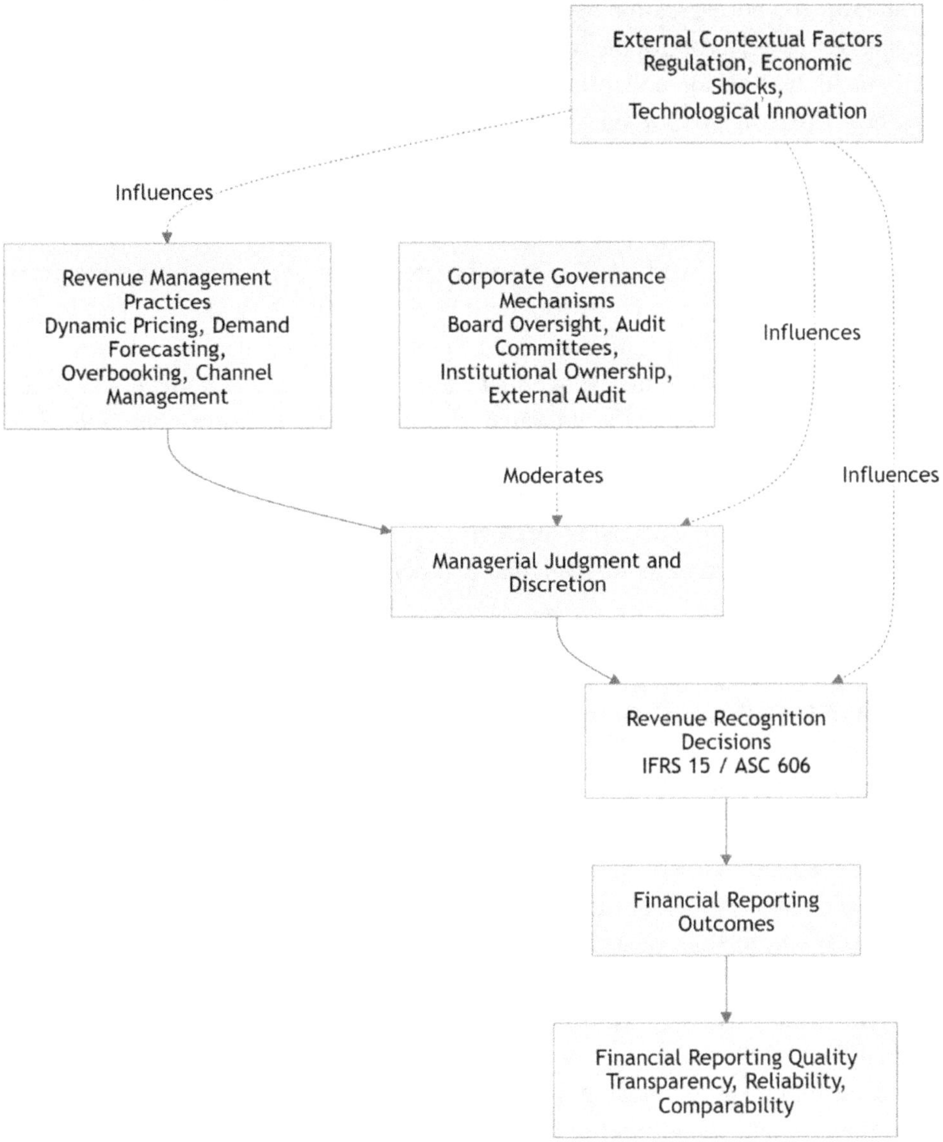

Authors compilation using mermaid

HOTEL REVENUE CREATION MODELS

Literature on hotel creation of revenue is largely based on the concept of revenue management (RM) as one of the strategic functions to maximize the prices, capacity, and demand distribution under the condition of demand uncertainty and perishable inventory (Li & Ma, 2015; Zaki, 2025). The main RM practices are dynamic pricing, yield management, overbooking, channel management and demand forecasting that in turn affect the key performance indicators average daily rate (ADR), revenue per available room (RevPAR), and revenue (Herath et al., 2023; Matviienko, 2019).

Other more recent works build upon the previous model of room-centric models and expand on them to cover food and beverage, ancillary service, and loyalty program and digital distribution platform quota-driven revenue models, owing to a general trend towards total revenue management (ug'li, 2022; Remy et al., 2023). New technological tools, such as data analytics and machine learning, have increased the capabilities of RM by making the use of the machine more accurate in predicting the demand and offering price responsiveness (Zaki, 2025; Bastos, 2023). These changes emphasize the increasing strategic significance of RM in determining the operational effectiveness as well as financial performance.

DIGITAL TRANSFORMATION IN REVENUE MANAGEMENT AND FINANCIAL REPORTING

In spite of these developments, the literature is predominantly concerned with revenue creation, as an operational phenomenon, or a strategic phenomenon with insufficient attention to how the patterns of RM-based revenue practice is reflected into the accountancy recognition and financial reporting. This detachment is especially relevant in light of the fact that hospitality includes more components of a bundled service and the multi-period revenue flow that makes it tough to match the economic activity with revenue values reported (Taliani, 2015; Goncalves et al., 2024).

The current technological developments have largely reshaped the revenue management practices within the hospitality industry. Hotels that use digital platforms, predictive analytics, and pricing systems based on artificial intelligence are becoming more popular in the modern world of hotels to optimize the way receipts are generated and the ability to predict the demand. Such technologies combine data about many sources, such as reservation systems, customer behaviour analysis, demand forecasts, and competitor rates, and help hotels to make more dynamic and analytic pricing decisions.

There are also implications of using the sophisticated revenue management systems on the accounting-based recognition of revenue and financial reporting. Pricing algorithms and integrated property management systems create real time transactional data which can enhance better measurement system and reporting of revenue. Nevertheless, the application of sophisticated digital systems can also bring new issues regarding the managerial controls, internal controls and transparency in the revenue recognition.

Also, the growing use of data analytics can affect managerial judgment during revenue recognition decisions. In as much as digital systems offer greater forecasting opportunities, managers are still very essential in interpreting algorithm outcomes and identifying how revenue should be realized according to accounting principles including IFRS 15 and ASC 606. Digital transformation might, therefore, not only increase the quality of reporting, but it will also introduce significant new points of managerial discretion that will have to be controlled through a properly functioning governance.

REVENUE RECOGNITION STANDARDS AND TROUBLES

The body of research in the field of recognition of the revenue in the hospitality industry is mostly placed in the context of the general accounting literature, in relation to the effect of the new standards (IFRS 15 and ASC 606) on the timing and measurement of the revenue (Myers et al., 2022; Lu and Wang, 2018). These are based on identifying the performance obligations, distribution of price on transactions, and recognition of revenue when the obligation is fulfilled-norms that are specifically difficult in application by the hotel industry with regards to bundling of product, customer reward programs, advance reservation and variable consideration.

A number of investigations emphasize the fact that the enhanced flexibility in accordance with principle-based standards helps improve the relevance of the targeted revenues but also increases the discretion of the managers in the estimates of the transaction price and recognition of revenue (Srivastava, 2013; Lu and Wang, 2018). With hospitality environments, this subjectivity is enhanced by the existence of advanced payments, deferred revenues and modification of contracts which add up the risk of recognition of revenues early or opportunistically (Caylor, 2008; Giedt, 2017).

Although the study of accounting presents a good contribution to the understanding of recognition mechanisms, the analysis of hospitals is still narrow. The literature presents an overview of little or no research that views RM practices into the analysis of the accounting recognition of revenue, thus creating a partiality of how the operational pricing and capacity decisions impact accounting performance

(Burnett et al., 2021; Goncalves et al., 2024). This disconnect shows the necessity of industry-specific models that capture the nature of the economic reality of hotel accommodation generation.

Although there is an increasing number of research papers looking into revenue recognition standards, including those like IFRS 15 and ASC 606, most authors look at the impact that the standards have on operations of hospitality companies rather than how they relate to the technical aspects of the standards. Although accounting research notes the greater discretion of the managerial discretion tied with principle-based standard, a comparatively lesser focus has been given to the role of revenue management strategies on determining the time of recognition and measure of the recognition of the revenues. The interaction between the operational pricing decisions and the accounting recognition rules is specifically important in the context of hospitality industry where the bundled services, loyalty programs, and advance booking are often practiced. It implies that the current literature could be underscoring the degree to which accounting outcomes are predetermined by the operational revenue strategies. This means that integrative research is required, which will study the joint impact of revenue management practices and accounting standards on the financial reporting behavior in the hotel firms.

FINANCIAL REPORTING AND DISCLOSURE PRACTICES

Transparency, comparability, and the quality of disclosed information are the aspects of financial reporting in the hospitality business that are highlighted by literature due to underlying complexity of the revenue systems and various ownership patterns (Jiao and Lu, 2019; Hu, 2010). Research records high inconsistency in the reported revenues practices by firms and jurisdiction, especially segment reports, deferred revenue, and explanations narratives of revenue drivers.

The empirical evidence indicates that earnings management activities have a negative impact on the quality of reporting in the hospitality sector, and benchmark-oriented reporting is the common practice of hospitality-related companies in order to prevent losses or loss of profits (Esteban and Devesa, 2011; Paiva and Lourenco, 2016). Nevertheless, other studies hold that, in a particular governance environment that is well-preserved, it is true that managerial discretion when used in reporting can make financial statements more informative, thus making them more relevant (Myers et al., 2022; Lu and Wang, 2018).

New accounting standards and digital RM tools have also impacted reporting that has been both mixed in terms of the effect it has on earnings informativeness and comparability (Jang et al., 2023; Talon-Ballestero et al., 2023). On the whole, the literature shows that not only accounting rules can influence the financial reporting in the hospitality industry, but also certain incentives of the manager and forms of governance.

Even as there has been increased literature on financial reporting within hospitality firms over the past years, a lot of research has been done on the identification of reporting patterns as opposed to giving critical consideration to the processes underlying the practices. Research often records disclosure quality differences, revenue reporting, and earnings management behavior, difference across hospitality companies, although there is not much agreement on the factors that affect the quality of reporting the most. Specifically, the study of the connection between operational revenue management decisions and the financial reporting outcomes has not been empirically studied in detail. Consequently, the available literature offers a partial insight into the influence of managerial incentives, operation strategies and governance systems on the financial reporting practice of the hospitality industry. To close this gap, there is need to undertake more integrative studies that give both operations and accounting aspects into account when assessing financial transparency among hotel companies.

MANAGERIAL JUDGMENT AND DISCRETION ROLE

The concept of managerial judgment becomes the focus of both accounting and hospitality studies, when it comes to the area of revenue recognition estimates, accrual decisions, and decisions concerning real activities (Myers et al., 2022; Burnett et al., 2021). Managers of hotel companies are significantly laissez faire when it comes to recognizing revenues, allocating transaction prices, capitalizing or expensing, and pricing policies associated with RM goals (Lee, 2014; Taliani, 2015).

The empirical evidence shows that the incentive system, the pressures of performance of the firm, and the contractual agreements, such as the management contracts to compensate for reported earnings or revenue-related metrics, determine managerial discretion (Turner and Guilding, 2011; Turner, 2013). Although discretion has the effect of upgrading faithful reporting of complex economic dealings, it has provided chances of earnings manipulation especially in settings where monitoring is weak or the financial distress (Caylor, 2008; Syahputri et al., 2023).

The literature also separates accrual-based and real earnings management and in it, the managers are observed as using mechanisms that are strategic in addition to regulatory constraints as well as the type of firm and its ownership structure (Gim and Jang, 2023; Evans et al., 2012). These results highlight the dual role of managerial judgment as a requirement of the accounting practice, as well as a possible cause of reporting risk.

Although the fact that managerial discretion is significant to the recognition of revenue and the financial reporting is widely recognized in the literature, the consequences of the discretion have been disputed. Other studies claim that managerial discretion makes the financial statements more informative since managers are able to capture the complicated economic transactions. Conversely, there are other studies that indicate the danger of such discretion encouraging opportunistic reporting behaviour especially where there are minimal monitoring systems or high performance expectations. In the hospitality sector, these strains can be even stronger based on the fact that the industry is grounded on a complex service structure, unpredictable demand trends and management contracts that tie compensation to financial performance indicators. These features indicate that managerial judgment is not only a required accounting process, but it can be a source of reporting risk, which supports the importance of analyzing the effect of governance structures on the exercise of managerial discretion.

EARNINGS MANAGEMENT RISKS OF HOSPITALITY

The management of earnings has been widely reported within the hospitality sector, and the research findings have revealed both accrual-based and actual earnings management to achieve earnings standards, smooth earnings or react to contract incentives (Esteban and Devesa, 2011; Goncalves et al, 2024). The cyclical nature of the industry and the fluctuating nature of the demand and the structure of assets offer special incentives and opportunities to operate in such manner.

Science emphasizes that hotel companies use the revenue acceleration, manipulation of the deferred revenues, sale of assets, and adjustment of discretionary expenses to regulate the reported performance (Sohn et al., 2011; Habětínek, 2020). The times of crisis have increased the use of real earnings management, where the managers are attempting to retain liquidity and express resilience when faced with increased uncertainty (Syahputri et al., 2023; Yassin et al., 2022).

Notably, the management of the earnings traits differ on the type of firms and the ownership structures. As an example, lodging REITs are more likely to practice real earnings management, as the regulations and the reports have certain limitations, C-corporations more often manipulate accruals (Gim & Jang, 2023). Such findings indicate that the risks of earnings management in the hospitality sphere are dependent on a context and are closely tied to the governance and institutional settings.

Despite the fact that the existence of earnings management in the hospitality industry has been sufficiently reported, the literature shows that there is a lot of diversity in the mechanisms through which the practice takes place. There are studies that focus on the issue of accrual-based earnings management techniques and some that argue the rise in real earnings management using operational decisions like asset disposal, discretionary spending or price changes. Nonetheless, the existing body of research did not investigate many studies concerning the hypothesis of how the revenue management strategies themselves can indirectly assist the earnings manipulation by affecting the timing and the structure of reported revenues. This weakness implies that the connection between operation revenue maximization and financial reporting practices is not well comprehended. Subsequent studies can further enhance the same by investigating the relationship between revenue management systems and accounting discretion to generate chances of informative and opportunistic reporting practices.

GOVERNANCE, AUDIT AND REGULATORY OVERSIGHT

Corporate governance mechanisms are always recognised by the literature as important in limiting earnings management and improving financial reporting quality in hospitality companies (Al-Okaily et al., 2019; Beattrice, 2015). Tracing of some of the key governance attributes, the board composition, efficacy of the audit committee, institutional ownership, and the quality of external audit have been analyzed.

It has been shown through empirical studies that the existence of the stronger governance structure- independent boards, active audit committees and existence of institutional investors- diminishes discretionary accruals and premature revenue recognition (Hu, 2010; Tehranian et al., 2006; Bashir et al., 2024). The additional contributions to monitoring the discretion of the managers and enhancing credibility in reports are audit-related factors such as auditor reputation and auditor fees (Larker and Richardson, 2004).

Nevertheless, the effectiveness of governance within the hospitality sector is usually dependent on the ownership as well as contractual affairs. The nature of the hotel management contracts addresses the complex agency relationships, which undermine the orthodox governance restriction instruments and requires the contemporary customized oversight apparatus (Turner, 2013; Turner and Guilding, 2011). Recent research also identifies the intervention of the risk management committees and reputational factors in taming the earnings management, especially in times of financial distress (Suhaemi & Hidayah, 2025; Musa & Ibrahim, 2024).

All the 6 lenses are telling me that the creation of hotel revenues, accounting-based recognition of revenues and financial reporting are also strongly intertwined based on the managerial judgment and restrained by the governance systems. Although the concept of revenue management has been observed to increase the operational performance, the implication of revenue management in the context of accounting recognition and the quality of reporting are not well incorporated in available studies. The governance structures are vital in the balancing of discretion in the hands of managers and transparency but they are not effective in both institutional and contractual settings. It is based on this synthesis that a critical analysis of the conceptual framework is then developed to suit the hospitality industry.

The data on corporate governance in the literature continues to point out governance of a corporation as one of the most effective mechanisms of limiting opportunistic financial reporting behavior, with empirical evidence being divided on the effectiveness of this mechanism. Whereas a number of studies indicate that good governance mechanisms, including independent boards, activeness and independence of audit committees and quality of external audit systems can limit earnings management, other studies suggest that management mechanism may not necessarily work effectively in sectors with complex ownership and contractual programs. Within the hospitality industry, multi-layered agency relationships exist between the owners and operators due to management contracts, asset-light business models, and which may compromise traditional forms of governance. The following structural features indicate that nation-specific governance structures are required that are designed in line with institutional and contractual specificities of the hospitality industry. The operation of the system of governance at these levels is therefore a critical area of learning that would enhance the transparency and accountability of the financial reporting.

CRITICAL ANALYSIS AND SYNTHESIS

It is a critical synthesis of the results of the six thematic lenses that is used to establish a consistent objective of the interrelationships between the hotel revenue creation process and the process of revenue management and the accounting-based revenue recognition process, the risk of managing earnings and earnings management, and the mechanism of governance. The analysis does not duplicate the standpoint findings of individual research, but instead, synthesizes converging and divergent insights, judges the approach and situational constraints and discovers cross-cutting findings that manage the level of financial reporting in the hospitality sector.

REVENUE MANAGEMENT AND ACCOUNTING- BASED REPORTING

In the literature reviewed, there is a well-founded agreement that the practices of revenue management are central to the strategic performance of the hotel in terms of the maximization of prices and capacity utilization, and the distribution of demands (Herath et al., 2023; Zaki, 2025). Nonetheless, a major shortcoming is revealed in the fact that little empirical skills have been integrated on the revenue management and the accounting-based recognition of revenue and financial reporting. However, even though RM-based decision-making directly affects the timing and scale of reported revenues, a majority of the literature considers RM operationally independent of accounting procedures and makes it analytically divorced between economic activity and financial reported performance (Taliani, 2015; Goncalves et al., 2024). Such segregation limits the comprehension of how revenue maximization tactics can be reflected in accounting recognition decisions and disclosure common sense, especially where there are complex and packages hotel services.

MANAGERIAL JUDGMENT AS A KEY MEDIATING PROCESS

Managerial judgment is the most important mediating variable in the synthesis of revenue management practices to financial reporting outcomes. The literature in accounting proves that discretion in revenue recognition might make financial statements necessarily relevant and informative when applied in the framework of properly designed reporting systems (Myers et al., 2022; Lu and Wang, 2018). This discretion is enhanced in hospitality environment by volatile demand, advance bookings and management contracts which mean greater exposure on opportunistic earnings management (Caylor, 2008; Turner & Guilding, 2011). The literatures therefore demonstrate a dual purpose of managerial judgment which is that it is an indispensable tool in accurately reflecting the intricate transactions and also can provide an avenue of earnings manipulation where there are misaligned incentives or lax regulation.

CONTEXTUAL SENSITIVITY AND EARNINGS MANAGEMENT RISKS

The critical synthesis of earnings management studies tells that, marketed by different firms depending on the type of firms and ownership structure and external conditions, hospitality firms have heterogeneous earnings management behavior patterns. Research always records the accrual-based as well as real earnings management practices to attain earnings standards or contractual objectives (Esteban and Devesa, 2011; Goncalves et al., 2024). Notably, crisis situations, especially the COVID-19 crisis, have increased the level of use of real earnings management as the manager is responding to liquidity pressures and increased uncertainty (Syahputri et al., 2023; Yassin et al., 2022). These results show the contingency of the earnings management risk and indicate that the conventional methods of governance or accounting models might fail in the dynamic managerial reactions to the hospitality settings.

MODERATING FORCES OF GOVERNANCE MECHANISMS

The received literature supports the argument of the moderation of the relationship between managerial judgment and earnings management by the corporate governance mechanisms, and thus, affecting the quality of the financial reporting. The general correlations that are related to lower levels of discretionary reporting and premature revenue recognition are board independence, audit committee independence, institutional ownership, and audit quality (Al-Okaily et al., 2019; Hu, 2010; Bashir et al., 2024). However, governance does not work equally. The agency formations in the hospitality industry, especially the one that is based on management contracts and plural form business strategies, is able to blur the traditional forms of controlling ownership and creates the complexity of reporting, which underpins the earnings manipulation (Turner, 2013; Poretti et al., 2024). This inconsistency highlights the necessity of the governance structures, which are specific to the structural features of hotels firms.

LIMITATIONS OF THE EXISTING RESEARCH METHODOLOGY AND THEORY

Methodological limitations of the synthesis complement it to limit cumulative knowledge development as well. Another significant part of the literature is based on cross-sectional designs and accrual-based proxies, constraining causation and dynamic interaction between revenue management and accounting discretion and time, as well as between revenue management and governance (Larcker and Richardson, 2004; Goncalves et al., 2024). Besides, theoretical frameworks frequently are taken on board without significant modification to the hospitality setting because of borrowing general accounting or corporate governance literature. Consequently, the prevailing models poorly explain industry specific aspects of service bundling, seasonality and owner-operator separation.

CONCEPTUAL APPROACH

Drawing these inferences together, the literature identifies a gap in the literature of interdependent conceptual lens where revenue management practices affect financial reporting performances as a result of managerial discretion where governance mechanisms serve as factors of constraint or facilitation of discretion. Quality of financial reporting becomes a product of this interaction and it is influenced by institutional, contractual or crisis related factors. This line of thought extends beyond the analysis which is usually fragmented and gives the theoretical basis of hospitality specific development that matches the economic and organisational reality of the industry.

In general, the critical analysis shows that the financial reporting in the hospitality industry must be viewed beyond the individual studies of the revenue management, earnings management, and governance. Rather, it demands integrative frameworks by which they can realize dynamic interactions, with the result of a much finer and policy-focused view of the subject of financial transparency and accountability in hotel companies.

IMPLICATION

The discussion presented in this section is anchored on theoretical and practical implications of integrated synergistic synthesis on literature published on the creation of hotel revenue, revenue management, the accounting recognition of revenue, judgement of managers, management of earnings, and the governance mechanisms. The chapter contributes to the development of the theory in the hospitality sectors, besides providing practical details that can be applied by marketers, to the regulators, and the same stakeholders.

THEORETICAL IMPLICATIONS

First, the results can add to the existing body of literature in accounting and hotel management by opposing the traditional notion that more room in deciding on revenue recognition in such a way that financial reporting quality is bound to suffer. In line with the latest accounting studies, the hospitality evidence implies that, when used in the framework of strong governance, the managerial judgment may allow increasing the relevance and informativeness of reported revenues (Myers et al., 2022; Lu and Wang, 2018). This subtle perspective is an extension of the revenue recognition theory as it puts more emphasis on how the outcomes of discretion are conditional with the influence of governance.

Second, the synthesis supports and builds the agency theory in the hospitality performance. Agreency conflicts between owners and operators are enhanced by the high level of management contracts and asset-light business models, resulting in different incentives to manage the earnings issue that is not present with vertically integrated firms (Turner, 2013; Turner and Guilding, 2011). The results indicate that the traditional models of agency should be adjusted to generate the impact of plural form business and multi-layered governance structure, which dominate hotel companies.

Third, the chapter also adds to the research on earnings management since it shows how hospitality firms logically prefer to choose between accrual and real-based earnings management methods depending on the type of the firm, regulations, and external factors. The fact that lodging REITs prefer real versus C-corporations that use more accrual manipulation would prove to be important in indicating the circumstances under which institutional and organizational settings matter in the formation of managerial behavior (Gim & Jang, 2023). This observation complements signaling and precautionary motive views by putting earnings management decisions in industry-specific context.

Fourth, the revenue management literature research combined with the accounting theory would develop the hospitality management literature by not only determining revenue management as an operational optimization tool but also a condition that determines financial reporting results. Current revenue management models are performance-based and focused on efficiency (Li & Ma, 2015; Zaki, 2025), but a synthesis showing that revenue management choices have accounting implications, which affect the quality and disclosure of earnings, has been made. It is on the basis of this view that interdisciplinary frameworks bridging the operational strategy, accounting discretion and governance are developed.

Lastly, the results highlight the moderating effect of corporate governance on a financial reporting performance, which should be part of governance-adjusted frameworks of earnings management distinguishing opportunistic and informative discretion (Kheirollah, 2014; Beattrice, 2015). The chapter adds to the governance theory by underscoring conditional effectiveness of governance mechanism in hospitality context with regard to the necessity of sector sensitive governance designs.

PRACTICAL IMPLICATIONS

To the owners of hotels and the boards, the results highlight the need to customize structure of governance to counter the type of agency problem that exists in contracts of hotel management. To reduce the threat of earnings management, increasing board independence, and aligning bonuses with long-term performance results may reduce financial reporting fraud and enhance audit committee independence (Al-Okaily et al., 2019; Bashir et al., 2024).

To the revenue management practitioners, this chapter shows the importance of considering the accounting and reporting issues alongside the revenue optimization decision. Although the use of advanced analytics and pricing algorithms has permitted the improvement in revenues, the results need to be interpreted within the accounting systems in order to prevent the unintended distortions of the reported revenues and revenues (Avi, 2022; Zaki, 2025). Revenue managers and accounting departments should hence work closely with each other.

To regulators and standard setters, the conflicting evidence on the implications of higher discretion in the revenue recognition whether it is IFRS 15 or ASC 606 would indicate that complementary disclosure would be necessary and that such governance should be controlled. This may be achieved by enhancing the level of transparency of performance obligations, variable consideration and deferred revenues to minimize information asymmetry and maintain the relevance of financial reports (Myers et al., 2022; Lu and Wang, 2018).

To investors and analysts, the results imply that there is a need to weigh the reported financial performance of hospitality firms in the context of the quality of governance, ownership, and contractual structure. These contextual elements may enhance the evaluation of earnings sustainability and risk and this is best done through awareness of the same especially when there is uncertainty on economic issues.

Lastly, in the context of the greater hospitality sector, the application of digital and AI-driven tools of revenue management has a broad potential to become more efficient and decision-making. Nevertheless, to achieve these benefits, it is necessary to invest together in governance, inner-control, and reporting to make sure that technological innovations do not weaken or eliminate financial transparency and confidence of stakeholders (Remy et al., 2023; Bastos, 2023).

LIMITATIONS AND FUTURE RESEARCH

Although there has been a surge in research investigating the prerogatives of revenue management, earnings management, and governance on hospitality industry, the available literature has various limitations, which limit the depth and generalisability of the available knowledge. Such limitations are important concepts that should be realized to put the findings of this review into perspective and to point to other areas of priority in future research.

LIMITATIONS OF THE LITERATURE REVIEW

The main weakness in the literature is that it is scattered in the various fields. Research into hotel revenue management is mostly centred in the field of hospitality and operations research with research on revenue recognition, earnings management as well as governance all being based on accounting and finance. The disciplinary divide created has led to the lack of empirical data on the integration of revenue management practices with accounting-based revenues recognition and financial reporting, as well as critical interactions have remained under-researched (Goncalves et al., 2024; Taliani, 2015).

Secondly, cross-sectional designs and accruals-based earnings management proxies are highly concentrated in its methodology. Although these methods offer useful information, they cannot explain the dynamism and situation-specificity of managerial decision-making in hospitality companies especially when there is a downturn in the economy or when regulations change (Larcker and Richardson, 2004; Syahputri et al., 2023). The occasioned use of longitudinal, mixed-method, and case-based study is limiting the causal and temporal indication of changes in revenue recognition and effectiveness of governance.

Third, there is a geographic and institutional bias in the literature, that is, a disproportionate coverage of a particular country or region and publicly emerging or large hotel companies. This small focus of the empirical study restricts the ability of findings to be generalized and ignores the different ownership models, regulatory factors, and market factors that describe the global hospitality market (Paiva and Lourenco, 2016; Kliestik et al., 2022).

Fourth, despite much research on governance mechanisms, the issues of governance specific to the hospitality industry, especially those stemming out of management contracts and the plural form business strategies were not theorized or empirically under-investigated. Board independence and audit committees are considered as remarkable traditional governance variables that might not be versatile enough to reflect the depth of owner-operative relationships in hotel companies (Turner, 2013; Turner and Guilding, 2011).

Lastly, there is yet to be a research touching on the situation of crises, such as the COVID-19 pandemic, which is still at an early and scattered stage. Although the change in the behavior of earnings management in crisis is still being reported in recent studies, what happens in the long term with terms of the quality of financial reporting, adaptation to the need to adjust its governance, and trust of any stakeholder is not yet fully comprehended (Syahputri et al., 2023; Yassin et al., 2022).

CONCLUSIONS

The following chapter aimed to give a synthesis of the literature review on the interaction between hotel revenue creation and management practices based on revenue management and financial reporting and accounting with special emphasis on the area of managerial judgments, risks of earnings management, and mechanisms of governance in the hotel and hospitality industry. Through the combination of research streams that conventionally developed independently, the chapter contributes to a holistic insight of how the operation-based strategies concerning revenue formation come to bear on the reported financial results in the intricate organizational and institutional settings.

In the synthesis, the revenue management has developed to become more of a strategic capability rather than a tactical pricing role that not only is the force behind the operational efficiency, but also financial performance of hotel companies. Nevertheless, even though the issue has a direct effect on the trend in revenue, the management of revenues has not been integrated adequately with accounting-based revenue recognition models in credible studies. This gap restricts the comprehensiveness of both scholars and practitioners as to the impact the revenue optimization decision will have on the timing, measurement, and disclosure of reported revenues especially where bundled services, advance booking and variable consideration are present, as is characteristic of hospitality operations.

Managerial judgment is found out as one of the key mediating factors between revenue management practice and financial reporting. Even though the discretion in the revenue recognition is required to reflect the complex economic transactions in a faithful manner, the literature shows that the discretion also provides the chances to manage the earnings under the conditions of misaligned managerial motivation or ineffective monitoring mechanisms. The behaviors of earnings management in the hospitality industry have been found to be a heterogeneous phenomenon as far as they differ by the different types of firms, ownership, contracts and the economic environment with the crisis periods intensifying the dependency on real activity manipulations.

The dynamics are moderately important to corporate governance structures. The reviewed evidence suggests that the governance systems of opportunity parts of the world, including board composition, audit committees, institutional ownership, and audit quality, tend to limit the opportunistic reporting behavior and increase the financial reporting quality. However, the efficiency of the mechanisms is extremely contextual, especially when applied in a hospitality industry that enables business strategies featured by management contracts and plural forms of business that present a distinct challenge of agency. Such results highlight the necessity to establish governance structures exclusive to cognitive realities of the hotel sector and not exclusively based on generic approaches to corporate governance.

In a larger sense, the chapter provides great relevance and considerable significance of integrative and interdisciplinary methods of researching financial reporting in the hospitality industry. The accounting standards and regulatory frameworks give great limits under which revenue can be realized but this is reliant on the conduct of the manager and the effectiveness of governance. The revenue management through various technological solutions such as digitalization and AI-based analytics contribute to the complexity of these relations introducing the new approaches to decisions and information streams, which proves the necessity of a coordinated operating, accounting and governance systems.

To sum up, the chapter adds the literature in hospitality and accounting because it develops a specific conceptual approach to the study of hospitality, tying together the relationship among revenue management, managerial discretion, the earnings management and governance into one conceptual framework. Through explaining these interdependencies, the chapter also presents the theoretical implications that expand on the current models and practical advice on how financial reporting integrity, regulatory oversight, and strategic decision making can be improved at hotel firms. With the hospitality industry keeping on changing with features of change in a technological setting, overshadowed by economic uncertainty, such integrative frameworks will be a key in promoting transparency, accountability and sustainable performance.

FUTURE RESEARCH DIRECTIONS

On the basis of these limitations, there are a number of likely avenues that the future research might take.

Firstly, upcoming research must aim at undertaking integrated empirical studies that directly interrelate the hotel revenue management practice in empowering the accounting-based hotel recognition of revenue alongside the financial reporting results. Integration of data on the detailed operations with financial statements data would allow making a more accurate estimate of the effect that the pricing, capacity, and demand decisions have on the reported revenues and the quality of the earnings.

Second, it is necessary to have their ownership and contract sensitive studies on the variation of managerial judgment in revenue recognition by different forms of hotel ownership, such as REITs, C-corporations, family-owned firms, and management contracts. Such studies would further investigate the agency issues and incentive to report in the hotel industry.

Third, researchers ought to establish and experiment hospitality-specific governance systems to the agency issues that exist in hotel management contracts. Further studies may examine the efficacy of different governance mechanisms e.g. performance-based contracts, risk management and employee committees as well as, and improved disclosure requirements in eliminating the earnings management risk.

Fourth, longitudinal and crisis studies are required to capture the nature of developments of earnings management behaviors and effectiveness of governance with respect to time especially before, during the time of, and after economic shocks.

These kinds of analyses would give information about how resilient the reporting practices would be under stressful conditions, and how adaptable they would be.

Fifth, the increasing usage of digital and the AI-based systems of revenue management raises an urgent field of study. The future studies must investigate how these technologies affect the managerial judgments, revenue recognition decisions, and governance inspection, and its effects on the transparency and accountability.

Lastly, the cross-country comparative research by integrating institutional, legal, and cultural factors would contribute to the comprehension of the manner in which regulatory traditions are characterized by regulatory environments and the nature of earnings management and governance results of the hospitality industry. Using interdisciplinary and multi-method techniques, further studies will facilitate more holistic and context-specific theories of reporting on financial performances in the hospitalities sector.

REFERENCES

Al-Okaily, J., Dixon, R., & Salama, A. (2019). Corporate governance quality and premature revenue recognition: Evidence from the UK. Social Science Research Network. https://doi.org/DOI: 10.2139/ssrn

Arimany, N., Fitó, M. A., & Orgaz, N. (2015). *Economic consequences of accounting standards in the hotel industry: Lobbying arguments versus expected impact.* Social Science Research Network.

Avi, M. S. (2022). Revenue managers in hotels: Is revenue focus enough? *International Journal of Tourism and Hotel Management, 4*(2), 55–74. DOI: 10.22271/27069583.2022.v4.i2a.58

Bashir, B., Rashid, M., & Bashir, Z. (2024). Impact of ownership structure and corporate governance on earnings management. *SEISENSE Journal of Management, 7*(1), 1–20. Advance online publication. DOI: 10.33215/c1qkdq06

Bastos, B. P. D. (2023). *Determinants of revenue management frameworks as enablers for cloud and e-commerce hospitality management.* Sustainability in Tourism., DOI: 10.54517/st.v4i2.2486

Beattrice, V. A. (2015). Corporate governance mechanisms and earnings management: A state-of-the-art review. *Annals of the Faculty of Economics, 1*(1), 982–990.

Burnett, B. M., Martin, G. W., & Reppenhagen, D. A. (2021). Managerial discretion in revenue recognition amidst financial restatements and implications for GAAP compliance. *Journal of Business Finance & Accounting, 48*(7–8), 869–894. DOI: 10.1111/jbfa.12504

Campos, F. C. D. A., Gomes, C., Cardoso, L., & Santos, L. L. (2022). Management accounting practices in the hospitality industry: The Portuguese background. *International Journal of Financial Studies, 10*(4), 88. DOI: 10.3390/ijfs10040088

Campos, F. C. D. A., Santos, L. L., Gomes, C., & Cardoso, L. (2022). Management accounting practices in the hospitality industry: A systematic review and critical approach. *Tourism and Hospitality, 3*(1), 243–264. DOI: 10.3390/tourhosp3010017

Caylor, M. L. (2008). Strategic revenue recognition to achieve earnings benchmarks. Social Science Research Network. https://doi.org/DOI: 10.2139/ssrn.885368

Esteban, L. P., & Devesa, M. J. S. (2011). Determinants of earnings benchmarks in the Spanish hotel industry. *Tourism Economics, 17*(1), 53–72. DOI: 10.5367/te.2011.0024

Esteban, L. P., & Devesa, M. J. S. (2011). Earnings management in the Spanish hotel industry. *Cornell Hospitality Quarterly*, *52*(4), 466–479. DOI: 10.1177/1938965511402930

Evans, M. E., Houston, R. W., Peters, M., & Pratt, J. H. (2012). The financial reporting environment, reporting discretion, and earnings management: US GAAP versus IFRS. *The Accounting Review*.

Giedt, J. Z. (2017). The roles of receivables and deferred revenues in revenue management. Social Science Research Network. https://doi.org/DOI: 10.2139/ssrn.2424848

Gim, J., & Jang, S. (2023). Earnings management practices of the lodging industry: Diverging behaviors of lodging REITs and lodging C-corporations. *Tourism Economics*. Advance online publication. DOI: 10.1177/13548166231189142

Gonçalves, B., Coelho, L. S., & Pinto, P. (2024). Earnings management in the hospitality industry: A systematic literature review. *Tourism & Management Studies*, *20*(1), 65–77. Advance online publication. DOI: 10.18089/tms.20240105

Habětínek, J. (2020). Is revenue management to meet earnings benchmarks informative? *The Journal of Hospitality Financial Management*.

Herath, R., Tham, J., Khatibi, A., & Azam, S. M. F. (2023). Revenue management practices and financial performance in star-rated hotels in Sri Lanka. *Journal of Law and Sustainable Development*, *11*(11), e1538. DOI: 10.55908/sdgs.v11i11.1538

Hu, L. (2010). Corporate governance and earnings management: Evidence from Singapore. *Journal of International Accounting Research*.

Jang, Y., Liu, C. H., Weinbaum, D., & Yehuda, N. (2023). Performing up to par? Hospitality firms after ASU 2016-02. Social Science Research Network. https://doi.org/DOI: 10.2139/ssrn.4549994

Jiao, F., & Lu, L. W. (2019). Earnings management, benchmarks, and market valuation: Evidence from hospitality firms. *Journal of Accounting and Finance*, *19*(3). Advance online publication. DOI: 10.33423/jaf.v19i3.2034

Kheirollah, A. (2014). Governance-adjusted earnings management and information asymmetry. Social Science Research Network. https://doi.org/DOI: 10.2139/ssrn.2578657

Kliestik, T., Hrosova, L., Valaskova, K., & Svabova, L. (2022). Do firms in the tourism sector manage earnings? Evidence from V4 countries. Journal of Tourism and Services. https://doi.org/DOI: 10.29036/jots.v13i25.376

Larcker, D. F., & Richardson, S. A. (2004). Fees paid to audit firms, accrual choices, and corporate governance. *Journal of Accounting Research, 42*(3), 625–658. DOI: 10.1111/j.1475-679X.2004.t01-1-00143.x

Lee, S. H. (2014). Managerial process of discount decision-making in the lodging industry. *International Journal of Hospitality Management.*

Li, M., & Ma, S. (2015). Hotel revenue management performance influencing mechanisms: A theoretical framework. *International Journal of Contemporary Hospitality Management.*

Lu, H., & Wang, S. (2018). Does lifting the objective-price constraint in revenue recognition increase value relevance? *Asian Review of Accounting, 26*(4), 545–570. DOI: 10.1108/ARA-08-2017-0126

Matviienko, M. (2019). *The financial aspect of revenue management in hospitality.* Economics and Management of Tourism. DOI: 10.31375/2226-1915-2019-4-119-130

Musa, A., & Ibrahim, M. T. (2024). Does the effectiveness of risk management committee mitigate earnings management practices? Journal of International Business [JIBE]. *Economics and Entrepreneurship, 9*(1), 84–99.

Myers, L. A., Schmardebeck, R., Seidel, T. A., & Stuart, M. D. (2022). The impact of managerial discretion in revenue recognition: A reexamination. *Contemporary Accounting Research, 39*(3), 2130–2174. DOI: 10.1111/1911-3846.12775

Paiva, I., & Lourenço, I. (2016). Determinants of earnings management in the hotel industry: An international perspective. *Corporate Ownership and Control, 14*(1), 449–457. DOI: 10.22495/cocv14i1c3p5

Poretti, C., Jérôme, T., & Das, P. (2024). Plural form business strategy and financial reporting quality in hospitality firms. *Journal of Hospitality and Tourism Management, 59*, 60–69. DOI: 10.1016/j.jhtm.2024.03.008

Remy, D., Boo, H. C., & Tee, S. W. W. (2023). From traditional to new hotel revenue management metrics. *Tourism and Hospitality Management, 29*(2), 221–233. DOI: 10.20867/thm.29.2.6

Sohn, J., Tang, C., & Jang, S. (2011). Asset sales and earnings management in the U.S. hotel industry. *The Journal of Hospitality Financial Management.*

Srivastava, A. (2013). Selling-price estimates in revenue recognition and earnings informativeness. Social Science Research Network. https://doi.org/DOI: 10.2139/ssrn.1078584

Suhaemi, U., & Hidayah, N. (2025). Earnings management: The role of corporate governance, reputation, and financial distress. *Neraca Keuangan, 20*(2), 353–359. DOI: 10.32832/neraca.v20i2.19840

Syahputri, W. D., Midiastuty, P. P., Suranta, E., & Putra, D. A. (2023). Earnings management before, during, and after COVID-19 in the hospitality sector. *Ilomata International Journal of Tax and Accounting*, *5*(1), 60–76. DOI: 10.52728/ijtc.v5i1.1000

Taliani, E. C. (2015). *Revenue management impact on management control systems*. Revista de la Facultad de Ciencias Econ6micas., DOI: 10.18359/rfce.1623

Tal6n-Ballestero, P., González-Serrano, L., Flecha-Barrio, M. D., & Orea-Giner, A. (2023). Revenue management strategies during the COVID-19 crisis. *International Marketing Review*. Advance online publication. DOI: 10.1108/IMR-12-2021-0387

Tehranian, H., Cornett, M. M., Marcus, A. J., & Saunders, A. (2006). Earnings management, corporate governance, and true financial performance. Social Science Research Network. https://doi.org/DOI: 10.2139/ssrn.886142

Turner, M. J. (2013). Hotel management contracts: A particularly rich research context. Journal of Hotel and Business Management. https://doi.org/DOI: 10.4172/2169-0286.1000e107

Turner, M. J., & Guilding, C. J. (2011). Motivations of hotel owners and operators to engage in earnings management. *Qualitative Research in Accounting & Management*, *8*(4), 358–381. DOI: 10.1108/11766091111189882

Yassin, M. M., Shaban, O. S., Al-Sraheen, D. A. O., & Daoud, K. A. A. (2022). Revenue standards and earnings management during COVID-19: IFRS versus GAAP. *Journal of Governance and Regulation*, *11*(2), 80–93. DOI: 10.22495/jgrv11i2art7

Zaki, K. (2025). Revenue management reinvented: Leveraging technical know-how to unlock hotel efficiency. *Tourism and Hospitality Management*, *32*(1). Advance online publication. DOI: 10.20867/thm.32.1.9

Chapter 2
Bridging the Gap: Integrating Financial and Managerial Accounting for Decision-Making in Hospitality

James Meersman
http://orcid.org/0009-0004-0853-4821
Texas A&M University, USA

ABSTRACT

This chapter bridges the critical gap between financial and managerial accounting in hospitality, transforming raw data into strategic decision-making tools. Hospitality leaders often treat metrics like labor costs and food variances as compliance burdens rather than actionable intelligence. Using the Uniform System of Accounts for the Lodging Industry (USALI), the text reconceptualizes accountants as business partners who interpret numbers through cost behavior analysis, contribution margins, break-even calculations, and sensitivity modeling. Real-world case studies, from menu engineering for restaurant profitability to food waste reduction and dynamic pricing, all demonstrate 10-20% margin improvements. By evolving from scorekeepers to strategic advisors, professionals can navigate volatile demand and fixed costs for sustainable competitive advantage.

INTRODUCTION

In the bustling corridors of a five-star hotel, every decision carries financial weight. When a front desk manager approves a room upgrade, when a chef redesigns the menu, when housekeeping adjusts staffing levels, it all has financial implications. Each action ripples through the property's financial statements. Despite this, most

DOI: 10.4018/979-8-3373-9479-4.ch002

hospitality professionals navigate these decisions with limited understanding of the financial architecture beneath their operations.

This chapter addresses a fundamental disconnect in the hospitality industry: the silos that separate financial accounting from managerial accounting. In many hospitality organizations, financial accounting focuses on external reporting and historical accuracy, while managerial accounting concentrates on internal planning and future-casting. This artificial separation prevents managers from leveraging their accounting systems as strategic tools. Instead, they treat financial data as a compliance burden rather than a compass for decision-making (Sari & Wibowo, 2025).

The core premise of this chapter is simple: in a hotel, every number is an action. A labor cost percentage is not merely a metric to report to investors; it is a signal about productivity, service quality, and staffing alignment. A food cost variance is not just a variance; it is a diagnostic indicator of waste, pricing misalignment, or menu engineering failures. By reconceptualizing accounting data as actionable intelligence, hospitality leaders can transform their operations and competitive positioning.

This transformation requires a fundamental change in mindset. Modern hospitality professionals must evolve from being simple collectors of financial data or scorekeepers into partners who actively shape strategy through financial analysis. This evolution demands understanding not just what the numbers are, but what they mean and what they should prompt us to do. Research confirms that Strategic Innovation Management Accounting (SIMA) adoption significantly influences decision-making processes in hospitality settings, with organizational structure, environmental factors, and information system quality playing crucial moderating roles (Sari & wibowo, 2025).

The foundation for this transformation exists in the industry's most powerful tool, namely, the Uniform System of Accounts for the Lodging Industry (USALI). While many view USALI as a static compliance framework, it is fundamentally a diagnostic tool. By the end of this chapter, you will understand how to transform raw departmental data into what we call a "managerial story." This process results in developing a compelling narrative that drives staffing decisions, shapes resource allocation, and justifies pricing pivots. The integration of USALI principles with contemporary management accounting practices creates a robust framework for financial decision-making (Harea & Harea, 2025).

THE INTERPRETIVE ROLE OF THE HOSPITALITY ACCOUNTANT: FROM SCOREKEEPER TO BUSINESS PARTNER

To understand the modern hospitality accountant's role, we must first examine the nature of accounting information systems in hotel operations. Accounting Information Systems (AIS) function as the nervous system of a hotel, connecting the guest's profile to the owner's balance sheet. This metaphor captures the essential reality that accounting data flows through every operational decision point. Research demonstrates that contemporary Management Accounting Practices (MAPs) play a crucial role in optimizing resource allocation and enhancing operational efficiency (**Leonandri & Erpurini, 2025**). These efficiencies primarily relate to cost analysis, budget forecasts, and performance reports.

Consider what happens when a guest checks in and receives room service. A series of transactions cascades through the system: the front office records the room revenue; the food and beverage department logs the service revenue; housekeeping records the room's occupancy status; and administrative overhead is allocated proportionally to revenue-generating activities. Each of these data points eventually contributes to departmental profit and loss statements, occupancy metrics, and ultimately, the property's gross operating profit. Studies on AIS user satisfaction reveal that system quality, information quality, and service quality significantly influence how effectively financial and accounting executives can perform their roles (**Diavastis et al., 2024**).

Yet in many hotels, this rich information stream is treated as noise rather than signal. Financial data is collected, aggregated, and reported, but the deeper stories embedded within remain untold. A food and beverage department might report a 35% food cost percentage, a metric that seems acceptable on the surface. But buried within that aggregate number might be stories of tremendous waste in the steak section, underpriced appetizers, or labor scheduling misalignment. The difference between a scorekeeper and a business partner lies in the willingness to interrogate these numbers and convert them into operational insights.

The shift from scorekeeper to business partner requires three essential capabilities:

First, the capacity to interpret. Numbers alone are meaningless; their significance emerges from context. A 10% decline in restaurant covers might signal the need for marketing intervention, but it could also indicate service quality deterioration, menu misalignment with guest preferences, or competitive pressure. The business partner accountant asks clarifying questions and synthesizes operational context with financial data. Recent research on the impact of accounting on business decision-making demonstrates that accounting serves not only as a regulatory tool but also as a strategic partner in pricing, investment, and long-term planning decisions (Avdylaj & Asllanaj, 2023).

Second, the ability to anticipate. While financial accounting looks backward (reporting what has already occurred), business partnership requires forward-looking analysis. What will happen to departmental profit if we reduce labor by 10%? What revenue increase would offset a 2% increase in labor costs? These "what-if" questions require managerial accounting tools and a deep understanding of cost behavior. Managerial accounting information significantly enhances financial performance and decision-making in enterprises of all sizes, particularly through improved cost efficiency and profitability (Suwandi et al., 2024).

Third, the courage to recommend. Scorekeepers report; business partners advise. This requires moving beyond the passive presentation of data into active consultation on operational decisions. The modern hospitality accountant must be willing to sit at the decision-making table and provide perspective on the financial implications of proposed changes. Studies examining the intersection of accounting practices and operational management reveal that an integrated approach in which accounting professionals actively participate in strategy formation will consistently outperform traditional financial reporting models (Zhyvko et al., 2023).

THE USALI FRAMEWORK: STRENGTHS, LIMITATIONS, AND STRATEGIC APPLICATION

The Uniform System of Accounts for the Lodging Industry (USALI) represents a remarkable achievement in standardization. Developed over decades through industry collaboration, USALI provides a globally recognized framework that allows hotel properties, management companies, and investors to compare financial performance across properties, brands, and markets. This standardized language is invaluable for external stakeholders seeking to evaluate hotel financial performance. The historical evolution of USALI demonstrates how the uniforming movement has shaped hospitality accounting practices since 1926, with successive versions continuously adapting to industry needs.

However, this same standardization that creates external transparency often becomes a barrier to internal strategic thinking. USALI was designed primarily as an external reporting framework, the purpose of which was to communicate hotel financial performance to investors, lenders, and industry analysts. When organizations treat USALI as merely a compliance requirement, they miss the diagnostic power embedded within its structure. Research on USALI implementation reveals significant associations between hotel features and USALI usage patterns, with data suggesting that properties utilizing comprehensive USALI analysis practices charge premium prices compared to their less analytical counterparts (Nunes & Machado, 2020).

The framework's usefulness lies in its departmental approach. Rather than presenting hotel financials as a single, undifferentiated entity, USALI breaks the organization into revenue-generating departments (e.g. Rooms, Food & Beverage, Telecommunications, etc.) and support departments (e.g. Maintenance, Administrative, Security, etc.). This departmental segregation enables what we might call the "Lobby to Bottom Line" analysis. Understanding this flow is essential for strategic thinking.

When you maintain the oil in a hotel's housekeeping van, you're not directly generating revenue, but you're preventing the far more expensive consequence of equipment breakdown. When you staff the front desk with exceptionally skilled team members, you are creating opportunities for upsells and loyalty development that extend far beyond the immediate transaction. When you maintain the property's exterior, you're protecting the intangible asset of brand perception.

USALI's departmental structure allows managers to trace these connections. Schedule 1 (Rooms Department) and Schedule 2 (Food & Beverage Department) capture direct departmental results. But the organization's true profitability story emerges only when you account for how support departments (i.e. Maintenance, Administrative, Engineering, Security, Information Technology) distribute their costs across revenue-generating activities. This distribution is not arbitrary; it is a sophisticated calculation that reveals the true cost of generating revenue through each department.

Advanced analytical approaches using USALI data enable hotels to identify temporal relationships between specific USALI components and gross operating profit, revealing patterns that traditional accounting review might miss. Predictive modeling using nonlinear autoregressive approaches on USALI data can capture both linear and nonlinear trends in profitability, enabling more sophisticated forecasting. (Labanowski, Frcz, Wotzka, & Foltys, 2024).

Despite the advantages this frameworks brings, USALI also has critical limitations, particularly for modern hospitality operations. The framework was designed with a specific hotel model in mind: a property with clearly delineated departments operating relatively independently. This model increasingly fails to capture the complexity of contemporary hospitality. Overhead allocation practices vary significantly across the hospitality industry, with many properties still relying on traditional cost allocation methods rather than modern activity-based approaches (**Pajrok, 2022**).

Consider a hybrid working and hotel space, where the same physical infrastructure serves simultaneously as a guest room, office space, and collaborative work environment. USALI's departmental structure struggles to allocate revenue and costs appropriately. Or consider a luxury resort where the distinction between F&B and

Rooms revenue blurs. For instance, a guest's meal during their room stay, a third-party visitor's meal in the same restaurant, and an off-site client's meal in the private dining room all would require different accounting treatments. An additional example could include a shared service centers in which a single team handles guest services, concierge services, and back-office operations. This creates allocation challenges that USALI's traditional structure doesn't elegantly address. Thankfully, forward-thinking hospitality organizations are extending USALI's framework rather than abandoning it. When done correctly, they maintain USALI compliance for external reporting while creating parallel analytical frameworks that capture operational complexity. This dual approach preserves the standardization required by external stakeholders while enabling the diagnostic capability essential for internal strategy.

COST BEHAVIOR AND CONTRIBUTION MARGIN ANALYSIS: THE FOUNDATION OF MANAGERIAL DECISIONS

Before we can effectively use accounting data to drive decisions, we must understand one of managerial accounting's most fundamental concepts: how costs behave in response to changes in volume. This understanding underlies nearly every strategic decision in hospitality operations.

Hospitality organizations are characterized by an unusual cost structure. High fixed costs combine with volatile demand to create a complex financial dynamic. Consider a 300-room hotel. The property has a building (fixed cost), mortgage or lease obligations (fixed cost), a permanent management team (largely fixed cost), and essential infrastructure (security, concierge, and administrative services). Many of these costs remain essentially unchanged whether the hotel operates at 40% or 100% occupancy.

Against these substantial fixed costs, the hotel generates revenue that fluctuates wildly based on seasonality, market conditions, and competitive dynamics. In peak season, a room might generate $300 in revenue; in shoulder season, $180; in low season, $120. This dramatic revenue volatility combined with rigid fixed costs creates both opportunity and peril. Research on financial planning and budget management in hospitality demonstrates that effective financial planning serves as a key tool to mitigate market risks and minimize negative consequences of economic instability (Nedzvedskyi et al., 2024).

This cost structure makes contribution margin analysis essential for strategic decision-making. Contribution margin is the revenue remaining after subtracting variable costs. That is, the amount of each revenue dollar that “contributes” to covering fixed costs and generating profit. In the Rooms Department, contribution margin might be 80% (after accounting for linens, toiletries, and housekeeping labor). In Food & Beverage, contribution margin might be 65% (after accounting for food costs and direct service labor).

Consider a real-world scenario that illustrates why this matters. During low season, a hotel faces a choice: operate the restaurant at a loss or close it temporarily. From a traditional accounting perspective, this seems like an easy decision. If the restaurant will lose money, close it. But a contribution margin perspective reveals complexity. If the restaurant has $200,000 in monthly revenue, 35% food and direct labor costs, and $100,000 in allocated fixed costs (rent on the restaurant space, depreciation on equipment, supervisory salaries), the P&L shows a $35,000 loss.

However, if the hotel closes the restaurant, it doesn't eliminate the $100,000 in fixed costs; it merely reallocates them elsewhere or operates with lower capacity. More importantly, the closed restaurant loses the $130,000 in contribution margin ($200,000 revenue × 65% contribution margin) that was being applied to overall property profitability. From a managerial decision-making perspective, continuing to operate the restaurant often makes financial sense despite it losing money.

This is the insight that transforms accounting from scorekeeper to business partner. The scorekeeper reports: "The restaurant lost $35,000 last month." The business partner says: "The restaurant generated $130,000 in contribution margin toward covering property fixed costs and generating profit, despite reporting a departmental loss. Closing it would eliminate that $130,000 contribution without proportionally reducing fixed costs, ultimately harming property profitability."

Understanding contribution margin enables increasingly sophisticated managerial decisions. Rather than asking "Is this department profitable?" (a binary, somewhat simplistic question), managers can ask:

- Does this activity generate positive contribution margin? If yes, continuing it generally improves property profitability, even if it reports a departmental loss.
- What is the contribution margin per unit of the constrained resource? If labor is the constraint, what's the contribution margin per labor hour? If kitchen capacity is the constraint, what's the contribution margin per kitchen-hour?
- What would contribution margin look like with different operational models? Operating a restaurant at different hours, with reduced capacity, or with different pricing would each generate different contribution margin mathematics.

Empirical research demonstrates that accurate cost estimation, reliable sales forecasting, and flexible cost structures play an important role in improving the reliability of CVP analysis outcomes (Rafi et al., 2025). The more accurate the estimations and forecasts, and the more adaptable the cost structure, the more effective contribution margin analysis becomes in supporting profit planning and operational strategy.

This analytical framework, grounded in understanding cost behavior, becomes the foundation for decisions about service offerings, pricing, staffing levels, and resource allocation.

BREAK-EVEN ANALYSIS AND SENSITIVITY ANALYSIS: NAVIGATING UNCERTAINTY

One of managerial accounting's most valuable tools for hospitality leaders is break-even analysis. This is the point at which revenues exactly equal costs, generating neither profit nor loss. In an industry characterized by high fixed costs and volatile demand, break-even analysis becomes essential strategic thinking. Research on CVP analysis in hospitality settings demonstrates that continuous cost management and monitoring are essential for long-term profitability (Shakya, 2025).

For hospitality operations, break-even analysis typically operates at two levels: the occupancy level required to break even, and the average daily rate (ADR) required to break even, both of which are fundamental for strategic decision making.

Occupancy-Based Break-Even Analysis

Consider a 200-room hotel with the following cost structure: - Fixed costs: $40,000 per day (mortgage, salaries, insurance, utilities, maintenance) - Variable cost per occupied room: $40 (housekeeping, toiletries, linens, utilities) - Average daily rate: $150

To calculate the occupancy percentage required to break even:

Contribution margin per room = ADR - Variable cost per room = $150 - $40 = $110

Break-even occupancy = Fixed costs ÷ (Contribution margin per room × Number of rooms) = $40,000 ÷ ($110 × 200) = $40,000 ÷ $22,000 = 1.82 rooms per night × 200 rooms = 36.4% occupancy

This reveals that the hotel needs approximately 37% occupancy just to cover fixed costs. Any occupancy above 37% generates profit; any occupancy below generates losses.

ADR-Based Break-Even Analysis

But occupancy-based break-even tells only part of the story. The same hotel might alternatively consider: what ADR is required to break even at a given occupancy level? This question becomes relevant when considering pricing strategies during different seasons.

Assume the hotel expects 70% occupancy during the upcoming season and wants to understand the minimum ADR required to break even:

Daily occupied rooms = 200 × 70% = 140 rooms

Break-even ADR = (Fixed costs + (Variable cost × Occupied rooms)) ÷ Occupied rooms = ($40,000 + ($40 × 140)) ÷ 140 = ($40,000 + $5,600) ÷ 140 = $45,600 ÷ 140 = $325.71

This reveals that at 70% occupancy, the hotel needs an ADR of approximately $325.71 to break even. This becomes the floor for pricing decisions. Any rate above this threshold generates profit; any rate below erodes profitability.

Sensitivity Analysis: What-If Thinking

Break-even analysis becomes genuinely strategic when combined with sensitivity analysis. Sensitivity analysis is a systematic exploration of how changes in key assumptions affect break-even points and profitability. Applied research on CVP analysis reveals that modeling carried out by entrepreneurs can be risky because pessimistic conditions could result in losses, while optimistic conditions could generate very large profits (Nugraha & Arifin, 2023).

Returning to our example, management might ask:

- *What if we reduce fixed costs by 10% through operational efficiencies?* The new break-even occupancy would decline from 37% to 33%, significantly improving financial resilience.
- *What if we increase ADR by 5%, to $157.50?* At the same 37% break-even occupancy, every room sold above that threshold now generates $117.50 in contribution margin (instead of $110), accelerating profit growth.
- *What if we increase variable costs by 8% due to labor inflation?* The contribution margin per room would decline to $102, pushing the break-even occupancy up to 38.6%, reducing financial flexibility.
- *What if we adopt a dual-pricing strategy, offering some rooms at $120 and others at $180?* This requires recalculating average contribution margin, but it might optimize revenue capture across different market segments.
- *What if we close the property for 30 days of maintenance?* Fixed costs would continue, reducing the available revenue-generating days and requiring higher occupancy rates during operating periods.

These what-if scenarios move break-even analysis from a static calculation into a dynamic tool for exploring strategic options. Managers can systematically evaluate different scenarios, understanding the financial implications of decisions before implementation. Research on food cost control demonstrates that identifying the causes of high food costs requires detailed CVP analysis. This is true in a variety of contexts (e.g. ineffective food cost control processes, food production control challenges, raw material price fluctuations, etc.).

Sensitivity analysis also reveals which assumptions most significantly impact profitability. In our hotel example, ADR carries a great deal of leverage. A 10% ADR increase has far greater impact on profitability than a 10% variable cost reduction. Conversely, for a property where food costs are high, food cost management might be the highest-leverage intervention. By understanding which variables matter most, management directs improvement efforts toward the highest-impact opportunities.

TRANSLATING RATIOS INTO ACTIONABLE INSIGHTS: BEYOND THE NUMBERS

A key concern in hospitality accounting is that organizations often become trapped with issues relating to paralysis by analysis. The more data that is being reported, the more complicated it can be to properly interpret. The gap between data reporting and data interpretation represents one of the most significant missed opportunities in hospitality management.

Consider labor cost percentage, one of the most commonly cited metrics in hospitality. The formula is straightforward:

Labor Cost Percentage = Total Labor Costs ÷ Total Department Revenue

A typical hotel General Manager knows their property's labor cost percentage and knows industry benchmarks. If they're at 30% and the benchmark is 28%, they know they're on the upper end of the range. But knowing the number without understanding the story beneath it leads to blunt interventions (e.g. cutting labor by 10%). This approach often damages service quality, guest experience, and ultimately, revenue. It is important to note that this impact could be the exact opposite of the actual intended outcome.

The business partner asks deeper questions:

- **Is our productivity misaligned with our service standard?** A high labor cost percentage might reflect either excessive staffing for the service level being delivered, or inadequate pricing for the labor-intensive service standard being offered. If the property competes on personalized service, higher labor costs might be strategically appropriate and should be reflected in premium pricing.

- **What is our labor cost percentage by department?** Rooms Department labor costs might be 15% of room revenue (appropriate), while Food & Beverage labor costs might be 35% of F&B revenue (also appropriate for full service). When consolidated into a single property metric, these departmental realities get obscured.
- **How has labor cost percentage trended over time?** A 10-percentage-point increase is far more concerning than a percentage point or two. Trends reveal whether the issue is structural (requiring strategic response) or temporary (possibly requiring only monitoring).
- **How do our staffing patterns align with demand fluctuations?** A property operating at 40% occupancy might need proportionally fewer staff than one operating at 80%, but accounting systems often mask this relationship.
- **What is our labor cost per occupied room and per revenue-generating transaction?** These metrics sometimes tell different stories than percentage metrics, particularly when revenue mix shifts.

One particularly valuable tool for translating financial data into actionable insights is flow-through analysis. This measures how much of an incremental revenue increase translates into incremental profit. Consider a property that increased room revenue by $1 million through a combination of rate increases and occupancy gains. The question becomes: how much of that $1 million actually improved bottom-line profitability?

The calculation proceeds as follows:

New revenue: $1,000,000

Less: Incremental variable costs (say 20% of incremental revenue) = $200,000

Less: Incremental operating costs (labor, supplies, maintenance): $150,000

Less: Incremental departmental overhead: $80,000

= Incremental flow-through to GOP: $570,000

This reveals a 57% flow-through rate. In other words, 57 cents of every dollar of incremental revenue flows through to gross operating profit. This metric is far more meaningful than topline revenue growth because it captures the cost implications of that growth.

Flow-through analysis becomes even more powerful in different scenarios:

- **For operational improvements:** If management achieves a 5% reduction in food costs through menu engineering, what's the bottom-line impact? By isolating the cost reduction and accounting for any offsetting changes in volume or pricing, managers see the true value of their efforts.
- **For capital investments:** If a $500,000 technology investment reduces labor costs by $150,000 annually, what's the payback period and ROI? Flow-

through analysis helps answer this question by isolating the incremental impact.

- **For pricing decisions:** If reducing rates by 10% increases occupancy by 20%, what's the bottom-line effect? By calculating incremental revenue, variable costs, and overhead, managers understand whether the trade-off improves or erodes profitability.

The discipline of asking "How much of this change actually impacts bottom-line profitability?" forces managers to think more rigorously about their decisions and moves accounting from a reporting function into a strategic tool.

CASE STUDY 1: MENU ENGINEERING AND RESTAURANT PROFITABILITY TRANSFORMATION

To illustrate how integrated financial and managerial accounting can transform operations, consider a detailed case study of a full-service hotel facing declining margins in its signature restaurant.

The Problem

The Riverside Hotel, a 250-room upscale property in an urban market, operated a 120-seat restaurant that had become a significant profit drag. The property's most recent monthly financials showed:

Figure 1. Restaurant P&L Summary (Month)

Line Item	Amount	% of Revenue
Revenue	$180,000	100%
Food Costs	$81,000	45%
Beverage Costs	$18,000	10%
Direct Labor	$54,000	30%
Supplies & Other	$9,000	5%
Departmental Profit	$18,000	10%
Allocated Admin & Overhead	$36,000	20%
Net Departmental Loss	**($18,000)**	**-10%**

The restaurant was losing money. A scorekeeper would recommend closure. A business partner accountant would investigate further.

The Accounting Lens: Menu Engineering and Prime Cost Analysis

Rather than accepting the aggregate numbers, the accounting team performed a granular analysis, starting with menu engineering, which is a technique that analyzes each menu item's contribution to profitability. Research demonstrates that menu engineering provides an integrated management tool combining principles of managerial accounting, marketing analytics, and behavioral economics, with systematic application contributing to improved restaurant profitability without significant operational cost increases (Ivanenko, 2025).

Menu engineering analysis involves evaluating each menu item's popularity (sales volume) and profitability (contribution margin), then classifying items into four categories: Stars (high popularity and profitability), Plowhorses (high popularity but low profitability), Puzzles (low popularity but high profitability), and Dogs (low popularity and low profitability) (Hidayat & Suyasa, 2024).

The analysis revealed stark variance across the menu:

High-Performing Items:

- Salmon Entrée: $28 price, $8 food cost, $5 direct labor, $15 contribution per item, sold 240 times/month
- Chicken Breast Entrée: $22 price, $5 food cost, $4 direct labor, $13 contribution per item, sold 380 times/month

Low-Performing Items:

- Beef Ribeye Entrée: $38 price, $18 food cost, $6 direct labor, $14 contribution per item, but only 95 times/month
- Signature Pasta: $16 price, $7 food cost, $4 direct labor, $5 contribution per item, sold 210 times/month (lower quality signal)

Beyond menu pricing, the analysis revealed operational waste. The Ribeye, despite strong contribution per item, was plated inconsistently. Some plates featured 8-ounce portions; others, 12-ounce portions. The inconsistency in portion control meant that the restaurant was sometimes giving away its margin.

Prime cost analysis:

Examining food cost plus direct labor cost as a percentage of revenue revealed an even more concerning pattern. For the restaurant overall, prime cost was 75%

($81,000 + $54,000 = $135,000 ÷ $180,000). But this obscured departmental variation:

- During breakfast service (low-volume, staff-intensive), prime cost exceeded 85%
- During lunch service (moderate volume, established routines), prime cost was 70%
- During dinner service (highest volume, full staffing), prime cost was 72%

The breakfast service, despite theoretical potential for revenue generation from hotel guests, was operationally challenged.

The analysis also examined labor scheduling. The restaurant maintained fixed staffing levels across all service periods, not proportionally adjusting for volume variation. During slow periods, the same number of servers, kitchen staff, and support personnel remained on duty, creating inefficiency.

The Intervention: Menu Redesign and Operational Restructuring

Based on this analysis, management implemented a comprehensive intervention employing menu engineering strategies documented in recent hospitality research. Studies demonstrate that incorporating menu engineering principles enables restaurants to identify areas for cost control and revenue optimization (Mashige et al., 2025).

Menu Restructuring:

1. Repositioned the signature Pasta dish (the lower-value item), either reducing its portion size and dropping its price to $12 (converting it into a lower-revenue but more-profitable appetizer category) or removing it entirely.
2. Expanded the Salmon and Chicken offerings, recognizing their superior contribution profitability.
3. Redesigned the Ribeye presentation, implementing strict portion control and using a higher-margin preparation style that reduced food waste.
4. Introduced a Prix Fixe "Chef's Special" pricing model during slower service periods, optimizing revenue for the anticipated demand pattern.

Operational Changes:

1. Restructured breakfast service into a simplified operation—eliminating full-menu availability during breakfast and replacing it with a limited, high-contribution breakfast menu.

2. Implemented dynamic labor scheduling, varying staffing levels based on historical covers forecasts.
3. Introduced standardized recipes and portion-control tools to reduce waste variance.
4. Cross-trained some line kitchen staff on point-of-sale and inventory management to improve accountability.

Results: The Transformation

Six months after implementation, the restaurant's financials had transformed dramatically:

Figure 2. Restaurant P&L Summary (Month) - Post-Intervention

Line Item	Amount	% of Revenue
Revenue	$190,000	100%
Food Costs	$76,050	40%
Beverage Costs	$18,050	9.5%
Direct Labor	$47,500	25%
Supplies & Other	$8,000	4%
Departmental Profit	$40,400	21.3%
Allocated Admin & Overhead	$36,000	19%
Net Departmental Profit	**$4,400**	**2.3%**

The intervention generated a 15% improvement in departmental profit (from $18,000 to $40,400), moved the restaurant from a loss position to profitability, and accomplished this without raising guest-facing prices on most items. Revenue increased modestly from improved mix, but the real driver was improved cost efficiency. Research on menu performance analysis confirms that applying multiple analysis models simultaneously enables in-depth analysis of profitability and identification of strategies to improve menu performance. Examples of these models include but are not limited to the Kasavana-Smith Menu Engineering Matrix, Miller's Menu Analysis, and Pavesic's Cost-Margin Model (Gomes et al., 2025).

More importantly, the analysis revealed what had actually been problematic: not low sales (sales were actually respectable at $180,000/month), but rather un-managed waste and poor labor scheduling. These operational failures were buried within aggregate financial metrics until accounting analysis interrogated the data and revealed the underlying story. Time-driven activity-based costing research demonstrates that associating labor costs with specific food production activities provides more detailed understanding of idle capacities and labor productivity than traditional methods (Enes & Koşan, 2024).

The Broader Lesson

This case study illustrates why integrated financial and managerial accounting matters so profoundly. Without managerial accounting analysis, management would have closed the restaurant based on a departmental loss. This decision would have eliminated $135,000 in monthly contribution margin and worsened property profitability. With holistic financial analysis and operational understanding, management identified and corrected the specific operational failures that were destroying value.

The restaurant's improvement also illustrates a critical principle: financial problems are almost always operational problems. They manifest in the numbers, but their roots lie in operations. Effective use of accounting information requires the discipline to dig beneath the aggregate metrics, understand operational reality, and connect financial symptoms to operational causes.

CASE STUDY 2: FOOD WASTE MANAGEMENT AND COST CONTROL OPTIMIZATION IN A LUXURY RESORT

The Problem

The Grand Palm Resort, a 400-room luxury property in a tropical destination, operated an extensive food and beverage operation spanning a main kitchen, three specialty restaurants, a swimming pool café, and in-room dining. Despite generating $2.8 million in F&B revenue annually, the property was struggling with its food cost percentage, which had climbed to 38% of revenue. This represents performance significantly above the industry standard of 32-34% for luxury resorts. More troubling, management had no clear visibility into where waste was occurring or how much food was being discarded.

The property's executive chef reported that the purchasing department was ordering based on historical patterns rather than actual demand forecasts, and no systematic tracking existed for food waste. The executive team suspected that the F&B operation was losing profitability not through pricing problems (rates were competitive) but through operational inefficiency.

The Financial Challenge

At $2.8 million in annual F&B revenue with a 38% food cost percentage, the property was spending $1.064 million on food costs annually. Using industry standards, they should have been at $902,000 (32% of revenue), representing a $162,000 annual opportunity. Additionally, waste disposal costs were running $18,000 annually, and disposal represented a non-revenue-generating expense that compounded the problem.

The challenge was multifaceted: Hotels implementing structured food waste management strategies such as a FIFO costing systems, just-in-time procurement systems, and flexible menu planning, can achieve significant food cost efficiency and support sustainability principles through the Triple Bottom Line approach (economic, environmental, and social).

The Accounting Analysis: Identifying Waste Points

Rather than accepting the aggregate 38% food cost figure, the accounting team conducted a detailed waste audit and procurement analysis. Research on food procurement procedures demonstrates that ineffective food cost control processes, inadequate quality checks on received goods, and non-compliant storage practices contribute significantly to increased food costs, with some properties experiencing food cost percentages exceeding 36%, well above standards of 34.58%.

The analysis involved three key phases:

Phase 1: Waste Identification and Quantification

Working with the executive chef and kitchen staff, the team conducted a one-week intensive waste tracking exercise. Using digital scales at the point of discard, they measured waste from each kitchen area:

- **Preparation waste** (vegetable trim, spoilage, trim): 45 kg/day
- **Spoilage and expiration losses** (food stored beyond usability): 28 kg/day
- **Plate waste** (guest-returned food): 12 kg/day
- **Production error waste** (incorrect preparations, over-production): 18 kg/day
- **Total daily waste**: 103 kg/day, or approximately 37,595 kg/year

At an average cost per kilogram of $2.85, this waste represented approximately $107,000 annually in pure loss.

Phase 2: Procurement and Receiving Procedures Assessment

The accounting team reviewed procurement procedures and found significant gaps: Research on food procurement with cluster discounts demonstrates that collaborative purchasing arrangements can reduce food costs significantly while maintaining ingredient quality and supporting operational standards. Additionally, sustainable procurement initiatives that prioritize local products, apply stringent supplier selection criteria, and minimize single-use plastics have proven effective in keeping food and beverage expenses within acceptable limits while advancing environmental stewardship (Yoga et al., 2025). These procedures include:

- Purchase orders were submitted without clear demand forecasts
- Receiving procedures lacked quality inspection protocols
- Food storage did not consistently follow FIFO principles
- Inventory turnover metrics were not monitored

Phase 3: Root Cause Analysis

Through detailed analysis, three primary problems emerged:

1. **Demand forecasting failures** (35% of waste): The kitchen was preparing dishes based on "typical" demands without accounting for seasonal variations, group bookings, or weather patterns.
2. **Supplier and specification issues** (28% of waste): Some suppliers were delivering inconsistent quality, requiring rejection. Additionally, order quantities didn't align with shelf life for certain perishables.
3. **Operational deficiencies** (37% of waste): Overcooking during prep periods, poor portion controls, and inadequate staff training on waste reduction contributed significantly.

The Intervention: Comprehensive Food Waste Management Program

Based on this analysis, the resort implemented a multi-faceted intervention. Research demonstrates that artificial intelligence technologies significantly reduce food waste through improved inventory control, personalized menu planning, and automated waste tracking, with real-time monitoring enabling swift corrective actions (Vukolić et al., 2025). This is particularly true when these systems target inventory management, process automation, and waste tracking.

Strategic Initiatives Implemented:

1. **Demand Forecasting System**
   - o Integrated booking system data with kitchen planning
   - o Implemented weekly demand forecasts based on occupancy, event schedules, and historical patterns
   - o Adjusted prep quantities based on forecasts rather than historical averages
2. **Procurement Optimization**
   - o Established just-in-time procurement for highly perishable items
   - o Renegotiated supplier contracts to include quality guarantees and appropriate order quantities
   - o Implemented supplier cluster purchasing to reduce per-unit costs (through a purchasing consortium with other luxury properties)
3. **Inventory Management**
   - o Implemented FIFO inventory discipline with staff training
   - o Established shelf-life tracking for all perishables
   - o Created a "salvage menu" to utilize items nearing their expiration dates
4. **Employee Training and Accountability**
   - o Conducted kitchen staff training on portion control and waste reduction
   - o Implemented daily waste tracking reports
   - o Tied annual bonuses partially to waste reduction targets
5. **Menu Redesign for Waste Reduction**
   - o Reformulated menus to reduce preparation waste through vegetable selection
   - o Created standardized portions to reduce cutting waste
   - o Developed sustainable uses for preparation byproducts (vegetable stocks, etc.)

Results: Financial Transformation

Within nine months of implementation:
Waste Reduction:

- Daily waste declined from 103 kg to 38 kg (63% reduction)
- Annual food waste decreased from 37,595 kg to 13,870 kg
- Financial value of waste reduced from $107,000 to $39,500 annually ($67,500 annual savings)

Food Cost Improvement: - Food cost percentage declined from 38% to 31.8% of revenue - Actual food costs fell from $1.064 million to $890,400 annually - Total food cost reduction: $173,600 annually

Figure 3. Cost Structure Changes:

Metric	Before	After	Change
Food cost %	38.0%	31.8%	-6.2 pts
Waste disposal costs	$18,000	$6,500	-63.9%
Procurement efficiency	85%	96%	+12.9%
Food cost per revenue $	$0.380	$0.318	-16.3%
Actual waste (kg/year)	37,595	13,870	-63.1%

Overall Impact: The combined initiatives generated approximately **$184,000 in annual cost savings** without reducing service quality or guest satisfaction. The property accomplished this through operational excellence and financial rigor rather than compromising on guest experience.

The Broader Strategic Insight

This case demonstrates a crucial principle in hospitality financial management: Structured interventions including enhanced staff education, improved portion management strategies, and active guest engagement are essential for reducing food waste in the tourism sector (Evliyağolu et al., 2025). Moreover,the food waste hierarchy serves as an important strategy for hotels, helping them reduce food waste at the generation point while reducing food costs and protecting the environment through structured integration of food distribution processes (Srijuntrapun et **al., 2022**).

The restaurant's success also illustrates the power of integrated financial and operational management. The problem was never purely financial, meaning you cannot account away waste. Instead, waste elimination required:

- Understanding the operational root causes through detailed analysis
- Connecting financial metrics to operational behaviors
- Implementing systematic controls and monitoring
- Building accountability throughout the organization
- Recognizing that small operational improvements compound into significant financial results

The accounting analysis provided the diagnostic foundation, but the operational implementation delivered the value.

CASE STUDY 3: REVENUE MANAGEMENT AND DYNAMIC PRICING STRATEGY FOR SEASONAL DEMAND OPTIMIZATION

The Problem

The Metropolitan Hotel, a 180-room mid-scale urban property in a business district, faced a classic hospitality challenge: significant fluctuations in occupancy and revenue between peak and low seasons. During the week, with business travelers, the property maintained 85%+ occupancy at strong average daily rates (ADR). But weekends and seasonal valleys created significant capacity underutilization, with occupancy dropping to 35-45% during slow periods.

Despite strong revenue during peak periods, the property's overall annual profitability was limited by its inability to effectively manage pricing during low-demand periods. The property's General Manager knew that simply reducing rates to fill rooms often just reduced profitability without significantly improving occupancy. Yet maintaining high rates during low-demand periods meant empty rooms and lost revenue.

The Financial Challenge

The property's core financial metrics revealed the challenge:

Current Pricing Model (Static ADR):

- Weekday ADR (Business): $165
- Weekend ADR (Leisure): $125
- Annual occupancy: 62%
- Annual room revenue: $6.6 million
- Annual operating profit: $1.2 million

The challenge was mathematical: At 62% occupancy, the property was leaving 180 rooms × 0.38 (empty rate) × 365 days = 24,990 room nights unsold annually. Even if repositioning these rooms at a lower rate but higher contribution margin could increase occupancy and overall profit, management lacked a framework for optimal pricing decisions.

The Analytical Foundation: Break-Even and CVP Analysis

The accounting team conducted a detailed break-even and contribution margin analysis to understand the dynamics:

Room Department Cost Structure (Monthly):

- Fixed costs (housekeeping staff, maintenance, utilities): $95,000/month - Variable cost per occupied room (linens, toiletries, etc.): $22/room
- Current room revenue: $550,000/month (at 62% occupancy × $145 average ADR)

Contribution Margin Analysis:

At current pricing and occupancy:

- Occupancy: 62% (average 111.6 rooms/night)
- Average ADR: $145 - Variable cost per room: $22
- Contribution per room: $123
- Monthly contribution: 111.6 × $123 × 30 = $411,948
- Fixed costs: $95,000 - Monthly profit: $316,948

Break-Even Analysis:

Break-even occupancy = Fixed costs ÷ (Contribution per room × Rooms × Days) = $95,000 ÷ ($123 × 180 × 1) = $95,000 ÷ $22,140 = 4.3% occupancy (or 7.7 rooms/night)

This revealed a critical insight: The property could generate significant losses before reaching break-even. However, more importantly, it showed the sensitivity of profitability to both pricing and occupancy:

Scenario Analysis:

If the property reduced ADR by 10% (to $130.50) during low-demand periods but achieved 70% occupancy (vs. current 62%), what would happen?

- New occupancy: 70% (126 rooms/night)
- New ADR: $130.50 (blended: 65% at $145 weekday + 35% at $110 weekend)
- Contribution per room: ($130.50 - $22) = $108.50
- Monthly contribution: 126 × $108.50 × 30 = $410,130

Result: Nearly identical monthly contribution ($410,130 vs. $411,948), but with 14.4 additional occupied rooms nightly. This scenario analysis demonstrated that moderate rate reductions could maintain profitability while improving occupancy.

The Challenge: Dynamic Pricing Strategy Development

Rather than continuing with static pricing, management recognized the need for (Mei, 2026) dynamic pricing strategies driven by deep reinforcement learning and advanced analytics, which integrate real-time data streams with predictive analytics to create responsive pricing systems. More practically, research demonstrates that dynamic pricing significantly increases hotel room occupancy and revenue by analyzing specific dates and times when occupancy is expected to peak (Hidayati et al., 2025).

The accounting team helped develop a comprehensive dynamic pricing framework: Hotels adopting dynamic pricing based on real-time demand, market segmentation, and targeted promotions (e.g. corporate travel packages, repeat guest discounts, etc.) optimize revenue while managing the challenges of rate parity across distribution channels and customer satisfaction (Dornyoh et al., 2026).

Implementation: Four-Tier Dynamic Pricing Model

Tier 1: Peak Season Pricing (Monday-Thursday, high occupancy forecast: 80%+)

- ADR: $165 (maintain existing rate)
- Target: Maximize per-room revenue
- Customer segment: Business travelers, corporate accounts

Tier 2: Strong Demand Pricing (Friday-Sunday, moderate occupancy forecast: 65-80%)

- ADR: $135
- Target: Optimize revenue while stimulating weekend leisure demand
- Customer segment: Mixed business/leisure

Tier 3: Moderate Demand Pricing (Off-peak weekdays, occupancy forecast: 45-65%)

- ADR: $110
- Target: Fill rooms with positive contribution margin
- Customer segment: Leisure travelers, extended-stay guests

Tier 4: Low-Demand Pricing (Seasonal valleys, occupancy forecast: <45%)

- ADR: $95

- Target: Maximize occupancy while maintaining positive contribution margin
- Customer segment: Deep-discount seekers, package deals

Pricing Logic: For each tier, the contribution margin per room remained above the break-even threshold of $73 (variable cost of $22 + required contribution of $51 to cover per-room share of fixed costs). By maintaining positive contribution margin even in the most aggressive pricing tier, every occupied room improved overall profitability compared to leaving it empty.

Advanced Revenue Management: Overbooking and Length-of-Stay Control

Beyond basic dynamic pricing, the team implemented additional revenue management techniques: Research on hotel revenue stream profitability reveals that while different departments contribute differently to overall profitability, integrated revenue management and cost control strategies tailored to each revenue stream optimize overall financial performance (Bhattacharya, 2025).

Overbooking Strategy:

Historical data showed a 7% cancellation rate. By overbooking by 6-8% during high-demand periods, the property could fill more rooms while accounting for cancellations. Careful overbooking calculations ensured that walk-outs (unavoidable room denials due to overbooking) remained below 2%, while still capturing the incremental rooms that cancellations would otherwise leave empty.

Length-of-Stay (LOS) Controls:

Rather than accepting any booking regardless of length of stay, the property implemented inventory controls:

- Peak periods: Minimum 2-night stay (maximizes rate and occupancy)
- Strong demand: 1-night minimum (fills rooms at good rates)
- Moderate demand: No minimum (fills rooms at any length)
- Low demand: Encourage longer stays through tiered pricing

Integration with Capital Allocation Decisions

The financial analysis also informed capital investment decisions. Value chain-oriented cost control approaches in hotels reveal that cross-departmental collaboration contributes 1.7 times more to total-factor productivity than isolated technological investment (Han, 2025).

The hotel invested in:

- **Revenue management software** ($80,000): Automated pricing optimization and inventory management
- **Guest analytics system** ($45,000): Tracked customer behavior, lifetime value, and segment profitability
- **Dynamic rate display system** ($15,000): Updated rates in real-time across all channels
- **Total investment**: $140,000

Results: Revenue Optimization Without Price Increases

Over a 12-month period following implementation:

Figure 4. Occupancy Improvements:

Metric	Before	After	Change
Annual occupancy	62%	71%	+9 percentage points
Avg occupied rooms/night	111.6	127.8	+16.2 rooms
Annual room nights sold	40,734	46,647	+5,913

Figure 5. Revenue Changes:

Metric	Before	After	Change
Annual room revenue	$6,600,000	$7,156,000	+$556,000 (+8.4%)
Average ADR	$162	$153	-$9 (-5.6%)
RevPAR	$100.50	$108.85	+$8.35 (+8.3%)

Profit Impact: The increase in occupancy from 62% to 71% generated additional monthly contribution margin:

Additional occupied rooms: 16.2/night Average contribution per room: $108 (blended across all pricing tiers)

Additional monthly contribution: 16.2 × $108 × 30 = $52,488

Less: Additional variable costs already accounted for: $0 (already in contribution margin calculation)

Net additional monthly profit: $52,488 Annual profit improvement: **$629,856**

Cost of implementation: $140,000 Payback period: 2.67 months First-year net benefit: $489,856

Customer Satisfaction and Loyalty Considerations

One potential risk with aggressive dynamic pricing is customer resentment if pricing appears arbitrary or unfair. Research on ethical considerations in revenue management reveals that while dynamic pricing and price discrimination are powerful tools, they can negatively impact perceived fairness, customer satisfaction, and loyalty if not implemented carefully (Hristov et al., 2023). Hotel managers must identify and define strategies to prevent and mitigate guest dissatisfaction from pricing manipulations. In this case, the following was implemented:

1. **Transparent communication**: Guests understood that rates varied based on demand, similar to airlines
2. **Loyalty rewards**: Frequent guests received rate guarantees or upgrades
3. **Value bundling**: Lower-priced packages included value-added services (breakfast, parking) rather than appearing as "cheap" rooms
4. **Advance booking discounts**: Guests booking 14+ days in advance received predictable discounts

Guest satisfaction metrics remained stable despite lower weekend rates, and overall guest loyalty actually improved due to the expanded market reaching new customer segments.

Strategic Insights and Broader Implications

This case illustrates several critical principles in hospitality financial management:

First, the mathematical reality of fixed costs: The role of artificial intelligence in revenue management and pricing strategies significantly enhances hotel financial performance and operational efficiency through improved demand forecasting and dynamic pricing, leading to increased revenue per available room (RevPAR) and average daily rates (ADR) (Gatera, 2024).

When fixed costs are substantial (as they are in hospitality), occupancy rates matter more than rate premiums. Filling 71% of rooms at $153 ADR generates more profit than filling 62% of rooms at $162 ADR. This is true even when the per-room rate is lower.

Second, the importance of contribution margin thinking: The property could safely reduce rates because each room still generated positive contribution margin toward covering fixed costs. This margin-based thinking prevents the common error of refusing to sell capacity because the selling price is below full average cost (which includes allocated fixed costs).

Third, the power of integrated analysis: The solution required combining three analytical tools: break-even analysis (to understand the fixed cost burden), CVP analysis (to model scenarios), and revenue management principles (to understand how pricing and volume interact). None of these alone would have been sufficient.

Fourth, the need for ongoing monitoring and adjustment: Dynamic pricing is not "set it and forget it." The system required continuous monitoring of:

- Booking pace relative to forecasts
- Competitive pricing in the market
- Customer mix and segment profitability
- Occupancy vs. profit trade-offs

The property's accounting system was reconfigured to provide real-time reporting on these metrics, enabling rapid adjustments to pricing strategies as market conditions changed.

COST-VOLUME-PROFIT ANALYSIS AND STRATEGIC PRICING DECISIONS

Beyond analyzing historical performance, managerial accountants help hospitality leaders make forward-looking decisions about pricing, service offerings, and operational structure. Cost-Volume-Profit (CVP) analysis provides a framework for this decision-making. Research on CVP analysis for pricing determination reveals that accurate cost-volume-profit analysis enables companies to calculate total costs, products, and expected profits for future periods, supporting optimal managerial performance (Nababan et al., 2025).

In hospitality, CVP analysis often centers on pricing strategy questions. Consider a luxury resort evaluating its conference and meeting business. The conference center has significant fixed costs (staff, facilities maintenance, utilities) and variable costs (catering, audiovisual support, laundry). Management is considering a pricing strategy change: reduce conference room rental rates by 15% to increase volume, betting that incremental volume will more than offset the rate reduction.

CVP analysis helps evaluate this decision quantitatively:

Current State:

- Conference room rental revenue: $500,000/month
- Banquet catering revenue: $300,000/month

- Total variable costs: 40% of revenue = $320,000/month
- Departmental contribution margin: 60% of revenue = $480,000/month
- Fixed costs: $200,000/month
- Departmental profit: $280,000/month

Proposed Strategy (Assuming 25% Volume Growth):

Conference room rental revenue: $425,000/month (15% rate reduction) × 1.25 (25% volume growth) = $531,250

Banquet catering revenue: $300,000 × 1.25 = $375,000

Total revenue: $906,250

Total variable costs: 40% of revenue = $362,500

Departmental contribution margin: 60% of revenue = $543,750

Fixed costs: $200,000/month (assuming no increase)

Departmental profit: $343,750/month

The CVP analysis shows that the pricing reduction, if it achieves 25% volume growth, would increase departmental profit from $280,000 to $343,750. This represents a 23% improvement. This justifies the strategy. However, if volume increases only 15%, the profit improvement shrinks to $305,000 (9% improvement), still positive but far less compelling. If volume increases less than 10%, the strategy could erode profitability.

The analytical framework thus allows management to evaluate: At what volume growth rate does this pricing strategy break even (i.e., maintain current profitability)? The calculation proceeds:

Required revenue = $906,250 needed to generate prior profit of $280,000

$280,000 = (Required revenue × 60% contribution margin) - $200,000 fixed costs $480,000 = Required revenue × 60% Required revenue = $800,000

This means that the pricing reduction needs to generate $800,000 in revenue to maintain prior profitability. Given that current revenue is $800,000 monthly, the pricing reduction needs approximately 12% volume growth to break even.

This analysis transforms what might have been an intuitive decision ("We should reduce rates to grow volume") into a disciplined forecast: "We believe rate reduction will drive volume growth. We need at least 12% volume growth to break even financially. Do we believe the market will respond with at least 12% volume growth? What evidence supports this?"

THE FUTURE OF FINANCIAL THINKING: INTEGRATION, LITERACY, AND LEADERSHIP

The final challenge facing modern hospitality organizations is ensuring that financial literacy becomes a core leadership trait throughout the organization. The integration of financial and managerial accounting is not simply a technical accounting matter; it is fundamentally a leadership and culture issue. Research on Big Data integration into managerial accounting decision-making reveals that while data analytics significantly enhance forecasting accuracy and responsiveness, effective implementation is hindered by skill gaps among accounting professionals, fragmented systems, and lack of cultural readiness (Uyun, 2025).

Too often, financial thinking is siloed within the accounting department. Operations leaders focus on guests, service, and logistics. Revenue management teams focus on pricing and demand. Human resources teams focus on recruitment, training, and retention. Finance operates separately, reporting results but disconnected from strategic decision-making. This fragmentation wastes the organization's most valuable resource: integrated information about how operational decisions create financial outcomes.

This fragmented approach is increasingly untenable. Research on sustainable cost management and managerial accounting innovations demonstrates that organizations embracing integrated approaches. These approaches include combining advanced costing methodologies like Activity-Based Costing (ABC) and Environmental Management Accounting (EMA) with strategic frameworks like the Balanced Scorecard. Doing so effectively integrate sustainability goals with business objectives, promoting long-term financial and environmental benefits (Hossain & Hasan, 2024).

The future of hospitality organizations depends on financial literacy becoming distributed throughout leadership. A General Manager must understand not just what their property's labor cost percentage is, but how operational decisions (staffing levels, service model, training investments) drive that metric. A Director of Sales must understand not just how to maximize revenue, but the cost implications of different revenue-generating strategies. A Director of Engineering must understand how maintenance quality and proactive investment decisions create value through extended equipment life and improved guest satisfaction.

This distributed financial literacy doesn't require every leader to have accounting expertise. It requires understanding several key concepts: fixed versus variable costs, contribution margins, break-even thinking, and the flow-through impact of decisions. With this foundation, leaders throughout the organization can evaluate decisions not just on operational merit, but on financial impact.

The path to this financial literacy requires investment. Many hospitality organizations lack the depth of managerial accounting analysis discussed in this chapter.

Implementing robust CVP analysis, menu engineering, and contribution margin analysis requires analytical capability that many properties don't currently possess. Developing this capability requires either hiring specialized talent or developing existing team members through training and mentoring. Additionally, organizations must invest in information systems capable of providing real-time financial data and analytics dashboards. Research on dashboard-driven decision-making reveals that organizations balancing dashboard functionality with usability, while prioritizing training and governance, maximize benefits of dashboard-driven decision-making and achieve enhanced operational efficiency and competitive advantage.

Yet this investment pays dividends. Properties that develop strong financial analysis capabilities consistently outperform competitors, not because they operate in better markets or have more guests, but because they make better decisions (Metwalli, 2025). They recognize which guests are most profitable, which service offerings create the most value, which cost reductions matter most, and which investments create the greatest returns.

CONCLUSION: BRIDGING THE GAP, CREATING VALUE

The central premise of this chapter is straightforward but profound: hospitality organizations that integrate financial and managerial accounting into their decision-making processes create significantly more value than those that treat accounting as a compliance function. Research on cost management and strategic decision-making demonstrates that organizations adopting advanced cost management techniques enhance cost information accuracy, facilitating more informed strategic decisions regarding pricing, product mix, and process improvements (Susilowati, 2023).

The practical tools exist. USALI provides a standardized framework for comparing financial performance. Cost-volume-profit analysis enables rigorous evaluation of pricing and operational decisions. Contribution margin analysis guides resource allocation. Menu engineering identifies which offerings drive profitability. Flow-through analysis captures the bottom-line impact of operational changes.

Yet tools are only valuable if they're properly understood and applied. Many hospitality organizations have sophisticated accounting systems but limited analytical use of the data. The accountants can generate reports, but the reports don't drive decisions. Financial data are available, but the business-relevant interpretations remain hidden beneath the surface of aggregate numbers.

The transformation from this current state to a future where financial data actively guide strategic decision-making requires three elements:

First, a clear understanding of what financial data actually means. Numbers without interpretation are merely noise. The skills to translate labor cost percentages into questions about productivity and service standards, to convert food cost metrics into menu engineering insights, and to convert contribution margin analysis into resource allocation decisions must be developed and distributed throughout leadership. Integration of Big Data and Business Intelligence technologies enables more timely anomaly detection, performance prediction, and strategic recommendations while minimizing human error risk. However, this only takes place when organizations prepare digital roadmaps including HR training, information system audits, and data protection policies with top management commitment (Narulita et al., 2025).

Second, the discipline to interrogate the data. When a metric seems outside expected range, the business partner accountant asks “Why?” They dig beneath aggregate numbers to find departmental patterns, they analyze variance over time, and they connect financial symptoms to operational causes. Research on environmental management accounting for strategic decision-making reveals that organizations initially adopting EMA for legitimacy gradually recognize its benefits in guiding proactive, solution-oriented managerial decisions (Swalih et al., 2024). This demonstrates that iterative refinement of analytical approaches enhance their strategic value.

Third, the willingness to act on financial insights. Understanding that a restaurant is unprofitable is insufficient; the insight must translate into operational change. Whether that change involves menu redesign, labor restructuring, pricing adjustment, or strategic repositioning depends on the specific situation. But understanding how financial and operational levers interact enables more confident decision-making.

The integration of financial and managerial accounting is ultimately about creating a culture where decisions are made with full appreciation of their financial implications. It's about recognizing that in a hotel, every number truly is an action, and every action creates a number. By closing the artificial gap between financial and managerial accounting, hospitality organizations position themselves to navigate an era of rising labor costs and inflationary pressures with greater confidence and effectiveness.

The opportunity lies not in new accounting tools. The opportunity lies in applying these tools with the rigor, creativity, and business focus that the modern hospitality environment demands. Characteristics of successful organizations include companies that embrace this integrated approach where financial accountants and managerial accountants work together to inform strategy, where operating leaders understand financial implications of their decisions, and where financial literacy is distributed throughout the organization. Those that maintain the artificial silos will increasingly struggle to compete.

REFERENCES

Avdylaj, A., & Asllanaj, R. (2023). The impact of accounting on business decision-making: A case study of the hotel industry in Kosovo. *Multidisciplinary Science Journal, 6*(6), 2024100. DOI: 10.31893/multiscience.2024100

Bhattacharya, A. (2025). A study on profitability analysis of different revenue streams in a hotel: Rooms, food and beverage (F&B), and events. *International Journal of Scientific Research in Engineering and Management, 9*(5), 1–9. DOI: 10.55041/IJSREM49057

Diavastis, I. E., Chrysafis, K. A., & Papadopoulou, G. C. (2024). Determinants of accounting information systems success: The case of the Greek hotel industry. *International Journal of Financial Studies, 12*(2), 42. DOI: 10.3390/ijfs12020042

Dornyoh, E., Moore, M. A., Yeboah, R., Ocloo, A. T., & Dacosta, F. D. (2026). The science and speculations driving revenue management decisions in hotels in Cape Coast. *International Journal of Hospitality & Tourism Management, 10*(1), 7–21. DOI: 10.11648/j.ijhtm.20261001.12

Enes, K., & Koşan, L. (2024). Using time-driven activity-based costing in restaurant business: Levelled application of a case study. *Heliyon, 10*(4), e25157. DOI: 10.1016/j.heliyon.2024.e25157 PMID: 38370254

Evliyaoğlu, G., Keskin, E., & Sert, A. N. (2025). The role of orange flag application in preventing food waste in tourism enterprises. Journal of multidisciplinary academic tourism, 10(2), 241-249.

Gatera, A. (2024). Role of artificial intelligence in revenue management and pricing strategies in hotels. *Journal of Modern Hospitality, 3*(2), 14–25. DOI: 10.47941/jmh.1957

Gomes, C., Malheiros, C., Lima Santos, L., & Campos, F. (2025). Ascertaining restaurant financial sustainability by analyzing menu performance. *Tourism and Hospitality, 6*(1), 47. DOI: 10.3390/tourhosp6010047

Han, X. (2025). Value Chain-Oriented Cost Control in Tourist Hotels: A Data-Driven Performance Evaluation Using DEA and AHP. [IJISSS]. *International Journal of Information Systems in the Service Sector, 16*(1), 1–15. DOI: 10.4018/IJISSS.397669

Harea, R., & Harea, R. (2025). Aspects regarding the accounting of tourism and hotel services. In Învă ământul superior contabil: Provocări i solu ii: Culegere de teze tiin ifice (pp. 105–107). Academia de Studii Economice din Moldova. DOI: 10.53486/isc2025.29

Hidayat, S. J., & Suyasa, I. G. W. (2024). Menu engineering analysis: An industrial reference for tourism students. *Proceeding of The International Global Tourism Science and Vocational Education*, 1(1), 43–62.

Hidayati, S., Nata, J. H., Reindrawati, D. Y., & Huda, M. N. (2025). The influence of dynamic pricing in enhancing room occupancy and room revenue in Bintan Island Resort. [The International Journal of Applied Business]. *TIJAB*, *9*(1), 38–50. DOI: 10.20473/tijab.v9.I1.2025.58812

Hossain, M. Z., & Hasan, L. (2024). Sustainable cost management and green business: The role of managerial accounting innovations. *European Modern Studies Journal*, *8*(4), 464–484. DOI: 10.59573/emsj.8(4).2024.24

Hristov, S. B., Đorđević, A., Kovačević, I., & Zečević, B. (2023). Ethical dilemmas as a result of the impact of revenue management on hotel guest behavior. *Marketing*, *54*(4), 258–263. DOI: 10.5937/mkng2304258H

Ivanenko, V. (2025). Menu engineering as an effective analytical tool for enhancing restaurant performance. Economics. Management. *Innovations*, *2*(37), 294–315.

Labanowski, L., Fracz, P., Wotzka, D., & Dabrowski, I. (2024). Studying The Interrelations Between USALI Parameters And GOP Through Wavelet Coherence Analysis. In ECMS (pp. 70-76). DOI: 10.7148/2024-0070

Labanowski, L., Fracz, P., Wotzka, D., & Foltys, J. (2024). Application Of The Nonlinear Autoregressive Model With Exogenous Inputs For Predicting The Gross Operating Product Based On USALI Data. In ECMS (pp. 77-83). DOI: 10.7148/2024-0077

Leonandri, D. G., & Erpurini, W. (2025). The Qualitative Study on the Use of Managerial Accounting Information in Resource Allocation Decision-Making in Hotels. JASa (Jurnal Akuntansi, Audit Dan Sistem Informasi Akuntansi), 9(1), 12-20.

Mashige, R., Hewson, D., & Mabaso, C. (2025). The influence of cultural cuisine on restaurant revenue: Implications for financial sustainability. *African Journal of Hospitality, Tourism and Leisure*, *5*(14), 989. DOI: 10.46222/ajhtl.19770720.685

Mei, Z. (2026). Dynamic pricing strategy driven by deep reinforcement learning with empirical analysis on the collaborative optimization of hotel revenue management and customer satisfaction. *International Journal of High Speed Electronics and Systems*, *35*(06), 2540865. DOI: 10.1142/S0129156425408654

Metwalli, M. Z. (2025). The Impact of Accounting Principles on Managerial Decision-Making in Small and Medium Enterprises. *International Journal of Accounting and Management Sciences*, *4*(3).

Nababan, D. R., Situmorang, E., & Zelmiyanti, R. (2025). An analysis of the implementation of the job costing method in pricing determination at PT Banana Cake. *Journal Research of Social Science, Economics, and Management*, *5*(4), 3954–3964. DOI: 10.59141/jrssem.v5i4.1180

Narulita, F. D., Baderi, R., & Hidayati, C. (2025). The use of Big Data and business intelligence in management accounting decision making. *Journal of Advances in Accounting, Economics, and Management*, *2*(4), 1–18. DOI: 10.47134/aaem.v2i4.706

Nedzvedskyi, Y., Baneva, I., Kushniruk, V., Velychko, O., & Cherven, I. (2024). Financial planning and budget management in hospitality and dining establishments: Navigating the financial landscape of the hotel and restaurant sector.

Nugraha, A. J. A., & Arifin, B. M. E. (2023). Financial and Cost-Volume-Profit Models in Developing a Hotel. Journal of Economics. *Management and Trade*, *29*(12), 81–89.

Nunes, C. R., & Machado, M. J. C. V. (2020). Benchmarking in the hotel industry: The use of USALI. *International Journal of Process Management and Benchmarking*, *10*(3), 382–396. DOI: 10.1504/IJPMB.2020.107939

Pajrok, A. (2022). Issue of allocation of overheads-the practice of the Hungarian hotel industry= Питання розподілу накладних витрат-практика готельної індустрії Угорщини= Általános költségek felosztásának kérdésköre-a magyar szállodaipar gyakorlata. *ACTA ACADEMIAE BEREGSASIENSIS-ECONOMICS*, (1), 297–311. DOI: 10.58423/2786-6742/2022-1-297-311

Rafi, M. I. A., Aprelianingrum, A., Indraswari, S. A. D. T., Erong, E. A. E., Wicaksono, F., Putriani, A. A. Y., & Yovita, M. (2025). Hubungan Cost Estimation Reliability, Sales Volume Forecasting, Dan Cost Structure Flexibility Terhadap Keberhasilan Cost-Volume-Profit Analysis Sebagai Alat Perencanaan: The Relationship of Cost Estimation Reliability, Sales Volume Forecasting, and Cost Structure Flexibility to the Success of Cost-Volume-Profit Analysis as a Planning Tool. Citizen. *Jurnal Ilmiah Multidisiplin Indonesia*, *5*(6), 1680–1689.

Sari, M. P., & Wibowo, W. A. (2025). Empirical analysis of hotel strategic management accounting practices. *Advances in Accounting Innovation*, *1*(2), 167–177. DOI: 10.69725/aai.v1i2.192

Shakya, J. (2025). Cost-volume-profit analysis for profit planning and control in hospitality industry: A study of Aloft, Kathmandu, Thamel. *MVIC Journal of Management and Information Technology*, *1*(1), 63–76. DOI: 10.3126/mvicjmit.v1i1.77320

Srijuntrapun, P., Sukwong, P., & Marshall, A. (2022). The role of food waste hierarchy as Thai hotels seek to fulfill their corporate social responsibility. *Heliyon, 8*(10), e11201. DOI: 10.1016/j.heliyon.2022.e11201 PMID: 36303920

Susilowati, E. (2023). Cost management and strategic decision making: The role of managerial accounting. Atestasi. *Jurnal Ilmiah Akuntansi, 6*(1), 457–473.

Suwandi, S., Manurung, R., & Ibrokhimov, N. (2024). The role of managerial accounting information in enhancing financial performance and decision-making of micro enterprises. Harmoni Economics. *International Journal of Economics and Accounting, 1*(1), 1–10.

Swalih, M. M., Ram, R., & Tew, E. (2024). Environmental management accounting for strategic decision-making: A systematic literature review. *Business Strategy and the Environment, 33*(7), 6335–6367. DOI: 10.1002/bse.3828

Uyun, L. (2025). The role of big data in managerial accounting decision-making: A literature review. Count: Journal of Accounting. *Business and Management, 3*(2), 78–88.

Vukolić, D., Gajić, T., Cabral, Ó., Veljović, S., & Knežević, S. (2025). Revolutionizing the hospitality industry: The impact of AI technologies on efficient food management and reduction of food waste. Journal of Tourism Futures, 1-29.

Zhyvko, Z., Rodchenko, S., & Holovach, T. (2023). EFFECTIVENESS OF INFORMATION SUPPORT FOR MANAGERIAL COLLABORATION AMONG HOSPITALITY INDUSTRY ENTERPRISES. Economics. *Finance and Management Review*, (4), 108–123.

Chapter 3
From Fixed Costs to Dynamic Revenues:
Financial Structure and Earnings Logic in Contemporary Hotel Operations

Rismawati Rismawati
http://orcid.org/0000-0001-8046-6764
Universitas Muhammadiyah Palopo, Indonesia

Whedy Prasetyo
http://orcid.org/0009-0000-8772-5634
Universitas Jember, Indonesia

Mohammad Azizurrohman
http://orcid.org/0000-0002-8559-5685
Sekolah Tinggi Pariwisata Mataram, Indonesia

Husmaruddin Husmaruddin
Universitas Muhammadiyah Palopo, Indonesia

ABSTRACT

This chapter elucidates that modern hotel profitability relies not solely on revenue augmentation but also on a "earnings logic" that facilitates the transformation of dynamic revenues into earnings, given the constraints of perishable capacity, elevated fixed-cost intensity, and asymmetric cost adjustment. It incorporates three interrelated systems: (1) cost and financial architecture (operating leverage and cost stickiness), (2) revenue architecture (pricing, segmentation, and multi-channel distribution economics), and (3) measurement coherence (USALI-oriented internal

DOI: 10.4018/979-8-3373-9479-4.ch003

reporting aligned with IFRS 15 judgments regarding bundles and principal-agent considerations). The chapter offers a decision-useful managerial guide that focuses on break-even analysis, flexible budgeting, net-contribution governance by channel and segment, and a reconciliation framework to avoid conflicting performance indicators in bundled and intermediated transactions.

1. INTRODUCTION

Hotel profitability operates under a structural paradox: revenue can rise while earnings fall. Unlike many service businesses, hotels commit large amounts of capital before a single room is sold. Property costs, core staffing contracts, and service infrastructure persist whether occupancy stands at 30% or 90%. When demand fluctuates and in hospitality it always does the cost base responds sluggishly while revenues move sharply. The result is pronounced operating leverage: a given percentage shift in revenue translates into a disproportionately larger shift in operating profit.

This structural sensitivity has grown more complicated as hotel distribution has become more layered. Contemporary hotels sell through a mix of direct channels, loyalty programs, corporate accounts, and online travel agencies (OTAs). Each channel imposes its own acquisition costs, cancellation rates, and contractual constraints. Research consistently shows that OTA participation can sustain or lift occupancy-based metrics such as RevPAR, yet profitability outcomes vary substantially once commission costs, promotional discounts, and demand-management frictions are accounted for (O'Connor et al., 2025; Lima Santos et al., 2024). A property that appears to be recovering at the topline may simultaneously be experiencing margin erosion driven by distribution economics a distinction that standard gross performance metrics obscure.

To bridge this gap, this chapter develops an "earnings logic" framework for modern hotel operations. Earnings logic refers to the structured understanding of how three interdependent systems cost architecture, revenue configuration, and measurement design jointly determine whether and how hotel revenues convert into sustainable profits. The central argument is that hotels operating under high fixed-cost intensity must manage not just revenue volume but also the net contribution quality of that revenue, and must do so through measurement systems coherent enough to surface the true earnings implications of pricing, packaging, and channel decisions.

The chapter is deliberately bounded in scope. The discussion applies to full-service and select-service hotels where capacity-related fixed costs are substantial and where multi-channel distribution and bundled offerings are strategically significant. The chapter does not aim to cover all hospitality subsectors comprehensively, but to provide a focused analytical lens connecting revenue decisions to earnings outcomes. The intended audience is academics, graduate students, and practitioners in hotel finance, revenue management, and managerial accounting who want a coherent framework that goes beyond top-line metrics.

1.1 Chapter Objectives

This chapter aims to:

1. Explain how fixed-cost intensity and operating leverage create asymmetric earnings outcomes when demand fluctuates.
2. Demonstrate how channel economics can produce margin erosion even when RevPAR improves.
3. Show how misalignment between internal departmental reporting (USALI) and external revenue recognition (IFRS 15) distorts managerial decision-making in dynamic revenue environments.
4. Provide practical, decision-useful tools contribution thresholds, channel P&L logic, bundle allocation policies, and reconciliation frameworks to operationalize earnings-logic management.

2. BACKGROUND

2.1 Fixed-Cost Intensity, Operating Leverage, and Cost Stickiness

Hotels are often described as high-fixed-cost businesses, but the more precise and analytically useful concept is fixed-cost intensity: the degree to which capacity commitments property costs, core staffing, technology subscriptions, management fees persist regardless of short-term demand shifts. Under these conditions, operating leverage becomes the dominant driver of earnings sensitivity. A given percentage change in revenue translates into a larger percentage change in operating profit because a substantial portion of the cost base does not adjust proportionally with occupancy.

Empirical work on hotel financial performance confirms this dynamic. Kizildag et al. (2023) document how small lodging establishments with limited cost flexibility experienced severe earnings compression during the COVID-19 demand shock, while Cengiz et al. (2025) demonstrate that cost system sophistication-the ability to understand and manage cost behavior at a granular level-correlates meaningfully with hotel profitability. Broader management accounting evidence likewise suggests that management accounting system effectiveness becomes especially important when uncertainty makes performance interpretation difficult (Abu Afifa & Saleh, 2021). Demydyuk and Carlbäck (2024) provide further evidence that short-term pricing decisions made without adequate attention to cost structures can undermine long-term profitability, even when they appear to stabilize occupancy.

What is frequently underappreciated in practitioner discussions is that hotel costs are not simply fixed or variable but frequently exhibit stepwise, semi-variable, and sticky behavior. Costs often decline more slowly when activity falls than they rise when activity recovers a pattern driven by labor contract rigidity, minimum service commitments, and deliberate managerial choices to preserve brand standards. This asymmetric cost response means that demand recovery does not automatically translate into earnings recovery, and demand decline triggers margin compression more quickly than traditional budgeting models predict. Operationally, this creates two distinct management problems: understanding how much additional revenue is needed before it converts into meaningful profit that is, knowing where break-even lies under realistic cost behavior assumptions and identifying which costs can be rendered more elastic without compromising the guest experience.

2.2 Revenue Architecture: From Pricing and Segmentation to Channel Economics

The revenue architecture of hotels has shifted substantially over the past two decades. Revenue management, traditionally concerned with room pricing and inventory controls for a capacity-constrained, perishable product, now encompasses dynamic pricing across multiple market segments, ancillary revenue optimization, and distribution strategy across a complex ecosystem of direct and intermediated channels. A substantial body of research documents the pricing and demand-forecasting dimensions of this evolution (Chen et al., 2023; Zaki, 2022; Guo et al., 2024; Yang et al., 2022). More recently, the focus has broadened to include the profitability consequences of distribution decisions.

The central insight of channel economics research is that channels are not neutral conduits for demand. They carry acquisition costs and contractual constraints that directly affect the net revenue retained by the hotel. O'Connor et al. (2025) provide US-focused empirical evidence that OTA participation has a complex relationship with hotel profitability: while OTAs can sustain occupancy during demand troughs, their commission structures and the demand behaviors they attract—higher cancellation rates, promotional dependency can erode net margins even as gross top-line metrics improve. Lima Santos et al. (2024) similarly document how hospitality firms navigating crises face a structural dilemma between accepting distribution costs to maintain cash flow and protecting contribution quality.

This body of evidence motivates the earnings logic framework developed in this chapter. Managing revenue effectively in a high-fixed-cost environment requires attention not just to volume and gross pricing, but to the net contribution generated after distribution costs and to how measurement systems reveal or conceal those distinctions. The following section examines three interconnected issues that arise when hotels fail to manage these relationships explicitly.

3. MAIN FOCUS OF THE CHAPTER: ISSUES, CONTROVERSIES, AND PROBLEMS

This section identifies three interconnected issues in modern hotel performance management. Each issue captures a practical managerial dilemma, a theoretical failure point in common assumptions, and a measurement risk that can mislead managers and owners. Together, they explain why hotels may appear healthy by conventional topline metrics while simultaneously experiencing margin erosion and earnings volatility.

3.1 Issue 1: Operating Leverage and Cost Stickiness Why Demand Shocks Create Asymmetric Earnings Outcomes

The Management Dilemma

Hotel managers face a recurring choice: when demand falls, should they defend rates or protect occupancy? Should service levels be maintained at cost, or reduced to manage margins? The practical difficulty is that these decisions seemingly tactical carry significant financial consequences in a high-fixed-cost environment. When a large share of costs is committed (property expenses, baseline staffing, technology contracts, brand fees), short-term revenue shifts produce disproportionate profit swings. Aggressive discounting to maintain occupancy may stabilize cash flow but can lock the property into low-contribution demand patterns that fail to cover fixed costs at meaningful levels.

To make this concrete, consider a hypothetical 200-room full-service hotel with an annual fixed-cost base of USD 4 million and variable costs of USD 40 per occupied room-night. At an ADR of USD 150 and 65% annual occupancy (47,450 room-nights), the property generates USD 7.1 million in room revenue. After variable costs of USD 1.9 million, the gross contribution from rooms is approximately USD 5.2 million sufficient to cover fixed costs and generate a modest operating surplus. At 55% occupancy (40,150 room-nights), room revenue falls to USD 6.0 million and variable costs decline to USD 1.6 million, but fixed costs remain at

USD 4 million. The operating surplus narrows sharply. At 45% occupancy (32,850 room-nights) with the same ADR, the property falls below break-even. A ten-percentage-point occupancy movement common in seasonal or disrupted markets can move the property from surplus to loss, not because management failed, but because the fixed-cost architecture amplifies demand volatility.

The Theoretical Dispute

The prevailing management assumption is that costs respond symmetrically to demand—that they fall proportionally when occupancy drops and rise proportionally when it recovers. Hospitality accounting research challenges this view. Costs exhibit stickiness: they decline by less when activity falls than they increase when activity rises. The sources of stickiness include labor contract minimums, service commitments to franchise standards, lease obligations, and deliberate decisions to preserve quality during downturns. As a result, a given occupancy decline produces a larger earnings shortfall than a symmetrical model would predict, while recovery is slower because some costs rise before revenues fully recover (Cengiz et al., 2025; Kizildag et al., 2023).

Measurement Risk

The reporting failure occurs when performance dashboards treat all costs as proportionally variable or mask the effects of cost stickiness inside aggregate expense categories. When managers cannot distinguish volume effects from efficiency effects in their profit reports, they may misdiagnose under-performance: attributing a profit shortfall to operational inefficiency when its root cause is the structural amplification of demand decline through operating leverage. The remedy requires both a better cost classification framework and a flexible budgeting discipline that adjusts expected costs to actual activity levels before assessing management accountability.

3.2 Issue 2: Channel Profitability Illusions When RevPAR Improves but Margins Erode

The Management Dilemma

Hotels allocate demand across direct channels (voice reservations, website, loyalty programs) and intermediated channels (OTAs, global distribution systems, wholesalers) as a matter of routine. Each channel decision affects not just how much room inventory is sold, but at what effective price after acquisition costs are deducted. The problem is that most hotel commercial teams optimize against gross top-line metrics primarily RevPAR that do not capture the acquisition cost burden embedded in intermediated demand.

A concrete illustration makes the point clearly. Suppose a hotel sells the same room category at USD 150 ADR through two different channels on the same night: a direct booking with a direct acquisition cost (web infrastructure, loyalty point allocation) of USD 8 produces a net room revenue of USD 142; an OTA booking at the same ADR with an 18% commission of USD 27 produces a net room revenue of USD 123. Both bookings register identically in a RevPAR calculation, yet the net contribution per room-night differs by USD 19 a 13.4% difference that compounds across thousands of room-nights annually. At 10,000 OTA room-nights per year, the channel cost differential represents approximately USD 190,000 in forgone net contribution. If OTA bookings also carry a structurally higher cancellation rate a pattern empirically documented in O'Connor et al. (2025) the effective net contribution gap is larger still when expected-value adjustments are applied.

The Theoretical Dispute

The core problem is the dominance of RevPAR as the industry's primary performance benchmark. RevPAR is a meaningful market performance indicator: it captures how effectively a hotel converts its capacity into revenue relative to competitors. But it is a gross metric. It does not deduct distribution costs, reflect cancellation patterns, or account for the incremental service costs associated with certain demand segments complimentary breakfast inclusions, loyalty redemptions, systematic upgrade patterns. Consequently, a property can improve its RevPAR while simultaneously deteriorating in net contribution per available room if that RevPAR growth is driven by acquiring commission-intensive or discount-dependent demand (O'Connor et al., 2025; Lima Santos et al., 2024).

Measurement Risk

The reporting risk arises when distribution costs are aggregated into a general "Sales and Marketing" expense category rather than attributed to specific channels and segments. Under this presentation, the link between a particular channel mix decision and its contribution outcome is invisible in management dashboards. Commercial teams optimizing against RevPAR targets may pursue demand that hurts net margins, while finance teams see the cost consequences but cannot trace them to their source. This structural blindspot is compounded when incentive structures reward gross revenue outcomes, creating organizational incentives that systematically erode contribution quality while appearing, superficially, to be delivering strong revenue performance.

3.3 Issue 3: Bundles, Principal–Agent Judgments, and Measurement Misalignment USALI versus IFRS 15 in Dynamic Revenue Environments

The Management Dilemma

Hotels increasingly sell packaged offerings room plus breakfast, dining credits, spa access, resort amenities to differentiate their product and capture incremental willingness-to-pay. These bundles create a practical accounting problem: how to attribute the package price across its component parts, and how that attribution affects departmental performance measurements.

Consider a package priced at USD 300 that includes a room night, breakfast for two, and a USD 50 resort credit. Under internal USALI-based departmental reporting, this package revenue must be allocated across Rooms, Food and Beverage, and ancillary departments. If the allocation is arbitrary, departmental profit statements become unreliable. If Rooms captures the full USD 300, the F&B department appears to underperform because its delivery cost is recognized without corresponding revenue credit. Under IFRS 15 for external reporting, the five-step model requires identification of performance obligations, estimation of stand-alone selling prices (SSPs) for each component, and proportional allocation of the total transaction price. If the hotel estimates SSPs as: Room USD 225, Breakfast USD 45, Resort Credit USD 50 (total SSP USD 320), the IFRS 15 allocation ratios are approximately 70%, 14%, and 16% allocating about USD 211 to Rooms, USD 42 to F&B, and USD 47 to ancillaries. If internal USALI reporting instead allocates the room's rack rate (say USD 250) to Rooms and the remainder to F&B, departmental profit comparisons are immediately distorted, and any cross-period benchmarking becomes unreliable (Barone et al., 2026; Coetsee et al., 2022).

The Theoretical Dispute

The structural tension lies between two legitimate but different purposes. IFRS 15 is designed to ensure consistency and comparability in external revenue recognition: its allocation logic follows economic substance and contractual terms as interpreted through observable or estimated SSPs. USALI is designed to support internal management control and inter-property benchmarking through standardized departmental cost and revenue classifications. These two frameworks can coexist productively, but only if their respective allocation methods are documented, reconciled, and consistently applied. Hotels that have not formally addressed this alignment face a latent risk: management decisions made on internally reported figures may rest on allocations that misrepresent the economic contribution of individual departments and bundle components.

Measurement Risk

Beyond bundles, the principal–agent dimension of channel arrangements adds further complexity. When hotels distribute services through third-party operators tours, transfers, activities the hotel may act as either a principal (controlling the service and recognizing gross revenue) or an agent (facilitating the transaction and recognizing only its net commission). This distinction affects both external revenue presentation and the internal indicators used to evaluate distribution relationships. Hotels that do not document and consistently apply principal-agent assessments for significant arrangements risk working from incompatible definitions of revenue for the same transaction across different reports and periods.

Synthesis: Why These Three Issues Must Be Addressed Together

The three issues are structurally connected. Operating leverage amplifies the earnings consequences of demand composition (Issue 1). Channel economics determines whether incremental demand generates net contribution or destroys margin (Issue 2). Measurement systems determine whether management can accurately perceive these dynamics or is misled by metrics that confound volume with contribution, gross revenue with net, and external recognition standards with internal operational realities (Issue 3). Addressing any one issue without the others is insufficient. The following section translates this integrated diagnosis into a practical management framework.

4. SOLUTIONS AND RECOMMENDATIONS

This section translates the three issues into a decision-supportive management framework. The recommendations address (i) operating leverage and cost stickiness through flexible cost structures and adaptive tools, (ii) channel profitability illusions through net-contribution analytics and governance, and (iii) measurement misalignment through USALI discipline aligned with IFRS 15 principles. Table 1 presents the full playbook. Figure 1 illustrates how these recommendations connect to produce coherent earnings outcomes.

Figure 1. Integrated Framework for Modern Hotel Profitability: Connecting Fixed-Cost Management, Revenue Configuration, and Measurement Coherence

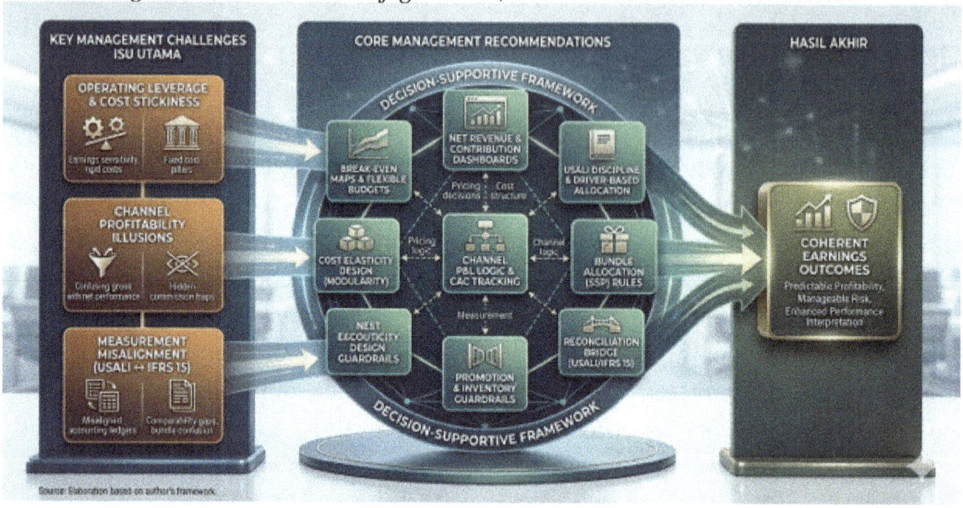

Figure 1 maps the complete earnings logic framework, showing how each key management challenge operating leverage and cost stickiness, channel profitability illusions, and measurement misalignment (USALI ↔ IFRS 15) connects directly to a set of decision-supportive tools that, taken together, produce coherent earnings outcomes: predictable profitability, manageable risk, and enhanced performance interpretation. Table 1 below operationalizes this framework as a detailed playbook, specifying for each intervention the managerial objective, recommended tools and routines, key output metrics, and critical implementation risks that practitioners should anticipate.

Table 1. Issue-to-Solution Playbook for Earnings Logic Management

Issue (Main Focus)	Managerial Objective	Recommended Tools / Routines	Key Metrics / Outputs	Implementation Notes / Risks
Issue 1: Operating leverage + cost stickiness	Make earnings sensitivity visible and manageable	Break-even map by occupancy bands (low/base/peak) incorporating step, semi-variable, and sticky costs	Break-even occupancy bands; contribution margin bands	Requires disciplined cost classification (capacity vs step vs variable). Avoid textbook fixed/variable splits that misrepresent operational reality.
	Separate demand effects from controllable efficiency	Flexible budgeting + variance decomposition (volume vs spending/efficiency)	Volume variance; spending variance; service-level variance	Needs stable drivers (rooms sold, covers, labor hours). Without driver integrity, variance analysis becomes noise.
	Increase cost elasticity without damaging brand/service promise	Cost elasticity design: workforce modularity, cross-training, outsourcing terms, service modularization	Adjustable cost share; step-cost triggers; labor productivity indicators	Risk: cost cutting that erodes guest experience. Use service-protection rules to define what must not flex.
	Prevent low-contribution business from harming earnings conversion	Contribution thresholds by demand state + displacement logic in peak periods	Minimum contribution per segment/channel; displacement/opportunity cost	Must be tied to break-even bands. Risk: thresholds too high in low demand (lost cash contribution) or too low in peaks (foregone margin).
Issue 2: Channel profitability illusions	Move from gross KPIs to net-contribution decision-making	Net revenue & net contribution dashboard by channel/segment (after commissions, CAC, cancellations)	Net ADR / Net RevPAR (conceptual); contribution by channel/segment; cancellation-adjusted contribution	Requires data integration across PMS-channel manager-CRM-finance. If CAC is not traceable, results will be disputed.
	Make channel economics visible and contestable	Channel P&L logic: trace commissions, paid media, loyalty costs, merchant/transaction fees to channels	Channel contribution statement; CAC per booking; commission ratio	Avoid over-allocation of general overhead. Focus on costs economically caused by channel decisions.
	Prevent systematic margin dilution from promotions and parity constraints	Promotion and inventory guardrails: approval based on expected contribution; rate-fence design; parity exception log	Promotion ROI (contribution-based); mix shift indicators; price fence compliance	Risk: governance too slow for dynamic markets. Use a two-tier rule (pre-approved playbooks vs exceptions).

continued on following page

Table 1. Continued

Issue (Main Focus)	Managerial Objective	Recommended Tools / Routines	Key Metrics / Outputs	Implementation Notes / Risks
	Align incentives so topline wins do not erode profit	Incentive alignment: commercial and ops metrics tied to net outcomes; shared targets for contribution	Net contribution KPIs; GOPPAR proxy; contribution variance	Risk: gaming and metric overload. Keep a small set of primary metrics plus diagnostic metrics.
	Institutionalize learning and reduce repeated mistakes	Post-action reviews (expected vs realized contribution) for major campaigns, channel shifts, packages	Forecast error in contribution; realized vs planned contribution gap	Requires a documented assumption sheet (commissions, cancel rate, service costs). Otherwise learning is not cumulative.
Issue 3: Measurement misalignment (USALI ↔ IFRS 15)	Improve comparability and internal interpretability of performance	USALI discipline + targeted costing sophistication (driver-based allocations where necessary)	Departmental contribution consistency; classification integrity checks	Risk: false precision. Use targeted sophistication only where decisions require it (channels/ bundles), not everywhere.
	Make bundle economics measurable and defensible	Bundle allocation policy anchored in stand-alone selling prices (SSP) and documented estimation rules	SSP-based allocated revenue by component/ department; allocation audit trail	SSP estimation is judgment-heavy; document method and update rules when product design changes.
	Prevent gross/ net reporting confusion for intermediated elements	Principal-agent documentation for key arrangements + consistent internal presentation rules	Gross vs net rules; reconciliation notes; comparability adjustments	Risk: inconsistent treatment across properties/periods. Use centralized policy, cross-functional sign-off (finance-revenue-ops).
	Ensure internal reporting and external logic remain coherent	Reconciliation bridge: IFRS 15 allocation to internal departmental view + monthly reconciliation pack	Reconciliation pack; exception log for complex cases	Needs governance ownership (who signs off). Without a routine cadence, coherence decays as bundles and channel terms evolve.

Source: Author elaboration

4.1 Managing Operating Leverage and Cost Stickiness

4.1.1 Build a break-even map anchored in realistic cost behavior

The first priority is making operating leverage visible. This means constructing a break-even analysis that separates (a) committed capacity costs fixed within the planning period, (b) step-costs that change at defined occupancy thresholds for example, additional staffing bands required above certain occupancy levels and (c) genuinely variable costs such as consumables and commissions. The break-even map should be calibrated to the property's actual cost structure, not industry averages or textbook classifications, so that managers can identify the occupancy levels at which profitability transitions from loss to surplus. The operational value extends beyond budget planning: a pricing or channel decision that sustains occupancy at or above break-even thresholds will have different earnings implications than one that keeps occupancy slightly below those thresholds, even if the RevPAR difference appears modest.

4.1.2 Implement flexible budgeting and variance decomposition

Flexible budgeting complements break-even analysis by adjusting expected cost levels to actual activity, enabling managers to determine whether profit shortfalls reflect demand deficiencies (a structural operating leverage effect) or controllable operational inefficiencies (a management accountability issue). Without this separation, management responses to under-performance risk being misdirected: indiscriminate cost-cutting during demand troughs may damage service standards and delay recovery, while attributing all cost variances to operational failures ignores the structural cost amplification inherent in the hotel's fixed-cost architecture.

4.1.3 Design elasticity into the cost structure

Reducing cost stickiness requires deliberate design rather than reactive cost-cutting. Hotels can increase cost elasticity through multi-skilling and cross-training that reduce staffing step-sizes, variable scheduling models calibrated to demand forecasts, selective outsourcing arrangements with activity-based contract provisions, and service modularization the distinction between core service standards that must be maintained at all occupancy levels and supplementary service layers that can be scaled with demand. The goal is not to eliminate fixed costs but to reduce the asymmetry of adjustment so that the property can reduce operational intensity as demand falls and restore it as demand recovers, without incurring disproportionate friction costs in either direction.

4.1.4 Embed contribution thresholds in pricing and inventory decisions

To bridge cost management and revenue decisions, hotels should establish contribution thresholds that define the minimum acceptable incremental contribution per room-night across demand states and channels. These thresholds should be anchored in the break-even map: during low-demand periods, the threshold should reflect cash contribution above variable costs; during peak periods, it should reflect the opportunity cost of displacing high-contribution demand. By linking pricing and inventory decisions explicitly to contribution thresholds calibrated to the cost structure, the hotel prevents two common failure modes: accepting low-margin OTA demand during constrained periods to fill rooms, and over-discounting during recovery phases when fixed costs are largely covered and rate integrity has the greatest earnings impact.

4.2 Correcting Channel Profitability Illusions with Net-Contribution Analytics

4.2.1 Shift to a net-revenue and net-contribution dashboard

The primary diagnostic tool for channel profitability illusions is a net-contribution dashboard that supplements gross KPI reporting. At minimum, this dashboard should show: room revenue by channel after commissions and transaction fees; customer acquisition costs attributed by channel; cancellation-adjusted contribution per channel incorporating expected cancellation rates and rebooking costs; and significant incremental service costs associated with specific demand segments including inclusive offerings, loyalty redemption costs, and systematic upgrade patterns. The output contribution by channel and segment becomes the primary decision metric for inventory allocation, channel investment, and promotion approval.

4.2.2 Introduce channel P&L logic

Implementing the net-contribution dashboard at a governance level requires what this chapter terms “channel P&L logic”: an internal profitability statement that assigns economically attributable revenues and costs to each distribution channel. This should include commissions, paid media and metasearch spending, loyalty subsidies, merchant fees, and chargeback costs costs that are economically caused by channel decisions and should therefore be reflected in the evaluation of those decisions. Channel P&L reports produced monthly for governance review and weekly as flash summaries for operational decisions create a fact base for commercial discussions: whether a particular OTA relationship generates net contribution sufficient to justify its visibility costs, and how cancellation behavior differs by channel and affects realized contribution.

4.2.3 Establish contribution-based guardrails for promotions and inventory allocation

Channel ecosystems create systematic pressure toward volume and visibility, which can gradually erode margins through promotional escalation, discount platforms, and parity constraints. Evidence from daily-deal participation shows why short-term demand stimulation must be evaluated against contribution quality, not volume alone (Chen et al., 2024). Hotels should establish governance protocols requiring contribution assessment before major promotional commitments: promotions should be approved only when expected net contribution, after acquisition costs and expected cancellation rates, exceeds a pre-defined threshold. Inventory allocation during constrained periods should prioritize high-contribution demand by segment and channel, reserving lower-threshold business for periods when occupancy risk exceeds the contribution cost of acceptance.

4.2.4 Align incentive structures with net-contribution outcomes

Channel profitability illusions persist partly because incentive structures reward gross metrics. Commercial teams compensated primarily on RevPAR or room nights have organizational reasons to pursue high-volume, commission-intensive demand that inflates gross metrics while undermining net margins. A more coherent incentive architecture ties a meaningful portion of commercial performance evaluation to net contribution indicators channel contribution per available room, GOPPAR proxies, or contribution margin variance from plan while calibrating operational performance metrics to account for demand-driven volume effects rather than penalizing cost outcomes that result from the demand decisions made by other functions.

4.3 Restoring Measurement Coherence Through USALI Discipline and IFRS 15 Alignment

4.3.1 Strengthen USALI implementation with targeted costing sophistication

USALI provides an essential framework for internal control, benchmarking, and departmental accountability. Strengthening its utility in dynamic revenue environments requires consistent classification of distribution-related costs, clear delineation of departmental versus undistributed expenses, and channel-specific cost tracking rather than aggregation into general commercial expense categories. Where bundled revenue and segmentation complexity have grown substantially, hotels may need to augment standard USALI reporting with driver-based cost allocations for specific overhead categories that are demonstrably driven by revenue mix decisions, such as variable loyalty program costs driven by reward redemption patterns. Environmental and management accounting research similarly shows that measurement systems must be aligned with strategic priorities rather than added after operational decisions have already been made (Gunarathne & Lee, 2021).

4.3.2 Develop a bundle revenue allocation policy based on stand-alone selling prices

For hotels with significant bundled offerings, a formal internal policy for bundle revenue allocation is essential for both external reporting accuracy and internal managerial coherence. The policy should follow IFRS 15 principles: identify performance obligations within each bundle type, establish observable or estimated SSPs for each component, and allocate total transaction price to departments proportionally. SSP estimates should be documented, reviewed annually or when product design changes significantly, and applied consistently. When SSPs are not directly observable, the estimation method and its key assumptions should be documented so that the allocation can be defended in an audit and understood by operational managers.

4.3.3 Document principal-agent assessments for intermediated arrangements

For arrangements where third-party service providers are involved, hotels should formally assess and document whether they act as principal or agent for each significant arrangement type. This affects both external gross-versus-net revenue presentation and the internal metrics used to evaluate distribution relationships. Documentation ensures consistency across reporting periods and prevents the benchmarking distortions that arise when the same economic arrangement is treated differently across periods.

4.3.4 Build a reconciliation bridge between IFRS 15 and USALI reporting

A practical solution to measurement misalignment is to establish a formal reconciliation bridge: a periodic analysis that explains how IFRS 15 recognition and allocation results translate into the USALI-based departmental view. The bridge should document how bundle allocations are reflected in departmental revenue lines, how variable consideration elements affect period comparability, and how channel cost presentations in management accounts relate to gross-or-net revenue distinctions in external reporting. The value is not to make internal reports identical to external ones, but to make them coherent: managers should be able to explain the difference between what their departmental reports show and what the external financial statements present, and those differences should trace to documented, principled decisions. Figure 2 presents this reconciliation bridge as a structured five-step process: (1) tracing bundled revenue to USALI departments based on SSP allocations; (2) reconciling gross-or-net channel transaction presentations; (3) analyzing variable consideration and cancellation impacts on period comparability; (4) maintaining a documented 'assumption sheet' for estimation rules; and (5) producing a monthly reconciliation pack with cross-functional sign-off. The end result is a coherent earnings view that enables informed managerial accountability while preserving full compliance with external reporting requirements.

Figure 2. USALI–IFRS 15 Reconciliation Bridge: A Five-Step Process for Achieving Coherent Earnings Reporting

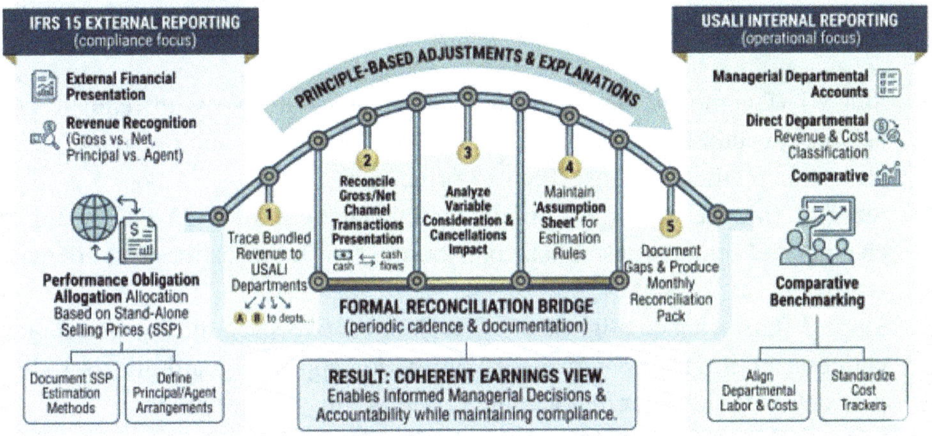

As depicted in Figure 2, the reconciliation bridge connects IFRS 15 external reporting requirements on the left encompassing performance obligation allocation, SSP estimation, and principal–agent determinations with USALI internal departmental reporting on the right, which governs direct departmental revenue classification and comparative benchmarking. The five numbered steps at the center of the bridge translate abstract compliance principles into concrete managerial actions. Critically, the process is designed for periodic repetition rather than one-time implementation:

as bundle configurations evolve, channel terms change, and new variable consideration patterns emerge, the reconciliation pack must be refreshed to maintain the coherent earnings view that underpins sound governance. Section 4.3.5 explains how this process is embedded into the hotel's standard planning and control routines to ensure that measurement coherence is sustained over time.

4.3.5 Integrate measurement coherence into standard management routines

Measurement alignment should be embedded in the hotel's planning and control calendar rather than treated as a periodic accounting task. Budgeting should apply SSP-based allocation rules to planned bundle volumes; forecasting should incorporate expected cancellation and variable consideration impacts on recognized revenue; and monthly management reporting should include standardized commentary on material changes in channel mix, bundle composition, or allocation methods that affect comparability with the prior period.

4.4 Integrated Implementation Roadmap

Hotels can organize these recommendations into four sequential stages:

- Stage 1 (Diagnostic clarity): Build the break-even map with realistic cost behavior; establish a baseline channel P&L statement; audit current bundle allocation methods against IFRS 15 principles.
- Stage 2 (Metric redesign): Implement the net-contribution dashboard by channel and segment; establish contribution thresholds calibrated to demand states.
- Stage 3 (Governance alignment): Revise incentive structures to incorporate net-contribution metrics; formalize promotion approval guardrails; introduce post-action reviews for major channel and pricing interventions.
- Stage 4 (Measurement coherence): Formalize the bundle allocation policy; document principal-agent assessments for key arrangements; establish the USALI–IFRS 15 reconciliation bridge.

This sequencing ensures that measurement infrastructure is built before governance protocols are tightened, and that governance is in place before incentive structures are redesigned. The common thread across all four stages is the earnings logic framework: fixed-cost architecture limits earnings conversion capacity; revenue configuration determines net contribution; and measurement systems determine whether management can accurately perceive and act on these relationships.

5. LIMITATIONS

This chapter makes several assumptions that define the boundaries of its analytical framework and should be acknowledged explicitly. First, the framework is most applicable to full-service and select-service hotels with substantial fixed-capacity commitments and multi-channel distribution. Budget properties with simpler cost structures and limited bundling, or resort properties where revenue mix is heavily ancillary-driven, may require adaptation of the specific mechanisms, even if the underlying earnings-logic principles remain applicable.

Second, the recommendations in this chapter are conceptually derived and illustrated with hypothetical examples. Empirical validation of the specific thresholds, relationships, and causal mechanisms proposed for example, the contribution impact of channel mix shifts under different operating leverage conditions remains an important agenda for future research, as discussed in the following section.

Third, implementing the recommended tools requires significant data integration across property management systems, channel management platforms, CRM systems, and financial reporting infrastructure. Many hotel organizations, particularly smaller independents, may lack the technical infrastructure or analytical capacity for full implementation. The recommendations should be understood as a target architecture toward which implementation can progress incrementally rather than a minimum standard requiring immediate adoption.

Fourth, the principal-agent and bundle allocation recommendations draw on IFRS 15 as the relevant external reporting standard. Hotels reporting under US GAAP (ASC 606) will encounter equivalent requirements with largely consistent principles, though specific application guidance differs in some areas. The framework is intended to be substantively applicable across reporting standards, but practitioners should apply the relevant standard's detailed guidance in their specific jurisdictions.

6. FUTURE RESEARCH DIRECTIONS

The earnings logic framework advanced in this chapter generates several productive research questions across empirical validation, channel economics, measurement design, and algorithmic governance.

6.1 Empirical Validation of Operating Leverage and Contribution Dynamics

This chapter illustrates the theoretical relationship between fixed-cost intensity, channel mix, and earnings outcomes through hypothetical examples and conceptual argument. Direct empirical investigation would strengthen the framework considerably. Panel studies using hotel-level financial data could examine whether properties with greater cost elasticity-measured by the adjustable cost share of total cost structures-demonstrate more stable earnings-to-revenue conversion across occupancy cycles. Research could also investigate whether the adoption of contribution-based pricing governance produces measurable improvements in GOPPAR or margin persistence relative to properties relying primarily on RevPAR-based management (Abu Afifa & Saleh, 2021; Nowotny et al., 2022). Participatory evaluation designs used in tourism intervention research may also help researchers study how earnings logic tools are adopted, adapted, and learned within operating properties (Suno Wu et al., 2024).

6.2 Channel Economics: Net Revenue Metrics and Earnings Quality

The gap between gross and net revenue metrics is conceptually well-established but empirically understudied at scale. Research designs using matched-sample approaches across hotels with varying OTA dependence, direct channel investment, and cancellation patterns could examine the relationship between channel mix and net ADR, contribution per available room, and earnings stability across demand cycles. Such research would provide an empirical foundation for the Net RevPAR concept introduced in this chapter and contribute to broader debates about optimal distribution strategy under different competitive and cost conditions (Mao et al., 2023; Guillet et al., 2026).

6.3 Measurement Design: USALI Sophistication, IFRS 15 Implementation, and Decision Quality

A third research opportunity lies at the intersection of managerial accounting and hospitality performance measurement. Surveys of USALI implementation practices, combined with performance data, could examine whether greater costing sophistication-driver-based overhead allocation, channel-specific cost attribution, SSP-based bundle allocation-is associated with better financial outcomes or stronger management decision quality. Research could also examine how the USALI-IFRS 15 alignment challenge is managed in practice, what reconciliation mechanisms hotels employ, and whether standardized guidance from USALI's standard-setting bodies could reduce the implementation burden (Abu Afifa & Saleh, 2021; Barone et al., 2026; Coetsee et al., 2022; Saleh et al., 2023).

6.4 Algorithmic Pricing, Automation, and Governance

A forward-looking research stream concerns the governance implications of increasingly automated revenue management. As dynamic pricing and channel allocation migrate to algorithmic systems operating in near-real time, the governance challenge shifts from manual decision oversight to monitoring and auditing of automated decision logic. Research questions include: how should accountability be allocated between human managers and algorithmic systems in automated pricing environments? What disclosure requirements are appropriate for algorithmic revenue management decisions that affect owner–operator financial arrangements? How do automated systems handle the contribution threshold logic advocated in this chapter, and should such thresholds be hard-coded into pricing algorithms as floor conditions (Chen et al., 2023; Zaki, 2022)?

7. CONCLUSION

This chapter has developed an earnings logic framework for modern hotel profitability, arguing that hotels function as earnings-conversion systems in which three structural factors jointly determine whether revenue growth produces proportional profit improvement. Fixed-cost intensity and cost stickiness mean that demand shocks create asymmetric earnings outcomes that standard volume-focused metrics fail to reveal. Channel economics mean that gross revenue indicators like RevPAR can improve while net contribution per available room erodes a profitability illusion that persists wherever distribution costs are not attributed to the channels and segments that generate them. Measurement misalignment between internal USALI-based reporting and IFRS 15 revenue recognition requirements compounds both problems by distorting departmental profitability signals, bundle economics, and the interpretation of intermediated revenue arrangements.

The chapter's practical contribution is to translate this diagnostic framework into an actionable management toolkit: break-even mapping, flexible budgeting, net-contribution dashboards, channel P&L logic, contribution thresholds, SSP-based bundle allocation policies, and USALI–IFRS 15 reconciliation frameworks. These tools are not independent innovations; they are components of a coherent earnings logic architecture that connects cost management, revenue configuration, and measurement design into a unified approach to hotel performance management.

The broader implication is conceptual: in dynamic revenue environments, managing revenue and managing earnings are not the same activity. Hotels that optimize for gross topline metrics without attending to the net contribution quality of their demand, the cost behavior implications of their channel decisions, and the coherence of their measurement systems risk pursuing revenue strategies that appear successful at the gross level while progressively undermining their financial resilience and governance integrity. The earnings logic framework offers a structured way to keep these connections visible and to manage them deliberately.

REFERENCES

Abu Afifa, M. M., & Saleh, I. (2021). Management accounting systems effectiveness, perceived environmental uncertainty and companies' performance: The case of Jordanian companies. *The International Journal of Organizational Analysis*, *30*(2), 259–288. DOI: 10.1108/IJOA-07-2020-2288

Barone, E., Mason, S., Mora, A., & Procházka, D. (2026). Changing the paradigm for revenue recognition: Literature review on intended and unintended effects of IFRS 15 and ASC 606. *Accounting in Europe*, *23*(2), 218–245. DOI: 10.1080/17449480.2025.2528899

Cengiz, E., Kaynakci, E., Nanu, L., & Cavusoglu, M. (2025). Optimizing hotel profitability: How cost system sophistication drives financial performance in the hotel industry. *Journal of Quality Assurance in Hospitality & Tourism*, •••, 1–15. DOI: 10.1080/1528008X.2025.2601706

Chen, J., Xu, Y., Yu, P., & Zhang, J. (2023). A reinforcement learning approach for hotel revenue management with evidence from field experiments. *Journal of Operations Management*, *69*(7), 1176–1201. DOI: 10.1002/joom.1246

Chen, M. M., Beaufort, C., & Earl-Erpelding, K. (2024). Should independent upmarket hotels work with daily deals platforms? An empirical case study from Switzerland. *Tourism and Hospitality Research*, •••, 14673584241311294. DOI: 10.1177/14673584241311294

Coetsee, D., Mohammadali-Haji, A., & Van Wyk, M. (2022). Revenue recognition practices in South Africa: An analysis of the decision usefulness of IFRS 15 disclosures. *South African Journal of Accounting Research*, *36*(1), 22–44. DOI: 10.1080/10291954.2020.1855886

Demydyuk, G. V., & Carlbäck, M. (2024). Balancing short-term gains and long-term success in lodging: The role of customer satisfaction and price in hotel profitability model. *Tourism Economics*, *30*(4), 844–875. DOI: 10.1177/13548166231199156

Guillet, B. D., Zhang, Y. R., Madanoglu, M., & Gao, L. (2026). Attribute-based pricing in hotels: Analyzing industry, customer, and behavioral insights. *International Journal of Hospitality Management*, *133*, 104445. DOI: 10.1016/j.ijhm.2025.104445

Gunarathne, N., & Lee, K. H. (2021). Corporate cleaner production strategy development and environmental management accounting: A contingency theory perspective. *Journal of Cleaner Production*, *297*, 126050. DOI: 10.1016/j.jclepro.2021.127402

Guo, Q., Cheng, S., & Zhao, P. (2024). How to introduce a livestreaming channel: A case of the hotel at a fixed capacity. *International Transactions in Operational Research, 31*(5), 3531–3552. DOI: 10.1111/itor.13259

Kizildag, M., Weinland, J. T., & Demirer, I. (2023). Financial sensitivity analysis of small lodging establishments during COVID-19. *Journal of Hospitality and Tourism Insights, 6*(5), 2257–2272. DOI: 10.1108/JHTI-05-2022-0176

Lima Santos, L., Gomes, C., Malheiros, C., Crespo, C., & Bento, C. (2024). Factors influencing hotel revenue management in times of crisis: Towards financial sustainability. *International Journal of Financial Studies, 12*(4), 112. DOI: 10.3390/ijfs12040112

Mao, Z., Liu, T., & Li, X. (2023). Pricing mechanism of variable opaque products for dual-channel online travel agencies. *Annals of Operations Research, 329*(1), 901–930. DOI: 10.1007/s10479-021-04163-4

Nowotny, S., Hirsch, B., & Nitzl, C. (2022). The influence of organizational structure on value-based management sophistication. *Management Accounting Research, 56*, 100797. DOI: 10.1016/j.mar.2022.100797

O'Connor, P., Assaker, G., & Haddad, R. E. (2025). Online travel agency participation: An empirical investigation of its financial contribution to US hotel profitability. *Cornell Hospitality Quarterly, 66*(4), 527–538. DOI: 10.1177/19389655251318185

Saleh, M. M. A., Jawabreh, O., & Abu-Eker, E. F. M. (2023). Factors of applying creative accounting and its impact on the quality of financial statements in Jordanian hotels. *Journal of Sustainable Finance & Investment, 13*(1), 499–515. DOI: 10.1080/20430795.2021.1962662

Suno Wu, J., Barbrook-Johnson, P., Font, X., & Torres-Delgado, A. (2024). Combining realist evaluation and appreciative inquiry: A participatory, learning-focused methodology for tourism interventions. *Annals of Tourism Research Empirical Insights, 5*(2), 100152. DOI: 10.1016/j.annale.2024.100152

Yang, Y., Nieto García, M., Viglia, G., & Nicolau, J. L. (2022). Competitors or complements: A meta-analysis of the effect of Airbnb on hotel performance. *Journal of Travel Research, 61*(7), 1508–1527. DOI: 10.1177/00472875211042670

Zaki, K. (2022). Implementing dynamic revenue management in hotels during COVID-19: Value stream and wavelet coherence perspectives. *International Journal of Contemporary Hospitality Management, 34*(5), 1768–1795. DOI: 10.1108/IJCHM-08-2021-1043

KEY TERMS AND DEFINITIONS

Channel Economics: The analysis of how direct and intermediated distribution channels affect retained revenue after commissions, acquisition costs, cancellation effects, and service costs.

Cost Stickiness: An asymmetric cost behavior pattern in which costs decline more slowly when activity falls than they rise when activity increases.

Earnings Logic: A structured view of how cost architecture, revenue configuration, and measurement design jointly determine whether hotel revenue converts into sustainable profit.

Fixed-Cost Intensity: The degree to which a hotel's capacity-related costs remain committed regardless of short-term changes in occupancy or demand.

Net RevPAR: A managerial metric concept that adjusts revenue per available room for channel-related acquisition costs and other contribution-relevant deductions.

Operating Leverage: The amplification effect through which a change in revenue produces a larger proportional change in operating profit because fixed costs remain largely unchanged.

Stand-Alone Selling Price (SSP): The observable or estimated selling price of each distinct component in a bundled offer, used to allocate transaction price under IFRS 15 logic.

USALI-IFRS 15 Reconciliation Bridge: A management reporting bridge that explains how external revenue-recognition outcomes connect to internal USALI-based departmental reporting.

Chapter 4
Key Performance Indicators (KPIs) in Hotel Revenue Management: A Critical and Educational Literature Review

Markos Kourgiantakis
http://orcid.org/0000-0002-2392-6952
Hellenic Mediterranean University, Greece

Panagiotis Kyriakogkonas
http://orcid.org/0009-0006-2351-3409
University of Western Macedonia, Greece

Alexandros Garefalakis
http://orcid.org/0000-0001-7980-3743
Hellenic Mediterranean University, Greece

Ioannis Passas
http://orcid.org/0000-0002-1261-2878
Hellenic Mediterranean University, Greece

ABSTRACT

Key Performance Indicators (KPIs) are central to hotel Revenue Management (RM) because they translate complex demand, pricing, and inventory-control decisions into measurable outcomes for managerial learning, accountability and benchmarking. For decades, the hotel sector relied heavily on a small canon of room-centric metrics. Yet contemporary hospitality markets challenge the sufficiency of traditional KPIs. Distribution costs and digital intermediaries make gross revenue measures

DOI: 10.4018/979-8-3373-9479-4.ch004

less decision-relevant. Total Revenue Management broadens RM beyond rooms into food and beverage, function space, and ancillaries. In parallel, customer-centric measurement is rising but remains operationally constrained by data fragmentation and organizational silos. This chapter provides a comprehensive, educational and critical review of KPIs used in hotel RM. It traces the roots of major indicators and evaluates what each KPI reveals and conceals. The chapter proposes a modern KPI portfolio—rooms, net, total, and profit metrics complemented by process KPIs.

INTRODUCTION

Revenue Management (RM) has become one of the most influential managerial disciplines in the hospitality industry (Cross, 1997; Kimes, 1989). Originating from the principles of yield management developed in the airline sector, RM seeks to maximize revenue and profitability from fixed, perishable, and capacity-constrained inventory through the strategic management of pricing, demand forecasting, inventory allocation, distribution channels, and customer segments (Ivanov & Zhechev, 2012). Over the past four decades, advances in technology, data availability, and analytical capabilities have transformed RM from a tactical pricing function into a sophisticated decision-support discipline that influences a wide range of commercial decisions across hospitality organizations.

Despite these developments, the effectiveness of RM ultimately depends on measurement (González-Serrano & Talón-Ballestero, 2022). Revenue managers continuously make decisions regarding pricing, inventory controls, distribution strategies, customer segmentation, and demand management. The quality of these decisions can only be evaluated through appropriate performance indicators that translate complex commercial outcomes into actionable managerial information. Consequently, Key Performance Indicators (KPIs) occupy a central role in RM practice, serving as tools for performance evaluation, benchmarking, forecasting, decision support, and continuous improvement.

The importance of KPIs extends beyond simple performance reporting. Well-designed indicators help managers identify revenue opportunities, assess the effectiveness of pricing and inventory decisions, evaluate competitive positioning, monitor customer value, and diagnose weaknesses within the RM process itself. At the same time, inappropriate or overly narrow performance measures may encourage suboptimal decision-making and provide an incomplete picture of organizational performance. For example, a hotel may achieve strong occupancy performance while sacrificing pricing power or generate high revenues through costly distribution channels that ultimately reduce profitability. As a result, the selection and interpretation of KPIs represent critical managerial challenges.

A further complication arises from the multidimensional nature of hospitality performance (Abad et al., 2019). Hotels simultaneously pursue objectives related to revenue generation, profitability, market share, customer value, operational efficiency, and long-term sustainability (Arnejo & Sarsale, 2025). No single indicator can capture all these dimensions. While metrics such as Occupancy, Average Daily Rate (ADR), and Revenue per Available Room (RevPAR) remain among the most widely used measures in the industry, contemporary hospitality organizations increasingly rely on broader sets of indicators that encompass total revenue performance, ancillary revenue generation, profitability, competitive benchmarking, customer-centric value creation, and the effectiveness of RM processes.

Against this background, the purpose of this chapter is to provide a comprehensive review of the most important KPIs used in hotel RM. Beyond presenting individual metrics, the chapter examines their managerial relevance, strengths, limitations, and appropriate applications within contemporary hospitality environments. Attention is given to the distinction between outcome-oriented indicators, which measure the results of RM decisions, and process-oriented indicators, which evaluate the effectiveness of the RM system itself.

To achieve this objective, the chapter first outlines the historical evolution of RM performance measurement and the factors that have shaped the development of contemporary KPI frameworks. It then reviews the principal KPI families used in hotel RM, including room-centric indicators, total revenue measures, competitive benchmarking metrics, ancillary revenue indicators, process KPIs, and emerging future-oriented measures. The chapter concludes by discussing future directions in RM performance measurement and the growing importance of profitability, customer value, artificial intelligence, and sustainability considerations in KPI design.

BACKGROUND NOTE: THE HISTORICAL EVOLUTION OF REVENUE MANAGEMENT KPIS

A KPI can be considered RM-relevant when it satisfies three fundamental conditions: (a) it reflects performance within a capacity-constrained and perishable inventory environment (Talluri & Van Ryzin 2004); (b) it is interpretable, measurable, and repeatable over time (Parmenter, 2015); and (c) it supports managerial decision-making. RM-related KPIs typically normalize outcomes by a capacity unit, such as room nights, seat-hours, or available space, and capture the trade-offs that lie at the heart of RM, including price versus volume, acceptance versus rejection, and availability versus restriction (Kimes, 1989).

The evolution of RM performance measurement closely mirrors the evolution of RM. Early yield management theory focused primarily on maximizing revenue from fixed and perishable capacity through the allocation of inventory across different customer segments and demand types. Although hotels gradually adopted these principles, performance measurement initially remained rooted in traditional operational indicators such as occupancy and average room rate. Over time, however, the limitations of using these indicators independently became increasingly apparent. This led to the development of composite productivity measures, most notably RevPAR, which combined occupancy and pricing performance into a single metric and eventually became the dominant performance indicator in hotel RM.

As the discipline matured, two structural developments further expanded the scope of RM performance measurement. First, growing hotel owner and investor emphasis on profitability shifted attention beyond revenue generation toward profit outcomes (Schwartz et al., 2017). This transition contributed to the adoption of profitability-oriented indicators such as Gross Operating Profit Per Available Room (GOPPAR), supported by accounting frameworks such as Uniform System of Accounts for the Lodging Industry (USALI), which facilitated greater standardization and comparability of financial performance (Hospitality Financial and Technology Professionals et al., 2024).

Second, the rapid growth of online distribution channels transformed the economics of hotel bookings. The emergence of Online Travel Agencies (OTAs), metasearch platforms, and paid digital marketing significantly increased customer acquisition and distribution costs, highlighting the limitations of traditional gross revenue measures. As a result, cost-adjusted indicators such as Net Revenue per Available Room (NRevPAR) emerged to evaluate not only revenue generation but also the efficiency with which revenue is retained after distribution-related expenses (Boo et al., 2025).

Technological advancements also enabled hotels to monitor competitors more systematically and in real time (Haynes, 2016). This development increased the importance of relative rather than purely absolute performance measurement, leading to the widespread adoption of competitive benchmarking indicators such as the Market Penetration Index (MPI), Average Rate Index (ARI), and Revenue Generation Index (RGI). These metrics shifted managerial attention toward market share, pricing power, and competitive positioning.

The next major evolutionary stage was the emergence of Total Revenue Management (TRM). Unlike traditional RM, which focuses primarily on guestrooms, TRM extends performance measurement across multiple revenue-generating assets and departments (Noone et al. 2017). This broader perspective led to the development of indicators such as Total Revenue Per Available Room (TRevPAR) and Total Revenue per Occupied Room (TRevPOR), and capacity-specific measures including Revenue per Available Seat Hour (RevPASH). These metrics reflect the growing recognition that hospitality organizations create value through a portfolio of revenue streams rather than accommodation services alone.

More recently, scholars and practitioners have recognized that effective RM requires measuring not only outcomes but also the quality of the decision-making process itself. Consequently, this chapter adopts a distinction between outcome KPIs and process KPIs. Outcome KPIs evaluate the results of RM decisions and include indicators such as RevPAR, NRevPAR, GOPPAR, and TRevPAR. Process KPIs, by contrast, evaluate how effectively the RM system operates and include measures such as forecast accuracy, forecast bias, pickup, pace, denials, regrets, unconstrained demand and Average Length of Stay (ALOS). These indicators provide valuable diagnostic information and support continuous improvement of the RM process.

Taking together, these developments illustrate the progressive evolution of RM performance measurement—from occupancy and pricing metrics to revenue and profitability indicators, to customer-centric, total-revenue, and process-oriented measures. Reflecting this evolution, the following section presents the most important RM KPIs, organized into six broad categories: (1) Room-Centric KPIs, (2) Total Revenue / Profit - Centric KPIs, (3) Competitive Benchmarking KPIs, (4) Ancillary Services-Centric KPIs, (5) RM Process KPIs, and (6) Emerging and Future-Oriented KPIs.

KEY PERFORMANCE INDICATOR FAMILIES IN HOTEL REVENUE MANAGEMENT

1. Room-Centric KPIs

Occupancy

Occupancy (OCC) or occupancy rate is defined as the proportion of available rooms that are sold or occupied during a specific period and is calculated as follows:

$$\text{Occupancy} = \frac{\text{Rooms Sold}}{\text{Number of Available Rooms}} \times 100$$

Occupancy is arguably the oldest and most widely recognized performance indicator in the hotel industry, predating the formal emergence of RM. Its enduring popularity is largely attributable to the simplicity and intuitiveness of its calculation, as well as its usefulness in reflecting demand intensity and capacity utilization.

Despite its operational value, occupancy is considered a limited performance indicator within contemporary RM theory and practice (Sainaghi, 2010; Arnejo & Sarsale, 2025). The primary limitation of OCC is that it does not account for pricing effectiveness, distribution costs or profitability. A hotel may achieve very high occupancy levels while simultaneously generating suboptimal financial performance, particularly when occupancy is driven by aggressive room discounting strategies or by distribution channels associated with high acquisition costs. Consequently, occupancy alone provides little insight into the quality of revenue generated.

For this reason, occupancy is best interpreted not as a standalone indicator of commercial success, but rather as an indicator of capacity utilization and operational constraints. High occupancy levels become strategically meaningful only when evaluated in conjunction with other dimensions of performance, such as ADR, net revenue contribution, channel mix, and the opportunity cost associated with displaced higher-value demand. Although hotel practitioners frequently continue to perceive high occupancy as synonymous with strong performance, contemporary RM logic emphasizes that maximizing occupancy does not necessarily equate to maximizing revenue, profitability, or long-term customer value.

Average Daily Rate

Average Daily Rate (ADR) is defined as the average revenue per room sold during a specific period (e.g. per day) and it is calculated as follows:

$$\text{ADR} = \frac{\text{Rooms Revenue}}{\text{Rooms Sold}}$$

ADR is one of the most widely used pricing indicators in the hotel industry, as it reflects the average realized room price achieved by a hospitality property (Vinod, 2022). Within the context of RM, ADR is commonly interpreted as an indicator of pricing effectiveness, since higher ADR values generally suggest that the hotel has been successful in selling rooms at higher average prices.

Despite its strategic importance, ADR presents significant limitations when used as a standalone performance indicator. Most importantly, ADR focuses exclusively on the rooms sold and completely ignores unsold inventory. As a result, ADR may increase even when total sales volume and overall revenue performance decline substantially. In other words, a hotel may report a high ADR while simultaneously experiencing low occupancy levels and poor capacity utilization.

For example, a hotel generating $100 in rooms revenue from the sale of a single room may report a higher ADR than another hotel generating $3,000 in total rooms revenue from 25 occupied rooms. Although the first property achieves a higher average room price, the second property demonstrates significantly greater overall revenue productivity. This example highlights a fundamental limitation of ADR: the indicator evaluates pricing performance but fails to capture the relationship between price and volume. Consequently, ADR cannot independently represent the overall productivity or financial effectiveness of a hotel's RM strategy.

In addition, ADR completely ignores the cost dimension associated with generating room revenue, particularly distribution and acquisition costs. In the contemporary hotel distribution environment, where Online Travel Agencies (OTAs), metasearch platforms, and third-party intermediaries play a dominant role, the nominal room price achieved does not necessarily reflect the actual economic value retained by the hotel. For example, if a hotel sells a room at a rate of \$180 through an OTA channel, the reported ADR is nominally \$180. However, the hotel does not retain the full amount, as a proportion of the revenue is typically deducted in the form of commissions, transaction fees, marketing contributions, or other distribution-related costs. Consequently, the effective revenue captured by the hotel may be substantially lower than the nominal ADR reported in operational systems.

This limitation has led both practitioners and scholars to increasingly recognize the importance of cost-adjusted pricing indicators such as Net ADR. Net ADR refers to the average net room revenue retained by the hotel after deducting distribution and channel-related costs from rooms revenue. It can be calculated as follows:

$$\text{Net ADR} = \frac{\text{Rooms Revenue} - \text{Distribution Costs}}{\text{Rooms Sold}}$$

Net ADR provides a more economically meaningful representation of pricing performance because it incorporates channel efficiency and acquisition cost considerations into the evaluation of room pricing outcomes. Particularly in highly intermediated markets, Net ADR may offer superior managerial insight compared to traditional ADR, as it reflects not only the nominal selling price but also the actual revenue contribution generated for the property.

For the aforementioned reasons, ADR should not be interpreted as a sufficient standalone indicator of hotel performance, especially when calculated at the aggregate property level. Its analytical value becomes substantially greater when it is applied at a more disaggregated level, such as by market segment, distribution channel, customer type, or room category. Segment-level and channel-level ADR analysis allows revenue managers to evaluate pricing effectiveness, customer mix quality, and channel profitability more accurately, thereby supporting more informed strategic and tactical RM decisions.

Revenue per Available Room

Revenue per Available Room (RevPAR) is widely regarded as the most influential and extensively used performance indicator in hotel RM. Indeed, among hospitality practitioners, RevPAR is often considered the "gold standard" of revenue performance measurement because it captures the combined effects of pricing and occupancy decisions within a single metric (Remy et al., 2023). RevPAR is defined as the rooms revenue generated per available room during a specific period and is calculated as follows:

$$\text{RevPAR} = \frac{\text{Rooms Revenue}}{\text{Number of Available Rooms}}$$

Alternatively, RevPAR can be expressed as:

$$\text{RevPAR} = \text{ADR} \times \text{Occupancy}$$

The second formulation illustrates the fundamental strength of RevPAR: it integrates the two principal dimensions of hotel revenue performance—price (ADR) and volume (occupancy)—into a single productivity indicator. Consequently, RevPAR provides a more comprehensive assessment of rooms revenue performance than either ADR or occupancy when considered independently.

From both a managerial and educational perspective, RevPAR should be understood primarily as a capacity-normalized productivity metric. Unlike ADR, which considers only rooms sold, or occupancy, which focuses solely on capacity utilization, RevPAR allocates total rooms revenue across the entire inventory available for sale. In doing so, it evaluates how effectively a hotel converts its available room capacity into revenue.

The conceptual logic of RevPAR can be illustrated through a simple example. Consider a hotel with 100 available rooms. On Monday, the revenue manager sells 70 rooms and achieves a RevPAR of $180. On Friday, 80 rooms are sold, but RevPAR decreases to $160. Although Friday exhibits higher occupancy, the Monday performance is superior from rooms revenue perspective because each available room generated, on average, $180 in revenue compared to only $160 on Friday. RevPAR therefore shifts managerial attention away from sales volume alone and toward the overall productivity of the available inventory.

This characteristic of RevPAR lies at the heart of one of the longest-standing debates in hotel management. Traditionally, many hotel managers and owners have favored strategies aimed at maximizing occupancy, often through aggressive discounting. Such approaches are frequently driven by concerns regarding unsold inventory, the perceived risk of "lost sales," or the expectation that additional guests will generate ancillary revenues through food and beverage outlets, spa services, parking, or other complementary offerings. RM, however, challenges this occupancy-oriented mindset by emphasizing the trade-off between price and volume. RevPAR explicitly captures this trade-off and demonstrates that superior rooms performance is often achieved through stronger pricing power rather than through occupancy growth alone. In many cases, a hotel can generate substantially higher revenue productivity by maintaining a higher ADR, even at somewhat lower occupancy levels.

This does not imply that occupancy is unimportant. Rather, RM seeks to optimize the balance between occupancy and price. The ideal outcome is a hotel that simultaneously achieves both high occupancy and high ADR, thereby maximizing RevPAR. Nevertheless, when a trade-off between the two dimensions becomes necessary, RevPAR provides a framework for evaluating which combination generates the greatest rooms revenue productivity.

Another important advantage of RevPAR is its ability to support benchmarking and comparative performance analysis. Because RevPAR normalizes revenue by room capacity, it allows meaningful comparisons among properties of different sizes. As a result, RevPAR is extensively used to compare competing hotels within the same market, evaluate performance against competitive sets, and assess individual property performance within hotel chains and management portfolios. This benchmarking role has significantly contributed to its widespread adoption as the dominant KPI in hotel RM.

Despite its importance, RevPAR is not without limitations. The first and most frequently cited limitation is its rooms-only perspective. RevPAR considers exclusively rooms revenue and ignores all other revenue streams generated by the property. This limitation is particularly relevant in full-service hotels, resorts, conference hotels, and integrated hospitality complexes, where significant portions of total revenue may originate from restaurants, bars, meeting facilities, spas, golf courses, casinos, or other ancillary services. Consequently, a hotel may achieve a strong RevPAR while underperforming in terms of total revenue generation. This shortcoming has contributed to the emergence of Total Revenue Management (TRM) and related indicators such as Total Revenue per Available Room (TRevPAR).

A second limitation is the absence of cost considerations. RevPAR is a gross revenue measure and therefore does not account for the costs associated with generating revenue. Distribution expenses, OTA commissions, digital marketing expenditures, loyalty program costs, and other customer acquisition expenses are completely excluded from the calculation. Consequently, two hotels with identical RevPAR values may exhibit substantially different levels of profitability depending on their channel mix and cost structures. This limitation has stimulated growing interest in net revenue indicators such as Net RevPAR (NRevPAR).

A third limitation concerns strategic ambiguity. Identical RevPAR values can result from very different combinations of occupancy and ADR. For example, a hotel operating with high occupancy and low ADR may generate the same RevPAR as another hotel operating with lower occupancy and higher ADR. While the resulting RevPAR is identical, the strategic implications may differ significantly in terms of market positioning, brand image, customer mix, operational workload, and long-term pricing power. RevPAR therefore measures the outcome of pricing and inventory decisions without fully revealing the underlying strategy that produced that outcome.

In summary, RevPAR represents one of the most valuable and influential indicators in hotel RM because it captures the overall revenue productivity of available room inventory. Nevertheless, RevPAR should be viewed as a highly useful—but inherently partial—indicator of rooms revenue performance that must be complemented by profitability, distribution-efficiency, customer-value, and total-revenue metrics in order to provide a holistic assessment of hotel performance.

Net Revenue per Available Room

Net Revenue per Available Room (NRevPAR) emerged as a response to one of the most frequently cited criticisms of traditional RM performance measurement: the inability of revenue-based metrics to account for the costs associated with generating revenue. While RevPAR remains the dominant indicator of room revenue productivity, it evaluates gross revenue generated from available room inventory and therefore ignores the distribution, acquisition, and transaction costs required to produce that revenue. As hotel distribution systems became increasingly complex and dependent on online intermediaries, many practitioners and researchers began questioning whether gross room revenue alone remained an adequate measure of commercial performance.

NRevPAR attempts to address this limitation by measuring the net room revenue retained by the hotel after deducting distribution-related expenses. It is generally calculated as follows:

$$\text{NRevPAR} = \frac{\text{Room Revenue} - \text{Distribution Costs}}{\text{Number of Available Rooms}}$$

Alternatively:

$$\text{NRevPAR} = \text{Net ADR} \times \text{Occupancy}$$

where distribution costs may include OTA commissions, global distribution system (GDS) fees, transaction costs, channel-specific marketing expenditures, loyalty program expenses, metasearch advertising costs, and other customer acquisition expenses directly associated with generating room revenue.

Conceptually, NRevPAR can be understood as the net-revenue equivalent of RevPAR. Whereas RevPAR evaluates how effectively a hotel converts available room inventory into gross room revenue, NRevPAR evaluates how effectively the same inventory generates revenue that is actually retained by the property (Boo et al., 2025). This distinction has become increasingly important in contemporary hospitality markets, where distribution costs may vary substantially across channels.

The growing relevance of NRevPAR is closely linked to the transformation of hotel distribution systems. Historically, hotels relied heavily on direct bookings, telephone reservations, travel agents, and corporate agreements, resulting in relatively limited distribution costs. The rapid expansion of OTAs, metasearch platforms, affiliate networks, and paid digital marketing has significantly altered this landscape. While these channels often contribute valuable demand, they also impose acquisition costs that can substantially reduce the economic value of a booking.

For example, consider two hotels generating an identical RevPAR of $120. Hotel A obtains most of its reservations through direct channels, whereas Hotel B relies heavily on OTA bookings associated with 20% commission costs. Although both hotels report identical RevPAR values, Hotel A retains substantially more revenue. NRevPAR captures this difference and therefore provides a more economically meaningful assessment of commercial performance.

One of the principal strengths of NRevPAR is its ability to support channel-management decisions. Revenue managers increasingly evaluate not only whether a booking generates revenue, but also whether it generates profitable revenue. By incorporating acquisition costs into performance measurement, NRevPAR encourages a more balanced assessment of distribution effectiveness and customer acquisition efficiency.

NRevPAR is also particularly useful when comparing market segments and booking channels. Certain channels may generate high booking volumes but relatively low net contribution due to commissions and marketing expenses. Others may produce lower volumes but substantially higher retained revenue. Consequently, NRevPAR can support more informed decisions regarding channel mix optimization, direct booking strategies, and customer acquisition investments.

Despite its advantages, NRevPAR presents several limitations. The first limitation concerns the lack of standardization in cost allocation (Barten, 2024). Different organizations include different cost categories when calculating net revenue. Some hotels deduct only OTA commissions, whereas others also incorporate digital marketing expenditures, loyalty program costs, transaction fees, and customer acquisition expenses. Consequently, direct comparisons of NRevPAR across organizations may be problematic unless calculation methodologies are clearly specified.

A second limitation relates to managerial controllability. While NRevPAR improves upon RevPAR by incorporating distribution costs, it still focuses exclusively on revenue generation rather than overall profitability. Operational expenses, labor costs, utility costs and departmental expenditure remain excluded from the calculation. Therefore, NRevPAR should not be interpreted as a substitute for profitability measures such as GOPPAR.

A third limitation concerns data availability and attribution. Accurately assigning acquisition costs to individual channels, segments, and reservations can be challenging, particularly when marketing expenditures support multiple distribution channels simultaneously. Consequently, the reliability of NRevPAR depends heavily on the quality of managerial accounting and distribution analytics systems.

From an educational perspective, NRevPAR represents an important milestone in the evolution of RM measurement. It reflects the industry's transition from revenue maximization toward revenue quality and commercial efficiency. In many respects, NRevPAR serves as a bridge between traditional revenue-based indicators such as RevPAR and profitability-oriented indicators such as GOPPAR. Nevertheless, because it remains a net-revenue rather than a profit-based measure, it should be interpreted alongside complementary indicators such as RevPAR, GOPPAR, and contribution-based metrics in order to provide a comprehensive assessment of hotel performance (Noone et al. 2017).

2. Total Revenue/ Profit - Centric KPIs

Total Revenue per Available Room

Total Revenue per Available Room (TRevPAR) emerged as a response to one of the most frequently cited limitations of traditional hotel RM metrics: their exclusive focus on rooms revenue. While indicators such as Occupancy, ADR, and RevPAR provide valuable insights into the performance of a hotel's room inventory, they fail to capture the broader revenue-generating capacity of hospitality properties, particularly those that derive substantial income from ancillary services. As the hospitality industry evolved toward more integrated and diversified business models, researchers and practitioners increasingly recognized the need for performance indicators that reflect the contribution of all revenue streams rather than room sales alone. Within this context, TRevPAR has become one of the most widely discussed metrics associated with the concept of TRM.

TRevPAR is defined as the total revenue generated by a hotel divided by the number of available rooms during a specific period and is calculated as follows:

$$\text{TRevPAR} = \frac{\text{Total Hotel Revenue}}{\text{Number of Available Rooms}}$$

Total hotel revenue includes all operating revenue streams generated by the property, such as rooms, food and beverage outlets, meeting and conference facilities, spa and wellness services, parking, retail operations, resort fees, and other ancillary activities.

Conceptually, TRevPAR extends the logic of RevPAR from a room-centric perspective to a property-wide perspective. While RevPAR evaluates how effectively room inventory generates room revenue, TRevPAR evaluates how effectively room inventory supports the generation of total hotel revenue. The underlying assumption is that the room functions as the primary gateway through which guests access the broader portfolio of hotel services. Consequently, every available room represents not only a potential room-night sale but also an opportunity to generate additional spending throughout the property.

From a strategic perspective, TRevPAR aligns closely with the philosophy of TRM (Santos et al., 2020). Traditional RM primarily seeks to optimize room revenue through pricing and inventory control decisions. TRM, by contrast, recognizes that guests generate value across multiple departments and that maximizing room revenue does not necessarily maximize total hotel revenue. For example, a hotel may decide to accept a lower room rate from a guest who is expected to generate significant expenditure in restaurants, bars, spa facilities, or conference services. Such decisions may appear suboptimal from a RevPAR perspective but highly beneficial from a TRevPAR perspective.

The relevance of TRevPAR is particularly evident in full-service hotels, resorts, convention hotels, integrated hospitality complexes, and luxury properties, where non-room revenue streams often represent a substantial share of total revenue. In many resort environments, food and beverage operations, wellness facilities, recreational services, and premium experiences can contribute a significant proportion of total revenues (Santos et al., 2020). In such cases, relying exclusively on RevPAR may lead managers to underestimate the true economic contribution of guests and market segments.

To illustrate this point, consider two hotels with identical RevPAR values of $150. Hotel A is a limited-service property where guests primarily consume the room product, while Hotel B is a luxury resort where guests regularly purchase spa treatments, premium dining experiences, and recreational activities. Although both properties exhibit identical room revenue productivity, Hotel B may generate substantially higher total revenue per available room. TRevPAR reveals this difference, whereas RevPAR does not.

Another important advantage of TRevPAR is its ability to encourage cross-departmental thinking and reduce organizational silos. Traditional hotel structures often separate rooms, food and beverage, events, and ancillary operations into distinct departments with different objectives and performance measures. TRevPAR promotes a more holistic perspective by emphasizing the overall economic performance of the property rather than the performance of individual departments. As a result, it supports strategic coordination among commercial, operational and marketing functions.

Although TRevPAR provides a more comprehensive view of hotel revenue generation, it is primarily a revenue-based indicator rather than a profitability measure. By incorporating all revenue streams, it captures the commercial contribution of the entire property but does not consider the costs incurred in generating those revenues. As a result, departments with substantially different cost structures are treated as equally valuable from a revenue perspective. For example, food and beverage operations often generate lower profit margins than room sales because of higher labor, inventory, and operating costs. Consequently, improvements in TRevPAR do not necessarily translate into improved financial performance, as hotels may increase total revenue by expanding low-margin activities while simultaneously reducing overall profitability.

The second limitation of TRevPAR concerns comparability across hotel types. The composition of total revenue varies considerably among hospitality properties. A limited-service hotel, a city-center business hotel, a luxury resort, and an integrated resort destination may generate fundamentally different revenue mixes. Therefore, comparing TRevPAR across different property categories can be misleading because differences in the indicator may reflect structural business model characteristics rather than managerial effectiveness.

A third limitation relates to managerial interpretation and controllability. Unlike RevPAR, which is directly linked to pricing and inventory decisions, TRevPAR reflects the combined performance of multiple departments, each influenced by different operational and strategic factors. Consequently, changes in TRevPAR may be difficult to attribute to specific managerial actions. A rise in TRevPAR may result from stronger room sales, improved restaurant performance, successful conference business, or increased ancillary spending, making diagnostic analysis more complex.

A fourth limitation is the implicit assumption that available rooms constitute the most appropriate denominator for all hotel revenue streams. While rooms are the primary capacity unit of most hotels, some departments operate under different capacity constraints. Restaurants are constrained by seats and table turnover, conference facilities by available meeting space, and spas by treatment rooms and appointment slots. As a result, some scholars argue that capacity-specific productivity indicators, such as Revenue per Available Seat Hour (RevPASH) for restaurants, may provide more accurate performance assessments for individual departments than TRevPAR alone.

These limitations have contributed to the ongoing development of more sophisticated TRM metrics, including profitability-oriented measures such as Gross Operating Profit per Available Room (GOPPAR) and emerging contribution-based indicators. Nevertheless, TRevPAR remains one of the most important milestones in the evolution of hotel performance measurement because it shifts managerial attention beyond room revenue and encourages a broader understanding of value creation within hospitality organizations.

From an educational perspective, TRevPAR should be viewed as the natural evolution of RevPAR within the TRM paradigm. Whereas RevPAR answers the question, "How effectively does the hotel convert its room inventory into room revenue?", TRevPAR addresses the broader question, "How effectively does the hotel convert its room inventory into total property revenue?" This distinction is particularly important in contemporary hospitality environments where guests increasingly engage with multiple products and services during their stay.

Total Revenue per Occupied Room

Total Revenue per Occupied Room (TRevPOR) is a performance indicator that focuses on the economic value generated by each occupied room. As such, it shifts managerial attention from inventory productivity toward guest spending behavior and revenue extraction per occupied room.

TRevPOR is defined as the total revenue generated by the hotel divided by the number of occupied rooms during a specific period and is calculated as follows:

$$\text{TRevPOR} = \frac{\text{Total Hotel Revenue}}{\text{Rooms Sold}}$$

where total hotel revenue includes all operating revenue streams generated during the period, such as rooms revenue, food and beverage sales, conference and event revenue, spa and wellness services, parking, retail operations, resort fees, and other ancillary revenues.

From an RM perspective, TRevPOR is particularly valuable because it recognizes that guests differ significantly in their overall economic contribution to the hotel. Traditional room-based metrics implicitly assume that the room transaction is the primary source of value creation. However, many guests generate substantial revenues beyond accommodation. A guest staying in a resort may purchase spa treatments, dine in hotel restaurants, consume beverages, participate in recreational activities, and purchase premium experiences. Similarly, a business traveler attending a conference may contribute revenue through meeting facilities, catering services, and ancillary purchases. TRevPOR captures these broader economic effects and therefore provides a more comprehensive measure of guest value than ADR alone.

The strategic significance of TRevPOR becomes evident when comparing market segments. Consider two guests who both pay an ADR of \$200. The first guest uses only the room product and generates no additional spending. The second guest spends an additional \$150 on food and beverage services and \$100 on spa treatments. Although both guests contribute equally to ADR, their overall contribution to hotel revenue differs substantially. TRevPOR allows managers to identify these differences and evaluate guest segments based on their total spending patterns rather than solely on room rates. For this reason, TRevPOR is associated with the broader philosophy of TRM.

Another important application of TRevPOR concerns market segmentation and customer relationship management. By calculating TRevPOR across different customer groups, hotels can identify high-value segments that may not necessarily pay the highest room rates. For example, leisure travelers, conference attendees, loyalty program members, and package tourists may exhibit very different spending behaviors across hotel departments. Consequently, TRevPOR can support more informed pricing, marketing, and customer acquisition decisions by highlighting the segments that generate the highest overall value for the property.

Furthermore, TRevPOR can be particularly useful when evaluating upselling, cross-selling, and ancillary revenue strategies. Many contemporary hospitality organizations invest heavily in pre-arrival upselling campaigns, personalized offers, and experience-based marketing initiatives designed to increase guest spending beyond accommodation. TRevPOR provides a direct measure of the effectiveness of these initiatives by capturing their impact on total revenue generated per occupied room.

Notwithstanding its advantages, TRevPOR exhibits several shortcomings. Firstly, like TRevPAR, it remains a revenue-based rather than a profit-based measure. Certain ancillary services may involve substantial operational costs, labor requirements, or commission expenses. Consequently, a higher TRevPOR does not necessarily imply higher profitability. A guest who generates significant food and beverage revenue may not be more profitable than a guest who primarily purchases high-margin room products.

A second limitation concerns its dependence on occupancy levels. Because the denominator of the metric is occupied rooms rather than available rooms, TRevPOR does not capture inventory utilization. A hotel may increase TRevPOR by attracting higher-spending guests while simultaneously experiencing lower occupancy levels. Consequently, TRevPOR should not be interpreted as a measure of overall property productivity. Unlike TRevPAR, it provides no information regarding how effectively the hotel converts its available capacity into revenue. For example, a hotel selling 50 rooms and generating $20,000 in total revenue would achieve a TRevPOR of $400. Another hotel selling 90 rooms and generating $30,000 in total revenue would report a TRevPOR of only $333. Although the first hotel appears superior according to TRevPOR, the second hotel generates substantially higher total revenue and may exhibit stronger overall financial performance.

A third limitation relates to managerial attribution. Because TRevPOR aggregates revenue from multiple departments, it may be difficult to determine which specific operational activities contributed to changes in the indicator. An increase in

TRevPOR could result from higher room rates, increased restaurant spending, successful upselling initiatives, conference business growth, or enhanced ancillary revenue programs. Consequently, while TRevPOR provides a useful overall measure of guest value, it often requires supplementary analysis to identify the underlying drivers of performance.

Another shortcoming relates to comparability across different hotel types and business models. Hotels with extensive ancillary facilities naturally tend to achieve higher TRevPOR values than limited-service properties. Resorts, integrated hospitality complexes, and luxury hotels often generate substantial non-room revenue, whereas economy and limited-service hotels rely primarily on accommodation revenue. Therefore, direct comparisons of TRevPOR across different hotel categories should be interpreted with caution.

These limitations have led some scholars and practitioners to advocate for even more customer-centric measures, including guest profitability indicators, customer lifetime value (CLV), and contribution-based metrics. Nevertheless, TRevPOR remains an important intermediary step in the evolution from traditional room-focused RM toward broader customer-value and TRM frameworks.

From an educational perspective, TRevPOR can be understood as the total revenue equivalent of ADR. While ADR answers the question, "How much room revenue does the average occupied room generate?", TRevPOR addresses the broader question, "How much total hotel revenue does the average occupied room generate?" This distinction is particularly relevant in contemporary hospitality environments where ancillary spending represents an increasingly important component of guest value.

Revenue per Available Guest (RevPAG)

Revenue per Available Guest (RevPAG) is an emerging customer-centric performance indicator that reflects the ongoing evolution of RM from a room-focused discipline toward a broader customer-value management perspective.

RevPAG is generally defined as the total revenue generated by a hotel divided by the total number of available guests within a defined customer population during a specific period. Conceptually, it may be expressed as follows:

$$\text{RevPAG} = \frac{\text{Total Revenue}}{\text{Available Guests}}$$

At first glance, RevPAG appears to be the customer-equivalent of RevPAR. Just as RevPAR measures the revenue generated from the available room inventory, RevPAG seeks to measure the revenue generated from the available guest base. In this sense, the indicator attempts to transfer the fundamental logic of RM from physical inventory management to customer portfolio management.

The emergence of RevPAG is closely associated with broader developments in Customer Relationship Management (CRM), data analytics and TRM. Historically, hotels focused on optimizing room inventory because rooms represented the primary capacity constraint and customer-level data were limited. Advances in technology have transformed this reality. Contemporary hospitality organizations now possess extensive customer databases, loyalty program records, behavioral profiles, and transaction histories, enabling managers to analyze performance from the perspective of customer relationships rather than solely from the perspective of room inventory.

From a strategic standpoint, RevPAG reflects the idea that hospitality organizations should not only maximize the productivity of their rooms but also maximize the productivity of their customer base. The underlying premise is that guests differ significantly in their economic value. Some guests may purchase only accommodation services, while others generate substantial spending across restaurants, bars, spas, conference facilities, recreational activities, and other ancillary services. Consequently, two hotels with identical RevPAR values may generate very different levels of total customer value depending on the spending behavior of their guests.

The managerial relevance of RevPAG can be illustrated through a simple example. Consider two hotels that each generate total revenues of $1,000,000 during a given period. Hotel A generates this revenue from a customer base of 5,000 available guests, while Hotel B generates the same revenue from a customer base of 10,000 available guests. The resulting RevPAG values would be $RevPAG_A$=$200 and $RevPAG_B$=$200. Although both hotels generate identical revenues, Hotel A extracts twice as much revenue from each available guest. From a customer monetization perspective, Hotel A therefore demonstrates superior performance. RevPAG thus provides insights that cannot be captured by traditional room-based indicators.

One of the principal strengths of RevPAG is its ability to support customer-centric decision-making. RM has traditionally focused on optimizing room availability and pricing decisions. RevPAG broadens this perspective by emphasizing the economic value generated by guests. This makes the indicator particularly relevant in environments where customer data is abundant and where hospitality organizations seek to personalize pricing, marketing, loyalty programs, and ancillary revenue strategies.

Furthermore, RevPAG aligns closely with the philosophy of TRM. Whereas RevPAR focuses exclusively on room revenue productivity, RevPAG encourages managers to evaluate the total revenue contribution of guests across all revenue-generating departments. As a result, it can support more sophisticated customer segmentation strategies based on total value rather than accommodation expenditure alone. High-value guests may be identified not because they pay the highest room rates but because they generate substantial total spending throughout the property.

RevPAG may also contribute to the evaluation of customer acquisition and retention strategies. Hotels increasingly invest in loyalty programs, personalized marketing campaigns, digital engagement initiatives, and customer relationship management systems. By measuring revenue generated relative to the available guest base, RevPAG provides insight into the effectiveness of these investments in converting customer potential into actual revenue.

Despite its conceptual appeal, RevPAG faces several important limitations that currently restrict its widespread adoption. The first and most significant limitation concerns the definition of the denominator itself. Unlike RevPAR, where the concept of an "available room" is universally understood and operationally measurable, the notion of an "available guest" remains ambiguous. Different organizations may define available guests in different ways. Some may consider all customers included in a CRM database as available guests. Others may use loyalty program members, active customers, target market populations, or previous guests. Consequently, the calculation of RevPAG may vary substantially across organizations, reducing comparability and standardization. This lack of conceptual clarity represents one of the major reasons why RevPAG has not yet achieved the same level of acceptance as traditional RM metrics. While the room is a clearly defined capacity unit, the customer base is often fluid, dynamic, and difficult to delimit precisely. Therefore, two hotels reporting identical RevPAG values may be using fundamentally different definitions of available guests.

A second limitation relates to the indicator's lack of capacity awareness. RM was originally developed to optimize the utilization of constrained and perishable inventory. RevPAR, ADR, and Occupancy directly reflect this reality because they are linked to room capacity. RevPAG, by contrast, focuses on customer value rather than inventory utilization. Consequently, a hotel may achieve a high RevPAG while simultaneously operating with poor occupancy levels and inefficient use of its available room inventory. For this reason, RevPAG cannot replace traditional capacity-based RM indicators.

A third limitation concerns profitability. Similar to RevPAR and TRevPAR, RevPAG is fundamentally a revenue measure rather than a profit measure. It does not account for customer acquisition costs, loyalty program expenses, marketing expenditures, commissions, or service delivery costs. A guest segment may generate a high RevPAG while simultaneously exhibiting low profitability due to high acquisition or servicing costs. Therefore, RevPAG should be complemented by profitability-oriented metrics whenever possible.

A fourth limitation is its relatively limited adoption within industry practice. While indicators such as RevPAR, ADR, Occupancy, TRevPAR, and GOPPAR are widely used and supported by benchmarking systems, RevPAG remains largely confined to conceptual discussions and emerging research. Industry standards and benchmarking databases have not yet fully incorporated customer-based indicators, limiting their practical applicability and comparability.

From an educational perspective, RevPAG represents an important illustration of the future direction of RM. Traditional RM metrics evaluate the productivity of physical inventory, whereas RevPAG evaluates the productivity of customer relationships. This transition reflects a broader shift in hospitality management toward customer-centricity, personalization, and value-based commercial strategies. In many respects, RevPAG can be viewed as a bridge between RM, Customer Relationship Management and TRM.

Nevertheless, the indicator should currently be regarded as an emerging rather than a mature KPI. Its conceptual foundations are compelling, but significant challenges remain regarding standardization, measurement consistency, and managerial applicability. Future research is likely to focus on refining the definition of available guests, integrating customer profitability considerations, and linking RevPAG with customer lifetime value (CLV) and other relationship-based metrics.

As RM evolves toward customer-centric value management, several related indicators have emerged alongside RevPAG. One such metric is Revenue per Available Customer (RevPAC), which shifts the unit of analysis from hotel guests to customer relationships. Whereas RevPAG focuses on the revenue generated by guests staying at the property, RevPAC evaluates revenue generated by the broader customer base, including repeat customers, loyalty members, and CRM-managed relationships. Consequently, RevPAC is more closely aligned with Customer Relationship Management (CRM) and customer portfolio management than with traditional RM.

A related measure is Average Revenue per Account (ARPA), widely used in subscription-based and digital businesses and increasingly adopted in hospitality analytics. ARPA measures the average revenue generated per customer account and is particularly useful when evaluating corporate clients, loyalty-program members, travel agencies, tour operators, and other account-based customer groups. Unlike RevPAG, which remains closely connected to guest activity, ARPA focuses on customer-account monetization and relationship value.

Although these indicators differ in their precise units of analysis, they share a common objective: shifting performance evaluation from physical inventory toward customer value creation. For this reason, they can be viewed as complementary extensions of customer-centric RM rather than as replacements for traditional inventory-based KPIs.

Gross Operating Profit per Available Room

Gross Operating Profit per Available Room (GOPPAR) has emerged as one of the most important profitability-oriented indicators in contemporary hotel performance measurement. While the more traditional RM metrics, such as Occupancy, ADR and RevPAR, focus primarily on revenue generation, GOPPAR extends the analysis by incorporating the cost dimension and evaluating the profit generated by a hotel relative to its available room inventory (Schwartz et al., 2017). As a result, GOPPAR is often regarded as one of the most owner-oriented and financially meaningful performance indicators in the hospitality industry. GOPPAR is defined as the Gross Operating Profit (GOP) generated by a hotel divided by the total number of available rooms during a specific period and is calculated as follows:

$$\text{GOPPAR} = \frac{\text{Gross Operating Profit (GOP)}}{\text{Number of Available Rooms}}$$

GOPPAR represents the profit generated from hotel operations after deducting both departmental and undistributed operating expenses from total revenue, but before fixed charges, interest, taxes, depreciation, and amortization. The calculation of GOP is typically based on the framework established by the *Uniform System of Accounts for the Lodging Industry (USALI)*, which has become the dominant accounting standard within the global hotel industry.

From a managerial perspective, GOPPAR can be interpreted as the amount of operating profit generated by each room available for sale, regardless of whether that room was occupied. Similar to RevPAR, GOPPAR normalizes performance by room inventory, allowing meaningful comparisons across properties of different sizes.

The strategic significance of GOPPAR becomes evident when comparing hotels that exhibit similar revenue performance but different cost structures. Consider two hotels, each generating a RevPAR of $150. At first glance, their rooms revenue performance appears identical. However, if Hotel A relies heavily on OTA channels, operates with higher labor costs, and incurs significant marketing expenditures, while Hotel B generates more direct bookings and maintains a more efficient cost structure, the two hotels may report substantially different GOPPAR values. In such a scenario, GOPPAR reveals differences in economic performance that remain hidden when relying solely on revenue-based indicators.

For this reason, many hotel owners, investors, asset managers, and financial analysts consider GOPPAR superior to RevPAR when evaluating overall business performance (Lee et al., 2019). While RevPAR answers the question, "How much revenue did the hotel generate from its room inventory?", GOPPAR addresses the arguably more important question, "How much profit did the hotel generate from its room inventory?". From an ownership perspective, profit generation rather than revenue generation ultimately determines the economic success and long-term sustainability of a hospitality operation.

Despite its strengths, GOPPAR is not without limitations. The first limitation concerns managerial controllability. Revenue managers directly influence room pricing, inventory controls, and distribution strategies, but many of the cost elements included in GOP are beyond their immediate control. Labor expenses, utility costs, maintenance expenditures, procurement policies, and administrative overheads are often determined by operational managers or corporate policies. Consequently, GOPPAR reflects the performance of the entire hotel organization rather than the effectiveness of the RM function alone.

A second limitation is the lack of standardization in cost structures across properties. Although USALI provides a common accounting framework, hotels operating in different markets, ownership structures, and service categories may allocate costs differently or face substantially different operating conditions. As a result, direct comparisons of GOPPAR across properties should be interpreted cautiously, particularly when comparing hotels from different segments or geographic regions.

A third limitation relates to timeliness and managerial responsiveness. Revenue-based indicators such as ADR, Occupancy and RevPAR can be monitored and adjusted daily, allowing revenue managers to make rapid tactical decisions. GOPPAR, by contrast, is often calculated monthly or quarterly because it requires complete financial information. Consequently, it functions primarily as a strategic and financial performance indicator rather than as a day-to-day operational control metric.

Furthermore, GOPPAR does not fully isolate the contribution of individual revenue streams. A hotel may achieve strong GOPPAR through exceptional food and beverage profitability while experiencing weak rooms performance, or vice versa. Therefore, while GOPPAR provides a valuable overall profitability perspective, it does not identify the specific sources of operational success or failure.

These limitations have led some researchers and practitioners to advocate for even more refined performance measures, including Contribution per Available Room (ConPAR) and departmental profitability indicators that more closely align responsibility with controllable outcomes (Kimes, 2017). Nevertheless, GOPPAR remains one of the most widely accepted profitability measures in hotel performance analysis.

In educational terms, GOPPAR can be viewed as the profitability equivalent of RevPAR. Whereas RevPAR evaluates the productivity of room inventory in generating revenue, GOPPAR evaluates the productivity of room inventory in generating operating profit. The distinction is critical because revenue generation and profit generation are not synonymous. A hotel may achieve outstanding revenue performance while simultaneously generating disappointing profit margins, particularly in environments characterized by high acquisition costs, rising labor expenses, or inefficient operations.

3. Competitive Benchmarking KPIs

The emergence of MPI, ARI, and RGI reflects the increasing importance of competitive benchmarking within hotel RM (Haynes, 2016). Unlike traditional performance indicators that evaluate internal performance, these indices assess a hotel's ability to capture its fair share of market demand, pricing power, and revenue generation relative to competitors. Previous research has emphasized that hotel performance should be interpreted within a competitive context rather than through absolute measures alone (Enz, Canina, & Walsh, 2001; Enz, Canina, & Lomanno, 2004). Consequently, benchmarking indicators have become central components of contemporary RM systems and are extensively used in both academic research and industry practice (Sainaghi, 2010).

Market Penetration Index

Market Penetration Index (MPI), also known as Occupancy Index, is one of the most widely used competitive benchmarking indicators in the hotel industry. While occupancy measures the percentage of available rooms sold within a property, MPI evaluates occupancy performance relative to a predefined competitive set (comp set). Consequently, MPI shifts the analytical focus from internal performance measurement to market positioning. MPI is calculated as follows:

$$\text{MPI} = \frac{\text{Hotel Occupancy}}{\text{Competitive Set Occupancy}} \times 100$$

An MPI value of 100 indicates that the hotel achieves the same occupancy performance as its competitive set. Values above 100 indicate that the hotel captures a larger share of available demand than its competitors, whereas values below 100 suggest underperformance relative to the market. For example, if a hotel reports an occupancy rate of 80% while its competitive set achieves an average occupancy of 70%, the resulting MPI is 114.3 and indicates that the hotel is capturing approximately 14% more room demand than the average competitor.

The primary advantage of MPI is that it contextualizes occupancy performance. An occupancy rate of 70% may appear satisfactory when viewed in isolation; however, if competitors achieve 85% occupancy, the hotel's relative market performance is weak. Conversely, a 60% occupancy rate may represent excellent performance during periods of market-wide demand decline.

Despite its usefulness, MPI inherits many of the limitations associated with occupancy itself. Most importantly, it focuses exclusively on volume and ignores pricing effectiveness, profitability, and distribution costs. A hotel may achieve a very high MPI by aggressively discounting room rates, thereby gaining market share at the expense of revenue and profitability. Consequently, MPI should not be interpreted as a standalone measure of commercial success.

From a RM perspective, MPI is best viewed as an indicator of demand capture effectiveness. It reveals how successfully a hotel attracts room demand relative to competitors but provides no information regarding the quality or profitability of that demand.

Average Rate Index

Average Rate Index (ARI) evaluates a hotel's pricing performance relative to its competitive set. Whereas MPI focuses on occupancy share, ARI focuses on rate positioning and pricing power. ARI is calculated as follows:

$$ARI = \frac{\text{Hotel ADR}}{\text{Competitive Set ADR}} \times 100$$

An ARI value of 100 indicates parity with competitors, while values above 100 indicate that the hotel achieves higher average room rates than its competitive set. For example, if a hotel achieves an ADR of \$180 while the competitive set reports an average ADR of \$150, the ARI is calculated as 120 and indicates that the hotel achieves room rates approximately 20% higher than the market average.

ARI is frequently interpreted as a measure of pricing power, brand strength, perceived quality, and market positioning. Luxury hotels, boutique properties, and strongly differentiated brands often maintain ARI values significantly above 100 because customers are willing to pay premium prices.

From a strategic perspective, ARI provides valuable information regarding the hotel's ability to command rate premiums. However, similar to ADR, ARI ignores volume effects. A hotel may achieve an exceptionally high ARI while suffering from low occupancy levels and poor overall revenue performance. Consequently, ARI should not be interpreted as evidence of superior RM performance on its own. It merely indicates that the hotel achieves higher or lower average room rates relative to competitors.

This limitation is particularly important because managers sometimes become excessively focused on maintaining rate premiums. While premium pricing may strengthen brand positioning, excessively high rates may reduce demand and ultimately diminish total revenue generation. Therefore, ARI is most useful when analyzed alongside occupancy-related indicators such as MPI and revenue productivity measures such as RGI.

Revenue Generation Index

Revenue Generation Index (RGI), sometimes referred to as RevPAR Index, is generally regarded as the most comprehensive of the three competitive benchmarking indicators. RGI evaluates a hotel's RevPAR performance relative to its competitive set and therefore combines both occupancy and pricing dimensions into a single measure of competitive effectiveness. RGI is calculated as follows:

$$RGI = \frac{\text{Hotel RevPAR}}{\text{Competitive Set RevPAR}} \times 100$$

An RGI value of 100 indicates that the hotel achieves the same RevPAR performance as its competitive set. Values above 100 indicate revenue outperformance, whereas values below 100 indicate underperformance. For example, if a hotel reports a RevPAR of $120 while its competitors achieve an average RevPAR of $100, then RGI=120 and indicates that the hotel generates 20% more room revenue per available room than the average competitor.

Because RevPAR incorporates both occupancy and ADR, RGI effectively captures the combined outcome of pricing and demand-management decisions. For this reason, it is often considered the most important competitive benchmarking KPI in contemporary RM practice. From a managerial perspective, RGI answers a simple but strategically critical question: "Is the hotel generating more or less room revenue than its fair share of the market?". Consequently, many hotel companies establish explicit RGI targets and use RGI as a key performance criterion for general managers and revenue managers.

One of the greatest strengths of RGI is that it reduces the ambiguity associated with MPI and ARI. A hotel may have a lower occupancy than competitors but compensate through superior pricing. Conversely, a hotel may maintain lower ADR but achieve exceptional occupancy. RGI consolidates these effects and evaluates the overall outcome.

However, RGI is not without limitations. First, RGI remains fundamentally a rooms revenue indicator. It ignores food and beverage revenue, conference income, spa revenue, and other ancillary streams that may be strategically important, particularly in full-service hotels and resorts. Second, RGI is a gross revenue metric and therefore ignores distribution costs, acquisition expenses, and profitability differences among channels. Two hotels may report identical RGI values while exhibiting significantly different levels of profit performance. Third limitation is that RGI is highly dependent on the composition of the competitive set. A poorly defined comp set may distort benchmarking results and lead to misleading managerial conclusions. Consequently, the validity of RGI depends heavily on the quality of competitive benchmarking practices.

4. Ancillary Services – Centric KPIs

Ancillary revenues encompass all revenues generated beyond accommodation, including food and beverage sales, spa and wellness services, meeting and event facilities, golf operations, parking, retail outlets, recreational activities, resort fees, and a wide range of other guest services. In many hospitality businesses, these revenue streams contribute substantially to overall financial performance and may account for a significant share of total revenue and profit.

As a result, RM has gradually expanded beyond guestrooms to include the optimization of ancillary products and services. This evolution has stimulated the development of a distinct family of ancillary RM KPIs designed to evaluate the effectiveness, productivity, and profitability of non-room revenue sources. The KPIs presented in this section can be broadly categorized into four groups: (a) guest-based ancillary revenue indicators (e.g., ARPOR and ARPG), (b) service utilization indicators (e.g., Capture Rate and Conversion Rate), (c) capacity-based productivity indicators (e.g., RevPASH, RevPATH, and RevPAM), and (d) profitability-oriented ancillary KPIs (e.g. Ancillary Contribution Margin). Collectively, these measures reflect the broader transition from traditional room-centric RM toward a TRM perspective that seeks to optimize value creation across the entire hospitality ecosystem.

Ancillary Revenue per Occupied Room

Ancillary Revenue per Occupied Room (ARPOR) measures the average ancillary revenue generated by each occupied room during a given period and it is calculated as follows:

$$ARPOR = \frac{\text{Ancillary Revenue}}{\text{Occupied Rooms}}$$

As is easily understood, this indicator evaluates the effectiveness of a hotel's ability to generate additional revenue from guests beyond accommodation purchases. It is particularly useful for assessing upselling, cross-selling, and guest engagement strategies. For example, if a hotel generates $50,000 in ancillary revenue from 1,000 occupied rooms, then the ARPOR is $50, i.e. each occupied room generates, on average, $50 in ancillary revenue.

From a managerial perspective, ARPOR provides a simple and intuitive measure of ancillary monetization effectiveness. However, it assumes that all occupied rooms have equal ancillary spending potential and therefore may conceal significant variation among guest segments.

Ancillary Revenue per Guest

While ARPOR focuses on occupied rooms, Ancillary Revenue per Guest (ARPG) evaluates ancillary spending at the individual guest level. It is calculated as follows:

$$ARPG = \frac{\text{Ancillary Revenue}}{\text{Number of Guests}}$$

ARPG is particularly relevant in resorts, all-inclusive properties, cruise operations and family-oriented destinations where room occupancy may vary considerably. For example, if the ancillary revenue is $100,000 and it is generated from 2,500 guests, ARPG suggests that each guest spends an average of $40 on ancillary services. Compared with ARPOR, ARPG provides a more customer-centric perspective because it recognizes that revenue is generated by guests rather than rooms.

Capture Rate

Capture Rate measures the proportion of eligible guests who use a specific service and it isa calculated as follows

$$Capture\ Rate = \frac{\text{Guests Using the Service}}{\text{Eligible Guests}} \times 100$$

For example, if from 1,000 hotel guests the 250 became spa users, the spa capture rate is 25%. Capture rate can be widely used in restaurants, spa facilities, golf operations, parking services, etc. From a RM perspective, Capture Rate reflects market penetration within the existing customer base.

Conversion Rate

Conversion Rate measures the effectiveness of marketing, sales, and upselling initiatives in converting opportunities into purchases.

$$Conversion\ Rate = \frac{\text{Transactions}}{\text{Offers Presented}} \times 100$$

For example, after 500 spa offers were presented, the hotel had 100 spa bookings so the conversion rate is 20%. This indicator helps managers evaluate the effectiveness of ancillary revenue campaigns and personalized guest offers.

Revenue per Available Seat Hour

RevPASH is perhaps the most established ancillary revenue KPI and is often described as the restaurant equivalent of RevPAR. Originally developed by Kimes (1999), RevPASH is calculated as:

$$RevPASH = \frac{\text{Restaurant Revenue}}{\text{Available Seat Hours}}$$

The indicator incorporates both physical capacity (seats) and time utilization (hours). RevPASH enables restaurant managers to evaluate the effectiveness of seating management, reservation systems, table turnover, and pricing strategies. Because restaurant inventory is highly perishable, RevPASH closely mirrors the logic of traditional RM.

Revenue per Available Treatment Hour

Revenue per Available Treatment Hour (RevPATH) applies the same productivity concept to spa operations and it is calculated as follows:

$$RevPATH = \frac{\text{Spa Revenue}}{\text{Available Treatment Hours}}$$

Alternative RevPATH can be calculated by multiplying the treatment room occupancy by the average treatment-related expenditure per person. Kimes & Singh (2009) propose a framework for implementing a spa RM strategy based on RevPATH.

The indicator measures the revenue productivity of spa capacity and helps managers optimize therapist scheduling, treatment pricing, appointment allocation, promotional campaigns. Usually, RevPATH is used in luxury resorts and wellness-focused hospitality businesses.

Revenue per Available Square Meter

Revenue per Available Square Meter (RevPAM) extends capacity-based measurement to physical space.

$$RevPAM = \frac{\text{Revenue}}{\text{Available Square Meters}}$$

It is particularly relevant for conference facilities, event venues, retail spaces, co-working areas, exhibition halls. RevPAM supports strategic decisions regarding facility utilization and space allocation.

Ancillary Contribution Margin

Ancillary Contribution Margin measures the profit contribution generated by ancillary services after deducting variable costs.

$$\text{Ancillary Contribution Margin} = \frac{\text{Ancillary Revenue} - \text{Variable Costs}}{\text{Ancillary Revenue}} \times 100$$

The indicator reveals the economic quality of ancillary revenue. For example, spa services often exhibit high contribution margins, whereas food and beverage operations may generate substantial revenue but lower margins.

Ancillary GOP Contribution

Hotels increasingly analyze the contribution of ancillary services to Gross Operating Profit.

$$\textit{Ancillary GOP Ratio} = \frac{\text{Ancillary GOP}}{\text{Total GOP}} \times 100$$

This KPI evaluates the extent to which ancillary operations contribute to overall property profitability. From an ownership perspective, this measure is often more meaningful than ancillary revenue itself.

Although ancillary revenue KPIs provide valuable insights, several limitations should be acknowledged. First, there is currently no universally accepted standardization comparable to RevPAR. Different organizations define ancillary revenues, guest counts, and capacity units differently, reducing benchmarking consistency. Second, many ancillary KPIs remain department-specific and may not fully capture cross-departmental customer value creation. Third, revenue-based indicators frequently ignore profitability considerations. A hotel may increase ancillary revenues while simultaneously reducing margins through excessive discounting or promotional activity. Fourth, ancillary revenue metrics are often highly dependent on hotel type. Resorts, luxury properties, and convention hotels naturally exhibit greater ancillary revenue potential than limited-service hotels, making cross-property comparisons challenging.

5. RM Process KPIs

Whereas outcome KPIs evaluate what happened, RM process KPIs evaluate how effectively the RM system operates. They measure the quality of forecasting, the responsiveness of demand monitoring systems, the effectiveness of inventory controls, and the ability of revenue managers to identify and react to changing market conditions. In this sense, process KPIs can be viewed as indicators of RM capability rather than RM outcomes. Among the most widely used process KPIs are forecast accuracy indicators, pickup and pace measures, denial and regret statistics, and estimates of unconstrained demand.

Average Length of Stay

Average Length of Stay (ALOS) is one of the most widely monitored demand-structure indicators in hotel RM. ALOS does not directly evaluate revenue or profitability outcomes, but instead, it describes a fundamental characteristic of demand by measuring the average number of nights guests remain at a property during a specific period. It is calculated as follows:

$$ALOS = \frac{\text{Occupied Room Nights}}{\text{Number of Bookings}}$$

For example, if a hotel records 1,000 occupied room nights generated from 250 reservations during a month, the resulting ALOS equals four nights. This indicates that guests stay, on average, four nights per booking.

Although simple in its calculation, ALOS plays a critical role in RM because length-of-stay patterns directly influence inventory availability, forecasting accuracy, overbooking decisions, and inventory control strategies. Revenue managers are concerned not only with how many rooms are sold, but also with how long those rooms remain occupied. Consequently, ALOS provides important information regarding the structure and behavior of demand.

From a forecasting perspective, ALOS is a key determinant of future inventory consumption. Demand forecasts based solely on arrival volumes may significantly underestimate or overestimate future occupancy if changes in average stay duration are ignored. For example, an increase in the number of arriving guests does not necessarily imply a proportional increase in room-night demand if average stay duration simultaneously declines. Similarly, relatively stable arrival volumes may generate substantial increases in occupancy when ALOS rises.

For this reason, many Revenue Management Systems (RMS) monitor ALOS continuously and incorporate length-of-stay patterns into forecasting models. Changes in ALOS often provide early indications of shifts in market behavior, customer preferences, seasonality patterns, or segment composition (Atsız et al.,2022). Business travelers typically exhibit shorter stays than leisure travelers, while resort destinations frequently experience longer average stays than urban hotels (Ivanov,

2014). Consequently, fluctuations in ALOS may reveal important changes in demand mix and customer behavior.

The strategic importance of ALOS becomes particularly evident in inventory control decisions. Length-of-stay restrictions such as Minimum Length of Stay (MinLOS), Closed to Arrival (CTA), and Closed to Departure (CTD) are explicitly designed to influence booking patterns and optimize inventory utilization. These controls aim to maximize the value extracted from limited room inventory by encouraging booking behaviors that improve occupancy distribution across high-demand periods.

For example, during periods of anticipated peak demand, a hotel may impose a minimum stay requirement to avoid selling valuable inventory to short-stay guests who could displace more profitable multi-night bookings. In such situations, understanding historical and forecasted ALOS becomes essential for evaluating the effectiveness of inventory-control strategies.

ALOS is also closely associated with displacement analysis (Talluri & Van Ryzin, 2004). Revenue managers frequently evaluate whether accepting a booking request may prevent the hotel from accommodating future demand with greater revenue potential. Because displacement calculations depend heavily on the number of room nights consumed by each reservation, average stay duration becomes an important factor in assessing opportunity costs and optimizing booking acceptance decisions.

Another important application of ALOS concerns overbooking management. Longer stays consume inventory over multiple nights and may create different risk profiles than short-stay reservations. Consequently, understanding length-of-stay distributions improves the accuracy of occupancy forecasts and supports more effective overbooking decisions.

Despite its importance, ALOS presents several limitations. First, it is a descriptive rather than evaluative indicator. A higher ALOS is not inherently better or worse than a lower ALOS. The managerial implications depend heavily on market conditions, business models, seasonality, and strategic objectives. For example, extended stays may increase occupancy stability and reduce acquisition costs, but they may also limit pricing flexibility during high-demand periods. Second, ALOS does not provide direct information regarding revenue generation, profitability, or customer value. Two hotels may exhibit identical average stay durations while generating substantially different ADR, RevPAR, or GOPPAR performance levels. Consequently, ALOS should not be interpreted as a standalone measure of commercial success. Third, aggregate ALOS values may conceal substantial variation across market segments, booking channels, customer types, and seasons. Segment-level analysis is therefore often more informative than property-level averages. For example, corporate travelers, leisure tourists, group bookings, and long-stay guests frequently exhibit significantly different stay patterns that may require distinct RM strategies.

From an educational perspective, ALOS can be viewed as a bridge between demand forecasting and inventory control. Whereas many traditional KPIs evaluate the outcomes of RM decisions, ALOS helps explain the underlying demand characteristics that shape those decisions. In this sense, it functions less as a performance metric and more as a demand-intelligence indicator that supports forecasting, inventory optimization, and capacity management.

Forecast Accuracy and Forecast Bias

Forecasting lies at the heart of RM. Virtually every RM decision—including pricing, inventory allocation, overbooking controls, length-of-stay restrictions, and channel management—depends on expectations regarding future demand. As a result, the quality of demand forecasts directly influences the quality of RM decisions.

Forecast accuracy indicators evaluate the extent to which forecasted demand corresponds with actual demand. Common measures include Mean Absolute Error (MAE), Mean Absolute Percentage Error (MAPE), Root Mean Squared Error (RMSE), and Weighted Absolute Percentage Error (WAPE). Although each metric has specific advantages and limitations, their common objective is to quantify forecasting precision.

A related concept is forecast bias, which evaluates whether forecasting errors occur systematically in one direction. A positive bias indicates consistent overestimation of demand, whereas a negative bias indicates systematic underestimation. Unlike random forecasting errors, forecast bias suggests structural weaknesses in forecasting models, data quality, or managerial assumptions.

From an RM perspective, forecasting errors can generate substantial revenue consequences (Weatherford & Kimes, 2003). Overestimation of demand may lead to excessive rate increases, restrictive inventory controls, and missed sales opportunities. Underestimation may result in unnecessary discounting, premature inventory release, and displacement of higher-value demand. Consequently, forecast accuracy is often regarded as one of the most important indicators of RM process quality.

Importantly, forecasting performance should not be evaluated solely at the aggregate property level. Forecast accuracy often varies considerably across market segments, distribution channels, room types, and booking windows. Segment-level forecasting diagnostics therefore provide more actionable managerial insights than aggregate accuracy measures alone.

Pickup and Pace Analysis

Pickup and pace indicators provide real-time visibility into booking behavior and represent some of the most frequently monitored operational metrics in hotel RM.

Pickup refers to the change in reservations or revenue accumulated for a future arrival date over a specified period. For example, if bookings for a future Saturday increase from 80 to 100 room nights over a seven-day period, the pickup equals 20 room nights.

Pace compares current booking levels with historical benchmarks, most commonly the same booking horizon from the previous year. In other words, pace analysis answers the question *"Are bookings accumulating faster or slower than expected?"*.

These indicators are particularly valuable because they provide early signals regarding future demand conditions. Strong pickup may indicate accelerating demand, suggesting opportunities for price increases, inventory restrictions, or channel optimization. Weak pickup may signal the need for promotional activity, pricing adjustments, or increased distribution exposure.

One of the greatest strengths of pickup and pace analysis is their operational responsiveness. Unlike monthly financial indicators, pickup and pace can be monitored daily, allowing revenue managers to identify demand shifts quickly and adjust pricing and inventory strategies accordingly.

However, pickup and pace measures should be interpreted carefully. Changes in booking behavior may reflect alterations in customer booking windows, market uncertainty, competitor actions, or distribution-channel dynamics rather than changes in total demand itself (Heo et al., 2024; Ampountolas & Bai, 2026). Therefore, these indicators are most effective when analyzed alongside forecasting and market intelligence data.

Denials, Regrets, and Unconstrained Demand

Denials and regrets represent some of the most theoretically important—but often underutilized—process indicators in RM.

A denial occurs when a booking request cannot be accommodated because the requested inventory is unavailable or restricted. In contrast, a regret occurs when a customer declines to book after observing the offered price, restrictions, or perceived value proposition.

These concepts originate from the foundations of yield management and are central to understanding demand unconstrained by inventory limitations.

Denials reveal situations where demand exceeded available capacity. High denial levels may indicate successful demand stimulation and justify future price increases or inventory expansion. However, they may also suggest overly restrictive controls that unnecessarily reject profitable demand.

Regrets provide insight into price resistance and customer willingness to pay. Rising regret levels may indicate that pricing strategies exceed market acceptance thresholds, potentially reducing conversion rates and long-term demand.

Both measures contribute to the estimation of unconstrained demand, defined as the demand that would have materialized if no inventory limitations, booking restrictions, or capacity constraints had existed. Unconstrained demand estimation is fundamental to advanced RM systems because it enables managers to distinguish between observed demand and latent market demand.

From a strategic perspective, denials, regrets, and unconstrained demand provide information that traditional revenue KPIs cannot capture. RevPAR may reveal how much revenue was generated, but denial and regret indicators help explain how much additional revenue might have been generated under different pricing and inventory decisions.

To facilitate comparison, Table 1 provides a comparative summary of the principal RM KPIs discussed in this chapter, including their formulas, primary purposes, strengths, limitations, and typical applications.

Table 1. Comparative Summary of Key Performance Indicators in Hotel Revenue Management

KPI	Formula	Primary purpose	Main strengths	Main limitations	Best application
Occupancy (OCC)	Occupied Rooms / Available Rooms	Measure capacity utilization	Simple, intuitive, reflects demand intensity	Ignores price, costs and profitability	Capacity monitoring and demand analysis
ADR	Room Revenue / Rooms Sold	Measure average room price	Indicates pricing effectiveness	Ignores unsold rooms and acquisition costs	Pricing evaluation by segment or channel
Net ADR	Net Room Revenue / Rooms Sold	Measure average retained room revenue after distribution costs	Incorporates channel efficiency into pricing evaluation	Depends on consistent allocation of distribution costs and does not capture capacity utilization	Segment- and channel-level pricing analysis
RevPAR	Room Revenue / Available Rooms (or ADR × OCC)	Measure room revenue productivity	Balances price and occupancy; industry benchmark	Excludes ancillary revenues and costs	Overall room performance and benchmarking

continued on following page

Table 1. Continued

KPI	Formula	Primary purpose	Main strengths	Main limitations	Best application
NRevPAR	(Room Revenue – Distribution Costs) / Available Rooms	Measure net room revenue productivity	Incorporates channel efficiency and acquisition costs	Limited standardization of cost allocation	Distribution and channel management
TRevPAR	Total Hotel Revenue / Available Rooms	Measure total hotel revenue productivity	Supports Total Revenue Management; captures all revenue streams	Ignores profitability; affected by hotel business model	Full-service hotels, resorts, TRM
TRevPOR	Total Hotel Revenue / Occupied Rooms	Measure guest spending per occupied room	Highlights guest value and ancillary spending	Does not measure inventory productivity	Guest value and ancillary revenue analysis
RevPAG	Total Revenue / Available Guests	Measure customer revenue productivity	Customer-centric perspective	Lack of standardized denominator; limited adoption	CRM and customer portfolio analysis
GOPPAR	Gross Operating Profit / Available Rooms	Measure operating profitability	Incorporates costs; owner-oriented	Influenced by non-RM operational decisions	Profitability and investment evaluation
MPI	Hotel OCC / Comp Set OCC ×100	Measure market share in occupancy	Competitive benchmarking	Ignores pricing and profitability	Competitive demand analysis
ARI	Hotel ADR / Comp Set ADR ×100	Measure pricing power	Evaluates relative pricing	Ignores occupancy	Rate positioning
RGI	Hotel RevPAR / Comp Set RevPAR ×100	Measure overall competitive performance	Combines occupancy and pricing	Room-focused; depends on comp-set quality	Strategic competitive benchmarking
ARPOR / ARPG	Ancillary Revenue / Occupied Rooms or Guests	Measure ancillary revenue generation	Evaluates cross-selling and upselling	Revenue rather than profit	Ancillary revenue management
RevPASH / RevPATH / RevPAM	Revenue / Capacity Unit	Measure departmental productivity	Capacity-specific optimization	Department-specific; limited comparability	Restaurant, spa and event RM
Forecast Accuracy	MAPE, MAE, RMSE, etc.	Evaluate forecasting quality	Improves pricing and inventory decisions	Depends on data quality	Forecast evaluation

continued on following page

Table 1. Continued

KPI	Formula	Primary purpose	Main strengths	Main limitations	Best application
Pickup / Pace	Booking accumulation measures	Monitor booking trends	Early demand signals	Sensitive to booking-window changes	Tactical RM decisions
Denials / Regrets	Booking requests rejected or declined	Estimate unconstrained demand	Supports inventory optimization	Difficult to measure consistently	Advanced RM systems

EMERGING KPI IDEAS AND FUTURE KPI DIRECTIONS

The evolution of hotel RM has been accompanied by a parallel evolution in performance measurement. Early RM systems emerged within a context where the primary objective was maximizing room revenue from a fixed and perishable inventory. Consequently, the industry's dominant performance indicators—Occupancy, ADR and RevPAR—were designed to evaluate room inventory productivity. For several decades, these metrics provided an effective foundation for monitoring and benchmarking hotel performance.

However, the contemporary hospitality environment presents challenges that increasingly expose the limitations of traditional KPI frameworks. Hotels operate within highly digitalized distribution ecosystems, face growing customer acquisition costs, generate substantial ancillary revenues and increasingly compete through personalized customer experiences rather than room products alone. Simultaneously, hotel owners and investors have become more focused on profitability, asset performance, and return on investment than on revenue growth alone. These developments have stimulated growing interest in next-generation KPIs capable of capturing dimensions of performance that remain largely invisible to traditional RM indicators.

The future of RM measurement is therefore likely to be characterized by three interconnected transitions: from revenue to profit, from rooms to customers, and from retrospective reporting to predictive intelligence.

From Revenue Metrics to Contribution-Based Metrics

One of the most important future directions concerns the growing emphasis on contribution-based performance measures. Traditional indicators such as RevPAR and TRevPAR evaluate revenue productivity but ignore the costs required to generate that revenue. In an environment characterized by OTA commissions, metasearch advertising costs, loyalty program expenses, digital marketing investments, and rising labor costs, gross revenue increasingly provides an incomplete representation of commercial performance.

This limitation has already encouraged the adoption of NRevPAR and GOPPAR. Nevertheless, many researchers argue that even these indicators do not fully align accountability with managerial controllability. Revenue managers influence pricing decisions, channel allocation, and customer mix, but they do not directly control many operating costs incorporated within profitability measures.

For this reason, future KPI development is increasingly expected to focus on contribution-based metrics, such as ConPAR, which deduct variable operating and distribution costs while excluding costs outside the direct influence of commercial decision makers. Such indicators may provide a more accurate representation of the value generated by RM decisions and better align performance measurement with organizational accountability structures.

From Room-Centric to Customer-Centric KPIs

A second major trend concerns the gradual transition from room-centric performance measurement toward customer-centric performance measurement (Talón-Ballestero et al., 2018). Historically, rooms represented the primary unit of analysis because guestrooms constituted the principal capacity constraint within hotel operations. However, advances in Customer Relationship Management (CRM), data analytics, loyalty systems, and artificial intelligence have enabled hotels to measure performance at the individual customer level.

Emerging indicators such as RevPAG, ARPA and Customer Lifetime Value (CLV) reflect this shift. These metrics recognize that customers, rather than rooms, are the ultimate generators of value. Two guests paying identical room rates may generate dramatically different levels of total revenue, ancillary spending, loyalty engagement, and long-term profitability.

Future RM systems are therefore likely to place increasing emphasis on customer portfolio optimization rather than inventory optimization alone. Under such an approach, booking decisions may be evaluated not only according to room revenue contribution but also according to expected customer lifetime value, ancillary spending behavior, acquisition cost, and retention potential.

This evolution may ultimately blur the traditional boundaries between RM, Customer Relationship Management, Marketing Analytics, and Customer Success functions, creating more integrated approaches to value management.

Total Revenue and Multi-Capacity Performance Measurement

The expansion of TRM has also created demand for more sophisticated performance indicators capable of evaluating multiple revenue-generating assets simultaneously.

Traditional RM relies heavily on room-based productivity measures because guestrooms represent the primary capacity unit. Yet hospitality organizations increasingly generate value through restaurants, conference facilities, spas, golf courses, wellness centers, co-working spaces, and entertainment venues, each characterized by distinct capacity constraints.

The success of measures such as RevPASH in RM suggests that future KPI frameworks may increasingly incorporate capacity-specific indicators tailored to the operational characteristics of individual departments. Similar approaches are already emerging through metrics such as RevPATH and RevPAM.

Future TRM systems may ultimately integrate these measures into unified dashboards capable of evaluating how effectively the entire hospitality ecosystem converts available capacity into revenue and profit.

AI-Enabled and Predictive KPIs

Perhaps the most transformative development concerns the growing influence of artificial intelligence, machine learning, and advanced analytics on RM measurement (Pereira & Cerqueira, 2022; Bulchand-Gidumal et al., 2024). Traditional KPIs are largely retrospective in nature. They evaluate performance after outcomes have occurred. Future KPI systems are increasingly expected to become predictive rather than descriptive. AI-enabled RM systems can continuously process large volumes of internal and external data, including booking patterns, search behavior, competitor pricing, online reputation metrics, weather forecasts, event calendars, flight capacity, and macroeconomic indicators. This capability creates opportunities for the development of entirely new classes of indicators.

Future AI-enabled RM systems may generate new categories of predictive and decision-support indicators. Potential examples include forecast confidence measures, dynamic pricing effectiveness indicators, AI recommendation acceptance rates, booking conversion probability scores, and other real-time opportunity assessment metrics. While such measures are not yet standardized across the industry, they illustrate the likely transition from retrospective performance measurement toward predictive and prescriptive analytics.

Sustainability and Value-Based KPIs

An emerging area of interest involves the integration of sustainability and long-term value creation into RM performance measurement.

Historically, RM focused almost exclusively on short-term revenue optimization. However, hospitality organizations increasingly operate under pressure to balance financial performance with environmental sustainability, social responsibility, and stakeholder value creation (Voukkali et al., 2023; Khalil et al., 2024; Mensah et al., 2026).

Future KPI frameworks are likely to expand beyond traditional revenue and profit metrics by incorporating sustainability and stakeholder-value considerations. Potential directions include carbon-adjusted revenue productivity measures, resource-efficiency indicators, guest-level environmental impact metrics and guest profitability measures. In addition, operational sustainability metrics—such as energy and water consumption per occupied room, waste diversion rates, green Return-on-Investment (ROI), and guest sustainability satisfaction measures—may increasingly complement financial KPIs by linking environmental efficiency with long-term value creation (Reem et al., 2022; Bruns-Smith et. al, 2015). Together, these indicators reflect a broader transition from short-term revenue optimization toward sustainable value creation, responsible resource management, and long-term customer relationship performance.

CONCLUSIONS

Key Performance Indicators occupy a central position within hotel RM because they translate complex pricing, forecasting, inventory allocation, and customer management decisions into measurable outcomes. Over the past four decades, the evolution of RM has been accompanied by a parallel evolution in performance measurement, reflecting broader changes in hospitality business models, technology, distribution systems, and managerial priorities.

This chapter reviewed the major KPI families used in hotel RM and critically examined their theoretical foundations, managerial applications, and limitations. The analysis demonstrates that no single indicator is capable of capturing the multidimensional nature of hotel performance. Traditional metrics such as Occupancy and ADR provide valuable insights into capacity utilization and pricing effectiveness, yet each offers only a partial perspective when interpreted independently. RevPAR emerged as the dominant industry metric because it combines pricing and occupancy into a single measure of rooms revenue productivity. Nevertheless, RevPAR remains fundamentally a rooms-focused and revenue-oriented indicator that ignores both profitability and customer value considerations.

The expansion of TRM has further challenged the adequacy of traditional room-centric measures. Indicators such as TRevPAR and TRevPOR reflect the growing recognition that hospitality organizations generate value through multiple revenue streams rather than accommodation services alone. Similarly, profitability-oriented measures such as GOPPAR demonstrate the increasing importance of evaluating not only revenue generation but also the efficiency with which revenue is converted into operating profit (Noone et al. 2017).

The chapter also highlighted the importance of competitive benchmarking indicators such as MPI, ARI, and RGI, which place hotel performance within a market context and support strategic positioning decisions. Equally important are process-oriented KPIs, including forecast accuracy, pickup, pace, denials, and regrets. These measures evaluate the effectiveness of the RM process itself and provide leading indicators of future performance. In many respects, process KPIs reveal the quality of the RM "engine", whereas traditional outcome KPIs merely reveal its results.

A critical theme emerging throughout the chapter is the growing inadequacy of single-metric approaches to performance evaluation. The longstanding industry tendency to prioritize one dominant indicator—whether occupancy, ADR, RevPAR, or even GOPPAR—risks oversimplifying commercial performance and encouraging suboptimal managerial behavior. Modern RM increasingly requires a portfolio approach in which multiple KPIs jointly capture revenue productivity, profitability, customer value, operational effectiveness, and strategic competitiveness.

The review further suggests that RM is currently undergoing a significant conceptual transformation. More broadly, the historical development of RM KPIs reflects wider changes in managerial priorities, technological capabilities, and conceptions of value creation within hospitality organizations.

The first phase may be characterized as the **Room Productivity Era**, during which performance measurement focused primarily on the efficient utilization and monetization of room inventory. Indicators such as Occupancy, ADR, and RevPAR were dominant, reflecting the central objective of maximizing revenue from a fixed and perishable capacity.

The second phase can be described as the **Total Revenue and Profitability Era**, characterized by the emergence and widespread adoption of indicators such as TRevPAR, NRevPAR and GOPPAR. During this stage, performance measurement expanded beyond room revenue productivity to incorporate total revenue generation, distribution economics, and profitability considerations.

A third phase is currently emerging, which may be described as the **Customer Value and Intelligence Era**. In this environment, the focal point of RM is gradually shifting from inventory optimization alone toward customer value creation and data-driven decision intelligence. Indicators such as RevPAG, customer-centric performance measures, process KPIs, and AI-enabled predictive metrics reflect this transition.

For practitioners, the primary implication is clear: effective RM requires moving beyond reliance on a single performance indicator and adopting balanced KPI portfolios aligned with organizational objectives. For researchers, important opportunities remain in developing and empirically validating contribution-based measures, customer profitability indicators, AI-enabled performance metrics, and standardized frameworks capable of supporting TRM environments.

At the same time, the review highlights a significant gap in existing academic literature regarding the empirical investigation of KPI adoption and use in hotel RM. Although many contemporary KPIs are widely discussed and applied in industry practice, the supporting academic evidence remains relatively limited, with much of the available knowledge originating from professional reports, industry publications, and practitioner-oriented sources. This observation underscores the need for more large-scale empirical studies examining the actual adoption, perceived usefulness, and managerial impact of RM KPIs across different hotel contexts, extending industry surveys such as that of Kimes (2017).

Ultimately, the evolution of hotel RM can be understood as progression from managing rooms, to managing revenue and profit, and increasingly to managing customer value and commercial intelligence. The future of RM measurement will therefore depend not on identifying a new universal "super KPI," but on developing integrated performance systems capable of capturing how hospitality organizations create, capture, and sustain value in increasingly complex commercial environments.

REFERENCES

Abad, P., De la Fuente-Cabrero, C., González-Serrano, L., & Talón-Ballestero, P. (2019). Determinants of successful revenue management. *Tourism Review, 74*(3), 666–678. DOI: 10.1108/TR-07-2018-0091

Ampountolas, A., & Bai, Y. (2026). Optimizing hotel demand forecasting through ensemble models: A Modern Portfolio Theory approach. *Tourism Management, 113*, 105314. Advance online publication. DOI: 10.1016/j.tourman.2025.105314

Arnejo, A., & Sarsale, M. (2025). Measuring hotel financial performance: A bibliometric review. *Hotel and Tourism Management, 13*(2), 117–135. DOI: 10.5937/menhottur2500017A

Atsız, O., Öğretmenoğlu, M., & Akova, O. (2022). A bibliometric analysis of length of stay studies in tourism. *European Journal of Tourism Research, 31*, 3101. Advance online publication. DOI: 10.54055/ejtr.v31i.2305

Barten, M. (2024, June 04). *NRevPAR explained: Net revenue per available room.* Revfine. https://www.revfine.com/nrevpar

Boo, H. C., Remy, D., & Lee, K.-H. (2025). Drivers, barriers, and challenges in NREVPAR and REVPAC adoption – towards a revenue management adoption scale. *International Journal of Hospitality Management, 127*, 104116. Advance online publication. DOI: 10.1016/j.ijhm.2025.104116

Bruns-Smith, A., Choy, V., Chong, H., & Verma, R. (2015). Environmental sustainability in the hospitality industry: Best practices, guest participation, and customer satisfaction. *Cornell Hospitality Report, 15*(3), 6-16, https://hdl.handle.net/1813/71174

Bulchand-Gidumal, J., William Secin, E., O'Connor, P., & Buhalis, D. (2024). Artificial intelligence's impact on hospitality and tourism marketing: Exploring key themes and addressing challenges. *Current Issues in Tourism, 27*(14), 2345–2362. DOI: 10.1080/13683500.2023.2229480

Cross, R. G. (1997). *Revenue management: Hard-core tactics for market domination*. Broadway Books.

Enz, C. A., Canina, L., & Lomanno, M. (2004). Why discounting does not work: The dynamics of rising occupancy and falling revenue among competitors. *The Cornell Hotel and Restaurant Administration Quarterly, 45*(1), 59–71. DOI: 10.1177/0010880403260103

Enz, C. A., Canina, L., & Walsh, K. (2001). Hotel-industry averages: An inaccurate tool for measuring performance. *The Cornell Hotel and Restaurant Administration Quarterly, 42*(6), 22–32. DOI: 10.1177/0010880401426002

González-Serrano, L., & Talón-Ballestero, P. (2022). Revenue management and e-tourism: The past, present, and future. In Xiang, Z., Fuchs, M., Gretzel, U., & Höpken, W. (Eds.), *Handbook of e-Tourism* (pp. 1261–1288). Springer., DOI: 10.1007/978-3-030-48652-5_76

Haynes, N. (2016). The evolution of competitor data collection in the hotel industry and its application to revenue management and pricing. *Journal of Revenue and Pricing Management, 15*(3–4), 258–263. DOI: 10.1057/rpm.2016.7

Heo, C. Y., Viverit, L., & Pereira, L. N. (2024). Does historical data still matter for demand forecasting in uncertain and turbulent times? An extension of the additive pickup time series method for SME hotels. *Journal of Revenue and Pricing Management, 23*(1), 39–43. DOI: 10.1057/s41272-023-00421-1

Hospitality Financial and Technology Professionals. American Hotel & Lodging Association, & Global Finance Committee. (2024). *Uniform system of accounts for the lodging industry, available at* https://usali.hftp.org/

Ivanov, S. (2014). *Hotel revenue management: From theory to practice*. Zangador. DOI: 10.13140/RG.2.1.2714.8960

Ivanov, S., & Zhechev, V. (2012). Hotel revenue management: A critical literature review. *Tourism: An International Interdisciplinary Journal, 60*(2), 175–197. DOI: 10.2139/ssrn.1977467

Khalil, N., Che Abdullah, S. N., Haron, S. N., & Hamid, M. Y. (2024). A review of green practices and initiatives from stakeholder's perspectives towards sustainable hotel operations and performance impact. *Journal of Facilities Management, 22*(4), 653–682. DOI: 10.1108/JFM-03-2022-0025

Kimes, S. E. (1989). Yield management: A tool for capacity-considered service firms. *Journal of Operations Management, 8*(4), 348–363. DOI: 10.1016/0272-6963(89)90035-1

Kimes, S. E. (1999). Implementing restaurant revenue management: A five-step approach. *The Cornell Hotel and Restaurant Administration Quarterly, 40*(3), 16–21. DOI: 10.1177/001088049904000315

Kimes, S. E. (2017). *The future of hotel revenue management. Cornell Hospitality Report, 17*(1), 3–10. https://vtechworks.lib.vt.edu/items/c390bff0-cf5a-4a7c-bd68-ce7112de1c75?utm_source=chatgpt.com

Kimes, S. E., & Singh, S. (2009). Spa revenue management. *Cornell Hospitality Quarterly*, *50*(1), 82–95. DOI: 10.1177/1938965508324868

Lee, S., Pan, B., & Park, S. (2019). Revpar vs. Goppar: Property- and firm-level analysis. *Annals of Tourism Research*, *76*, 180–190. DOI: 10.1016/j.annals.2019.04.006

Mensah, P. O., Mensah, H. K., Osei, B. A., & Iddris, F. (2026). Antecedents of Sustainable Performance in Hotels: The Mediating Role of Green Innovation Strategy. *International Journal of Hospitality & Tourism Administration*, *27*(3), 568–592. DOI: 10.1080/15256480.2025.2494591

Noone, B. M., Enz, C. A., & Glassmire, J. (2017). Total hotel revenue management: A strategic profit perspective. *Cornell Hospitality Report*, *17*(8), 3–14. https://hdl.handle.net/1813/70992

Parmenter, D. (2015). *Key Performance Indicators: Developing, Implementing, and Using Winning KPIs* (3rd ed.). Wiley. DOI: 10.1002/9781119019855

Pereira, L. N., & Cerqueira, V. (2022). Forecasting hotel demand for revenue management using machine learning regression methods. *Current Issues in Tourism*, *25*(17), 2733–2750. DOI: 10.1080/13683500.2021.1999397

Reem, M., Rasoolimanesh, S., & Wijesinghe, S. N. R. (2022). Sustainability indicators in hotels: A systematic literature review. *Asia-Pacific Journal of Innovation in Hospitality and Tourism*, *11*(1), 149–178.

Remy, D., Tan, S., Boo, H. C., & Tee, S. (2023). Revenue Management Metrics Study (Version 1). Singapore Institute of Technology. DOI: 10.25447/sit.24145212.v1

Sainaghi, R. (2010). Hotel performance: State of the art. *International Journal of Contemporary Hospitality Management*, *22*(7), 920–952. DOI: 10.1108/09596111011066617

Santos, L., Malheiros, C., Gomes, C., & Guerra, T., 2020. TRevPAR as hotels performance evaluation indicator and influencing factors in Portugal. *EATSJ - Euro-Asia Tourism Studies Journal*, 1, 93–105. DOI: 10.58345/KQMJ7114

Schwartz, Z., Altin, M., & Singal, M. (2017). Performance measures for strategic revenue management: Revpar versus goppar. *Journal of Revenue and Pricing Management*, *16*(4), 357–375. DOI: 10.1057/rpm.2016.23

Talluri, K. T., & Van Ryzin, G. J. (2004). *The theory and practice of revenue management*. Springer., DOI: 10.1007/b139000

Talón-Ballestero, P., González-Serrano, L., Soguero-Ruiz, C., Muñoz-Romero, S., & Rojo-Álvarez, J. L. (2018). Using big data from Customer Relationship Management Information Systems to determine the client profile in the hotel sector. *Tourism Management, 68*, 187–197. DOI: 10.1016/j.tourman.2018.03.017

Vinod, B. (2022). Introduction to hotel revenue management. *Management for Professionals*, 1–50. DOI: 10.1007/978-3-031-14302-1_1

Voukkali, I., Papamichael, I., Loizia, P., & Zorpas, A. A. (2023). The importance of KPIs to calibrate waste strategy in hospitality sector. *Energy Nexus, 11*, 100211. Advance online publication. DOI: 10.1016/j.nexus.2023.100211

Weatherford, L. R., & Kimes, S. E. (2003). A comparison of forecasting methods for hotel revenue management. *International Journal of Forecasting, 19*(3), 401–415. DOI: 10.1016/S0169-2070(02)00011-0

Chapter 5
Integrating Accounting Information and Revenue Management for Strategic Decision Making in Hospitality

Mohammad Taqi
Bahrain Polytechnic, Bahrain

Friday Ogbu Edeh
http://orcid.org/0000-0001-8041-1317
Kampala International University, Uganda

Rizwan Khan
http://orcid.org/0000-0002-3942-9985
Haji Taufeeq Ali Mahavidyalaya, India

ABSTRACT

This chapter examines how the integration of accounting information with revenue management enhances strategic decision-making in the hospitality sector. In a highly dynamic and demand-driven environment, hotels increasingly rely on real-time financial and operational data to optimize pricing, capacity utilization, and profitability. The chapter highlights the role of accounting systems in providing cost insights and performance metrics, such as RevPAR, ADR, and occupancy rates, which support effective revenue strategies. It further discusses how combining financial data with forecasting and segmentation techniques enables more informed and responsive decisions. While integration offers significant benefits in improving efficiency and

DOI: 10.4018/979-8-3373-9479-4.ch005

competitiveness, challenges such as data fragmentation, system limitations, and skill gaps persist. The chapter concludes that a coordinated approach to accounting and revenue management is essential for achieving sustainable profitability and long-term strategic advantage in the hospitality industry.

1. INTRODUCTION

1.1 Concept of Revenue Management in Hospitality

The hospitality industry is characterised by high fixed costs, fluctuating demand, and perishable inventory, making effective pricing and capacity utilisation essential for profitability. In this context, revenue management (RM) has emerged as a strategic approach aimed at maximising revenue by selling the right service to the right customer at the right time and at the right price (Kimes, 1989).

Originally developed in the airline industry, RM has since been widely adopted across hotels, resorts, and other hospitality sectors where unsold inventory cannot be stored for future sale. Key RM practices include demand forecasting, market segmentation, and dynamic pricing. Performance is typically evaluated using key indicators such as Revenue per Available Room (RevPAR), Average Daily Rate (ADR), and occupancy rate, which assist managers in making pricing decisions.

Empirical evidence from the global hotel industry suggests that even a 1% increase in RevPAR can significantly enhance profitability due to the sector's high operating leverage (Ivanov & Zhechev, 2012). These metrics provide valuable insights into demand patterns and enable real-time pricing adjustments based on market conditions.

However, traditional RM approaches have primarily focused on revenue maximisation rather than profitability. This limitation underscores the need to integrate revenue management with cost and financial considerations, ensuring that pricing strategies contribute not only to increased revenue but also to sustainable profit margins.

1.2 Role of Accounting Information in Decision-Making

Accounting information forms the backbone of organisational decision-making by providing structured, reliable, and timely insights into financial performance and operational efficiency. In the hospitality industry, management accounting systems generate both financial and non-financial information that supports planning, control, and strategic decision-making (Horngren et al., 2014).

This includes cost data, departmental performance reports, and profitability analyses across different service segments such as rooms, food and beverage, and ancillary services. Key financial indicators such as Gross Operating Profit per Available Room (GOPPAR), cost per occupied room, and Return on Investment (ROI), are essential for evaluating the financial health of hospitality businesses.

While RM metrics are predominantly forward-looking, accounting information incorporates both historical and current data to assess efficiency and guide resource allocation. For example, distinguishing between fixed and variable costs enables managers to determine minimum acceptable pricing levels and avoid loss-making decisions.

Advancements in Accounting Information Systems (AIS), particularly through Enterprise Resource Planning (ERP) platforms, have enhanced data accuracy, accessibility, and integration. These systems facilitate real-time reporting and cross-functional coordination, offering a comprehensive view of organisational performance. Consequently, accounting information is increasingly utilised not only for compliance and reporting but also as a strategic tool in competitive decision-making environments.

1.3 Need for Integration in a Dynamic Service Environment

Despite their individual importance, revenue management and accounting information systems have traditionally operated in silos within hospitality organisations. Revenue managers typically rely on market data and forecasting models, whereas accounting functions focus on cost control and financial reporting. This separation can lead to suboptimal decisions for instance, pricing strategies that maximise occupancy but reduce overall profitability due to high variable costs.

The growing complexity and volatility of the hospitality industry necessitate a more integrated approach. Factors such as digital transformation, the proliferation of online distribution channels, and evolving customer preferences demand real-time, data-driven decision-making. Integrating RM with accounting information enables organisations to align pricing strategies with cost structures, thereby shifting the focus from revenue maximisation to profit optimisation.

For example, incorporating cost data into pricing models helps identify the most profitable customer segments and distribution channels. The importance of such integration was particularly evident during the COVID-19 pandemic, when global hotel occupancy rates declined by more than 50% (UNWTO, 2021). Organisations with integrated data systems were better positioned to adjust pricing strategies, control costs, and manage cash flows under conditions of extreme uncertainty.

The convergence of RM and accounting information, facilitated by advanced analytics and digital technologies enhances decision-making quality, operational efficiency, and long-term competitiveness. In this context, the present chapter examines how the integration of accounting information and revenue management can support strategic decision-making in the hospitality sector. It aims to provide a comprehensive understanding of their interrelationship and highlight the importance of a unified, data-driven approach in a dynamic business environment.

2. THEORETICAL FOUNDATIONS AND CONCEPTUAL FRAMEWORK

2.1 Revenue Management Theory: Pricing, Demand Forecasting, and Capacity Utilization

Revenue Management (RM) theory is grounded in microeconomic principles such as price discrimination, demand elasticity, and marginal revenue maximisation. The core objective is to maximise revenue from a fixed and perishable inventory such as hotel rooms by adjusting prices in response to fluctuations in demand (Kimes, 1989).

In the hospitality industry, efficient capacity utilisation is critical, as unsold inventory (e.g., an unoccupied room for a night) cannot be recovered. Demand forecasting is a central component of RM and involves analysing historical data, seasonality patterns, booking trends, and external factors such as economic conditions or local events to predict customer behaviour. Accurate forecasting enables firms to segment customers and apply differentiated pricing strategies. For instance, business travellers tend to be less price-sensitive than leisure travellers, allowing hotels to charge premium rates during high-demand periods.

Dynamic pricing is another key element of RM, whereby room rates are continuously adjusted based on real-time demand and supply conditions. This approach relies heavily on data analytics and algorithm-driven models to optimise pricing decisions. Empirical evidence suggests that firms adopting advanced RM systems can achieve revenue improvements of approximately 5% to 10% compared to traditional pricing approaches (Ivanov & Zhechev, 2012).

Capacity utilisation strategies, such as overbooking, are also widely employed to mitigate the impact of cancellations and no-shows, thereby maintaining optimal occupancy levels. However, such strategies must be implemented carefully to avoid negative customer experiences and reputational risks.

Overall, RM provides a robust framework for revenue maximisation; however, its primary focus on top-line growth highlights the need for integration with cost and profitability considerations for more comprehensive decision-making.

2.2 Role of Management Accounting in Service Industries

Management accounting plays a crucial role in supporting both strategic and operational decision-making within service industries, particularly hospitality. Unlike financial accounting, which is externally oriented, management accounting focuses on internal processes by providing detailed insights into cost behaviour, resource utilisation, and performance measurement (Horngren et al., 2014).

The cost structure in hospitality is typically characterised by high fixed costs such as property maintenance and staff salaries and relatively low variable costs per additional customer. This makes cost-volume-profit (CVP) analysis particularly relevant, as it helps managers determine break-even points and assess the profitability implications of pricing decisions. For example, during periods of low demand, a hotel may reduce room rates provided that prices cover variable costs and contribute towards fixed cost recovery.

Management accounting also supports budgeting and variance analysis, enabling organisations to compare actual performance with planned targets and identify deviations. Techniques such as Activity-Based Costing (ABC) further enhance cost accuracy by allocating costs to specific activities, thereby improving profitability analysis across services and customer segments.

Additionally, performance measurement systems in hospitality increasingly incorporate both financial and non-financial indicators, including customer satisfaction, service quality, and employee productivity. This broader perspective aligns operational performance with strategic objectives and ensures that short-term profitability does not compromise long-term value creation.

Thus, management accounting provides the necessary financial perspective to evaluate RM decisions and ensures that revenue-maximising strategies are aligned with long-term profitability and sustainability goals.

2.3 Linkages Between Financial Data and Operational Decisions

The integration of financial data with operational decision-making represents a significant advancement in modern hospitality management. Traditionally, operational decisions such as pricing, inventory allocation, and service offering were made independently of detailed financial analysis. However, the increasing availability of real-time data and advanced information systems has enabled stronger alignment between these functions.

Accounting systems provide critical financial insights, including cost per room, departmental profitability, and cash flow metrics, which can significantly enhance RM strategies. For instance, incorporating cost data into pricing models allows managers to identify the most profitable customer segments rather than simply focusing on revenue generation. This shift from revenue maximisation to profit optimisation is essential in a competitive and cost-sensitive environment.

Integrated systems such as Enterprise Resource Planning (ERP) platforms and business intelligence dashboards facilitate this alignment by consolidating data from multiple sources into a unified view of organisational performance. Managers can simultaneously monitor key metrics such as RevPAR, occupancy rates, and gross operating profit, thereby enabling more informed and timely decision-making.

The conceptual framework underlying this integration is summarised in Table 1.

Table 1. Conceptual Linkages Between Revenue Management and Accounting Information

Dimension	Revenue Management Perspective	Accounting Information Perspective	Integrated Outcome
Objective	Revenue maximisation	Cost control and profitability	Profit optimisation
Data Type	Market and demand data	Financial and cost data	Holistic performance data
Decision Focus	Pricing and capacity allocation	Budgeting and cost management	Strategic decision-making
Time Orientation	Future-oriented	Historical and current	Real-time and predictive insights

Source: Developed by the author

As illustrated in Table 1, the integration of RM and accounting information bridges the gap between market-driven and internally focused decision-making. This alignment enhances organisational agility and supports strategic objectives such as sustainable profitability and competitive advantage.

In conclusion, while RM and management accounting independently offer valuable insights, their integration through a well-defined conceptual framework enables hospitality firms to leverage both market intelligence and financial data. This combined approach improves decision quality and contributes to superior organisational performance.

3. ACCOUNTING INFORMATION SYSTEMS IN HOSPITALITY

3.1 Nature and Types of Accounting Information: Financial vs. Managerial

In the hospitality industry, Accounting Information Systems (AIS) are designed to collect, process, and report data that support both internal decision-making and external reporting. Due to the service-oriented nature of hospitality businesses, AIS must manage high transaction volumes, multiple revenue streams (e.g., rooms, food and beverage, events), and complex cost structures.

Accounting information can broadly be classified into two categories: financial accounting information and managerial accounting information, each serving distinct yet complementary purposes.

Financial accounting information focuses on the preparation of standardised reports such as income statements, balance sheets, and cash flow statements, in accordance with established accounting standards and regulatory requirements. These reports provide insights into the organisation's financial performance over a given period, enabling stakeholders including investors, regulators, and creditors to assess financial health and compliance (Weygandt et al., 2019). In the hospitality industry, financial accounting also facilitates benchmarking against industry standards, such as those prescribed by the Uniform System of Accounts for the Lodging Industry (USALI).

In contrast, managerial accounting information is internally oriented and supports planning, control, and strategic decision-making. It includes detailed cost data, departmental profitability reports, variance analyses, and forecasts. For example, a hotel may evaluate the profitability of its rooms division separately from its food and beverage operations to identify areas for improvement. Managerial accounting also enables the application of techniques such as budgeting, Cost-Volume-Profit (CVP) analysis, and Activity-Based Costing (ABC), which provide deeper insights into cost behaviour and resource utilisation (Horngren et al., 2014).

In the hospitality context where timely and detailed information is essential for decisions related to pricing, staffing, and service offerings, understanding the distinction between these two types of accounting information is critical. Financial accounting ensures transparency and accountability, while managerial accounting enhances flexibility and responsiveness. Together, they form the foundation of an effective AIS.

3.2 Key Performance Indicators (KPIs) in Hospitality

Performance measurement in the hospitality industry relies heavily on a combination of financial and operational Key Performance Indicators (KPIs). These metrics are integral to both revenue management and accounting systems, as they provide quantifiable measures of efficiency, profitability, and market performance.

Among the most widely used KPIs are:

- **Revenue per Available Room (RevPAR):** Measures revenue generated per available room and is calculated as total room revenue divided by the number of available rooms.

- **Average Daily Rate (ADR):** Indicates the average revenue earned per occupied room.
- **Occupancy Rate:** Reflects the percentage of available rooms that are occupied over a given period.

These indicators are interrelated and collectively provide a comprehensive view of hotel performance. For instance, a high occupancy rate combined with a low ADR may indicate underpricing, whereas a high ADR with low occupancy may suggest overpricing or weak demand.

In addition to these core metrics, hospitality firms increasingly utilise profit-oriented KPIs such as Gross Operating Profit per Available Room (GOPPAR) and Net Profit Margin, which incorporate cost considerations into performance evaluation. Relying solely on RevPAR can be misleading, as it does not account for cost efficiency; therefore, integrating financial KPIs is essential for a more accurate assessment of overall performance (Chen & Rothschild, 2010).

The significance of these KPIs lies in their ability to integrate operational and financial perspectives, enabling managers to align pricing strategies with profitability objectives.

3.3 Use of Real-Time Data and Digital Accounting Systems

The rapid advancement of digital technologies has significantly transformed Accounting Information Systems in the hospitality industry, enabling the use of real-time data and integrated platforms for enhanced decision-making. Traditional AIS, which relied on periodic reporting, are increasingly being replaced by cloud-based systems and Enterprise Resource Planning (ERP) solutions that provide continuous access to financial and operational data.

Real-time data integration allows hospitality managers to monitor key performance indicators dynamically and respond promptly to changes in demand, pricing, and cost structures. For example, a hotel can adjust room rates in response to current occupancy levels, competitor pricing, and booking trends, while simultaneously considering cost implications. This capability is particularly valuable in volatile market conditions where demand fluctuates rapidly.

Digital accounting systems also facilitate integration with other functional platforms, including Property Management Systems (PMS), Customer Relationship Management (CRM) systems, and revenue management software. This integration creates a unified data ecosystem that supports comprehensive analysis and informed decision-making. For instance, combining customer data with financial information enables the identification of high-value customer segments and supports the development of targeted pricing and service strategies.

Furthermore, emerging technologies such as artificial intelligence (AI) and big data analytics are enhancing AIS capabilities. Predictive analytics improves the accuracy of demand forecasting, while automation reduces errors and increases the efficiency of financial reporting processes. Industry evidence suggests that organisations adopting integrated digital systems experience notable improvements in both operational efficiency and financial performance (Davenport & Harris, 2017).

However, the adoption of digital AIS also presents challenges, including high implementation costs, data security concerns, and the need for skilled personnel. Despite these challenges, the transition towards real-time, data-driven systems is essential for maintaining competitiveness in the modern hospitality environment.

In summary, Accounting Information Systems in the hospitality industry have evolved from basic reporting tools to strategic enablers of decision-making. By integrating financial and managerial data, leveraging KPIs, and utilising real-time digital technologies, AIS play a critical role in strengthening the integration between accounting and revenue management, ultimately enhancing organisational performance.

4. REVENUE MANAGEMENT PRACTICES IN HOSPITALITY

4.1 Dynamic Pricing and Demand-Based Pricing Strategies

Dynamic pricing represents a central component of revenue management (RM) in the hospitality industry, enabling firms to adjust prices in real time in response to fluctuations in demand, market conditions, and customer behaviour. Unlike traditional pricing models that rely on fixed rates, dynamic pricing utilises data analytics and forecasting tools to continuously optimise room rates. This approach is particularly relevant in hospitality due to the perishable nature of inventory and the variability of demand (Kimes, 1989).

Demand-based pricing strategies are grounded in the concept of price elasticity, which measures the responsiveness of customers to changes in price. For example, business travellers are generally less price-sensitive than leisure travellers, allowing hotels to charge premium rates during weekdays while offering lower rates during weekends or off-peak periods. Similarly, peak demand periods such as holidays and major events, enable hotels to increase room rates in response to higher demand levels.

Advancements in technology have further enhanced dynamic pricing through automated RM systems. These systems analyse large datasets, including historical booking patterns, competitor pricing, and online search trends, to recommend optimal pricing decisions. Empirical evidence suggests that hotels implementing dynamic pricing strategies can achieve revenue improvements of approximately 5–10% compared to those using static pricing models (Ivanov & Zhechev, 2012).

However, while dynamic pricing contributes to revenue growth, it must be aligned with cost structures to ensure profitability. Excessive discounting to increase occupancy may negatively affect profit margins, highlighting the importance of integrating pricing strategies with accounting information.

4.2 Segmentation and Forecasting Techniques

Market segmentation and demand forecasting are fundamental components of effective revenue management in the hospitality sector. Segmentation involves categorising customers into distinct groups based on characteristics such as purpose of travel (business versus leisure), booking behaviour, price sensitivity, and geographic location. This enables hotels to design tailored pricing and service strategies that maximise revenue across different customer segments.

For instance, corporate clients may be offered negotiated rates and value-added services, while leisure travellers may be targeted through promotional packages and seasonal discounts. Advanced segmentation techniques also incorporate behavioural and psychographic factors such as booking lead time and preferred distribution channels allowing for greater precision in targeting and personalisation.

Demand forecasting involves predicting future demand using historical data, market trends, and external factors such as economic conditions, seasonality, and local events. Accurate forecasting is essential for effective pricing and inventory allocation decisions. Common forecasting techniques include time-series analysis, regression models, and increasingly, machine learning algorithms capable of processing large and complex datasets.

The accuracy of demand forecasts has a direct impact on revenue performance. Overestimating demand may result in overpricing and reduced occupancy, whereas underestimating demand can lead to underpricing and lost revenue opportunities. Research indicates that even marginal improvements in forecasting accuracy can significantly enhance revenue outcomes in the hospitality industry (Song & Li, 2008).

By integrating segmentation and forecasting techniques, hospitality firms can better anticipate demand patterns and proactively adjust their strategies, leading to improved revenue performance and enhanced customer satisfaction.

5. INTEGRATION OF ACCOUNTING INFORMATION WITH REVENUE MANAGEMENT

5.1 Aligning Cost Structures with Pricing Decisions

A critical dimension of integrating accounting information with revenue management (RM) is the alignment of cost structures with pricing decisions. Traditional RM practices emphasise revenue maximisation through dynamic pricing and demand optimisation; however, without incorporating cost data, such strategies may lead to suboptimal or even loss-making outcomes.

In the hospitality industry characterised by high fixed costs (e.g., property, salaries) and relatively low marginal costs understanding cost behaviour is essential for effective pricing decisions. Management accounting provides detailed insights into fixed, variable, and semi-variable costs, enabling managers to determine minimum acceptable pricing levels.

For example, during off-peak periods, hotels may reduce room rates to increase occupancy; however, such pricing must at least cover variable costs and contribute towards fixed cost recovery. This aligns with Cost-Volume-Profit (CVP) principles, which emphasise the relationship between sales volume, costs, and profitability (Horngren et al., 2014).

Furthermore, techniques such as Activity-Based Costing (ABC) enable more accurate allocation of indirect costs to specific services or customer segments. This allows hotels to identify high-cost and low-margin segments and adjust pricing strategies accordingly. For instance, bookings through certain distribution channels (e.g., online travel agencies) may generate high revenue but lower margins due to commission costs.

Integrating these cost considerations into RM systems shifts the focus from revenue maximisation to profit optimisation, which is more aligned with long-term strategic objectives. To illustrate the practical importance of integrating revenue management with accounting information, Table 2 presents key performance indicators across different market phases.

Table 2. Integrated Revenue and Cost Performance Metrics in Hospitality

Metric	Pre-Pandemic (2019)	Pandemic Impact (2020)	Recovery Phase (2022)	Decision Insight
Occupancy Rate (%)	68%	35%	62%	Demand fluctuation affects pricing strategies
Average Daily Rate (ADR) ($)	130	95	125	Price adjustments reflect demand elasticity
RevPAR ($)	88.4	33.3	77.5	Combined effect of occupancy and pricing
GOPPAR ($)	52	10	45	Profitability declined more sharply than revenue
Cost per Occupied Room ($)	60	72	65	Costs increased during low occupancy
Distribution Cost (%)	18%	22%	20%	Higher OTA dependency during crisis
Net Profit Margin (%)	22%	-5%	15%	Highlights need for cost-revenue integration

Source: Adapted from industry reports (STR Global, UNWTO, Deloitte Hospitality Insights); values presented for academic illustration.

As shown in Table 2, while occupancy and RevPAR declined sharply during the pandemic, profitability indicators such as GOPPAR and net profit margin experienced a more severe contraction. This demonstrates that revenue-focused strategies without cost alignment can significantly affect financial sustainability.

5.2 Use of Accounting Data for Demand Forecasting and Budgeting

Accounting information plays a critical role in enhancing the accuracy and reliability of demand forecasting and budgeting, two essential components of RM practices. While RM systems traditionally rely on historical booking data and market trends, the integration of financial data such as past revenue patterns, cost behaviour, and seasonal profitability significantly improves forecasting accuracy.

For example, analysis of historical financial statements can reveal seasonal variations in both costs and revenues, thereby supporting more informed projections of future demand and profitability. By integrating such data, managers can develop forecasts that account not only for expected occupancy and pricing but also for associated cost implications. This is particularly important in the hospitality sector, where demand is influenced by economic conditions, tourism trends, and local events (Song & Li, 2008).

In terms of budgeting, the integration of accounting and RM data facilitates the development of more realistic and flexible budgets. Traditional static budgets are increasingly being replaced by rolling forecasts and dynamic budgeting approaches that are continuously updated based on real-time data. For instance, if demand forecasts indicate a decline in occupancy, managers can proactively adjust pricing strategies and cost structures such as staffing levels or marketing expenditures to maintain profitability.

Moreover, incorporating accounting data into forecasting models supports scenario analysis, enabling organisations to evaluate the financial implications of different pricing and demand scenarios. This enhances strategic planning and improves responsiveness to market changes.

5.3 Role of Analytics and Dashboards in Integrated Decision-Making

Advanced analytics and digital dashboards play a crucial role in facilitating the integration of accounting information with revenue management by providing real-time, data-driven insights for decision-making. Modern hospitality organisations increasingly rely on technologies such as business intelligence (BI) systems, Enterprise Resource Planning (ERP) platforms, and cloud-based analytics tools to consolidate financial and operational data into a unified system.

Dashboards are particularly valuable as they present key performance indicators (KPIs) including RevPAR, ADR, occupancy rate, and gross operating profit in a visually accessible format. This enables managers to monitor performance across multiple dimensions simultaneously and make timely, informed decisions. For example, a dashboard may highlight a scenario where occupancy rates are high but profitability is declining, prompting a review of pricing strategies or cost structures.

Predictive analytics further enhances decision-making by using historical and real-time data to forecast future outcomes. Machine learning algorithms can identify complex patterns in customer behaviour, price sensitivity, and cost fluctuations, thereby improving demand forecasting and pricing accuracy (Davenport & Harris, 2017). Additionally, prescriptive analytics can recommend optimal actions such as pricing adjustments or inventory allocation based on predefined objectives.

These analytics tools also promote cross-functional integration by consolidating data from accounting, marketing, operations, and RM systems. This reduces information silos and ensures alignment in decision-making across departments.

For instance, marketing initiatives can be evaluated not only in terms of booking volumes but also based on their impact on overall profitability.

In summary, the integration of accounting information with revenue management represents a significant advancement in hospitality management practices. By aligning cost structures with pricing decisions, leveraging accounting data for forecasting and budgeting, and utilising advanced analytics tools, organisations can enhance decision-making quality. This integrated approach not only improves revenue performance but also ensures sustainable profitability and long-term competitive advantage.

6. STRATEGIC DECISION MAKING IN HOSPITALITY

6.1 Pricing, Investment, and Capacity Decisions

Strategic decision-making in the hospitality industry is inherently complex due to demand uncertainty, high cost structures, and the perishable nature of inventory. Among the most critical decisions are those related to pricing, investment, and capacity management, all of which require the integration of revenue management (RM) insights and accounting information.

Pricing decisions should extend beyond short-term revenue objectives and align with long-term strategic goals such as brand positioning and market competitiveness. While RM systems enable dynamic pricing based on demand fluctuations, accounting information ensures that such pricing decisions remain financially viable. For example, determining optimal room rates requires an understanding of customer willingness to pay, alongside a clear assessment of cost structures and target profit margins (Kimes, 1989).

Investment decisions in hospitality such as property expansion, renovation, or technology adoption are capital-intensive and involve long-term commitments. These decisions rely on financial evaluation techniques including Net Present Value (NPV), Internal Rate of Return (IRR), and payback period analysis. Integrating RM data into these evaluations enhances their reliability by incorporating demand forecasts and revenue potential. For instance, decisions to expand room capacity should consider projected occupancy rates and pricing trends to ensure financial feasibility.

Capacity decisions are equally significant, as they influence the utilisation of available resources. Given the relative rigidity of capacity in the short term, effective allocation of inventory across customer segments and time periods is essential. Techniques such as overbooking and length-of-stay controls are commonly employed to maximise occupancy and revenue. However, these strategies must be supported by accounting data to assess their implications for cost and profitability.

Overall, the integration of pricing, investment, and capacity decisions facilitates a comprehensive strategic approach that aligns revenue opportunities with long-term financial sustainability.

6.2 Cost Control and Profitability Analysis

Cost control and profitability analysis are fundamental to strategic decision-making in the hospitality industry, where even minor inefficiencies can significantly impact overall performance. Management accounting provides the tools necessary to monitor costs, evaluate performance, and identify opportunities for improvement.

Effective cost control involves continuous monitoring of both fixed and variable costs. Major cost components in hospitality include labour, utilities, maintenance, and distribution channel commissions. Techniques such as standard costing and variance analysis enable managers to identify deviations between actual and budgeted costs. For example, higher-than-expected labour costs may indicate inefficiencies in staffing or scheduling, requiring corrective action.

Profitability analysis extends beyond cost control by evaluating the financial contribution of different services, departments, and customer segments. Metrics such as Gross Operating Profit per Available Room (GOPPAR) provide a more comprehensive measure of performance compared to revenue-based indicators like RevPAR, as they incorporate cost considerations. Segment-level profitability analysis may reveal that certain customer groups or booking channels, despite generating high revenue, contribute less to overall profit due to higher associated costs.

The integration of RM with accounting information enhances profitability analysis by linking pricing and demand decisions with cost implications. For instance, discount pricing strategies may increase occupancy but reduce overall profitability if not carefully managed. By incorporating cost data into RM models, hospitality firms can identify pricing strategies that optimise profit rather than merely maximising revenue (Drury, 2018).

Furthermore, advanced analytics tools enable real-time monitoring of cost and profitability metrics, allowing managers to make timely adjustments. This proactive approach is essential for maintaining competitiveness in a dynamic market environment.

6.3 Enhancing Customer Value and Competitive Advantage

In the contemporary hospitality landscape, strategic decision-making increasingly focuses on enhancing customer value as a means of achieving sustainable competitive advantage. Customer value extends beyond pricing and encompasses the overall service experience, including quality, convenience, and personalisation.

The integration of accounting information with RM supports value-based strategies by enabling organisations to design pricing and service offerings that meet customer expectations while maintaining profitability. For example, data-driven insights can help identify high-value customer segments and support the development of tailored offerings such as personalised packages, loyalty programmes, and targeted promotions. These initiatives contribute to higher customer satisfaction and retention, which are critical for long-term success.

Organisations that effectively integrate financial and operational data are better positioned to respond to market changes and outperform competitors. The use of data analytics and digital platforms enhances capabilities in demand forecasting, pricing optimisation, and resource allocation. According to Porter's competitive strategy framework, such capabilities support both cost leadership and differentiation, thereby contributing to sustained competitive advantage (Porter, 1985).

Moreover, transparency in pricing and value delivery strengthens customer trust and brand reputation. In an environment where customers have access to extensive information, maintaining alignment between price and perceived value is essential. Accounting information ensures that value-enhancing strategies remain financially viable, while RM ensures responsiveness to market dynamics.

7. CASE STUDY: REVENUE MANAGEMENT AND FINANCIAL INTEGRATION IN HOSPITALITY

A real-world case study is presented to provide practical insights into the integration of accounting information and revenue management (RM). This case illustrates how a global hotel organisation utilised integrated systems to enhance strategic decision-making and improve financial performance.

Marriott International is one of the largest hotel chains globally, operating more than 8,000 properties across over 130 countries. The company has been an early adopter of advanced RM systems, supported by robust accounting and financial reporting frameworks. Its business model focuses on optimising pricing, occupancy, and distribution strategies while maintaining profitability across diverse markets.

Prior to the COVID-19 pandemic, Marriott's RM practices emphasised dynamic pricing, segmentation, and channel optimisation to maximise Revenue per Available Room (RevPAR). Simultaneously, its accounting systems provided detailed insights into cost structures, margins, and overall financial performance. However, the pandemic exposed the limitations of treating these systems as partially independent functions.

Problem Statement

The global hospitality industry experienced an unprecedented downturn in 2020. According to company and industry reports, Marriott's global occupancy rates declined significantly, while RevPAR decreased by approximately 50% in 2020 compared to 2019.

Although the company implemented aggressive pricing strategies to stimulate demand, these measures were insufficient to sustain profitability due to high fixed costs and reduced international travel. This situation highlighted a critical issue: revenue-focused strategies, when not aligned with cost considerations, are insufficient to ensure financial sustainability.

To stabilise operations and support recovery, Marriott needed to align its pricing, distribution, and operational decisions with real-time financial data.

Strategic Response and Integration Approach

To address these challenges, Marriott strengthened the integration between its RM systems and accounting information through several key initiatives:

- **Adoption of Profit-Based Metrics:** The company shifted its focus from RevPAR to more comprehensive indicators such as Gross Operating Profit (GOP) and Adjusted EBITDA, ensuring that pricing decisions aligned with profitability objectives.
- **Cost-Integrated Pricing Models:** Pricing strategies were recalibrated by incorporating cost data, including labour, utilities, and distribution channel commissions, thereby reducing the risk of margin erosion due to excessive discounting.
- **Advanced Analytics and Forecasting:** AI-driven forecasting tools were utilised to analyse booking patterns, customer behaviour, and market trends. These tools were integrated with financial systems to support holistic decision-making.
- **Digital Transformation and Centralised Systems:** Marriott enhanced its use of centralised data platforms by integrating property-level financial data with global RM systems, enabling real-time monitoring of both revenue and cost performance.
- **Channel and Cost Optimisation:** The company prioritised direct bookings through its loyalty programme (Marriott Bonvoy), reducing reliance on high-cost online travel agencies (OTAs) and improving net margins.

Performance Outcomes

The impact of this integrated approach is summarised in Table 3. The strategy contributed significantly to Marriott's recovery during the period 2021–2023.

Table 3. Integrated Revenue and Profitability Metrics in Hospitality

Metric	2020 (Crisis)	2022 (Recovery)	Insight
Occupancy Rate (%)	36%	65%	Demand recovery supported by pricing strategy
RevPAR Change	-50%	Near pre-pandemic levels	Revenue recovery achieved
Adjusted EBITDA ($ Billion)	0.3	3.3	Strong profitability rebound
Net Income ($ Billion)	Loss	2.4	Return to profitability
Direct Booking Share (%)	Increased	Significantly higher	Lower distribution costs

Source: Marriott Annual Reports (2020–2023), STR Global

As shown in Table 3, the firm experienced substantial improvements in both revenue and profitability metrics following the adoption of integrated RM and accounting strategies.

Analysis and Key Insights

The Marriott case highlights several important insights for hospitality management:

- **Integration Enhances Resilience:** Aligning RM with accounting data enabled the organisation to respond effectively to demand shocks and cost pressures.
- **Shift from Revenue to Profit Optimisation:** The adoption of profit-based metrics ensured that pricing decisions supported long-term financial sustainability.
- **Role of Technology:** AI-driven analytics and integrated data platforms significantly improved forecasting accuracy and decision-making speed.
- **Importance of Channel Strategy:** Increasing direct bookings reduced distribution costs and enhanced profit margins.

Managerial Implications

- Hospitality firms should adopt integrated RM–accounting frameworks rather than treating them as separate functions.
- Decision-making should prioritise profitability metrics (e.g., GOP, EBITDA) rather than focusing solely on revenue.
- Investment in digital infrastructure and analytics capabilities is essential for sustaining competitive advantage.

In conclusion, the experience of Marriott International demonstrates that the integration of accounting information with revenue management is critical for navigating uncertainty and achieving sustainable growth. By aligning pricing strategies with cost structures and leveraging advanced analytics, hospitality firms can enhance both operational efficiency and financial performance in an increasingly complex global environment.

This case reinforces the theoretical discussion presented in earlier sections, particularly the importance of integrating revenue management with accounting information to achieve long-term competitive advantage.

In conclusion, the integration of customer-centric strategies with financial discipline enables hospitality organisations to balance revenue growth, cost efficiency, and service excellence. This holistic approach to strategic decision-making enhances both short-term performance and long-term competitiveness in an increasingly complex and digitalised industry.

8. CHALLENGES AND EMERGING TRENDS

8.1 Data Integration Issues and System Incompatibility

Despite significant technological advancements, integrating Accounting Information Systems (AIS) with revenue management (RM) platforms remains a major challenge in the hospitality industry. One of the primary issues is data fragmentation, where information is stored across multiple systems that are not fully interoperable. These include Property Management Systems (PMS), Enterprise Resource Planning (ERP) tools, Customer Relationship Management (CRM) platforms, and standalone RM software.

Such systems are often developed by different vendors, resulting in inconsistencies in data formats, structures, and reporting standards. System incompatibility disrupts the seamless flow of information, leading to errors, delays, and inefficiencies in decision-making. For instance, discrepancies between financial data in accounting systems and operational data from RM tools may result in inaccurate performance evaluations. This lack of synchronisation undermines the effectiveness of integrated decision-making and may lead to suboptimal pricing and cost management strategies.

Furthermore, the absence of standardised data governance frameworks exacerbates these challenges. Without clearly defined protocols for data collection, validation, and sharing, organisations may struggle to maintain data accuracy and reliability. Research indicates that poor data quality can significantly hinder the effectiveness of analytics-driven decision-making, particularly in data-intensive sectors such as hospitality (Davenport & Harris, 2017).

To address these issues, hospitality organisations are increasingly adopting integrated platforms and cloud-based solutions that enable real-time data sharing and accessibility. However, transitioning to such systems requires substantial investment and careful implementation planning, making it a complex and gradual process.

8.2 Skill Gaps and Organizational Resistance

Another critical challenge in integrating accounting information with RM is the presence of skill gaps and organisational resistance. Effective utilisation of integrated systems requires professionals with a combination of financial expertise, analytical capabilities, and technological proficiency. However, many hospitality organisations face a shortage of such multidisciplinary talent.

Traditionally, accounting and RM functions have operated independently, with specialists in each domain. Accountants may have limited exposure to data analytics and forecasting techniques, while revenue managers may lack in-depth knowledge of cost structures and financial reporting. This lack of cross-functional expertise can hinder collaboration and reduce the effectiveness of integrated decision-making.

In addition to skill gaps, organisational resistance to change poses a significant barrier. Employees may be reluctant to adopt new technologies or processes due to concerns about job security, increased workload, or unfamiliarity with advanced systems. Resistance may also stem from organisational cultures that emphasise departmental autonomy over cross-functional integration.

Addressing these challenges requires targeted training and capacity-building initiatives. Organisations should invest in continuous professional development programmes focused on data analytics, digital tools, and integrated decision-making frameworks. Furthermore, fostering a culture of collaboration and innovation can help reduce resistance and encourage the adoption of integrated practices.

Leadership plays a crucial role in managing this transition. By clearly communicating the strategic benefits of integration and providing adequate support, management can facilitate smoother implementation and enhance employee engagement.

8.3 Impact of Digital Transformation, AI, and Big Data Analytics

Digital transformation is rapidly reshaping the hospitality industry, creating both opportunities and challenges for the integration of accounting information and RM. Technologies such as artificial intelligence (AI), machine learning, and big data analytics are driving a shift towards more sophisticated, data-driven decision-making processes.

Big data analytics enables hospitality organisations to analyse large volumes of structured and unstructured data, including customer preferences, booking patterns, and market trends. This enhances the accuracy of demand forecasting and supports more effective pricing and segmentation strategies. For example, predictive analytics can identify patterns in customer behaviour, allowing hotels to anticipate demand and adjust pricing proactively (Song & Li, 2008).

Artificial intelligence further extends these capabilities by automating complex decision-making processes. AI-powered RM systems can evaluate multiple variables simultaneously and recommend optimal pricing and inventory allocation strategies in real time. Similarly, AI-driven accounting tools can automate routine tasks such as data entry, reconciliation, and reporting, thereby improving efficiency and reducing the likelihood of errors.

However, the adoption of these technologies also introduces new challenges, including data privacy concerns, cybersecurity risks, and ethical considerations. Increased reliance on automated systems raises questions regarding transparency and accountability in decision-making. Additionally, the high cost of implementation and the need for specialised skills may limit the adoption of advanced technologies, particularly among smaller hospitality firms.

Table 4. Challenges and Emerging Trends in Integration

Area	Key Issues	Implications for Hospitality Firms
Data Integration	System incompatibility, data silos	Inefficient decision-making
Human Resources	Skill gaps, resistance to change	Reduced effectiveness of integration
Digital Transformation	AI, big data, automation	Enhanced analytics but increased complexity
Risk and Governance	Data privacy, cybersecurity	Need for stronger controls and policies

Source: Developed by the author

In conclusion, while the integration of accounting information and revenue management offers substantial strategic benefits, it is accompanied by several challenges that must be carefully managed. Addressing data integration issues, bridging skill gaps, and navigating the complexities of digital transformation are critical for successful implementation.

At the same time, emerging technologies such as AI and big data analytics present significant opportunities to enhance decision-making and drive innovation in the hospitality industry. Organisations that effectively manage these challenges while leveraging technological advancements will be better positioned to achieve sustainable growth and long-term competitive advantage.

9. CONCLUSION, POLICY IMPLICATIONS, AND FUTURE RESEARCH SCOPE

This chapter has examined the critical role of integrating accounting information with revenue management (RM) in enhancing strategic decision-making within the hospitality industry. The analysis demonstrates that while RM focuses on demand forecasting, pricing strategies, and capacity utilisation, accounting information provides essential insights into cost structures, profitability, and overall financial performance. When these two domains operate in isolation, decision-making tends to be incomplete and potentially inefficient. However, their integration enables a more comprehensive and balanced approach, shifting the focus from revenue maximisation to profit optimisation and long-term value creation.

The chapter highlights that contemporary hospitality environments are increasingly data-driven, requiring real-time information and cross-functional coordination. Accounting Information Systems (AIS), supported by digital technologies, facilitate the generation and dissemination of relevant financial and operational data. Simultaneously, RM practices such as dynamic pricing, segmentation, and demand forecasting depend on accurate and timely information to remain effective. The integration of these systems allows organisations to align pricing decisions with cost structures, improve forecasting accuracy, and enhance overall performance.

Furthermore, the discussion on strategic decision-making emphasises the importance of combining financial discipline with market responsiveness. The chapter also identifies key challenges, including data integration issues, skill gaps, and organisational resistance, while recognising the transformative potential of emerging technologies such as artificial intelligence and big data analytics. Overall, the findings underscore that integration is not merely a technological requirement but a strategic necessity for achieving sustainable competitive advantage in the hospitality sector.

From a managerial perspective, hospitality organisations should prioritise the development of integrated information systems that consolidate accounting and RM data into a unified platform. The adoption of Enterprise Resource Planning (ERP) systems and Business Intelligence (BI) tools can significantly enhance data accessibility, accuracy, and real-time decision-making capabilities.

Managers should also focus on developing profitability-based performance metrics, such as Gross Operating Profit per Available Room (GOPPAR), alongside traditional revenue-based indicators. This shift ensures that decision-making aligns with long-term financial sustainability rather than short-term revenue gains.

Investment in human capital is equally critical. Organisations should provide continuous training programmes to develop multidisciplinary skills in accounting, data analytics, and revenue management. Encouraging cross-functional collaboration between finance and RM teams can further improve decision quality and organisational alignment.

From a policy perspective, industry regulators and professional bodies should promote the standardisation of accounting and performance measurement frameworks within the hospitality sector. The adoption of systems such as the Uniform System of Accounts for the Lodging Industry (USALI) can enhance transparency and comparability across organisations.

Additionally, policies that support digital transformation such as incentives for technology adoption and investments in data infrastructure can facilitate integration, particularly for small and medium-sized enterprises (SMEs). Data governance also requires significant policy attention. As reliance on digital platforms increases, organisations must implement robust frameworks to ensure data accuracy, security, and privacy. Clear regulatory guidelines can help mitigate risks associated with data breaches and misuse.

While this chapter provides a comprehensive conceptual analysis of the integration between accounting information and revenue management, several avenues remain open for further research.

First, empirical studies are needed to examine the impact of integration on financial performance, operational efficiency, and customer satisfaction. Such research can provide evidence-based insights into the effectiveness of integrated systems across different categories of hospitality organisations.

Second, future research can explore the role of emerging technologies such as artificial intelligence, machine learning, and blockchain, in enhancing integration and decision-making processes. Investigating their practical implementation across diverse organisational contexts would offer valuable insights.

Third, the behavioural and organisational dimensions of integration warrant further attention. Factors such as leadership, organisational culture, and change management practices can significantly influence the adoption and success of integrated systems. Understanding these aspects can help organisations design more effective implementation strategies.

Finally, comparative studies across regions and market segments can provide insights into how contextual factors such as regulatory environments, technological readiness, and market maturity affect integration practices. This is particularly relevant for emerging markets, where resource constraints and institutional differences may pose additional challenges.

In conclusion, the integration of accounting information with revenue management represents a significant advancement in hospitality management, enhancing efficiency, profitability, and competitiveness. By addressing existing challenges and leveraging emerging opportunities, both practitioners and policymakers can contribute to building a more resilient and data-driven hospitality industry.

REFERENCES

Chen, C. F., & Rothschild, R. (2010). An application of revenue management in the hotel industry. *The Journal of Hospitality Financial Management, 18*(1), 45–60. DOI: 10.1080/10913211.2010.10653887

Davenport, T. H., & Harris, J. G. (2017). *Competing on analytics: The new science of winning*. Harvard Business Review Press.

Drury, C. (2018). *Management and cost accounting* (10th ed.). Cengage Learning.

Horngren, C. T., Datar, S. M., & Rajan, M. (2014). *Cost accounting: A managerial emphasis* (15th ed.). Pearson.

Ivanov, S., & Zhechev, V. (2012). Hotel revenue management: From theory to practice. *Tourism Review, 67*(1), 45–56.

Kimes, S. E. (1989). The basics of yield management. *The Cornell Hotel and Restaurant Administration Quarterly, 30*(3), 14–19. DOI: 10.1177/001088048903000309

Song, H., & Li, G. (2008). Tourism demand modelling and forecasting: A review of recent research. *Tourism Management, 29*(2), 203–220. DOI: 10.1016/j.tourman.2007.07.016

UNWTO. (2021). *International tourism and COVID-19 impact report.* World Tourism Organization.

Weygandt, J. J., Kimmel, P. D., & Kieso, D. E. (2019). *Financial accounting* (10th ed.). Wiley.

Chapter 6
Revenue Management Concepts and Pricing Logic in Hotels:
From Algorithmic Optimization to Strategic Value-Based Pricing

Gaye Deniz
http://orcid.org/0000-0002-9980-8506
Nevşehir Hacı Bektaş Veli University, Turkey

ABSTRACT

Strategic management focuses on decisions shaping the future of businesses, while revenue management functions as a key strategic link within the value chain. In the tourism sector, traditional pricing approaches based on cost and demand have evolved due to the active role of guests in value creation. Perceived value, willingness to pay, and market positioning significantly influence pricing decisions, making it a multidimensional and multi-actor process. Therefore, relying solely on traditional indicators such as RevPAR, ADR, and occupancy rates is insufficient to explain today's strategic pricing logic. Although artificial intelligence and algorithmic systems enhance pricing efficiency, human judgment remains essential, especially in uncertain and crisis contexts. This chapter emphasizes the need to integrate analytical tools with managerial reasoning, offering a more holistic and strategic perspective on revenue management and pricing in accommodation businesses.

DOI: 10.4018/979-8-3373-9479-4.ch006

INTRODUCTION

Revenue management, a management approach that is strategically important, was first used in the airline industry. In fact, the differentiating characteristics inherent to the service sector, which distinguish it from other sectors, made this management strategy necessary. This is because, in the service sector, capacity cannot be increased immediately in the short term. Moreover, demand for the service offered is highly uncertain, and services that cannot be provided today cannot be stored to be offered tomorrow (Buzacott, 2000). Due to its structural characteristics, this mindset, based on revenue management and dynamic pricing strategies first applied in the 1980s in airlines to maximize revenue in the tourism sector, is based on Dr. Robert Crandall, who developed these strategies while working at American Airlines (Boyd, 2007). The idea of optimizing a product's price based on capacity limitations later became widespread through Talluri. He approached revenue management as an academic discipline through his studies in the field (Baltazar, 2008). Revenue management, which aims to maximize revenue by optimizing prices with a fixed capacity (Smith et al., 1992), has over time been adapted to the hospitality sector. In hospitality businesses, revenue management is based on dynamically adjusting prices, regularly forecasting demand, and deciding how to allocate service capacity (Kimes et al., 1998; Talluri & Van Ryzin, 2004).

The fundamental characteristics of the service sector that distinguish it from other sectors are the main factors that make revenue management important for hospitality businesses. The characteristics of hotel businesses and the characteristics of services show parallels with each other through the features of non-storability, intangibility, simultaneity, and lack of ownership (Koşan & Türkseven, 2022). Every room that a hotel cannot sell on a given day, along with every restaurant table and chair, and every spa service that cannot be sold, means that revenue is lost for that day (Martin et al., 2019; Minor et al., 2025; Tranter et al., 2009). Hotel businesses must keep their costs at a minimum and maximize their revenues in order to survive in conditions of increasing competition. Therefore, businesses need to consider all elements related to costs and revenues (Didin & Köroğlu, 2008). Investments in accommodation businesses are largely made in fixed costs (Moon & Sharma, 2014). Additionally, there is a capacity limitation with respect to the number of sellable rooms (Farouk El Gayar et al., 2011). Therefore, demand must be forecasted both at the right time and at the right price (Emeksiz, 2001; Ören, 2005). Within this framework, revenue management is a multifaceted decision-making process that also encompasses demand, customer segmentation, and capacity optimization (Kimes, 2000).

Revenue management is a topic that should be approached both technically and strategically. However, due to this perspective, which is mostly neglected in the literature, revenue management has so far mostly been conducted through mathematical algorithms, optimization models, and methods used to forecast demand (Eren et al., 2024; Ivanov & Zhechev, 2012; Petricek et al., 2021; Tse & Poon, 2012). Yet, in order to price accurately in hospitality businesses, the underlying different variables must also be taken into account. For example, perceived value allows the consumer to make an assessment regarding the benefit of a product they receive. It is the total value judgment formed in the customer's mind by comparing the benefits (quality, status, experience) of a product or service with the costs (price, time, effort) (Zeithaml, 1988). Therefore, perceived value is one of the important variables to be considered in pricing decisions. Another is perceptions regarding how the brand is positioned. Brand positioning is the strategy that ensures the product occupies a unique value in the consumer's mind, different from competitors (Kotler & Keller, 2016). Price, on the other hand, is the most tangible indicator of this perception. Depending on the success of brand positioning, the product's price is shaped not only by market conditions but also by the brand's value. In this way, the business can gain control over the product's price and determine the initial price (Strauss, 2009). There are also numerous studies on the effect of customer experience on the price that customers are willing to pay (Çifçi & Kızılırmak, 2025; Setiawan & Saptutyningsih, 2022; Wang et al., 2018). Since all these variables are directly related to price, trying to explain revenue management only with technical and analytical methods is not sufficient and does not adequately reflect decision-making mechanisms.

Accordingly, this chapter argues that revenue management in hospitality should no longer be viewed solely as a technical optimization mechanism driven by algorithms and historical demand patterns. Instead, it should be conceptualized as a strategic and value-oriented managerial capability shaped by customer perception, brand positioning, experiential value creation, and managerial reasoning. In this context, the chapter proposes a hybrid revenue management perspective in which artificial intelligence-supported analytical systems and human managerial judgment operate in an integrated manner rather than as competing mechanisms.

Revenue management in the hospitality industry is increasingly evolving into a data-driven and artificial intelligence-supported structure. Thanks to artificial intelligence and big data analytics, revenue management has become more scientific and forecast-based (Millauer & Vellekoop, 2019). However, threats such as data security and cyber risks have emerged. Similarly, machine learning and real-time data analysis provide significant competitive advantages in revenue optimization (Talal et al., 2025). Ramos et al. (2015) highlighted the role of big data systems, which form the infrastructure of this transformation, in increasing decision quality. Therefore, it can be stated that revenue management has become even more complex in recent years. Data-driven dynamic pricing strategies play a decisive role in revenue optimization, especially in businesses dominated by intense competition and variable cost structures (Ding, 2025). Despite this, in the sector where pricing decisions have not yet been fully automated, the experience and intuition of managers come to the forefront, especially in uncertain environments experienced during crisis periods (Denizci Guillet & Chu, 2021; Hallin & Marnburg, 2008; Ho et al., 2025). Revenue management encompasses the fundamental processes related to pricing, demand forecasting, and capacity allocation. Beyond the application of analytical pricing methods aimed at maximizing a company's revenue or profit (Chen & Hu, 2023), it requires significant managerial judgment and expertise (Talluri & Van Ryzin, 2006).

Revenue management aims to maximize revenue by using a series of strategies to optimize the financial performance of a facility. In order for business managers to master the main principles of revenue management, they need to know forecasting methods, be able to apply different pricing according to segments, and prevent potential revenue loss. However, as in every component of tourism, one of the processes that guests evaluate perceptually in accommodation establishments is pricing. Studies indicate that guests who feel unfairly treated regarding prices have a lower likelihood of making subsequent purchases and later express their dissatisfaction through word of mouth (Choi & Mattila, 2004; Heo & Lee, 2011; Kimes & Wirtz, 2003). For this reason, businesses need to be careful about pricing. It should be approached not only from the perspective of optimization logic but also as a strategic decision-making process. Therefore, revenue management also represents relationship management beyond what is visible (Méatchi & Camus, 2020; Meatchi et al., 2021; Palmer & McMahon-Beattie, 2008). In this context, it should be considered not only with the goal of revenue maximization but also from the perspective of long-term customer relationships and brand value.

It is also an important element for businesses to be able to correctly position their brand in the market they operate in. Strategic price positioning affects the revenue performance of accommodation businesses (Noone et al., 2011). However, since pricing is not merely a cost- or demand-based decision process (Hinterhuber, 2004), it should reflect the value offered to the customer and be handled in an integrated manner with customer perception, value proposition, organizational capabilities, and market dynamics (Hallberg, 2008; Johansson & Andersson, 2012). In the context of tourism, pricing decisions are too complex to be reduced to a standard model. Therefore, they should be shaped by managerial reasoning in conjunction with contextual factors (Pellinen, 2003). In this context, the value creation process has become more dynamic with digitalization and algorithmic pricing (Nunan & Di Domenico, 2022).

Although the revenue management literature has significantly expanded in recent years, existing studies have predominantly approached the subject from a technical and optimization-oriented perspective, focusing mainly on forecasting models, dynamic pricing systems, and algorithmic efficiency. Comparatively limited attention has been devoted to the strategic, behavioral, ethical, and value-based dimensions of pricing decisions in hospitality businesses. In particular, the interaction between artificial intelligence-supported pricing systems, managerial reasoning, customer perception, pricing transparency, and long-term brand positioning remains underexplored in the hospitality literature. Furthermore, while AI-supported revenue management systems are becoming increasingly widespread, discussions concerning algorithmic ethics, transparency, fairness, and customer trust are still fragmented and insufficiently integrated into strategic hospitality management research. In this respect, the present chapter seeks to address these gaps by proposing a multidimensional and strategic perspective on revenue management in hospitality.

This study aims to examine how pricing decisions in hospitality businesses are shaped not only by analytical models but also within the framework of consumer perception, value creation processes, and strategic positioning dynamics, by addressing revenue management from a multidimensional perspective. Based on this idea, the chapter seeks answers to some research questions. Firstly, the nature of revenue management and pricing logic from the perspective of accommodation enterprises has been questioned. In this context, both structural and strategic antecedents affecting revenue management have been outlined. In addition, it has been discussed that pricing decisions are not only algorithmic calculations, but beyond that, they require an integrated structure of correct managerial thinking. Although traditional criteria are the cornerstones of performance evaluation, they may not be sufficient on their own in the pricing process. While these indicators provide a snapshot of performance, they may not align with long-term strategic goals, especially in today's competitive environment. Therefore, the importance of value-based pricing logic, especially in hotel businesses, has been emphasized. From this point, it is no coincidence that dynamic pricing is extensively utilized in the tourism sector. The unforgettable experience offered in the industry aims to create a loyal customer base. If businesses maintain this perception in the long term, it will strengthen their brand position. For this reason, since the applied pricing policy affects the perception of quality, trust, and uniqueness, dynamic pricing logic needs to be well-managed in revenue management. Especially from a managerial perspective, even the decision-making mechanisms of businesses necessitate the correct operation of this system. Ultimately, the section provides a holistic contribution with its recommendations both academically and sectoral.

BACKGROUND

The Definition and Evolution of Revenue Management

The foundations of revenue management were laid with Littlewood's (1972) capacity control model and Belobaba's (1987) studies on airline revenue optimization, and after the 1979 deregulation, its area of application rapidly expanded. After the deregulation in 1979, the airline industry effectively began looking for ways to compete and developed different approaches to revenue management. Since then, airlines have expanded their efforts in the field of revenue management to increase their revenues. Revenue management was commonly defined by Kimes (1989) as "selling the right seat, to the right customer, at the right time, for the right price," in other words, "the process of allocating the right type of capacity to the right customer at the right price in order to maximize revenue or yield." Similarly, Smith and others (1992) stated that the purpose of revenue management is to sell the right product to the right customer at the right time and at the right price. Revenue management is the application of systematic analytical methods that predict consumer behavior at the micro-market level and optimize product supply and pricing to maximize revenue (Cross et al., 2009). In a segmented market, capacity utilization is also optimized by offering different prices to customers in each segment. Revenue management is used in various transportation sectors such as car rental, ferries, railways, tour operators, cargo, and cruise lines, as well as in other areas such as hotels, resorts, healthcare services, clothing manufacturing, and companies producing perishable goods (Siddappa, 2006). Today, it plays a central role in the strategic decision-making processes of businesses in the hospitality sector.

Revenue management essentially consists of complementary components such as demand forecasting, capacity allocation, pricing, and the management of distribution channels. Initially, revenue management focused on the allocation of capacity for units at risk of losing value in inventory, but later different perspectives were developed and revenue management research gained depth. It has become particularly important for businesses operating with fixed capacity to accurately predict and control demand. Additionally, considering their roles, especially in the service sector, it has become necessary to use distribution channels in a way that enhances performance. Differentiated pricing practices based on target markets created through market segmentation have also constituted an important step in revenue management (Coulter, 2001; Denizci Guillet, 2020). According to Cross and others (2009), revenue management represents a holistic perspective that includes not only the optimization of revenue from rooms, but also other facilities offered by the business. Therefore, beyond being an operational function, revenue management has become a strategic function.

However, the successful implementation of revenue management at the sectoral level also brings some conditions with it. Among these conditions, which can be considered structural factors, are fixed capacity (Cesaret & Katok, 2025) that cannot be changed within a certain period or cannot be increased in a short time, and demand uncertainty (Petrick et al., 2012), which refers to the situation where future demand for a product or service cannot be known with certainty. Additionally, due to the fact that the product, which particularly restricts the service sector, cannot be physically produced and stored, capacity offered when there is no demand leads to an irreplaceable capacity loss (non-storability/perishability) and cannot be instantly met in cases of excess demand (Caldentey & Wein, 2002). When approached from a marketing perspective, one of the factors that facilitates revenue management is the ability to segment and apply different prices to each customer segment (Bodea & Ferguson, 2014; Vives et al., 2018). This situation is explained in the literature by price discrimination practices. Therefore, approaching revenue management solely from a technical standpoint may lead to a limited consideration of the topic, and it should be evaluated by integrating it with the structural and strategic characteristics of the business.

Structural Characteristics of Hotel Operations

The revenue management system successfully applied in the aviation sector has gradually begun to be used in different sectors that exhibit similar characteristics based on the products they produce. The accommodation sector within the tourism industry is one of them (Koşan & Türkseven, 2022). Hotel enterprises are facilities arranged according to certain standards for the purpose of temporary relocation and accommodation (Erdem, 2010). The main basis of hotel management is human labor. In hotel enterprises serving a dynamic area that sells time, services are provided within specific time periods. The sale of services only begins upon the guests' request to the enterprise, and room sales, which are the most important source of revenue, have a distinct feature. The sector, where the risk factor is quite high, continuously benefits from technological innovations. The services provided require close cooperation and mutual assistance between departments and personnel. In hotel businesses that also meet various needs such as food, drink, and entertainment, sales are generally made in cash, and credit cards are commonly used for payments. In addition to these basic characteristics, a large portion of the capital in hotel businesses is allocated to fixed assets (Demirtaş, 2010). In this context, revenue management practices are extremely common in four- and five-star hotel businesses with a fixed capacity and departmental structure (Brotherton & Mooney, 1992). For hotel businesses that have to operate at a fixed capacity, managing demand accurately also becomes a necessity. Looking at the fundamental dynamics behind the change in industry, the last-minute trend is not a coincidence but rather a reflection of the new priorities of the modern consumer. Therefore, taking a position before demand increases becomes a necessity. However, since demand is extremely variable, the most realistic way to deal with this uncertainty is the effective implementation of revenue management. While revenue management makes it possible to gain a competitive advantage over competitors in very short periods of time, it enables focusing on revenue and profitability optimization instead of occupancy rates, while also allowing different price responses for different segments (Cross et al., 2009; Kimes, 1989).

The most fundamental structural feature of hotel businesses is that they have a fixed capacity. The number of rooms in a hotel cannot be increased in the short term (Kimes, 1989). It is especially impossible to expand capacity during periods of high demand. This situation makes the efficient use of capacity critical and distinguishes hotels from manufacturing businesses, directly affecting strategic decisions (Güzel et al., 2022). In hotel businesses operating with fixed capacity, where demand is flexible, the use of revenue management systems increases revenues (Koşan & Türkseven, 2022).

The structure of demand in hotel businesses varies greatly. Demand quickly perceives changes in the environment and responds rapidly. Being able to control demand with this structure is related to the high speed of decision-making and flexibility of hotel businesses (Bozkurt & Göral, 2013). For example, crisis-creating situations in tourist attraction centers have different types of impacts on tourist demand, and depending on the significance of the event, noticeable and serious declines in demand may occur (Aydın & Akyol, 2013). Similarly, during the COVID-19 pandemic, it was observed that health and safety concerns reduced demand, negatively affecting the sector (Karadeniz et al., 2020). Many factors such as seasonality, events, economic fluctuations, and digital visibility can change the structure of demand quickly and unpredictably (Talluri et al., 2004). Therefore, demand uncertainty in hotel businesses is one of the most important dynamics affecting revenue.

One of the important foundations in revenue management is that it provides the opportunity for price differentiation. The ability to control capacity through pricing in demand management remains a characteristic feature of revenue management practices in today's airline industry (Van Ryzin & Talluri, 2005). Price differentiation refers to offering the same product or service at different prices to different customer segments, time periods, or channels (Yiğit, 2024). The main goal here is to maximize profit by increasing capacity utilization through optimizing demand and generating revenue that matches each customer segment's willingness to pay (Cross et al., 2009). Especially in the tourism sector, the fact that different customer segments have different willingness to pay makes it possible to offer the same product at different prices (Kimes, 2000). This situation is particularly evident in the differences in price sensitivity between customers traveling for business and those traveling for leisure.

One of the important structural features of hotel businesses is that it requires segmentation of the target audience, which is necessary for price differentiation. In revenue management, decisions are made regarding which sales format, which market segmentation or differentiation mechanism will be used, how products will be grouped, how product categories will be priced, how prices will change over time, how much capacity will be allocated to different market segments, when the product will be closed for sale and when it will be sold again (Akmeşe & Güderoğlu, 2017). One of the decisions here, separating customers according to their behavioral and demographic characteristics, is important in that it enables the development of pricing and sales strategies suitable for each segment. However, the proliferation of digital platforms and the increase in price transparency are making the boundaries between these segments increasingly permeable and turning revenue management practices into a more complex structure (Noone et al., 2011).

Features such as intangibility, heterogeneity, shared experience, simultaneous production and consumption, perishability, high fixed or sunk costs, demand seasonality, fixed capacity, and multiple market segments in hospitality (Bull, 2006) make it impossible to establish conditions of perfect competition in the accommodation sector (Mitra, 2020). Developing a management framework that guides strategic thinking in changing markets is becoming increasingly critical for researchers and managers to cope with the complex and rapidly changing global business environment (Cravens et al., 2009). In this context, hotels should make the effects of performance factors efficient for effective revenue management by correctly managing capacity and modeling consumer behaviors (Ampountolas et al., 2021). Additionally, since the market can be divided into narrow customer segments, they can benefit from differentiated pricing for various segments (Yelkur & Nêveda DaCosta, 2001). Revenue optimization provides a consistent approach to pricing decisions with the aim of offering the right price to the right customer segment for the right product through the right channel at the right time (Sun et al., 2011).

Performance Metrics and Limitations

The most important performance indicators used in hotel businesses are occupancy rates and revenue. The number of rooms to be sold and the revenue to be obtained from these rooms constitute the first stage of planning. In revenue management, financial success is measured by achieving maximum efficiency through optimizing the occupancy-price balance based on the correlation between the realized average daily rate (ADR), the revenue per available room (RevPAR) reflecting capacity efficiency, and the potential average rate level showing pricing discipline (Koşan & Türkseven, 2022).

Room sales are the main product of hotels and at the same time a major source of revenue. The room price is consistent with the services provided in hotels as much as it is high. Ratio showing the average room rate (ADR) sold in hotels over a one-month period are calculated (Oses et al., 2016). It can also provide an indirect indicator of price competition (Jayanti, 2021). Comparing the average daily room rate (ADR) with the potential maximum revenue that could be achieved if all rooms were sold on a daily basis and over specific periods ensures the control of pricing efficiency (Koşan & Türkseven, 2022). ADR, calculated by dividing the total room revenue by the number of rooms sold within a specific time period, helps hotels understand their pricing performance, track revenue trends, and make data-driven pricing and strategic decisions. Hotels can increase the average room price by offering strategic pricing, segmentation, upselling, packaging, and value-added amenities or experiences (Yurtlu & Ateş, 2019).

RevPAR, or revenue per available room, is one of the most commonly used performance metrics when evaluating a hotel's performance. RevPAR (Revenue Per Available Room) is a financial ratio that indicates how much revenue a hotel generates based on the total number of rooms it has over a specific period of time (Osmanoğlu, 2019). There are two main methods to calculate RevPAR; based on total revenue and based on ADR and occupancy. RevPAR is an important indicator of operational efficiency. It allows for competitive analysis, determines return on investment, and provides important insights into strategic performance (Güzel et al., 2022; Schwartz et al., 2017). Guest satisfaction and repeat visits play a decisive role on RevPAR (Ho & Kim, 2025). However, hoteliers have also recognized the limitations of RevPAR and have developed other alternative performance metrics. Gross Operating Profit per Available Room (GOPPAR) has become popular as an alternative performance metric because it addresses the limitations of RevPAR (Lee et al., 2019). While offering aggressive discounts to increase occupancy can temporarily improve RevPAR by boosting demand in the short term, it limits the profitability of businesses in the long term due to the pressure it creates on the average daily room rate and the value attributed to the brand. Continuous promotional strategies that disrupt price parity can change customer behavior, complicate revenue management, increase operational costs, and create negative effects on RevPAR (Kim et al., 2019; Yıldıztekin, 2010). Evaluating revenue management solely through quantitative, measurable performance indicators (KPIs) such as RevPAR, ADR, or occupancy rate can lead to the neglect of strategic processes and result in faulty decisions. Therefore, revenue management should be assessed through strategic processes.

Pricing generally serves as a cue for perceived value, quality, and affordability (Yiğit, 2024). Nagle and Müller (2018) also add willingness to pay to this. Therefore, when setting prices, it is necessary to provide a value-based perspective beyond traditional performance indicators. This is because a management strategy that focuses solely on making decisions based on classic indicators such as RevPAR, ADR, and occupancy rates carries the risk of missing a competitive advantage in the long term. Hence, it is clear that performance indicators alone are not sufficient. Revenue management should be considered a multidimensional decision-making area that is not limited to measurement tools but rather includes strategic reasoning, value perception, and brand positioning beyond these measurements.

Overall, the literature reviewed in this section demonstrates that revenue management in hospitality cannot be adequately explained through operational metrics and technical optimization models alone. The multidimensional nature of pricing decisions, together with increasing market complexity, technological transformation, and changing customer expectations, requires a broader strategic perspective. In this respect, the following section discusses revenue management and pricing logic through strategic, behavioral, and value-oriented dimensions beyond traditional analytical frameworks.

MAIN FOCUS OF THE CHAPTER

In this section, revenue management and pricing logic are approached from a strategic, behavioral, and value-focused perspective. It is argued that the pricing process in hotel operations is influenced by different determinants, moving beyond the analytical framework discussed in the literature to date. In this context, this section addresses target market segmentation based on demand forecasting and under conditions of uncertainty, as well as the related price differentiation strategies. Additionally, the dependence of pricing decisions on distribution channels is evident. Since there are two systems that need to be managed together, correct pricing decisions should be implemented with the right channel for the right customer segment to achieve maximum revenue and profitability. In pricing, while algorithms answer the question of what should be done, managers are the ultimate decision-making authority on what is more appropriate to do. Therefore, an integrated decision-making system based on human–algorithm interaction is a topic that should be considered holistically in revenue management. This section presents an approach that goes beyond the numerical optimization processes of revenue management and aims to create value in the market. In this approach, strategic decisions are shaped based on consumer perception. In this respect, the chapter moves beyond the conventional understanding of revenue management as a purely algorithmic optimization process. Instead, it introduces a hybrid revenue management framework in which data-driven analytical systems, dynamic pricing algorithms, and artificial intelligence applications are strategically balanced with managerial intuition, contextual interpretation, ethical considerations, and long-term brand positioning objectives. Therefore, pricing decisions are conceptualized not merely as numerical outputs generated by algorithms, but as multidimensional strategic judgments shaped by organizational, behavioral, and experiential dynamics.

Pricing Logic as a Strategic Construct

Determining a pricing strategy enables business owners to decide how much to charge for a product or service. Successful pricing should be based on establishing a harmonious connection between cost, demand, and competition (Kasapoğlu, 2007). Prices are determined either by setting a margin above costs to achieve certain turnover, market share, or capacity utilization, or based on the value created for customers. The subject of pricing has so far been based on analytical and cost-based approaches. However, in the service economy of the modern world, this cost-focused view does not fully meet the desired outcome. A well-designed pricing strategy can help shape consumer perception while promoting brand loyalty and willingness to pay (Zeithaml, 1988). One of the fundamental concepts that is often overlooked here is perceived value. However, value-based pricing is defined as the strategy of setting the product price according to the value that the consumer assigns to the product, rather than determining the price based on the product's cost, market price, or competitors' prices (Ural, 2008). While traditional methods overlook the potential to sell the product at a higher price, value-based pricing allows for the realization of this potential. Among pricing strategies, it is acknowledged that the customer value-based pricing approach can produce more effective results in many cases. Additionally, it is emphasized that value-based pricing can lead to higher profitability and customer satisfaction by focusing on the value perceived by customers (Hinterhuber, 2008). When value is emphasized, the willingness to pay that forms in the consumer in response to the perception of the product or service in question becomes decisive (Nagle & Müller, 2018). When it comes to the service sector, this criterion becomes even more prominent. For example, there is a difference in the value attributed between a guest who comes to a hotel for vacation and a guest who is there for a business trip. While experience and satisfaction may be more prominent for one, the other may have preferred a location where they can manage their time. Therefore, the price that consumers are willing to pay varies according to different perceptions of value. These differences in perception are also the answer to why customer segmentation is done when making pricing decisions in hotel businesses.

Economists, psychologists, and marketing researchers rely on measurements of consumers' willingness to pay when predicting demand for a product or service and designing optimal pricing programs (Wertenbroch & Skiera, 2002). In practice, their willingness to pay means that customers are willing to pay more for the features of a preferred product compared to competing products (Aaker, 1996, Netemeyer et al., 2004), and it is at the center of pricing logic. Here, the highest price that consumers are willing to pay varies according to many factors. Foremost among these are economic factors. However, psychological, social, and experiential elements beyond these can also shape the price that consumers are willing to pay. When individuals achieve psychological satisfaction, come together with their social circles, and experience situations according to specific interests, the price they are willing to pay can become flexible (Temel & Anbarcı, 2025). One of the most striking examples in the context of hotel businesses is the opportunity to stay in luxury cave hotels offered alongside balloon tourism in the Cappadocia destination. The unforgettable tourism experience stems from the fact that it has psychological, social, and experiential characteristics. Therefore, it is difficult for two hotels located in the same destination, one offering superior service and the other unable to meet this criterion, to achieve a sustainable competitive advantage. This is because it is directly related to price, brand value, and perceived quality (Aktepe & Candemir, 2024). In the tourism sector, where the tourist becomes a fully-fledged actor in creating their own experience and the roles of tourism professionals and tourists need to be redefined; tourists want to experience new, different, and unforgettable experiences during their holidays compared to their daily lives (Thanh & Kirova, 2018), and certain tourist segments may be willing to pay higher prices (Hwang & Han, 2018).

In the experience economy, a new form of economy that can meet various experiential needs of people (Pine & Gilmore, 1998; 1999), consumers consume products and services not only for their functional reasons but also to have unique, memorable, extraordinary, and unforgettable experiences (Oh et al., 2007; Morgan et al., 2009; Hosany & Witham, 2010). In this context, price holds strategic importance specifically for hotel businesses. Prices offered to modern consumers, who seek memorable experiences alongside the service while purchasing, vary. This is valid not only for businesses but also in terms of destination characteristics (Pike & Mason, 2011). Hotel businesses located in destinations that have tourist appeal worldwide, especially those with natural and cultural heritage value, have a high pricing power. For hotels in the luxury segment of the tourism sector, setting a high price is an important revenue management policy. While a high price can be perceived as a reputation indicator in the long term, at the same time, short-term discounted pricing policies can also undermine the market position of businesses.

One of the necessary factors for addressing pricing in hotels from a strategic perspective is the element of competition. According to Porter, cost leadership and differentiation strategy are two different approaches used to achieve competitive advantage. While the cost leadership strategy aims to achieve above-average returns against competitors through low prices by reducing costs in all components, the differentiation strategy seeks to create competitive advantage by offering unique products characterized by valuable features such as innovation, quality, and customer service (Mirzayeva & Türkay, 2016). Competitors are an important factor due to price-level competition through the quality and variety of services they offer. The ease with which customers can compare prices via online sales channels or bargaining on the internet is also a significant factor (Kılıç & Uslu, 2019). Therefore, in the tourism sector, where the number of digital platforms is extremely high, price transparency causes competition to intensify. Based on this idea, implementing price-based differentiation strategies in hotel businesses has become more difficult. One of the points to be noted is that businesses that continuously set competitive prices experience value erosion in the long term. For this reason, when pricing, businesses should focus on competition while simultaneously acting proactively with strategic pricing decisions. From this perspective, pricing logic constitutes an important component of revenue management, which is also the focus of this section. Businesses need to view the price not as a technical optimization but as a strategic decision-making method. Therefore, for the long-term success of businesses, in addition to quantitative methods, qualitative factors should also be evaluated together with brand value and destination dynamics.

These discussions indicate that pricing in hospitality businesses is not merely a numerical decision process but a strategic mechanism shaped by customer perception, competitive positioning, and experiential value creation. However, the successful implementation of such strategic pricing decisions also depends heavily on the ability of businesses to anticipate demand accurately under conditions of uncertainty. Therefore, demand forecasting becomes one of the central pillars supporting effective revenue management practices.

Demand Forecasting and Uncertainty

Revenue management examines the relationship between the concepts of time, price, and product. The goal of revenue management is to maximize revenues by making the best use of available capacity (Gür & Yıldız, 2016). The effectiveness of the system largely depends on the most accurate possible forecasting of demand. Accurate forecasting of tourist arrivals emerges as a strategic necessity in terms of the planning, operation, and management of tourist destinations. According to Talluri and Van Ryzin (2004), the accuracy of forecasts determines which customer segment, at what time, and at what price sales will be made. In revenue management, historical data and current reservation practices are used as much as possible to forecast future demand. For example, demand can be forecasted by examining the status of past reservations through automation systems within the front office system (Koşan & Türkseven, 2022). Additionally, many hotel chains around the world increase their revenues by using demand forecasting algorithms and dynamic pricing software (Şeker, 2025). Demand forecasting, evaluated together with capacity allocation in hotel operations, forms the basis of pricing policies. Therefore, in hotel operations, demand forecasting should be seen as a strategic decision-making mechanism rather than an analytical optimization.

As previously mentioned, the service sector faces certain structural problems due to its nature. When evaluated on a sectoral basis, uncertainties arising from seasonality, special events, and economic fluctuations, as well as from geopolitical developments and numerous factors such as visibility on digital platforms, are extremely influential on demand forecasting. Hotel businesses struggle most with seasonal demand fluctuations (Bulgan & Soybali, 2011). Seasonality, which allows for predicting reservation requests that are higher or lower in certain periods, affects pricing decisions and, consequently, revenue management. The seasonality characteristic of tourism necessitates the creation of demand forecasts for businesses to make the most of available resources (Kaman & Bölükbaş, 2024). Although there is no single model that works comprehensively and accurately to consistently predict demand in tourism, using both quantitative and qualitative forecasting approaches together by also utilizing seasonal and cyclical analyses of tourism yields better results (Song & Li, 2008). For example, platforms like Airbnb and Booking.com use predictive analyses to adjust prices based on factors such as demand, seasonality, and competitor pricing (Sönmez Karapınar, 2024). On the other hand, special event periods at destinations create short-term but intense increases in demand, particularly in hotel operations. In this case, more dynamic and flexible forecasts are required, as pricing and capacity planning are directly affected by these forecasts (Barreda, 2017; Depken & Stephenson, 2018; Falk & Vieru, 2021; Kamola & Arabas, 2020). One of the periods when uncertainty is most intensely experienced is during times of economic fluctuations. In these periods, it directly affects demand forecasts as a factor influencing both tourists' intentions to travel and their willingness to spend. It is especially necessary to act cautiously and foresightedly during economic downturns (Kruhlyanko et al., 2025; Minich, 2025). This is because the tourism sector largely depends on consumers' disposable income and therefore needs to respond very sensitively to economic fluctuations (Lee et al., 2016). Geopolitical risks, which affect perceptions of safety in destinations and cause uncertainty in demand by changing tourist flows, also occur from time to time (Balli et al., 2019; Papagianni et al., 2024). As a requirement of today's technology, visibility on digital platforms also increases access to potential customers and reservation volume. This situation ensures that demand forecasts are made more accurately and based on data (Smithson et al., 2011; Suwitri et al., 2025). In addition to these factors that can change demand quickly and unpredictably, destination image and external environmental factors, beyond business performance, also affect this situation. Therefore, demand forecasting should not be considered a deterministic process, and it should always be thought to contain a certain margin of error (Ivanov & Zhechev, 2012).

One of the challenges the industry faces in demand forecasting is the limitations caused by missing, outdated, or low-quality data. This situation prevents accurate demand forecasting and, therefore, leads to incorrect decisions in both pricing and capacity planning (Magnini et al., 2003). Big data is transforming businesses in their strategic decision-making processes. By analyzing data, consumer behaviors, price sensitivity, booking habits, and demand forecasts can be determined more accurately. Thus, revenue management practices become more dynamic (Özsoy Erarslan, 2025). Through the analysis of multidimensional data sets, the accuracy of forecasts is improved, thereby enhancing the success of pricing decisions as well (Guizzardi et al., 2021; Henriques & Pereira, 2024). It has become possible, especially based on past bookings, to predict tourist behavior and generate forecasts based on market conditions. However, since all these calculations are based on past data, they may not produce entirely reliable results. Businesses experience uncertainty due to unforeseeable events such as natural disasters, economic crises, epidemics, and wars (Canöz, 2022). From this point, because the validity of the data is affected, it may not be a sufficient indicator on its own in demand forecasting. Therefore, forecast methods based on past data alone may not be sufficient, as they can limit the flexibility of businesses.

Price ensures measurability and establishes a balance between supply and demand (Tek, 1999). In a variable and competitive environment, especially in the tourism sector, which is quickly affected by changes, dynamic pricing is a highly effective pricing strategy to keep supply and demand balanced at all levels (Tarakçı & Göktaş, 2020). The analysis of past data provides a basis for dynamic pricing strategies, enabling more accurate demand forecasts and ensuring revenue optimization. Dynamic pricing helps businesses understand the current and future supply-demand balance in the face of experienced or potential unexpected changes, such as when supply decreases, when there is a major event in the city on a weekend, or as in 2020, when a pandemic affected many sectors worldwide. Indeed, the underlying assumption here is that past trends will continue in the future. However, the tourism market today is unpredictable due to the aforementioned uncertainty factors. Unlike many other sectors, the tourism sector has a relatively more fragile structure against environmental impacts (Pekdemir & Küçükaltan, 2024). For example, at the point reached today, digitalization has also changed tourist behavior. In particular, booking periods have shortened and last-minute decisions have increased. Therefore, past static forecasting methods have proven to be insufficient. Flexible forecasting methods based on real-time data have now gained importance (Noone et al., 2011).

There is no single method used for demand forecasting. Since the purpose of demand forecasting is to develop a useful forecast from available information using a technique suitable for different demand structures, businesses may use different methods in different situations (Ulucan & Kızılırmak, 2018). Demand forecasting is generally considered in two main groups: qualitative methods based on expert opinion (Delphi, scenario analysis, etc.) and quantitative methods based on historical data and statistical models (time series, exponential smoothing, ARIMA, etc.) (Krajewski et al., 2013). However, demand forecasting should not be regarded solely as a technical process carried out through numerical models. Non-numerical demand forecasting encompasses methods in which managers develop future projections based more on knowledge, experience, intuition, and expert opinion during periods of uncertainty arising from the nature of the industry (Ergün & Şahin, 2017). For example, the dates of a major event such as the UEFA Champions League Final, past year's occupancy rates, and price increase trends can be predicted in advance by data models. However, the impact of an upcoming event on demand or possible changes in competitors' pricing strategies may not always be fully captured by data models. In the case of the Cappadocia Balloon Festival, there may be an unexpected surge in demand due to content suddenly going viral on social media or influencer posts. This unpredictable increase may not be forecasted through data models based on numerical methods. For all these reasons, it is important to consider both methods together when implementing revenue management in hotel operations.

Since revenue management decisions are central, it is necessary to make demand forecasts as accurately as possible; however, in an environment of uncertainty and with existing limitations, it may not be possible to make decisions with absolute accuracy. Therefore, a demand forecasting model that maximizes revenue needs to be flexible. From this perspective, for the sustainability of revenue management applied in hotel operations, it is important to consider not only forecasts based on past data but also the market's variability along with an insight system that analyzes market dynamics.

Accurate demand forecasting not only supports pricing decisions but also enables businesses to identify which customer groups generate value under different market conditions. In this context, segmentation and differentiated pricing strategies emerge as critical mechanisms for aligning demand characteristics with revenue optimization objectives.

Segmentation and Differential Pricing

Revenue management and pricing analytics applications analytically calculate demand forecasts using past sales data. These forecasts are then used in optimization models to determine and update the capacity (or prices) offered to specific customer segments through various channels, with the aim of maximizing profit (Bodea & Ferguson, 2014). Segmentation and differentiated pricing are fundamental building blocks of revenue management, and when not applied correctly, the effectiveness of the system is significantly weakened.

Due to different customer groups having different price sensitivities (price elasticity) and willingness to pay (Kimes, 2000), the same service is offered at different prices to different segments in revenue management. This differentiated pricing technique strategically aims to maximize revenue. Different customer groups vary in terms of the value they assign to a business's products. The process of identifying these different customer groups is generally referred to as customer segmentation (Çilkara, 2024; Doğanlı, 2025). Segmentation is defined as dividing the market into different sections in order to offer a different marketing mix to each section, based on the fact that consumers' wants, needs, and behaviors will differ (Kotler, 1996). Businesses can choose the entire market as their target market without segmenting the market, or they can segment the market and target specific market segments. The two most important segmentation strategies are customer-based and product-based (De Larrea & Gregory, 2020; Sarvari et al., 2016). Customer-based segmentation is when a business offers exactly the same product at different prices to two or more different customers based on specific customer characteristics, such as age, gender, or nationality. Product-based segmentation involves creating higher or lower quality versions of a product. This allows a different price to be assigned to each version. However, sales from higher-priced versions cannibalizing lower-priced versions are minimized (Bodea & Ferguson, 2014).

Among the most common segment types in the accommodation sector are business travelers, leisure travelers, group reservations, and customers coming through online travel agencies (OTAs) (Crawford-Welch, 1990; Morritt & Weinstein, 2012). Tourists in the business travel segment generally have low price elasticity. Service quality, price affordability, and the location of the establishment create a partially or jointly significant effect on customer satisfaction. This effect is further strengthened with increased price alignment (Risnawati et al., 2019). Tourists who place more importance on factors such as time constraints, location advantage, and service quality may accept higher prices. In contrast, tourists with free time traveling for leisure purposes have higher price sensitivity. It aims to provide relaxation and renewal through experiential, sustainable, and health-focused activities such as taking a break from daily routines, engaging in cultural exploration, or enjoying a sea-sand-sun holiday. Booking decisions are shaped by price advantages such as promotions, early booking opportunities, and package offers. This segment plays an important role in tourism demand (Balińska & Olejniczak, 2022; Mercan & Sandıkcı, 2024). Research shows that business travelers generally have lower price sensitivity, whereas leisure travelers differ among the three segments (Kim et al., 2020). For instance, business travelers tend to prefer flying because they value their time more. As travel expenses are mostly covered by the company, they are not as sensitive to price as vacation travelers. In contrast, vacation travelers are much more sensitive to price.

Revenue management is not only about pricing, but also a capacity allocation problem. Group bookings are the most critical element that disrupts this balance yet also creates opportunities. In this segment, the discussion is about price based on total volume. Since unit prices are set at lower levels, occupancy rates increase and may provide revenue growth. Aziz and others (2008) analyze the impact of group bookings on revenue management in hotel operations, showing that capacity allocation decisions should be optimized not only based on individual bookings, but also taking into account group size and demand scenarios. Therefore, the group segment should be considered as a strategic tool to optimize capacity usage, especially during low demand periods (Talluri & Van Ryzin, 2004).

One of the most notable segments in recent years is customers of online travel agencies (OTAs). Hardy (2020) defined online travel agencies as third-party intermediaries and meta-search platforms that buy, promote, and market trips, hotels, cars, flights, vacation packages, and similar services provided or organized by others. The widespread use of digital platforms has increased price transparency and enabled consumers to easily compare different hotels (Noone et al., 2011). Customers of online travel agencies have high price sensitivity. Therefore, they base their decisions largely on price comparisons. This allows hotel businesses to reach a broad customer base. However, at the same time, price competition intensifies and puts pressure on profit margins. Additionally, reverse auction platforms like priceline.com and price prediction sites like farecast.com also pose a great challenge for the pricing of both suppliers and intermediaries (Doğan & Eker, 2022).

Differentiated pricing is a system based on a multi-tiered pricing structure that relies on segmentation-focused price management and allows different prices to be set for the same product (Yiğit, 2024). The aim here is to facilitate business operations and increase revenues depending on customers' demand for the product. In order for businesses to reach their targeted sales volumes and profits, they need to set the correct price and make appropriate price differentiation by considering many factors such as consumers' price sensitivity, price awareness levels, and willingness to pay (Çolak & Koşan, 2018). Prices are adjusted upward during periods of high demand and relaxed downward during periods of low demand. The most typical example of this is coastal hotels, increasing their prices during holiday seasons and official holidays when the season is suitable, while keeping prices lower at the beginning and end of the winter months. If the economic, social, and psychological structures of the consumers creating the demand are different, different prices can be applied for room and food and beverage services in hotel businesses (Denizer, 1991).

The heterogeneous structure of different segments forms the basis of price differentiation strategies. However, this process is not only about setting prices according to segments. It also requires the creation of conditions that allow different prices to be applied to different customer groups. For example, an early booking opportunity offered before the season starts is quite advantageous for both hotels and customers. Making a reservation during the winter months to avoid the high accommodation prices during the season creates a perception of a price discount for tourists, while hotel operators benefit from the advantage of being able to anticipate occupancy months in advance. In non-refundable reservations, there is a prepaid service offered at a lower price where the amount paid cannot be refunded in case of cancellation or changes. This situation reduces the occupancy risk for the hotel. While it carries risk for the consumer, it can also offer significant price advantages. The minimum length of stay during periods of high demand is a restriction applied to those making reservations in order to sell all rooms for all days. In other words, it means imposing a minimum stay requirement to persuade guests interested in the hotel to stay for more nights than they planned and supporting it with suitable campaigns. Applying different prices to different customer segments depends on the correct analysis of price elasticity. Price elasticity refers to the response of demand to price changes and varies for each segment. Incorrect segmentation or pricing decisions can lead to the loss of customers with high willingness to pay or to an overrepresentation of low-priced segments. Although this may increase occupancy rates in the short term, it can lead to revenue loss and brand value erosion in the long term (Ivanov & Zhechev, 2012). Therefore, because revenue management is a strategic decision area, segmentation and differentiated pricing are important. In the context of hotel businesses, when customer segments are correctly identified and value-based price differentiation is applied according to segments, the likelihood of revenue management achieving success will increase. From this perspective, customer segmentation, which may seem like a specialty of the marketing department, also plays an important role in revenue-related decision-making at the management level. This situation will also contribute to the long-term positioning of businesses.

While customer segmentation and differentiated pricing strategies enable hotels to target varying willingness-to-pay levels, the effectiveness of these strategies also depends on how prices are communicated and distributed across sales channels. Therefore, distribution channels play a decisive role in shaping both pricing dynamics and customer perceptions within contemporary revenue management systems.

Distribution Channels and Pricing Interaction

The importance of distribution channels in hotel businesses and determining these channels, careful and meticulous market segmentation, and creating necessary strategies are essential for the continuity of the business (Çalık, 2023). Because for hotel businesses, distribution channels are important intermediaries that both make sales and determine pricing strategies for the sector. At the point technology has reached today, especially online travel agencies hold a significant share of these sales. Online travel agencies promote the hotel, sell hotel rooms through their own website, and receive commission from the hotel for the sold rooms (Ling et al., 2014). The existing literature focuses on hotels' online distribution procedures, pricing strategies for different segments, and room availability issues (Gazzoli et al., 2008).

Price is one of the most important tools that hoteliers have to adjust supply and demand in the short term. Dynamic pricing is the practice of changing the price demanded for a product over time (Fernandez et al., 2014). In the industry, pricing strategies have turned into more complex processes, and this transformation has influenced revenue management practices (Noone et al., 2011). Since profit is the main motivation factor for both hoteliers and distribution channels, most channel conflict problems arise from the misalignment of objectives surrounding pricing strategies (Tan & Dwyer, 2014).

The transparency strategy includes design choices that affect the accessibility and availability of information about businesses' products and prices. Information transparency is an external variable determined by the environment (Jiang & Wen, 2020; Xiao et al., 2025). The greatest impact of online travel agencies on the accommodation sector is that they increase price transparency beyond expectations. Therefore, from the consumer's perspective, it provides the opportunity to simultaneously compare customer reviews that determine both service quality and reputation for many different hotels on the same platform. Granados and others (2003) developed decision support models for pricing online mechanisms with different levels of transparency. In their studies, they experimentally analyzed the transparent price levels set by airlines through online travel agencies and showed that businesses could increase their profits by either increasing price differences or affecting OTA transparency differences. In reality, OTAs' transparency strategies move away from the classic pricing strategies that have been applied since the past. The increasing transparency created by online travel agencies and digital platforms has fundamentally transformed pricing competition in hospitality by enabling real-time price comparisons and increasing consumer awareness regarding pricing differences across channels (O'Connor, 2020). For businesses aiming to take the largest share of the market in a competitive market, this situation can make it difficult to implement differentiation strategies. For example, the faster comparison of many hotels in the same destination compared to the past results in a speeding up of the decision-making process. In this case, it is seen that price is not the only determinant of competition among hotels. Studies further demonstrate that consumers' hotel choices are increasingly influenced not only by room prices but also by non-price information such as online reviews, reputation signals, and digital visibility across platforms (Noone & McGuire, 2013). The price, which varies according to both the brand value of businesses and their reputation based on reviews, as well as the quality of the experiences they offer, is a multidimensional and important signal for businesses (Çetiner & Yaylı, 2020; Koçoğlu & Yurt, 2020; Orhan, 2025). Online travel agencies provide access to larger audiences and thus can contribute to an increase in demand. This is particularly important for access to markets that small and independent hotel businesses would find difficult to reach on their own. However, the commissions requested by OTAs and, to some extent, the reduction of control over pricing, also negatively affect businesses. Collaborations with OTAs require a balanced strategic decision to enable proper revenue management (Raab et al., 2018; Shah, 2025).

The transformation of consumer behavior over time has also been influenced by price transparency. Consumers process the information they have found and compare options. In online booking environments, perceived trust and value significantly influence consumers' purchase intentions and booking decisions, particularly when customers evaluate price transparency and platform reliability simultaneously (Ponte et al., 2015). They evaluate the product's price, quality, quantity, brand image, and other factors, and generally prefer the option with the best price-performance ratio (Kiani Mavi et al., 2022). According to Voss et al. (1998), when price fluctuations, which are common in many service industries applying demand-oriented pricing, combine with heterogeneity, they largely lead to varying price-performance combinations. In a service exchange, the level of price-performance consistency affects the relationship between performance expectations and subsequent performance and satisfaction judgments. In this context, tourists evaluate the price–performance balance together. Faced with these factors affecting their decisions, hotel businesses are compelled to clearly demonstrate the differentiated value they offer in a competitive market. If a business tries to outperform its competitors solely based on price reduction strategies, it will, in the long term, face the risk of both reducing its profit margin and weakening its brand value (Ivanov & Zhechev, 2012).

For effective revenue management, it is important to make contracts with distribution channels, promotion and marketing, direct sales, the effectiveness of websites, staff empowerment, customer relationship management, and dynamic pricing (Arikan & Parlakkaya, 2020). Direct sales channels, in particular, have strategic importance. User-friendly, secure, transparent, and customizable websites not only ensure that customers choose them again but also reduce dependency on OTAs by using strategies such as 'best price guarantee' to encourage bookings directly through hotels' own websites (Ibrahim et al., 2021). This way, both customer relationship management becomes easier and greater control over pricing is achieved.

However, the user experience offered by hotel businesses, the trust they provide, consumers' brand perception, as well as their digital visibility are factors that bring success in revenue management. In particular, the interaction that businesses establish with users on digital platforms (social media, websites, mobile applications, etc.) increases brand visibility. Along with user experience such as likes, comments, and shares, sales, reservations, and the value obtained per customer also tend to increase (Mishra & Vijayvargy, 2025). Additionally, customers who are loyal to the brand attribute a unique value to the brand that no other brand can match. This is due to increasing trust in the reliability of the brand or the more positive effect that occurs when they use the brand (Chaudhuri & Holbrook, 2001). Customers' trust in the brand, emotional connections, purchase loyalty, and attitudinal loyalty play an important role when making hotel reservations (Lee et al., 2022). In this respect, a hotel with a good brand image will have higher direct booking rates. This is the main reason why businesses with weak brand awareness are dependent on OTAs. Therefore, there is a strong link between distribution channels and brand strategy for hotel businesses. In this context, a successful revenue management approach requires establishing a balanced structure between OTAs and direct sales channels, integrating pricing strategies with this multi-channel structure, and considering price not only as a competitive tool but also as a strategic positioning element.

Algorithmic Pricing vs Managerial Reasoning

One of the central debates in contemporary revenue management is whether pricing decisions should be delegated primarily to algorithmic systems or strategically interpreted through managerial reasoning. While artificial intelligence and dynamic pricing systems provide unprecedented analytical capabilities, hospitality pricing decisions often involve contextual, experiential, ethical, and reputational dimensions that cannot be fully captured through data alone. In recent years, the field that has experienced the greatest transformation is technology. Today, the areas of application of algorithms, which play an important role especially in decision-making processes, are spreading to many significant societal areas such as health, banking, security, e-commerce, and access to information, and are increasing gradually (Ünal & Sezgin, 2021). It is known that companies use artificial intelligence technologies in different dimensions such as customer experience, operational efficiency, financial analysis, image processing, and human resources (Sarnıç, 2025). One of the profound changes that digital transformation has created in the field of management is understanding the language of big data analytics. The big data analyses included in business decision-making mechanisms enable companies to take precautions in advance by predicting potential risks. Data analytics plays a very important role in modern business decision-making processes by enabling organizations to transform raw data into valuable insights (Tiwari, 2024). This situation has also been benchmarked by hotel businesses, making managers' work somewhat easier, especially in pricing decisions. This change, which is an important step in terms of sectoral development, has taken the traditional statistical methods used from past to present one step further. Although it provides meaningful results with small and medium-sized data, it has become a mechanism that can offer stronger predictions against traditional methods that struggle with big data analytics (Sheng et al., 2021). However, in such situations, there must be step-by-step instructions to follow in order to solve a problem (Tonidandel et al., 2018). For these processes to work effectively, algorithms need to be based on certain rules and data structures.

Optimizing hotel revenue management through dynamic pricing algorithms and data analysis models enables the analysis of factors for dynamically adjusting room rates and allows revenue optimization according to demand and market conditions (Gao, 2025). Algorithmic pricing is the process of determining optimal prices by using the power of machine learning and artificial intelligence, programmed to maximize revenue (Aydan & Atılgan, 2023). The main feature of a pricing algorithm is to monitor the market and then reprice products (Kloostra, 2022). In this sense, it has greatly strengthened the analytical dimension of revenue management through dynamic pricing and personalized pricing methods. In particular, with the use of AI-supported systems, it has made it possible to maximize revenue by dynamically adjusting room prices according to real-time demand, market trends, and competitor actions (Gao, 2025).

However, leaving the decision entirely to algorithmic systems when pricing also poses a risk for businesses. Recent studies emphasize that AI-supported pricing systems may create challenges related to transparency, customer trust, and ethical accountability, particularly when algorithmic decision-making processes are not sufficiently explainable to consumers (Huang & Rust, 2021). Because issues such as ethical oversight, which used to be less important, have become more significant. Therefore, the removal of human supervision from this process will disrupt strategic decisions made in management. In particular, the fundamental requirement underlying the establishment of a proper system is that the datasets at the disposal of businesses are sufficiently accurate. Today, by analyzing large-volume datasets through big data analysis, sectoral trends can be detected early, helping to make accurate decisions (Chatterjee et al., 2023; Islam et al., 2024). Businesses that benefit from big data gain an advantage over others both in terms of time and economically (Uladi & Arı, 2023). However, it may be limited in situations such as sudden demand changes, unexpected crises, or market disruptions, and especially in environments of uncertainty (Ivanov & Zhechev, 2012).

Algorithms can be used in pricing systems that show continuous variation depending on different variables. However, one of the important limitations to consider is that algorithms cannot sufficiently account for intuition-based knowledge. For example, the impact of a major event occurring at a destination on demand, social media trends, or competitors not yet disclosed strategic moves may not be fully reflected in the data sets (Song et al., 2008). In such cases, managers' market knowledge, experience, and intuitive assessments play a critical role (Kahneman & Klein, 2009). While analytical scenarios serve as a guide, their effectiveness in assessing potential outcomes based on current information and expectations remains limited unless supported by managerial judgment. This underscores the need to establish a complementary relationship between "human intelligence" and "artificial intelligence" in revenue management. Özdemir and Hekim (2018) define Industry 5.0 as a meaning-creating partnership between human intelligence and artificial intelligence. A growing concern in artificial intelligence-supported revenue management system applications is algorithmic bias (Kafetzi, 2025). Since these systems are based on historical data and predictive analytics, they can unintentionally reproduce existing inequalities. An effective revenue management system should be built on a hybrid structure that combines the analytical power provided by algorithms with the strategic vision of managers. Considering ethical and perceptual aspects as well, it is especially necessary to correctly interpret its value from the consumer's perspective. Therefore, the approach to algorithmic systems is an important issue that should be evaluated for its long-term contribution to businesses.

Recent empirical studies have increasingly demonstrated that consumers are highly sensitive to issues of pricing transparency and perceived fairness in AI-supported dynamic pricing systems. Research indicates that opaque algorithmic pricing practices may negatively affect customer trust, satisfaction, and repurchase intention, particularly when consumers perceive price discrimination as unfair or manipulative (Xiang et al., 2021; Huang & Rust, 2021). Similarly, studies on AI ethics emphasize that algorithmic systems lacking transparency and explainability can create reputational risks for hospitality businesses and weaken long-term customer relationships (Buhalis et al., 2019). Therefore, discussions regarding ethical responsibility, transparency, and consumer trust have become central issues in the strategic implementation of AI-driven revenue management systems.

Issues, Controversies, Problems

Revenue management and the associated pricing processes in hotel businesses are carried out with rational and data-driven decisions. However, even though this is the case in theory, different dynamics emerge in practice. Because even in routine operations, conflicts may occasionally arise. Especially when discussed with one of today's topics, the ethical dimensions, various problems emerge. The logic that has been applied in revenue management from past to present is that this is a price optimization process. However, this thought has nowadays turned into a tool that needs to be considered strategically. Faced with this tension, traditional methods create an argument for increasing both occupancy rates and short-term revenue in the pricing process. Modern approaches, on the other hand, progress more with a focus on brand value and competitive advantage. This second approach, which is considered strategically (Nagle & Müller, 2018), becomes more important and prominent especially in destinations where competition is intense. The stance of traditionalists is to offer discounted prices during periods of low demand to achieve occupancy targets. While being a rational approach, in the long run it can harm the strategic position of the business. Therefore, the first criticism is that the pricing logic in revenue management should have a long-term rather than short-term perspective.

Although it is an important performance indicator in the industry, focusing excessively on RevPAR is also problematic. Price discounts made to increase the current revenue per room may seem to increase occupancy in the short term. However, as the process extends, it can negatively affect the price perception because it will actually lower the average daily rate (Ivanov & Zhechev, 2012). The problem here is the mismatch between measurement results and decision-making processes. Hotel businesses explain operational performance through key indicators such as RevPAR. However, it is not known what kind of strategy is followed in the decision-making results based on the measurements. Therefore, for managers who do not seek short-term solutions, a value-focused perspective can be considered a more appropriate approach. It can be said that, in this sense, managers should make pricing decisions from the perspective of brand value and customer perception rather than traditional performance indicators.

With the conveniences provided in daily life thanks to artificial intelligence, significant transformations are also occurring in industrial sectors (İmamoğlu et al., 2023). AI-supported algorithms provide managers with predictive capabilities to understand consumer behavior. With the aim of creating the optimal price to attract the customer and with the support of big data analytics, real-time access to customer data is achieved, and this data is processed into personalized dynamic pricing decisions (Karaman, 2021). However, with the reflection of artificial intelligence in business processes, discussions on ethics and trust have also arisen. Although revenue management provides a profit margin to businesses by offering the service to different customers, at different times, and at different prices, this situation can be interpreted by some customers as the unfairness of the system. With the frequent change of prices in hotels being inevitable, this situation also reflects on purchasing behaviors. It is important that the prices customers will pay for the services they purchase create trust. For consumers who cannot understand the rationale behind paying different prices for the same product, doubts may arise towards the pricing system. Although it is possible to increase turnover in the short term, as the process progresses, it may lead to a deterioration of the sense of loyalty. Additionally, transparency is an important indicator of the reliability of technological systems established in businesses. If the opposite occurs, decisions taken in businesses will not be sufficiently understood by customers, and discussions regarding ethical issues will deepen. From this perspective, it can be stated that hotel businesses should consider revenue management together with concepts such as fairness, transparency, and trust, beyond economic efficiency. Recent hospitality research also highlights that ethical concerns surrounding artificial intelligence-supported decision systems increasingly influence customer perceptions, digital trust, and the long-term reputational sustainability of hospitality businesses (Buhalis et al., 2019).

Travel agencies are the most commonly used marketing tools in the tourism industry, and with the development of the internet, the importance of online travel agencies is increasing. This rise brings both opportunities and risks for hotel businesses (Sönmez Karapınar, 2024). Their biggest advantage is their dominance over the overall market and their ability to create demand. However, over time, hotels have become overly dependent on these online platforms (Noone et al., 2011). This dependency is a factor that limits hotel businesses in controlling their own prices. Rate agreements among online platforms are a handicap for hotels that want to apply different prices. Moreover, when it comes to OTAs, high commission costs and decreasing direct bookings occur (Yadav, 2025). Therefore, pricing decisions are indirectly shaped by platform dynamics. However, as mentioned at the beginning, revenue management is a topic that should be approached strategically. Yet, the aforementioned challenges make its implementation difficult. One of the encountered challenges is that the distribution method is multi-channel and causes conflicts. Although hotel businesses expand their portfolios through OTAs, on the other hand, they want to strengthen their direct booking channels. However, this situation poses a problem not only for customers who encounter different prices from each channel but also for stakeholders. Customers frequently highlighted in platform ads may also experience distrust when they see the possibility of getting the same service cheaper from a different channel after making a direct booking. All these opportunities and threats show why hotel businesses have to proceed in alignment with channels when implementing revenue management and why they need to manage customers' perceptions carefully.

One of the biggest limitations in hospitality is the attempt to achieve performance in the short term. This limitation also guides pricing processes in revenue management. Managers, feeling obliged to increase occupancy rates, tend to make price reductions. Reducing room rates can alleviate the cumulative occupancy loss it causes. However, this discount can delay the recovery periods of both occupancy and RevPAR (Kim et al., 2019). The erosion occurring in ADR over time can also damage brand value. For a hotel that constantly lowers its prices, a weakening of its reputation may occur. That is, the profile of customers willing to pay, an important segment, may be lost (Nagle & Müller, 2018). Therefore, it is necessary to see the price as an element that forms the brand identity.

All these discussions show that revenue management is a complex decision area that, beyond being a technical and analytical process, also has ethical, strategic, and managerial dimensions. Balancing pricing decisions between short-term performance goals and long-term value creation, using algorithmic systems within ethical boundaries, and strategically managing distribution channels are among the most critical issues in this field. Therefore, revenue management should be approached from a multi-dimensional perspective, and not only how much revenue is generated, but also how and with what strategic logic this revenue is obtained should be questioned.

Taken together, these discussions demonstrate that the challenges associated with revenue management in hospitality are not limited to operational inefficiencies or technical forecasting problems alone. Rather, they emerge from the increasingly complex interaction between pricing strategies, customer perception, ethical concerns, technological transformation, distribution channel dynamics, and long-term brand positioning. Consequently, addressing these multidimensional challenges requires moving beyond traditional revenue optimization logic toward more integrated, flexible, and strategically oriented management approaches. In this respect, the following section presents a set of strategic solutions and recommendations aimed at enhancing the sustainability, effectiveness, and ethical grounding of revenue management practices in hospitality businesses.

SOLUTIONS AND RECOMMENDATIONS

Given the multidimensional and strategic nature of the challenges discussed above, revenue management solutions in hospitality should not be limited to technical improvements alone. However, solutions to any kind of problems, whether structural or strategic, as well as issues arising from an ethical standpoint, lie in focusing on topics such as brand value and customer perception during pricing processes. When approached with a strategic perspective beyond analytical thinking, revenue management can be given a more strategic structure. Accordingly, in this section, a set of recommendations is also offered to both academia and industry managers.

Hotel businesses need to focus not only on segmentation but also on customer-based value estimation analyses. In the literature, it is emphasized that pricing strategies that consider the long-term value of the customer provide more sustainable profitability compared to short-term revenue maximization (Kumar & Reinartz, 2016). In this context, developing different pricing and privilege strategies especially for loyal customers strengthens the value-based approach. Moreover, the strong relationship between online reviews and rating systems and price is also an important indicator of value-based pricing. Research shows that highly rated hotels can demand higher prices compared to low-rated hotels with similar characteristics (Anderson, 2012).

This situation indicates that the customer's perceived value can directly translate into pricing power. Therefore, hotels need to focus not only on price competition but also on creating a price premium by enhancing the quality of the experience. In addition, the effectiveness of value-based pricing can be further increased with real-time data analytics and dynamic pricing systems. Hotels that utilize big data analytics can analyze customer behaviors, booking patterns, and demand fluctuations to determine different 'willingness-to-pay' levels for different segments (Phillips, 2021). This allows the same product to be offered to different customers at different values, contributing to revenue optimization. In terms of the sustainability of value-based pricing, hotels need to focus not only on economic but also on experiential and emotional value creation. Especially in the tourism sector, customers pay for the experience they have rather than the tangible service. Therefore, storytelling, original experience design, and personalized services increase the perceived value of the customer, reduce price elasticity, and provide a competitive advantage to the business (Pine & Gilmore, 1999).

In order to ensure the sustainability of revenue management, hotel operations need to focus not only on short-term performance indicators but also on multidimensional performance metrics. It is known that RevPAR alone is not sufficient; instead, TRevPAR (Total Revenue), GOPPAR (Gross Operating Profit Per Available Room), and customer-based value measurements should be evaluated together (Ivanov & Zhechev, 2012). This finding indicates that revenue management should focus not only on room revenue but also on the overall experience and profitability structure. Furthermore, the effectiveness of AI-supported systems is directly related to data quality and organizational learning capacity. Data-driven decision systems provide sustainable competitive advantage only when supported by a learning culture and knowledge sharing within the organization (Mariani et al., 2023). Therefore, it is not sufficient for hotels to invest only in technology. At the same time, they need to invest in human resources capable of interpreting these systems and in corporate learning mechanisms. Additionally, during periods of uncertainty (pandemics, crises, geopolitical risks, etc.), it is observed that forecast models based solely on historical data are limited, and therefore scenario-based revenue management approaches gain importance. In this context, it becomes a critical factor in risk management for managers to develop flexible pricing and capacity strategies based on different demand scenarios (Talluri & Van Ryzin, 2004). This approach makes the integration of AI system predictions and managerial intuition even more meaningful.

Effective management of distribution channels is not limited to channel selection alone, but also requires systematic analysis of channel profitability. Despite the visibility advantage provided by OTAs, it is stated that high commission rates (between 15%–30%) put serious pressure on hotel profitability (Garrigos-Simon et al., 2017). Therefore, it is recommended that hotels adopt a channel-based revenue optimization approach by analyzing the net income obtained from each channel. Moreover, one of the most effective tools in increasing direct bookings is loyalty programs and personalized offers. Customers who are members of loyalty programs are more likely to make direct bookings. Therefore, it can be said that their price sensitivity is lower (Noone et al., 2011). Current studies show that customers use multiple channels during the booking process (for example, researching on OTA and booking directly on the website) (Verhoef et al., 2015). Therefore, channel management should prioritize inter-channel integration and holistic management of the customer journey rather than competition between channels. To increase the success of direct channels, not only technical infrastructure but also trust and brand reputation play a critical role. It has been shown that when online trust and brand perception are high, customers are more inclined to make direct bookings (Bilgihan et al., 2016). In this context, user experience, data security, and transparent pricing policies should be considered as the fundamental building blocks of direct sales strategies.

The effectiveness of hybrid revenue management models depends not only on the use of technology but also on the proper design of human–machine interaction. Due to the "black box" nature of algorithmic decision systems, it is emphasized that it is risky for managers to implement them without scrutiny at all times, and therefore human oversight (human-in-the-loop) is a critical element (Shrestha et al., 2019). This approach reveals that systems where artificial intelligence provides recommendations but the final decision is made by humans produce more reliable and sustainable results. Moreover, the success of AI-supported pricing systems depends not only on algorithmic accuracy but also on data diversity and contextual data integration. When external data such as weather, event schedules, flight data, and social media trends are integrated into the model, it significantly increases the accuracy of demand forecasts (Ivanov & Webster, 2017). This situation reveals that artificial intelligence systems should be operated not in isolation but within a broad data ecosystem. In addition, another advantage of hybrid models is the management of ethical and brand reputation risks. Fully algorithmic pricing systems can create perceptions of 'opportunism' during excessive price fluctuations or crisis periods. Therefore, managerial intervention ensures that pricing decisions consider not only profitability but also fairness, transparency, and customer perception dimensions (Xiang et al., 2021). In terms of the sustainability of hybrid revenue management systems, hotels need not only to invest in technology but also to train managers with high analytical literacy and data interpretation skills. Such human resources can create strategic advantages by critically evaluating the suggestions from artificial intelligence rather than implementing them without critical assessment. This situation ensures that revenue management transforms from being a technical function into an organizational capability.

Pricing decisions should be considered not only as a tool for revenue maximization but also as a mechanism for market positioning and signaling quality. Within the framework of signaling theory, it is particularly noted in the service sector that price is perceived as an important indicator of quality, and low-price strategies can weaken perceived quality (Rao & Monroe, 1989). This situation necessitates that hotel businesses operating in the luxury segment act more cautiously regarding pricing. However, the literature frequently emphasizes that although aggressive discount strategies may increase demand in the short term, they cause erosion of brand value and increased price sensitivity in the long term (Kotler & Keller, 2016). In businesses that continually offer discounts, customers' perception of reference prices decreases, and this situation makes it difficult for the business to return to its normal price level. Therefore, pricing decisions should be made not only based on immediate occupancy targets but also taking long-term brand positioning into account. Additionally, in luxury hotel operations, value enhancement and packaging strategies are recommended instead of direct discounts in order to maintain the price level. In this approach, while the room price is kept constant, the perceived value for the customer is increased by expanding the scope of services offered (Nagle & Müller, 2018). In this way, both the positive effect of the price level on brand prestige is preserved, and customer satisfaction and experience quality are enhanced. To manage the relationship between pricing and brand perception, hotels need to invest in online reputation management and customer experience design. Research shows that hotels with high online ratings can charge higher prices, and this directly reflects on revenue performance (Anderson, 2012). For this reason, pricing strategies should be considered not only with cost and demand factors, but also integrated with perceived value and digital reputation.

FUTURE RESEARCH DIRECTIONS

Revenue management has entered a process of paradigm shift. In this context, future research must focus not only on the question "How can we generate more revenue?" but also on the questions "Under what conditions, within what boundaries, and for which stakeholders is value created?" AI-powered pricing systems provide significant accuracy and speed advantages in demand forecasting and price optimization processes, while also bringing important ethical discussions such as algorithmic discrimination, price fairness, and transparency. Dynamic pricing applications make it possible to offer the same service at different prices to different consumers, which directly affects the perceived price fairness by consumers. Research shows that price differentiation is perceived as fair by consumers only under certain conditions (for example, when it is based on time or demand intensity) (Bolton et al., 2003). Therefore, it is important that future studies focus on questions such as in which contexts algorithmic pricing is acceptable, how the level of transparency affects trust, and how regulatory frameworks should be established. In this respect, it is expected that the revenue management literature will systematically incorporate the dimension of ethical sustainability, going beyond economic efficiency.

Sustainability is becoming increasingly decisive in the tourism sector, and this situation is directly reflected in pricing strategies. In particular, green pricing approaches are redefining the relationship between environmental value and economic value. Empirical studies show that eco-friendly practices can increase consumers' willingness to pay, but this effect is directly related to reliability and transparency (Han et al., 2019). In this context, future research should focus on the pricing of carbon-neutral services, the mechanisms by which sustainability investments translate into price premiums, and the effects of these strategies on brand value. In this way, pricing can be repositioned not only as an economic tool but also as a means of generating environmental and social value.

Digitalization and big data analytics are transforming revenue management from static and historical models into real-time and predictive adaptive systems. Recent research shows that dynamic pricing systems using real-time data significantly improve revenue performance (Phillips, 2021). However, an increase in data flow speed does not automatically enhance decision quality; on the contrary, it also brings risks of information overload and misinterpretation. Therefore, future studies need to examine the limits of data speed on decision quality, the optimal balance of human–machine interaction, and the organizational integration of adaptive systems.

Another critical expansion area of the revenue management literature is the behavioral dimension. While traditional models are based on the assumption of rational decision-makers, recent studies show that managers make decisions under cognitive biases, risk perception, and performance pressures. It is particularly known that short-term RevPAR pressure can trigger pricing decisions that may harm long-term brand value. In this context, the behavioral revenue management approach should analyze the interaction of intuitive and analytical decision-making processes, the impact of managerial biases on pricing, and consumers' psychological responses to dynamic pricing. This approach transforms revenue management from a technical tool into a human-centered strategic management field.

One of the main limitations of the existing literature is that revenue management is largely addressed at the firm level. However, the tourism sector inherently exhibits a multi-stakeholder structure, and pricing decisions create significant externalities at the destination level. Therefore, a destination-level revenue management approach is one of the critical research areas expected to emerge in the future. In this context, inter-firm price coordination, the impact of price competition on destination image, and public–private partnership models should be examined. Especially in destinations experiencing overtourism, the role of pricing strategies on demand management and sustainability becomes even more critical.

CONCLUSION

Theoretical Contributions

This chapter contributes to the revenue management literature by extending the dominant technical and optimization-oriented perspective toward a more strategic, behavioral, and value-centered framework. Unlike traditional approaches that predominantly focus on demand forecasting, pricing algorithms, and capacity optimization, this study conceptualizes revenue management as a multidimensional managerial capability shaped by customer perception, brand positioning, experiential value creation, and contextual managerial reasoning. In this respect, the chapter contributes to the literature by proposing a hybrid revenue management paradigm in which artificial intelligence-supported analytical systems and human managerial judgment operate in an integrated and complementary manner. Furthermore, the study expands the conceptual boundaries of revenue management by linking pricing logic with long-term brand value, customer trust, ethical sensitivity, and destination competitiveness.

Managerial Implications

From a managerial perspective, the chapter highlights that pricing decisions in hospitality businesses should not be evaluated solely through short-term financial performance indicators such as ADR, RevPAR, or occupancy rates. Instead, managers should approach pricing as a strategic positioning mechanism directly associated with customer perception, brand reputation, and long-term competitive advantage. The study also emphasizes that while AI-supported systems provide significant analytical advantages in demand forecasting and dynamic pricing, managerial intuition and contextual interpretation remain indispensable, particularly under conditions of uncertainty and crisis. Therefore, hotel businesses are encouraged to adopt hybrid revenue management systems that combine analytical intelligence with human judgment. In addition, the chapter underlines the strategic importance of balancing OTA dependency with direct booking strategies, strengthening value-based pricing approaches, and integrating customer experience into revenue management decisions.

This section challenges the prevailing technical and algorithmic perspective on revenue management and pricing, demonstrating that the subject must be addressed within a much broader and multidimensional framework. In particular, the unique structural characteristics of the hospitality industry limit attempts to explain revenue management solely through numerical optimization models. In this context, the study argues that revenue management should be repositioned not as a technical tool, but as a strategic way of thinking. Pricing decisions are shaped by the interaction of numerous factors—such as perceived value, customer experience, brand positioning, and distribution channels—that go beyond mere cost and demand variables. This situation reveals that traditional performance indicators like RevPAR, ADR, and occupancy rate are limited in explaining the actual performance of businesses and their long-term competitive strength. Therefore, revenue management practices are expected to answer not only the question of 'how much revenue was generated' but also 'through which value proposition and strategic positioning this revenue was produced.'

This study also shows that while it is acknowledged that revenue management has become more data-driven with digitalization and artificial intelligence, this transformation has not fully evolved into an automation process and still requires significant human intervention. On the contrary, especially during periods of crisis, uncertainty, and sudden changes in demand, managerial intuition, experience, and contextual assessment play a critical role. In this context, it is argued that one of the most effective approaches is a hybrid revenue management model where artificial intelligence-supported systems and human intelligence are used together. This model allows for more balanced and sustainable decisions by complementing the speed and accuracy advantages of algorithms with the strategic foresight and contextual interpretation ability of managers.

On the other hand, the value-based pricing approach emphasized in the chapter indicates a critical paradigmatic shift for the future of revenue management. The fact that price is not only an economic variable but also a tool for perception, positioning, and value creation becomes even more evident, particularly in the tourism sector, where the experience economy stands out. In this context, structuring hotel pricing strategies based on the value customers are willing to pay, rather than cost- or competition-based approaches, can provide a sustainable advantage in terms of both profitability and brand loyalty.

This section contributes to redefining the boundaries of revenue management and treats it not merely as a technical optimization problem but as a strategic, behavioral, and value-oriented management paradigm. This approach aims not only to enhance business performance but also to strengthen long-term brand value, customer relationships, and destination competitiveness. In this aspect, the study provides a conceptual expansion to the revenue management literature while also presenting a more holistic and sustainable strategic framework for industry practitioners.

Ultimately, the future of revenue management in hospitality does not lie in choosing between artificial intelligence and managerial judgment, but in establishing a strategic hybrid structure where analytical intelligence and human reasoning complement one another. Therefore, revenue management should evolve from being a technical pricing function into a multidimensional strategic capability centered on value creation, customer perception, ethical sensitivity, and long-term competitive positioning.

DISCLOSURE OF DELEGATION TO GENERATIVE AI

The authors declare the use of generative AI in the research and writing process. According to the GAIDeT taxonomy (2025), the following tasks were delegated to GAI tools under full human supervision:

- Evaluation of the novelty of the research and identification of gaps
- Proofreading and editing
- Summarizing text
- Adapting and adjusting emotional tone
- Translation
- Reformatting

The GAI tool used was: ChatGPT Plus.

Responsibility for the final manuscript lies entirely with the authors.

GAI tools are not listed as authors and do not bear responsibility for the final outcomes.

REFERENCES

Aaker, D. A. (1996). *Building strong brands.* Free Press.

Akmeşe, H., & Güderoğlu, M. (2017). Konaklama İşletmelerinde Bir Yönetim Muhasebesi Uygulamasi Olarak Gelir Yönetiminin Müşteri Algisi. [JSHSR]. *International Journal of Social and Humanities Sciences Research, 4*(15), 1896–1909.

Aktepe, H. S., & Candemir, Z. (2024). Algılanan Değer Modeli (Perceived Value Model). *Tüketici Davranışlarında Kullanılan Modeller: Geçmişten Günümüze Tüketici Davranışlarını Belirlemede Kullanılan Modeller*, 137.

Ampountolas, A., Shaw, G., & James, S. (2021). Examining the relationships between market indicators and hotel pricing approaches. *Tourism Economics, 27*(8), 1591–1614. DOI: 10.1177/1354816620925225

Anderson, C. K. (2012). The impact of social media on lodging performance. *Cornell Hospitality Report, 12*(15), 6–11.

Arıkan, E., & Parlakkaya, R. (2020). Beş Yıldızlı Otel İşletmelerinde Gelir Yönetimi Uygulamalarina İlişkin Nitel Bir Araştirma. *Elektronik Sosyal Bilimler Dergisi, 19*(75), 1255–1274. DOI: 10.17755/esosder.552750

Aydan, G., & Atılgan, K. Ö. (2023). Tüketicilerin kişiselleştirilmiş fiyatlandırma ile dinamik fiyatlandırma uygulamalarına yönelik tutumlarının incelenmesi. *Pamukkale Üniversitesi İşletme Araştırmaları Dergisi, 10*(1-Prof. Dr. Feyzullah EROĞLU Armağan Sayısı), 243-256.

Aydın, B., & Akyol, Ş. (2013). Otel işletmelerinin kriz dönemlerinde uyguladıkları pazarlama stratejileri: İstanbul'da faaliyet gösteren beş yıldızlı otel işletmelerinde nitel bir araştırma. *Seyahat ve Otel İşletmeciliği Dergisi, 10*(1), 23–35.

Aziz, H. A., El Gayar, N., Saleh, M., & El Shishiny, H. (2008). A randomized model for group reservations in a hotel's revenue management system. *Proceedings of the 6th International Conference on Informatics and Systems (INFOS 2008)*, Cairo, Egypt.

Balińska, A., & Olejniczak, W. (2022). Aplikacje turystyczne w ocenie użytkowników. *Studia Periegetica, 39*(3), 23–38. DOI: 10.5604/01.3001.0016.0762

Balli, F., Uddin, G. S., & Shahzad, S. J. H. (2019). Geopolitical risk and tourism demand in emerging economies. *Tourism Economics, 25*(6), 997–1005. DOI: 10.1177/1354816619831824

Baltazar, M. B. (2008). Revenue marketing and its application within the hospitality industry: History and future development. In *Pricing Perspectives: Marketing and Management Implications of New Theories and Applications* (pp. 175–205). Palgrave Macmillan UK. DOI: 10.1057/9780230594890_8

Barreda, A. (2017). Financial marketing decisions in the hospitality industry. In *Routledge Handbook of Hospitality Marketing* (pp. 132–147). Routledge. DOI: 10.4324/9781315445526-11

Belobaba, P. P. (1987). Air travel demand and airline seat inventory management. *PhD Dissertation*, Massachusetts Institute of Technology.

Bilgihan, A., Okumus, F., Nusair, K., & Kwun, D. J. (2016). Information technology applications and competitive advantage in hotel companies. *Journal of Hospitality and Tourism Technology*, *7*(1), 102–118.

Bodea, T., & Ferguson, M. (2014). *Segmentation, revenue management and pricing analytics*. Routledge. DOI: 10.4324/9780203802151

Bolton, L. E., Warlop, L., & Alba, J. W. (2003). Consumer perceptions of price fairness. *The Journal of Consumer Research*, *29*(4), 474–491. DOI: 10.1086/346244

Boyd, A. E. (2007). The future of pricing: How airline ticket pricing has inspired a revolution. In Yeoman, I., & McMahon-Beattie, U. (Eds.), *Revenue management and pricing: Case studies and applications* (pp. xx–xx). Thomson Learning.

Bozkurt, Ö., & Göral, M. (2013). Otel işletmelerinde yenilik stratejileri. İçinde M. Mesci & Ö. Bozkurt (Ed.), *Otel işletmelerinde yenilik yönetimi* (ss. 91–108). Sidas.

Brotherton, B., & Mooney, S. (1992). Yield management—Progress and prospects. *International Journal of Hospitality Management*, *11*(1), 23–32. DOI: 10.1016/0278-4319(92)90033-R

Buhalis, D., Harwood, T., Bogicevic, V., Viglia, G., Beldona, S., & Hofacker, C. (2019). Technological disruptions in services: Lessons from tourism and hospitality. *Journal of Service Management*, *30*(4), 484–506. DOI: 10.1108/JOSM-12-2018-0398

Bulgan, G., & Soybali, H. H. (2011). Antalya Belek Bölgesindeki Beş Yıldızlı Otel Işletmelerinde Düşük Sezonda Konaklayan Alman Müşterilerin Hizmet Beklentilerinin Ve Memnuniyet Düzeylerinin Değerlendirilmesi. *Journal of Yasar University*, *21*(6), 3572–3597.

Bull, A. O. (2006). Industrial economics and pricing issues within tourism enterprises and markets. *International handbook on the economics of tourism*, 138.

Buzacott, J. A. (2000). Service system structure. *International Journal of Production Economics, 68*(1), 15–27. DOI: 10.1016/S0925-5273(99)00133-4

Caldentey, R. A., & Wein, L. M. (2002). Revenue management of a make-to-stock queue. *Manufacturing & Service Operations Management, 4*(1), 4–6. DOI: 10.1287/msom.4.1.4.288

Çalık, Ü. (2023). Otel İşletmelerinde Pazarlama Stratejileri Üzerine Bir Değerlendirme. *Selçuk Üniversitesi Akşehir Meslek Yüksekokulu Sosyal Bilimler Dergisi,* (16), 57–77.

Canöz, F. (2022). *Üst düzey otel yöneticilerinin dönemsel krizleri değerlendirmesi...* (Doktora tezi). Necmettin Erbakan Üniversitesi.

Cesaret, B., & Katok, E. (2025). A behavioral study of capacity allocation in revenue management. *The Journal of the Operational Research Society, 76*(3), 514–527. DOI: 10.1080/01605682.2024.2370872

Çetiner, H., & Yaylı, A. (2020). Animasyon aktivitelerinde deneyim kalitesinin otel işletmelerinin imajı, konukların değer algısı ve tekrar satın alma niyetine etkisi. *İşletme Araştırmaları Dergisi, 12*(1), 749-768.

Chatterjee, S., Chaudhuri, R., Gupta, S., Sivarajah, U., & Bag, S. (2023). Assessing the impact of big data analytics on decision-making processes, forecasting, and performance of a firm. *Technological Forecasting and Social Change, 196*, 122824. DOI: 10.1016/j.techfore.2023.122824

Chaudhuri, A., & Holbrook, M. B. (2001). The chain of effects from brand trust and brand affect to brand performance: The role of brand loyalty. *Journal of Marketing, 65*(2), 81–93. DOI: 10.1509/jmkg.65.2.81.18255

Chen, N., & Hu, M. (2023). Frontiers in service science: Data-driven revenue management: The interplay of data, model, and decisions. *Service Science, 15*(2), 79–91. DOI: 10.1287/serv.2023.0322

Choi, S., & Mattila, A. S. (2004). Hotel revenue management and its impact on customers' perceptions of fairness. *Journal of Revenue and Pricing Management, 2*(4), 303–314. DOI: 10.1057/palgrave.rpm.5170079

Çifçi, H., & Kızılırmak, İ. (2025). Vegan Restoranlarda Müşteri Deneyimi Bileşenlerinin Netnografi Analiziyle İncelenmesi: Tripadvisor Örneği. *Aydın Gastronomy, 9*(2), 353–373. DOI: 10.17932/IAU.GASTRONOMY.2017.016/gastronomy_v09i2007

Çilkara, S. U. (2024). *Müşteri segmentasyonu ve fiyatlandırma stratejileri. Tüketici davranışlarında kullanılan teoriler: Geçmişten günümüze tüketici davranışlarını belirlemede kullanılan teoriler içinde (ss.* Eğitim Yayınevi.

Çolak, O., & Koşan, L. (2018). Fiyat Farklilaştirma Araci Olarak Fiyat Duyarlilik Ölçümü: Bir Otel İşletmesinde Uygulama. *Çukurova Üniversitesi Sosyal Bilimler Enstitüsü Dergisi, 27*(2), 137-153.

Coulter, K. S. (2001). Decreasing price sensitivity involving physical product inventory: A yield management application. *Journal of Product and Brand Management, 10*(5), 301–317. DOI: 10.1108/EUM0000000005846

Cravens, D. W., Piercy, N. F., & Baldauf, A. (2009). Management framework guiding strategic thinking in rapidly changing markets. *Journal of Marketing Management, 25*(1-2), 31–49. DOI: 10.1362/026725709X410025

Crawford-Welch, S. (1990). Market segmentation in the hospitality industry. *Hospitality Research Journal, 14*(2), 295–308. DOI: 10.1177/109634809001400232

Cross, R. G., Higbie, J. A., & Cross, D. Q. (2009). Revenue management's renaissance: A rebirth of the art and science of profitable revenue generation. *Cornell Hospitality Quarterly, 50*(1), 56–81. DOI: 10.1177/1938965508328716

De Larrea, G. L., & Gregory, A. M. (2020). Informing timeshare exchange services on the drivers of customer-driven co-production. *International Journal of Hospitality Management, 91*, 102645. DOI: 10.1016/j.ijhm.2020.102645

Demirtaş, N. (2010). *Otel işletmeciliği.* Ankara Üniversitesi Uzaktan Eğitim Merkezi.

Denizci Guillet, B. (2020). An evolutionary analysis of revenue management research in hospitality and tourism: Is there a paradigm shift? *International Journal of Contemporary Hospitality Management, 32*(2), 560–587. DOI: 10.1108/IJCHM-06-2019-0515

Denizci Guillet, B., & Chu, A. M. C. (2021). Managing hotel revenue amid the COVID-19 crisis. *International Journal of Contemporary Hospitality Management, 33*(2), 604–627. DOI: 10.1108/IJCHM-06-2020-0623

Denizer, D. (1991). Konaklama işletmelerinde fiyatın önemi ve fiyat farklılaştırması. *Anatolia: Turizm Araştırmaları Dergisi, 2*(5), 23–25.

Depken, C. A.II, & Stephenson, E. F. (2018). Hotel demand before, during, and after sports events: Evidence from Charlotte, North Carolina. *Economic Inquiry, 56*(3), 1764–1776. DOI: 10.1111/ecin.12572

Didin, S., & Köroğlu, Ç. (2008). Konaklama işletmelerinin satışlar-maliyetler bakımından rekabet edebilme durumu ve gelecekten beklentileri. *Uluslararası Yönetim İktisat ve İşletme Dergisi, 4*(7), 109–118.

Ding, Z. (2025). The Correlation between Data-driven Dynamic Pricing Strategies and Revenue Optimization for Technology Enterprises. *American Journal Of Big Data, 6*(05), 37–44. DOI: 10.71465/ajbd3430

Doğan, S., & Eker, Ş. (2022). Geleneksel seyahat acentelerinin çevrim içi seyahat acentelerini tercihi üzerine bir araştırma. *Journal of Recreation and Tourism Research, 9*(1), 16–32.

Doğanlı, B. (2025). Dijital pazarlama kampanyalarında müşteri davranışlarının dönüşüm oranları üzerindeki etkisi: Veri analitiği ve random forest modeli yaklaşımı. *Politik Ekonomik Kuram, 9*(2), 596–610. DOI: 10.30586/pek.1605496

Emeksiz, M. (2001). *Beş yıldızlı otel işletmeleri için getiri yönetimi uygulama modeli* (Yayımlanmamış doktora tezi). Anadolu Üniversitesi.

Erdem, B. (2010). Otel endüstrisinde yeni bir trend: Dizayn oteller. *Gazi Üniversitesi Ticaret ve Turizm Eğitim Fakültesi Dergisi*, (1), 115–132.

Eren, E. C., Zhang, Z., Rauch, J., Kumar, R., & Kallesen, R. (2024). Revenue management without demand forecasting: A data-driven approach for bid price generation. *Journal of Revenue and Pricing Management, 23*(6), 499–516. DOI: 10.1057/s41272-023-00465-3

Ergün, S., & Şahin, S. (2017). İşletme talep tahmini üzerine literatür araştırması. *Ulakbilge, 5*(10), 469–487. DOI: 10.7816/ulakbilge-05-10-11

Falk, M. T., & Vieru, M. (2021). Short-term hotel room price effects of sporting events. *Tourism Economics, 27*(3), 569–588. DOI: 10.1177/1354816620901953

Farouk El Gayar, N., Saleh, M., Atiya, A., El-Shishiny, H., Alkes Youhanna Fayez Zakhary, A., & Abdel Aziz Mohammed Habib, H. (2011). An integrated framework for advanced hotel revenue management. *International Journal of Contemporary Hospitality Management, 23*(1), 84–98. DOI: 10.1108/09596111111101689

Fernandez, N. O., Gerrikagoitia, J. K., & Alzua-Sorzabal, A. (2014). Dynamic pricing patterns on an Internet distribution channel: The case study of Bilbao's hotels in 2013. In *Information and Communication Technologies in Tourism 2015* (pp. 735–747). Springer.

Gao, J. (2025). Optimizing hotel revenue management through dynamic pricing algorithms and data analysis. *Journal of Computational Methods in Sciences and Engineering, 25*(2), 1200–1209. DOI: 10.1177/14727978241298467

Garrigos-Simon, F. J., Narangajavana, Y., & Palacios-Marqués, D. (2017). The power of social media in the tourism industry. *Tourism Management Perspectives, 21*, 65–73.

Gazzoli, G., Kim, W. G., & Palakurthi, R. (2008). Online distribution strategies and competition: Are the global hotel companies getting it right? *International Journal of Contemporary Hospitality Management, 20*(4), 375–387. DOI: 10.1108/09596110810873499

Granados, N., Gupta, A., & Kauffman, R. J. (2003). Online and offline demand and price elasticities: Evidence from the air travel industry. *Information Systems Research, 14*(4), 379–395. DOI: 10.1287/isre.14.4.379.24899

Guizzardi, A., Pons, F. M. E., Angelini, G., & Ranieri, E. (2021). Big data from dynamic pricing: A smart approach to tourism demand forecasting. *International Journal of Forecasting, 37*(3), 1049–1060. DOI: 10.1016/j.ijforecast.2020.11.006

Gür, Ç., & Yıldız, M. S. (2016). Gelir yönetimi uygulamaları: Ankara'daki otel işletmelerinde bir araştırma. *Düzce Üniversitesi Sosyal Bilimler Dergisi, 6*(2), 15–36.

Güzel, S. Ö., Uzut, İ., Mengü, C., & Şahin, M. A. (Eds.). (2022). *Turizm işletmelerinde gelir yönetimi.* Yalın Yayıncılık.

Hallberg, N. L. (2008). *Pricing capability and its strategic dimensions* (Doctoral dissertation, Lund University).

Hallin, C. A., & Marnburg, E. (2008). Knowledge management in the hospitality industry: A review of empirical research. *Tourism Management, 29*(2), 366–381. DOI: 10.1016/j.tourman.2007.02.019

Han, H., Yu, J., & Kim, W. (2019). Environmental corporate social responsibility and customer responses. *International Journal of Hospitality Management, 76*, 16–26.

Hardy, A. (2020). *Tracking tourists.* Goodfellow Publishers., DOI: 10.23912/9781911635383-4277

Henriques, H., & Pereira, L. N. (2024). Hotel demand forecasting models and methods using artificial intelligence: A systematic literature review. *Tourism & Management Studies, 20*(3), 39–51. DOI: 10.18089/tms.20240304

Heo, C. Y., & Lee, S. (2011). Influences of consumer characteristics on fairness perceptions of revenue management pricing in the hotel industry. *International Journal of Hospitality Management, 30*(2), 243–251. DOI: 10.1016/j.ijhm.2010.07.002

Hinterhuber, A. (2004). Towards value-based pricing: An integrative framework for decision making. *Industrial Marketing Management, 33*(8), 765–778. DOI: 10.1016/j.indmarman.2003.10.006

Hinterhuber, A. (2008). Customer value-based pricing strategies: Why companies resist. *The Journal of Business Strategy, 29*(4), 41–50. DOI: 10.1108/02756660810887079

Ho, D. H., & Kim, H. S. (2025). Examining the influence of customer satisfaction and occupancy rates on RevPAR: Insights from 5-star hotels in Da Nang. *Culinary Science & Hospitality Research, 31*(2), 42–55. DOI: 10.20878/cshr.2025.31.2.006

Hosany, S., & Witham, M. (2010). Dimensions of cruisers' experiences, satisfaction, and intention to recommend. *Journal of Travel Research, 49*(3), 351–364. DOI: 10.1177/0047287509346859

Huang, M. H., & Rust, R. T. (2021). A strategic framework for artificial intelligence in marketing. *Journal of the Academy of Marketing Science, 49*(1), 30–50. DOI: 10.1007/s11747-020-00749-9

Hwang, J., & Han, H. (2018). A study on the application of the experience economy to luxury cruise passengers. *Tourism and Hospitality Research, 18*(4), 478–491. DOI: 10.1177/1467358416682068

Ibrahim, Y., Abbas, T., & Kamal, M. (2021). The use of electronic customer relationship management (e-CRM) features through hotel websites to enhance customer loyalty and brand image. *Journal of Association of Arab Universities for Tourism and Hospitality, 21*(1), 103–125. DOI: 10.21608/jaauth.2021.79828.1190

İmamoğlu, S. Z., Erat, S., & İnce, H. (2023). *Yönetim biliminde yapay zekâ*. Nobel Akademik Yayıncılık.

Islam, M. S., Ali, M., & Azizzadeh, F. (2024). Consumer decision-making processes in digital environments: A psychological perspective. *Applied Psychology Research, 3*(1), 1362. DOI: 10.59400/apr.v3i1.1362

Ivanov, S., & Webster, C. (2017). Adoption of robots, artificial intelligence and service automation by travel, tourism and hospitality companies. *International Journal of Contemporary Hospitality Management.*

Ivanov, S., & Zhechev, V. (2012). Hotel revenue management: A critical literature review. *Tourism: An International Interdisciplinary Journal, 60*(2), 175–197.

Jayanti, R. K. (2021). An institutional theory perspective on retailer loyalty. *Journal ofRelationship Marketing, 20*(2), 156–176. DOI: 10.1080/15332667.2020.1756025

Jiang, Y., & Wen, J. (2020). Effects of COVID-19 on hotel marketing and management: A perspective article. *International Journal of Contemporary Hospitality Management, 32*(8), 2563–2573. DOI: 10.1108/IJCHM-03-2020-0237

Johansson, M., & Andersson, L. (2012). Pricing practices and value creation logics. *Journal of Revenue and Pricing Management, 11*(1), 64–75. DOI: 10.1057/rpm.2011.43

Kafetzi, F.-C. (2025). *Evaluation of contemporary revenue management systems in the tourism industry* (Master's thesis, University of Macedonia).

Kahneman, D., & Klein, G. (2009). Conditions for intuitive expertise: A failure to disagree. *The American Psychologist, 64*(6), 515–526. DOI: 10.1037/a0016755 PMID: 19739881

Kaman, G. S., & Bölükbaş, R. (2024). Konaklama işletmelerinde getiri yönetiminin uygulanması. *Üçüncü Sektör Sosyal Ekonomi Dergisi, 59*(3), 1248–1261.

Kamola, M., & Arabas, P. (2020). Improving time-series demand modeling in hospitality business by analytics of public event datasets. *IEEE Access : Practical Innovations, Open Solutions, 8*, 53666–53677. DOI: 10.1109/ACCESS.2020.2980501

Karadeniz, E., Beyaz, F. S., Ünlübulduk, S. N., & Kayhan, E. (2020). COVID-19 salgınının turizm sektörüne etkilerinin ve uygulanan stratejilerin değerlendirilmesi: Otel yöneticileri üzerinde bir araştırma. *Türk Turizm Araştırmaları Dergisi, 4*(4), 3116–3136. DOI: 10.26677/TR1010.2020.554

Karaman, Ö. (2021). Yapay zeka destekli kişiselleştirme algoritmalarının tüketici zihninde filtre balonu yaratma etkisinin incelenmesi. *Süleyman Demirel Üniversitesi Vizyoner Dergisi, 12*(32), 1339–1351. DOI: 10.21076/vizyoner.896059

Kasapoğlu, V. (2007). *Maliyet temeline dayalı fiyatlandırma yöntemleri* (Yüksek lisans tezi). Sakarya Üniversitesi.

Kiani Mavi, R., Kiani Mavi, N., Olaru, D., Biermann, S., & Chi, S. (2022). Innovations in freight transport: A systematic literature evaluation and COVID implications. *International Journal of Logistics Management, 33*(4), 1157–1195. DOI: 10.1108/IJLM-07-2021-0360

Kılıç, B., & Uslu, T. (2019). Porter'in rekabet modelinin İstanbul'daki zincir otel işletmelerinde incelenmesi. *Uluslararası Global Turizm Araştırmaları Dergisi, 3*(2), 83–98.

Kim, D., Hong, S., Park, B. J., & Kim, I. (2020). Understanding heterogeneous preferences of hotel choice attributes: Do customer segments matter? *Journal of Hospitality and Tourism Management, 45*, 330–337. DOI: 10.1016/j.jhtm.2020.08.014

Kim, M., Roehl, W., & Lee, S. K. (2019). Effect of hotels' price discounts on performance recovery after a crisis. *International Journal of Hospitality Management, 83*, 74–82. DOI: 10.1016/j.ijhm.2019.04.006

Kimes, S. E. (1989). Yield management: A tool for capacity-considered service firms. *Journal of Operations Management, 8*(4), 348–363. DOI: 10.1016/0272-6963(89)90035-1

Kimes, S. E. (2000). Revenue management on the links: Applying yield management to the golf-course industry. *The Cornell Hotel and Restaurant Administration Quarterly, 41*(1), 120–127. DOI: 10.1177/001088040004100129

Kimes, S. E., Chase, R. B., Choi, S., Lee, P. Y., & Ngonzi, E. N. (1998). Restaurant revenue management: Applying yield management to the restaurant industry. *The Cornell Hotel and Restaurant Administration Quarterly, 39*(3), 32–39. DOI: 10.1177/001088049803900308

Kimes, S. E., & Wirtz, J. (2003). Has revenue management become acceptable? Findings from an international study on the perceived fairness of rate fences. *Journal of Service Research, 6*(2), 125–135. DOI: 10.1177/1094670503257038

Kloostra, J. (2022). Algorithmic pricing: A concern for platform workers? *European Labour Law Journal, 13*(1), 108–126. DOI: 10.1177/20319525211060360

Koçoğlu, C. M., & Yurt, B. Ç. (2020). Otel tercihleri kapsamında fiyat algısı bileşenlerinin ilişkisi üzerine bir araştırma. *Uluslararası İktisadi ve İdari İncelemeler Dergisi, 27*, 179–192.

Koşan, L., & Türkseven, Y. Ç. (2022). Otel işletmelerinde gelir yönetimi süreci üzerine bir değerlendirme. *Turizm Ekonomi ve İşletme Araştırmaları Dergisi, 4*(1), 71–90.

Kotler, P., & Keller, K. L. (2016). *A framework for marketing management* (6th ed.). Pearson.

Krajewski, L. J., Ritzman, L. P., & Malhotra, M. K. (2013). *Operations management: Processes and supply chains* (10th ed., global ed.). Pearson.

Kruhlyanko, A., Peniuk, V., Ursakii, Y., & Verstiak, O. (2025). Mathematical modeling for enhancing business strategies in the hotel and restaurant industry: Implications for economic stability. *Advances in Nonlinear Variational Inequalities, 28*(3s, 3S), 386–400. DOI: 10.52783/anvi.v28.3066

Kumar, V., & Reinartz, W. (2016). Creating enduring customer value. *Journal of Marketing*, *80*(6), 36–68. DOI: 10.1509/jm.15.0414

Lee, S., O'Neill, J. W., & McGinley, S. (2016). Effects of economic conditions and other factors on hotel sale prices. *International Journal of Contemporary Hospitality Management*, *28*(10), 2267–2284. DOI: 10.1108/IJCHM-07-2014-0363

Lee, S., Pan, B., & Park, S. (2019). RevPAR vs. GOPPAR: Property- and firm-level analysis. *Annals of Tourism Research*, *76*, 180–190. DOI: 10.1016/j.annals.2019.04.006

Lee, S. H., Deale, C. S., & Lee, J. (2022). Does it pay to book direct? Customers' perceptions of online channel distributors, price, and loyalty membership on brand dimensions. [Sayfa aralığı doğrulanmalı]. *Journal of Revenue and Pricing Management*, *21*(6), 657–670. DOI: 10.1057/s41272-022-00382-x

Ling, L., Guo, X., & Yang, C. (2014). Opening the online marketplace: An examination of hotel pricing and travel agency online distribution of rooms. *Tourism Management*, *45*, 234–243. DOI: 10.1016/j.tourman.2014.05.003

Littlewood, K. (1972). *Forecasting and control of passenger bookings*. In *Proceedings of the 12th AGIFORS Symposium* (pp. 95–117). American Airlines.

Magnini, V. P., Honeycutt, E. D.Jr, & Hodge, S. K. (2003). Data mining for hotel firms: Use and limitations. *The Cornell Hotel and Restaurant Administration Quarterly*, *44*(2), 94–105. DOI: 10.1016/S0010-8804(03)90022-X

Mariani, M. M., Baggio, R., Fuchs, M., & Höepken, W. (2023). Business intelligence and big data in hospitality and tourism: A systematic literature review. *International Journal of Contemporary Hospitality Management*.

Martin, I. W., Lopez, J. L., & Olsen, L. (2019). Policy design and the politics of city revenue: Evidence from California municipal ballot measures. *Urban Affairs Review*, *55*(5), 1312–1338. DOI: 10.1177/1078087417752474

Méatchi, S., & Camus, S. (2020). Revenue management pricing in the hotel sector: Reducing perceived unfairness to encourage willingness to pay. [English Edition]. *Recherche et Applications en Marketing*, *35*(3), 102–123. DOI: 10.1177/2051570720954760

Meatchi, S., Camus, S., & Lecointre-Erickson, D. (2021). Perceived unfairness of revenue management pricing: Developing a measurement scale in the context of hospitality. *International Journal of Contemporary Hospitality Management*, *33*(10), 3157–3176. DOI: 10.1108/IJCHM-11-2020-1344

Mercan, R., & Sandıkcı, M. (2024). Bleisure tourism: Business and leisure together. In *Future tourism trends volume 1: Tourism in the changing world* (pp. 3–15). Emerald Publishing Limited.

Millauer, T., & Vellekoop, M. (2019). Artificial intelligence in today's hotel revenue management: Opportunities and risks. *Research in Hospitality Management, 9*(2), 121–124. DOI: 10.1080/22243534.2019.1689702

Minich, I. (2025). Hotel revenues under economic instability: Adaptation strategies. *Ekonomichnyy Analiz, 35*(1), 484–492. DOI: 10.35774/econa2025.01.484

Minor, K., Ivanov, S., & Bratec, M. (2025). Hotel daily deals: A revenue management perspective. *Tourism and Hospitality Management, 31*(3), I–XII. DOI: 10.20867/thm.31.3.10

Mirzayeva, G., & Türkay, O. (2016). Rekabet stratejilerinin değerlendirilmesi: Bakü'deki otel işletmeleri üzerine bir araştırma. *Uluslararası Türk Dünyası Turizm Araştırmaları Dergisi, 1*(1), 74–83.

Mishra, D., & Vijayvargy, L. (2025). Smart tourism supply chains: Integrating AI, advanced analytics, and robotics for enhanced customer experiences. In *Handbook of Business Analytics* (pp. 196–218). CRC Press. DOI: 10.1201/9781003514282-11

Mitra, S. K. (2020). An analysis of asymmetry in dynamic pricing of hospitality industry. *International Journal of Hospitality Management, 89*, 102406. DOI: 10.1016/j.ijhm.2019.102406

Moon, J., & Sharma, A. (2014). Franchising effects on the lodging industry: Optimal franchising proportion in terms of profitability and intangible value. *Tourism Economics, 20*(5), 1027–1045. DOI: 10.5367/te.2013.0336

Morgan, M., Elbe, J., & de Esteban Curiel, J. (2009). Has the experience economy arrived? The views of destination managers in three visitor-dependent areas. *International Journal of Tourism Research, 11*(2), 201–216. DOI: 10.1002/jtr.719

Morritt, R., & Weinstein, A. (2012). *Segmentation strategies for hospitality managers: Target marketing for competitive advantage*. Routledge. DOI: 10.4324/9780203050095

Nagle, T. T., & Müller, G. (2018). *The strategy and tactics of pricing* (6th ed.). Routledge.

Netemeyer, R. G., Krishnan, B., Pullig, C., Wang, G., Yagci, M., Dean, D., & Wirth, F. (2004). Developing and validating measures of facets of customer-based brand equity. *Journal of Business Research, 57*(2), 209–224. DOI: 10.1016/S0148-2963(01)00303-4

Noone, B. M., & McGuire, K. A. (2013). Pricing in a social world: The influence of non-price information on hotel choice. *Journal of Revenue and Pricing Management, 12*(5), 385–401. DOI: 10.1057/rpm.2013.13

Noone, B. M., McGuire, K. A., & Rohlfs, K. V. (2011). Social media meets hotel revenue management: Opportunities, issues and unanswered questions. *Journal of Revenue and Pricing Management, 10*(4), 293–305. DOI: 10.1057/rpm.2011.12

Nunan, D., & Di Domenico, M. (2022). Value creation in an algorithmic world: Towards an ethics of dynamic pricing. *Journal of Business Research, 150*, 451–460. DOI: 10.1016/j.jbusres.2022.06.032

O'Connor, P. (2020). Online tourism and hospitality distribution: A perspective article. *Tourism Review, 75*(1), 290–293. DOI: 10.1108/TR-06-2019-0216

Oh, H., Fiore, A. M., & Jeoung, M. (2007). Measuring experience economy concepts: Tourism applications. *Journal of Travel Research, 46*(2), 119–132. DOI: 10.1177/0047287507304039

Orhan, B. K. (2025). SERVQUAL modeli çerçevesinde yüksek ve düşük fiyatlı otellerdeki olumsuz yorumların karşılaştırmalı analizi. *Ankara Hacı Bayram Veli Üniversitesi Turizm Fakültesi Dergisi, 28*(2), 99–130. DOI: 10.55931/ahbvtfd.1800722

Oses, N., Gerrikagoitia, J. K., & Alzua-Sorzabal, A. (2016). Modelling and prediction of a destination's monthly average daily rate and occupancy rate based on hotel room prices offered online. *Tourism Economics, 22*(6), 1380–1403. DOI: 10.5367/te.2015.0491

Osmanoğlu, Ş. (2019). *Konaklama işletmeleri rekabet ortamında getiri yönetimi uygulamaları* (Yüksek lisans tezi). İstanbul Üniversitesi, Sosyal Bilimler Enstitüsü.

Özdemir, V., & Hekim, N. (2018). Birth of industry 5.0: Making sense of big data with artificial intelligence, the internet of things and next-generation technology policy. *Omics : A Journal of Integrative Biology, 22*(1), 65–76. DOI: 10.1089/omi.2017.0194 PMID: 29293405

Özsoy Erarslan, A. (2025). Getiri yönetimi. İçinde G. Deniz (Ed.), *İtibar ve getiri yönetimi: Büyük veri ve stratejik yaklaşımlarla teoriden uygulamaya* (ss. 16–23). Nevşehir Hacı Bektaş Veli Üniversitesi Yayınları.

Palmer, A., & McMahon-Beattie, U. (2008). Variable pricing through revenue management: A critical evaluation of affective outcomes. *Management Research News, 31*(3), 189–199. DOI: 10.1108/01409170810851285

Papagianni, E., Evgenidis, A., Tsagkanos, A., & Megalooikonomou, V. (2024). Tourism demand in the face of geopolitical risk: Insights from a cross-country analysis. *Journal of Travel Research, 63*(8), 2094–2119. DOI: 10.1177/00472875231206539

Pekdemir, T., & Küçükaltan, E. G. (2024). Organizational resilience and crisis management relationship on hospitality businesses. *İşletme Araştırmaları Dergisi, 16*(1), 206–222.

Pellinen, J. (2003). Making price decisions in tourism enterprises. *International Journal of Hospitality Management, 22*(2), 217–235. DOI: 10.1016/S0278-4319(03)00019-7

Petricek, M., Chalupa, S., & Melas, D. (2021). Model of price optimization as a part of hotel revenue management: Stochastic approach. *Mathematics, 9*(13), 1552. DOI: 10.3390/math9131552

Petrick, A., Steinhardt, C., Gönsch, J., & Klein, R. (2012). Using flexible products to cope with demand uncertainty in revenue management. *OR-Spektrum, 34*(1), 215–242. DOI: 10.1007/s00291-009-0188-1

Phillips, R. (2021). *Pricing and revenue optimization* (2nd ed.). Stanford University Press.

Pike, S., & Mason, R. (2011). Destination competitiveness through the lens of brand positioning: The case of Australia's Sunshine Coast. *Current Issues in Tourism, 14*(2), 169–182. DOI: 10.1080/13683501003797523

Pine, B. J., & Gilmore, J. H. (1998). The experience economy. *Harvard Business Review, 76*(6), 18–23. PMID: 10181589

Pine, B. J., & Gilmore, J. H. (1999). *The experience economy*. Harvard Business School Press.

Ponte, E. B., Carvajal-Trujillo, E., & Escobar-Rodríguez, T. (2015). Influence of trust and perceived value on the intention to purchase travel online: Integrating the effects of assurance on trust antecedents. *Tourism Management, 47*, 286–302. DOI: 10.1016/j.tourman.2014.10.009

Raab, C., Berezan, O., Christodoulidou, N., Jiang, L., & Shoemaker, S. (2018). Creating strategic relationships with online travel agents to drive hotel room revenue: An OTA perspective. *Journal of Hospitality and Tourism Technology*, *9*(1), 125–140. DOI: 10.1108/JHTT-10-2016-0069

Ramos, C. M. Q., Correia, M. B., Rodrigues, J. M. F., Martins, D., & Serra, F. (2015). Big data warehouse framework for smart revenue management. In *Advances in Environmental Science and Energy Planning* (pp. 13–22). *(Yayıncı bilgisi doğrulanmalı)*

Rao, A. R., & Monroe, K. B. (1989). The effect of price, brand name, and store name on buyers' perceptions of product quality. *JMR, Journal of Marketing Research*, *26*(3), 351–357.

Risnawati, H., Sumarga, H. E., & Purwanto, S. (2019). The effect of service quality, prices, and location of companies on customer satisfaction and its implications for customer loyalty. [Sayfa aralığı doğrulanmalı]. *International Review of Management and Marketing*, *9*(6), 38–45. DOI: 10.32479/irmm.8736

Sarnıç, A. (2025). İşletme zekâsından yapay zekâya: Türkiye'nin hızlı büyüyen firmalarında yapay zekâ uygulamaları üzerine bir içerik analizi. *Nevşehir Hacı Bektaş Veli Üniversitesi SBE Dergisi*, (Sosyal Bilimlerde Yapay Zeka: Kuram, Uygulama ve Gelecek Perspektifleri), 300-319.

Sarvari, P. A., Ustundag, A., & Takci, H. (2016). Performance evaluation of different customer segmentation approaches based on RFM and demographics analysis. *Kybernetes*, *45*(7), 1129–1157. DOI: 10.1108/K-07-2015-0180

Schwartz, Z., Altin, M., & Singal, M. (2017). Performance measures for strategic revenue management: RevPAR versus GOPPAR. *Journal of Revenue and Pricing Management*, *16*(4), 357–375. DOI: 10.1057/rpm.2016.23

Şeker, A. (2025). Stratejik öneriler ve yol haritası. İçinde G. Deniz (Ed.), *İtibar ve getiri yönetimi* (ss. 67–78). Nevşehir Hacı Bektaş Veli Üniversitesi Yayınları.

Setiawan, F., & Saptutyningsih, E. (2022). Willingness to pay for destination quality improvement: Case study of Baru Beach, Yogyakarta. *Journal of Economics Research and Social Sciences*, *6*(1), 31–43. DOI: 10.18196/jerss.v6i1.13363

Shah, M. S. M. (2025). A study on determinants of hotels' strategic choices: Collaboration or competition with OTAs in Srinagar. *The Quintessential*, 21–33. *(Dergi bilgisi doğrulanmalı)*

Sheng, J., Amankwah-Amoah, J., Khan, Z., & Wang, X. (2021). COVID-19 pandemic in the new era of big data analytics: Methodological innovations and future research directions. *British Journal of Management, 32*(4), 1164–1183. DOI: 10.1111/1467-8551.12441

Shrestha, Y. R., Ben-Menahem, S. M., & von Krogh, G. (2019). Organizational decision-making structures in the age of artificial intelligence. *California Management Review, 61*(4), 66–83. DOI: 10.1177/0008125619862257

Siddappa, S. (2006). *Statistical modeling approach to airline revenue management with overbooking* (Doctoral dissertation, The University of Texas at Arlington).

Smith, B. C., Leimkuhler, J. F., & Darrow, R. M. (1992). Yield management at American Airlines. *Interfaces, 22*(1), 8–31. DOI: 10.1287/inte.22.1.8

Smithson, S., Devece, C. A., & Lapiedra, R. (2011). Online visibility as a source of competitive advantage for small- and medium-sized tourism accommodation enterprises. *Service Industries Journal, 31*(10), 1573–1587. DOI: 10.1080/02642069.2010.485640

Song, H., & Li, G. (2008). Tourism demand modelling and forecasting: A review of recent research. *Tourism Management, 29*(2), 203–220. DOI: 10.1016/j.tourman.2007.07.016

Song, H., Witt, S. F., & Li, G. (2008). *The advanced econometrics of tourism demand.* Routledge. DOI: 10.4324/9780203891469

Sönmez Karapınar, E. (2024). Dijital pazarlama. İçinde Ş. Karaca (Ed.), *Turizm ve dijital pazarlama: Teori ve uygulamalar* (s. 35). Özgür Yayınları. https://doi.org/ DOI: 10.58830/ozgur.pub603.c2539

Strauss, A. K. (2009). *Optimisation in choice-based network revenue management.* Lancaster University.

Sun, X., Jiao, Y., & Tian, P. (2011). Marketing research and revenue optimization for the cruise industry: A concise review. *International Journal of Hospitality Management, 30*(3), 746–755. DOI: 10.1016/j.ijhm.2010.11.007

Suwitri, S. A. N., Gede, I. G. K., & Wajdi, M. (2025). Enhancing hospitality business visibility through strategic search engine optimization (SEO) implementation in digital marketing platforms. *Journal of Commerce, Management, and Tourism Studies, 4*(2), 272–286. DOI: 10.58881/jcmts.v4i2.370

Talal, M., Garfan, S., Qays, R., Pamucar, D., Delen, D., Pedrycz, W., & Simic, V. (2025). A comprehensive systematic review on machine learning application in the 5G-RAN architecture: Issues, challenges, and future directions. *Journal of Network and Computer Applications, 233*, 104041. DOI: 10.1016/j.jnca.2024.104041

Talluri, K. T., & Van Ryzin, G. J. (2004). *The theory and practice of revenue management.* Springer. DOI: 10.1007/b139000

Tan, J., & Dwyer, L. (2014). Managing distribution channel conflict in the hotel industry. [Sayfa aralığı doğrulanmalı]. *International Journal of Marketing & Business Communication, 3*(1), 1–10.

Tarakçı, İ. E., & Göktaş, B. (2020). Turizm işletmelerinde hizmet hataları ve hizmet telafisi yöntemlerinin müşteri memnuniyeti üzerindeki etkisi: Bir uygulama. *Türk Turizm Araştırmaları Dergisi, 4*(1), 259–278. DOI: 10.26677/TR1010.2020.311

Tek, Ö. B. (1999). *Pazarlama ilkeleri.* Beta Yayınları.

Temel, E., & Anbarcı, M. (2025). Yoksa rasyonel tüketici eğilimleri de esasında hedonik mi? Tüketicilerin rasyonel satın alma eğilimleri ve haz üzerine fenomenolojik bir çözümleme. *Kapadokya Akademik Bakış, 9*(1), 38–70. DOI: 10.69851/car.1660721

Thanh, T. V., & Kirova, V. (2018). Wine tourism experience: A netnography study. *Journal of Business Research, 83*, 30–37. DOI: 10.1016/j.jbusres.2017.10.008

Tiwari, V. (2024). Role of data analytics in business decision making. *Knowledgeable Research A Multidisciplinary Journal, 3*(01), 18-27.

Tonidandel, S., King, E. B., & Cortina, J. M. (2018). Big data methods: Leveraging modern data analytic techniques to build organizational science. *Organizational Research Methods, 21*(3), 525–547. DOI: 10.1177/1094428116677299

Tranter, K. A., Stuart-Hill, T., & Parker, J. (2009). *An introduction to revenue management for the hospitality industry: Principles and practice for the real world.* Pearson.

Tse, T. S., & Poon, Y. T. (2012). Revenue management: Resolving a revenue optimization paradox. *International Journal of Contemporary Hospitality Management, 24*(4), 507–521. DOI: 10.1108/09596111211226798

Uladi, A. İ., & Arı, E. S. (2023). Büyük veri, büyük veri analizi ve uygulama alanları. *Yönetim Bilişim Sistemleri Dergisi, 9*(1), 1–14.

Ulucan, E., & Kızılırmak, İ. (2018). Konaklama işletmelerinde talep tahmin yöntemleri: Yapay sinir ağları ile ilgili bir araştırma. *Seyahat ve Otel İşletmeciliği Dergisi, 15*(1), 89–101. DOI: 10.24010/soid.415343

Ünal, S., & Sezgin, A. A. (2021). Büyük veri (big data)'nin yapay zeka uygulamalarında toplumsal sınıflandırmaya yönelik kaygılar. *AJIT-e: Academic Journal of Information Technology, 12*(44), 47–70. DOI: 10.5824/ajite.2021.01.004.x

Ural, T. (2008). Değer temelli fiyatlama: Ürünün tüketici değer algısına göre fiyatlanması. *Anadolu Üniversitesi Sosyal Bilimler Dergisi, 8*(2), 1–16.

Van Ryzin, G. J., & Talluri, K. T. (2005). An introduction to revenue management. In *Emerging theory, methods, and applications* (pp. 142–194). Informs.

Verhoef, P. C., Kannan, P. K., & Inman, J. J. (2015). From multi-channel retailing to omni-channel retailing. *Journal of Retailing, 91*(2), 174–181. DOI: 10.1016/j.jretai.2015.02.005

Vives, A., Jacob, M., & Payeras, M. (2018). Revenue management and price optimization techniques in the hotel sector: A critical literature review. *Tourism Economics, 24*(6), 720–752. DOI: 10.1177/1354816618777590

Voss, G. B., Parasuraman, A., & Grewal, D. (1998). The roles of price, performance, and expectations in determining satisfaction in service exchanges. *Journal of Marketing, 62*(4), 46–61. DOI: 10.1177/002224299806200404

Wang, Z., Dong, X., & Yin, J. (2018). Antecedents of urban residents' separate collection intentions for household solid waste and their willingness to pay: Evidence from China. *Journal of Cleaner Production, 173*, 256–264. DOI: 10.1016/j.jclepro.2016.09.223

Wertenbroch, K., & Skiera, B. (2002). Measuring consumers' willingness to pay at the point of purchase. *JMR, Journal of Marketing Research, 39*(2), 228–241. DOI: 10.1509/jmkr.39.2.228.19086

Xiang, Z., Schwartz, Z., Gerdes, J., & Uysal, M. (2021). What can big data and text analytics tell us about hotel guest experience? *International Journal of Hospitality Management.*

Xiao, Z., Li, Y., Liu, X., & Gong, X. (2025). The impact of compensation information transparency on guest booking behavior in the home-sharing economy: An asymmetric information perspective. *International Journal of Contemporary Hospitality Management, 37*(12), 3897–3916. DOI: 10.1108/IJCHM-01-2025-0138

Yadav, S. J. (2025). Digital Platforms and Open Innovation: How Online Travel Agencies Shape the Future of Hospitality. In *Open Innovation and Technology in Tourism and Hospitality* (pp. 75-92). IGI Global Scientific Publishing.

Yelkur, R., & Nêveda DaCosta, M. M. (2001). Differential pricing and segmentation on the Internet: The case of hotels. *Management Decision, 39*(4), 252–262. DOI: 10.1108/00251740110391411

Yiğit, B. B. (2024). Fiyatlandırma stratejileri. İçinde Ö. S. Aykaç & A. Yılmaz (Ed.), *Pazarlama ve perakendecilik: Dijital çağın dönüşümleri* (ss. 103–130). Özgür Yayınları.

Yıldıztekin, İ. (2010). Konaklama hizmetlerinde maliyete dayalı fiyatlama ve fiyat değişiminin bölüm karlılığına etkileri. *Atatürk Üniversitesi İktisadi ve İdari Bilimler Dergisi, 23*(4), 215–240.

Yurtlu, M., & Ateş, A. (2019). Online kanal yöneticisiyle otel oda fiyatlandırmada verim yönetimi. *Seyahat ve Otel İşletmeciliği Dergisi, 16*(2), 207–228. DOI: 10.24010/soid.471106

Zeithaml, V. A. (1988). Consumer perceptions of price, quality, and value: A means-end model and synthesis of evidence. *Journal of Marketing, 52*(3), 2–22. DOI: 10.1177/002224298805200302

ADDITIONAL READING

Buhalis, D., & Leung, R. (2018). Smart hospitality: Interconnectivity and interoperability towards an ecosystem. *International Journal of Hospitality Management, 71*, 41–50. DOI: 10.1016/j.ijhm.2017.11.011

Dolgui, A., Ivanov, D., & Sokolov, B. (2020). Reconfigurable supply chain: The X-network. *International Journal of Production Research, 58*(13), 4138–4163. DOI: 10.1080/00207543.2020.1774679

Hayes, D. K., Hayes, J. D., & Hayes, P. A. (2021). *Revenue management for the hospitality industry*. John Wiley & Sons.

Ivanov, S. (2014). *Hotel revenue management: From theory to practice*. Zangador.

Kotler, P., Bowen, J. T., Makens, J. C., & Baloglu, S. (2006). *Marketing for hospitality and tourism* (4th ed.). Prentice Hall.

Mariani, M., Baggio, R., Fuchs, M., & Höepken, W. (2018). Business intelligence and big data in hospitality and tourism: A systematic literature review. *International Journal of Contemporary Hospitality Management, 30*(12), 3514–3554. DOI: 10.1108/IJCHM-07-2017-0461

Schwartz, Z., Stewart, W., & Backlund, E. A. (2012). Visitation at capacity-constrained tourism destinations: Exploring revenue management at a national park. *Tourism Management, 33*(3), 500–508. DOI: 10.1016/j.tourman.2011.05.008

Zhang, Z., Ye, Q., & Law, R. (2011). Determinants of hotel room price: An exploration of travelers' hierarchy of accommodation needs. *International Journal of Contemporary Hospitality Management, 23*(7), 972–981. DOI: 10.1108/09596111111167551

KEY TERMS AND DEFINITIONS

Algorithmic Pricing: It is the dynamic pricing process automatically determined according to demand, competition, and market conditions using data analytics and artificial intelligence algorithms.

Demand Forecasting: It is the systematic analysis process carried out using historical data and analytical models to predict future customer demand.

Differential Pricing: It is a pricing approach aimed at revenue optimization, which refers to offering the same service at different prices to different customer segments.

Pricing Logic: It is a decision framework based on perceived value, willingness to pay, and brand positioning, which refers to the strategic reasoning process behind pricing decisions.

Revenue Management: It is a strategic management approach aimed at maximizing revenue by selling to the right customer at the right time at the right price in service businesses with fixed capacity.

RevPAR (Revenue Per Available Room): It is one of the key financial indicators used to measure revenue per available room and to evaluate hotel performance.

Value-Based Pricing: It is a pricing approach where the price is determined based on the value perceived by the customer and their willingness to pay rather than on costs.

Chapter 7
Revenue Optimization and the Role of Dynamic Pricing in Hospitality Accounting

Medha Tiwari
http://orcid.org/0009-0004-3301-0923
Amity University, Gurgaon, India

Rajnish Shukla
http://orcid.org/0000-0003-0202-9133
Amity University, Noida, India

Manish K. Sharma
http://orcid.org/0000-0002-1440-3252
Amity University, Noida, India

ABSTRACT

Hotel pricing techniques have shifted from cost-plus models to dynamic, data-driven strategies. In the present era of digital selling platforms with real-time analytics, fixed pricing has become obsolete in hospitality industry. The main objective of this chapter is to break down the complexities of pricing logic by providing an easy-to-understand framework and explain how people's irrational behaviors affect the perception of "fair" pricing. This chapter adopts a conceptual and analytical approach to breakdown complexity through offering a structured framework for the revenue management process. The discussions combine dynamic pricing with operational strategies to show how revenue management strategy achieves high occupancy rates and strong revenue performance. In 2026, values come from a mix of

DOI: 10.4018/979-8-3373-9479-4.ch007

rigorous data analysis and a deep understanding of human psychology. Successful companies use revenue management not only to maximize prices but also to provide maximum value, creating a win-win for both customers and the firm.

INTRODUCTION

For centuries, retail commerce relied on two main methods, individual bargaining or a fixed price. The fixed price model was the only way to maintain steady business year after year until the 20th century. This approach lowered transaction costs and built customer trust and loyalty. However, it also prevented companies from capturing customer surplus and caused losses during peak demand periods, which could greatly affect gross operating profit. This model became especially vulnerable for asset-heavy and capital-intensive organizations.

Even one unsold room night loses all economic value the moment the next day begins. Today, dynamic pricing, which adjusts prices based on real-time changes in supply, demand, and competition, has become the leading strategy for maximizing revenue in the hospitality industry. In competitive markets characterized by fluctuating demand, limited inventory, and price-sensitive customers, businesses increasingly depend on pricing strategies to boost revenue and profits. Revenue management, originally called yield management, arose in response to the US Airline Deregulation Act of 1978 (Kimes, 2016). American Airlines led the way with the first automated yield management system, DINAMO (Dynamic Inventory Optimization and Maintenance). Instead of simply matching discount fares, American Airlines used statistical forecasting to categorize inventory on the same aircraft. By limiting the number of low-fare seats available and reserving the rest for late-booking, price-sensitive business travellers, American matched People Express's prices on certain seats while protecting high-paying corporate accounts. This innovation allowed American Airlines to increase revenue by hundreds of millions of dollars, ultimately driving under-optimized, low-cost competitors into bankruptcy.

Over the time the same logic was adopted by hotels, car rentals, cruise lines. At the core of revenue management lies the concept of dynamic pricing, a price strategy where the prices are continuously watched and adjusted as per the market conditions, demand, time, competition and in the end the customer purchasing behaviour. Dynamic pricing is often misunderstood as merely raising the prices during periods of high demand (El Haddad et al., 2015). Whereas it is much more than just raising the prices. It is a sophisticated decision-making process grounded in economics, customer psychology, demand forecasting and market response. The main logic behind dynamic prices is that the customer's willingness to pay varies across time, situation, customer segment, season and most importantly, the need to travel. Yet for all its strategic projection, dynamic pricing is not merely a marketing or operational matter. Its effect propagates immediately and materially into the accounting systems of a hospitality enterprise, shaping revenue recognition timing, distorting traditional cost per occupied room - CPOR analysis, complicating loyalty liability calculations and demanding new approaches to management reporting. It is often colloquially summarized as selling the right product to the right customer at the right time for the right price (Lima Santos et al., 2024).

Despite the extensive body of literature on revenue management and dynamic pricing, existing studies have predominantly examined these concepts from operational, marketing, and technological perspectives. Comparatively limited attention has been devoted to understanding how dynamic pricing decisions influence financial reporting, revenue recognition, managerial accounting, and performance evaluation within hospitality organisations. As hotels increasingly adopt AI-enabled pricing systems and integrated digital platforms, the interaction between pricing decisions and accounting practices has become strategically important. This chapter addresses this gap by examining dynamic pricing through an accounting-oriented lens, integrating contemporary revenue management theory with financial reporting principles, managerial accounting considerations, and emerging digital technologies. In doing so, it provides a more holistic understanding of how pricing decisions influence both operational performance and financial outcomes in modern hospitality enterprises. It explores the theoretical foundation, key principles, pricing mechanisms, technologies, advantages, challenges, ethical concerns, and applications within the hospitality industry. It will also highlight how dynamic pricing contributes not only to revenue optimisation but also to long-term profitability and competitive advantage (Kimes, 2016). It provides a rigorous examination of dynamic pricing from an accounting perspective, addressing how revenues generated under variable rate structures are recognized, measured, reported, and evaluated. It draws on the provisions of ASC 606, FASB 2014, and IFRS15, IASB, 2014 for revenue recognition, integrates the Uniform System of Accounts for the Lodging Industry (USALI) framework, HFTP - Hospitality Financial and Technology Professionals 2014, and situates dynamic pricing within the contemporary Revenue Management (RM) literature. (Dimitrova, 2025)

RESEARCH GAP AND CHAPTER FOCUS

Even though the dynamic pricing and revenue management have been extensively studied from operational, marketing, and technological perspectives, comparatively limited research has examined their implications for financial reporting, revenue recognition, managerial accounting, performance evaluation, and regulatory compliance in hospitality. This gap has become increasingly significant with the adoption of AI-enabled pricing systems and integrated digital platforms. Accordingly, this chapter adopts an accounting-oriented perspective to integrate contemporary revenue management with financial reporting, managerial accounting, and emerging technologies, providing a holistic understanding of how dynamic pricing influences both operational and financial performance. This chapter addresses these gaps by focusing on two objectives.

1. To critically examine the accounting and financial implications of dynamic pricing in hospitality, with particular emphasis on revenue recognition, managerial reporting, and financial performance measurement.
2. To develop an integrated perspective linking contemporary revenue management and AI-enabled dynamic pricing with accounting practices, financial reporting, and strategic decision-making in hospitality organisations.

LITERATURE REVIEW

Revenue management can be defined as the process of using data analytics, forecasting and pricing strategies based on the history and current demand levels to sell the right product to the right customer at the right time for the right price and through the right distribution channel. It is basically the application of disciplined analytics to predict consumer behaviour at the micro market level and to optimise the availability and price of perishable products to maximize revenue growth. The key objective is not only to increase the occupancy levels, but at the same time, the profitability and viability of that business from the available inventory. Revenue management is adopted by various industries that are dealing with Fixed and Perishable inventory, High fixed cost and low variable cost, Fluctuating demands, Different Sources and segments of business and requirement of Timely consumption. Any hotel room that remains unsold even for one night represents lost revenue that cannot be recovered later. Therefore, it becomes even more important for hotels to optimize by using revenue management techniques for rooms/F&B pricing. Revenue management is not only about changing the room prices as mentioned earlier. It includes various functions like - understanding historical data, understanding current happenings in the market, forecasting demand, managing inventory, market segmentation, channel/source management & customer history and behaviour.

Progressively now the traditional revenue management approach of measuring just the room prices has evolved into a wider perspective known as Total Revenue Management. Which includes all revenue generating rooms, restaurants, banquets, SPA etc (Altin et al., 2017; Kimes, 2016). The Economic Logic of Dynamic Pricing is a part of microeconomic theory of Price Discrimination. It is the result of Supply, demand and the customer willingness to pay. In a stable market, where the demand is the same and the supply is constant, dynamic pricing is impossible. However, in hospitality these both keeps changing along with the time. The same category of room is sold at a different rate when the city occupancy is down, whereas if there is a conference or an event happening in the city, the hotel can sell the same room at double the price. The challenge for pricing strategy is to validate these fluctuations in rate structures that are profitable (Bandalouski et al., 2021; Guizzardi et al., 2022).

When demand increases, as compared to the available inventory the prices will increase and similarly when demand reduces the prices also reduces (Guizzardi et al., 2022).

This principle can be represented through the demand function:

$$Q_d = f(P)$$

Where:

Q_d= Quantity demanded

P= Price

In Hospitality, the room supply is always fixed; pricing is the only tool to maximize yield. For Eg: During long weekends and vacations and conference time, the demand for rooms increases and hotels tend to take advantage of this and increase prices. During Wedding dates, the banquet prices are high. During the off-season, there are promotions and discounts offered by hotels to induce demand(Abrate & Viglia, 2016).

Perishable commodity: One of the strongest justifications for revenue management is the perishability. Hotel Rooms, Event Tickets, Restaurant Table, Spa treatment loose all the value if there is no consumption on the same day. Any unsold room cannot be sold in future and it's a permanent loss. Hence the pressure is on both Occupancy and average selling price for yield optimization (Altin, 2017). Revenue performance in hotels for rooms is measured by calculating revenue per available room or RevPAR.

RevPAR = ADR x Occupancy Rate, *Where: ADR = Average Daily Rate*

The key challenge remains with having the right balance in occupancy and the pricing. Selling all rooms at low prices will bring down the GOP whereas if the prices are too high, then the probability of having vacant rooms is high.

Market Segmentation: For a successful revenue management system, it is very important to divide the market into various segments depending on their purpose to travel. Each of the key segments in hotels like - corporate/ business Travelers, leisure travellers, online travel agent's customer, group bookings, loyalty program members and walk-ins or direct website bookings, have different booking patterns and price sensitivity. Revenue management system studies their patterns and then determines the different price strategies suiting the requirement for difference segments Each of the above segment have different booking patterns and price sensitivity. Revenue management system studies their patterns and then determines the different price strategies suiting the requirement for difference segments (Moula et al., 2024) (Altin et al., 2017).

Demand Forecasting: Demand Forecasting is the predictive process of estimating or budgeting the future revenues and profits (Anshori, Katias, et al., 2025). Accurate demand forecasting can help in controlling expenses, making sure that the hotels are equipped with the required supplies if the demand is high. (Ma et al., 2024). Forecasting methods includes study of historical data and trends, time series, regression analysis, competition study, future events/ weddings in the city and market intelligence. Based on the above, the hotel does forecast the future occupancy levels, revenue expected, booking PACE, market demand and competition Pricing. Major Errors like underestimating the demand results in selling rooms at lower prices and overestimating may have unsold inventories at hand and these may significantly affect the profitability. For this reason, now days all modern revenue management systems are equipped with AI (Artificial Intelligence) and big data to support the outcome and improving the accuracy of forecasting (Kumari & Raj, 2025).

MODERN DYNAMIC PRICING SYSTEMS DESIGNS

Dynamic pricing depends on various factors like time-based pricing, demand-based pricing, direct competition effect, and buyer-based pricing (Lima Santos et al., 2024). Time Based Pricing depends on the Seasonality, Weekday/ Weekend, Time of arrival and Holidays/ Long Weekends/ Festivals etc for the price variation. Hotels in Leisure destination will increase the rates during Holiday season whereas the hotels in corporate locations will decrease the rates during the same period. Demand Based Pricing will watch for the events and activities in the location and have the price going up and down as per the demand. When the demand is high the rates will increase and when the demand is low the rates will decrease. Pricing through direct competition effect will monitor their competition closely and adjust pricing to maintain a fair share of the market. They mainly consider hotel market position, competition's occupancy and rate levels, and look at their service quality, guest reviews and branding. Buyer-based pricing is one of the most important and is becoming increasingly common now. It focuses on the buying behaviour of the customer and considers loyalty Programs, customer data analytics, past purchase patterns along with the booking channels and market segments.

Currently the dynamic pricing in hotel industry is delivered through integrated technology which gets connected to property management system (PMS), Central reservation system (CRS), Revenue management system (RMS) and Channel management platforms. The revenue management system products such as IDeaS G3, Duetto Gamechanger, or Infor EzRMS, sits at the heart of the pricing decision process, ingesting data from multiple sources (Gao, 2025): historical occupancy and rate patterns, forward-looking pickup reports, competitive rate intelligence gathered through rate shopping tools, event calendars, weather forecasts, and increasingly, social media sentiment and macroeconomic indicators (Anshori, Herlambang, et al., 2025). The output of these revenue management systems (RMS) is into rate recommendations. This could be typically one BAR rate (Best available rate) or rates with different discounting for different segments. There are other aspects as well when it comes to deciding the BAR rates like minimum length of stay (MLOS), Close to Arrival (CTA) non-refundable booking etc. These recommendations are automatically given by the RMS or prompted by human intervention. In this case it is described as assisted automated pricing (Haynes & Egan, 2023).

Dynamic Pricing in Hospitality: Dynamic Pricing for hotels is a strategic revenue management practice, and it is applied across all revenue-generating departments, but major focus remains in areas like Room categories, distribution channels, customer segments, booking periods and location. Key Strategies for Revenue management includes (Alrawadieh et al., 2021)

1. Best Available Rate (BAR)/ Rate of the day (ROTD) - This is the lowest benchmark rate that is calculated according to the market demand.
2. Length of stay controls (LOS) - This is to encourage guests staying for longer duration as it reduces cost and helps in better yield.
3. Overbooking strategies - The level up to which the hotels can overbook themselves to compensate for last-minute cancellations and no shows.
4. Channel Optimisation: Hotels generally distribute and allocate the number of rooms to be sold across various channels, so that the more rooms are not consumed by anyone low-paying channel like - Direct website, OTA, Travel Agents, Corporate Contracts and FIT/Walk-in

Revenue Management Metrics: Several performance indicators measure Revenue Management system's effectiveness and increasingly hotel companies now focus on profitability metrics such as GOPPAR rather than occupancy alone (Schwartz et al., 2017).

Average Daily Rate (ADR) $ADR = \frac{Total\ Room\ Revenue}{Rooms\ Sold}$

Occupancy Rate $Occupancy\ Rate = \frac{Rooms\ Sold}{Rooms\ Available} \times 100$

Revenue Per Available Room (RevPAR) $RevPAR = \frac{Total\ Room\ Revenue}{Rooms\ Available}$

Gross Operating Profit Per Available Room (GOPPAR) $GOPPAR = \frac{Gross\ Operating\ Profit}{Rooms\ Available}$

ACCOUNTING IMPLICATIONS OF DYNAMIC PRICING IN HOSPITALITY

Dynamic pricing has traditionally been examined from operational and marketing perspectives, with emphasis on demand forecasting, inventory optimisation, and revenue maximisation. However, its implications extend well beyond pricing decisions and significantly influence financial reporting, revenue recognition, cost allocation, and managerial accounting within hospitality organisations (HFTP & AHLA, 2026). As hotels increasingly adopt AI-enabled revenue management systems capable of adjusting room rates in real time, accounting systems must accurately capture, measure, and report the financial effects of these continuously changing transactions. Consequently, dynamic pricing has become an important accounting consideration rather than merely a commercial strategy.

One of the most significant accounting implications of dynamic pricing relates to revenue recognition. Under IFRS 15, revenue is recognised to depict the transfer of promised goods or services to customers in an amount reflecting the consideration to which the entity expects to be entitled (IASB, 2014) In the hotel industry, although a reservation may be confirmed weeks or months before arrival, the revenue from accommodation is generally recognised only when the guest actually occupies the room. Dynamic pricing introduces variability into the transaction price because room rates fluctuate according to booking time, demand levels, customer segment, distribution channel, seasonality, and market conditions (MCA 2020; IASB 2014). Therefore, accounting systems must ensure that the final recognised revenue accurately reflects the contractual transaction price after considering any modifications, discounts, promotional offers, upgrades, or cancellations. This requires close integration between the revenue management system (RMS), property management system (PMS), and financial accounting system to maintain compliance with financial reporting standards.

Another important accounting issue concerns non-refundable advance reservations. Hotels frequently offer discounted rates in exchange for non-refundable bookings made several weeks or months before arrival. Although cash is received at the time of booking, accounting standards require that the amount initially be recognised as a contract liability (deferred revenue) because the hotel has not yet fulfilled its performance obligation. Revenue is recognised only when the guest checks in and the accommodation service is provided. If the reservation is modified because of changes in pricing policies, upgrades, or rescheduled stay dates, the accounting system must appropriately adjust the deferred revenue balance before recognising revenue. Dynamic pricing therefore increases the complexity of contract accounting by requiring continuous monitoring of transaction prices and contractual obligations throughout the booking cycle.

Dynamic pricing also affects distribution channel accounting. Hotels distribute inventory through multiple channels, including direct websites, online travel agencies (OTAs), global distribution systems (GDS), corporate contracts, wholesalers, and travel agents. Although two guests may occupy identical rooms on the same night, the accounting treatment may differ depending on the booking channel. Direct bookings generally generate higher net revenue because commission expenses are minimal, whereas OTA bookings involve commission payments that reduce net profitability. Consequently, management accounting should evaluate not only total revenue generated by each channel but also its contribution margin after deducting distribution costs. Integrating revenue management information with accounting reports enables managers to identify the most profitable booking channels rather than focusing solely on occupancy or gross revenue.

The growing importance of customer loyalty programmes introduces additional accounting complexities under dynamic pricing (*How to Optimize Your Loyalty Program through Data and Technology: PwC*, n.d.) (Ha, 2026). Many hotel chains reward repeat customers through loyalty points that can later be redeemed for complimentary accommodation or other hospitality services (Applying IFRS: Disclosure of Accounting Policy Information | EY - Global, 2022) (Lentz et al., 2022). According to IFRS 15, these loyalty benefits represent a separate performance obligation because the customer receives a material right that extends beyond the current transaction. Accordingly, a portion of the transaction price must be allocated to the loyalty obligation and recognised as deferred revenue until redemption or expiry of the points. Dynamic pricing influences this valuation because the fair value of future room redemptions varies according to prevailing room rates, occupancy levels, seasonal demand, and promotional campaigns. Consequently, accounting systems must periodically reassess loyalty liabilities to ensure accurate financial reporting while supporting effective revenue management decisions.

Dynamic pricing further influences managerial accounting and profitability analysis. Revenue management performance has traditionally been evaluated using indicators such as Average Daily Rate (ADR), Occupancy Rate, Revenue per

Available Room (RevPAR) (HFTP; AHLA 2026), and Gross Operating Profit per Available Room (GOPPAR). However, accounting analysis extends beyond revenue measurement to examine the relationship between pricing decisions and operating costs. For example, higher occupancy achieved through discounted pricing may increase housekeeping expenses, laundry costs, utilities, guest amenities, and labour requirements, thereby affecting the Cost per Occupied Room (CPOR). Conversely, premium pricing strategies may generate higher revenue while maintaining relatively stable operating costs, resulting in improved profitability. Therefore, management should evaluate pricing decisions using an integrated set of financial and operational performance indicators rather than relying solely on occupancy or RevPAR.

The integration of artificial intelligence into revenue management systems further reinforces the need for stronger collaboration between commercial and accounting functions. Modern RMS platforms continuously analyse booking pace, competitor pricing, demand forecasts, customer behaviour, and market conditions to recommend optimal room rates. These pricing decisions influence revenue recognition, deferred revenue balances, channel profitability, forecasting accuracy, budgeting, and financial reporting. Accordingly, hospitality organisations require seamless integration between pricing algorithms, operational systems, and accounting information systems to ensure that commercial decisions are accurately reflected in financial statements and managerial reports.

Overall, dynamic pricing should be viewed not merely as a revenue optimisation technique but as an accounting-sensitive managerial practice that influences multiple aspects of financial reporting and organisational performance. As hospitality organisations increasingly rely on data-driven pricing decisions, integrating revenue management with accounting processes has become essential for ensuring regulatory compliance, improving financial transparency, and supporting strategic decision-making. Such integration enables managers to evaluate not only whether revenue has increased but also whether pricing decisions have enhanced long-term profitability, operational efficiency, and sustainable business performance.

ADVANTAGES OF REVENUE MANAGEMENT AND DYNAMIC PRICING

At its core, revenue management is all about selling right room to the right guest at the right price and most importantly through the right channel and at the right time. Whereas dynamic pricing or variable pricing is the tactical engine behind this. Hotel industry has gradually moved away from the static and seasonal room rates to a real time inventory and rates based on the current market conditions. Effective revenue management offers several strategic benefits like enhanced forecasting to improve planning and operational efficiency, better inventory management to reduce loss from unsold inventory along with, revenue maximisation by adjusting the pricing opportunities as per the demand variables. It can also help in customer segmentation which helps in focusing on more productive and profitable segments rather than increasing/decreasing rates for all segments and thus brings the profitability boost by balancing the occupancy with best rates, which in turn improves the profitability of the hotel (Altin et al., 2017).

CHALLENGES AND ETHICAL CONSIDERATIONS IN DYNAMIC PRICING

Despite its potential to enhance profitability, dynamic pricing presents significant managerial, technological, and ethical challenges. Excessive reliance on automated and algorithmic pricing may lead to consumer backlash, brand erosion, forecasting uncertainty, technology dependency, skill gaps, competitive price wars, and regulatory and compliance concerns. Ethical considerations are particularly important because customers assess price changes against perceived reference prices and expectations of fairness. The Ethics of dynamic pricing in hospitality is a questionable and debatable issue between the price increase and the necessity of the usage(Qi et al., 2024). Kimes and Wirtz (2003) introduced the concept of 'price fairness' to the revenue management literature, drawing on dual-entitlement theory to argue that consumers evaluate price changes not in absolute terms but relative to a 'reference price' anchored to their prior experience or expectations. From a legal point of view, several jurisdictions have been proposed to cap the increase during the high-demand periods or during declared emergencies (Talón-Ballestero et al., 2022) (Wamsler et al., 2022).

Therefore, hospitality organisations must balance revenue optimisation with transparency, customer trust, regulatory requirements, and responsible pricing practices

THE FUTURE OF DYNAMIC PRICING

The future of revenue management is evolving past traditional revenue management systems, rule-based automation, to a hyper-personalised and autonomous revenue systems(Yeoman, 2025). With real time decision making with the real time inputs and integration with the property management systems, the feed will directly help in getting the best-selling price. It is now a mix of both predictive analytics, generative AI and agentic systems and shifting away from historical methods (Alrawadieh et al., 2021). Key Future trends may include use of artificial intelligence and machine learning. The new AI-driven systems will automate pricing decisions and will prompt the best available rate and offer personalised pricing based on past data, history and trend of their expenses in the hotel (Wamsler et al., 2022). Moving towards the total revenue management, the focus is now shifting from RevPAR to the total revenue per available room (TRevPAR). In this profitability race, the sustainability cannot be forgotten, and all hotels need to integrate the sustainability considerations into the pricing as going forward this will be an important point while selecting the hotel (Talón-Ballestero et al., 2022)

The future of dynamic pricing in the hospitality industry is being shaped by rapid advances in artificial intelligence (AI), machine learning, cloud computing, big data analytics, and integrated property technologies. Traditional revenue management systems relied primarily on historical booking patterns and manual pricing decisions. Contemporary revenue management, however, has evolved into an intelligent decision-support ecosystem capable of analysing vast volumes of structured and unstructured data in real time. This transformation enables hotels to move beyond reactive pricing strategies toward predictive and prescriptive revenue optimization. At the same time, the growing integration between revenue management, accounting information systems, and customer relationship management is redefining how hospitality organisations evaluate profitability, operational efficiency, and long-term financial sustainability. Future developments in dynamic pricing are therefore expected to enhance not only revenue optimisation but also strategic financial planning and organisational decision-making.

ARTIFICIAL INTELLIGENCE AND MACHINE LEARNING

Artificial intelligence and machine learning are transforming revenue management by enabling pricing decisions that continuously learn from changing market conditions. Modern Revenue Management Systems (RMS) analyse historical reservations, booking pace, cancellation behaviour, competitor pricing, local events, weather conditions, customer preferences, and macroeconomic indicators to recommend optimal room prices(Gao, 2025; Mohammed & Denizci Guillet, 2026). Unlike traditional rule-based pricing systems, AI-powered algorithms continuously improve forecasting accuracy through adaptive learning, allowing hotels to respond more effectively to fluctuations in demand.

Machine learning also supports anomaly detection by identifying unusual booking patterns or sudden market disruptions that may require immediate pricing adjustments. As AI technologies continue to evolve, hotels are expected to adopt increasingly autonomous pricing systems capable of recommending or implementing pricing decisions with minimal human intervention while maintaining managerial oversight and governance.

PERSONALIZED PRICING

The growing availability of customer data has accelerated the shift toward personalised pricing strategies. Rather than offering identical prices to all customers, hotels increasingly tailor pricing according to customer profiles, booking behaviour, loyalty status, travel purpose, purchase history, and willingness to pay (Talón-Ballestero et al., 2022b).Personalised pricing enables organisations to improve customer value while simultaneously increasing revenue opportunities.

However, personalised pricing also introduces important ethical and regulatory considerations(Cohen et al., 2025). Excessive price discrimination or lack of pricing transparency may negatively influence customer perceptions of fairness and trust. Consequently, future pricing systems must balance commercial optimisation with responsible pricing practices, ensuring transparency, fairness, data privacy, and compliance with applicable consumer protection regulations (Qi et al., 2024).

TOTAL REVENUE MANAGEMENT

The scope of revenue management is expanding beyond guestrooms toward a comprehensive Total Revenue Management (TRM) approach(Tuomi et al., 2026). Instead of optimising room revenue alone, hotels increasingly integrate pricing decisions across multiple revenue-generating departments, including restaurants, banquets, spa services, meetings and events, parking, recreation, and ancillary guest services. This integrated approach enables hospitality organisations to maximise the overall profitability of each guest rather than focusing exclusively on Average Daily Rate (ADR) or Revenue per Available Room (RevPAR). Consequently, performance measurement is gradually shifting toward broader financial indicators such as Total Revenue per Available Room (TRevPAR), Gross Operating Profit per Available Room (GOPPAR), and customer lifetime value. Such integration also strengthens collaboration between revenue management, finance, sales, and operations, allowing strategic decisions to be based on enterprise-wide financial performance rather than departmental outcomes.

REAL-TIME DECISION MAKING

Real-time pricing represents one of the most significant developments in hospitality revenue management. Advances in cloud computing, Internet of Things (IoT) technologies, and system integration allow pricing decisions to be updated almost instantaneously in response to changes in market conditions. Integrated Property Management Systems (PMS), Central Reservation Systems (CRS), Channel Managers, and Revenue Management Systems (RMS) continuously exchange operational and financial information, enabling hotels to adjust room rates dynamically as demand changes throughout the booking cycle. Real-time analytics also improve forecasting accuracy, inventory allocation, budgeting, and financial planning by providing management with immediate access to operational performance indicators. As hospitality organisations continue their digital transformation, real-time decision support is expected to become a standard component of strategic revenue management rather than a competitive advantage available only to large hotel chains.

SUSTAINABILITY

Sustainability is emerging as an important consideration within contemporary pricing strategies (Vrionis & Varelas, 2026). Increasingly, travellers consider environmental responsibility, energy efficiency, and sustainable business practices when selecting accommodation providers. Hotels are therefore integrating sustainability objectives into broader revenue management decisions by encouraging environmentally responsible consumption patterns, reducing operational waste, and optimising resource utilisation.

Dynamic pricing can contribute to sustainability by influencing demand distribution across different periods, thereby reducing pressure during peak occupancy while improving resource utilisation during low-demand periods (de Bastos, 2023). In addition, improved forecasting accuracy helps minimise unnecessary operational costs associated with staffing, utilities, food production, and inventory management. Future revenue management strategies are therefore expected to balance financial performance with environmental and social sustainability objectives, supporting the hospitality industry's transition toward more responsible business practices.

ILLUSTRATIVE INDUSTRY CASE: AI-DRIVEN DYNAMIC PRICING AT MARRIOTT INTERNATIONAL

An illustrative example of contemporary dynamic pricing can be observed in Marriott International, one of the world's largest hospitality companies. Marriott has invested extensively in digital transformation by integrating sophisticated revenue management technologies with property management systems, customer relationship management platforms, and loyalty programme data to support data-driven pricing decisions. Rather than relying solely on historical occupancy patterns, the company's revenue management process incorporates multiple variables, including booking pace, competitor pricing, seasonal demand, local events, customer segmentation, distribution channels, and market trends to recommend optimal room rates across its global portfolio.

From an accounting perspective, AI-supported pricing influences several financial reporting processes. Variable room rates generated through dynamic pricing require accurate transaction price determination for revenue recognition under IFRS 15 and ASC 606 (*Revenue Recognition*, n.d.). Advance bookings, promotional discounts, room upgrades, cancellations, and loyalty programme redemptions must all be reflected appropriately within accounting records to ensure compliance with financial reporting standards. Furthermore, reservations received through different distribution channels generate varying commission expenses and contribution margins, requiring management accounting systems to evaluate channel profitability rather than gross revenue alone.

The integration of revenue management systems with accounting information systems also enhances financial planning and performance evaluation. Pricing decisions influence key financial indicators such as Average Daily Rate (ADR), Revenue per Available Room (RevPAR), Gross Operating Profit per Available Room (GOPPAR), deferred revenue balances, and customer loyalty liabilities. Consequently, revenue optimisation decisions increasingly require collaboration between revenue managers, finance professionals, and operational managers to ensure that pricing strategies improve not only revenue generation but also long-term profitability and financial sustainability.

The Marriott example demonstrates that contemporary dynamic pricing extends far beyond operational revenue optimisation. It represents an integrated managerial process in which artificial intelligence, accounting information systems, financial reporting, and strategic decision-making operate collectively to enhance organisational performance. As hospitality organisations continue adopting AI-enabled revenue management technologies, similar integrated approaches are expected to become standard industry practice, reinforcing the strategic relationship between pricing decisions and financial management.

CONCLUSION

Dynamic pricing is neither a passing trend nor a purely technical revenue management tool. Together, they have transformed the modern business strategy, particularly in the hotel industry. It is a fundamental restructuring of the relationship between supply, demand and price. Rather than relying on fixed pricing structures, firms are now using real-time data, forecasting models, customer and competition insights to maximise profitability. This chapter debates for an integrated approach to dynamic pricing that not only focuses on revenue optimization, but at the same time focuses on contribution margins, displacement cost or customer loyalty. The logic of dynamic pricing lies in the economic principles of demand, scarcity, and most importantly, willingness to pay (Choi et al., 2023).

Successful revenue management requires more than algorithmic pricing, more important if this is in hospitality industry. It demands strategic market segmentation, technological integration, ethical sensitivity and Customer relationship management. The way forward requires close working relation between revenue management and accounting and sales functions, which in current scenario is undergoing a lot of changes and most of the companies are encouraging this amalgamation. It requires investments in robust system which are integrated to the Property management systems (PMS) to allow seamless data flows from pricing systems to accounting systems. As digital technologies. Artificial Intelligence and consumer data analytics continue to evolve; dynamic pricing will become increasingly intelligent and personalised (Fresno-Aranda et al., 2025; Ma et al., 2024).

The organisations need to balance profitability with fair pricing, keeping in mind the long-term customer trust (Alderighi et al., 2022). The future of Revenue management lies not only with short-term revenue gain, but in creating value for customers through informed pricing and keeping in mind the sustainability goals.

REFERENCES

Abrate, G., & Viglia, G. (2016). Strategic and tactical price decisions in hotel revenue management. *Tourism Management, 55*, 123–132. DOI: 10.1016/j.tourman.2016.02.006

Alderighi, M., Nava, C. R., Calabrese, M., Christille, J. M., & Salvemini, C. B. (2022). Consumer perception of price fairness and dynamic pricing: Evidence from Booking.com. *Journal of Business Research, 145*, 769–783. DOI: 10.1016/j.jbusres.2022.03.017

Alrawadieh, Z., Alrawadieh, Z., & Cetin, G. (2021). Digital transformation and revenue management: Evidence from the hotel industry. *Tourism Economics, 27*(2), 328–345. DOI: 10.1177/1354816620901928

Altin, M. (2017). A taxonomy of hotel revenue management implementation strategies. *Journal of Revenue and Pricing Management, 16*(3), 246–264. DOI: 10.1057/s41272-017-0077-1

Altin, M., Schwartz, Z., & Uysal, M. (2017). "Where you do it" matters: The impact of hotels' revenue-management implementation strategies on performance. *International Journal of Hospitality Management, 67*, 46–52. DOI: 10.1016/j.ijhm.2017.08.001

Anshori, M. Y., Herlambang, T., & Abu Yaziz, M. F. (2025). Optimizing occupancy of hospitality sector using Support Vector Regression and Genetic Algorithm. *Journal of Revenue and Pricing Management 2025 25:3, 25*(3), 243–249. DOI: 10.1057/s41272-025-00539-4

Anshori, M. Y., Katias, P., Herlambang, T., Meutia, N. S., Othman, Z. B., & Azmi, M. S. (2025). Predicting hotel revenue using gradient boosting regression and support vector regression: a comparative analysis. *Journal of Revenue and Pricing Management 2025 25:3, 25*(3), 274–283. DOI: 10.1057/s41272-025-00557-2

Applying IFRS: Disclosure of accounting policy information | EY - Global. (n.d.). Retrieved September 3, 2026, from https://www.ey.com/en_gl/technical/ifrs-technical-resources/applying-ifrs-disclosure-of-accounting-policy-information

Bandalouski, A. M., Egorova, N. G., Kovalyov, M. Y., Pesch, E., & Tarim, S. A. (2021). Dynamic pricing with demand disaggregation for hotel revenue management. *Journal of Heuristics 2021 27:5, 27*(5), 869–885. DOI: 10.1007/s10732-021-09480-2

Choi, S., Song, M., & Jing, L. (2023). Let your algorithm shine: The impact of algorithmic cues on consumer perceptions of price discrimination. *Tourism Management, 99*, 104792. Advance online publication. DOI: 10.1016/j.tourman.2023.104792

Cohen, M. C., Miao, S., & Wang, Y. (2025). Dynamic Pricing with Fairness Constraints. *Operations Research, 73*(6), 3027–3043. DOI: 10.1287/opre.2023.0123

de Bastos, B. P. (2023). Contribution of hotels' revenue management for supply chain sustainability. *Journal of Revenue and Pricing Management, 22*(4), 294–305. DOI: 10.1057/s41272-022-00380-z

Dimitrova, T. (2025). Certain highlights on the major changes in the uniform system of accounts for the lodging industry 12th revised edition. *Economics and Computer Science, 11*(2), 13–18. https://eknigibg.net/ojs/index.php/ecs/article/view/28

El Haddad, R., Hallak, R., & Assaker, G. (2015). Price fairness perceptions and hotel customers' behavioral intentions. *Journal of Vacation Marketing, 21*(3), 262–276. DOI: 10.1177/1356766715573651

Fresno-Aranda, R., Fernandez, P., Gamez-Diaz, A., Duran, A., & Ruiz-Cortes, A. (2025). Pricing4APIs: A rigorous model for RESTful API pricings. *Computer Standards & Interfaces, 91*, 103878. Advance online publication. DOI: 10.1016/j.csi.2024.103878

Gao, J. (2025). Optimizing hotel revenue management through dynamic pricing algorithms and data analysis. *Journal of Computational Methods in Sciences and Engineering, 25*(2), 1200–1209. DOI: 10.1177/14727978241298467

Guizzardi, A., Ballestra, L. V., & D'Innocenzo, E. (2022). Hotel dynamic pricing, stochastic demand and covid-19. *Annals of Tourism Research, 97*, 103495. DOI: 10.1016/j.annals.2022.103495 PMID: 36311899

Ha, H. Y. (2026). When rewards buffer service failures: The role of residual value in loyalty programs. *Journal of Hospitality and Tourism Management, 68*, 101530. DOI: 10.1016/j.jhtm.2026.101530

Haynes, N., & Egan, D. (2023). Transient price setting in the era of automated systems: the 'hands-on' hotel general manager lives on! *Journal of Revenue and Pricing Management 2023 23:1, 23*(1), 28–38. DOI: 10.1057/s41272-023-00447-5

How to optimize your loyalty program through data and technology: PwC. (n.d.). Retrieved September 2, 2026, from https://www.pwc.com/us/en/services/audit-assurance/risk-modeling-services/loyalty-programs.html

IFRS - IFRS 15 Revenue from Contracts with Customers. (n.d.). Retrieved September 2, 2026, from https://www.ifrs.org/issued-standards/list-of-standards/ifrs-15-revenue-from-contracts-with-customers/

Indian Accounting Standard (Ind AS) 115 | Companies Act Integrated Ready Reckoner|Companies Act 2013|CAIRR. (n.d.). Retrieved September 2, 2026, from https://ca2013.com/indian-accounting-standard-ind-115-2/

Kimes, S. E. (2016). The evolution of hotel revenue management. *Journal of Revenue and Pricing Management, 15*(3–4), 247–251. DOI: 10.1057/rpm.2016.27

Kumari, V. P., & Raj, S. A. (2025). Optimizing revenue and pricing for UPI transactions using AI-based dynamic pricing models. *Journal of Revenue and Pricing Management 2025 25:4, 25*(4), 395–408. DOI: 10.1057/s41272-025-00561-6

Lentz, M., Berezan, O., & Raab, C. (2022). Uncovering the relationship between revenue management and hotel loyalty programs. *Journal of Revenue and Pricing Management, 21*(3), 306–320. DOI: 10.1057/s41272-021-00331-0

Lima Santos, L., Gomes, C., Malheiros, C., Crespo, C., & Bento, C. (2024). Factors Influencing Hotel Revenue Management in Times of Crisis: Towards Financial Sustainability. *International Journal of Financial Studies 2024, Vol. 12, Page 112, 12*(4), 112. DOI: 10.3390/ijfs12040112

Ma, H., Zhang, H., Tian, D., Yue, D., & Hancke, G. P. (2024). Optimal demand response based dynamic pricing strategy via Multi-Agent Federated Twin Delayed Deep Deterministic policy gradient algorithm. *Engineering Applications of Artificial Intelligence, 133*, 108012. Advance online publication. DOI: 10.1016/j.engappai.2024.108012

Mohammed, I., & Denizci Guillet, B. (2026). Stakeholder perspectives on integrating explainable artificial intelligence into hotel revenue management system. *Tourism Economics, 32*(4), 804–824. DOI: 10.1177/13548166251382289

Moula, H. S., Yaghoubyan, S. H., Malekhosseini, R., & Bagherifard, K. (2024). Customer type discovery in hotel revenue management: A data mining approach. *Journal of Revenue and Pricing Management, 23*(3), 238–248. DOI: 10.1057/s41272-024-00474-w

Qi, R., Jin, D., Chen, H., Mou, X., & Ali, F. (2024). Strategic-level perceived fairness of hotel dynamic pricing: the role of cues and the asymmetric moderating effect of inflation attribution. *Journal of Revenue and Pricing Management 2024 23:3, 23*(3), 249–261. DOI: 10.1057/s41272-024-00479-5

Revenue Recognition. (n.d.). Retrieved September 2, 2026, from https://fasb.org/projects/recently-completed-projects/revenue-recognition-summary?utm_source=chatgpt.com

Schwartz, Z., Altin, M., & Singal, M. (2017). Performance measures for strategic revenue management: RevPAR versus GOPPAR ra. *Journal of Revenue and Pricing Management, 16*(4), 357–375. DOI: 10.1057/rpm.2016.23

Talón-Ballestero, P., Nieto-García, M., & González-Serrano, L. (2022). The wheel of dynamic pricing: Towards open pricing and one to one pricing in hotel revenue management. *International Journal of Hospitality Management, 102*, 103184. DOI: 10.1016/j.ijhm.2022.103184

Tuomi, A., Ashton, M., & Ivanov, S. (2026). Dynamic price differentiation in restaurant revenue management. *International Journal of Revenue Management, 16*(5), 10080199. Advance online publication. DOI: 10.1504/IJRM.2026.10080199

Uniform System of Accounts for the Lodging Industry | HFTP. (n.d.). Retrieved September 2, 2026, from https://usali.hftp.org/

Vrionis, I. A., & Varelas, S. (2026). Implementing Sustainable Habits in Dynamic Pricing Through Revenue Management Strategies in the Hotel Industry—A Literature Review. *Springer Proceedings in Business and Economics*, 761–768. https://doi.org/DOI: 10.1007/978-3-032-12968-0_83/SAVE-RESEARCH

Wamsler, J., Natter, M., & Algesheimer, R. (2022). Transitioning to dynamic prices: Should pricing authority remain with the company or be delegated to the service employees instead? *Journal of Business Research, 139*, 1476–1488. DOI: 10.1016/j.jbusres.2021.10.067

Yeoman, I. (2025). Expanding the frontiers of revenue and pricing management. *Journal of Revenue and Pricing Management, 24*(6), 503–505. DOI: 10.1057/s41272-025-00563-4

Chapter 8
Profit-Driven Pricing: Bridging Accounting and Revenue Strategy

Siriyama Kanthi Herath
http://orcid.org/0000-0002-6443-9739
Clark Atlanta University, USA

ABSTRACT

This chapter proposes a profit-driven pricing framework that integrates managerial accounting with revenue management in the hospitality industry. Traditional metrics such as occupancy, ADR, and RevPAR emphasize revenue performance but overlook rising labor costs, distribution commissions, and customer acquisition expenses. As a result, revenue growth no longer guarantees profitability. Building on contribution margin analysis, break-even logic, and flow-through measurement, the chapter introduces profit-based metrics including Net Revenue per Available Room (NRevPAR), Gross Operating Profit per Available Room (GOPPAR), and Profit per Available Room (ProPAR). Through applied models and displacement analysis, it demonstrates how distribution strategy, ancillary revenue, and cost behavior influence true financial performance and concludes with a practical framework for implementation.

1. INTRODUCTION

Hotel room pricing has traditionally been grounded in revenue management principles, in which quality is emphasized over quantity, and the business is centered on short-term revenue management (Kimes, 1989; Talluri & Van Ryzin, 2004). Performance measurement models, revenue management models, and incentive schemes have always been centered on metrics like occupancy, Average Daily Rate,

DOI: 10.4018/979-8-3373-9479-4.ch008

and Revenue Per Available Room (Hayes & Miller, 2011). These metrics are still relevant. Yet they are only relevant insofar as they are based on an implicit assumption that an increase in revenues automatically translates into an increase in profits (Horngren et al., 2015). This assumption is no longer valid in the contemporary hospitality environment.

The labor market, energy costs, distribution costs, and competition have profoundly changed the fundamental relationship between revenues and costs (Eyster & deRoos, 2011). Hotels now operate in conditions where incremental revenue gains are often matched, or even surpassed, by incremental cost increases (Horngren et al., 2015). In this context, focusing solely on revenue growth can weaken profitability, distort strategic decisions, and mask the true economic value of demand (Hayes & Miller, 2011).

At the same time, accounting in hospitality enterprises has traditionally been a retroactive function, focused on financial statement preparation, variance analysis, and cost management after revenue management decisions have been made (Jagels, 2010). This temporal and conceptual disconnection between revenue management decisions and accounting insights has led to a lack of organizational integration of financial information for strategic decision-making (Eyster & deRoos, 2011). Revenue managers price demand without accounting insight into cost behavior, and accountants report results without any input into revenue management decisions.

This chapter proposes that these simultaneous approaches need to be integrated into a single profit-driven pricing paradigm. By incorporating managerial accounting ideas directly into revenue management practice, the hospitality industry can shift from revenue growth to value creation (Kaplan & Cooper, 1998; Horngren et al., 2015). This chapter sees profit-driven pricing as a strategic development that combines pricing with contribution margin reasoning, flow-through thinking, and financial viability.

Despite the extensive literature on revenue management and hospitality accounting, these two areas have traditionally developed separately rather than in an integrated manner. Revenue management literature has mainly concentrated on demand forecasting and price optimization. Managerial accounting literature has concentrated on cost control and reporting. Revenue management has developed in conjunction with digital distribution systems and e-tourism technology (Gonzalez-Serrano & Talon-Ballestero, 2022). As argued by Ivanov & Zhechev (2012), relatively little research has attempted to integrate cost information into price decisions in the context of the hospitality industry. This chapter addresses this gap by proposing a conceptual framework that integrates managerial accounting logic with revenue management decision-making to support profit-driven pricing strategies.

The aim of this chapter is threefold. First, it integrates revenue management and managerial accounting literature to provide a common conceptual basis (Talluri & Van Ryzin, 2004; Horngren et al., 2015). Second, it proposes profit-driven performance measures such as Net RevPAR (NRevPAR), Gross Operating Profit per Available Room (GOPPAR), and Profit per Available Room (ProPAR) as more effective decision-making tools in cost-intensive environments (Hayes & Miller, 2011; Eyster & deRoos, 2011). Third, it offers practical frameworks and managerial insights for hospitality managers, asset managers, and researchers.

The rest of the chapter is organized as follows. The next section discusses the history of revenue management and its inadequacies when practiced independently of accounting insights. The following sections cover managerial accounting ideas pertinent to pricing, an integrated profit-driven framework, performance metrics, technology enablement, ethics, and future research streams.

This chapter contributes to the body of knowledge in hospitality management by offering a conceptual framework that combines the concepts of managerial accounting with revenue management decision-making. While this chapter does not offer a technically focused revenue management optimization model, it does offer a managerially focused model that emphasizes the role of cost structures, distribution economics, and contribution margin analysis in pricing decisions.

2. THE EVOLUTION OF REVENUE MANAGEMENT AND ITS STRUCTURAL LIMITATIONS

Revenue management was developed in the latter part of the twentieth century as a reaction to the specific economic properties of service sectors, especially airlines and hotels (Kimes, 1989; Talluri & Van Ryzin, 2004). The service sectors have some defining properties, such as fixed capacity, perishable products, high fixed costs, and variability of demand over time (Kimes, 1989). The first revenue management systems were developed to react to these properties by maximizing the allocation of fixed capacity to different customers paying different amounts (Talluri & Van Ryzin, 2004).

In its earliest incarnation, commonly referred to as yield management, the practice was purely focused on inventory (Kimes, 1989). Hotels aimed to preserve high-paying demand by limiting cut-rate inventory during peak periods and driving demand through lower rates during off-peak periods. The decisions were based on historical booking curves, length of stay controls, and forecasted occupancies. Success was largely measured in terms of improvements in hotel occupancies and average daily rates (Hayes & Miller, 2011).

Revenue management evolved into a more analytical and strategic process (Kimes, 1989; Kimes, 2011; Talluri & Van Ryzin, 2004). Dynamic pricing tools, real-time forecasting techniques, and competitive intelligence in rates helped hotels make more informed decisions in terms of pricing. This second phase of revenue management, or Revenue Management 2.0, was all about maximizing revenues from all possible sources (Cross et al., 2009). RevPAR was a popular tool because it allowed hoteliers to measure their room rates and occupancies comparably (Hayes & Miller, 2011).

However, despite the technological improvements, the fundamentals of revenue management have remained the same (Talluri & Van Ryzin, 2004). The success of pricing strategies was still measured based on their ability to generate room revenues, without necessarily considering the cost of revenues (Horngren et al., 2015). Distribution commissions, marketing, labor, and service costs remain fixed or external variables, and not variables that can be manipulated via channel management and pricing strategies (Ivanov & Zhechev, 2012).

That loss of focus became even more pronounced when the industry shifted into a period of diminishing margins. With the development of online travel agencies, the markets were expanded, but the commission costs also became very high (Ivanov & Zhechev, 2012). At the same time, higher labor expenses, higher regulatory expenses, and erratic energy markets further decreased operating margins (Eyster & deRoos, 2011). In the same context, it is important to note that incremental revenue growth does not necessarily imply higher profitability (Horngren et al., 2015).

The conventional revenue management systems could not handle the complexities (Talluri & Van Ryzin, 2004). RevPAR is an important tool that could be used as an effective measure of revenue management performance. However, it does not offer any scope for assessing revenue profitability (Hayes & Miller, 2011). Two hotels that perform equally well on RevPAR could have completely different profitability outcomes based on their respective cost structures and revenue management strategies (Eyster & deRoos, 2011). Revenue management strategies based on RevPAR could be counterproductive and might lead to strategies that enhance revenues while damaging the long-term financial health of the hotels.

This misalignment was also reflected in the division between the conventional revenue management and accounting systems (Jagels, 2010). Forecasts of demand were traditionally developed without taking into consideration the cost factors. Pricing outcomes were also not examined using the contribution margin analysis (Horngren et al., 2015). This division of labor between revenue management and accounting indicated that revenue management was essentially focused on efforts that could enhance demand. On the other hand, the accounting function was also examined in a way that was constrained to influence pricing outcomes retroactively.

This led to the emergence of literature that highlighted the misalignment between the two and emphasized the need for an integrated approach to performance measurement (Cross et al., 2009; Hayes & Miller, 2011). Revenue management research has also extended beyond the hotel industry and has included the camping and outdoor sector (Grande & Haynes, 2025). Contemporary literature emphasizes the need to consider the cost factors while developing revenue management strategies (Gupta & Lehmann, 2003). However, the extent of the same is quite variable within the sector.

The limitations of traditional revenue management practices make it essential to construct a new conceptual framework. Traditional revenue optimization models are largely geared towards the maximization of revenues through dynamic pricing and demand forecasting (Talluri & Van Ryzin, 2004). Although these models have proven successful in managing the allocation of resources among different groups of customers, these models generally treat the cost aspect as a standalone entity. On the other hand, the profit-oriented model discussed in the chapter of this dissertation stands apart in the way managerial accounting disciplines, such as contribution margin, acquisition costs of customers, and departmental structures of costs are factored into the assessment of the effectiveness of pricing strategies in terms of profits as well as revenues. The profit-oriented pricing strategy is a simple solution for dealing with these problems by integrating accounting knowledge into the pricing strategy (Horngren et al., 2015). Instead of considering cost as a given in the pricing strategy, the framework views cost behavior as a variable input in the decision-making process. The following section will identify the managerial accounting principles that are the basis of the integrated strategy.

3. FOUNDATIONS OF MANAGERIAL ACCOUNTING FOR PRICING DECISIONS

Managerial accounting introduces the system of analysis required to be used to assess the financial implications of decisions that bring about revenue (Horngren et al., 2015). In contrast to financial accounting, managerial accounting is concerned with internal decision-making, cost behavior, and performance analysis (Kaplan & Cooper, 1998). These are the characteristics of managerial accounting that make it a useful model for application in pricing decisions in the hospitality industry, which is characterized by high fixed costs and variable prices that adjust according to demand levels (Jagels, 2010).

Managerial accounting is founded on the difference between fixed costs and variable costs (Horngren et al., 2015). Fixed costs consist of property taxes, insurance, and lease payments. They remain constant and do not vary with occupancy in the short term. Variable costs comprise housekeeping, laundry, guest supplies, utilities, and distribution commissions, which directly depend on the level of demand and the nature of the customer (Jagels, 2010). This difference may be pivotal for the actual profitability of additional revenue.

Break-even analysis also introduces the time factor in pricing decisions (Horngren et al., 2015). Fixed costs are allocated within an accounting period, and changes in pricing are made daily, and in some cases, hourly. When managers understand their current position relative to the break-even point, they can make more sound decisions. A loss-making business can be justified if it results in increased profitability after passing the break-even point. When operating below the break-even point, the contribution margin must be maintained even at lower occupancy levels (Jagels, 2010).

The integration of break-even logic into revenue management systems represents an evolution from market-based pricing. Instead of asking how much business can be secured at any given price, the manager whose concern is profit wants to know if that business will get the property closer to achieving its financial goals (Horngren et al., 2015).

The understanding of step costs' trends also enables managers to realize when costs might increase disproportionately and therefore increase price floors before margins are adversely affected (Kaplan & Cooper, 1998).

Another aspect that underlies profit-driven pricing in the hotel industry is break-even analysis. While contribution margin analysis controls the viability of pricing decisions, break-even analysis controls the minimum viability required to meet fixed operating costs (Horngren et al., 2015). At the smallest operating unit in any hotel facility, the smallest unit of performance can be expressed in terms of rooms sold or occupied, or revenue expressed in terms of rooms available. Identifying the break-even point enables hotel managers to control how much business must be secured before additional revenue goes into profit instead of covering fixed costs like service costs, management costs, and base salaries (Jagels, 2010).

From the accounting point of view, the break-even point is the total fixed expenses divided by the contribution margin per unit (Horngren et al., 2015). From the pricing point of view, the equation highlights the danger of the discount pricing strategy during the low season. While the ADR reduction may result in higher occupancy levels, the contribution margin may be lower. Consequently, the number of rooms required to break even may be much higher. This is the reason why hotels may report high occupancy levels and yet have poor operating profits. Volume measures in a market with high variable and acquisition costs cannot be a reliable indicator of performance (Hayes & Miller, 2011).

It demands much more coordination between the revenue management function, the accounting function, and the operations function. All aspects of the hotel are important areas that provide valuable information that may be the basis of an informed performance appraisal (Eyster & deRoos, 2011). It demands the development of integrated information systems that can capture costs at the reservation level and the departmental levels (Hayes & Miller, 2011). Without the development of these systems, profit measures may easily turn out to be historical reporting vehicles instead of decision-support vehicles.

Profit measures redefine the concept of success in the present-day hospitality business environment. They are the quantitative measures necessary to evaluate the effectiveness of pricing strategies in the present-day hotel industry marked by increasing expenses, distribution complexities, and increasing pressures on profit margins (Eyster & deRoos, 2011). In the following sections, profit metrics are the basis for further analysis in terms of customer acquisition cost, channel economics, and displacement.

While the last section identified the principles on which profit-oriented decisions are made, the following section will discuss how these principles are used to measure the performance of a hospitality business through profit-based measures such as NRevPAR, GOPPAR, and ProPAR, which can be used to assess the financial impact of pricing strategies.

4. PROFIT-BASED PERFORMANCE METRICS IN HOSPITALITY

The limitation of the above revenue management metrics is best illustrated when the evaluation of performance is decoupled from the cost structure (Hayes & Miller, 2011). The performance metrics of occupancy rates, average daily rates (ADR), and revenue per available room (RevPAR) were originally developed in a context in which the labor market was relatively stable, the cost of utilities could be forecasted, and the complexity of the distribution channel was negligible. Within such a context, the maximization of room revenues would be a reasonable surrogate for the maximization of profits (Kimes, 1989). However, as the stability of the cost structure and the cost of customer acquisition have diminished, the above metrics have increasingly become poor surrogates for the actual performance of hotel operations (Horngren et al., 2015).

RevPAR is the most widely accepted performance metric in the hotel industry (Hayes & Miller, 2011). RevPAR emerged as a performance metric combining occupancy and ADR to evaluate room revenue efficiency, particularly in capacity-constrained environments (Kimes, 1989). It aggregates the metrics of occupancy rates and ADR into a single measure, allowing managers to compare revenue performance across time periods and competing properties. While widely accepted as a performance metric, RevPAR remains primarily a revenue management metric because it evaluates revenue performance without considering the cost structure associated with generating that revenue (Kimes, 1989; Horngren et al., 2015). It treats all revenues equally without regard to the distribution channel through which the revenue is earned or the variable costs of servicing the revenue (Ivanov & Zhechev, 2012). Consequently, two hotels that report the same performance on the RevPAR metric may report significantly different profitability outcomes depending on the composition of the respective revenue streams (Eyster & deRoos, 2011).

The inherent limitation of the above metric has led to the development of profit-based performance metrics that attempt to integrate the insights of accounting into the field of revenue management (Hayes & Miller, 2011). Among the most widely accepted of these metrics are Net Revenue per Available Room (NRevPAR), Gross Operating Profit per Available Room (GOPPAR), and Profit per Available Room (ProPAR) (Eyster & deRoos, 2011). These steps are a movement towards increasingly combining pricing intelligence and financial results, and managerial emphasis is no longer on revenue volume but on sustainable creation of value (Kaplan & Cooper, 1998).

Net Revenue per Available Room (NRevPAR) is a variation of the traditional RevPAR metric, where the cost of distribution and customer acquisition is subtracted from total room revenue, and the outcome is divided by the number of available rooms (Ivanov & Zhechev, 2012). NRevPAR has emerged in both academic and practitioner discussions to adjust RevPAR for distribution costs. These deductions may normally include commissions of online travel agencies, commissions of global distribution systems, transaction fees and deductions on redeeming loyalty programs. With the introduction of such costs, NRevPAR demonstrates the true economic effectiveness of the distribution strategy of a hotel.

On a managerial level, NRevPAR forms a standardized tool of analysis between the revenue management and accounting functions (Hayes & Miller, 2011). This metric reduces organizational silos and aligns pricing decisions with overall financial goals.

Gross Operating Profit per Available Room (GOPPAR) further extends the performance analysis from the rooms division to the entire property by factoring in the operating expenses of all other hotel departments (Eyster & deRoos, 2011). GOPPAR is derived by dividing the gross operating profit by the total number of available rooms, thus accounting for the net impact of revenue and expense management at the hotel level. Unlike RevPAR and NRevPAR, which are essentially room revenue metrics, GOPPAR accounts for the operational viability of food and beverage operations, spa operations, administrative, and support departments (HFTP, 2014).

In terms of ownership and asset management, GOPPAR is a superior metric for financial performance (Eyster & deRoos, 2011). Consequently, GOPPAR has become a more crucial metric for investors, lenders, and asset managers who are more interested in long-term profitability than short-term revenue maximization.

For example, in practice, there are many hotel organizations and asset management organizations that utilize profit-oriented performance measurement metrics such as GOPPAR to evaluate the operational performance of the hotels they own. Asset management organizations tend to utilize the hotel GOPPAR to evaluate the operational efficiency and cost management of the hotels they own, especially when the hotels they own operate in markets with different labor costs and structures. In the same way, revenue management organizations have started utilizing net revenue management metrics that consider the cost of the distribution structure when evaluating the performance of the hotels they own.

Profit per Available Room (ProPAR) is an even more precise metric of financial performance, which specifically focuses on profit after deducting variable and fixed operating expenses, without including non-operating items such as depreciation, interest, and taxes (Horngren et al., 2015). ProPAR definitions vary in practice but generally refer to net operating profit per available room before financing and tax effects. ProPAR is a way of translating financial statements into an operationally relevant metric that can be tracked alongside other revenue metrics daily.

The strategic relevance of ProPAR is its ability to affect managerial attitudes. When revenue managers are measured using ProPAR instead of RevPAR, their key performance indicators will automatically change to focus on profit margins, channel management, and demand quality (Kaplan & Cooper, 1998).

As shown in Figure 1, this chapter introduces a pricing framework driven by profits, which illustrates how gross room revenue is progressively evaluated by accounting filters to assess the true profitability of each room booking. Gross room revenue is poured into the top of the funnel, followed by subtractions for acquisition and distribution expenses to arrive at net room revenue. Variable operating expenses are then subtracted to arrive at contribution margin, which then contributes to gross operating profit (Horngren et al., 2015).

NRevPAR, GOPPAR, and ProPAR collectively represent a paradigm shift in hospitality performance measurement (Eyster & deRoos, 2011). The profit measures are not substitutes for traditional measures but rather offer perspective and complement traditional measures.

The shift to profit-sensitive indicators has serious organizational consequences (Hayes & Miller, 2011). It requires a far more coordinated strategy in terms of revenue management, accounting, and operations (Eyster & deRoos, 2011).

Success in the current hospitality business environment is also redefined by profit metrics. They provide the quantitative foundation which is required to determine the effectiveness of pricing strategy in an environment of rising costs, distribution complexity, and profit margin issues (Horngren et al., 2015).

Although the profit-based measures may improve the "visibility of performance," the true significance of these measures may be grasped when the economics of the distribution channels are analyzed. The next section will discuss the role of the distribution channels in relation to net revenue and profit in the modern hotel operation.

5. DISTRIBUTION COSTS, CUSTOMER ACQUISITION, AND NET REVENUE LOGIC

In the modern hotel management field, the knowledge of the costs of distribution and the dynamics of customer acquisition is of primary importance when it comes to the application of profit-driven pricing (Ivanov & Zhechev, 2012; Hayes & Miller, 2011). Hotels are no longer dependent on direct business; a significant percentage of their business is being generated through online travel agencies (OTAs), global distribution systems (GDS), and meta-search engines (Guillet & Mohammed, 2015). Although these channels are a gateway to the market for hotels, they are associated with excessive costs, which affect profitability (Ivanov & Zhechev, 2012). While revenue managers were once concerned about the gross room revenue to the point of ignoring the net value of the actual reservation, the importance of Net Revenue per Available Room (NRevPAR) now calls for the consideration of all acquisition costs (Hayes & Miller, 2011).

Customer acquisition cost (CAC) not only includes the commission charged by online travel agencies (OTAs) but also encompasses marketing expenses, loyalty redemption expenses, and transaction expenses (Gupta & Lehmann, 2003). Customer acquisition costs in hospitality have increased due to the growing importance of online distribution intermediaries and digital marketing channels (Guillet & Mohammed, 2015; Ivanov & Zhechev, 2012). This indicates the rising importance of the distribution strategy as a determinant of net profitability. While pricing decisions are being made, one cannot afford to look at ADR alone; instead, there is a need to look at the net revenue after all acquisition costs have been taken care of (Horngren et al., 2015). A hotel may have a high ADR but an expensive distribution strategy. However, net profitability may be lower compared to a hotel with a lower ADR and a lower corporate booking strategy (Ivanov & Zhechev, 2012).

Segment-level analysis can also be employed to further reinforce this assessment. Different segments of the market, such as corporate contracts, leisure transient customers, groups, and online travel agency customers, may have different profiles of contribution margin. Corporate customers may have stable demand but at contracted rates, while leisure customers may have higher ancillary revenue opportunities. OTA customers may have high occupancy but low margins due to commissions. By analyzing contribution margins at a segment level, revenue managers can identify which segments are most profitable to sell to.

Table 1 shows a comparison between two hypothetical distribution scenarios for a 100-room boutique hotel. In Scenario A, an OTA booking is made for \$200 with a 20% commission. In Scenario B, a direct booking is made for \$175 with minimal transaction costs. The table calculates the net revenue, variable cost per occupied room (CPOR), and profit contribution in total.

Table 1. Profit Comparison of Distribution Scenario

Component	Scenario A (OTA)	Scenario B (Direct)
Gross Room Rate (ADR)	$200	$175
Distribution Commission / Fee	$40	$5
Net Room Revenue	$160	$170
Variable Cost per Occupied Room	$30	$30
Contribution Margin per Room	$130	$140

As presented in Table 1, the ADR for the OTA booking scenario is higher than the ADR for the direct booking scenario. However, the profit for the direct booking scenario is $10 higher. This emphasizes the importance of accounting knowledge in revenue management (Horngren et al., 2015). Revenue managers may consider net profit contribution instead of revenue to maximize profit contribution (Hayes & Miller, 2011).

Revenue managers may consider the pricing flexibility of the distribution channels. For instance, when the commission rates are high, revenue managers may need to consider a higher ADR to maximize contribution margin. However, considering a higher ADR may be a problem in terms of market competition (Talluri & Van Ryzin, 2004). Nevertheless, the advantage of the low-cost booking channel is the improved adaptability of the pricing in terms of discounts without compromising profitability (Ivanov & Zhechev, 2012).

Scenario analysis is a powerful tool for evaluating the fiscal impact of the strategies of the distribution channels (Horngren et al., 2015). Revenue managers may evaluate the net profitability of the different distribution channels by using different strategies for each distribution channel. Revenue managers may apply the managerial accounting knowledge discussed in Section 3 to evaluate the actual profit potential of the different distribution channels and the different booking channels (Jagels, 2010).

Moreover, the emergence of meta-search engines and pricing algorithms requires hotels to monitor their CAC and net contribution on a real-time basis (Guillet & Mohammed, 2015). This is because meta-search engines can change their display and pricing based on the commission rates offered by the hotels. As such, hotels need to have flexible pricing structures that are not only sensitive to market demand but also to the cost of each marketing channel. Otherwise, hotels will end up with "profitless volume" (Hayes & Miller, 2011).

Displacement analysis and the maximization of ancillary revenue can also be based on the intersection of distribution strategy, cost of acquisition, and net revenue logic (Talluri & Van Ryzin, 2004). The information on the actual profit that the segment and revenue-generating channel have realized will allow the revenue managers to decide wisely on what bookings to take, reject, and combine in a manner that will benefit high-margin consumption (Horngren et al., 2015). These concerns, which will be discussed in more detail in Section 6, are the use of the profit-driven pricing model.

Altogether, Section 5 demonstrates the importance of the distribution cost analysis and CAC awareness integration concerning the modern revenue management reality. Net revenue logic enables revenue managers to appropriately assess the true economic worth of each booking, channel strategy optimization, and profitability in a dynamic and costly setting (Ivanov & Zhechev, 2012). It is critical for this implementation of displacement analysis, TrevPAR optimization, and other sophisticated profit-based models that will be discussed in the subsequent sections.

Whereas, Section 5 discussed the financial consequences of distribution channels and customer acquisition cost, the following discussion expands this logic to the allocation of inventory. One of the areas that accounting insight and revenue management overlap is displacement analysis.

6. DISPLACEMENT ANALYSIS: THE ACCOUNTING-REVENUE NEXUS

Displacement analysis is the crossroads of revenue management insight and accounting acumen (Kimes, 1989; Talluri & Van Ryzin, 2004). It occurs when the demand for hotels exceeds the supply. In this case, the revenue managers are required to evaluate the net profitability of accepting lower-rated groups compared to the profitability of the higher-rated transients. This involves the calculation of the revenue and variable cost of the two alternatives. It also involves the evaluation of the revenue opportunities (Horngren et al., 2015).

6.1 Displacement Logic and Formula

The general formula for displacement analysis compares the net profit potential of a group with the profit potential of the displaced transients (Talluri & Van Ryzin, 2004; Yao et al., 2012):

Group Net Contribution must exceed Displaced Transient Net Contribution.

Where:

- Group Net Contribution = Sum (Room Revenue + F&B Revenue + Other Revenue) – Sum (Variable Costs + Commissions)
- Displaced Transient Net Contribution = (Rooms Displaced × Net ADR) – Variable Costs

The accountant's job is to correctly identify and measure all cost and margin items, enabling the revenue manager to make decisions based on more than just the top-line revenue figure, as Jagels (2010) states.

6.2 Multi-Departmental Displacement Analysis

Hotels are a series of interrelated profit centers (HFTP, 2014). A group may produce substantial F&B sales but also provide lower room rates than transient business. A comparative displacement analysis is shown in Table 2, using 100 room nights, to illustrate the significance of departmental contribution margins.

Table 2. Comparative Displacement Analysis (100 Room Nights)

Revenue Stream	**Transient (Displaced)**	**Group (Proposed)**	**Margin %**
Room Revenue	$25,000 ($250 ADR)	$18,000 ($180 ADR)	80%
F&B Revenue	$2,000	$10,000	30%
Other (Spa/Misc.)	$1,000	$500	50%
Gross Revenue	**$28,000**	**$28,500**	—
Net Profit (GOP)	**$21,100**	**$17,650**	—

In this example, the group sales increase gross revenue by $500 but also decreases net profit by $3,450, reflecting the reduced margins in F&B sales compared to room sales. Without this combined view, the revenue manager may choose the group sale solely based on total volume, thereby decreasing the overall profitability of the property (Kaplan & Cooper, 1998).

6.3 Practical Applications

Displacement analysis helps to make decisions about accepting guaranteed low-rate groups during peak periods, focusing on high-margin transient business, and designing mixed-use packages (Kimes, 1989). The application of this analysis will make sure that room inventory is assigned in such a way that it can maximize contribution margin, and not the occupancy (Horngren et al., 2015). In addition, the CAC and variable cost analysis can be combined and, therefore, help the managers identify which channels or segments generate higher flow-through (Hayes & Miller, 2011).

6.4 Decision-Making Workflow

Displacement analysis should include the following steps in its decision-making workflow:

1. Calculation of Group Net Contribution that includes all the associated variable costs and ancillary revenues.
2. Approximation of lost temporary revenue and contribution margin.
3. Comparison of net contributions to determine the option that will make the best profit.
4. Assumptions, margins, and sensitivity analysis documentation are to be clear so that the financial statements can be prepared for post-event analysis (Horngren et al., 2015).

When displacement analysis is integrated into the revenue workflow, the hotels can switch their decision-making approach to profit-centric instead of occupancy-centric (Talluri & Van Ryzin, 2004). The theme presented in the workflow is the integration of managerial accounting, operating knowledge, and revenue management strategies in a bid to optimize financial performance.

Aside from profitability in inventory allocation, profitability also has a bearing on the revenue structure of the hotel. This is discussed in the following sections.

7. ANCILLARY REVENUE AND TOTAL REVENUE PERFORMANCE (TREVPAR)

Revenue management strategy toward 2026 increasingly emphasizes the importance of the total revenue performance, which goes beyond the rooms division (Noone et al., 2011). TrevPAR or Total Revenue per Available Room refers to the sum of money received by all hotel activities, including rooms division, food and beverage (F&B), spa, events, and ancillary services divided by the total number of available rooms (Hayes & Miller, 2011). Though traditional RevPAR analysis provides useful data on the efficiency of the room revenue, it does not consider the large revenue that is produced by the ancillary departments that does not contribute significantly to overall profitability (Eyster & deRoos, 2011). By combining TrevPAR analysis with cost accounting analysis, hotel managers can separate high-volume, low-margin activities from revenue streams that make a meaningful contribution to net profits (Kaplan & Cooper, 1998).

7.1 Activity-Based Contribution Margin Analysis

Activity-based costing (ABC) plays a pivotal role in determining the actual profitability of ancillary businesses (Kaplan & Cooper, 1998). Every revenue-generating department has variable costs such as labor, materials, and supplies, which need to be properly assigned to determine contribution margins (Horngren et al., 2015). For instance, F&B may record high revenue but lower margins because of high costs of goods and service labor, while the rooms department typically records higher margins because the variable cost per occupied room is lower and more stable (HFTP, 2014). By determining contribution margins for every department, revenue managers can identify and focus on marketing promotions, packages, and pricing initiatives that drive the greatest flow-through to gross operating profit (GOP) (Hayes & Miller, 2011).

Table 3. Departmental Contribution Margins

Department	Incremental Revenue	Variable Cost	Contribution Margin	Margin %
Rooms	$100	$20	$80	80%
F&B	$100	$70	$30	30%
Spa	$100	$60	$40	40%

As shown in Table 3, not all revenue is equal. While a sales manager may be interested in landing a big F&B-scale gala, the accounting rationale indicates that $1,000 in room revenue drives more than twice the profit of $1,000 in F&B revenue (Kaplan & Cooper, 1998). This difference is at the heart of Total Revenue Management (TRevPAR): optimizing the business mix to drive the greatest total property contribution (Noone et al., 2011).

7.2 Integrating TrevPAR and GOPPAR

Although TrevPAR is a measure of total revenue efficiency, it does not take into consideration operating expenses. GOPPAR takes into consideration both revenue and operating expenses, giving a more realistic view of profitability (Eyster & deRoos, 2011). A more holistic view is to take a volume measure in TrevPAR and a measure of success in GOPPAR.

7.3 Risk of Ancillary Over-Reliance

According to HVS (2025), many hotels have increasingly relied on ancillary revenue streams to support profitability. However, these services often require significant labor input, which can offset the financial benefits of additional revenue. Over-reliance on low-margin or labor-intensive ancillary services can therefore negatively impact profitability (Eyster & deRoos, 2011).

While the analysis of ancillary revenues emphasizes the need to understand departmental contribution margins, the effectiveness of profit-driven pricing in business is increasingly subject to the dictates of technology integration and managerial governance. The next section of this paper will explore how data systems, ethics, and emerging trends facilitate the implementation of profit-oriented pricing strategies in business.

8. Technology Enablement, Ethics, and Future Research

How can profit-based pricing be taken from conceptual harmonization to a true technological and ethical infrastructure for supporting advanced real-time decision-making?

8.1 Technology Enablement and Data Integration

The distinction between revenue management and accounting in hospitality businesses has traditionally been supported by a fragmented approach to technology infrastructure. Digital transformation is increasingly enabling integrated decision-making across hospitality organizations (Chakraborty, 2025). Property Management Systems (PMS), Enterprise Resource Planning systems (ERP), and Revenue Management Systems (RMS) traditionally function as separate systems with little real-time communication between them (Hayes & Miller, 2011). As discussed in Section 4, traditional revenue management metrics such as RevPAR focus on revenue performance while ignoring the cost structures associated with generating that revenue. This limitation highlights the need for integrated decision-support systems that combine revenue management data with accounting information. Historically, revenue management decisions were often taken in isolation from cost considerations, while accounting focused on financial reporting after pricing decisions had already been implemented (Eyster & deRoos, 2011).

The current ability of Business Intelligence (BI) systems, cloud computing environments, and Application Programming Interfaces (APIs) to integrate operational, financial, and market data into a unified decision support environment provides a potential solution for hospitality businesses (Davenport & Harris, 2007; Mariani, 2020). Additionally, artificial intelligence, business intelligence systems, and big data analytics play a significant role in influencing the decision-making of hospitality organizations (Mariani et al., 2018). Today, technology is helping hospitality businesses incorporate dynamic cost elements, like labor costs, energy costs, or distribution costs, directly into revenue optimization models (Eyster & deRoos, 2011; Kimes, 2011; Gao, 2025). Therefore, revenue management systems can establish price floors informed by cost structures and contribution margin analysis, rather than relying solely on forecasted demand (Talluri & Van Ryzin, 2004).

The integration of such systems enables the automation of profit-based performance measures such as Net Revenue per Available Room (NRevPAR), Gross Operating Profit per Available Room (GOPPAR), and Profit per Available Room (ProPAR). Moreover, the integration of cost intelligence into the price calculation model enables hotels to avoid the acceptance of bookings where the revenue generated does not contribute sufficiently to the overall profit, a situation commonly known as "profitless volume" in the context of revenue management in the hospitality industry (Hayes & Miller, 2011).

8.2 Ethical Issues in Profit-Driven Pricing

While profit-driven pricing strategies provide tremendous benefits in terms of economic gains, the increasing use of algorithm-based price management and real-time price optimization creates several ethical concerns. Pricing in service industries is highly correlated with the perception of price fairness by consumers (Xia, Monroe, & Cox, 2004). Hotels and other service providers in the industry are likely to face situations where prices are increased significantly during periods of high demand such as during events, natural disasters, and other public emergencies. Such price increases are perceived as unfair and exploitative by consumers.

In this context, research on price fairness has shown that consumers consider the price of a service as well as the perceived justification for the price in relation to the specific situations and experiences (Bolton, Warlop, & Alba, 2003). In the context of the hospitality industry, such situations are more likely to result in damage to the reputation of the brands and the relationship with the customers over time (Kotler & Keller, 2016).

Thus, ethical pricing strategies involve transparent communication, realistic surge limits, and consideration of the long-term relationship between the hotel and the guests. For instance, loyalty program members may expect some level of "perceived value" or "preferential treatment" instead of "margin extraction." From a strategic management viewpoint, achieving a sustainable level of profitability demands that the organization be able to draw upon a form of "trust equity" in the brand.

8.3 Future Research Directions: Toward Customer Lifetime Value (CLV)

While the focus of this chapter has been on operational profit measures such as ProPAR and TrevPAR, it is suggested as a direction for future research to consider how Customer Lifetime Value (CLV) might be incorporated into profit-based pricing models in the hospitality industry. Customer Lifetime Value is defined as the net present value of the long-run profit contribution of a customer relationship (Gupta & Lehmann, 2003). If profit-based pricing models are able to take account of Customer Lifetime Value, then pricing decisions will consider the long-run profit contribution of repeat customers.

For example, it might make business sense to accept a reduced contribution margin for a guest in one stay if they are expected to provide significant repeat business in the long term. In addition, profit maximization strategies might reduce long-run profit if they discourage repeat business, even if the contribution margin for the stay is high.

Another area of research is how profit-based pricing models can consider Customer Lifetime Value and how it might be achieved in the future. In addition, with the rise of the sharing economy and peer-to-peer rentals, there are now diverse types of business models in the hospitality industry with different cost structures and less fixed capital requirements (Guttentag, 2015). How profit-based pricing models might apply in such business models is another area for future research.

While technology integration increases the analytical power of revenue systems and accounting systems, the effectiveness of a profit-driven pricing strategy still depends on managerial reasoning and organizational mindset. While even the most advanced systems cannot compensate for biases in managerial decisions, which are based on occupancy instead of profitability, the next section of this paper will examine the potential of avoiding the so-called "occupancy trap."

9. MANAGERIAL REASONING: ESCAPING THE OCCUPANCY TRAP

Although the industry has largely adopted sophisticated revenue management systems, many hotel managers are still impacted by a psychological phenomenon that favors high occupancy (Hayes & Miller, 2011). The "Occupancy Trap" is the situation where property management thinks that the higher the occupancy levels, the better the performance of the property, without considering the profitability implications of variable costs, distribution channels, and the concept of marginal profitability (Horngren et al., 2015). This type of thinking will lead to volume-based decisions. As a result of this thinking, the net profit will deteriorate despite the higher RevPAR and ADR (Eyster & deRoos, 2011).

9.1 Understanding the Cost Structure

The most important aspect of avoiding the "Occupancy Trap" is the understanding of the various types of costs, which include the fixed costs and the variable costs. The fixed costs include debt repayment, property taxes, insurance, and salaries, among others. The variable costs include the guest services, housekeeping labor costs, laundry, and utilities. The variable costs vary directly with the occupancy levels. Overtime and promotional expenses will be semi-variable costs that contain an element of both fixed and variable costs. The interrelation of the costs is important since it is essential in the allocation of the costs and the pricing of the property to avoid the "profitless occupancy" (Kaplan & Cooper, 1998).

Another key factor to be considered while determining pricing strategies, in terms of their effect upon costs, is labor market pressure. Hospitality markets are often characterized by rising labor costs, and this has been a major factor in determining the costs of operations, particularly in areas such as housekeeping, food and beverage service, and other services. Labor costs are often one of the largest variable or semi-variable costs of operations for hotels, and therefore, rising labor costs would have a direct effect upon the cost per occupied room (CPOR) and, therefore, upon the minimum required profit for operations. Therefore, while determining profit-driven pricing strategies, it would be necessary to consider demand fluctuations, as well as regional labor market conditions, which may affect costs for operations.

9.2 Break-Even Pricing and Marginal Contribution

Break-even analysis is a critical tool in determining the minimum price at which occupancy will positively impact profitability (Horngren et al., 2015). Contribution margin per occupied room can be calculated as:

CM = Price (ADR) – Variable Cost per Occupied Room (CPOR)

Jagels (2010) advises against setting rates below CPOR, as this will drive occupancy at the expense of cash flow and overall profitability. Even with high occupancy, there may be insufficient positive net contribution if acquisition expenses and variable costs exceed revenue (Hayes & Miller, 2011).

9.3 Occupancy vs. Flow-Through

The relationship between occupancy, total revenue, variable cost, and net contribution for a hypothetical hotel example is shown in Table 4. This shows that a lower occupancy strategy can result in higher net profit when marginal costs are considered (Horngren et al., 2015).

Table 4. Pricing Sensitivity and Flow-Through

ADR	Occupancy	Total Revenue	Total Variable Cost	Net Contribution
$150	60%	$9,000	$2,700	$6,300
$100	90%	$9,000	$4,050	$4,950

Table 4 above shows that while total revenue is the same for both pricing strategies, the 60% occupancy pricing strategy results in $1,350 more net contribution than the 90% occupancy pricing strategy. This example highlights the need to focus on flow-through and contribution margin, rather than simply focusing on occupancy (Eyster & deRoos, 2011).

9.4 Decision Framework for Profit-Driven Occupancy

A decision framework can be used by hotel managers to avoid the occupancy trap as follows:

1. Compute CPOR: Estimate accurate variable costs per room, including department-specific allocations (Jagels, 2010).
2. Analyze Acquisition Costs: Analyze commission and marketing expenses related to each booking source (Ivanov & Zhechev, 2012).
3. Estimate Net Contribution: Use the formula CM = ADR – CPOR – CAC for each possible booking (Horngren et al., 2015).
4. Prioritize High-Margin Bookings: Accept bookings that generate the highest net contribution, regardless of occupancy (Hayes & Miller, 2011).
5. Monitor Flow-Through: Regularly track the percentage of incremental revenue reaching the profit line to ensure the success of pricing initiatives (Eyster & deRoos, 2011).

9.5 Managerial Implications

To escape the occupancy trap, there must be a cultural change in the property, which focuses on profit rather than volume (Kaplan & Cooper, 1998). Incentives must be designed to encourage efforts that contribute to net profit, not total room sales or occupancy (Hayes & Miller, 2011). By utilizing accounting knowledge within revenue management strategies, managers can make operational decisions that are consistent with long-term financial viability within the property (Horngren et al., 2015). The profit-oriented approach is also beneficial for enhancing the effectiveness of displacement analysis, TrevPAR optimization, as well as channel management strategies that are presented within Sections 5-7 of this chapter (Talluri & Van Ryzin, 2004).

In conclusion, it is evident from this section that occupancy is not necessarily a measure of profitability. By utilizing knowledge of cost as well as concepts of contribution margin, managers can break free from the occupancy trap by utilizing strategies that are focused on profitable growth (Eyster & deRoos, 2011).

The managerial principles presented in this section demonstrate the practical implications of accounting logic in pricing strategies. In the following section, concepts that are presented within this chapter will be utilized to develop a framework that is applicable within the hospitality industry of 2026.

10. Proposed Profitability Framework

The application of knowledge in the field of accounting and revenue management represents a paradigm shift for hotels operating in the tough 2026 scenario (Hayes & Miller, 2011; Santos et al., 2026). The findings from the theoretical framework and case studies reveal that the application of the traditional metrics of RevPAR and ADR is not adequate for property performance analysis (Kimes, 1989). Building on the limitations of RevPAR discussed in Section 4, the conceptual framework presented in this chapter emphasizes profit-based metrics such as NRevPAR, GOPPAR, and ProPAR as more comprehensive indicators of hotel performance. These metrics incorporate cost structures and operational efficiency, enabling hotel managers to evaluate the financial impact of pricing decisions more accurately (Eyster & deRoos, 2011).

10.1 Net RevPAR as a Leading Indicator

NRevPAR, which is net room revenue after distribution costs, loyalty overrides, and transaction fees, divided by total available rooms, highlights the impact of channel management on profitability (Ivanov & Zhechev, 2012). By applying NRevPAR as a primary performance metric, hotel executives will be able to concentrate revenue management efforts on net financial results rather than gross occupancy or ADR

(Hayes & Miller, 2011). This will ensure that marketing and distribution plans have a positive impact on flow-through and the bottom line (Horngren et al., 2015).

10.2 GOPPAR and ProPAR for Holistic Analysis

GOPPAR takes the analysis to all operating departments and considers variable and fixed costs that are controllable (Eyster & deRoos, 2011). ProPAR also makes the analysis more accurate, as the net profit per available room is measured and provides a clear picture of the effectiveness of pricing and cost management plans (Horngren et al., 2015). The combination of these two measures helps hotel management with pinpointing areas in which incremental revenue may not always help to increase net profit and modify operational or pricing strategies (Kaplan & Cooper, 1998).

10.3 Integration of Managerial Accounting and Revenue Strategy

In the results, it is evident that any hotel that has embraced an integrated accounting and revenue strategy approach will always outperform others regarding profitability (Talluri & Van Ryzin, 2004). This approach conquers the issue of profitless volume, biases based on occupancy, and financial survival in the long-term (Hayes & Miller, 2011).

10.4 Key Takeaways

1. Profit Growth: In high-cost operating environments, there is no guarantee that ADR or occupancy growth will result in higher net profit because of higher variable costs or commission costs (Horngren et al., 2015).
2. Channel strategy also matters: Direct sales are more lucrative than OTA sales with big commissions, and analysis of net revenues is required (Ivanov & Zhechev, 2012).
3. Additional Revenue Required: TrevPAR reports total revenue, but this can be misleading due to the presence of revenue in low-profit departments that can hurt overall profitability unless their contribution margin is considered (Noone et al., 2011).
4. Analysis of group sales and transient sales is crucial: Analyzing group and transient sales is critical to ensure maximum net contribution in inventory distribution, as opposed to volume (Kimes, 1989).

10.5 Implementing the Profitability Framework

To pursue the profitability framework, the 2026 profitability framework suggests the following step-by-step process.

Profitability Framework: Step-by-Step Implementation

1. **Compute CPOR and Departmental Variable Costs**

Accurate calculation of variable cost per occupied room (CPOR) and variable costs is critical to ensure a strong cost base (Jagels, 2010).

2. **Calculate Customer Acquisition Costs (CAC)**

Calculating acquisition costs for each sales channel is crucial to ensure accurate costs for OTA commissions, GDS costs, and marketing expenses (Ivanov & Zhechev, 2012).

3. **Compute Net Contribution per Sale**

Evaluate each booking using NRevPAR and contribution margin analysis to measure true economic value (Horngren et al., 2015).

4. **Conduct Displacement Analysis**

Compare the profitability of group versus transient business to ensure inventory allocation maximizes net contribution (Talluri & Van Ryzin, 2004).

5. **Track Total Revenue and Departmental Margins**

Monitor TrevPAR alongside departmental contribution margins to optimize ancillary revenue performance (Kaplan & Cooper, 1998).

6. **Integrate Property-Level Profit Metrics**

Use GOPPAR and ProPAR to assess overall operational profitability and align pricing decisions with financial performance objectives (Eyster & deRoos, 2011).

10.6 Strategic Implications

The 2026 profitability model will enable property managers to make productive decisions that will balance the revenue and expenditure. Hotels can also be profitable even in a tough marketplace environment by focusing on net contribution and flow-through, rather than on occupancy or revenue, reducing the effect of rising labor and utility expenses, and allocating the marketing budget fully based on possible ROI (Horngren et al., 2015). In addition, the model allows the accounting and revenue managers to work harmoniously based on the utilization of the same set of tools and measures, which are aligned with real-time performance (Hayes & Miller, 2011).

Overall, the results of this chapter allow the conclusion that profit-driven pricing is not reactive but proactive (Talluri & Van Ryzin, 2004). Hotels with the capacity to utilize skills in accounting, management of costs, and revenue are in a better position to handle the profitability issues in 2026 (Eyster & deRoos, 2011).

While the conceptual framework provides an insight into the applicability of profit-oriented metrics in decision-making, its true worth could be realized by applying it in the context of real-life operational scenarios. The following learning case study aims to illustrate the applicability of the principles of NRevPAR, contribution margin analysis, and displacement analysis in day-to-day revenue management decisions.

11. LEARNING CASE STUDY: THE WEEKEND SCENARIO

The following simplified scenario illustrates how accounting insight can influence pricing decisions. To illustrate the principles of profit-oriented pricing, NRevPAR, and displacement analysis, the following case study presents a hypothetical scenario of a 100-room boutique hotel (Hayes & Miller, 2011). The purpose is to show how combining accounting insight with revenue management improves operational decisions (Horngren et al., 2015).

This example illustrates that gross ADR alone does not determine profitability. Instead, the net contribution generated by each booking provides a more meaningful measure of financial performance (Jagels, 2010).

Flow-through measures how much incremental revenue translates into profit (Eyster & deRoos, 2011).

This reinforces that profit-driven pricing evaluates each booking's total financial effect, including ancillary income and long-term value (Gupta & Lehmann, 2003).

The case study shows how profit-oriented thinking can influence individual decision-making in pricing strategies. However, for this thinking to take hold at the organizational level, it is necessary to redefine the performance indicators for organizational success. Thus, the next section will focus on the evolution of hospitality key performance indicators in relation to profit-oriented thinking.

12. EVOLUTIONARY KPIs: DEFINING SUCCESS IN 2026

As discussed earlier in Section 4, traditional metrics such as Occupancy, ADR, and RevPAR measure revenue efficiency but provide limited insight into profitability. Consequently, recent developments in hospitality performance measurement emphasize profit-based indicators that integrate managerial accounting insights with revenue management practices (Hayes & Miller, 2011; Eyster & deRoos, 2011). Accordingly, the development in the field of measuring performance in the hospitality industry has shifted more focus on profitability measures through the integration of managerial accounting and revenue management (Talluri & Van Ryzin, 2004).

12.1 GOPPAR vs. RevPAR

RevPAR measures rooms revenue efficiency only (Kimes, 1989). GOPPAR incorporates departmental operating expenses, providing a broader picture of financial performance (Eyster & deRoos, 2011).

12.2 NRevPAR and ProPAR

NRevPAR reflects true channel efficiency by accounting for OTA commissions, GDS fees, and loyalty costs (Ivanov & Zhechev, 2012).

ProPAR measures net operating profit per available room after all operating expenses (Horngren et al., 2015).

12.3 Strategic Application

Modern KPIs enable managers to:

1. Align incentives with profit instead of volume (Kaplan & Cooper, 1998).
2. Optimize distribution using NRevPAR insights (Ivanov & Zhechev, 2012).
3. Prioritize high-margin departments via TrevGOP (Eyster & deRoos, 2011).
4. Focus on long-term customer value through CLV (Gupta & Lehmann, 2003).

12.4 Data-Driven Management

The evolution of KPIs requires integrated technology, real-time dashboards, and unified analytics (Hayes & Miller, 2011). Profit-based metrics allow proactive management of both revenue growth and cost control (Horngren et al., 2015).

However, it should be understood that in order to move forward to profit-oriented KPIs, there also needs to be proper data consistency between all systems of operation. Hence, it is understood that without proper data flow, it is impossible to act on these profit-oriented KPIs in any meaningful manner. Therefore, in the next section of this discussion, it will be understood how modern technology platforms provide a unified "single source of truth."

13. Technology and the Single Source of Truth

While Section 8 discussed the conceptual role of technology in enabling profit-driven pricing, this section focuses on how integrated data systems create a "single source of truth" within hospitality organizations. Historically, data fragmentation separated accounting and revenue management (Hayes & Miller, 2011). By 2026, integrated systems increasingly eliminate this barrier by connecting operational, financial, and market data across hospitality platforms. A single source of truth ensures consistent, real-time information across departments, enabling managers to align pricing decisions with cost structures and profitability objectives (Eyster & deRoos, 2011).

13.1 Integrated Technology Stack

- PMS: Central reservation and guest data
- RMS: Demand forecasting and dynamic pricing (Talluri & Van Ryzin, 2004)
- ERP: Cost tracking for labor, utilities, and supplies (Horngren et al., 2015)
- BI Dashboards: Real-time display of NRevPAR, ProPAR, GOPPAR, and departmental margins (Hayes & Miller, 2011)

13.2 Predictive Accounting

Machine learning can anticipate cost increases (e.g., 15% rise in linen costs) and automatically adjust minimum ADR thresholds. Pricing decisions thus reflect both demand conditions and operational realities (Talluri & Van Ryzin, 2004; Horngren et al., 2015).

13.3 Benefits

- Improved accuracy
- Greater efficiency
- Real-time decision-making
- Advanced scenario modeling (Kaplan & Cooper, 1998)

13.4 Implementation Steps

1. Audit existing systems
2. Integrate PMS, RMS, and ERP
3. Establish data governance
4. Train cross-functional teams
5. Refine predictive models continuously (Hayes & Miller, 2011)

Moreover, integrated technology enables profit-oriented pricing to become operational rather than a theoretical concept (Talluri & Van Ryzin, 2004).

Technology enables more precise analysis as well as quicker decision-making; however, there are important ethical implications related to algorithms within pricing. The subsequent section will discuss how profit-oriented pricing can be achieved without compromising fairness and transparency within a business relationship.

14. ETHICAL PRICING AND LONG-TERM VALUE

Profit-focused pricing must be balanced with ethical responsibility. Aggressive dynamic pricing during high-demand periods can damage brand trust and customer loyalty (Xia et al., 2004).

Besides ethical considerations, the pricing strategies in a profit-driven model must also be compliant with the regulations and guidelines on pricing transparency and taxation. Hospitality businesses operate in a framework where resort fee practices, dynamic pricing, and customer disclosure regulations are under regulatory scrutiny. This may impact on pricing strategies and profit calculations, especially in situations where taxes, service charges, and mandatory fees must be factored in to arrive at the final customer price. Therefore, the pricing strategies in a profit-driven model must be compliant with regulations and transparent in customer communication.

14.1 Algorithmic Pricing Ethics

This could lead to an increase in price gouging. This might be profitable in the short term but could ultimately harm the Customer Lifetime Value (CLV) and increase customer churn rates (Gupta & Lehmann, 2003; Xia et al., 2004).

The manager needs to consider the price decisions using both margin and reputational risk analysis (Xia et al., 2004).

The ethical implications of the profit-driven pricing policy need to be considered in the context of the luxury hospitality environment. Customer perceptions of ethical and unfair practices will be higher. For example, the customers of luxury hotels may have low price elasticity of demand in the presence of inelastic demand. However, unfair practices could ultimately lead to negative impacts on customer loyalty and the reputation of the firm. Research on price fairness perceptions suggests that customers do not just consider the price levels but also the perceived justification of price variations (Xia et al., 2004). Therefore, it is proposed that the profit-driven pricing policy needs to be considered not just as an optimization problem but also as an aspect of customer relationship management.

14.2 Long-Term Considerations

1. Customer Retention (Gupta & Lehmann, 2003)
2. Brand Equity (Eyster & deRoos, 2011)
3. Sustainable Profitability (Horngren et al., 2015)

14.3 Practical Actions

1. Integrate CLV into pricing models (Gupta & Lehmann, 2003)
2. Set maximum surge thresholds
3. Monitor guest sentiment
4. Train teams in ethical decision-making

Thus, profitability and ethics are not mutually exclusive. Both need to be balanced to ensure success (Xia et al., 2004). After analyzing the concepts related to the operational, technological, and ethical sides of profit-driven pricing, the following section includes discussion questions that invite the reader to reflect critically on how these concepts can be applied in different scenarios related to the hospitality industry.

15. DISCUSSION QUESTIONS

The following discussion questions invite the reader to apply concepts related to profit-driven pricing in scenarios related to revenue, distribution, technology, and ethics. These questions challenge status-quo thinking and instead emphasize margin logic, evaluation, and strategy (Kaplan & Cooper, 1998; Hayes & Miller, 2011).

The above questions invite analytical reflection on the concepts and themes developed throughout the current chapter. The next section includes managerial implications that can be applied to support profit-driven pricing concepts.

16. MANAGERIAL IMPLICATIONS: PROFIT-STRATEGY CHECKLIST

Transitioning to profit-driven pricing requires cultural and structural change (Kaplan & Cooper, 1998). Key actions include:

Unified dashboards (Hayes & Miller, 2011)

1. Cross-functional pricing decisions (Talluri & Van Ryzin, 2004)
2. Margin-based incentives (Horngren et al., 2015)
3. Weekly Profit-Performance Meetings
4. Dynamic CPOR updates (Jagels, 2010)
5. Channel net-back analysis (Ivanov & Zhechev, 2012)
6. Ancillary margin monitoring (HFTP, 2014)
7. Organizational culture must shift from occupancy pride to profitability discipline (Eyster & deRoos, 2011).

Although the managerial checklist provides a list of key organizational changes needed, the transition to a profit-driven pricing approach must also include a process for implementation. The following roadmap provides a step-by-step approach to the implementation of accounting insights and revenue management practices.

The following is a key managerial implication of profit-driven pricing: the incentive system must be modified to emphasize profitability over volume. For example, revenue managers in many hotels have traditionally been assessed based on occupancy and RevPAR. For revenue managers to be assessed based on new profit-driven measures, such as NRevPAR and ProPAR, there is a need to modify their assessment systems. Managers should be evaluated based on profitability rather than volume.

However, the transition toward profit-based metrics may encounter organizational resistance, particularly from revenue managers whose performance has historically been evaluated using RevPAR or occupancy targets. Shifting toward metrics such as NRevPAR or ProPAR requires change management efforts that include staff training, revised performance incentives, and cross-functional communication between revenue management, finance, and operations teams. Without these organizational adjustments, profit-oriented metrics may remain theoretical rather than operational tools.

It should be noted that while many of the examples mentioned in this chapter assume that hotels have access to advanced revenue management systems or integrated analytics platforms, profit-driven pricing is just as relevant to smaller hotels or boutique hotels with limited technological capabilities. For instance, a boutique hotel may attempt to determine its revenue streams from various booking channels by analyzing its net revenue earned from each of those channels after deducting commission costs and calculating its variable cost per occupied room (CPOR) using data from its various departments. While hotels may not have access to advanced pricing models or systems to determine optimal prices, they may still attempt to increase profitability through profit-driven pricing by focusing on higher margin revenue streams and increasing floor prices to match current operating costs.

17. STRATEGIC IMPLEMENTATION ROADMAP

A strategic, multi-phased approach is necessary for a successful transition from a revenue-focused to a profit-focused hospitality industry (Talluri & Van Ryzin, 2004). As a guide to the organization in the effective implementation of integrated pricing strategies within 12 months, a four-phased approach is proposed as follows:

One of the most important implementation challenges facing the organization as it undertakes this transition is that of organizational resistance to change. The revenue management teams, as well as sales teams, may be resistant to change from traditional metrics such as occupancy and RevPAR, especially if these metrics have historically been tied to bonuses as well as other performance management activities. To ensure effective implementation of this strategy, it is important that management can communicate to the teams the importance of metrics such as profit-based metrics. In addition to this, training programs that can educate teams on contribution margin logic are important to ensure a smooth transition from a volume-oriented approach to a profitability-oriented approach.

17.1 Phase 1: Data Normalization (Months 1–3)

Goal: To ensure that the costs and revenues are accurately tracked at the reservation level (Jagels, 2010).

To-Do: Review the P&L statement to uncover concealed or inaccurately allocated distribution expenses (commissions, GDS fees, loyalty overrides) (Ivanov & Zhechev, 2012).

1. Set up procedures for allocating variable and fixed expenses per department (Horngren et al., 2015).
2. Determine Net ADR and NRevPAR for past periods to set up historical baselines (Hayes & Miller, 2011).

17.2 Phase 2: Integrated Technology Alignment (Months 4–6)

Goal: To integrate the PMS, RMS, and ERP systems for a common data platform (Hayes & Miller, 2011).

To-Do: Develop API interfaces between RMS and ERP systems to enable real-time cost inputs into pricing models (Talluri & Van Ryzin, 2004).

1. Verify that the RMS considers variable CPOR and acquisition costs in determining the Price Floor (Horngren et al., 2015).
2. Develop BI dashboards to monitor NRevPAR, ProPAR, and departmental contribution margins in real-time (Eyster & deRoos, 2011).

17.3 Phase 3: Incentive Re-Engineering (Months 7–9)

Goal: Align team incentives with profit, not revenue (Kaplan & Cooper, 1998).

Actions: Modify Sales and Revenue Management bonus plans to emphasize meeting target GOPPAR, not overall revenue (Eyster & deRoos, 2011).

1. Introduce departmental contribution margin goals for F&B and Spa managers (HFTP, 2014).
2. Educate staff on understanding integrated key performance indicators to inform profit-driven operational decisions (Hayes & Miller, 2011).

17.4 Phase 4: Total Revenue Optimization (Months 10–12)

Goal: Apply profit-centric strategies to all other non-room departments (Noone et al., 2011).

Actions: Apply Activity-Based Costing (ABC) analysis to meeting rooms, F&B outlets, and other ancillary services (Kaplan & Cooper, 1998).

1. Analyze high margin configurations and options for priority in marketing and dynamic pricing strategies (Horngren et al., 2015).
2. Analyze quarterly performance for better prediction models and ensure that the "Price Floor" reflects labor and utility market volatilities correctly (Talluri & Van Ryzin, 2004).

After implementation, a system of reviews must be put in place to assess whether profit-driven pricing strategies are yielding desired financial results. Regular audits of NRevPAR, GOPPAR, and departmental contribution margins can be conducted to check for discrepancies between actual results and projections. These reviews can be conducted to ensure that the pricing models are updated regularly according to market changes.

By implementing this structured approach, an organization can progress from data silos to an integrated financial mindset. This process ultimately leads to the establishment of a new industry standard where profit, not volume, defines success (Eyster & deRoos, 2011).

In addition to organizational processes, visualizing the interaction between revenue and cost data can help managers better understand how profit-driven pricing operates in practice. The next section introduces a conceptual model that illustrates this interaction.

An operational challenge that may arise while adopting profit-driven pricing is that, even after adopting profit-driven pricing strategies, revenue managers may still be using traditional performance measurement systems that are based on volume metrics such as occupancy and RevPAR. In such cases, there is every possibility that revenue managers may get conflicting information from profit metrics such as NRevPAR and contribution margin, which may advise rejecting low-margin bookings, and volume metrics such as RevPAR and occupancy, which may still be indicating volume growth for the hotel. While adopting profit-driven pricing strategies, hotels may also experience lower occupancies for a short period because the hotel is using pricing strategies that are more focused on higher-margin bookings.

18. VISUALIZING THE PROFIT ENGINE

Figure 1 presents the conceptual architecture of the proposed profit-driven pricing framework. The framework shows the way in which market demand information from revenue management systems interacts with accounting intelligence on the behavior of costs, customer acquisition costs, and contribution margins to arrive at profit-sensitive prices.

To better comprehend the link between accounting intelligence and revenue management, it is important to conceptualize the profit engine and its data flow process within the hotel (Horngren et al., 2015). This allows the reader to better understand the relationship between market inputs, cost structures, and profit goals.

Figure 1. Profit-Driven Pricing Decision Framework (Hospitality Profit Engine)

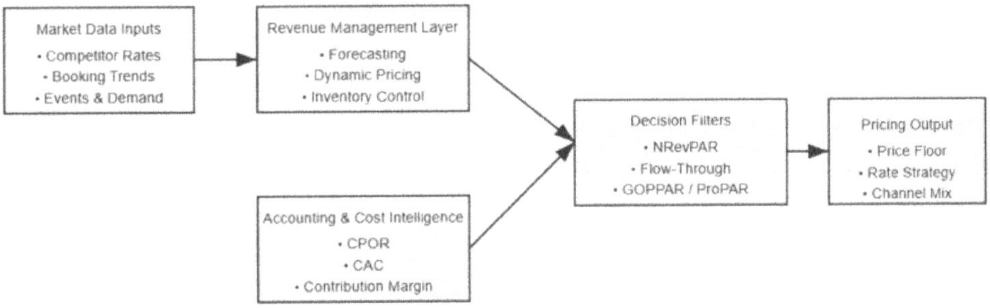

Source: Developed by the author

As a conceptual model, this illustrates the way information about market demand, as reported through the systems of revenue management, in conjunction with managerial intelligence in terms of costs of acquiring customers, variable costs of operation, and contribution margin, impacts profit-sensitive pricing decisions as indicated through metrics including NRevPAR, GOPPAR, and ProPAR.

18.1 Components of the Profit Engine

1. Market Data Inputs: This includes competitor pricing, local events, past booking trends, and projected occupancy levels (Talluri & Van Ryzin, 2004).
2. Revenue Management Layer: This uses predictive modeling to analyze demand, assign room inventory, and provide dynamic pricing strategies (Kimes, 1989).
3. Accounting and Cost Intelligence Layer: This includes CPOR, fixed and variable departmental expenses, acquisition costs, and contribution margins (Horngren et al., 2015).

4. Decision Filters: These use flow-through, NRevPAR, ProPAR, and GOPPAR to measure the net value of each booking (Hayes & Miller, 2011).
5. Actionable Pricing Output: This provides the Price Floor, suggested rate, and room inventory for each market and segment (Talluri & Van Ryzin, 2004).

18.2 Operational Implications

The Profit Engine is “a mechanism that links top-line demand with bottom-line accounting intelligence to ensure that occupancy translates into actual cash flow.” Profit Engine's visualization helps the manager identify where the “leakage” is, and that is between the Revenue Management layer and the accounting core, due to the lack of visibility into distribution costs and variable costs (Ivanov & Zhechev, 2012).

The Profit Engine is a conceptual and operational mechanism that integrates market data, cost structures, and decision filters into one system. Embracing this holistic approach, hotel managers can move from a reactive approach to pricing and into an informed and timely approach that can lead to optimal decisions in terms of net contribution and asset value (Eyster & deRoos, 2011).

The success of the Profit Engine, therefore, depends entirely on the profile of the leadership that guides it. This, in turn, requires an entire review of the skills that are required from today's hospitality leader (Hayes & Miller, 2011).

The conceptual model illustrates the operational mechanics of profit-driven pricing. To effectively manage such an approach, there is an emerging requirement for today's hospitality executive. This is addressed in the following section.

19. THE NEW HOSPITALITY EXECUTIVE

The path to 2026 is a complete paradigm shift in professional identity (Eyster & deRoos, 2011). The distinction between “Accounting Department” and “Revenue Office” is becoming obsolete (Hayes & Miller, 2011). In their place, a new single identity is emerging: the Hospitality Asset Strategist. This executive is more than a rate manager; he or she is a manager of the financial health of the property assets (Kaplan & Cooper, 1998).

19.1 From Transactional to Strategic Thinking

The Asset Strategist has a margin-based strategy instead of a volume-based strategy, as has been traditional (Horngren et al., 2015). This is a complete mind shift from past lagging indicators, such as historical ADR and occupancy, to leading profitability indicators like ProPAR and NRevPAR (Eyster & deRoos, 2011) - Table 5.

Table 5. Evolution from Revenue Manager to Asset Strategist

Traditional Revenue Manager	Hospitality Asset Strategist
Focused on "Heads in Beds" (Occupancy)	Focused on "Dollars in Bank" (Flow-through) (Hayes & Miller, 2011)
Views OTA commissions as a marketing expense	Views OTA commissions as a margin-erosion variable (Ivanov & Zhechev, 2012)
Responds to competitor rate movements	Forecasts the effects of variable CPOR on the price floor (Horngren et al., 2015)
Reports to the GM on top-line RevPAR	Collaborate with the CFO on property EBITDA (Eyster & deRoos, 2011)

19.2 The "Single Source of Truth" Mandate

The main role of the Hospitality Asset Strategist is to eliminate silos of data (Hayes & Miller, 2011). By ensuring the promotion of the integrated technology stack of (PMS + RMS + ERP), the Hospitality Asset Strategist ensures that all departments in the hotel, including Housekeeping and Sales, have a common financial reality (Talluri & Van Ryzin, 2004). It is a cross-functional role that ensures only high-margin segments are marketed, and operational costs are factored in with every dynamic price change (Horngren et al., 2015).

Pricing floors may also vary depending on the prevailing market conditions. During an economic downturn or recessionary phase, a hotel may agree to a lower contribution margin in exchange for a consistent cash inflow to meet a part of the fixed costs. On the other hand, during a boom or a supply-constrained market, a hotel may increase the price floors in line with the rising labor costs, energy costs, and distribution costs. Dynamic pricing of rooms based on the changing market conditions would therefore involve changing the price floors in line with the changing costs.

19.3 Custodian of Ethical Profitability

Lastly, the Asset Strategist is the ethical custodian of the property. The Asset Strategist understands that while algorithms will ultimately drive short-term profitability, they will also destroy long-term brand value if they are not correctly optimized (Xia et al., 2004). By adding Customer Lifetime Value to the pricing equation, the Asset Strategist ensures that the guest relationship is profitable not just for the weekend, but for many years to come (Gupta & Lehmann, 2003).

The Asset Strategist will be unable to optimize that which they cannot measure. To bring leadership theory into day-to-day application, mathematical models must be applied to strip away the illusions of the income statement and uncover the hidden net values (Kaplan & Cooper, 1998).

To bridge the gap between strategic leadership and day-to-day decision-making, effective tools must be employed. A simple framework will be discussed in the following section to measure profitability in bookings using the concept of NRevPAR.

20. PRACTICAL TOOL: THE NREVPAR & FLOW-THROUGH CALCULATOR

To apply the principles of profit-driven pricing, a manager must have a systematic approach to remove top-line illusions (Horngren et al., 2015). The NRevPAR & Flow-Through Calculator is a decision-making tool that fills the gap between the Property Management System and the General Ledger (Hayes & Miller, 2011).

20.1 Purpose and Design

The purpose of this tool is to apply a focus on Net Contribution rather than Gross ADR (Jagels, 2010). By combining inputs from marketing (commissions), distribution (fees), and operations (CPOR), a manager can measure the net cash flow associated with any given booking or distribution channel (Ivanov & Zhechev, 2012).

20.2 The Profit-Driven Pricing Worksheet (Template)

The following worksheet illustrates the necessary logic to measure the efficiency of any given revenue stream (Horngren et al., 2015).

Table 6. Profit-Driven Pricing Worksheet (Template)

Category	Input Variable	Formula / Source	Value (Example)
Revenue	Gross ADR	PMS / Booking Engine	$200.00
Costs	OTA Commission %	Contract Agreement	20%
Costs	Transaction / GDS Fee	Accounting Records	$5.00
Calculation	Total Acquisition Cost	(Gross ADR × %) + Fee	$45.00
Metric	Net ADR	Gross ADR – Acquisition Cost	$155.00
Costs	Variable CPOR	USALI (Laundry + Labor) (HFTP, 2014)	$35.00
Calculation	Net Contribution	Net ADR – CPOR	$120.00
Metric	Flow-Through %	(Net Contribution ÷ Gross ADR)	60%

20.3 Applied Case Scenario: The "Direct vs. OTA" Pivot

To demonstrate the strength of this tool, we will apply the logic of the worksheet to a classic strategic question: a 100-room hotel considering a high-volume OTA flash sale to fill a slow weekend (Hayes & Miller, 2011).

Table 7. Comparative Strategic Pivot (Direct vs. OTA Scenario)

Metric	Current State (Direct)	Proposed State (OTA)	Variance
Occupancy	50%	80%	+30%
Gross ADR	$200	$170	($30)
OTA Commission (20%)	$0	$34	+$34
Variable CPOR	$35	$35	$0
Net Contribution (Per Room)	$165	$101	($64)
Total Net Contribution	$8,250	$8,080	($170)

As shown in Table 7, the "success" of the 30% increase in occupancy from the OTA sales channel has led to a $170 loss in total net profit. This is the mathematical proof of the Occupancy Trap (Horngren et al., 2015). By focusing on volume over profit, the hotel finds itself working harder (cleaning 30 more rooms) to make less money (Eyster & deRoos, 2011).

As shown in the "Direct vs. OTA" pivot, the first step to recovery is mathematical clarity. However, to implement these findings across an entire organization, more than a single calculation is required; it requires a long-term strategy for implementation (Kaplan & Cooper, 1998).

20.4 Strategic Interpretation

1. **High Flow-Through (>70%)**: Indicates efficient sales channels. These channels should be leveraged during peak demand periods to maximize Gross Operating Profit per Available Room (GOPPAR) (Eyster & deRoos, 2011).
2. **Low Flow-Through (<50%)**: Indicates that revenue is significantly reduced by third-party distribution expenses. These channels should be used selectively, primarily for distress inventory or in situations where the marginal cost of an empty room exceeds the net contribution generated (Ivanov & Zhechev, 2012).

With the use of this calculator, the Hospitality Asset Strategist can make informed decisions in real-time to safeguard the financial and operational integrity of the asset, ensuring that every pricing move made is for the bottom line (Hayes & Miller, 2011).

Although the analytical tools give us valuable insights into the individual booking decisions, the organizational impact of the price setting in the interest of profit depends on the systematic implementation of the price strategies across the different organizational departments. This is outlined in the following section.

21. CONCLUSION: THE INTEGRATED FINANCIAL MINDSET

This chapter demonstrates that reliance on revenue-based metrics such as RevPAR can obscure the true profitability of hotel operations. As operating environments become more complex and distribution costs increase, the limitations of traditional performance indicators become increasingly apparent. The hospitality industry's continued emphasis on RevPAR, ADR, and occupancy as measures of success can mask the unintended consequences of rising customer acquisition costs, labor expenses, and volatile operating conditions (Ivanov & Zhechev, 2012; Horngren et al., 2015). Consequently, the integration of managerial accounting insights with revenue management practices is essential for achieving sustainable profitability in the hospitality industry (Hayes & Miller, 2011).

21.1 Summary of Key Takeaways

To navigate the hospitality industry in 2026, the various frameworks and tools presented in this chapter provide a guideline on how these changes will integrate:

1. Profit Over Volume: NRevPAR, ProPAR, and GOPPAR enable hotel pricing decisions based on net profitability rather than gross revenue volume (Eyster & deRoos, 2011).
2. Flow-Through as a Decision Engine: Evaluating the percentage of revenue available to the profit line enables hotel managers to make informed decisions regarding channel and segment selection (Hayes & Miller, 2011).
3. Total Revenue Optimization: Evaluating contribution margin across ancillary departments ensures that food and beverage, spa, and meeting revenues have a material impact on the bottom line (Kaplan & Cooper, 1998).
4. The Technology Nexus: A "single source of truth" that links PMS, RMS, and ERP systems enables timely cost-sensitive pricing decisions (Talluri & Van Ryzin, 2004).

5. Strategic Displacement: Careful assessment of group versus transient demand patterns optimizes inventory distribution for net contribution instead of occupancy only (Kimes, 1989).

21.2 The Emergence of the Hospitality Asset Strategist

At the center of this convergence is a new professional role: the Hospitality Asset Strategist (Eyster & deRoos, 2011). The new role transcends traditional distinctions between revenue management and accounting by uniting market knowledge and accounting knowledge (Hayes & Miller, 2011). In this new world, market knowledge must be complemented by accounting knowledge (Horngren et al., 2015).

Ultimately, accounting intelligence-driven pricing for profit is the foundation of a viable hospitality business strategy (Kaplan & Cooper, 1998). By moving from top-line metrics to net contribution to profitability, hospitality managers can make informed decisions to protect the bottom line and ensure long-term asset viability (Gupta & Lehmann, 2003). In a world characterized by rising costs and competitive challenges, closing the gap between accounting and revenue management is no longer a best practice; it is the hallmark of the future-proof hospitality executive (Talluri & Van Ryzin, 2004)

REFERENCES

Bolton, L. E., Warlop, L., & Alba, J. W. (2003). Consumer perceptions of price (un) fairness. *The Journal of Consumer Research, 29*(4), 474–491. DOI: 10.1086/346244

Chakraborty, P. P. (2025). Digital transformation in hospitality. In Thaichon, P., Dutta, P. K., Haghi, A. K., & Dutta, S. (Eds.), *Digital disruption in hospitality, AI, and emerging technologies: A roadmap to personalized experiences, enhanced operations, and revenue growth* (pp. 157–188). Emerald Publishing Limited., DOI: 10.1108/978-1-83608-796-020251009

Cross, R. G., Higbie, J. A., & Cross, Z. N. (2009). Revenue management's renaissance: A rebirth of the art and science of profitable revenue generation. *Cornell Hospitality Quarterly, 50*(1), 56–81. DOI: 10.1177/1938965508328716

Davenport, T. H., & Harris, J. G. (2007). *Competing on analytics: The new science of winning*. Harvard Business School Press.

Eyster, J. J., & deRoos, J. A. (Eds.). (2011). *The Cornell School of Hotel Administration on hospitality: Cutting edge thinking and practice*. John Wiley & Sons.

Gao, J. (2025). Optimizing hotel revenue management through dynamic pricing algorithms and data analysis. *Journal of Computational Methods in Sciences and Engineering, 25*(2), 1200–1209. DOI: 10.1177/14727978241298467

González-Serrano, L., & Talón-Ballestero, P. (2022). Revenue management and e-tourism: The past, present, and future. In Z. Xiang, M. Fuchs, U. Gretzel, & W. Höpken (Eds.), *Handbook of e-tourism* (pp. 1261–1288). Springer. https://doi.org/ DOI: 10.1007/978-3-030-48652-5_76

Grande, K., & Haynes, N. (2025). Campsite revenue management decision-making: A semi-systematic review. *Tourism and Hospitality Research, 25*(2), 387–405. DOI: 10.1177/14673584231218111

Guillet, B. D., & Mohammed, I. (2015). Revenue management research in hospitality and tourism: A critical review of current literature and suggestions for future research. *International Journal of Contemporary Hospitality Management, 27*(4), 526–560. DOI: 10.1108/IJCHM-06-2014-0295

Gupta, S., & Lehmann, D. R. (2003). Customers as assets. *Journal of Interactive Marketing, 17*(1), 9–24. DOI: 10.1002/dir.10045

Guttentag, D. (2015). Airbnb: Disruptive innovation and the rise of an informal tourism accommodation sector. *Current Issues in Tourism, 18*(12), 1192–1217. DOI: 10.1080/13683500.2013.827159

Hayes, D. K., & Miller, A. A. (2011). *Revenue management for the hospitality industry*. John Wiley & Sons.

HFTP. (2014). *Uniform system of accounts for the lodging industry* (11th ed.). https://hftp.org/usali

Horngren, C. T., Datar, S. M., & Rajan, M. V. (2015). *Cost accounting: A managerial emphasis* (15th ed.). Pearson.

HVS. (2025). *HVS global perspectives: Our 2025 outlook, https://www.hvs.com/article/10107-hvs-global-perspectives-our-2025-outlooks

Ivanov, S., & Zhechev, V. (2012). Hotel revenue management: A critical literature review. *Tourism: An International Interdisciplinary Journal, 60*(2), 175–197. https://hrcak.srce.hr/file/125946

Jagels, M. G. (2010). *Hospitality management accounting* (9th ed.). John Wiley & Sons.

Kaplan, R. S., & Cooper, R. (1998). *Cost and effect: Using integrated cost systems to drive profitability and performance*. Harvard Business School Press.

Kimes, S. E. (1989). Yield management: A tool for capacity-constrained service firms. *Journal of Operations Management, 8*(4), 348–363. DOI: 10.1016/0272-6963(89)90035-1

Kimes, S. E. (2011). The future of hotel revenue management. *Journal of Revenue and Pricing Management, 10*(1), 62–72. DOI: 10.1057/rpm.2010.47

Kotler, P., & Keller, K. L. (2016). *Marketing management* (15th ed.). Pearson.

Mariani, M. (2020). Big data and analytics in tourism and hospitality: A perspective article. *Tourism Review, 75*(1), 299–303. DOI: 10.1108/TR-06-2019-0259

Mariani, M., Baggio, R., Fuchs, M., & Höpken, W. (2018). Business intelligence and big data in hospitality and tourism: A systematic literature review. *International Journal of Contemporary Hospitality Management, 30*(12), 3514–3554. DOI: 10.1108/IJCHM-07-2017-0461

Noone, B. M., McGuire, K. A., & Rohlfs, K. V. (2011). Social media meets hotel revenue management. *Journal of Revenue and Pricing Management, 10*(4), 293–305. DOI: 10.1057/rpm.2011.12

Santos, L. L., Silva, E., Gomes, C., & Malheiros, C. (2026). Rethinking revenue management in the tourism industry's new era. *International Journal of Marketing, Communication and New Media.* https://doi.org/DOI: 10.54663/2182-9306.2026.SpecialIssueCMTH.11-24

Talluri, K. T., & Van Ryzin, G. J. (2004). *The theory and practice of revenue management.* Springer. DOI: 10.1007/b139000

Xia, L., Monroe, K. B., & Cox, J. L. (2004). The price is unfair! A conceptual framework of price fairness perceptions. *Journal of Marketing, 68*(4), 1–15. DOI: 10.1509/jmkg.68.4.1.42733

Yao, D. Q., Wang, Z., Mukhopadhyay, S., & Cong, Y. (2012). Dynamic pricing strategy for subscription-based information goods. *Journal of Revenue and Pricing Management, 11*(2), 210–224. DOI: 10.1057/rpm.2010.48

Chapter 9
Transport as Part of the Hospitality Revenue Chain in Island Destinations:
Accounting Information, Pricing, and Managerial Decision-Making Under Uncertainty

Ioannis Sitzimis
http://orcid.org/0000-0001-7479-0883
Hellenic Mediterranean University, Greece

ABSTRACT

The accessibility of island destinations is subject to the cost, time and uncertainty involved in reaching them. Transportation is part of the hospitality economy, since it contributes to what island tourism offers to guests before a reservation is made. This chapter focuses on coastal shipping and air transportation as components of the hotel revenue chain and examines the impact of transport access on demand, accommodation prices, revenue forecasts and operations. Room rates do not only depend on the product or competition, but also on total travel cost, route reliability and perceived uncertainty. We underscore how accounting and financial information act as a bridge between external changes and internal management decisions. When access improves, pricing flexibility increases, whereas limited access puts accommodation, cash flow and operational organisation under pressure. Through

DOI: 10.4018/979-8-3373-9479-4.ch009

the embedded case study, we identify how transport disruption is connected with booking signals, managerial diagnosis, price formation, operational action and revenue resilience.

1. INTRODUCTION

Transportation is both an experience for tourists and an important contributor to the overall hospitality economy in many island destinations. The relationship between transportation and tourism is easy to see as it relates to the booking process. In instances where the journey to the destination becomes more difficult or more expensive, booking rates tend to slow, cancellation rates increase, the length of stay is altered and, ultimately, revenues are affected (Prideaux, 2000; Wardana et al., 2025).

Transportation forms part of the overall destination experience, but it is not under the direct control of the hotel. In other words, hotels have no say over how many ferries run or how many flights are offered. However, these factors still determine their demand during a given period of time, their rate of bookings, the pricing levels they can sustain, and how a hotel will be organised to accommodate these arrivals. For example, if the last ferry arrives at the same time as a number of guests, and their rooms are not ready, this could increase waiting times at the front desk.

The hospitality revenue chain starts before the hotel front desk, when the customer calculates the total cost of the trip, since the cost of tickets, luggage, local transport, time and possible delays affects the final decision. If access to the hotel represents a high percentage of the available budget, then there will be a great deal of pressure on hotels to charge a lower room rate. If the journey to the hotel is easy and dependable, most likely, the market will accept higher prices (Nagle & Müller, 2018; Prideaux, 2000).

Hotel managers have experienced this through practice. A route may change from time to time. The frequency may be decreased. Fares may be increased. Extra capacity may be added during peak season. Each of these changes can affect hotel bookings. Therefore, the hotel leadership team may need to change its pricing structure, minimum length of stay, cancellation policies, or operational plan. Often, the problem may not be whether there is demand, but whether the hotel can organise itself around the arrival of this demand.

The basis for making these kinds of decisions comes down to accounting information. Financial information is not merely a record of history, as it also depicts whether the assumptions made during forecasting were realistic, whether the rate of occupancy growth is sufficient and whether pricing provides an adequate margin (Kimes, 1989). It also shows the amount of resilience a business has to withstand an unexpected change. In an island environment, this is critical, since the hotel cannot directly control transportation, but it can monitor the effects of transportation on its business as early as possible and respond appropriately before these effects result in a larger problem (Figure 1).

Figure 1. The role of transport access in the hospitality revenue chain of island destinations

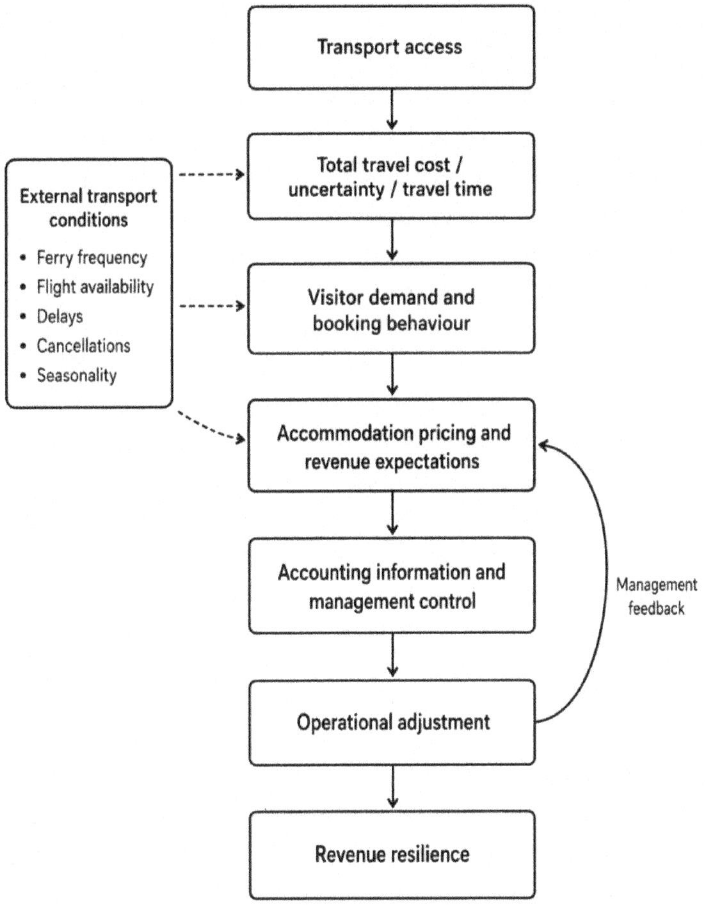

Source: Author's elaboration.

2. TRANSPORT AND TOURISM DEMAND IN ISLAND DESTINATIONS

The demand for tourism on islands can be sensitive to changes in access (Wardana et al., 2025), and changes in ferry frequency, flight availability and the cost of travel can alter the behaviour of visitors. The traveller considers not only the hotel or destination, but also how easy the trip will be, what options are available and how much time they have for the trip.

While both air and sea transport connect travellers to the island, they do not create the same type of demand (Button & Taylor, 2000; Sitzimis, 2026). Islands with frequent air service will generally have improved destination connectivity and more opportunities for short-term visits (Florido-Benítez, 2025; Forsyth, 2006), while sea transport may be more suitable for longer stays and more flexible travel planning.

Unreliable connections, cancellations or delays create greater feelings of risk for those travelling. Some people alter their travel plans altogether by travelling to different destinations. Others do not stay as long as they had originally planned or avoid times when transport is unreliable. So it is not just the number of visitors that may be reduced, but also the types of visitors who come to the area. A family with young children, for example, may choose not to visit a destination where there is uncertainty about getting back home. However, a young person with more time available may be willing to accept the same level of uncertainty.

The difference in the characteristics of visitors is very important for hotels. Visitors have different ways of booking accommodation, different lengths of stay and different levels of sensitivity to price. If short-term visitors are reduced, hotels will likely lose a portion of their weekend business. If families avoid times with uncertain travel, the types of visitors who stay at the hotel will differ. Therefore, the issue is not only about getting a specific number of arrivals to the hotel, but also about the type of guests who are coming to the area, when they are coming and how secure the reservations are.

An island's ability to be accessed easily, regularly and at an appropriate cost is also a factor in determining seasonality for the tourist industry, particularly for hotel operators. During low-demand times, there are fewer transportation options available to the destination, resulting in fewer routes and a less convenient travel experience. Additionally, destinations can appear less attractive when there are fewer transportation options. Thus, the number of arrivals to the island can be affected, but the overall operation of the hotel business can also change.

Although hotel owners may want to stay open for longer periods of time, limited connections through airlines or boats may make it difficult to justify the expenses required to remain open and operate.

3. TRANSPORTATION, TOTAL TRAVEL COST AND PERCEIVED VALUE

For travellers to island destinations, the journey to their accommodation, rather than the accommodation itself, can be a primary factor in choosing where to stay. The traveller will first consider the total cost of travel before assessing the price of lodging. This cost is more than just the fare (Button, 2010; Nagle & Müller, 2018). It includes:

- Cost of baggage
- Transfer costs to and from the port or airport
- Waiting and delays
- Costs associated with an overnight stay
- Loss of time associated with travel

Lost travel time matters to travellers. As travel time to the island increases, the perceived value of the island decreases.

Travelling to an island can also be a multiple-leg journey. For example, a traveller may have to transfer from a boat to a car or from an aircraft to a bus, and wait for or adjust to delays before reaching their accommodation. The more complex the journey is perceived to be, and/or the larger the amount of time lost, the greater the perceived cost to the traveller will be.

The perceived value of access to island accommodation is based on the cost of access relative to the expected experience. If the island is perceived as difficult to reach, uncertain or disproportionately time-consuming relative to the length of stay, the perceived value of the experience is lessened. This is especially true for short-term and weekend trips, when the relative burden of access costs is greater for the traveller.

The cost of the trip establishes a general target for the cost of accommodation. While it does not dictate room rates directly, it does determine the maximum rate that a traveller may consider acceptable for a particular room. When access is easy and reliable, there is more room in the rate range. If access is difficult or uncertain, there is much less room in that range (Nagle & Müller, 2018).

4. TRANSPORT UNCERTAINTY, CUSTOMER EXPECTATIONS AND BOOKING BEHAVIOUR

Travel-related uncertainty does not occur only on the travel day, but begins during the search and comparison period, when travellers evaluate price, accommodation and risks such as delay, cancellation, loss of time or difficulty of return (Prideaux, 2000; Silvestre et al., 2026).

Not all transport uncertainty leads to rejection of a destination. In fact, it more often leads travellers to postpone their trip. Therefore, travellers wait to see if they can travel by comparing available dates and monitoring inventory levels, while keeping alternative plans open. Demand does not go away. Rather, it is simply delayed in how it manifests itself and, therefore, becomes less predictable.

This affects how occupancy develops because reservations are not distributed evenly over time. Rather, they become concentrated closer to the date of arrival. Therefore, management has less visibility, forecasts become less reliable and bookings cannot be viewed as locked (Silvestre et al., 2026).

In this environment, flexibility has value. Guests place greater emphasis on cancellation policies, date changes and reservations without prepayment. Therefore, certainty of choice may, in fact, be more important than a small price discount. Travel uncertainty affects people differently. Those with less time available, families and those with work commitments have less tolerance for travel-related risks, whereas those who have greater flexibility with their time can more easily accommodate changes and/or delays. This also changes the demand mix.

5. TRANSPORTATION AND PRICING DECISIONS IN HOSPITALITY

Products and competition are often taken into account when determining a hospitality price. However, competitive pricing does not always have a direct relationship with the actual cost of the product. Access to the island greatly affects hospitality pricing and where customers fall along the price continuum based on that access.

The fundamental tenets of revenue management involve offering the right product to the right person, at the right time and at the right price (Kimes, 1989). On an island, the "right time" is highly correlated with the time and method by which a customer can reach the island. The more limited the access, the less likely it is that the price can increase.

Accommodation demand derives partly from travel demand (Kotler et al., 2017), and increases in total travel cost will be passed through to the accommodation industry. A hotel may choose either to decrease its accommodation price or to offer enhancements to its value-for-money proposition in order to maintain its attractiveness.

Hotel pricing decisions are based on booking trends, expected capacity and time of year. Increasing capacity on an airline flight or ferry route will contribute to an increase in expected demand; therefore, accommodation businesses may be able to take more aggressive pricing positions on the same nights as the new or expanded capacity. Conversely, when transport capacity or bookings are limited, hotels will generally take more conservative pricing positions.

Willingness to pay relates to more than just the hotel room; it is related to the whole journey (Nagle & Müller, 2018). If the guest feels that there is a large burden to reach the destination, then their willingness to pay a higher room rate will decrease, and this will also affect additional sales.

In reality, price is a tool for balancing external pressure. Since businesses cannot control transport, they can only control how they react. Thus, pricing, minimum length of stay requirements, restrictions and cancellation policies are tools for adapting and responding to these external pressures.

6. ACCOUNTING INFORMATION AND MANAGEMENT CONTROL

Pricing decisions are not only evaluated at the moment they are made, but also by seeing how they are reflected in financial results and how they perform under control measures after the fact. Accounting information is therefore one of the most important tools for a manager (Kimes, 1989).

Seasonality on the island has a significant impact. Often, the only significant period of peak demand during the year occurs over a few months. Therefore, any deviation during that short period can have a disproportionate effect on the overall season. For example, one week of lower occupancy or multiple cancellations can adversely affect the entire season.

When market conditions change, it is critical to reassess occupancy and revenue estimates. Occupancy is only used as a starting point when estimating revenues and should not be viewed as an end state. Just because there is high occupancy does not mean there is a positive revenue situation, especially if operating costs are high or inflexible.

Cash flow is critical to the organisation (Nagle & Müller, 2018). Delays, cancellations and changes in arrival dates will have an impact on incoming collections. In addition, collections can fluctuate significantly from month to month in a highly seasonal business. Therefore, tracking cash flow on a continuous basis allows for timely correction and reduced risk.

Accounting information not only reflects the company's financial performance, but also supports operational decisions, including staff planning and operational intensity by department. The link between financial information and management decisions is gaining wider importance as hotel businesses integrate ESG factors into their strategic and financial planning. Recent evidence from the Greek hotel industry shows that ESG implementation affects cost structure and stakeholder relations, reinforcing the importance of appropriate financial information for decision-making (Garefalakis et al., 2026). Cost information also affects the level of service provided. However, interpretation of indicators is necessary, since a change in an indicator may not reflect an internal problem, but rather a change in access or in the pattern of arrivals.

7. FROM ACCOUNTING INFORMATION TO MANAGEMENT DECISION

The functions of modern accounting include recording transactions and warning against potential issues. Any need for change will show in the volume of reservations, cancellations, pick-up and collections from customers. The movement of money will occur before there is a full and complete understanding of business conditions in the marketplace.

Management will be required to make decisions in an environment where it cannot be absolutely confident. Financial accounting data are often fragmented, dynamic and subject to change. Therefore, having information processed in a timely manner is very important, because it provides management with an early, though incomplete, warning of potential problems. Conversely, if information is processed too late, there may be no ability to make corrections (Broccardo et al., 2025).

The purpose of developing scenarios is not to predict future events. Scenarios provide concise methods for defining alternative courses of action. For example, if unusual events occur at the hotel, such as a decrease in guest arrivals, postponement of arrivals, or an increase in last-minute cancellations, each of these events will yield different results with respect to revenue, costs, working capital and organisational structure.

Information supports decisions when it is connected to an action lever, such as price, restrictions, shifts, supplies, service or cash priority. Each measure has a unique effect. For example, a price change is different from reducing a specific service or delaying a payment. It is imperative that management understands what can change quickly, what has an immediate effect on the business, and what may adversely affect customer experience.

Numbers do not dictate decisions, but managers do. However, when there is not enough timely and structured data to make a decision, the likelihood of making poor decisions increases. Control is not usually achievable over the transport of goods or services. Therefore, control lies in the business's response.

8. ADMINISTRATIVE LIMITS AND ORGANISATIONAL CONSEQUENCES OF TRANSPORT DEPENDENCY

Transport dependency affects the way management operates (Button, 2010; Prideaux, 2000). Access to islands is not easy. Travel to and between islands is restricted by limited schedules. Only a limited number of people can be moved from island to island at one time. The number of people who can be moved between islands changes significantly from season to season. The amount of time needed to get from one island to another can also vary significantly. On an island, some of the options normally available on the mainland can be very difficult to access.

One of the biggest administrative constraints is time itself. Changes in transportation access are quickly passed on to demand and operational levels. If management waits until all details are available before making arrangements, it can reduce the ability to control the operations of the organisation. By the time the access details are available, employees may have already been hired, supplies organised and services ordered.

Transportation constraints will also affect human resources. If an organisation has more employees than it needs due to access issues, its operating costs will increase. If an organisation has fewer employees than it needs, customer satisfaction will go down and employees will feel overworked. Suppliers and other external business partners also face similar challenges. Transportation problems do not affect visitors alone.

A management paradox therefore arises. A company is ultimately responsible for what happens, but the organisation does not control many factors that contribute to the variations. Transportation is therefore outside the organisation's immediate control. Consequently, management focuses on the output of the organisation, even though it does not always control the factors that shape those results. This does not relieve the organisation of accountability; it changes how that accountability is defined.

9. OPERATIONAL ADAPTATION AND MANAGEMENT RESPONSES

The daily operations of hotels will show the first signs of changes in access. These changes will appear in monthly reports at a later stage. Hotels respond to changes in access by monitoring the check-in time of their guests, evaluating delays in service, answering guest questions, and monitoring the need for last-minute changes (Prideaux, 2000).

The actual arrival may differ from the itinerary and can significantly affect hotel operations. When more guests arrive during a short time frame, the hotel must reassign staff, change its cleaning pace, and plan service coordination among its departments.

Transportation-related cancellations are a different type of cancellation from what might be considered a traditional demand cancellation. A transportation-related cancellation does not reflect the quality of the product being provided. The end result, in terms of hotel operation, is the same: empty hotel rooms, changes in the daily hotel operating schedule, and uncertainty regarding whether or not the vacancy will be filled.

Hotel management has practical responses to changes in access. It may adjust staffing or shift times according to daily operations. If the hotel has anticipated either a large number of arrivals or a late arrival, hotel management will increase staffing, adjust scheduling and/or modify the delivery of services.

Effective communication with customers is of increased importance, as customers are looking for information and practical solutions to a transportation problem that is not under their control. Front-line customer service staff require clear direction and inter-departmental coordination in order to ensure that the uncertainty of transportation does not lead to uncertainty regarding the guest experience.

10. REAL-WORLD EXAMPLES FROM ISLAND TOURISM MARKETS

The connection between transportation and accommodation becomes more evident through abrupt changes in access than through gradual changes. When transport is available but accommodation is not, or vice versa, demand for transport or accommodation can change immediately. In other words, demand adjusts quickly, while supply must also respond as fast as possible.

For example, when the Eyjafjallajökull volcano erupted in Iceland in 2010, there were widespread restrictions on airspace throughout Europe, which resulted in mass flight cancellations (European Commission, 2010). While this created considerable challenges for access to island destinations, it also caused an immediate shift in demand and required immediate replanning of operations related to both transportation and accommodation.

Similarly, in 2021, volcanic activity on La Palma temporarily closed the airport and resulted in flight cancellations (Reuters, 2021). In 2017, Bali experienced a similar disruption due to volcanic activity from Mount Agung, which resulted in airport closures, flight cancellations and stranded travellers (Reuters, 2017). In all these situations, uncertainty about transportation availability passed directly into the operation of hospitality businesses.

Transport reliance is not merely a constraint in the Maldives. It is also the system that connects resorts with the main international gateways. Seaplanes are the only access method for many resorts, and they fly only during daylight hours (Trans

Maldivian Airways, n.d.). Thus, if a visitor arrives at a particular time, they may have to stay until morning to take the next available flight. Furthermore, seaplane access influences how a resort coordinates guest arrivals, overnight stays and onward transfers.

Improved access can also help tourism market development. The development of low-cost carrier networks can expand destination accessibility and is closely connected to the evolution of travel demand (Efthymiou & Christidis, 2023). Similarly, the liberalisation of air transport in the Azores has been linked to improved accessibility and growth in travel and tourism (Silveira et al., 2023).

While access can create limitations, it can also open a new market for tourism.

11. EMBEDDED CASE STUDY: TRANSPORT DISRUPTION AND HOTEL RESPONSE IN AN ISLAND DESTINATION

11.1 Case Description and Operational Framework

The following case illustrates the above-mentioned argument in a more specific setting. It does not deal with a particular island, but represents the situation of a typical island destination which combines coastal and air transport. The aim is not to give a real example with specific numerical characteristics, but to illustrate the conversion of transport accessibility into hotel decisions, financial information and operational adjustment (Button, 2010; Prideaux, 2000).

The destination is characterised by significant seasonality in tourism. The peak of tourism demand occurs within a few months, and there is much less activity before and after the peak months of the high season. Visitors tend to prefer coastal transport when they travel for longer periods, travel with their family, use cars for travelling and have more flexible travel plans. At the same time, air transport works better for short trips when visitors stay for only a few days.

In this situation, the hotel usually has good occupancy during the high season, but there are difficulties when the connection is less reliable. Demand depends not only on the hotel's attractiveness. Accessibility to the destination is also very important for consumers. According to the literature on accessibility and tourism development, accessibility is an important condition, although it does not necessarily generate tourism growth on its own (Wardana et al., 2025).

The hotel has no influence on the ferry timetable, flight availability, or delays. However, these aspects influence the hotel's business. Management cannot define the number of trips that will be organised. Nevertheless, the hotel has to make decisions about its pricing strategies, personnel management, booking policy, and related issues. There is a clear distinction between external issues that the firm cannot control and internal issues that remain under its control.

11.2 The Transport Disruption Scenario

In this scenario, a change in access takes place at the beginning of the tourist season. This may result in a temporary reduction of frequencies, alteration of travel schedules and lower certainty for visitors. Air access remains possible but limited, more expensive on certain days and insufficient to remove travel uncertainty. Therefore, the destination is not totally cut off from the outside world. However, its access becomes less predictable.

This situation creates uncertainty for tourists. They may still be interested in travelling to the island but will usually postpone booking their holidays. They may also be inclined to find other, cheaper destinations. Demand for the island does not disappear altogether, but often remains only an intention to travel.

This also creates an interpretation problem for hotel management. If it thinks that demand is absent, it may be tempted to proceed with price-cutting too early. If there is only a delay in demand, price-cutting could be harmful for hotel revenues. On the contrary, if there is no real demand for the hotel in question but only expectations that demand will rise later, maintaining prices may also become risky.

Management should therefore examine more than the number of bookings. It should monitor the rate at which reservations are made, the time remaining until arrival, the number of cancellation inquiries, changes in dates and the progress of deposits. When bookings are concentrated closer to the arrival date, the business has less certainty in its planning. The importance of predicting cancellations and managing uncertainty in changing hotel conditions has also been highlighted in recent literature (Silvestre et al., 2026).

11.3 Effects on Demand Composition

The first effect of the disruption is not only the possible reduction in visitors, but also the change in the type of visitors who finally arrive. Families with young children are likely to be more sensitive to uncertainty, because a delayed return or a change in itinerary creates greater practical cost. Working visitors with limited days off may also avoid a trip that has an increased risk of delay. Visitors with greater time flexibility may accept the same uncertainty, especially if the destination remains attractive or if the accommodation price is adjusted.

This has a direct impact on the hotel. Short visits can decrease, whereas longer visits may remain stable, especially when guests visit for a week and have sufficient flexibility. The combination of guests may still yield the same occupancy. However, many short stays do not have the same operational and financial consequences as fewer longer stays.

The difference between air and sea access reinforces this point. Air access can support short visits because it reduces travel time and allows for specific arrival dates. Sea access may be more associated with longer trips, especially when the guest travels with a car or organises a trip involving several stages. Different modes of transport can generate different forms of tourism demand (Button & Taylor, 2000; Sitzimis, 2026), while air accessibility can support specific forms of tourism and destination connectivity (Florido-Benítez, 2025; Forsyth, 2006).

Hotel management must therefore interpret not only how many guests are coming, but which guests are coming. If the segment of guests with higher daily spending decreases, the business may see lower revenue even if occupancy does not decline sharply. If longer-stay but lower-daily-priced guests increase, the business may have stable occupancy but a different margin. If last-minute bookings increase, the business may need different staffing and advance payment policies.

11.4 Pricing Response Without Hasty Discounting

The most difficult point for management is price. When bookings appear later than expected, the first thought may be to reduce the price. However, this reaction may be wrong if the problem is not a lack of demand, but a delay in the decision due to uncertainty. Price should function as an adjustment tool, not as a mechanical response to every drop in the booking rate.

Management has different options in a situation like this one. It can keep its price constant, but at the same time offer more flexibility to its guests. It can allow its guests to change their arrival date without penalty. It can create packages that include a transfer from the airport to the hotel, without creating the perception of a direct discount on the hotel price. Thus, the company does not reduce its price, but rather makes its offer less risky for the customer.

Revenue management is not only about whether the price is too high or too low. It is more about the interrelation between product, customer, time, and price (Kimes, 1989). In the case of an island destination, time does not only include the date of stay. The concept of time also includes the ability of the guest to arrive and return. If transport is inconvenient, even the same room rate may be perceived as higher because the total expense has increased. Willingness to pay is affected by the entire perception of the trip (Nagle & Müller, 2018).

It is important that the hotel does not rely too much on last-minute discounts. If customers learn that uncertainty about transport will always allow them to pay less, they will wait longer before booking. This reduces management's ability to see demand in advance. The hotel can be more flexible without losing its pricing credibility. In particular, it can provide assurance to the customer, maintain its pricing policy and adjust prices only if there is evidence of a decrease in demand.

11.5 Reservation, Advance Payment and Cancellation Policy

Transport disruption affects reservation policy significantly. When a customer is unsure of their arrival time or return, a strict cancellation policy can act as a disincentive. On the other hand, when the policy is extremely flexible, it increases the risk for the business. Management should therefore strive to strike a balance between financial security and the commercial attractiveness of the business (Kimes, 1989; Nagle & Müller, 2018).

In view of seasonal variability, the company may develop a differentiated policy depending on the season. For example, in the high season, when it is easier to replace a cancelled reservation with another customer, the company can work with a stricter set of conditions. Conversely, in low-season periods, which are characterised by lower demand or transport disruptions, the company may turn towards a policy of greater flexibility. At the same time, flexibility should not be unlimited. Thus, changes in the booking date may be permitted once; the advance payment may be kept low but not symbolic; and cancellation of the booking may be free, but only within a specific time limit and not until the last moment.

The reservation policy should also be related to the reservation channel. Direct reservations may have more flexible conditions than reservations made through intermediaries, since they involve more direct communication with clients. Reservations made through intermediaries may impose different constraints, higher commission fees and less control over the client relationship. In times of transport uncertainty, direct communication is of greater value, since it allows the hotel to explain possible alternatives, suggest a postponement of the reservation and, thus, avoid total cancellation.

The function of the deposit for the hotel is twofold. It is used to support liquidity and reduce no-show problems. Besides this, the deposit can become a barrier for clients who are uncertain about their booking decisions. Therefore, hotel management should observe whether a decrease in the amount of the deposit will lead to an increase in the number of reservations or whether it will simply lead to more uncertain reservations made by clients.

11.6 Accounting Information as an Early Warning System

In this case, accounting information functions not only as a record of the past, but also as an early warning system. Management does not wait until the end of the month to see whether revenues have decreased. It monitors daily or weekly indicators that show whether transport disruption is affecting the business (Broccardo et al., 2025).

The key information is not limited to occupancy. It includes the rate of reservations, cancellations, date changes, the value of deposits, the speed of collection, the average room rate, revenue per available room, personnel costs, cleaning costs, cost per occupied room and cash needs. These indicators help management understand what kind of problem it is facing.

For example, if occupancy remains relatively high but revenues are declining, the problem may lie in advance payments or more relaxed payment policies. If occupancy is declining but the average price remains high, the problem may be related to the inability to attract customers in conditions of increased total travel cost. If reservations exist but dates are constantly changing, management may have a staffing problem and not necessarily a final demand problem. If cancellations increase after itinerary changes, the problem should be interpreted as a transport signal, not simply as a failure of the hotel product.

The importance of accounting data is based on their interpretation. Only the relationship between an indicator and the event to which it refers makes it valuable. An increase in the number of last-minute reservations may mean that customers are waiting for transport to be confirmed. A decrease in the number of advance payments might also indicate a decrease in the level of trust. A shorter average length of stay may correlate with flight schedules or ferry frequency. All this can help management differentiate a temporary change from a real drop in earnings (Figure 2).

The use of digital revenue management tools and smart tourism technologies in the hospitality industry can enhance managerial forecasting and pricing decisions. Unlike in the past, modern systems can capture changes in demand and support appropriate pricing decisions (Haynes & Egan, 2024). Real-time data can facilitate the decision-making process for hotel managers (Abdou, 2025). For islands, this feature becomes even more important, since internal business information can be combined with data concerning access and transport. Such systems do not remove uncertainty, but they can shorten the time between an unexpected event and its identification in business data.

Figure 2. Managerial response to transport disruption in an island hotel

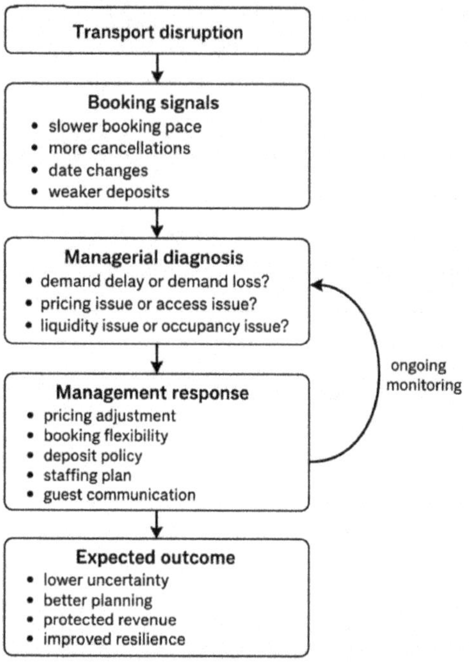

Source: Author's elaboration.

11.7 Operational Response and Internal Coordination

Disruption in transportation quickly affects the accommodation's daily operations. The late arrival of the ship creates an issue that goes beyond the delayed arrival of guests, because check-in requirements and staff availability may change, while the guest's first impression may also be affected. In such a situation, when many arrivals happen at the same time, the hotel may need more staff at reception, revised cleaning schedules and greater coordination among the departments providing services.

The ability to make such operational adjustments, however, also depends on the availability of human resources. Staff shortages can be a significant constraint for hotel businesses, especially in highly seasonal destinations, as they can increase work pressure and affect the business's ability to maintain the quality and authenticity of the hospitality provided (Konstantopoulos et al., 2026).

Operational change involves not only adding more employees, but also changing schedules, shifting some activities, preparing rooms earlier, offering flexible check-in options or changing the services provided on the arrival date. Reception becomes critical in the case of a difficult journey.

Procurement is also part of this reasoning. In an island destination, suppliers may experience the same transportation issues that visitors encounter. If there are any changes in the itinerary, there may be a delay in the delivery of products, cleaning supplies or equipment. Thus, management should not plan too tightly. However, that does not mean that inventory should be increased unnecessarily. Instead, it involves being aware of which items are important and knowing which suppliers are in a position to provide alternative delivery solutions.

It is also important that internal operations among the various departments are maintained effectively. Receptionists should be kept informed about any changes in arrivals, housekeeping should know of any changes in departures, and management should be aware of the reasons for cancellations.

11.8 Guest Communication and Trust Management

Under conditions of uncertainty in transport, communication with guests is not merely customer service; rather, it is a component of risk management. The guest who is anxious about arrival or departure needs not only information about the accommodation, but also an understanding of the available options if the schedule changes, the trip is prolonged, or there is a need to change the reservation. Uncertainty is mitigated when the guest receives assurance that the hotel has a procedure in this regard.

The hotel has various options that may be used to minimise the level of uncertainty. For instance, the hotel may provide guests with information about the route from the port or airport ahead of time. Such assistance can help guests understand the possibility of late arrival in advance. In addition, the hotel should have clear answers for guests in cases of route changes, or suggest alternative travel dates instead of cancellation of the arrangement.

Communication also influences guests' perception of value. If a guest feels that the hotel reduces uncertainty in their experience, they may perceive the pricing as acceptable. On the other hand, if they think that the risk lies entirely on their shoulders, then the same price appears too high. Thus, value does not emerge from the room alone, but also from the level of safety, information and practical assistance involved in the reservation process.

Trust management is significant for returning guests. If there are some issues with transport, but the guest receives good assistance from the hotel, they may still perceive the hotel positively. On the contrary, if difficulties with transport are accompanied by inflexibility, lack of relevant information and poor reception, the guest may associate the negative experience with the hotel, even though the hotel was not responsible for the transport issue.

11.9 Coordination with Local Destination Actors

Besides internal decisions made within the hotel, transport disruption also requires cooperation with local actors in the destination. The hotel cannot operate independently when there are transport problems. Ports, airports, taxis, tourist agencies and local government bodies may face similar transport difficulties at the same time. Thus, part of the managerial response is not only internal adjustment, but also coordination.

This coordination does not imply that the hotel controls the transport system. It means that the hotel is able to improve the quantity and timeliness of the information it receives. For instance, prior notice about ferry delays, changing arrival times, availability of taxis or overcrowded airports enables the management team to prepare reception, housekeeping and customer communication operations.

It is particularly relevant in the context of islands, because the impact of the same disruption can be felt across various facets of the visitor experience. For instance, problems with a ferry schedule can affect the timing of the check-in procedure, transfers, and restaurant operations, in addition to guests' perceptions of the destination. If a hotel is unable to receive information in time, it will only react; timely information allows for proactive management of such situations.

Moreover, participation in the local information network will allow hotels to ease the tension felt by tourists. A hotel that has reliable information related to transfers, alternative travel options, or delays becomes much more helpful to guests. It is not possible to completely eliminate transport uncertainty, but it is possible to ease some of the pressure associated with it. Therefore, the management of transport uncertainty should not be viewed only as a process taking place within the hotel, but also as depending on the ability of the hotel to be part of a broader information network at the destination.

This comprehensive coordination also requires openness and the active involvement of community members. In island destinations, access to data, participation in the decision-making process and the use of flexible governance methods can help destinations solve common problems and achieve fairer and more sustainable outcomes (Mirkova & Padrón-Fumero, 2025).

11.10 Lessons from the Case Study

This case indicates that transport disruption has consequences beyond the possibility of arrival. It has implications for timing, customer mix, reservation conditions, pricing, revenue collection and also the guest experience. While the hotel has limited influence over the transport process, the hotel can control how transport-related information is converted into management decisions.

Monitoring transport access represents the main lesson to be derived from this application. It is not enough for managers to be aware of hotel occupancy. They also have to know about the transport situation in terms of routes, frequency of travel services, delays and travel prices. A further implication concerns the evaluation of reservations, since booking terms should be assessed in connection with timing and certainty.

Pricing policy should also avoid a mechanical response. A price cut can be beneficial, but it can also hurt revenues if there is no loss of demand. Accounting information, in turn, has to be interpreted rather than treated only as descriptive information. Management must know whether the change in results is caused by market forces, transportation, pricing policies, or operating costs. Operational flexibility is equally important and represents one of the main conditions of resilience.

The value of the case lies in showing the role of transportation as part of management. In an island destination, transport access precedes accommodation, and its implications continue within accommodation as well. Transport has an impact on pricing, revenue collection procedures and other areas of hotel management. Therefore, it is important for hotel management in island destinations to consider transport not only as an issue of connectivity, but also as an integral part of the revenue chain.

12. FINANCIAL VOLATILITY AND REVENUE RESILIENCE

Island destination hospitality faces increased financial instability because of the variability of business revenues. A hospitality business may experience periods of high income, periods of very low activity, or sudden changes in its financial performance.

Access is an important factor creating demand variability and increased volatility for hospitality businesses located on islands. The vulnerability of island tourism destinations is also part of a wider context of environmental pressures, which reinforces the importance of environmental assessment tools for their sustainable planning and long-term resilience (Angelaki et al., 2026). Transport-related variability also creates revenue risk or uncertainty for maritime operators providing transport services. Transportation risks do not always create a complete loss of service. More often, they create unstable service, such as delays, cancellations, reductions in capacity, or schedule changes. All of these changes affect both the timing and the amount of revenue generated.

The ability of a hotel operation to be resilient to fluctuations in demand is critical. In addition to being defined by the amount of demand the hotel has, resilience also depends on its ability to absorb changes without creating disruption to its financial stability. Hotels that have sufficient liquidity, a clear understanding of their costs, and the ability to adjust their operations can better withstand volatility (Tascón et al., 2024).

Turbulence in transportation can continue to affect revenue composition. Booking lead times become shorter, prepayments decrease and more flexible policies are adopted. Revenues become more unpredictable, while many costs remain fixed and/or semi-fixed. As a result, the relationship between revenues and costs will become increasingly tenuous.

A resilient business is not one that maximises revenue under the best circumstances. Instead, it is one that maintains operational and financial balance under difficult conditions. In island destinations, this means understanding variability rather than just averages.

13. MICROECONOMIC VIEW OF ACCESS

The economic effects discussed above can be understood using basic microeconomic theory and transport economics (Button, 2010). At a microeconomic level, transport is an important constraint. It affects not only the level of demand, but also the options available to visitors and businesses.

For visitors, the trip to the island forms a component of the overall consumption cost associated with the trip. The cost of visiting the island includes many things besides the transport ticket. It also includes time, uncertainty and effort. These cost elements make up the overall cost of travelling to the island. As a result, they have a direct impact on the level of demand for accommodation on the island (Button, 2010; Nagle & Müller, 2018).

As accommodation demand is derived from travel demand (Prideaux, 2000), an increase in travel costs or a reduction in transport availability can reduce hotel sales, even though the hotel has no control over these changes.

The transportation system provides a selection mechanism. Some visitors leave the market, while others continue travelling but reduce their willingness to pay. Therefore, demand shifts and becomes more price elastic. A small change in prices can result in large changes in demand.

From the viewpoint of the business, accessibility affects the conditions under which the hotel seeks to maximise profit. The hotel has to make more than one decision regarding price. It also has to choose the level of operation, the level of service, and the level of flexibility. All of these decisions are made in an environment of limited capacity, seasonality and uncertainty.

14. DISCUSSION AND CONCLUSIONS

The transportation system on islands is more than a supporting component of the tourism industry. It is a foundation of the hospitality sector and drives demand for accommodation before a decision is made on where to stay. It also influences accommodation pricing and is quickly reflected in the financial and operational aspects of the lodging business.

Pricing is partly influenced by transport accessibility, since the ease and cost of reaching an island affect the room rates that hotels can sustain. Hotel operators therefore take into account total travel expenditure and the reliability of the available transport services.

Information generated from accounting systems allows the hotel operator to link the external environment to the internal environment and convert access-related changes into financial terms. It also assists the hotel operator in identifying how changes in demand will impact revenue, costs and cash flow. It does not eliminate uncertainty, but rather assists in managing it.

The operational dimension provides a more complete view of hospitality. Daily decisions are made in operations, including personnel, service, supply and customer experience. Access, demand, price, occupancy and operation are connected stages in the same overall process.

The embedded case study clarifies the managerial aspects of this process. To begin with, disruptions in transportation are expressed through booking signals, such as cancellations, date changes and doubts about demand for services. Afterwards, these signals should be interpreted through financial results and translated into action regarding service pricing, staffing and communication with clients.

The major contribution of this chapter lies in presenting a unified view of hospitality and transportation. If these sectors are separated, then the true picture is lost. In an island destination, transportation is part of the hospitality product and influences demand, pricing and operations.

Hospitality on islands faces both constraints and opportunities, and in both cases access is the starting point. Understanding how this system operates can lead to more realistic predictions, more flexible decision-making and more resilient businesses. Future research may provide empirical support for the relationships between booking patterns and transport supply systems in specific island destinations.

AI DISCLOSURE STATEMENT

ChatGPT and Grammarly were used for language editing, grammar, and readability. The author reviewed and approved all changes.

REFERENCES

Abdou, A. H. (2025). Smarter technologies, innovation, and managerial capabilities driving hotel sustainability: The integration of resource-based view and dynamic capabilities perspective. *Tourism and Hospitality*, *6*(5), 252. DOI: 10.3390/tourhosp6050252

Angelaki, E., Garefalakis, S., & Samaras, I. (2026). Environmental impact assessment in coastal and island tourism as a tool for sustainable development. *Sustainability Research in the Mediterranean*, *2*(2), 107–118. DOI: 10.13052/srm2795-0514.008

Broccardo, L., Ballesio, E., Yaqub, M. Z., & Mohapatra, A. K. (2025). A bridge to success: The role of management accountants' intellectual capital in driving organizational decision-making through knowledge management. *Journal of Knowledge Management*, *29*(5), 1365–1411. DOI: 10.1108/JKM-04-2024-0452

Button, K. (2010). *Transport economics* (3rd ed.). Edward Elgar.

Button, K., & Taylor, S. (2000). International air transportation and economic development. *Journal of Air Transport Management*, *6*(4), 209–222. DOI: 10.1016/S0969-6997(00)00015-6

Efthymiou, M., & Christidis, P. (2023). Low-cost carriers route network development. *Annals of Tourism Research*, *101*, 103608. DOI: 10.1016/j.annals.2023.103608

European Commission. (2010, April 27). *Volcanic ash cloud crisis: Commission outlines response to tackle the impact on air transport*. MEMO/10/152.

Florido-Benítez, L. (2025). Air transport: A complex perspective for US Disney and Universal theme parks. *Journal of the Air Transport Research Society*, *4*, 100051. DOI: 10.1016/j.jatrs.2024.100051

Forsyth, P. (2006). Martin Kunz Memorial Lecture. Tourism benefits and aviation policy. *Journal of Air Transport Management*, *12*(1), 3–13. DOI: 10.1016/j.jairtraman.2005.09.001

Garefalakis, A., Stratidaki, F., Angelaki, E., Antonaki, D., & Papademetriou, C. (2026). Governance and financial outcomes of ESG implementation in tourism enterprises: A case study from Greece. *International Journal of Financial Studies*, *14*(3), 61. DOI: 10.3390/ijfs14030061

Haynes, N., & Egan, D. (2024). Transient price setting in the era of automated systems: The 'hands-on' hotel general manager lives on! *Journal of Revenue and Pricing Management*, *23*(1), 28–38. DOI: 10.1057/s41272-023-00447-5

Kimes, S. E. (1989). Yield management: A tool for capacity-considered service firms. *Journal of Operations Management*, *8*(4), 348–363. DOI: 10.1016/0272-6963(89)90035-1

Konstantopoulos, G., Giannarakis, G., Xenaki, M., Thanasas, G., & Garefalakis, A. (2026). Operational labor shortages and authentic hospitality: Evidence from Greek hotels. *Tourism and Hospitality*, *7*(6), 180. DOI: 10.3390/tourhosp7060180

Kotler, P., Bowen, J. T., Makens, J. C., & Baloglu, S. (2017). *Marketing for hospitality and tourism* (7th ed.). Pearson Education.

Mirkova, I., & Padrón-Fumero, N. (2025). From vulnerability to resilience: Empowering stakeholder-driven just transitions in island tourism economies. *Energy Research & Social Science*, *121*, 103966. DOI: 10.1016/j.erss.2025.103966

Nagle, T. T., & Müller, G. (2018). *The strategy and tactics of pricing* (6th ed.). Routledge.

Prideaux, B. (2000). The role of the transport system in destination development. *Tourism Management*, *21*(1), 53–63. DOI: 10.1016/S0261-5177(99)00079-5

Reuters. (2017, November 29). Indonesia reopens Bali airport as wind clears volcanic ash. *Reuters*.

Reuters. (2021, September 26). Airport closed as La Palma volcano eruption intensifies. *Reuters*.

Silveira, L., Santos, N., & Moreira, C. O. (2023). The liberalisation of air transport and the impacts on travel and tourism: The case of the Azores Archipelago. *Sustainability (Basel)*, *15*(5), 4488. DOI: 10.3390/su15054488

Silvestre, P., Antonio, N., & Carrasco, P. (2026). Navigating uncertainty: Enhancing hotel cancellation predictions with adaptive machine learning. *Information Technology & Tourism*, *28*(1), 9. DOI: 10.1007/s40558-025-00349-9

Sitzimis, I. (2026). Air tourism as a driver of coastal and ferry transport demand in Greece: A quantitative assessment. *Case Studies on Transport Policy*, *23*, 101688. DOI: 10.1016/j.cstp.2025.101688

Tascón, M. T., Castro, P., & Valdunciel, L. (2024). Effects of financial restrictions on firms' financial resilience against the COVID-19 pandemic: Evidence from the European hospitality industry. *Applied Economics*, *56*(58), 8226–8241. DOI: 10.1080/00036846.2023.2289951

Trans Maldivian Airways. (n.d.). *Frequently asked questions*. Trans Maldivian Airways.

Wardana, W. W., Haryanto, T., Jamil, I. R., Ismail, N. A., Heriqbaldi, U., Correa, E., Rohmah, W. N., & Ajija, S. R. (2025). Does improved accessibility translate into tourism growth? A difference-in-differences analysis of bridge infrastructure in Indonesia. *Annals of Tourism Research Empirical Insights*, *6*(2), 100189. DOI: 10.1016/j.annale.2025.100189

Chapter 10
Corporate Governance and Internal Control Systems in Hotel Revenue Management

Panagiotis Kyriakogkonas
http://orcid.org/0009-0006-2351-3409
University of Western Macedonia, Greece

Markos Kourgiantakis
http://orcid.org/0000-0002-2392-6952
Hellenic Mediterranean University, Greece

Alexandros Garefalakis
http://orcid.org/0000-0001-7980-3743
Hellenic Mediterranean University, Greece

Ioannis Passas
http://orcid.org/0000-0002-1261-2878
Hellenic Mediterranean University, Greece

ABSTRACT

This chapter develops a theoretically grounded and integrative analysis of corporate governance and internal control systems in the context of hotel revenue management. Within this architecture, internal control systems are examined as process-based mechanisms that operationalize governance objectives through risk assessment, control activities, monitoring, and reporting structures. The chapter argues that hotel revenue presents a distinctive empirical setting for governance and control analysis due to its perishability, simultaneity of production and consumption,

DOI: 10.4018/979-8-3373-9479-4.ch010

decentralization across operational departments, and dependence on technology-mediated distribution channels. These characteristics intensify information asymmetries, increase exposure to opportunistic behavior, and amplify the need for robust control environments. Drawing on internationally recognized control frameworks and risk-based approaches, the chapter positions internal controls not merely as accounting safeguards but as embedded organizational processes shaped by cultural, technological, and governance determinants

INTRODUCTION

The hotel industry holds a particularly important position in modern economy. Singal (2015) highlights that it is a complex and dynamic industry with strong particularities. It is characterized by high capital intensity and significant operational uncertainty, and its organizational structures are multi-layered and often complex. Contractor and Kundu (1998) and Michael (1999) argue that expansion through hybrid forms, such as franchising and management contracts, intensifies this complexity. Relationships between owners, managers and brand owners are becoming more demanding. Kimes (1989) notes that the perishability of service capacity directly affects revenue. In addition, operation with limited capacity enhances this pressure. Thus, revenue becomes particularly sensitive to changes in demand. Cross et al. (2009) emphasize the role of revenue management systems in modern hotel operations. Moreover, Ivanov (2014) argues that multi-channel distribution increases the need for better coordination. Therefore, firms need more effective control mechanisms. In this context, understanding the relationship among corporate governance, revenue structure and control systems is particularly important. It is directly linked to the sustainable development of hotel firms. This chapter examines the role of corporate governance and Internal Control Systems in the hotel industry, with particular emphasis on governance complexity, monitoring mechanisms and revenue-related control challenges. It also discusses the importance of information quality and effective control systems in supporting operational effectiveness and long-term sustainability.

The Importance of Governance and Control in the Hotel Industry

In recent years, the hotel industry has been characterized by increasing organizational and institutional complexity. Firms are increasingly expanding through hybrid organizational forms such as franchising, management contracts and other forms of co-operation with no equity participation. Contractor and Kundu (1998) note that this shift from full-ownership models to contractual and cooperative relationships is essentially altering the structure of the industry. Michael (1999) argues that these new forms of organization increase the complexity of the relationships among the involved parties. As a result, corporate governance and control mechanisms are emerging as crucial factors. They contribute to ensuring the quality of services, brand consistency and long-term sustainability of hotel firms. Jensen and Meckling (1976) introduce agency theory as a key framework for understanding these relationships. This theory focuses on the interactions among principals and agents. Eisenhardt (1989) and Bergen et al. (1992) emphasize that these relationships are characterized by information asymmetry and divergent interests. In addition, the ability to monitor and evaluate performance is often limited. This is mainly due to the intangible and experiential nature of hospitality services. Brown et al. (2003) argue that, under these circumstances, the absence of effective governance mechanisms increases the risk of opportunistic behaviour. Moreover, Lafontaine and Blair (2005) emphasize that deviations from operational standards are enhanced. Combs et al. (2011) add that this may lead to a degradation in the quality of services and corporate reputation. This phenomenon is particularly pronounced in franchising and management contracts.

Eisenhardt (1989) suggests that corporate governance is not limited to the composition and operation of boards. Instead, it establishes a broader system of supervision and control. Dalton et al. (1998) add that this system includes internal control mechanisms and compliance procedures. In addition, Aguilera et al. (2008) highlight the role of contractual control mechanisms in shaping effective governance. Although much of the literature comes from interdisciplinary studies, these approaches are of particular importance in the hotel industry. This is because the operation through franchising networks and management contracts intensifies the information asymmetry issues. At the same time, it makes the allocation of control among the involved parties more complex. Brown et al. (2003) emphasize that, in these systems, governance mechanisms function as key coordination tools. In the same vein, Combs et al. (2011) argue that they contribute significantly to monitoring the behaviour of individual units. This enhances the coherence and efficient operation of hotel networks.

On this basis, sustainability practices and ESG factors are not treated as an independent field of analysis. On the contrary, they are part of the broader corporate governance and accountability system. Aguilera et al. (2008) highlight that the characteristics of corporate governance are positively linked to the environmental and social performance of firms. Moreover, Jo and Harjoto (2012) argue that stronger governance structures strengthen firms' commitment to responsible practises. In the hotel industry in particular, Jackson (2025) suggests that firms with more developed governance structures achieve higher levels of environmental responsibility. At the same time, they show better environmental performance compared to less structured firms. These findings reinforce the view that the quality of governance plays a key role and is directly linked to achieving sustainable results in the hospitality industry (Passas, 2024; Vortelinos et al., 2024).

The importance of corporate governance and control in the hotel industry becomes even more evident through the operation of Internal Control Systems. These systems are a key pillar of monitoring and accountability. Doyle et al. (2007) highlight that effective internal controls are linked to a higher quality of financial reporting. In addition, Ashbaugh-Skaife et al. (2009) emphasize that they contribute to reducing operational and financial risks. Moreover, Frias-Aceituno et al. (2013) highlight that investor and shareholder confidence is enhanced. Although these studies do not focus exclusively on the hotel industry, their conclusions are of particular importance. This is especially true in an environment such as hospitality, where operation through multiple legal entities and contractual arrangements are common. The need for transparent and effective control mechanisms is therefore increasing.

The mechanisms of governance and control in the relationships between franchisor and franchisee are of particular value. In these arrangements, the decentralisation of operation and the contractual autonomy of individual units increase complexity. In addition, they intensify the risks of conflict and opportunistic behaviour. Brickley and Dark (1987) argue that agency and monitoring considerations influence the choice and control of franchising arrangements. Lafontaine and Blair (2005) argue that risk allocation and risk management largely determine the design of control mechanisms. Combs et al. (2011) add that these factors also affect the stability of partnerships. At the same time, strong governance frameworks contribute significantly to reducing conflicts. In addition, they facilitate the alignment of incentives among the involved parties. Thus, trust is strengthened and the long-term performance of hospitality networks is supported.

Revenue Management, Operational Complexity and Control Challenges in the Hotel Industry

The hotel industry is characterized by a complex revenue structure and increased financial complexity. These characteristics differentiate it significantly from other service industries. This complexity is related to the volatility of demand, the international activity of hotel firms and the use of complex organizational and contractual structures. In addition, the use of complex contractual schemes further enhances this complexity. Singal (2015) highlights that hospitality firms have a higher degree of operational and financial complexity than other service industries. Kimes (1989) identifies that the perishability of service is a key characteristic of the industry. Unsold rooms cannot be transferred in subsequent periods. In addition, Singal (2015) emphasizes that this increases the pressure for efficient capacity and pricing management. As a result, hotel firms require effective monitoring and control mechanisms in order to manage operational uncertainty and support revenue stability.

In addition, strong reliance on labor intensity increases the complexity of cost management. Contractor and Kundu (1998) argue that the differences between franchising and management contracts create additional challenges. Moreover, Singal (2015) shows that these forms increase the difficulty of financial monitoring. Overall, the structural characteristics of the industry create greater operational complexity and reinforce the need for effective governance, monitoring and Internal Control Systems.

Kimes (1989) highlights that yield management plays a key role in revenue formation. This approach was originally developed for capacity-constrained service firms. It then evolved into modern revenue management. Cross et al. (2009) demonstrate that this development is closely linked to the adoption of dynamic pricing and demand forecasting practices. However, the growing reliance on demand forecasts and dynamic price adjustments poses new challenges. Hotel decision-making increasingly depends on the accuracy of forecasting models and the reliability of operational information (Cross et al., 2009). Consequently, the effective implementation of revenue management practices requires robust monitoring and internal control mechanisms.

Ivanov (2014) explains that the rooms are available through multi-channel distribution. These channels include both direct bookings and online travel agencies (OTAs). In addition, the coexistence of different channels affects pricing and revenue management strategies. As a result, operational coordination and monitoring requirements become more demanding.

The structural characteristics of the hotel industry create specific revenue risks and heighten operational control challenges. Kimes (1989) explains that the perishability of service capacity, combined with capacity-constrained service setting, makes revenue particularly sensitive to demand variations. In this context, revenue management has evolved as a key mechanism for addressing such risks. It is mainly based on dynamic pricing and demand forecasting. Furthermore, Aziz et al. (2011) emphasize that revenue optimization in hotel firms depends on the use of dynamic pricing models and accurate demand forecasting techniques. Thus, the quality of information and analytical tools directly affects the success of revenue management.

Multi-channel distribution further enhances the complexity of revenue management. Ivanov (2014) demonstrates that the growth of online travel agencies (OTAs) has significantly reshaped the competitive environment and pricing dynamics. At the same time, it makes it necessary to systematically monitor performance per channel. Moreover, the expansion of online distribution channels and OTAs has increased price transparency and intensified competition among hotel firms (Ivanov,

2014). As a result, the need for effective price consistency and distribution-channel controls is reinforced.

Control challenges are further intensified by fraud risk and deficiencies in internal monitoring and control mechanisms. According to Doyle et al. (2007) weaknesses in Internal Control Systems are linked to lower quality financial reporting. In addition, Ashbaugh-Skaife et al. (2009) indicate that the risk of errors and irregularities is increased. In the hospitality environment, these challenges become more intense. Transactions are conducted across multiple points of contact and digital channels, so the need for clear procedures and effective controls is increased. The segregation of duties and the systematic monitoring of operations are therefore of critical importance (Maravelaki et al., 2021; Passas, 2023b).

Finally, revenue risks are also affected by the form of governance. Contractor and Kundu (1998) argue that in franchising and management contracts, the allocation of control rights is more complex. Michael (1999) adds that this can lead to information asymmetry and conflicts of interest. Lafontaine and Blair (2005) underline the importance of contractual governance mechanisms in managing these relations. According to Combs et al. (2011), alignment of incentives is critical to maintaining the quality and overall performance of networks.

Objectives and Structure of the Chapter

The increasing intensity of competition within the hospitality industry has highlighted the importance of effective corporate governance and robust Internal Control Systems as essential components of organizational sustainability and performance. Hotel firms operate in highly dynamic environments characterized by complex organizational structures, diverse stakeholder relationships and extensive operational networks. Consequently, the need for transparency, accountability, and effective risk management has become increasingly significant.

Within this framework, corporate governance serves as a critical mechanism for aligning the interests of management and stakeholders, thereby reducing agency conflicts and mitigating information asymmetry. Effective governance practices contribute to improved transparency in decision-making processes, strengthen accountability, and support the achievement of organizational objectives.

At the same time, Internal Control Systems constitute a fundamental element of the governance framework by facilitating the identification, assessment, and management of risks that may affect organizational performance. Furthermore, well-designed internal controls enhance the reliability and accuracy of financial reporting and operational information, supporting informed decision-making and regulatory compliance. Therefore, the integration of effective corporate governance mechanisms with comprehensive internal control practices is essential for strengthening organizational resilience, improving operational efficiency, and promoting long-term value creation within hotel firms.

The hospitality industry exhibits distinctive operational characteristics that increase the importance of effective corporate governance and control mechanisms. The widespread adoption of sophisticated revenue management practices, the integration of multiple distribution channels, and the extensive use of franchising and management contract arrangements contribute to greater organizational complexity and reinforce the need for comprehensive oversight and monitoring processes. Furthermore, the quality of information, the effectiveness of information systems, and the adequacy of monitoring procedures play a critical role in supporting managerial decision-making and maintaining both operational efficiency and financial stability within hotel firms.

This chapter is structured into four main sections. The first section discusses the significance of corporate governance and control mechanisms in hotel firms, drawing on key theoretical perspectives, with particular emphasis on agency theory and the governance challenges associated with contemporary organizational structures in the hospitality industry. The second section examines the operational and organizational complexity of hotel firms, focusing on revenue management practices, distribution systems, and the increasing demand for effective monitoring and internal control mechanisms. The third section provides a detailed analysis of corporate governance practices within the hospitality industry and their contribution to organizational performance and accountability. Finally, the fourth section explores Internal Control Systems within the framework proposed by the Committee of Sponsoring Organizations of the Treadway Commission (COSO), emphasizing their role in risk management, financial reporting reliability, and the enhancement of operational effectiveness in hotel firms.

CORPORATE GOVERNANCE: CONCEPTUAL FOUNDATIONS

Definitions and Evolution of Corporate Governance

Corporate governance is a fundamental concept in modern business administration theory and practice, as it refers to the framework through which businesses are directed, monitored and held accountable. At institutional level, the G20/OECD Principles of Corporate Governance (2023) define corporate governance as an internationally recognized framework of principles regulating the allocation of rights and responsibilities between board of directors, management, shareholders and other stakeholders, as well as decision-making processes. According to Cadbury (1992) and OECD (2015,2023), governance is linked to concepts such as accountability, transparency and effective oversight, which are key pillars of modern control systems.

From a financial point of view, the concept of corporate governance acquires a more specific and operational content. Shleifer and Vishny (1997) define corporate governance as the set of mechanisms through which suppliers of finance ensure they get a return on their investment. La Porta et al. (1998, 2000) highlight the importance of institutional frameworks, investor protection and ownership structure for the smooth functioning of capital markets. In particular, they underline that the legal origin of a system and the quality of law enforcement have a decisive influence on the level of financial development, the dispersion of equity ownership and the functioning of corporate governance mechanisms. At micro-economy level, these effects are reflected in the way businesses are organized and operated. For this reason, many researchers have extensively examined the relationship of corporate governance to firm performance and ownership structure at international level (Shleifer and Vishny, 1997; Denis and McConnell, 2003), while recent studies focus particularly on the functioning of boards and decision-making processes (Zattoni et al., 2020).

The conceptual evolution of corporate governance is directly linked to the separation between ownership and control and the agency problem, which highlighted the need for governance monitoring mechanisms. Jensen and Meckling (1976) emphasize that, according to agency theory, the delegation of decision-making from the principals (owners) to agents (managers) can create conflicts of interest, which makes it necessary to have effective control mechanisms. Similarly, Fama and Jensen (1983) argue that a separation between decision management and decision control is a key organizational mechanism to reduce agency problems. Recent studies focus on board structure and board composition which are considered central internal mechanisms of corporate governance. In particular, they examine the relationship between the characteristics of the board, such as the independence of members and the size, as well as firm performance (Dalton et al., 1998; Bhagat and Black, 2001; Hermalin and Weisbach, 2001; Kiel and Nicholson, 2003; Post and Byron, 2015; Zattoni et al., 2020).

In addition, the literature indicates that corporate governance research has expanded beyond the narrow study of internal control mechanisms. More recent studies examine the cross-country differences in corporate governance and the role of legal and institutional systems in the adoption of governance mechanisms (La Porta et al., 1998; Denis and McConnell, 2003; Aguilera et al., 2008; Zattoni et al., 2020; Balios et al., 2024). In particular, La Porta et al. (1998) and Aguilera and Jackson (2010) highlight that the effectiveness of governance mechanisms is influenced by legal origin, ownership concentration and capital market structure. These differences contribute to the adoption of different models of corporate governance across countries and influence how firms organize their monitoring and control mechanisms.

More recent studies indicate the broadening of the corporate governance agenda towards sustainability, corporate social responsibility and ESG factors. This suggests that governance characteristics, such as board composition and ownership structure, are now examined in relation not only to firm performance but also to non-financial performance indicators and long-term value creation (Aguilera et al., 2019). In the same vein, recent systematic literature reviews confirm that Agency Theory continues to be the key theoretical framework in the study of corporate governance, often complemented by approaches such as the Stakeholder Theory and the Resource Dependence Theory (Zattoni et al., 2020) (Passas, 2024; Vortelinos et al., 2024).

More generally, the evolution of the corporate governance concept reflects the transition from a relatively narrow framework of Internal Control Systems and shareholder protection to a wider system of institutional monitoring, strategic orientation and risk management. According to Zattoni et al. (2020) and the OECD (2023), this system is dynamically shaped by the institutional environment and modern accountability requirements.

Separation of Ownership and Control in Modern Corporations

The need to establish corporate governance mechanisms is directly linked to the separation of ownership and control, which is a fundamental structural feature of contemporary business environments. Berle and Means (1932) find that in modern organizations, equity ownership is characterized by a high degree of dispersion, while decision control is exercised by professional managers. In this way, the potential for conflicts of interest between shareholders and management was highlighted and the basis for the study of control and monitoring mechanisms was laid.

Jensen and Meckling (1976) define the delegation of decision-making power from principals to agents as an agency relationship. The above-mentioned researchers argue that the existence of such a relationship gives rise to agency costs, which arise both from the need to monitor the management and from the risk of divergent interests. Fama and Jensen (1983) then define the decision-making process as a set of four functions — initiation, ratification, implementation and monitoring — and emphasize that the separation of decision management (initiation and implementation) and decision control (ratification and monitoring) is a key mechanism to reduce conflicts of interest. Consequently, the board of directors emerges as a central oversight and control body.

The relevant literature has highlighted cross-country differences in ownership and control separation. La Porta et al. (1999) demonstrate that in many economies ownership is concentrated and controlled by ultimate controlling shareholders, which alters the nature of conflicts of interest by shifting them from conflicts between shareholders and managers to conflicts between controlling and minority shareholders. Furthermore, Young et al. (2008), Claessens and Yurtoglu (2013), Aguilera and Crespi-Cladera (2016), and Zattoni et al. (2020) examine how ownership structure, ownership concentration, and the relationship between controlling and minority shareholders influence the effectiveness of corporate governance mechanisms and managerial behavior.

More recent studies emphasize that ownership and control separation remains a major issue, particularly in the context of the globalization of capital markets and changes in the ownership structure of organizations (Aguilera and Crespi-Cladera, 2016; Bebchuk and Hirst, 2019; Zattoni et al., 2020). According to Shleifer and Vishny, (1997) and Appel et al. (2016), strengthening the presence of institutional investors affects monitoring practices and management accountability, without, however, negating the fundamental separation between owners and managers. At the same time, the increasing concentration of ownership in large investment funds is reshaping the dynamics of the agency problem, without eliminating the need for effective control mechanisms (Aguilera et al., 2019; Zattoni et al., 2020).

In addition, Aguilera et al. (2019) link ownership and control separation to issues of long-term value creation and sustainable governance. Corporate governance structures play a central role in ensuring accountability and transparency, both contributing to sustainable value creation and enhancing investor confidence. In the same vein, Fatemi et al. (2018) and Chau et al. (2025) demonstrate that the incorporation of sustainability practices and the disclosure of ESG factors can have a positive impact on the long-term firm value and the firm's performance assessment. Finally, Sjåfjell and Tsagas (2022) argue that legal and regulatory frameworks can support the integration of sustainable long-term value creation into corporate governance structures and corporate decision-making processes.

In conclusion, the separation of ownership and control is a fundamental feature of modern organizations, which explains the need for corporate governance mechanisms, the effectiveness of which varies across institutional environments (Berle and Means, 1932; Jensen and Meckling, 1976; Fama and Jensen, 1983; Shleifer and Vishny, 1997; La Porta et al., 1998; Zattoni et al., 2020).

Corporate Governance in the Hospitality and Hotel Industry

Corporate governance in the hospitality industry and in particular in the hotel industry has attracted growing research interest in recent years, as the organizational structure of firms in the hotel industry differs significantly from that of other service sectors. According to Singal (2015), the hotel industry operates in an environment of high capital intensity and strong demand volatility, while also being influenced by external factors, such as economic crises, geopolitical developments and changes in international tourist flows. At the same time, firms in the hotel industry adopt asset-light strategies, in which the development of activities is based mainly on contractual arrangements, such as management contracts and franchising (Li and Singal, 2019). This development contributes to the emergence of complex governance structures. For this reason, property ownership, hotel operation and brand ownership are not necessarily concentrated in the same organization, but are distributed among different parties, such as investors, hotel operators and international hotel brands (Contractor and Kundu, 1998; Brown et al., 2003; Li and Singal, 2022). This multi-level structure creates complex relationships of control, responsibilities and accountability between stakeholders such as owners, operators, brand owners and franchisees. Since the day-to-day management of hotel properties is often carried out through franchising or management contracts, Contractor and Kundu (1998) and Michael (1999) argue that corporate governance mechanisms are critical for aligning incentives, monitoring performance and ensuring consistency in brand standards.

The complexity of these relationships in the hotel industry makes the agency theory a particularly useful theoretical framework for understanding corporate governance issues. Jensen and Meckling (1976) and Eisenhardt (1989) emphasize that this theory focuses on the principal-agent relationships, which arise when the principal delegates decision-making authority and resource management to the agent. Such relationships often result in information asymmetry issues and potential conflicts of interest, as the two sides may have different objectives or incentives. For this reason, organizations are adopting oversight and monitoring mechanisms, aimed at limiting opportunistic behavior and aligning interests. In the hotel industry, such agency relationships often occur between owners, operators, brand owners, franchisors and franchisees, as well as between shareholders and managers. Their importance is particularly accentuated in hotel firms operating through franchising or management contracts (Contractor and Kundu, 1998; Michael, 1999; Li and Singal, 2019).

Contractor and Kundu (1998) and Li and Singal (2019) highlight that the expansion of hotel firms through franchising and management contracts, together with the adoption of asset-light strategies, has strengthened the separation among ownership, operational management and brand ownership. Hotel property owners usually seek to maximize the return on their investment, while hotel management firms or franchisees are responsible for the day-to-day operations of hotel firms and the achievement of operational objectives, such as increasing revenue and improving occupancy levels. This differentiation of objectives may create conflicts of interest between the stakeholders involved, as owners and managers may evaluate firm performance based on different criteria, such as profitability, occupancy or retention of brand reputation (Michael, 1999; Brown et al., 2003). At this point, corporate governance mechanisms play a crucial role in aligning incentives and effectively monitoring the operation of firms in the hotel industry. Especially in franchising systems, Lafontaine and Blair (2005) and Combs et al. (2011) emphasize that governance and monitoring mechanisms are necessary to reduce agency problems and ensure consistency of operating standards across the network. Uyar et al. (2020) demonstrate that governance-related board characteristics are positively associated with CSR performance and financial performance in hospitality and tourism firms. In the same vein, Li and Singal (2022) emphasize the importance of governance mechanisms for effective oversight and organizational performance in the hospitality industry.

These challenges make it particularly important to have effective corporate governance mechanisms in hotel firms. According to Dalton et al. (1998), Doyle et al. (2007), and Li and Singal (2022), governance mechanisms include both internal governance mechanisms, such as boards and Internal Control Systems, and contractual mechanisms resulting from franchising and management contracts. Brickley and Dark (1987) and Lafontaine and Blair (2005) highlight that franchising arrangements require monitoring and control mechanisms to mitigate agency problems and align incentives between franchisors and franchisees. In international hotel networks, corporate governance mechanisms also contribute to maintaining common operational standards and ensuring the quality of service across all affiliated hotels. At the same time, Bergen et al. (1992) and Li and Singal (2022) emphasize that performance monitoring systems and evaluation processes allow hotel chains to monitor the operations of individual hotels, particularly when these hotels are managed by independent partners such as operators or franchisees. In the light of the agency theory, these practices contribute to reducing agency costs arising from the separation of ownership and management and enhance brand consistency and strengthen corporate reputation across the entire network (Aguilera et al., 2008; Zattoni et al., 2020).

Corporate governance mechanisms in hotel firms are implemented through a combination of contractual arrangements, monitoring procedures and operational standards applied across the network. In franchising and management contracts, hotel chains often use performance evaluation procedures, quality inspections and standard operating protocols to ensure that individual hotels comply with brand standards. Brown et al. (2003) and Combs et al. (2011) find that these practices act as control mechanisms that limit the information asymmetry between owners and managers and help maintain the consistency of services in international hotel networks. Furthermore, management accounting and performance monitoring systems provide hotel managers with information that supports decision-making, coordination and operational control (Mia and Patiar, 2001). In larger hotel networks, these mechanisms also facilitate monitoring and strategic coordination across organizational units (Li and Singal, 2022).

In addition to the contractual mechanisms implemented at the network level, internal management structures play an important role in the corporate governance of firms in the hotel industry. More specifically, boards of directors serve as a key governance mechanism, providing oversight and ensuring accountability to shareholders and other stakeholders (Bebchuk and Hirst, 2019; Yeh, 2019). Dalton et al. (1998), Hermalin and Weisbach (2001), and Zattoni et al. (2020) emphasize that, in the context of corporate governance, the composition, independence and functioning of boards of directors influence the effectiveness of managerial oversight and the strategic direction of firms. In the hotel industry, where firms often operate in international environments and through complex organizational structures, the role of boards of directors becomes crucial. Boards are not only limited to an oversight role, but also contribute to the coordination of strategic decisions, as well as to the monitoring of the performance of individual hotels within the network (Li and Singal, 2022).

At the same time, the ownership structure is another crucial factor in corporate governance. According to Shleifer and Vishny (1997) and Aguilera et al. (2008), ownership concentration, the presence of institutional investors and the participation of strategic shareholders can affect the effectiveness of oversight mechanisms and strategic decision-making in firms. In the hotel industry, differences in ownership structure are often associated with different growth strategies adopted by hotel firms (Contractor and Kundu, 1998; Yeh, 2019). In particular, the separation between asset-heavy and asset-light business models affects not only the way activities are organized but also the functioning of governance mechanisms and the strategic direction of hotel chains (Li and Singal, 2022).

Finally, in recent years, scholars have linked corporate governance in the hospitality industry to sustainability and ESG factors (Friede et al., 2015; Gillan et al., 2021). Corporate governance mechanisms appear to influence the adoption of environmental and social responsibility practices, as well as the level of transparency in the disclosure of sustainability-related information. In fact, Deng and Zhou (2022) and Jackson (2025) indicate that stronger governance structures are linked to higher levels of environmental performance and the integration of more sustainable strategies into the hospitality industry. Based on the above, corporate governance extends beyond managing relationships between owners and management and increasingly contributes to the development of long-term strategies that incorporate economic, social and environmental objectives.

Figure 1 presents a conceptual framework linking governance complexity, monitoring mechanisms and Internal Control Systems in the hotel industry.

Figure 1. Conceptual Framework of Governance and Internal Control in the Hotel Industry

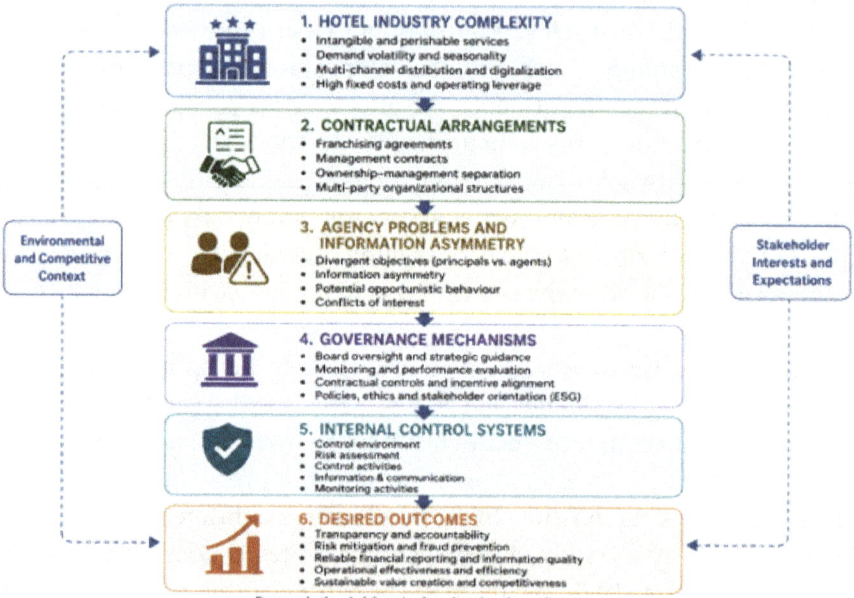

Source: Authors' elaboration based on the relevant literature.

INTERNAL CONTROL SYSTEMS: CONCEPTS, HOSPITALITY APPLICATIONS AND HOTEL REVENUE IMPLICATIONS

Internal Control Systems: Conceptual Foundations, Determinants and Effectiveness

Conceptual Foundations of Internal Control Systems

The importance of Internal Control Systems (ICS) in modern business administration has been significantly enhanced, as they are directly linked to corporate governance and risk management. ICS play a key role in ensuring the reliability of financial information, enhancing operational effectiveness and ensuring compliance with the current regulatory framework. The relevant literature, including Power (1997) and Spira & Page (2003), highlight that ICS have evolved from a traditional and limited control approach into a broader governance and oversight framework.

This evolution is also reflected in the context of the Committee of Sponsoring Organizations (COSO) (2013), where ICS are viewed as integrated and interconnected systems embedded within organizational processes. In addition, Doyle et al. (2007) and Ashbaugh-Skaife et al. (2009) demonstrate that the quality of ICS directly affects the reliability of financial reporting, while DeFond and Zhang (2014) emphasize their role in decision-making. Hence, ICS are not limited to a passive control function; rather, they have evolved into a critical mechanism that shapes the overall functioning of organizations (Kagias et al., 2024; Lampropoulos et al., 2025).

One of the most well-established theoretical frameworks for understanding ICS is the model of the Committee of Sponsoring Organizations of the Treadway Commission (2013), which approaches internal audit as a dynamic process influenced by the board, management and all staff. The purpose of this process is to provide reasonable assurance as to the achievement of the basic objectives of the organization. Internal audit is not seen as an individual function, but as a set of interrelated features that run horizontally across the firm. In particular, as highlighted by COSO (2013) and further documented by Feng et al. (2009), Novatiani et al. (2024), and Chen et al. (2025), the context consists of five main components: control environment, risk assessment, control activities, information and communication and finally monitoring. This distinction highlights the multi-dimensional character of ICS.

Figure 2. Internal Control Systems Framework based on COSO (2013)

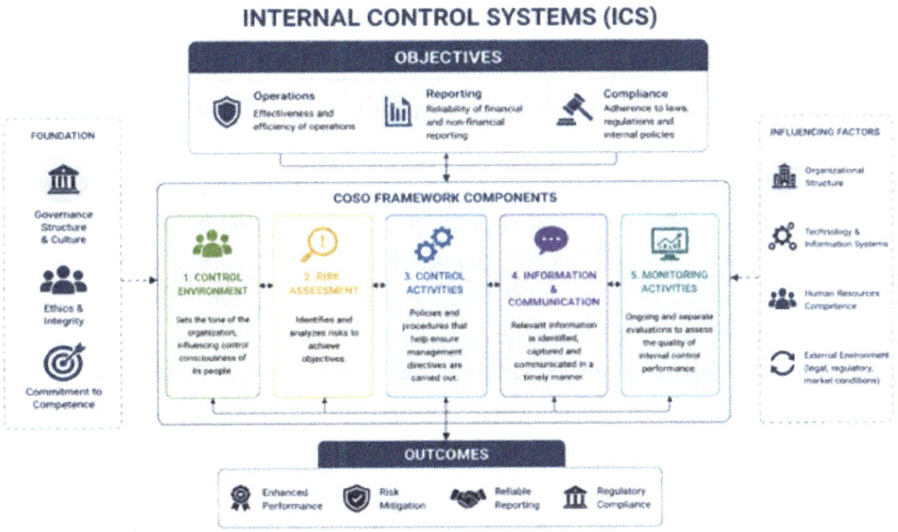

Source: Adapted from COSO (2013) – Internal Control – Integrated Framework.

Figure 2 illustrates the structure and functional integration of the core components of Internal Control Systems as defined in the Committee of Sponsoring Organizations of the Treadway Commission (2013). As illustrated, the five dimensions work interdependently, forming a coherent system that supports the achievement of organizational goals. At the same time, a clear distinction is made between the individual functions of the system and the intended outcomes, reflecting the orientation of internal audits towards the effectiveness of operations, the reliability of financial reporting and compliance with the regulatory framework. In addition, the role of organizational and environmental factors, which affect the overall operation of ICS and shape their degree of effectiveness, is highlighted. It is therefore appropriate to examine in more detail the individual components of the COSO context, which form the basis for the design and evaluation of ICS.

In particular, control environment is recognized as the fundamental component of ICS, as it defines the organizational culture, ethical values and administrative philosophy of the organization (COSO, 2013). In the same vein, Doyle et al. (2007), Ashbaugh-Skaife et al. (2009), Feng et al. (2009), and Ege (2015) demonstrate that the effectiveness of ICS is linked to the improvement of the quality of financial reporting and the reduction of failures and fraud risks. Similarly, Cheng et al. (2013) highlight that the quality of ICS is associated with increased investment efficiency and improved operational efficiency, while Hoitash et al. (2009) emphasize the key role of corporate governance and oversight by management bodies in enhancing the quality of internal controls.

The risk assessment component concerns the systematic identification, analysis and assessment of risks that may affect the achievement of the organization's strategic and operational objectives, as defined in the Committee of Sponsoring Organizations (2013). In an environment characterized by increased uncertainty and constant changes, effective risk management is becoming a critical factor for organizational resilience and long-term sustainability. Similarly, Gordon et al. (2009) and Arena et al. (2010) emphasize that the integration of risk management practices into ICS enhances the ability of organizations to respond in a timely manner to changing conditions, while contributing to improved overall performance. In the same vein, Hoitash et al. (2009) highlight that effective corporate governance and active oversight by competent bodies, such as audit committees, play a key role in enhancing both the quality of internal controls and the risk management process.

Control activities, on the other hand, form the operational part of ICS and include a set of policies and procedures that ensure the effective implementation of administrative decisions. These activities are integrated into the day-to-day operation of the organization and include practices such as segregation of duties, authorization and approval procedures, physical controls over assets, IT controls, as well as reconciliations and independent checks (COSO, 2013). According to Doyle et al. (2007)

and Ashbaugh-Skaife et al. (2009) effective implementation of control activities contributes significantly to reducing internal audit weaknesses and to limiting the risk of errors in financial reporting. At the same time, Ege (2015) highlights their role in enhancing transparency and reducing managerial misconduct. In addition, Goh and Li (2011) and Cheng et al. (2013) document that the high quality of ICS is linked to increased reliability of financial reporting and greater efficiency in investment decision-making.

The information and communication dimension concerns the processes of collecting, processing and disseminating reliable information within the organization, which are necessary to support effective decision-making (COSO, 2013). The availability of timely and high-quality information is considered particularly important for the operational effectiveness of organizations and for the effective functioning of internal control mechanisms. Granlund (2011), Appelbaum et al. (2017), and Alles (2015) underline that the development and integration of information systems and digital technologies significantly enhance the function of ICS. In particular, the use of technological tools helps to automate processes, improve data quality and reduce operational errors. At the same time, faster dissemination of information between organizational levels is facilitated, which enhances ability to respond promptly to potential risks and operational weaknesses.

The monitoring activities component is related to the ongoing and systematic evaluation of the effectiveness of ICS, with the aim of ensuring that internal control mechanisms operate effectively in accordance with their design and adapt in a timely manner to the changing conditions of the organizational environment (COSO, 2013). The monitoring process is carried out both through ongoing monitoring activities, which are integrated into the day-to-day operation of the organization and through separate evaluations, such as internal and external audit functions (COSO, 2013; Hoitash et al., 2009; Ege, 2015). Doyle et al. (2007) and Ashbaugh-Skaife et al. (2009) demonstrate that effective monitoring activities contribute to the early identification of organizational weaknesses and improve the quality of financial reporting. Through ongoing evaluation processes, organizations are able to identify deviations in a timely manner, reduce potential risks and adapt control mechanisms more effectively to the operational requirements of their environment. Therefore, the functioning of monitoring activities is not limited to assessing the effectiveness of ICS, but contributes more broadly to maintaining reliability, transparency and organizational stability.

Determinants of Internal Control Effectiveness

Beyond the framework of the Committee of Sponsoring Organizations, the theoretical approach to ICS has also expanded to examine the factors that affect their design and effectiveness in different organizational and institutional environments. Literature increasingly conceptualizes ICS not as static sets of processes, but as dynamic and adaptive systems that change according to the specific characteristics of the firm, its strategic orientation and the conditions of the external environment. Chenhall (2003), Otley (2016), and Hoai and Nguyen (2022) emphasize that the effectiveness of ICS depends significantly on their degree of adaptation to organizational needs and changing operational conditions. The operation of ICS is influenced by factors such as the firm size and structure, the level of organizational complexity, technological infrastructure, as well as the regulatory and institutional framework within which the firm operates.

In this context, factors such as firm size, operational complexity and organizational structure significantly affect the design and implementation of internal controls. Doyle et al. (2007), Feng et al. (2009), and Abernethy et al. (2023) show that larger and more complex organizations have increased control needs and therefore require more developed and standardized systems to effectively manage operational risks and organizational weaknesses resulting from the complexity of their activities. Apart from the structural characteristics of organizations, the role of organizational culture and management commitment to supporting internal control processes are also considered to be particularly important. Ashbaugh-Skaife et al. (2009), Feng et al. (2009), and Alzeban and Gwilliam (2014) argue that the effective operation of ICS depends largely on the level of compliance with control procedures, as well as on management's overall attitude toward control and accountability mechanisms.

The quality of corporate governance is also recognized as a crucial determinant of the effectiveness of ICS, as supervisory mechanisms such as boards of directors and audit committees play a key role in strengthening the internal audit function and ensuring the reliability of financial reporting. Ashbaugh-Skaife et al. (2009), Hoitash et al. (2009), and DeFond and Zhang (2014) emphasize that effective oversight enhances the quality of audit processes and contributes to improving the transparency and accountability of organizations. Similarly, an effective internal audit function enhances the ability of organizations to identify weaknesses, continuously improve control systems and limit managerial misconduct and fraud risks. Ege (2015) and Roussy and Brivot (2016) argue that the contribution of the internal audit is not limited to the evaluation of internal processes, but also extends to strengthening organizational monitoring and risk management frameworks.

At the same time, the development and integration of information systems and technological infrastructure have significantly enhanced the effectiveness of ICS, by enabling the automation the automation of critical processes, improving data quality and reliability and facilitating the early detection of errors and deviations. Granlund (2011), Appelbaum et al. (2017), and Alles (2015) emphasize that the use of digital technologies contributes significantly to enhancing the functionality and efficiency of control mechanisms. Furthermore, the adoption of advanced technologies such as data analytics improves the transparency and accuracy of financial reporting. Appelbaum et al. (2017), Alles (2015), and Vasarhelyi et al. (2015) demonstrate that these technological capabilities enable more efficient monitoring of procedures, faster detection of deviations and overall improvement of ICS operations (Ragazou et al., 2023).

Finally, the relevant literature highlights the key role of the external environment and the regulatory framework in shaping ICS. Doyle et al. (2007), Ashbaugh-Skaife et al. (2009), and COSO (2013) argue that regulatory requirements, accounting standards and pressures from regulatory and supervisory bodies directly affect the design and implementation of control mechanisms. In environments characterized by increased compliance requirements, organizations tend to adopt more stringent and standardized control systems, seeking to reduce the risk of errors and ensure compliance with the current regulatory framework. Altamuro and Beatty (2010), Doyle et al. (2007), and COSO (2013) emphasize that strengthening regulatory requirements often leads to more systematic monitoring, oversight and control processes, thereby strengthening the overall effectiveness of ICS. More generally, the effectiveness of ICS emerges through the dynamic interaction of organizational, technological and external factors. For this reason, ICS cannot be approached as static and uniform systems, but requires continuous adaptation to the specific conditions and needs of each organization, as well as to the environment in which it operates.

Internal Control Systems and Organizational Effectiveness

The effectiveness of ICS is directly linked to overall organizational performance, as it affects operational effectiveness, the reliability of financial reporting and compliance with the regulatory framework. According to COSO (2013) and Doyle et al. (2007), the existence of effective control mechanisms contributes significantly to improving organizational functioning and educing risks that may affect the achievement of operational objectives. In this context, ICS are not treated as isolated audit processes, but rather as integrated and interconnected system of mechanisms and practices embedded within all organizational functions. Romney and Steinbart (2018) emphasize that the functioning of ICS supports informed decision-making and contributes to the optimal utilization of available resources, while enhancing the overall effectiveness and stability of organizations.

The relevant literature shows that effective ICS contribute significantly to reducing organizational uncertainty and operational risks, while enhancing the accuracy, completeness and reliability of information supporting managerial processes. Goh and Li (2011) and Cheng et al. (2013) emphasize that the quality of ICS directly affects the ability of organizations to make more informed and effective decisions, improving overall organizational performance. Through the continuous monitoring of procedures and the implementation of appropriate control mechanisms, organizations are able to detect deviations at an early stage, correct operational errors and reduce fraud and managerial misconduct risks. Ege (2015) and DeFond and Zhang (2014) argue that an effective internal audit function significantly enhances transparency and limits information asymmetry, thereby contributing to the credibility and stability of organizations.

Furthermore, empirical studies highlight the positive relationship between the quality of ICS and key organizational performance indicators. Cheng et al. (2013) and Goh and Li (2011) demonstrate that strong control mechanisms enhance investment efficiency and enhance the quality of financial performance, thereby strengthening the overall operational and economic effectiveness of organizations. Ege (2015) emphasizes that effective audit mechanisms enhance transparency and improve overall organizational effectiveness, thereby creating a more reliable and stable operating environment.

Finally, technological development plays an increasingly important role in enhancing the effectiveness of ICS. Granlund (2011), Appelbaum et al. (2017), Alles (2015), and Vasarhelyi et al. (2015) emphasize that the integration of information systems and the use of advanced technologies, such as data analytics tools, enable the automation of audit processes, improve data quality and strengthen the reliability of financial reporting. Through these technological capabilities, organizations gain the ability to identify real-time deviations and operational weaknesses, strengthen the control process and make more timely and informed decisions. Therefore, ICS are no longer limited to traditional monitoring mechanisms, but are evolving into dynamic and technologically supported frameworks for risk management and organizational support, contributing significantly to maintaining organizational transparency, reliability, and overall effectiveness (Ragazou et al., 2023; Stavropoulou et al., 2023).

Internal Control Systems in the Hospitality and Hotel Industry

The role of ICS in the hospitality industry is particularly important due to the sector's operational complexity, high volume of transactions and strong dependence on human resources. Hotel firms operate in a dynamic and demanding environment characterized by multiple revenue streams, including room accommodations, food and beverage services and various ancillary services. Kimes (2011) and Ivanov and Zhechev (2012) emphasize that this complexity significantly increases the need for effective internal control mechanisms, as organizations must manage a wide range of operational and financial processes. In this context, ICS serve as a critical mechanism for ensuring operational efficiency, safeguarding assets, and enhancing the reliability of financial and managerial information. According to Doyle et al. (2007)

and COSO (2013), the effective implementation of ICS contributes significantly to reducing operational risks while promoting transparency, accountability, and sound governance within organizations (Vortelinos et al., 2025).

The hotel industry, however, has distinctive characteristics that significantly differentiate the requirements of ICS from those in other sectors. The decentralized nature of operations, the continuous interaction with customers and partners, as well as the high frequency of transactions increase the complexity of processes and may increase exposure to operational risks. Ivanov (2014), Kimes (2011), and Doyle et al. (2007) highlight that these conditions create a greater need for monitoring mechanisms and control procedures that can effectively support the operation of hotel firms. Previous studies by Doyle et al. (2007), Ashbaugh-Skaife et al. (2009), and Feng et al. (2009) demonstrate that weaknesses in ICS are linked to an increased likelihood of financial misstatements and problems in the quality of financial reporting. For this reason, the existence of effective control mechanisms is considered particularly important to ensure the transparency, accountability and overall reliability of hotel firms.

In addition, ICS are directly linked to the effective implementation of revenue management practices, one of the key success factors in the hotel industry. Kimes (2011) and Ivanov (2014) emphasize that revenue management is based on the ability of hotel firms to anticipate demand, dynamically adjust prices and optimize the use of available resources, with the aim of maximizing revenue. Effective implementation of pricing and inventory management strategies requires reliable, accurate and timely information to support the decision-making process. In this context, the increasing use of information systems and digital technologies further enhances the dependence of hotel firms on high-quality data. Law et al. (2020), Mariani (2020), and Sigala (2020) highlight that the digital transformation of the hotel industry has significantly increased the volume and importance of available data, while strengthening the need for effective control and monitoring mechanisms. In this environment, ICS play a key role in ensuring the accurate recording of transactions, the reliability of information and the overall quality of data used in the decision-making process. Appelbaum et al. (2017) demonstrate that the effective functioning of internal control mechanisms enhances the ability of organizations to make more effective use of available data and support more informed managerial decisions. The relationship between ICS and revenue management is discussed in more detail in the following sub-section.

Technological evolution has significantly affected the operation of ICS in the hospitality industry, transforming the way hotel firms organize and monitor their operational processes. The adoption of information systems, such as Property Management Systems (PMS), Point-of-Sale (POS) systems and Enterprise Resource Planning (ERP) systems, enables the automation of critical processes and strengthens control mechanisms. Law et al. (2020) indicate that these technological systems significantly enhance the efficiency of operational management and facilitate the collection and utilization of large volumes of data. At the same time, these systems contribute to reducing human error, improving transaction traceability and enhancing the transparency and accountability of organizational processes. Appelbaum et al. (2017) demonstrate that automation of control and audit procedures enables more effective monitoring of operations and enhances the overall reliability of information. In addition, the use of data analytics technologies strengthens the ability of organizations to continuously monitor operations and identify deviations or operational weaknesses in a timely manner. Vasarhelyi et al. (2015) and Appelbaum et al. (2017) highlight that the use of advanced data analytics tools enables organizations to identify potential risks more rapidly, strengthen control processes and support more effectively managerial decision-making.

Despite significant technological developments, the human factor continues to be a key element in the effectiveness of ICS in the hospitality industry. High work demands and continuous interaction with customers increase the likelihood of operational errors, procedural deviations and organizational weaknesses. Baum (2015) highlights that the particular working conditions in the hotel industry create greater demands for human resource management and effective monitoring of operational processes. Similarly, Alola et al. (2018) and Alzeban (2020) emphasize that staff training, clear allocation of responsibilities and strengthening organizational culture are crucial factors for the effective functioning of organizations and the strengthening of control mechanisms. The development of a culture of responsibility and compliance contributes significantly to reducing operational weaknesses and enhancing the credibility of internal processes. Consequently, the effectiveness of ICS does not depend solely on the processes or information systems used by organizations, but also on the attitudes, behaviors and commitment of employees towards control processes and organizational goals.

Corporate governance is one of the most important factors in enhancing the effectiveness of ICS in the hotel industry. Hoitash et al. (2009), Kagias et al. (2023), DeFond and Zhang (2014), Passas et al. (2023a), and Alzeban (2020) demonstrate that monitoring mechanisms, such as boards and audit committees, play a key role in ensuring compliance with regulatory frameworks and enhancing the credibility of financial reporting. Effective monitoring reduces instances of managerial misconduct while enhancing transparency and accountability, thereby contributing to improved organizational performance (Cheliatzidou et al., 2023; Kagias et al., 2024; Lampropoulos et al., 2025).

The role of the external environment and regulatory requirements in shaping ICS in the hospitality industry is particularly important. Hotel firms are required to comply with a complex set of regulations, including tax regulations, financial reporting standards, and health and safety requirements. Doyle et al. (2007) and Mesa-Pérez (2024) suggest that increased compliance requirements reinforce the need for more structured and standardized control systems capable of effectively supporting organizational functioning. In this environment, the adoption of stricter control mechanisms contributes to the reduction of operational and regulatory risks, while enhancing compliance, transparency and the overall operational efficiency of hotel firms.

Internal Control Systems and Hotel Revenue

Revenue management is one of the most important success factors in the hotel industry, as it directly affects the profitability and sustainability of firms. Kimes (2011) and Ivanov (2014) emphasize that the fundamental principle of revenue management is the optimization of pricing and the allocation of available resources through demand forecasting and dynamic price adjustment. In the highly competitive and ever-changing hospitality environment, these decisions are made in real time and are based on the processing of large volumes of complex, high-frequency data.

Information quality becomes a crucial factor in the effective implementation of revenue management practices. Hotel firms rely on information systems to collect, process and analyze data related to demand, bookings, customer behavior and market conditions. Law et al. (2020) and Mariani (2020) highlight that the growing reliance on digital systems and data has significantly altered the way businesses in the industry make strategic and operational decisions.

However, the credibility of these decisions depends largely on the accuracy, completeness and consistency of the information used, which highlights the importance of effective ICS. COSO (2013) and Appelbaum et al. (2017) emphasize that ICS play a key role in ensuring the quality of data and the reliability of information supporting the decision-making process. Through accurate transaction recording, systematic monitoring of procedures and the implementation of appropriate control mechanisms, ICS help to reduce errors and ensure information consistency. In addition, effective control mechanisms allow organizations to detect discrepancies in a timely manner, prevent irregularities and enhance the transparency of procedures, which are considered particularly critical for the effective implementation of revenue management practices and the optimization of hotel revenues.

The link between ICS and revenue management is particularly evident in decision-making, as pricing and inventory management strategies are based on data that must be reliable, accurate and available in a timely manner. Feng et al. (2009) and Cheng et al. (2013) indicate that weaknesses in ICS are linked to a lower quality of information and an increased likelihood of errors, which can negatively affect the decision-making process and the overall effectiveness of organizations. On the other hand, more recent studies indicate that strengthening control mechanisms and the use of technological tools contribute significantly to improving data quality and enhancing organizational transparency in the hospitality industry. Law et al. (2020), Mariani (2020), and Alzeban (2020) highlight that the increasing use of information systems and digital technologies enables more efficient monitoring of operations and greater reliability in information management. The importance of data quality becomes even greater in the hotel industry, where pricing decisions are made in real time and are based on complex, high-frequency data. Kimes (2011) and Ivanov (2014) argue that effective revenue management directly depends on the accuracy of the information used for demand forecasting and dynamic pricing. Mariani (2020) and Law et al. (2020) indicate that the use of inaccurate or incomplete data may lead to incorrect pricing strategies and inefficient demand management. Within this framework, ICS serve as a critical mechanism for supporting data reliability and information quality, thereby enhancing the effectiveness of revenue management practices and overall organizational performance. COSO (2013) and Appelbaum et al. (2017) highlight that the effective functioning of control mechanisms contributes significantly to improving transparency, accuracy of information and the overall decision-making process.

The relationship between ICS and revenue management can be interpreted from the perspective of agency theory, according to which information asymmetry between managers and owners creates an increased need for control and monitoring mechanisms. In the hotel industry, where a significant proportion of decisions are taken at a decentralized level and operational processes are highly complex, reliable accurate and timely information is particularly critical for reducing the risks associated with incorrect, ineffective, or opportunistic decisions. ICS serve as a key mechanism for mitigating information asymmetry, enhancing transparency, accountability and the reliability of organizational processes. DeFond and Zhang (2014) and Alzeban (2020) emphasize that the effective functioning of control mechanisms contributes significantly to improving the quality of information and strengthening monitoring, thus supporting more informed and effective managerial decisions.

The increasing complexity of the external business environment further enhances the importance of the relationship between ICS and revenue management in the hotel industry. Hotel firms operate in an environment characterized by a high degree of uncertainty, intense competition and constant changes in demand, making data management and information quality critical determinants of organizational success. Law et al. (2020) and Sigala (2020) emphasize that the increasing reliance on digital data and information systems has significantly enhanced the importance of the reliability and accuracy of available information. For this reason, the ability to make timely and informed decisions becomes a key factor in enhancing the competitiveness and operational performance of hotel organizations. Elbanna et al. (2022) indicate that the effective use of available information enables firms to respond more quickly to market changes, improve managerial decision-making, and enhance their overall operational and financial performance.

IT capabilities have a significant impact on the overall performance of hotel firms, as the effective integration of information systems into operational and managerial processes enhances data analytics capabilities and supports strategic decision-making. Law et al. (2020) and Shniekat et al. (2021) indicate that the use of technological infrastructure contributes significantly to improving organizational performance and the more efficient management of operational processes. However, the value of information systems depends largely on the reliability, accuracy and consistency of the data they manage. For this reason, ICS are particularly important as mechanisms for ensuring information quality and support effective decision-making. Appelbaum et al. (2017) demonstrate that the effective functioning of internal control mechanisms enhances the reliability of information and reduces the risk of inaccurate or incomplete data. At the same time, technological development and the increasing use of advanced data analytics tools, such as artificial intelligence and machine learning, have significantly transformed revenue management practices in the hotel industry. Webster and Ivanov (2020) and Sigala (2020) highlight that these technologies enhance organizational efficiency, support data-driven decision-making, and facilitate the implementation of more sophisticated revenue management practices. However, the growing reliance on information systems and digital technologies further reinforces the need for effective control mechanisms that ensure data reliability and information integrity.

The concept of a dynamic control environment is of particular importance in the hotel industry, where businesses operate in an environment of high volatility and constant changes in demand. Unlike traditional control systems, modern ICS incorporate sophisticated monitoring mechanisms, which enable the early detection of deviations and the immediate adaptation of operational and strategic processes. Vasarhelyi et al. (2015) emphasize that continuous monitoring of operations significantly enhances the ability of organizations to respond more quickly to changes in the external environment and to adapt decision-making processes more effectively. This is particularly important in revenue management, as it allows hotel firms to respond more effectively to fluctuations in demand and changes in market conditions. At the same time, data quality has become a critical factor in optimizing revenue management strategies. Hajli et al. (2020) and Mariani (2020) indicate that the use of inaccurate or incomplete data may lead to discrepancies between forecasts and actual results, negatively affecting the efficiency and operational effectiveness of hotel firms. Within this framework, ICS contribute significantly to ensuring the accuracy, completeness and consistency of data, thereby enhancing the credibility of the decision-making process. Appelbaum et al. (2017) demonstrate that effective internal control mechanisms support transparency and enhance the overall quality of organizational information, which is particularly critical for the effective functioning of revenue management systems. The contribution of ICS is not limited to ensuring information quality but also extends to reducing operational risks, protecting revenue, and enhancing the financial stability of organizations. Through continuous monitoring of processes and early detection of discrepancies, ICS serve firms to reduce potential revenue losses and enhance their operational resilience. Yemer & Chekol (2017) and Otoo et al. (2023) highlight that the effective operation of control mechanisms contributes significantly to maintaining organizational stability and improving overall operational performance.

However, the effectiveness of ICS does not depend solely on information systems or standard procedures, but is also significantly influenced by the human factor. Baum (2015) and Alzeban (2020) emphasize that employee training, experience and compliance with control procedures directly affect the effective implementation of internal control mechanisms and the overall operational efficiency of organizations. The importance of the human factor is even greater in the hotel industry, where direct interaction with customers is a key feature of service delivery and the overall hospitality experience. Baum (2015) indicates that employee behavior, accountability and consistency can significantly affect both revenue management and the quality of service provided. For this reason, the effective functioning of ICS requires not only the existence of appropriate technological infrastructure and control processes, but also the development of an organizational culture that enhances compliance, accountability and responsible operational behavior.

In the modern and highly competitive hospitality environment, the connection between ICS and revenue management is increasingly critical for the operational and financial stability of hotel firms. The effective functioning of ICS enhances the reliability of information, supports more informed managerial decisions and helps to reduce operational and organizational risks. Therefore, enhancing the effectiveness of ICS is not only a matter of compliance but also a key factor in enhancing competitiveness and promoting the sustainable development of hotel firms (Passas & Garefalakis, 2025).

CONCLUSION

The literature review of the previous chapters highlighted the key role of corporate governance and ICS in the operation, efficiency and sustainability of hotel firms. In an operational environment characterized by increased complexity, strong demand volatility, high capital intensity and complex organizational structures, governance and internal control mechanisms are not limited to formal administrative procedures.

On the contrary, they are critical strategic mechanisms that directly affect overall organizational efficiency and long-term financial stability of hotel firms. Jensen and Meckling (1976) and Singal (2015) argue that the effective operation of these mechanisms contributes significantly to risk management, improved accountability and enhanced organizational reliability.

In particular, the section 2 analysis showed that the concept of corporate governance has evolved significantly in recent decades, moving from a limited framework of shareholder protection and management oversight to a broader system of strategic supervision, risk management and accountability assurance. OECD (2023) and Zattoni et al. (2020) emphasize that modern corporate governance is now closely linked to strengthening organizational transparency, sustainability and effective management of operational risks. A central element of the relevant theoretical approach is the separation between ownership and control, which reinforces the problems of information asymmetry and creates an increased need for effective monitoring and control mechanisms. Berle and Means (1932) and Fama and Jensen (1983) argue that the existence of conflicts of interest between owners and management makes it necessary to implement mechanisms that ensure accountability and limit managerial opportunism. In the hotel industry, this need becomes even more acute due to the extensive use of asset-light strategies, franchising and management contracts, through which ownership, operational management and brand governance are distributed among different stakeholders, such as owners, operators, franchisees and international hotel chains. Contractor and Kundu (1998) and Li and Singal (2019) highlight that these complex forms of organization increase organizational complexity and reinforce the need for effective mechanisms of control, supervision and coordination.

Through this complex organizational structure, corporate governance emerges as a key mechanism for aligning incentives and limiting agency impacts. The existence of divergent objectives between owners, managers and franchisees makes it necessary to operate monitoring mechanisms, performance evaluation and ensuring consistency of operational standards and quality of services. Eisenhardt (1989) and Michael (1999) suggest that these mechanisms contribute significantly to reducing problems resulting from information asymmetry and conflicting interests among stakeholders.

In the same vein, Dalton et al. (1998) and Combs et al. (2011) argue that boards, control mechanisms, monitoring procedures and conventional governance mechanisms act as critical tools to limit opportunistic behavior and enhance accountability. The effective operation of these mechanisms enhances transparency, supports the maintenance of service quality and contributes to the overall stability of hotel firms. In addition, in literature it is shown that corporate governance is no longer exclusively linked to financial performance, but also extends to sustainability, ESG practices and long-term value creation issues. Aguilera et al. (2019) and Gillan et al. (2021)

suggest that modern corporate governance mechanisms are increasingly expected to incorporate not only economic, but also social and environmental objectives. In this way, corporate governance is now becoming multidimensional in the hotel industry, reflecting increasing requirements for sustainability, transparency, and responsible business operations.

Then, section 3 highlighted the importance of ICS as a key pillar of organizational and risk management in the hospitality industry. Through the analysis of the framework of the Committee of Sponsoring Organizations of the Treadway Commission (2013), ICS was presented as a dynamic and integrated system of processes and mechanisms, which is integrated into all functions of the organization and aims to ensure operational efficiency, the reliability of financial reporting and compliance with the regulatory framework. Doyle et al. (2007) and Ashbaugh-Skaife et al. (2009) demonstrate that the effective functioning of ICS contributes significantly to reducing organizational risks and improving information quality. The five key components of the framework — control environment, risk assessment, control activities, information and communication and monitoring — operate interdependently and form a coherent monitoring and control framework supporting overall organizational efficiency and managerial decision-making (COSO, 2013).

Chenhall (2003) and Hoitash et al. (2009) argue that the effectiveness of ICS is influenced by a wide range of organizational and external factors, such as the quality of corporate governance, organizational culture, technological capabilities and regulatory environment. The literature also highlights the important role of technology and information systems in the operation of modern control mechanisms. Granlund (2011) and Appelbaum et al. (2017) demonstrate that the integration of PMS, POS, ERP systems, data analytics and automated monitoring tools enhances the ability to continuously monitor operations, improves data quality and reduces operational errors and deviations. However, despite significant technological developments, Baum (2015) and Alzeban (2020) emphasize that the human factor remains a crucial element in the effective implementation of internal audits. Its importance is even greater in the hotel industry, where the provision of services is largely based on human interaction, operational decentralization and the management of complex daily processes. These authors further suggest that the training, experience and compliance of employees with audit procedures significantly affect the operational effectiveness of organizations and the overall reliability of internal control mechanisms.

The relationship between ICS and revenue management was also identified as a key theme in the literature. Kimes (2011) and Ivanov (2014) argue that revenue management in the hotel industry is based on dynamic pricing, demand forecasting and occupancy optimization processes, which are largely dependent on the quality and reliability of available information. In this context, ICS serve as a key mechanism to ensure the accuracy, completeness and consistency of the data used in the decision-making process. Feng et al. (2009) and Cheng et al. (2013) demonstrate that weaknesses in ICS may lead to inaccurate forecasts, ineffective pricing decisions and revenue losses, thereby negatively affecting overall organizational performance. On the contrary, Law et al. (2020) and Mariani (2020) highlight that high-quality data and effective information management enhance transparency, reduce information asymmetries and support the effective functioning of revenue management systems.

Overall, the analysis of sections 2 and 3 revealed that corporate governance and ICS are interrelated dimensions of modern hotel management. DeFond and Zhang (2014) and Li and Singal (2022) find that the effective operation of these mechanisms contributes significantly to reducing operational uncertainty, improving financial transparency, enhancing operational efficiency and ensuring the long-term sustainability of hotel firms. At the same time, the increasing complexity of the business environment, the digitalization of operations, increased accountability requirements and the integration of ESG practices reinforce the need for stronger governance mechanisms and ICS in the hospitality industry. Future studies could empirically investigate the relationship between corporate governance, internal control effectiveness, technological capabilities and organizational performance in the hotel industry, as well as on the role of new technologies and ESG strategies in shaping modern governance and control systems.

REFERENCES

Abernethy, M. A., Li, W., Zhang, Y., & Shi, H. (2023). Firm culture and internal control system. [Object Identifier] [DOI]. *Accounting and Finance*, *63*(3), 3095–3123. DOI: 10.1111/acfi.13020

Aguilera, R. V., & Crespi-Cladera, R. (2016). Global corporate governance: On the relevance of firms' ownership structure. *Journal of World Business*, *51*(1), 50–57. DOI: 10.1016/j.jwb.2015.10.003

Aguilera, R. V., Filatotchev, I., Gospel, H., & Jackson, G. (2008). An organizational approach to comparative corporate governance: Costs, contingencies, and complementarities. *Organization Science*, *19*(3), 475–492. DOI: 10.1287/orsc.1070.0322

Aguilera, R. V., & Jackson, G. (2010). Comparative and international corporate governance. *The Academy of Management Annals*, *4*(1), 485–556. DOI: 10.5465/19416520.2010.495525

Aguilera, R. V., Marano, V., & Haxhi, I. (2019). International corporate governance: A review and opportunities for future research. *Journal of International Business Studies*, *50*(4), 457–498. DOI: 10.1057/s41267-019-00232-w

Alles, M. G. (2015). Drivers of the use and facilitators and obstacles of the evolution of big data by the audit profession. *Accounting Horizons*, *29*(2), 439–449. DOI: 10.2308/acch-51067

Alola, U. V., Avci, T., & Ozturen, A. (2018). Organizational sustainability through human resource capital: The impacts of supervisor incivility and self-efficacy. *Sustainability (Basel)*, *10*(8), 2610. DOI: 10.3390/su10082610

Altamuro, J., & Beatty, A. (2010). How does internal control regulation affect financial reporting? *Journal of Accounting and Economics*, *49*(1–2), 58–74. DOI: 10.1016/j.jacceco.2009.07.002

Alzeban, A. (2020). The impact of audit committee, CEO, and external auditor quality on the quality of financial reporting. *Corporate Governance (Bradford)*, *20*(2), 263–279. DOI: 10.1108/CG-07-2019-0204

Alzeban, A., & Gwilliam, D. (2014). Factors affecting the internal audit effectiveness: A survey of the Saudi public sector. *Journal of International Accounting, Auditing & Taxation*, *23*(2), 74–86. DOI: 10.1016/j.intaccaudtax.2014.06.001

Appel, I. R., Gormley, T. A., & Keim, D. B. (2016). Passive investors, not passive owners. *Journal of Financial Economics, 121*(1), 111–141. DOI: 10.1016/j.jfineco.2016.03.003

Appelbaum, D., Kogan, A., Vasarhelyi, M., & Yan, Z. (2017). Impact of business analytics and enterprise systems on managerial accounting. *International Journal of Accounting Information Systems, 25*, 29–44. DOI: 10.1016/j.accinf.2017.03.003

Arena, M., Arnaboldi, M., & Azzone, G. (2010). The organizational dynamics of enterprise risk management. *Accounting, Organizations and Society, 35*(7), 659–675. DOI: 10.1016/j.aos.2010.07.003

Ashbaugh-Skaife, H., Collins, D. W., Kinney, W. R.Jr, & LaFond, R. (2009). The effect of SOX internal control deficiencies on firm risk and cost of equity. *Journal of Accounting Research, 47*(1), 1–43. DOI: 10.1111/j.1475-679X.2008.00315.x

Aziz, H. A., Saleh, M., Rasmy, M. H., & ElShishiny, H. (2011). Dynamic room pricing model for hotel revenue management systems. *Egyptian Informatics Journal, 12*(3), 177–183. DOI: 10.1016/j.eij.2011.08.001

Balios, D., Katsikis, V. N., Naoum, V. C., & Zaroulea, T. (2024). The effect of industry level characteristics and cross-country differences on earnings management: A European comparative perspective. *Journal of Governance & Regulation, 13*(2), 403–418. DOI: 10.22495/jgrv13i2siart16

Baum, T. (2015). Human resources in tourism: Still waiting for change? – A 2015 reprise. *Tourism Management, 50*, 204–212. DOI: 10.1016/j.tourman.2015.02.001

Bebchuk, L. A., & Hirst, S. (2019). Index funds and the future of corporate governance: Theory, evidence, and policy. *Columbia Law Review, 119*(8), 2029–2146.

Bergen, M., Dutta, S., & Walker, O. C.Jr. (1992). Agency relationships in marketing: A review of the implications and applications. *Journal of Marketing, 56*(3), 1–24. DOI: 10.1177/002224299205600301

Berle, A. A., & Means, G. C. (1932). *The modern corporation and private property*. Macmillan.

Bhagat, S., & Black, B. (2001). The non-correlation between board independence and long-term firm performance. *The Journal of Corporation Law, 27*(2), 231–274.

Brickley, J. A., & Dark, F. H. (1987). The choice of organizational form: The case of franchising. *Journal of Financial Economics, 18*(2), 401–420. DOI: 10.1016/0304-405X(87)90046-8

Brown, J. R., Dev, C. S., & Zhou, Z. (2003). Broadening the foreign market entry mode decision: Separating ownership and control. *Journal of International Business Studies, 34*(5), 473–488. DOI: 10.1057/palgrave.jibs.8400050

Cadbury, A. (1992). *Report of the Committee on the Financial Aspects of Corporate Governance*. Gee and Co Ltd.

Chau, L., Anh, L., & Duc, V. (2025). Valuing ESG: How financial markets respond to corporate sustainability. *International Business Review, 34*(3), 102418. DOI: 10.1016/j.ibusrev.2025.102418

Cheliatsidou, A., Sariannidis, N., Garefalakis, A., Passas, I., & Spinthiropoulos, K. (2023). Exploring Attitudes towards Whistleblowing in Relation to Sustainable Municipalities. *Administrative Sciences, 13*(9), 199. DOI: 10.3390/admsci13090199

Chen, H., Wang, S., Yang, D., & Zhou, N. (2025). COSO-based internal control and comprehensive enterprise risk management: Institutional background and research evidence from China. Encyclopedia, 5(3), Article 106.

Cheng, M., Dhaliwal, D., & Zhang, Y. (2013). Does investment efficiency improve after the disclosure of material weaknesses in internal control over financial reporting? *Journal of Accounting and Economics, 56*(1), 1–18. DOI: 10.1016/j.jacceco.2013.03.001

Chenhall, R. H. (2003). Management control systems design within its organizational context: Findings from contingency-based research and directions for the future. *Accounting, Organizations and Society, 28*(2–3), 127–168. DOI: 10.1016/S0361-3682(01)00027-7

Claessens, S., & Yurtoglu, B. B. (2013). Corporate governance in emerging markets: A survey. *Emerging Markets Review, 15*, 1–33. DOI: 10.1016/j.ememar.2012.03.002

Combs, J. G., Ketchen, D. J.Jr, & Short, J. C. (2011). Franchising research: Major milestones, new directions, and its future within entrepreneurship. *Entrepreneurship Theory and Practice, 35*(3), 413–425. DOI: 10.1111/j.1540-6520.2011.00443.x

Committee of Sponsoring Organizations of the Treadway Commission. (2013). *Internal control—Integrated framework*. COSO.

Contractor, F. J., & Kundu, S. K. (1998). Modal choice in a world of alliances: Analyzing organizational forms in the international hotel sector. *Journal of International Business Studies, 29*(2), 325–356. DOI: 10.1057/palgrave.jibs.8490039

Cross, R. G., Higbie, J. A., & Cross, D. Q. (2009). Revenue management's renaissance: A rebirth of the art and science of profitable revenue generation. *Cornell Hospitality Quarterly, 50*(1), 56–81. DOI: 10.1177/1938965508328716

Dalton, D. R., Daily, C. M., Ellstrand, A. E., & Johnson, J. L. (1998). Meta-analytic reviews of board composition, leadership structure, and financial performance. *Strategic Management Journal, 19*(3), 269–290. DOI: 10.1002/(SICI)1097-0266(199803)19:3<269::AID-SMJ950>3.0.CO;2-K

DeFond, M., & Zhang, J. (2014). A review of archival auditing research. *Journal of Accounting and Economics, 58*(2–3), 275–326. DOI: 10.1016/j.jacceco.2014.09.002

Deng, F., & Zhou, C. (2022). Sustainable development of corporate governance in the hospitality and tourism industry: The evolution and the future. *Sustainability (Basel), 14*(7), 4286. DOI: 10.3390/su14074286

Denis, D. K., & McConnell, J. J. (2003). International corporate governance. *Journal of Financial and Quantitative Analysis, 38*(1), 1–36. DOI: 10.2307/4126762

Doyle, J., Ge, W., & McVay, S. (2007). Determinants of weaknesses in internal control over financial reporting. *Journal of Accounting and Economics, 44*(1–2), 193–223. DOI: 10.1016/j.jacceco.2006.10.003

Ege, M. S. (2015). Does internal audit function quality deter management misconduct? *The Accounting Review, 90*(2), 495–527. DOI: 10.2308/accr-50871

Eisenhardt, K. M. (1989). Agency theory: An assessment and review. *Academy of Management Review, 14*(1), 57–74. DOI: 10.2307/258191

Elbanna, S., Kamel, H., Fatima, T., & Eid, R. (2022). An investigation of the causality links in the balanced scorecard: The case of the Gulf Cooperation Council hospitality industry. *International Journal of Contemporary Hospitality Management, 34*(7), 2594–2615.

Fama, E. F., & Jensen, M. C. (1983). Separation of ownership and control. *The Journal of Law & Economics, 26*(2), 301–325. DOI: 10.1086/467037

Fatemi, A., Glaum, M., & Kaiser, S. (2018). ESG performance and firm value: The moderating role of disclosure. *Global Finance Journal, 38*, 45–64. DOI: 10.1016/j.gfj.2017.03.001

Feng, M., Li, C., & McVay, S. (2009). Internal control and management guidance. *Journal of Accounting and Economics, 48*(2–3), 190–209. DOI: 10.1016/j.jacceco.2009.09.004

Frias-Aceituno, J. V., Rodríguez-Ariza, L., & García-Sánchez, I. M. (2013). The role of the board in the dissemination of integrated corporate social reporting. *Corporate Social Responsibility and Environmental Management, 20*(4), 219–233. DOI: 10.1002/csr.1294

Friede, G., Busch, T., & Bassen, A. (2015). ESG and financial performance: Aggregated evidence from more than 2000 empirical studies. *Journal of Sustainable Finance & Investment, 5*(4), 210–233. DOI: 10.1080/20430795.2015.1118917

Gillan, S. L., Koch, A., & Starks, L. T. (2021). Firms and social responsibility: A review of ESG and CSR research in corporate finance. *Journal of Corporate Finance, 66*, 101889. DOI: 10.1016/j.jcorpfin.2021.101889

Goh, B. W., & Li, D. (2011). Internal controls and conditional conservatism. *The Accounting Review, 86*(3), 975–1005. DOI: 10.2308/accr.00000041

Gordon, L. A., Loeb, M. P., & Tseng, C. Y. (2009). Enterprise risk management and firm performance: A contingency perspective. *Journal of Accounting and Public Policy, 28*(4), 301–327. DOI: 10.1016/j.jaccpubpol.2009.06.006

Granlund, M. (2011). Extending AIS research to management accounting and control issues. *International Journal of Accounting Information Systems, 12*(1), 3–19. DOI: 10.1016/j.accinf.2010.11.001

Hajli, N., Tajvidi, M., Gbadamosi, A., & Nadeem, W. (2020). Understanding market agility for new product success with big data analytics. *Industrial Marketing Management, 86*, 135–143. DOI: 10.1016/j.indmarman.2019.09.010

Hermalin, B. E., & Weisbach, M. S. (2001). Boards of directors as an endogenously determined institution: A survey of the economic literature (NBER Working Paper No. 8161).

Hoai, T. T., & Nguyen, N. P. (2022). Internal control systems and performance of emerging market firms: The moderating roles of leadership consistency and quality. *SAGE Open, 12*(3), 21582440221123509. DOI: 10.1177/21582440221123509

Hoitash, U., Hoitash, R., & Bedard, J. C. (2009). Corporate governance and internal control over financial reporting: A comparison of regulatory regimes. *The Accounting Review, 84*(3), 839–867. DOI: 10.2308/accr.2009.84.3.839

Ivanov, S. (2014). *Hotel revenue management: From theory to practice*. Zangador.

Ivanov, S., & Zhechev, V. (2012). Hotel revenue management: A critical literature review. *Tourism and Hospitality Management, 18*(2), 175–197.

Jackson, L. A. (2025). Corporate governance and environmental citizenship in global hospitality: A cross-national empirical study. *Sustainability (Basel), 17*(9), 3918. DOI: 10.3390/su17093918

Jensen, M. C., & Meckling, W. H. (1976). Theory of the firm: Managerial behavior, agency costs and ownership structure. *Journal of Financial Economics, 3*(4), 305–360. DOI: 10.1016/0304-405X(76)90026-X

Jo, H., & Harjoto, M. A. (2012). The causal effect of corporate governance on corporate social responsibility. *Journal of Business Ethics, 106*(1), 53–72. DOI: 10.1007/s10551-011-1052-1

Kagias, P., Garefalakis, A., Passas, I., Kyriakogkonas, P., & Sariannidis, N. (2024). Whistleblowing Based on the Three Lines Model. *Administrative Sciences, 14*(5), 83. DOI: 10.3390/admsci14050083

Kagias, P., Kourgiantakis, M., Passas, I., Ragazou, K., & Bakeas, S. (2023). CG and Prosperous Investment Decisions — The Paradigm of Mergers and Acquisitions. In Governance and Financial Performance: Current Trends and Perspectives (pp. 275–300). World Scientific Publishing Co. https://doi.org/DOI: 10.1142/9789811260506_0011

Kiel, G. C., & Nicholson, G. J. (2003). Board composition and corporate performance: How the Australian experience informs contrasting theories of corporate governance. *Corporate Governance, 11*(3), 189–205. DOI: 10.1111/1467-8683.00318

Kimes, S. E. (1989). Yield management: A tool for capacity-constrained service firms. *Journal of Operations Management, 8*(4), 348–363. DOI: 10.1016/0272-6963(89)90035-1

Kimes, S. E. (2011). The future of hotel revenue management. *Journal of Revenue and Pricing Management, 10*(1), 62–72. DOI: 10.1057/rpm.2010.47

La Porta, R., Lopez-de-Silanes, F., Shleifer, A., & Vishny, R. (1999). Corporate ownership around the world. *The Journal of Finance, 54*(2), 471–517. DOI: 10.1111/0022-1082.00115

La Porta, R., Lopez-de-Silanes, F., Shleifer, A., & Vishny, R. W. (1998). Law and finance. *Journal of Political Economy, 106*(6), 1113–1155. DOI: 10.1086/250042

La Porta, R., Lopez-de-Silanes, F., Shleifer, A., & Vishny, R. W. (2000). Investor protection and corporate governance. *Journal of Financial Economics, 58*(1–2), 3–27. DOI: 10.1016/S0304-405X(00)00065-9

Lafontaine, F., & Blair, R. D. (2005). *The economics of franchising*. Cambridge University Press.

Lampropoulos, S. D., Thanasas, G. L., Garefalakis, A., & Passas, I. (2025). Harmonizing Sustainability and Resilience: The Integral Role of Internal Audit in ESG Implementation—A Review. *International Journal of Financial Studies*, *13*(4), 194. DOI: 10.3390/ijfs13040194

Law, R., Leung, D., & Chan, I. C. C. (2020). Progression and development of information and communication technology research in hospitality and tourism: A state-of-the-art review. *International Journal of Contemporary Hospitality Management*, *32*(2), 511–534. DOI: 10.1108/IJCHM-07-2018-0586

Li, Y., & Singal, M. (2019). Capital structure in the hospitality industry: The role of the asset-light and fee-oriented strategy. *Tourism Management*, *70*, 124–133. DOI: 10.1016/j.tourman.2018.08.004

Li, Y., & Singal, M. (2022). Corporate governance in the hospitality and tourism industry: Theoretical foundations and future research. *Journal of Hospitality & Tourism Research (Washington, D.C.)*, *46*(7), 1347–1383. DOI: 10.1177/10963480211011718

Maravelaki, A., Zopounidis, C., Lemonakis, C., & Passas, I. (2021). Corporate Governance as a Tool for Fraud Mitigation. In Papadakis, S., Garefalakis, A., Lemonakis, C., & Zopounidis, C. (Eds.), *Machine Learning Applications for Accounting Disclosure and Fraud Detection* (pp. 1–15). IGI Global Scientific Publishing., DOI: 10.4018/978-1-7998-4805-9.ch001

Mariani, M. (2020). Big data and analytics in tourism and hospitality: A perspective article. *Tourism Review*, *75*(1), 299–303. DOI: 10.1108/TR-06-2019-0259

Mesa-Pérez, E. (2024). The rise of compliance systems? The evolution of internal control through the accounting literature. *Revista Española de Financiación y Contabilidad*, *53*(3), 302–322. DOI: 10.1080/02102412.2023.2255416

Mia, L., & Patiar, A. (2001). The use of management accounting systems in hotels: An exploratory study. *International Journal of Hospitality Management*, *20*(2), 111–128. DOI: 10.1016/S0278-4319(00)00033-5

Michael, S. C. (1999). The elasticity of franchising. *Small Business Economics*, *12*(4), 313–320. DOI: 10.1023/A:1008019418231

Novatiani, R. A., Kusumah, R. W. R., Yadiati, W., Rachmat, A. H., & Rachman, A. (2024). Internal auditor competence and internal control: Improving internal audit quality to prevent fraudulent financial statements. *Cogent Business & Management*, *11*(1), 2409339. DOI: 10.1080/23311975.2024.2409339

OECD. (2015). *G20/OECD principles of corporate governance*. OECD Publishing.

OECD. (2023). *G20/OECD principles of corporate governance*. OECD Publishing.

Otley, D. (2016). The contingency theory of management accounting and control: 1980–2014. *Management Accounting Research*, *31*, 45–62. DOI: 10.1016/j.mar.2016.02.001

Otoo, F. N. K., Kaur, M., & Rather, N. A. (2023). Evaluating the impact of internal control systems on organizational effectiveness. *LBS Journal of Management & Research*, *21*(1), 135–154. DOI: 10.1108/LBSJMR-11-2022-0078

Passas, I. (2023b). Accounting for integrity: ESG and financial disclosures: The challenge of internal fraud in management decision-making [Doctoral dissertation, Hellenic Mediterranean University]. DOI: 10.12681/eadd/55359

Passas, I. (2024). The Evolution of ESG: From CSR to ESG 2.0. *Encyclopedia*, *4*(4), 1711–1720. DOI: 10.3390/encyclopedia4040112

Passas, I., & Garefalakis, A. (2025). The Impact of Fraud Perception and ESG-Washing on Investment Trust: Integrating Corporate Governance Theory and Empirical Evidence. *Accounting and Auditing*, *1*(3), 9. DOI: 10.3390/accountaudit1030009

Passas, I., Ragazou, K., Giannopoulos, P., & Kagias, P. (2023a). CG and Viable Corporate Debt. In Governance and Financial Performance: Current Trends and Perspectives (pp. 155–170). World Scientific Publishing Co. DOI: 10.1142/9789811260506_0007

Post, C., & Byron, K. (2015). Women on boards and firm financial performance: A meta-analysis. *Academy of Management Journal*, *58*(5), 1546–1571. DOI: 10.5465/amj.2013.0319

Power, M. (1997). *The audit society: Rituals of verification*. Oxford University Press.

Ragazou, K., Passas, I., Garefalakis, A., Galariotis, E., & Zopounidis, C. (2023). Big Data Analytics Applications in Information Management Driving Operational Efficiencies and Decision-Making: Mapping the Field of Knowledge with Bibliometric Analysis Using R. *Big Data and Cognitive Computing*, *7*(1), 13. DOI: 10.3390/bdcc7010013

Romney, M. B., & Steinbart, P. J. (2018). *Accounting information systems* (14th ed.). Pearson.

Roussy, M., & Brivot, M. (2016). Internal audit quality: A polysemous notion? *Accounting, Auditing & Accountability Journal*, *29*(5), 714–738. DOI: 10.1108/AAAJ-10-2014-1843

Shleifer, A., & Vishny, R. W. (1997). A survey of corporate governance. *The Journal of Finance*, *52*(2), 737–783. DOI: 10.1111/j.1540-6261.1997.tb04820.x

Shniekat, N., Jawabreh, O., & Saleh, M. M. A. (2021). Efficiency and effect on the competitive advantage of management information systems (MIS) in classified hotels in the city of Petra. Academy of Strategic Management Journal, 20(Special Issue 2), 1–12.

Sigala, M. (2020). Tourism and COVID-19: Impacts and implications for advancing and resetting industry and research. *Journal of Business Research*, *117*, 312–321. DOI: 10.1016/j.jbusres.2020.06.015 PMID: 32546875

Singal, M. (2015). How is the hospitality and tourism industry different? An empirical test of some structural characteristics. *International Journal of Hospitality Management*, *47*, 116–119. DOI: 10.1016/j.ijhm.2015.03.006

Sjäfjell, B., & Tsagas, G. (2022). Integrating sustainable value creation in corporate governance: Company law, corporate governance codes and the constitution of the company. In Sjäfjell, B., Tsagas, G., & Villiers, C. (Eds.), *Sustainable value creation in the EU: Towards pathways to a sustainable future through crises* (pp. 209–236). Cambridge University Press. DOI: 10.1017/9781009243841.014

Spira, L. F., & Page, M. (2003). Risk management: The reinvention of internal control and the changing role of internal audit. *Accounting, Auditing & Accountability Journal*, *16*(4), 640–661. DOI: 10.1108/09513570310492335

Stavropoulou, E., Spinthiropoulos, K., Ragazou, K., Papademetriou, C., & Passas, I. (2023). Green Balanced Scorecard: A Tool of Sustainable Information Systems for an Energy Efficient Business. *Energies*, *16*(18), 6432. DOI: 10.3390/en16186432

Uyar, A., Kilic, M., Koseoglu, M. A., Kuzey, C., & Karaman, A. S. (2020). The link among board characteristics, corporate social responsibility performance, and financial performance: Evidence from the hospitality and tourism industry. *Tourism Management Perspectives*, *35*, 100714. DOI: 10.1016/j.tmp.2020.100714

Vasarhelyi, M. A., Kogan, A., & Tuttle, B. M. (2015). Big data in accounting: An overview. *Accounting Horizons*, *29*(2), 381–396. DOI: 10.2308/acch-51071

Vortelinos, D., Floros, C., Apostolakis, A., & Passas, I. (2025). Hotel Sales During COVID-19. In Dimotikalis, Y., & Skiadas, C. (Eds.), *Data Analysis and Related Applications 5: Models, Methods and Techniques* (Vol. 13, pp. 333–348). Wiley., DOI: 10.1002/9781394401604.ch21

Vortelinos, D., Passas, I., Floros, C., & Garefalakis, A. (2024). Corporate Social Responsibility and Country Governance: An International Comparative Study Amid the COVID-19 Pandemic. *International Journal of Financial Studies, 12*(4), 110. DOI: 10.3390/ijfs12040110

Webster, C., & Ivanov, S. (2020). Demographic change as a driver for tourism automation. *Journal of Tourism Futures, 6*(3), 263–270. DOI: 10.1108/JTF-10-2019-0109

Yeh, C. M. (2019). Ownership structure and firm performance of listed tourism firms. *International Journal of Tourism Research, 21*(2), 165–179. DOI: 10.1002/jtr.2250

Yemer, M., & Chekol, F. (2017). The effect of internal controls systems on hotels revenue: A case of hotels in Bahir Dar and Gondar cities. [Oman Chapter]. *Arabian Journal of Business and Management Review, 6*(6), 19–37.

Young, M. N., Peng, M. W., Ahlstrom, D., Bruton, G. D., & Jiang, Y. (2008). Corporate governance in emerging economies: A review of the principal–principal perspective. *Journal of Management Studies, 45*(1), 196–220. DOI: 10.1111/j.1467-6486.2007.00752.x

Zattoni, A., Dedoulis, E., Leventis, S., & Van Ees, H. (2020). Corporate governance and institutions: A review and research agenda. *Corporate Governance, 28*(6), 465–487. DOI: 10.1111/corg.12347

Chapter 11
Revenue Integrity: Mitigating Risks, Preventing Leakage, and Navigating Ethical Dilemmas

James Meersman
http://orcid.org/0009-0004-0853-4821
Texas A&M University, USA

ABSTRACT

This chapter redefines revenue management in hospitality from a purely growth-oriented function to a comprehensive "revenue integrity" framework. Modern hotels face a critical "Revenue-Governance Gap" between aggressive revenue generation and inadequate revenue protection. The chapter identifies key vulnerabilities across the fragmented digital distribution ecosystem, including price parity failures, OTA commission leakage, and PMS-RMS synchronization errors. It presents a governance framework featuring compensating controls for consolidated duties, human-in-the-loop algorithmic pricing, and the Revenue Control Matrix as a practical implementation tool. The chapter further addresses ethical dimensions of revenue management, including prohibitive dynamic pricing during emergencies and algorithmic bias risks.

INTRODUCTION: THE DUAL CHALLENGE OF MODERN HOSPITALITY REVENUE MANAGEMENT

The modern hotel industry faces a paradoxical challenge that requires a fundamental reimagining of how revenue is managed and protected. While hospitality professionals have become increasingly sophisticated in their ability to generate

DOI: 10.4018/979-8-3373-9479-4.ch011

revenue through dynamic pricing strategies and multi-channel distribution, they have simultaneously lagged in their capacity to protect and safeguard the revenue that these systems generate. This gap between aggressive revenue generation and adequate revenue protection has created what can be characterized as the "Revenue-Governance Gap", which is a dangerous space between ambitious sales targets and the internal controls required to ensure that those sales actually reach the hotel's bank account.

Traditional accounting frameworks recognize hotel revenue when a guest's stay is completed and the service is delivered. However, in the digital ecosystem where distribution occurs across numerous online channels, the vulnerability of revenue begins much earlier, at the moment a potential guest enters a search query into a search engine or an Online Travel Agency (OTA) platform. This temporal disconnect between when revenue risk originates and when it is formally recognized in accounting systems represents a fundamental blind spot in contemporary hospitality management practice. The complexity has intensified as the hospitality distribution landscape has become increasingly fragmented, with hotels now managing sales across Direct-to-Consumer (DTC) websites, Global Distribution Systems (GDS), dozens of Online Travel Agencies, and emerging alternative distribution channels (Dornyoh et al., 2026).

The primary mission of this chapter is to redefine "Revenue Management" from a purely growth-oriented function to a comprehensive "Revenue Integrity" function. This reconceptualization acknowledges that in the modern hospitality landscape, the complexity of distribution has created what can be aptly described as a "leaky bucket" effect. This leakage spans numerous areas including direct-to-consumer websites, global distribution systems, and online travel agencies, each of which presents unique vulnerabilities and control challenges. The purpose of this chapter is threefold: to identify the technical and operational touchpoints where revenue is lost; to provide a governance framework for internal controls that protects assets without stifling the agility of revenue managers; and to address the burgeoning ethical concerns regarding algorithmic pricing and consumer data transparency, providing managers with a moral compass for financial decision-making.

The applicability of the revenue integrity framework presented in this chapter requires important contextual considerations. The modern hospitality landscape encompasses diverse property types, from large chain hotels in major metropolitan areas to independent properties, seasonal resorts, and limited-service brands, each operate under distinct market conditions, technological capabilities, and revenue management complexities. While the Revenue-Governance Gap represents a universal challenge in contemporary hospitality, the magnitude of specific risks, the nature of distribution channels, and the feasibility of implementing various control mechanisms vary substantially based on hotel category, operational model, and geographic location. Throughout this chapter, readers should apply the governance principles and control frameworks with appropriate adaptation to their specific operational context. A large urban chain hotel with centralized revenue management and sophisticated system integration faces materially different risks than an independent property with limited staffing or a seasonal resort with highly volatile demand patterns. The case studies presented later in this chapter include diverse property types to illustrate how these principles manifest across different operational environments.

THE REVENUE-GOVERNANCE GAP: UNDERSTANDING THE VULNERABILITY OF THE HOSPITALITY REVENUE CYCLE

The gap between revenue generation and revenue protection is not only a theoretical concern. It represents a significant and measurable challenge in contemporary hospitality operations. To understand this vulnerability, it is essential to recognize that the hospitality revenue cycle in the digital age operates fundamentally differently from traditional revenue cycles in other industries. In traditional retail or service-based businesses, revenue recognition and revenue receipt are typically separated by short time periods. In hospitality, however, the separation between the booking moment (where revenue commitment occurs) and the stay fulfillment moment (where revenue is recognized) creates extended windows of vulnerability (Bimantari et al., 2025).

Consider the timeline of a hotel reservation in the digital ecosystem. A guest searches for a hotel using a search engine or OTA platform, potentially views the property's website, compares rates across channels, reviews competitor offerings, and eventually makes a booking. At each stage of this journey, from the initial search through the final booking confirmation, the hotel's revenue system is recording, tracking, and managing information. Yet the formal recognition of revenue in the accounting system may be days, weeks, or even months away. During this extended period, numerous risks emerge. Some of these include but are not limited to rates being inadvertently discounted across channels, commission structures being miscalculated, system synchronization errors occurring, or guests canceling their reservations with varying cancellation policies across different distribution channels (Mei, 2026).

The traditional conceptualization of revenue management focused almost exclusively on optimization and growth. Revenue managers were tasked with maximizing revenue through dynamic pricing, inventory management, and demand forecasting (ГРОМКО, 2025). These functions remain important, but they have been pursued often without corresponding attention to the control environment that ensures booked revenue actually materializes. The result has been a systematic underinvestment in the internal controls, audit procedures, and governance frameworks necessary to protect revenue from being eroded through various leakage mechanisms.

This vulnerability is compounded by the organizational structure typical in most hospitality properties. Unlike centralized business functions where a single person or team might manage an entire process, hotel revenue management is inherently decentralized. The Front Office generates room revenue, the Reservations department manages bookings, the Food and Beverage department controls ancillary revenue, the Spa or other departments generate additional income, and the Night Audit function attempts to reconcile all of these streams at day-end. Each of these departments operates with some degree of autonomy, uses different systems and procedures, and may have limited visibility into the operations of other departments. This decentralization, while necessary for operational efficiency, creates numerous failure points where revenue can be lost through misinterpretation, error, or lack of coordination (Bimantari et al., 2025).

Furthermore, the tools used to measure revenue success in many hotels have themselves created perverse incentives that mask underlying leakage. RevPAR (Revenue Per Available Room), which has become the standard metric for evaluating revenue performance, provides only a surface-level view of revenue success. A hotel might achieve excellent RevPAR growth while simultaneously experiencing significant erosion of actual profitability due to commission leakage, distribution costs, or unauthorized discounting (Gao, 2025). The chapter argues that managers must interpret RevPAR not merely as a success metric, but as a diagnostic tool. If RevPAR is high but Net RevPAR (i.e. revenue after deducting commissions and customer acquisition costs) is declining, a fundamental governance failure has likely occurred.

DISTRIBUTION LEAKAGE: THE FRAGMENTED CHANNEL ENVIRONMENT

Understanding revenue leakage requires a detailed examination of the modern distribution environment and the specific vulnerabilities inherent in each channel. The hotel industry's distribution landscape has fundamentally transformed over the past two decades, evolving from a relatively centralized system based on direct bookings and travel agent commissions to a highly fragmented ecosystem involving numerous intermediaries, each with their own booking rules, commission structures, and integration capabilities (Dornyoh et al., 2026).

Price Parity Failures and Margin Erosion

One of the most significant sources of distribution leakage stems from price parity failures. Most hotel agreements with Online Travel Agencies include "rate parity" clauses that require hotels to offer the same rates on the OTA's platform as they offer on their own direct channels. These clauses are intended to protect consumers from unfair price discrimination and to prevent arbitrage opportunities. However, in practice, maintaining true price parity across dozens of distribution channels simultaneously is extraordinarily difficult, and failures are commonplace (Xiao et al., 2024).

Price parity failures typically occur through several mechanisms. First, timing delays in updating rates across systems can create temporary parity violations. When a revenue manager updates rates on the hotel's direct website, it may take minutes, hours, or even longer for those updated rates to propagate to all connected distribution channels. During this window, a guest might find a lower rate on the hotel's website compared to an OTA, or vice versa. While individual parity violations may seem minor, they accumulate across thousands of bookings and can represent substantial margin erosion.

Second, technical errors in the rate distribution system itself can cause unintended discounts to be distributed across channels. For example, a revenue manager might intend to set a promotional rate of $189 for a specific date range on the hotel's direct website, but due to a data entry error or system bug, this rate might inadvertently be distributed to all OTA channels as well, creating unintended discounting across the entire distribution network. Third, the complexity of applying different rates to different customer segments, length-of-stay requirements, or booking windows can lead to errors where overly broad or incorrect rates are applied to larger customer populations than intended (Angelini et al., 2025).

Channel Management Systems: Automating Rate Parity Enforcement and Dynamic Inventory Control

While price parity failures represent a significant source of revenue leakage, the good news is that the hospitality technology industry has developed sophisticated solutions specifically designed to prevent these failures through automation and centralized control. Channel Management Systems (CMS) platforms serve as the technology backbone that enables hotels to maintain rate parity and implement sophisticated rate management strategies across fragmented distribution environments.

A well-implemented Channel Management System functions as a centralized nerve center that connects the hotel's Property Management System, revenue management system, and all external distribution channels—including the hotel's direct website,

Global Distribution Systems, Online Travel Agencies, and emerging alternative distribution channels. When a revenue manager updates a rate in the CMS, that update is transmitted simultaneously to all connected distribution channels, eliminating the timing delays that create temporary parity violations. Rather than waiting minutes, hours, or longer for rate updates to propagate across channels individually, a modern CMS updates all channels in near-real-time, typically within seconds.

Beyond simple rate distribution, mature CMS implementations enable revenue managers to implement sophisticated business rules that apply consistently across all channels. A hotel can specify that a promotional rate of $189 should apply only to bookings made on the direct website, not to OTA channels, and the CMS will automatically enforce this rule. Similarly, a hotel can implement rate rules that specify different rates for different length-of-stay requirements, different customer segments, or different booking windows, with the assurance that these rules will be applied consistently across all channels. This level of control is impossible to achieve through manual rate management but becomes routine through CMS implementation.

Modern Channel Management Systems also enable dynamic inventory management through automated rule application. When a hotel reaches a specified occupancy threshold—say, 85% occupancy—the CMS can be configured to automatically stop accepting reservations from lower-commission OTA channels while continuing to accept bookings on the direct website or high-value distribution channels. This capability allows revenue managers to allocate limited inventory to the most profitable distribution channels automatically, without requiring manual intervention. When occupancy drops below the threshold, the CMS automatically re-opens the lower-commission channels, ensuring that inventory is always being allocated to available distribution sources.

OTA Commission Structures and Overpayment

Beyond price parity failures, the commission structures inherent in OTA relationships present significant leakage risks. Most OTAs operate on a commission-based model where they take a percentage of the booking value (typically ranging from 15% to 30%, though commissions have been rising in recent years) in exchange for generating bookings for the hotel. Generally speaking, the OTA only profits when the hotel achieves bookings; so while this model aligns incentives in theory, in practice, these commission relationships are often insufficiently monitored and can result in substantial overpayments.

Commission leakage typically occurs when hotels fail to properly audit OTA invoices against actual performance. For instance, many OTAs assess commissions not only on completed stays but also on cancelled bookings, depending on the cancellation policy. If a guest cancels a reservation, the OTA might still retain its commission or charge cancellation fees unless the hotel actively disputes the charge. Similarly, if a guest fails to appear for a reservation ("no-show"), OTAs may charge commission differently based on the cancellation policies negotiated in the contract. Without rigorous reconciliation procedures, hotels may fail to detect and dispute these charges, resulting in significant commission leakage over time (Hyera et al., 2025).

Additionally, many hotels struggle with the complexity of tracking and verifying OTA commission rates across different room types, customer segments, and booking windows. An OTA contract might specify one commission rate for standard bookings but different rates for package deals, non-refundable rates, or bookings made within specific promotional windows. The administrative burden of tracking these variations and ensuring that commission invoices reflect the correct rates is substantial, and many hotels lack the systems and procedures necessary to perform these verifications effectively.

Systemic Mismatches Between PMS and RMS

A second major category of revenue leakage stems from synchronization errors between a hotel's Property Management System (PMS) and its Revenue Management System (RMS). These two critical systems, which are often operated by different vendors and are essential to hotel operations, must be tightly integrated to function properly (Saitta et al., 2024). The PMS maintains the hotel's inventory of rooms, tracks guest arrivals and departures, records charges to guest accounts, and manages the property's operational data. The RMS analyzes demand patterns, forecasts occupancy, recommends pricing strategies, and provides revenue managers with the information necessary to make dynamic pricing decisions.

When these systems are not properly synchronized, significant revenue leakage can occur. One common problem occurs when a hotel's PMS does not communicate availability information to the RMS and distribution channels in real time. For example, when a property reaches full occupancy for a particular night, this information must be communicated immediately to all distribution channels to prevent additional bookings from being accepted. However, if this communication is delayed or fails entirely, guests may be able to book rooms through various channels even though the property is already fully sold (Hidayati et al., 2025). This situation, known as overbooking, creates substantial costs for the hotel, including the expense of walking guests to competing hotels, providing compensation to inconvenienced guests, and managing the operational and reputational consequences of denying guests their reserved rooms.

Furthermore, the "sold out" status itself may not trigger simultaneously across all channels. A guest might still be able to book through an OTA or the hotel's direct website even though the PMS shows no available inventory. This asynchronous communication between systems results in overbooking costs that represent significant, yet often unrecorded, revenue losses. The full economic cost of an overbooking event includes not only the direct cost of the hotel accommodations provided to a competitor property but also the loss of ancillary revenue that the guest would have spent on food and beverage, parking, and other services. Additionally, the reputational damage from a negative guest experience resulting from overbooking can lead to reduced future bookings and negative reviews.

Technological Solutions: The Integrated PMS/RMS Platform and Real-Time Synchronization

The revenue leakage challenges stemming from PMS/RMS synchronization failures are themselves largely addressed through the adoption of modern integrated PMS/RMS platforms or through implementation of robust, real-time API integrations between separate best-of-breed systems. When these systems are properly implemented and configured, they eliminate the asynchronous communication that creates overbooking, unposted revenue, and inventory management failures.

A true integrated PMS/RMS platform maintains a single, unified database of property inventory, guest reservations, and revenue transactions. When the front desk agent confirms a reservation, the inventory count in the system immediately decrements by one room for that night. This updated inventory count is simultaneously pushed to all external distribution channels through the Channel Management System connection. A guest attempting to book through an OTA will see the property as fully sold immediately when true inventory reaches zero, rather than experiencing the delays that lead to overbooking situations.

Similarly, modern integrated systems include automated interfaces that connect departmental point-of-sale systems—from the restaurant and bar systems to the spa system, parking system, and other revenue-generating departments—directly to the guest accounting module within the PMS. When a guest charges a meal to room 412, that charge is automatically transmitted to and posted on guest 412's folio in real-time. The hotel no longer relies on manual data entry, batch transmission processes, or end-of-day reconciliation procedures. The risk of unposted revenue (i.e. charges that are entered in departmental systems but never reach the guest's folio) is dramatically reduced because the integration process is automatic and continuous rather than manual and periodic.

Net Rate Strategy and Data-Driven Distribution Channel Management

While gross room rate represents the headline price that a guest sees when booking a hotel, gross rate obscures the actual economic value of a booking once distribution costs are accounted for. The net rate (i.e. the gross room rate minus all OTA commissions, payment processing fees, marketing and customer acquisition costs) represents the true revenue contribution of a booking to the hotel's profitability. A comprehensive approach to net rate management requires that hotels: (1) systematically track net rate contribution by distribution channel; (2) use net rate data to make dynamic allocation decisions about inventory distribution; (3) establish net rate thresholds that inform which OTA channels are worth pursuing; and (4) regularly review whether each OTA relationship generates net rate contribution sufficient to justify the costs of channel integration and management.

For example, many hotels discover through net rate analysis that certain OTA channels, while generating high booking volume, actually destroy profitability due to high commission rates and customer acquisition costs. A boutique hotel might find that a particular OTA channel generates 8% of total bookings but consumes 15% of revenue due to commission structure. In such cases, hotels can make the strategic decision to reduce inventory allocation to that channel, to negotiate revised commission structures, or in some cases, to exit the channel entirely if the net rate contribution is fundamentally uneconomical.

GOVERNANCE AND INTERNAL CONTROLS: A STRATEGIC FRAMEWORK FOR REVENUE INTEGRITY, ENABLED BY TECHNOLOGY

Addressing the revenue leakage challenges outlined above requires the implementation of a comprehensive governance framework for revenue management that extends far beyond traditional internal control systems. The framework must simultaneously pursue two complementary strategies: (1) implementation of sophisticated, well-integrated technology systems that automate much of the leakage prevention process; and (2) development of robust governance procedures, audit mechanisms, and organizational accountability structures that ensure technology systems are functioning as designed and that human judgment is appropriately applied to decisions outside the scope of automation.

The critical insight is that technology and governance are complementary rather than substitutional. Technology alone is insufficient—a Channel Management System that is poorly configured or inadequately monitored will not prevent rate parity failures, and an integrated PMS/RMS platform that lacks proper audit trails and reconciliation procedures cannot ensure that the system is functioning correctly. Conversely, strong governance procedures operating in the absence of enabling technology place enormous demands on human staff and are inevitably vulnerable to human error and resource constraints (Amanamah et al., 2025; Salsabila & Islamudin, 2025).

The Challenge of Separation of Duties in a Paperless Environment

One of the foundational principles of internal control theory is the concept of "separation of duties". This ensures that no single individual has the power to execute a transaction, authorize it, and reconcile it (Yulianti et al., 2024). In traditional accounting environments with paper-based processes, maintaining separation of duties is relatively straightforward. In the paperless, automated hotel environment, however, maintaining appropriate separation of duties becomes significantly more challenging.

Consider the role of a hotel revenue manager in a contemporary property. This individual may have access to systems that allow them to modify room rates across all distribution channels, authorize discounts or rate adjustments for specific bookings, process manual room transfers between departments, adjust guest folios after initial posting, and produce the revenue reconciliation reports that are used to verify that the day's operations have been recorded correctly. In a traditional separation of duties framework, these various functions would be distributed across multiple individuals, with some serving in authorization roles, others in execution roles, and still others in verification roles (Muslim, 2025).

The consolidation of these functions in a single individual is often driven by legitimate operational necessities. In smaller and mid-size hotels, staffing constraints make it impractical to fully separate all revenue-related duties. Moreover, the agility required for effective revenue management in a dynamic pricing environment demands that revenue managers can make rapid adjustments to rates, apply targeted discounts, and respond to market conditions without requiring multiple approvals and authorization chains (Putra & Anggiriawan, 2025). The challenge, therefore, is not to enforce separation of duties in the traditional sense, but to implement compensating controls that mitigate the risks created by the consolidation of duties.

A key compensating control in a paperless environment is the maintenance of a comprehensive audit trail. Every change to a rate, every adjustment to a guest folio, every manual override of a system parameter, and every exception to normal procedures must be recorded with complete information about who made the change, when the change was made, what the change entailed, and the business justification for the change. These audit trails must be retained indefinitely and must be reviewed regularly by individuals other than those who made the original changes. Furthermore, these audit trail reviews should not be passive or perfunctory. Instead, they should be active, analytical reviews designed to identify potential exceptions, unusual patterns, or concerning activities that might indicate either errors or intentional misconduct (Dewi et al., 2025).

Automated Controls Versus Human Judgment: The Human-in-the-Loop Model

The risks associated with automated pricing algorithms present another significant governance challenge in contemporary revenue management. The sophistication of revenue management technology has increased dramatically over the past decade, with many hotels now using algorithms that automatically adjust pricing based on demand forecasts, competitive intelligence, inventory levels, and numerous other variables (Saitta et al., 2024). These algorithms can process vastly more information and make adjustments far more frequently than any human revenue manager could accomplish manually. Indeed, for sophisticated property types such as large urban hotels or resort properties, algorithmic pricing has become essential to achieving optimal revenue outcomes (Brar et al., 2025).

However, the implementation of sophisticated pricing algorithms creates new risks that must be actively managed. The danger of implementing an algorithm, allowing it to run without active human oversight (i.e. "setting and forgetting"), and assuming that it will continue to function correctly under all conditions represents a significant governance failure. Pricing algorithms are fundamentally designed based on historical data and historical patterns. When conditions deviate significantly from historical norms (i.e. "black-swan" events), algorithms may produce pricing recommendations that are economically unsound or even catastrophic (Mei, 2026).

Consider, for example, a scenario where a major event such as a natural disaster, public health emergency, or significant security incident occurs in a hotel's market. In such situations, demand patterns might swing dramatically in one direction or another, consumer sentiment might shift rapidly, and ethical and reputational considerations might make the price recommendations generated by an algorithm based on demand elasticity entirely inappropriate. Yet without adequate human oversight and decision-making authority, these algorithms might continue to recommend pricing strategies that are economically optimal in a narrow sense but ethically and strategically problematic in a broader context.

The governance framework proposed here advocates for a "Human-in-the-Loop" model of algorithmic pricing. Under this model, pricing algorithms remain active and generate pricing recommendations, but human revenue managers retain authority and responsibility for reviewing, approving, and implementing these recommendations. Importantly, a human revenue manager can deviate from algorithmic recommendations by either overriding a recommendation or making a different pricing decision based on factors not captured in the algorithm. When this happens, the decision must be documented and justified. This documentation serves multiple purposes: it creates an audit trail of human decision-making that can be reviewed for potential errors or misconduct; it allows the organization to understand why human decisions diverged from algorithmic recommendations, which can provide insights into factors that should be incorporated into the algorithm itself; and it ensures accountability for revenue management decisions.

The Revenue Control Matrix: A Practical Framework for Implementation

Moving beyond these conceptual frameworks, the chapter proposes a practical tool for implementing revenue integrity controls across a hotel property: the Revenue Control Matrix (RCM). This matrix serves as a standardized, comprehensive framework for identifying key revenue risks, defining control objectives, specifying the primary control activities that address each risk, and establishing monitoring and audit procedures to verify that controls are operating effectively.

The Revenue Control Matrix is organized around major revenue risk areas. For each risk area, the matrix specifies a control objective. This is the end state the hotel seeks to achieve in terms of preventing or mitigating the risk. Next, the matrix identifies the primary control activities that, if implemented and operating effectively, would achieve that control objective. Finally, the matrix specifies monitoring and audit procedures. These are the steps that should be taken regularly to verify that the primary control activities are operating as designed and are preventing or mitigating the identified risk (Belesis et al., 2025).

The RCM begins with **Price Parity Risk**. The control objective for price parity is to prevent margin erosion from unauthorized discounts on high-cost distribution channels. The primary control activity consists of automated channel manager systems that lock rates across all OTAs and the hotel's direct web channel, ensuring that any rate change is reflected simultaneously across all channels. The monitoring and audit procedures for price parity include weekly "mystery shop" audits where staff or service providers search for the hotel's rooms across various distribution channels and verify that displayed rates are consistent, and regular analysis of Rate Intelligence reports that compare rates across channels. If these monitoring procedures identify price parity failures, they trigger investigations to determine whether the failures resulted from technical glitches in the distribution system, human errors in rate entry, or other causes (Adekunle et al., 2024).

A second key risk area is **Folio Adjustment Risk**. Guest folios are electronic records of charges and credits to each guest's account. These items are frequently adjusted after initial posting due to various reasons: corrections for billing errors, application of authorized discounts that were not reflected at check-in, post-stay adjustments for damage or additional services, or corrections for payment processing errors. Each adjustment represents a potential revenue loss, and without appropriate controls, adjustments can be made inappropriately or without proper authorization. The control objective is to ensure that all guest folio adjustments are legitimate, properly authorized, and documented. The primary control activities include the use of system-enforced "reason codes" that require adjustment entries to be classified by type (billing error, authorized discount, damage charge adjustment, etc.) and the implementation of a mandatory managerial override requirement for any adjustment exceeding a specified dollar threshold (commonly $50 or more) (Bakker et al., 2024). The monitoring and audit procedure consists of a daily review of the adjustments report by the night auditor or controller, with particular attention to any adjustments that were not classified with appropriate reason codes or that required managerial override approval.

A third critical risk area is **Commission Leakage**. As discussed in detail earlier in the chapter, commission overpayments and undetected commission charges represent a significant source of revenue loss in many hotels. The control objective is to prevent overpayment of OTA fees for cancelled or "no-show" bookings. The primary control activity is the implementation of two-way integration between the hotel's PMS and the OTA platforms, which automatically flags cancellations and no-shows and initiates the process of commission reconciliation. Rather than relying on the OTA to provide accurate commission invoices, this primary control activity shifts to an active approach where the hotel system itself monitors for conditions that might trigger inappropriate commission charges and flags them for investigation. The monitoring and audit procedure involves a monthly matching of OTA commission invoices against a detailed report of actual guest stays that were completed, with particular attention to ensuring that commission was not assessed on cancelled bookings, no-show situations, or guest stays that did not meet the criteria specified in the OTA contract (Ehima & Amede, 2025).

A fourth important risk area is **Unposted Revenue**. In hospitality operations, numerous ancillary charges are generated throughout a guest's stay. Such charges may include spa services, food and beverage charges from restaurants and room service, minibar items, parking fees, and various other services. All of these charges must be transferred from the individual operating systems (the spa's point-of-sale system, the restaurant's point-of-sale system, the minibar system, etc.) to the hotel's property management system, where they are accumulated on the guest's folio and are ultimately included in the total revenue recorded when the guest checks out .

When this transfer process fails, significant unposted revenue results. Failures could be due to —either because the system interfaces between the individual point-of-sale systems and the PMS are not functioning correctly, or because charges were never entered in the individual systems to begin with— This represents revenue that was earned (the service was delivered and should have been charged to the guest) but was never captured in the hotel's accounting system, resulting in a complete loss of that revenue stream (Rohim et al., 2024).

The control objective for unposted revenue is to ensure that all ancillary charges generated throughout a guest's stay are captured in the property management system before the guest completes checkout. The primary control activity is the implementation of Interface Verification Checks (IFC)—automated processes that verify that the point-of-sale systems from all revenue-generating departments are communicating with the PMS in real time or near real-time. These checks alert system administrators when interfaces fail or data is not being transmitted properly. The monitoring and audit procedure consists of the production of a daily "Balance of Interface" report that identifies any charges that were entered in a departmental point-of-sale system but were not received by the PMS, or that were received but are missing key information (such as the guest room number, which is essential for posting the charge to the guest's folio). This report is reviewed daily, and any discrepancies are investigated immediately, with the goal of resolving them before the affected guests depart the property (Harahap et al., 2025).

THE ETHICS OF REVENUE DECISIONS: REDEFINING REVENUE MANAGEMENT'S MORAL COMPASS

The reframing of revenue management as revenue integrity necessarily includes serious engagement with the ethical dimensions of revenue decisions. The chapter explicitly acknowledges that the focus on controlling costs and protecting against loss is only one dimension of ethical revenue management. Equally important are the ethical implications of the revenue-generating strategies themselves and the obligation of hotel managers to consider the broader impact of their revenue decisions on guests, employees, communities, and the industry as a whole.

Dynamic Pricing and the Ethics of Price Gouging

Dynamic pricing has become a standard practice in hospitality, particularly in urban hotels, resort properties, and properties in markets with significant demand volatility. The fundamental principle underlying dynamic pricing is economically sound: hotels should charge higher prices during periods of high demand and lower prices during periods of low demand. This practice optimizes revenue and also allocates hotel inventory to guests who value it most highly (those willing to pay premium prices during peak periods). In normal market conditions, dynamic pricing is widely accepted and expected (Dornyoh et al., 2026; ГРОМКО, 2025).

However, dynamic pricing becomes ethically problematic when it is applied during periods of distress or when market conditions are highly constrained. Consider a scenario where a natural disaster evacuates a major portion of a city or region, forcing people to seek emergency accommodations. In such situations, hotels might face extraordinarily high demand from evacuees and displaced persons, at the same time that their competitors may have been damaged and capacity may be severely limited. Dynamic pricing algorithms might recommend significantly elevated rates during such periods because standard demand elasticity principles would suggest that the willingness to pay for scarce accommodations has increased dramatically. However, charging premium prices to people in situations of genuine emergency and hardship raises serious ethical concerns and carries significant reputational risks (Yarlagadda, 2025).

The reputational and brand risks associated with aggressive pricing during distress situations are themselves long-term financial liabilities. Social media and the internet allow information about pricing practices to spread rapidly and widely, and negative publicity regarding price gouging during emergencies can cause sustained damage to a brand, leading to reduced bookings, negative reviews, and diminished customer loyalty. Major hospitality brands have learned this lesson through painful experience—instances of aggressive pricing during natural disasters or public health emergencies have led to significant backlash and have resulted in long-term brand damage that far exceeds the incremental revenue that was captured through aggressive pricing during the distress period.

Algorithmic Bias and Discriminatory Pricing

A more subtle, but equally important, ethical concern emerging in contemporary revenue management is the risk of algorithmic bias and discriminatory pricing practices (Zhao, 2024). Many advanced revenue management systems now incorporate not only demand forecasting and pricing optimization algorithms but also customer analytics that attempt to predict individual customer "willingness to pay" based on customer characteristics. These systems analyze variables such as past booking behavior, customer demographics, booking channel, timing of booking, and numerous other factors to attempt to predict the maximum price an individual customer would pay for a given room.

While such personalized pricing systems can improve revenue by capturing additional value from customers willing to pay premium prices, they also create the risk of discriminatory pricing practices. For example, if a pricing algorithm incorporates demographic variables and if historical data reflects patterns of discrimination (e.g., if certain demographic groups have in the past been more willing to pay higher prices, either because they had greater means or because they faced greater difficulty finding accommodations), then allowing the algorithm to incorporate these demographic factors into pricing recommendations could lead to discriminatory pricing where similarly situated customers pay different prices based on protected characteristics such as race, national origin, religion, or other legally protected categories (Duani et al., 2024).

Discriminatory pricing practices are not only ethically problematic; they also expose hotels to significant legal liability under civil rights statutes and consumer protection regulations. More fundamentally, they represent a corruption of the revenue management function itself. The purpose of revenue management should be to allocate scarce hotel inventory to those who value it most highly, as measured by their demonstrated willingness to pay. Allowing pricing decisions to be influenced by customer demographic characteristics unrelated to the actual value that the customer places on the room violates this principle and instead uses pricing as a tool for discrimination (Grochowski et al., 2022).

The governance framework for ethical revenue management must therefore include explicit constraints on the factors that can be incorporated into pricing algorithms. Systems should be regularly audited to detect potential discrimination, and pricing recommendations should be regularly reviewed to identify patterns that might suggest discriminatory outcomes, even if not intentionally produced by the algorithm. Furthermore, managers should receive training in the ethical dimensions of algorithmic pricing and should understand both the legal risks and the ethical imperatives that flow from their role as stewards of revenue management systems.

Transparency and Financial Reporting Integrity

A third important ethical dimension of revenue management concerns transparency and the integrity of financial reporting. In recent years, the practice of assessing "resort fees," "destination fees," "facility fees," and similar ancillary charges has become increasingly common in the hospitality industry. These fees are often presented to customers separately from room rates, are assessed per night or per visit, and are frequently not disclosed until late in the booking process. These costs, at times, only appear on the final confirmation page after the customer has already entered payment information (Nazlan, 2024).

The use of these hidden or obscured fees raises serious ethical concerns. From a consumer perspective, these practices are arguably deceptive because they present the room rate as lower than the actual total cost of the accommodation. The widespread consumer frustration with these practices has led to regulatory scrutiny, with some jurisdictions and regulatory bodies requiring more transparent disclosure of all costs associated with a hotel booking (Toukabri & Chaouachi, 2025).

From a financial reporting perspective, the use of hidden fees creates distorted departmental performance metrics and makes it difficult to understand true departmental profitability. If a hotel property divides its revenue into "room revenue" (the explicit room rate) and "ancillary revenue" (which includes both legitimate ancillary services such as spa, dining, and parking, as well as facility fees), the use of facility fees to supplement room revenue creates confusion. Room revenue appears higher than it actually is, because some of the true room revenue is classified as ancillary. This "obfuscated revenue" creates a distorted view of departmental performance that makes it difficult for management to understand whether the property's room business is performing well or whether revenue per room is being artificially inflated through ancillary charges.

The ethical framework for revenue management must therefore emphasize transparency in all revenue practices. Customers should receive clear, complete information about the total cost of their accommodation before they are required to commit to the booking. Financial reporting should clearly distinguish between room revenue, legitimate ancillary services, and fee-based charges that are supplements to room revenue. Management reporting should include both gross revenue metrics and net, transparent revenue metrics that provide a true and complete picture of departmental financial performance.

CASE STUDY 1: THE SILENT LEAK OF UNRECONCILED COMMISSIONS

To illustrate the concepts and frameworks presented in this chapter with a concrete, real-world example, this section presents a detailed case study of a mid-scale hotel group that discovered and subsequently addressed a significant, previously undetected revenue leak stemming from unreconciled OTA commissions.

The Discovery Phase

The hotel group in question was a chain of eight upscale, limited-service hotels located in secondary and tertiary markets across the southern United States. The properties were well-managed, had strong occupancy rates, and maintained good customer satisfaction scores. The director of revenue for the group noticed, while reviewing year-end financial statements, that Net RevPAR (revenue after deducting commissions and distribution costs) had declined by approximately 2.5% during the final quarter of the year, even though gross RevPAR (revenue before deducting commissions and distribution) had remained stable.

This divergence between gross RevPAR and Net RevPAR is precisely the kind of diagnostic signal that careful financial analysis should detect. The director of revenue, using the interpretive approach to RevPAR that the governance framework recommends, immediately recognized that this pattern indicated a potential governance failure. Despite stable room demand and relatively consistent pricing, the property's bottom-line revenue performance was deteriorating. Rather than accepting this decline as a consequence of market conditions, the director initiated an investigation to identify the underlying cause.

The investigation began with a detailed examination of commission expenses for each property. Commission expenses were broken into categories for major OTAs: Booking.com, Expedia, and others, with Booking.com and Expedia accounting for approximately 80% of OTA-generated bookings. The director noticed that while the number of OTA-generated bookings had remained relatively stable, commission expenses had increased disproportionately. The commission rate as a percentage of OTA revenue had increased from approximately 20% (the contractual rate) to approximately 24-25% (an unexplained increase of 4-5 percentage points).

Root Cause Analysis

To investigate the source of this increase, the director's team obtained detailed booking reports from Booking.com for a sample month (October) and manually compared the hotel's internal records of completed stays with the Booking.com invoice for that month. They discovered a systematic discrepancy: Booking.com assessed approximately 12-15% of cancelled bookings and no-show reservations, contrary to the hotel's contractual understanding that commission would be assessed only on completed stays (Hyera et al., 2025).

Further investigation revealed that the hotels' PMS was not generating automated reports of cancellations and no-shows, and the revenue manager was not manually reconciling these cancellations against OTA invoices. As a result, when a Booking.com invoice arrived on the 15th of each month, the revenue manager would review it cursorily—ensuring that the invoice amount seemed reasonable relative to the previous month—and would process it for payment without detailed verification that each charge on the invoice corresponded to an actual completed stay.

The director's team reviewed OTA invoices for the past eight quarters and discovered that this pattern had been consistent throughout the entire period. By conservative estimate, undetected commission overcharges totaled approximately $34,000 over an eight-quarter period. For a hotel group of this size, this represented approximately 4% of total commission expenses—a material and previously undetected revenue leak.

Managerial Reasoning and Implementation

The discovery of this commission leakage prompted careful examination of the circumstances that had allowed it to persist undetected for such an extended period. The director's analysis revealed several contributing factors: (1) the PMS system in place at the properties did not have automated functionality to flag cancellations and no-shows in a format suitable for comparison with OTA invoices; (2) the revenue manager's job responsibilities had expanded significantly over the past two years as the group added additional properties, reducing the time available for detailed reconciliation work; (3) the revenue manager had not received training on the importance of OTA commission verification and the detailed procedures necessary to perform this function; and (4) the compensation structure for the revenue manager was based primarily on gross RevPAR growth, creating incentives focused on revenue generation rather than revenue protection.

The response to these findings involved implementation of multiple primary control activities and supporting procedures. First, the director authorized an upgrade to the PMS system to include functionality for generating detailed reports of all cancellations and no-shows, segregated by OTA source. Second, procedures were established requiring monthly reconciliation of OTA invoices against these cancellation and no-show reports, with particular attention to identifying any commission charges assessed on cancelled or no-show reservations. Third, a dedicated position of revenue analyst was created within the revenue department, with responsibility for OTA reconciliation and commission verification. Fourth, the revenue manager's compensation structure was revised to include performance metrics related to Net RevPAR and revenue protection, in addition to gross RevPAR growth.

Results and Impact

Implementation of these control activities and procedural changes produced measurable results. In the first full quarter following implementation of the new controls, the commission rate (as a percentage of OTA revenue) decreased from the previously elevated level of 24-25% back down to the contractual rate of approximately 20%. The hotel group was able to dispute and recover, through negotiation with Booking.com, approximately 60% of the overcharges identified in the historical analysis—approximately $20,400. The recovery of this amount, combined with the prevention of future overcharges, had a material impact on the group's Net RevPAR performance, with Net RevPAR increasing by approximately 3% in the quarter following implementation of the new controls.

Beyond the direct financial impact, the successful identification and correction of this revenue leak had several important secondary effects. First, it reinforced across the organization the importance of revenue protection and the need for robust internal controls. Revenue management went from being conceptualized as purely a revenue-generation function to being understood as encompassing both revenue generation and revenue protection. Second, it created a positive example of how careful financial analysis could uncover previously unknown problems and drive meaningful improvement. The success of the commission reconciliation initiative encouraged other members of the management team to scrutinize their areas of responsibility for potential revenue leaks. Third, it created a model and a template for addressing similar commission leakage issues in other OTA relationships, leading to the systematic auditing of all OTA agreements and reconciliation procedures (Hyera et al., 2025).

CASE STUDY 2: DYNAMIC PRICING AND BRAND REPUTATION MANAGEMENT

The second case study presented in this chapter illustrates the ethical challenges inherent in contemporary revenue management and demonstrates how inappropriate application of dynamic pricing can create long-term brand and financial damage that far exceeds any short-term revenue gains.

Background and Context

The property in this case study is a 180-room upscale boutique hotel located in a major metropolitan area that experienced a significant natural disaster (a severe ice storm) that disrupted electricity, water, transportation, and other essential services across a large portion of the city. The storm stranded tens of thousands of residents and visitors, with many forced to seek emergency accommodation. The hotel's property was largely unaffected by the storm and retained full capacity, while many competing hotels had been significantly damaged or were operating at reduced capacity due to damage or utilities disruption.

The hotel's revenue management system, which utilized dynamic pricing algorithms, immediately detected the extraordinary demand surge resulting from the storm emergency. The algorithm recommended substantial rate increases. Morning rates that had been $189 were adjusted upward to $389, and evening rates that had been $259 were adjusted to $499 or higher. These recommendations were based entirely on demand elasticity principles: perceived supply of available accommodations had been dramatically reduced due to competing properties being offline, and perceived demand had increased dramatically due to evacuees seeking emergency shelter (Mei, 2026).

The Decision Point

The challenge occurred when the hotel's revenue manager received algorithmic pricing recommendations and was required to make the decision of whether to implement them. The revenue manager understood that implementing these rates would have two effects: first, it would substantially increase the hotel's revenue for the emergency period; second, it would generate significant negative publicity and social media backlash for the practice of price gouging during a time of widespread distress and hardship (YARLAGADDA, 2025).

The revenue manager escalated the decision to the hotel's general manager and to the regional director of operations. In the discussion that ensued, the team grappled with the tension between revenue optimization and brand stewardship. The revenue manager and general manager argued that a more moderate rate increase (perhaps $50-75 per room above normal pricing) would be appropriate to reflect the genuine scarcity of accommodations and the increase in operational costs during the emergency period (many staff members had to be paid overtime or had to be provided with accommodations, certain supplies were more difficult to obtain, etc.), but that accepting the algorithmic recommendations for rates of $389-$499 would be price gouging and would create serious brand reputation risks.

The Decision and Its Consequences

The hotel ultimately implemented a middle path: rates were increased by approximately $40-50 per room (from $189 to approximately $230, and from $259 to approximately $300-310), representing a more modest increase than the algorithmic recommendations. This rate level was sufficient to ensure that the hotel's marginal costs and profit margins during the emergency period were appropriate while still being supportable from an ethical standpoint. The hotel also made a conscious decision to offer several rooms per night at normal pre-emergency rates to guests who could demonstrate that they had been displaced or were facing genuine hardship due to the storm.

The decision to forgo the substantial revenue that would have been captured through aggressive dynamic pricing during the emergency period created an opportunity cost. Based on occupancy levels and the algorithmic pricing recommendations, the hotel would have captured approximately $18,000-$22,000 in additional incremental revenue during the five-day emergency period. By choosing to implement more moderate pricing, the hotel sacrificed this incremental revenue.

However, the consequences of this decision became apparent in the months following the emergency. The hotel received substantial positive media coverage for its compassionate pricing during the emergency period and for providing discounted rooms to displaced residents. The hotel's online reviews and customer satisfaction scores increased notably, and there was a measurable increase in repeat bookings from guests who had stayed at the hotel during the emergency period and who explicitly mentioned in their booking notes that they appreciated the hotel's ethical behavior during the crisis. Customer loyalty metrics and brand perception indicators all improved in the post-emergency period (Dornyoh et al., 2026).

In a longer-term financial analysis, the decision to moderate pricing during the emergency period actually had a positive financial impact. The positive publicity and improved brand perception generated in the months following the emergency led to increased bookings and improved rate realization (higher average daily rates) across the six-month post-emergency period, resulting in incremental revenue that substantially exceeded the revenue sacrificed through more moderate pricing during the emergency itself. More importantly, the hotel avoided the potential brand damage that would have resulted from aggressive price gouging, damage that could have persisted for years.

Lessons and Implications

This case study illustrates several important lessons about the integration of ethical decision-making into revenue management practice. First, the availability of algorithmic pricing recommendations does not eliminate the need for human judgment and ethical reasoning. Algorithms can optimize narrow economic objectives (revenue during a specific period) without considering broader strategic and ethical concerns (long-term brand reputation and customer loyalty).

Second, the framework of revenue integrity encompasses not only protection against loss and fraud but also the affirmative commitment to ethical decision-making in revenue generation. The revenue manager in this case study was making a decision about how to apply revenue-generating authority in an ethical manner, not making a decision about how to prevent leakage or protect against fraud. Yet the principles of revenue integrity—the exercise of stewardship over revenue-related decisions and the consideration of broader impacts beyond narrow short-term financial metrics—applied equally to this decision.

Third, the integration of ethical decision-making into revenue management requires the alignment of performance metrics and compensation structures with the values and principles that the organization wants to embody. If the revenue manager's compensation had been based primarily on maximizing revenue during a specific period without any consideration for ethical factors or long-term brand implications, the decision to moderate pricing during the emergency might not have been made. By ensuring that the general manager and regional director were engaged in the decision-making process, and by implying through organizational behavior that ethical decision-making is valued and supported, the hotel created an environment in which the appropriate decision was made.

BUILDING A CULTURE OF REVENUE INTEGRITY

The identification and remediation of revenue leakage, the implementation of robust internal controls, and the integration of ethical decision-making into revenue management processes are all essential components of revenue integrity. However, these individual actions and systems, while necessary, are insufficient without a broader organizational culture that values and prioritizes revenue integrity as a core competency. Building such a culture requires deliberate action across multiple dimensions of organizational management, including training and development, performance evaluation, organizational structure, and leadership communication.

Training and Professional Development in Ethical Revenue Management

The contemporary hospitality management curriculum has traditionally emphasized revenue management techniques. This includes demand forecasting, pricing optimization, inventory allocation, and distribution channel management. While these technical skills remain essential, they are insufficient for the modern revenue professional. Formal training in revenue integrity should address several key topic areas: the specific revenue leakage risks most prevalent in each operating context; the use of data analytics to identify potential revenue leakage; the governance frameworks and control systems appropriate for the organization; and most importantly, the ethical dimensions of revenue management, including exposure to scenarios that present ethical challenges and opportunities to develop moral reasoning about revenue-related decisions.

Performance Evaluation and Compensation Alignment

Performance evaluation systems have traditionally focused heavily on gross revenue metrics such as RevPAR and occupancy percentage. A comprehensive approach to performance evaluation in an environment focused on revenue integrity must expand to include metrics that capture revenue protection and ethical decision-making. Net RevPAR, which deducts commissions and distribution costs from gross RevPAR, provides a more accurate picture of true revenue impact. Similarly, metrics related to the effectiveness of internal controls—such as the percentage of identified revenue leakage that is prevented through control activities—should be incorporated into performance evaluation. Compensation structures should be revised to reward both revenue generation and revenue protection, ensuring that revenue managers perceive that the organization values both dimensions of their role.

Leadership Communication and Organizational Values

Building a culture of revenue integrity requires explicit and consistent communication from organizational leadership about the importance of revenue integrity and about the organization's commitment to ethical, controlled, and well-governed revenue management practices. This communication must be reflected in the decisions that leaders make and the ways they respond to situations that present tensions between short-term revenue maximization and longer-term integrity concerns. When leaders face circumstances similar to those in Case Study 2—where revenue-maximizing decisions might conflict with ethical considerations or brand concerns—the decisions they make become powerful signals about what the organization actually values. If leaders consistently choose short-term revenue maximization at the expense of ethical considerations, employees will reasonably conclude that stated values are not authentic. Conversely, when leaders make decisions reflecting genuine commitment to revenue integrity even when doing so involves short-term revenue sacrifice, they send powerful signals about organizational values (Dornyoh et al., 2026).

CONCLUSION: VIEWING FINANCIAL DATA AS AN INTERPRETIVE TOOL

This chapter has presented a comprehensive framework for understanding revenue integrity in contemporary hospitality operations and for implementing governance systems and ethical practices that support revenue protection alongside revenue generation. The chapter directly supports the editors' overarching goal of viewing financial data as interpretive tools rather than as mere mechanistic outputs of business systems. By examining revenue management data carefully, managers can extract profound insights into the operational realities and managerial choices that produced the financial results reflected in the organization's statements and reports.

The two case studies presented in this chapter illustrate this interpretive approach in action. In Case Study 1, careful interpretation of the divergence between gross RevPAR and Net RevPAR led to the discovery of a previously undetected $34,000 revenue leak. In Case Study 2, the challenge facing revenue management required interpretation of what pricing decisions would mean. Revenue integrity is ultimately a function of managerial judgment and organizational governance rather than of complex mathematical models alone. While the technical tools (e.g.

the Revenue Control Matrix, the detailed audit procedures, the system integrations, the algorithmic pricing recommendations, etc.) all play important roles, they are most effective when deployed within an organizational context where managers understand that financial data provides windows into operational realities, where revenue management is valued as a form of stewardship over organizational assets, and where ethical decision-making is recognized as integral to professional excellence in hospitality management .

The shift from viewing revenue management as purely a growth-oriented function to viewing it as a comprehensive revenue integrity function requires sustained effort across multiple dimensions of organizational management. It requires investments in systems, procedures, and controls. It requires training and development of revenue management professionals. It requires alignment of organizational structures and compensation arrangements. And most fundamentally, it requires leadership commitment and authentic organizational values that reflect the importance of revenue protection, ethical decision-making, and stewardship alongside the traditional focus on revenue growth. When these elements come together, hospitality organizations can achieve both the revenue performance they seek and the operational excellence and ethical standards that reflect true professional competence in financial management and stewardship.

REFERENCES

Adekunle, B. I., Chukwuma-Eke, E. C., Balogun, E. D., & Ogunsola, K. O. (2024). Optimizing internal control systems through blockchain-based financial reporting: Opportunities and risks. *International Journal of Management and Organizational Research*, *3*(1), 213–222. DOI: 10.54660/IJMOR.2024.3.1.213-222

Amanamah, R. B., Anaman, P. D., Ahmed, I. A., Quayson, J. A., Akyen, B., & Donkor, C. (2025). Internal controls and financial reporting accuracy in hotels: The role of management commitment and employee training. *SEISENSE Business Review*, *5*(1), 29–49. DOI: 10.33215/65wnpf71

Angelini, G., Costa, M., & Guizzardi, A. (2025). Complex data in tourism analysis: A stochastic approach to price competition. *Big Data Research*, *40*, 100520. DOI: 10.1016/j.bdr.2025.100520

Bakker, C. C., Parawiyati, P., & Pangastuti, D. A. (2024). The effects of information systems and the utilization of information technology on the quality of financial reports with internal control as moderation. Journal of Economics. *Finance and Management Studies*, *7*(1), 476–482.

Belesis, N. D., Kampouris, C. G., Fousteris, A. E., & Varouxis, D. (2025). Evaluating the effectiveness of internal control systems: Evidence from financial and audit performance data. Corporate Board: Role. *Duties and Composition*, *21*(3), 76–86.

Bimantari, P. M. K., Arnawa, I. P., & Wiryanata, I. G. N. A. (2025). Analisis Peranan Income Audit Pada Pengendalian Internal Di Hotel The Westin Resort & Spa Ubud Bali. Jurnal Ekonomi. *Manajemen Pariwisata Dan Perhotelan*, *4*(3), 579–589.

Brar, V., Jha, P., Jain, S., Mehrotra, S., Kumar, A., Jha, C. K., & Gupta, D. (2025, July). Deep reinforcement learning for dynamic pricing strategies in revenue management. In 2025 3rd World Conference on Communication & Computing (WCONF) (pp. 1-5). IEEE. DOI: 10.1109/WCONF64849.2025.11233694

Dewi, N. K. M., Wiryanata, I. G. N. A., & Lilasari, L. N. T. (2025). Analisis dampak digital payment pada pengendalian internal penerimaan di Hotel Grand Hyatt Bali. Riset Ilmu Manajemen Bisnis dan Akuntansi, 3(4), 102–114. **https://doi.org/**DOI: 10.61132/rimba.v3i4.2236

Dornyoh, E., Moore, M. A., Yeboah, R., Ocloo, A. T., & Dacosta, F. D. (2026). The science and speculations driving revenue management decisions in hotels in Cape Coast. *International Journal of Hospitality & Tourism Management*, *10*(1), 7–21. DOI: 10.11648/j.ijhtm.20261001.12

Duani, N., Barasch, A., & Morwitz, V. (2024). Demographic pricing in the digital age: Assessing fairness perceptions in algorithmic versus human-based price discrimination. *Journal of the Association for Consumer Research, 9*(3), 257–268. DOI: 10.1086/729440

Ehima, E., & Amede, O. F. (2025). Effect of internal control components and revenue leakage: Evidence from financial institutions in Edo State, Nigeria. *Gusau Journal of Accounting and Finance, 6*(2), 94–109. DOI: 10.57233/gujaf.v6i2.07

Gao, J. (2025). Optimizing hotel revenue management through dynamic pricing algorithms and data analysis. *Journal of Computational Methods in Sciences and Engineering, 25*(2), 1200–1209. DOI: 10.1177/14727978241298467

Grochowski, M. F., JABLONOWSKA, A. A., Lagioia, F., & Sartor, G. (2022). Algorithmic price discrimination and consumer protection: a digital arms race?. Technology and regulation, 2022, 36-47.

Harahap, A. J. S., Vonita, R. N. S., Nuraeni, P., & Khairi, F. R. (2025). The role of accounting information systems in strengthening revenue budget management and village expenditure in Indonesia. *West Science Interdisciplinary Studies, 3*(12), 2248–2256. DOI: 10.58812/wsis.v3i12.2295

Hidayati, S., Nata, J. H., Reindrawati, D. Y., & Huda, M. N. (2025). The influence of dynamic pricing in enhancing room occupancy and room revenue in Bintan Island Resort. [The International Journal of Applied Business]. *TIJAB, 9*(1), 38–50. DOI: 10.20473/tijab.v9.I1.2025.58812

Hyera, D. W., Kadigi, M. L., & Ndyetabula, D. W. (2025). Internal control systems and the revenue collection performance among local government authorities (LGA) in Tanzania. *Journal of Policy and Development Studies (Editon), 4*(1), 1–15. DOI: 10.51317/jpds.v4i1.676

Mei, Z. (2026). Dynamic pricing strategy driven by deep reinforcement learning with empirical analysis on the collaborative optimization of hotel revenue management and customer satisfaction. *International Journal of High Speed Electronics and Systems, 35*(06), 2540865. DOI: 10.1142/S0129156425408654

Muslim, M. (2025). The failure of governance and internal controls in preventing fraud in the company. *Advances in Managerial Auditing Research, 3*(1), 15–29. DOI: 10.60079/amar.v3i1.418

Nazlan, N. H. (2024). The Effect of Price Transparency on Young Travellers' Choices: An Experimental Study of Resort Packages. *Information Management and Business Review, 16*(3), 1170–1179. DOI: 10.22610/imbr.v16i3S(I)a.4229

Putra, I. G. B. N. P., & Anggiriawan, I. P. B. (2025). Sustainable Hospitality in Bali: Synergy of Good Corporate Governance, Internal Control System, and Quadruple Bottom Line. *South Asian Journal of Social Studies and Economics*, *22*(11), 22–32. DOI: 10.9734/sajsse/2025/v22i111202

Rohim, N. I., Rose, M., & Mayardit, F. K. (2024). Accounting information systems as a tool for effective petty cash control: Evidence from a hotel case study. *Journal of Islamic Economics Perspectives*, *6*(2), 117–127. DOI: 10.35719/11mxed32

Saitta, S., D'Amico, V., & Farinella, G. M. (2024). Dynamic Price Prediction for Revenue Management System in Hospitality Sector. In DATA (pp. 218-228). DOI: 10.5220/0012707700003756

Salsabila, D., & Islamudin, A. (2025). Analisis Sistem Pengendalian Internal pada Penerimaan Kas dan Verifikasi Invoice pada Hotel XYZ. *Jurnal Riset Rumpun Ilmu Ekonomi*, *4*(2), 507–516. DOI: 10.55606/jurrie.v4i2.6157

Toukabri, M., & Chaouachi, M. (2025). Exploring the Influence of Corporate Social Responsibility, Blockchain Transparency, and Cultural Alignment on Consumer Trust and Premium Pricing Willingness for Local Food in Saudi Arabia. *Current Research in Nutrition and Food Science*, *13*(1), 304–316. DOI: 10.12944/CRNFSJ.13.1.20

Xiao, W., Zhang, S., Huang, Z., & Yu, Y. (2024, May). Multi-scenario pricing for hotel revenue management. In *Proceedings of the ACM Web Conference 2024* (pp. 3986-3994). DOI: 10.1145/3589334.3645350

Yarlagadda, K. C.KRISHNA CHAITANYA YARLAGADDA. (2025). AI-driven dynamic pricing: Optimizing revenue in digital marketplaces. *World Journal of Advanced Engineering Technology and Sciences*, *15*(02), 2147–2157. DOI: 10.30574/wjaets.2025.15.2.0681

Yulianti, R., Maryam, M., Hamdiah, C., Mahdi, M., & Khairuna, K. (2024). The role of internal control systems and good corporate governance in fraud prevention efforts: A literature review. *Frontiers in Business and Economics*, *3*(1), 39–54. DOI: 10.56225/finbe.v3i1.325

Zhao, Q. (2024). Exploration on the protection of consumer rights and interests in big data price discrimination. *International Journal of Frontiers in Sociology*, *6*(4), 15–20.

Chapter 12
Corporate Integrity and ESG in Hotel Revenue Management:
The Role of Internal Audit

Evangelia Pappa
http://orcid.org/0000-0003-0958-851X
European University of Cyprus, Cyprus

Theodora Zaroulea
http://orcid.org/0000-0002-9725-591X
Neapolis University Pafos, Cyprus

Anastasios Konstantinidis
University of Western Macedonia, Greece

Dimitrios Niklis
http://orcid.org/0009-0005-8376-4026
University of Western Macedonia, Greece

ABSTRACT

The global business environment is being called upon to adapt to constantly changing conditions influenced by market globalization, rapid technological advancement, economic crises, and geopolitical tensions, financial scandals, the COVID-19 pandemic, and climate change. The hotel industry is also affected by these conditions, facing challenges related to fluctuating demand, strong seasonality, environmental crises, and the increasing level of digitization and technological innovation. The hotel industry operates in a new environment where the values of information quality, transparency, and adaptation to modern consumer expectations are par-

DOI: 10.4018/979-8-3373-9479-4.ch012

amount. The purpose of this chapter is to examine revenue management in hotel businesses, based on ESG practices and internal audit. The chapter contributes to the literature by proposing a holistic governance framework that demonstrates how corporate integrity, ESG criteria, and internal audit can support effective revenue management, strengthen organizational resilience, and promote sustainable value creation in hotel businesses.

INTRODUCTION

Over the past decade, there have been many changes in the ever-evolving business landscape, with the hotel industry being called upon to adapt its role. The challenges arising from volatile demand, strong seasonality, the climate crisis, technological advances, and armed conflicts require digital personalization and flexibility (Kasavana and Brooks, 2020; AL Mushattat et al., 2025; Vukotić et al., 2026). At the same time, global geopolitical turmoil, economic uncertainty, and inflationary pressures are affecting both travel preferences and consumer psychology, while seasonality is forcing businesses to adopt strategies to extend the tourist season and maximize revenue (Papatheodorou and Tsiotsou, 2020). Furthermore, climate change and extreme weather conditions are altering travel patterns and tourism consumption, negatively affecting demand for hotel services (Becken and Hay, 2022). Finally, rising energy costs are intensifying the need to adopt sustainable practices and create environmentally responsible hotels that implement sustainability strategies (Mitev et al., 2025).

Hotel businesses are called upon to move away from short-term risk management and adopt strategies that focus on long-term sustainability and corporate responsibility (Szerb and Gábor, 2022). The integration of ESG (Environmental, Social, Governance) is becoming increasingly important for the hotel industry, as it strengthens competitive advantage, bolsters customer trust, and improves corporate reputation by promoting the circular economy and developing socially responsible initiatives (Chen et al., 2022; Yu et al., 2025). Furthermore, the adoption of sustainable practices improves the financial performance of hotels, ensuring their long-term growth and competitiveness (Zhang and Kim, 2022).

According to the Triple Bottom Line approach (Elkington, 1994) hotel businesses recognize that the assessment of their business performance is not limited solely to the economic dimension (profit), but must also include the social dimension and the well-being of people, as well as the environmental impacts of business activity (planet) (Gaio et al., 2022). The Triple Bottom Line transforms the traditional business model into a multidimensional tool for evaluating the "3 Ps," ensuring that profit is maximized while respecting social well-being and environmental protection.

Despite the importance of these frameworks, the literature is still dispersed because revenue management, corporate integrity, internal audit, and ESG are typically studied as distinct research streams. This fragmentation underscores the need for a more comprehensive conceptual approach that explains how various variables interact within hotel businesses to create sustainable value.

In this light, internal audit emerges as a key mechanism for ensuring the effective implementation of control procedures and internal safeguards related to the collection, recording, and reporting of revenue, thereby enhancing the transparency and accountability of the cash flow management system (Amanamah et al., 2025). Through the systematic monitoring of these cash flows, it helps prevent and detect fraud or other irregularities, while ensuring compliance with regulatory requirements, such as tax obligations and financial reporting. In this way, internal audit and ESG principles work in tandem, enhancing the accuracy and reliability of financial reporting, safeguarding revenue, preventing irregularities, and enhancing the integrity and credibility of hotel businesses in a highly competitive environment (Lu et al., 2025; Yu et al., 2025).

The objective of this chapter is to analyze the combined effect of ESG principles and internal audit on the revenue management of hotel businesses, examining how their implementation enhances transparency, corporate integrity, and financial efficiency. The methodological approach of this chapter includes a review of the literature on ESG, internal audit, and revenue management.

The chapter is structured as follows: Following the introduction, the second section analyzes the issue of integrity in the hotel industry. Next, the role of distinct ESG criteria in the organization and operation of hotel businesses is examined. The fourth section focuses on the relationship between internal audit and revenue management. Finally, the chapter concludes with a set of concluding recommendations.

INTEGRITY IN THE HOTEL BUSINESS

Integrity is a fundamental aspect of business ethics and plays a significant role in strengthening and maintaining effective governance, by fostering trust both in the principal-agent relationship (agency theory) and in the relationship between the company and its customers and other stakeholders (stakeholder theory). Business ethics refers to the set of values, rules, and principles that shape the objective behavior of individuals and organizations by defining the boundaries between ethically acceptable and unacceptable practices (Bian and Çalıyurt, 2018). Beyond mere compliance with the applicable legal framework, business ethics serves as a decision-making mechanism that promotes accountability, transparency, fairness, and respect for all stakeholders. In today's business environment, the application of ethical principles is not limited to a company's relationships with its customers and employees, but extends to the management of suppliers, investors, local communities, and the natural environment. From this perspective, business ethics is a key pillar of corporate governance, as it helps reduce conflicts of interest, strengthen accountability, and build relationships of trust with stakeholders.

At the same time, adopting ethical practices enhances a company's reputation, laying the groundwork for long-term sustainability and a competitive advantage in an environment of heightened demands for social and environmental responsibility. The "Six Pillars of Character" framework developed by the Josephson Institute of Ethics (2013) makes a significant contribution in this regard, identifying six fundamental values of ethical behavior: trustworthiness, respect, responsibility, fairness, caring, and citizenship. These values form the basis for the development of ethical judgment and responsible professional conduct, regardless of the field of activity.

The development of a strong culture of integrity in the hospitality industry can begin as early as the vocational training stage. Vallen and Casado (2000) argued that the teaching of business ethics should be an integral part of the education of future professionals. Drawing on the framework of the Josephson Institute of Ethics, the authors identified a set of ethical principles that can serve as guidelines for decision-making and the shaping of professional conduct in the hospitality industry. Those involved in the hospitality industry are expected to apply and uphold the following principles:

- Accountability: Building a culture of accountability and responsibility, from the hotel management down to the front-line staff.
- Commitment to excellence: Providing high-quality hotel services at the best possible price, adhering to the golden rule of 'value for money'.
- Concern for others: Focusing on understanding customer needs and protecting the rights of stakeholders.
- Fairness: Promoting a diverse and inclusive hospitality environment based on equality and acceptance (equity theory).
- Honesty: Speaking the truth regardless of how difficult it may be, and establishing free and open channels of communication.
- Integrity: Actions carried out with sincerity, objectivity, reliability, and independence - qualities that build trust among travelers.
- Law abiding: Compliance with regulatory requirements, bearing in mind that in many cases what is legal is not necessarily ethical.
- Leadership: Incorporating empathy, transparency, and fairness into the leadership style used in hotel management.

- Loyalty: Transforming customers into guests by meeting their expectations (expectation-confirmation theory) and strengthening employee reward programs.
- Promise keeping: Consistently adhering to decisions regarding the adoption of health protocols, environmental requirements, and operational regulations, as well as providing compensation in the event of failures.
- Reputation: Personalized handling of complaints and criticism and strengthening of the company's reputation, as the combination of corporate identity and corporate image.
- Respect for others: Creating equal opportunities for employment and development, and establishing policies against violence and harassment.

The adoption and systematic implementation of the above principles contribute significantly to the creation of an ethical and sustainable operating framework for hospitality businesses, enhancing organizational effectiveness, stakeholder trust, and their long-term competitiveness. However, the effective integration of ethical values into organizational operations requires the existence of institutionalized mechanisms that guide and monitor the professional conduct of employees and managers.

In this context, the development and implementation of a code of ethics -which serves as a tool for ethical governance and organizational guidance- takes on particular importance. Recognizing the need to establish common standards of professional conduct at the international level, the International Hospitality Institute (IHI)1 took the initiative to develop a unified code of ethics for the hospitality industry, publishing the Hospitality Code of Ethics (HCODE). This code aims to create a common framework of principles and guidelines that can be adopted by hospitality businesses regardless of size, geographic region, or business model.

The Hospitality Code of Ethics serves as a benchmark for promoting ethical conduct and professional integrity, combining both binding compliance requirements and voluntary practices, which fall under the category of so-called "soft law." The code sets forth the values, rules, and standards of conduct expected to govern companies' relationships with employees, customers, suppliers, local communities, and the natural environment. A clearly articulated code of ethics is an important management tool, as it helps establish a common understanding of acceptable and unacceptable behaviors within the organization. Simultaneously, it provides guidance to employees in managing ethical dilemmas that may arise in the course of their duties, promoting consistency in decision-making and reducing the risk of deviations from the company's core values.

Furthermore, the adoption of a comprehensive ethical and deontological framework is associated with significant organizational benefits. According to Pappa et al. (2022), the existence of clear rules of ethical conduct helps strengthen corporate reputation, improve the work environment, and foster trust between employees and management. In parallel, the systematic application of ethical principles enhances transparency, accountability, and the company's legitimacy in the eyes of its stakeholders, serving as a fundamental prerequisite for maintaining social acceptance and sustainable development in the modern hospitality industry.

IHI's Hospitality Code of Ethics (n.d.: 2-4) includes four sections that outline the specific responsibilities of hospitality professionals:

"Section I – Responsibility to customers

Be consistently kind and patient with customers, resolving issues effectively. Protect their personal information and maintain confidentiality, per legal requirements. Comply with laws on data handling, respect privacy, and communicate truthfully and constructively. Practice active listening and promote customer safety and wellbeing. Seek customer feedback on performance.

Section II – Responsibility to employers

Be honest, maintain confidentiality, communicate clearly, report unethical behavior or threats, protect employer's interests, avoid conflicts of interest and wrongdoing, follow the company handbook, work diligently, and seek professional development.

Section III – Responsibility to employees or students

Treat all employees with fairness, equality, and respect, acknowledging cultural, religious, and racial diversity. Avoid bullying and intimidation, fostering an ethical work atmosphere. Ensure a safe, healthy workplace and conduct sexual harassment training. Practice fair communication, timely reviews, and merit increases. Use power wisely, offering competitive wages and access to healthcare resources. Promote work-life balance, offer development opportunities, and uphold privacy. Adhere to equal employment practices and the Hospitality Code of Ethics. Recognize exceptional service and establish clear job responsibilities and performance metrics. Avoid retaliation and support environmental sustainability.

Section IV – Responsibility to colleagues, vendors, and other stakeholders

Treat all stakeholders with dignity and respect, valuing diversity. Avoid hurtful actions, be kind and ethical, promote positivity, collaborate, listen actively, communicate clearly, and welcome feedback while reporting unethical behavior."

The application of the Code of Ethics takes on particular importance in the context of revenue management—also known as yield management—since decisions related to pricing, demand management, and occupancy optimization directly affect both financial performance and the relationships of trust between the company and its customers (Kimes and Wirtz, 2003; Hayes and Miller, 2022). Therefore, revenue management cannot be viewed solely as a set of techniques for maximizing revenue, but rather as a managerial process that must operate within a framework of ethical principles, transparency, and accountability (Pappa et al., 2022).

In the hotel industry, the Finance Department plays a decisive role in the formulation and implementation of revenue management strategies, as it is responsible for financial planning, the oversight of financial activities, and the monitoring of the company's financial performance (Jagels and Coltman, 2004). Through its collaboration with the Accounting Department, the Credit Department, and the Food and Beverage Revenue and Cost Control Department, the collection and processing of reliable financial data are ensured; this data is a fundamental prerequisite for effective decision-making regarding pricing policy, demand forecasting, and the management of available capacity (Guilding et al., 2005; Hayes and Miller, 2022).

The importance of financial data integrity is particularly evident in the context of revenue management, as the quality of decisions depends on the accuracy and reliability of the information used. The existence of clear ethical standards and internal audit procedures reduces the risk of errors, misstatements, or improper practices, helping to ensure the transparency and reliability of financial reporting (COSO, 2013; Koutoupis and Pappa, 2018).

The link between the Code of Ethics and the formulation of pricing policy is of particular importance. Dynamic pricing, a key tool of revenue management, allows prices to be adjusted according to demand, availability, and market conditions (Kimes, 1989; Ivanov, 2014). However, its implementation must be guided by the principles of fairness, transparency, and equal treatment of customers. In this context, the Code of Ethics serves as a mechanism for ethical oversight, preventing practices that could be considered misleading or abusive, such as withholding critical information, misleading price presentation, or the exploitation of information asymmetry between the firm and the customer (Hwang and Wen, 2009; Noone and Mattila, 2009).

At the same time, the proper management of credits, collections, and financial obligations is directly linked to the principles of responsibility and accountability promoted by the Code of Ethics. The effective operation of the Credit Department and the Accounting Department contributes not only to maintaining the company's financial stability but also to strengthening the trust of its business partners (Jagels and Coltman, 2004). Similarly, revenue control procedures ensure the accurate recording of financial transactions and compliance with the principles of sound management and corporate governance (Anderson et al., 2017; Koutoupis and Pappa, 2018).

The growing use of information systems and data analytics technologies in revenue management makes it equally important to ensure the protection of personal data and the confidentiality of information. These systems provide critical information about customer preferences and behavior, which places increased demands on the ethical management of data. Compliance with data protection principles and the provisions of codes of conduct are essential prerequisites for maintaining customer trust and legitimizing the use of these technologies (Martin, 2019; OECD, 2023).

Consequently, the effectiveness of revenue management does not depend solely on the application of advanced analytical and forecasting techniques, but also on the integration of ethical principles into decision-making processes. Linking the Code of Ethics to revenue management helps create a framework for responsible management, which allows hotel businesses to pursue revenue maximization without undermining customer trust, transparency in transactions, and their long-term sustainability (Pappa et al., 2022; Kyriakogkonas et al., 2022).

ESG AND HOTEL INDUSTRY

Hotel businesses utilize ESG criteria as a key driver for promoting sustainable development (Kyriakogkonas, et al., 2022) and ethical corporate governance (Oh et al., 2024). According to Pappa et al. (2024), the systematic application of these criteria is observed primarily in developed countries and in the private sector, while it is less widespread in developing economies and in the public sector. At the same time, the level of maturity varies depending on the size of the company and the degree to which ESG criteria are integrated into business strategy. However, as noted by Lin et al. (2024) and Yu et al. (2025), few studies have examined the application of ESG criteria in the hospitality and tourism sector.

Meng and Shaikh (2023), Wibawa and Septianto (2024), and Passas (2024) emphasize that ESG criteria are an essential prerequisite for sustainability and business resilience, significantly influencing decision-making. Specifically, these criteria encompass a set of non-financial indicators that assess corporate performance across three dimensions. The first relates to the environmental dimension, which includes sustainability, reducing the environmental footprint, and utilizing renewable energy sources. The second pillar relates to the social dimension, which examines how organizations manage their relationships with employees and society, with an emphasis on labor rights. The final pillar refers to corporate governance, which encompasses the transparency, accountability, and integrity that govern the decision-making processes and administrative structures of hotel businesses.

The ESG framework encompasses a broad range of environmental, social and governance pillars that collectively shape the sustainable development and long-term performance of hotel firms. Figure 1 provides a conceptual overview of the three ESG pillars and their role in fostering sustainable hotel performance, competitive advantage and long-term value creation within the hospitality industry.

Figure 1. ESG Pillars and Their Contribution to Sustainable Hotel Performance, Competitive Advantage and Long-Term Value Creation

Source: *Authors' elaboration based on relevant ESG and hospitality management literature.*

The systematic adoption of ESG criteria offers substantial benefits to hotel businesses, which influence their long-term competitiveness. Specifically, Lee et al. (2016), emphasize that the integration of the aforementioned practices enhances companies' credibility and reputation, facilitating their access to financing sources on favorable terms and supporting their compliance with the regulatory environment. Furthermore, Muhammad et al. (2015) and Shaikh (2022) point out that the application of ESG criteria helps build relationships of trust with customers and other stakeholders, while increasing companies' ability to attract and retain highly knowledgeable and skilled personnel.

The impact of the above factors enhances the organizational effectiveness and operational efficiency of hotel businesses. Lu et al. (2025) highlight that high performance on ESG criteria is linked to improved financial results and greater access to resources, as these criteria serve as indicators of reliability for investors and stakeholders, thereby reducing risks and uncertainty. In the hospitality industry, the implementation of ESG criteria also influences consumer behavior. Bae (2022) and Zhang and Jung (2026) note that initiatives related to social responsibility help foster trusting relationships with customers, strengthening their commitment to the product. Furthermore, the growing trend of hotel chains publishing ESG reports reflects the gradual integration of sustainability into corporate strategic planning, a development that promotes transparency and accountability and improves reputation and financial performance.

The benefits associated with ESG adoption extend beyond environmental and social responsibility and increasingly influence the financial performance of hotel firms. ESG initiatives contribute to enhanced operational efficiency, stronger stakeholder relationships, improved resource utilization and reduced risk exposure, thereby creating multiple pathways through which sustainability-oriented practices generate measurable economic value. Through these mechanisms, ESG implementation can support revenue growth, profitability, access to capital and long-term business resilience. Figure 2 illustrates the principal pathways linking ESG practices to hotel financial performance and long-term value creation.

Figure 2. Pathways Through Which ESG Practices Influence Hotel Financial Performance and Long-Term Value Creation in the Hospitality Industry

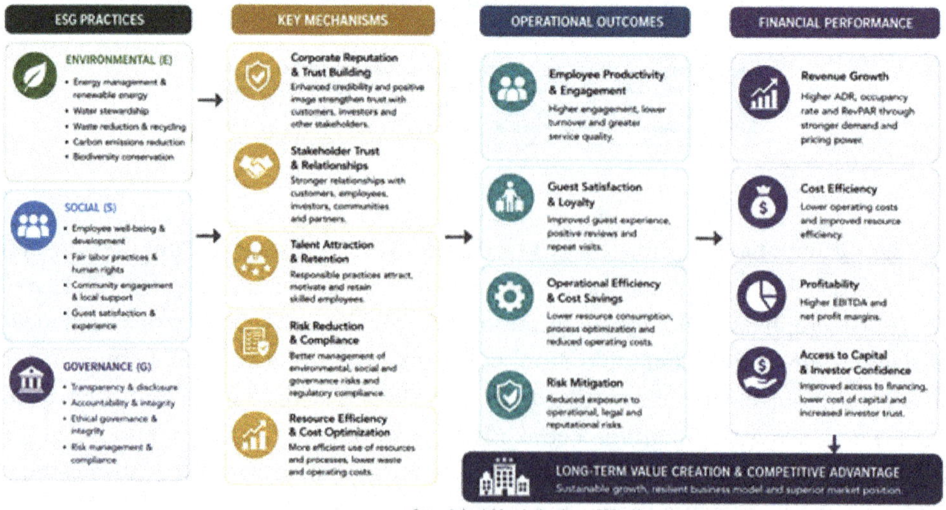

Source: Authors' elaboration based on the ESG and hospitality management literature.

The importance of ESG criteria in hotel revenue management is growing, as they ensure that decision-making is based on transparency, accountability, and sustainable development. According to Kyriakogkonas et al. (2022), the adoption of ESG practices in revenue management processes helps mitigate operational and financial risks while strengthening relationships of trust with customers, investors, and other stakeholders. Consequently, business stability is maintained and competitiveness is strengthened in a constantly evolving environment fraught with multiple challenges.

Notable examples of the application of ESG criteria demonstrate how sustainability principles can be integrated into the day-to-day operations of businesses and contribute both to reducing the environmental footprint and to the profitable management of of hotel businesses. Table 1 summarizes representative ESG practices implemented across the environmental, social and governance pillars within the hotel industry.

Table 1. Representative ESG Practices in the Hotel Industry

ESG Pillar	Area	Representative Practices
Environmental	Energy Management	LED lighting, energy-efficient appliances, heat pumps, CHP systems, smart energy meters, and Building Management Systems (BMS)
Environmental	Water Stewardship	Greywater reuse, rainwater harvesting, leak detection systems, low-flow fixtures, and wastewater recycling
Environmental	Waste Management	Recycling, food waste monitoring and reduction, composting, material reuse, and circular economy initiatives
Social	Community Development and Cultural Heritage	Collaboration with local suppliers, support for local communities, preservation of cultural heritage, and biodiversity protection
Social	Human Capital and Inclusion	Diversity and inclusion policies, human rights protection, employee training, and workforce well-being initiatives
Governance	Corporate Governance and Social Responsibility	Sustainability training, stakeholder engagement, Corporate Social Responsibility (CSR) initiatives, transparency, and regulatory compliance

Source: Authors' elaboration

According to a study by the Research Institute for Tourism (2024), the environmental dimension of ESG criteria is considered the most widespread aspect of sustainable development in the hotel industry. Initiatives in this area focus on reducing energy consumption and the use of natural resources through the application of technology. Energy-efficient lighting systems, high-efficiency appliances, heat pumps, and combined heat and power (CHP) systems are examples of how businesses can reduce their environmental footprint. At the same time, the use of automation and building management systems (BMS), smart energy meters, and electric vehicle charging stations enhances resource management and reduces the operating costs of hotel properties. Effective water management plays a prominent role in the environmental practices of hotel businesses, as high water consumption is one of the industry's most significant challenges.

For this reason, businesses reuse towels and linens, treat graywater, utilize rainwater and treated wastewater, and upgrade their biological treatment systems. Similarly, Butler (2008) emphasizes that waste management is a priority for hotel businesses. Promoting recycling, implementing circular economy practices, tracking food waste, composting organic waste, and utilizing surplus food all contribute to reducing waste.

Furthermore, under the "Environment" criterion, water-related actions focus on practices:

- water conservation, such as reusing towels, treating and reusing graywater for garden irrigation, creating a rainwater harvesting system, upgrading biological wastewater treatment and using treated wastewater for irrigation, installing water meters and systematically checking for leaks, planting drought-tolerant plants, installing flow reducers and sensors on faucets, showers, automated systems for controlled irrigation, reuse of bed linens, informational signs regarding water conservation in the hotel, and low-flow toilet flushes,
- water management in hotel swimming pools through the use of seawater and the reduction of leaks.

The social dimension of ESG criteria relates to the creation of social value and the development of relationships between hotel businesses, employees, and other stakeholders. The protection of cultural heritage, the conservation of biodiversity, the strengthening of the local economy through collaboration with local producers and suppliers, as well as the promotion of sustainable consumption patterns through the use of local, organic, and environmentally certified products strengthen social cohesion and promote sustainability throughout the supply chain. Equally beneficial is the adoption of policies that promote and defend equality, diversity, and inclusion and ensure human rights. Furthermore, as noted by Yu et al. (2024) note, hotel businesses invest in lifelong learning and in improving staff skills, taking employee satisfaction into account, which in turn fosters strong relationships of trust with both customers and local communities.

The corporate governance dimension is linked to the management, decision-making, and accountability processes of hotel businesses. The implementation of effective control systems ensures their ethical operation and sustainability. For this reason, companies take steps to raise staff awareness regarding sustainable development, environmental management, and corporate responsibility. Furthermore, the implementation of corporate social responsibility (CSR) practices, stakeholder engagement, and compliance with the institutional and regulatory framework enhance the credibility of businesses. Consequently, effective corporate governance fosters a climate of trust among investors, customers, and society. This creates the conditions for preserving long-term value and developing a sustainable competitive advantage.

Despite the significant and numerous benefits resulting from the adoption of ESG criteria, the challenges must be highlighted. Yébenes (2024) emphasizes that these challenges can affect investment decisions and the competitiveness of businesses. In particular, environmental risks are linked to the operations of hotel businesses and their impact on the natural environment. Greenwashing (Jamil and Wahyuni, 2024), dependence on natural resources (Jackson, 2025), pollution (Lin et al., 2024), and a negative impact on the customer experience are some of the phenomena that damage a company's image, especially at a time when the public is better informed and more aware of sustainability issues (Lunkes et al., 2025). Furthermore, social risks concern companies' relationships with all stakeholders and are linked to human rights violations, workplace discrimination, and failure to manage community relations. These issues are likely to lead to complaints, fines, and sanctions, which means that the company's reputation is at stake (Zientara, et al., 2025). Finally, corporate governance risks relate to how a hotel business is organized, managed, and monitored for quality. Bae (2022) notably emphasizes that its credibility can be negatively affected by a lack of transparency in decision-making, breaches of personal data, and a lack of compliance with tax, health, or other regulations.

INTERNAL AUDIT AND HOTEL REVENUE MANAGEMENT

The ultimate goal of every hotel business is to ensure the provision of high-quality services to its customers, through the most effective use of available resources, the lowest possible operating costs, within the framework of legality, excellent management, and sound financial management. A key factor in achieving this mission is the architectural structure of the governance and control system for its day-to-day operations, in accordance with the internal control framework of the Committee of Sponsoring Organizations of the Treadway Commission (COSO), the global standards for the professional practice of internal auditing (Standards), the Institute of Internal Auditors (IIA), and best practices (Koutoupis and Pappa, 2018; Balios et al., 2022).

The Internal Control System helps address the risks faced by the hotel business and provides only reasonable assurance to senior management that it will achieve its objectives, which are: (a) ensuring the effectiveness, economy, and efficiency of operations, including operational objectives, and providing reliable information for decision-making; preventing or discouraging waste, and protecting assets, information, and reputation, (b) the preparation of reliable and timely financial information;

and (c) compliance with the applicable legal and regulatory framework governing the company's operations and activities.

The structure of the Internal Control System is based on a three-level functional approach, known as the "three-lines model". This model distinguishes three levels of roles ("lines") that contribute to the achievement of objectives and facilitate strong governance and effective management of risks and threats. The first line pertains to the hotel's operational functions, activities, and internal controls, and includes all hotel employees, from waitstaff, housekeeping staff, and front desk employees to the floor manager, the food and beverage manager, and the general manager. The second line of defense concerns management mechanisms for risk management, ensuring compliance with laws and regulations, and overseeing and evaluating the controls for which the first line of defense is responsible. Specifically, it includes the information security officer, the quality manager, the compliance officer, the risk management officer, and the chief financial officer.

The third line refers to the Internal Audit Department, which monitors the first two lines in order to provide assurance to management that the governance framework, risk management, and the individual components and mechanisms of the Internal Control System are functioning effectively. It includes the chief internal auditor, internal auditors, and/or external partners in the case of outsourcing. To safeguard the independence and objectivity of the Internal Audit Department's operations, it must be organizationally separate from the entity's operational and administrative functions; and for this reason, it reports directly to the Board of Directors and the Audit Committee. The literature also identifies an additional line of defense involving external supervisory and auditing bodies of the hotel enterprise, such as certified public accountants, regulatory supervisory authorities, and even European or international regulatory compliance bodies.

From the above, it is clear that the internal control system should not be confused conceptually with the internal audit function as the latter is a component of the Internal Control System that evaluates the effectiveness and efficiency of its operations, the exercise of management's responsibilities, and the performance of the duties of the hotel company's staff, while providing recommendations for improvement. Consequently, internal audit—as an independent assurance and advisory activity conducted through a systematic and disciplined approach—is a critical tool for strengthening corporate governance and organizational effectiveness.

The value of internal audit stems from improving the chances of achieving organizational objectives, identifying operational changes, and/or reducing risk exposure, as well as from providing reasonable assurance and advisory services. The hotel company's senior management relies on the internal audit function to provide objective assurance and insight regarding the efficiency and effectiveness of the internal control system and related processes, such as reservation procedures, revenue management, and resource management. Consequently, the creation of added value is expressed through the three pillars of assurance, insight, and objectivity (Miller and Smith, 2011).

More specifically, as illustrated in Figure 3, internal audit provides reasonable assurance regarding governance, risk management, and control, in order to ensure the achievement of the hotel company's strategic, operational, financial objectives, as well as the hotel company's regulatory compliance objectives. Furthermore, the catalytic role of internal audit lies in identifying and understanding processes to improve the effectiveness and efficiency of the hotel business, providing information and recommendations based on analyses and evaluations of data and organizational processes. Finally, internal audit demonstrates a commitment to integrity and accountability, adding value to governing bodies and senior and top executives as an independent source of objective advice and guidance (Anderson et al., 2017).

Figure 3. Core Dimensions of Internal Audit Value Creation

Source: Pappa, 2024.

In the hotel industry, we have shifted from the traditional approach of maximizing profitability per service unit to optimizing revenue through dynamic pricing and the effective management of demand and available capacity. Kimes and Wirtz (2003) define revenue management as pricing the right product for the right customer at the right time through the right channel. Essentially, it is a support system for direct revenue-generating units such as the room division (Orkin, 2003), restaurants and bars (Heo, 2013), spas (Modica and Scanu, 2014), conference and event venues (Wang et al., 2015), casinos (Hendler and Hendler, 2004), and golf courses (Rasekh and Li, 2011). Furthermore, as a system, it requires data (occupancy rates, revenue per available room, no-shows) and information (business vs. leisure guests, demand forecasting), tools (pricing dashboards, channel management tools), and specific software (Cloudbeds, Opera) (Ivanov, 2014). Internal audit can intervene at any stage of the revenue management process, from data collection and analysis to the evaluation of the system as a whole.

Effective revenue management requires internal audits to be conducted across all business cycles of the hotel enterprise. Of course, the division of activities into cycles depends largely on the specific nature of each hotel business, while the importance of each cycle is determined by factors specific to each case. According to Table 2, business cycles are divided into primary cycles—such as business administration, procurement, production, and sales—and auxiliary cycles, such as human resources, fixed assets, finance, accounting and taxation, information technology, and specialized functions (legal services, public relations).

Table 2. Activity cycles

Main Cycles	**Supportive Cycles**
1. Management	5. Personnel
2. Procurement	6. Fixed assets
3. Production-Inventory	7. Finance
4. Sales	8. Accounting-Tax
	9. Computerization (Data Processing / IT Systems
	10. Special functions

Source: Filos (2004)

Each of the four main cycles of activity includes several functions, which are as follows (Filos, 2004):

1. Management: This cycle covers the activities of the Board of Directors and the General Assembly, the role of the CEO (or general manager), as well as specific management issues, such as project management and administrative support for the hotel business.
2. Procurement: This involves activities related to identifying procurement needs, conducting market research, evaluating bids, placing orders, and arranging for the transportation, insurance, and receipt of goods (raw materials, merchandise, supplies, etc.).

3. Production – Inventory: This involves the organization and control of the production process (e.g., food and beverage services), the storage and management of raw materials and finished products, as well as overall inventory management.
4. Sales: This involves marketing and pricing activities, including taking reservations and providing hospitality and food and beverage services.

Each of the six auxiliary activity cycles includes several functions, which, according to the structure of this Procedures Manual, are as follows (Filos, 2004):

5. Personnel: This involves assessing staffing needs, hiring, assigning responsibilities, training, evaluating, terminating, or retiring staff, and monitoring and processing payroll,
6. Fixed Assets: This involves assessing the hotel's needs for fixed assets (buildings, machinery, vehicles, etc., whether owned or leased) and managing the security, insurance, maintenance, and monitoring of these assets.
7. Finance: This cycle refers to activities related to meeting the business's financing needs and managing cash reserves and working capital, including payments and collections. This cycle also includes activities related to budgeting and reporting.
8. Accounting: This cycle refers to the tasks of updating the accounting ledgers, documenting the relevant work, monitoring tax matters, and preparing financial statements.
9. Computerization: This cycle refers to the tasks involved in supporting the company's operations from an IT perspective, to carry out the company's business activities and to fulfill accounting and tax obligations, as well as to meet management's information needs. Computerization efforts primarily involve issues related to equipment, systems, security, and support.
10. Special Functions: The last, but no less important, cycle of activities, which includes all functions not covered by previous cycles. For example, the legal support function may fall under this cycle. Similarly, the work of internal auditors—support work that spans all activity cycles—may also be included in this cycle. Other functions within this cycle include quality assurance, public relations, document management, etc.

CONCLUSIONS

The hotel industry currently operates in an increasingly complex environment shaped by the interplay of economic, social, technological, and environmental factors. The impacts of climate change, geopolitical turmoil, market uncertainty, the digitization of operations, and the ever-changing demands of travelers are creating a new operating environment for hotel businesses, which are being called upon to redefine how they create and sustain value (Kasavana and Brooks, 2020; Papatheodorou and Tsiotsou, 2020; Becken and Hay, 2022; Vukotić et al., 2026). In this context, effective management can no longer be limited to achieving short-term financial results but must incorporate the principles of sustainability, transparency, integrity, and accountability.

This chapter examines the interconnection between business integrity, ESG criteria, internal control, and revenue management in the hotel industry. The key finding is that these concepts do not function as independent practices but as interrelated elements of a comprehensive corporate governance framework, which enhances both the financial performance and the long-term sustainability of hospitality businesses. The interconnection of these four dimensions is particularly important in an industry where trust, reputation, service quality, and the customer experience are key factors in competitiveness.

The analysis of business integrity has shown that ethical behavior and responsible management are fundamental prerequisites for ensuring the effective operation of hotel businesses. Fostering a culture of organizational integrity, guided by the principles of honesty, fairness, accountability, and respect for stakeholders, helps build relationships of trust and minimize conflicts of interest. At the same time, the implementation of a code of ethics, such as the Hospitality Code of Ethics, provides a clear framework for ethical conduct for executives and employees in the industry, enhancing consistency in decision-making and compliance with the principles of good governance (Vallen and Casado, 2000; Pappa et al., 2022). From this perspective, integrity is not merely a moral obligation but a strategic asset that directly influences corporate reputation and competitiveness.

At the same time, the preceding analysis highlighted the strategic role of ESG criteria in modern hotel management. The systematic integration of environmental, social, and governance practices enhances businesses' ability to respond to market demands and effectively manage risks arising from the external environment. Initiatives related to reducing energy and water consumption, waste management, biodiversity conservation, promoting diversity and inclusion, and improving corporate governance mechanisms contribute to creating value not only for the company but also for all stakeholders (Kyriakogkonas et al., 2022; Oh et al., 2024; Pappa et al., 2024).

The relevant literature highlights that the adoption of ESG practices is not limited to compliance with sustainability requirements, but serves as a factor that strengthens organizational resilience, access to financing, corporate reputation, and the trust that the company enjoys from investors, customers, and other stakeholders (Lee et al., 2016; Meng and Shaikh, 2023; Wibawa and Septianto, 2024; Lu et al., 2025; Yu et al., 2025). For hotel companies, the adoption of ESG practices takes on particular strategic importance, given that customer trust, the destination's reputation, and the responsible management of natural resources are factors that directly influence both their competitiveness and their long-term profitability. Furthermore, ESG practices serve as risk prevention and management mechanisms, helping to maintain business continuity during periods of crisis and uncertainty.

Of particular importance was the highlighting of the relationship between ESG and the Triple Bottom Line approach. According to Elkington (1994), the assessment of business performance should not be limited solely to the financial dimension but should also include the social and environmental impacts of business activity. This approach takes on particular significance in the hospitality industry, as the success of hotel businesses depends to a large extent on the quality of the natural environment, the well-being of local communities, and their ability to build relationships of trust with guests. Therefore, the adoption of ESG criteria should not be viewed merely as a matter of compliance but as an integral part of the strategy for growth and value creation.

Another key focus of the chapter was the examination of the role of internal audit. The analysis demonstrated that internal audit is a critical mechanism for strengthening corporate governance and risk management. Through the independent and objective evaluation of procedures, the provision of reasonable assurance, and the formulation of recommendations for improvement, it helps ensure the effectiveness of operations, the reliability of financial reporting, and compliance with the applicable regulatory framework (Koutoupis and Pappa, 2018; Balios et al., 2022). At the same time, according to Miller and Smith (2011) and Anderson et al. (2017), the added value of internal audit is expressed through the three pillars of assurance, insight, and objectivity—elements that support evidence-based managerial decision-making.

The importance of internal audit becomes even more evident in the context of revenue management. Revenue management has evolved into one of the most important managerial functions in hotel enterprises, as it directly affects their profitability and financial sustainability. As Kimes and Wirtz (2003) argue, the essence of revenue management lies in providing the right product, to the right customer, at the right time, and at the right price. However, achieving this objective requires reliable data, effective information systems, and strong control mechanisms. The collection and analysis of data regarding demand, reservations, cancellations, no-shows, and customer preferences makes it necessary to have procedures that ensure the accuracy, completeness, and integrity of information.

From this perspective, internal control plays a pivotal role in ensuring the effectiveness of revenue management processes. The evaluation of information systems, verification of data reliability, assessment of compliance with pricing policies, and monitoring of reservation and distribution processes contribute to revenue protection and the reduction of operational risk (Orkin, 2003; Ivanov, 2014). At the same time, the increasing use of data analytics technologies and artificial intelligence applications makes it necessary to strengthen control mechanisms related to information security, the protection of personal data, and the reliability of algorithmic models.

A key conclusion emerging from the present analysis is that effective revenue management does not depend exclusively on demand forecasting techniques or advanced dynamic pricing models. On the contrary, the success of revenue management is substantially influenced by the quality of corporate governance, the maturity of internal control systems, organizational integrity, and the degree to which ESG standards are integrated into the firm's strategy. Hotel enterprises that successfully combine these elements are better able to manage risks, respond to market demands, and achieve profitability.

From a theoretical perspective, the contribution of this chapter lies in the integration of four fields of knowledge that are typically examined separately in the international literature: business integrity, ESG practices, internal audit, and revenue management. The majority of current research, however, continues to take a compartmentalized approach, which leaves out important interdependencies between these operational and governance aspects. By highlighting their interrelated roles within a cohesive governing framework for the hotel sector, this chapter overcomes this constraint. The synthesis of these concepts contributes to the development of a comprehensive managerial framework in which sustainability and corporate governance act as catalysts for long-term value creation and organizational resilience. At the same time, the chapter expands the relevant literature in the hospitality sector, where empirical and theoretical studies that simultaneously address these dimensions remain limited (Lin et al., 2024; Yu et al., 2025).

The present analysis highlights practical implications for hotel managers. The establishment of effective internal control mechanisms, the development of a strong culture of integrity, the systematic implementation of ESG criteria, and the integration of sustainability principles into revenue management strategies can significantly enhance operational efficiency, financial performance, and long-term resilience. Achieving sustainable competitiveness now requires collaboration across all business functions and the adoption of a holistic management approach that combines economic, social, and environmental objectives.

Finally, future research could empirically examine the relationship between ESG maturity, the effectiveness of internal control functions, and revenue management performance indicators such as Average Daily Rate (ADR), Revenue per Available Room (RevPAR), and Gross Operating Profit per Available Room (GOPPAR). In addition, particular interest lies in studying how artificial intelligence technologies, predictive analytics, and automated decision-making systems influence the interaction between ESG, corporate governance, internal audit, and revenue management. Investigating these issues is expected to contribute substantially to understanding the factors that will shape the future of sustainable and responsible management in the global hospitality industry.

DISCLOSURE OF DELEGATION TO GENERATIVE AI

The authors declare the use of generative AI in the research and writing process. According to the GAIDeT taxonomy (2025), the following tasks were delegated to GAI tools under full human supervision:

- Evaluation of the novelty of the research and identification of gaps
- Proofreading and editing
- Summarizing text
- Adapting and adjusting emotional tone
- Translation
- Reformatting

The GAI tool used was: ChatGPT Plus.

Responsibility for the final manuscript lies entirely with the authors.

GAI tools are not listed as authors and do not bear responsibility for the final outcomes.

REFERENCES

Al Mushattat, M. A. J., Al-Sulaiti, K., Al Halbusi, H., Alhitmi, H. K., & Al-Sulaiti, I. (2025). Investigating innovative tourism and hospitality sustainability: Modeling the moderating roles of mobile information technology and green human resource management. *Discover Sustainability, 6*(1), 1064. DOI: 10.1007/s43621-025-01811-8

Amanamah, R. B., Anaman, P. D., Ahmed, I. A., Quayson, J. A., Akyen, B., & Donkor, C. (2025). Internal controls and financial reporting accuracy in hotels: The role of management commitment and employee training. *SEISENSE Business Review, 5*(1), 29–49. DOI: 10.33215/65wnpf71

Anderson, U. L., Head, M. J., Ramamoorti, S., Riddle, C., Salamasick, M., & Sobel, P. J. (2017). *Internal auditing: Assurance and advisory services*. Institute of Internal Auditors Research Foundation.

Bae, J. H. (2022). Developing ESG evaluation guidelines for the tourism sector: With a focus on the hotel industry. *Sustainability (Basel), 14*(24), 16474. DOI: 10.3390/su142416474

Balios, D., Kalantonis, P., & Zaroulea, T. (2022). Corporate governance mechanisms and earnings management. *Journal of International Business and Entrepreneurship Development, 14*(3), 304–328. DOI: 10.1504/JIBED.2022.126950

Becken, S., & Hay, J. (2022). Sustainable tourism and the role of water resources. *Environmental Science & Policy, 128*, 49–56.

Bian, J., & Çalıyurt, K. T. (Eds.). (2018). *Regulations and applications of ethics in business practice*. Springer. DOI: 10.1007/978-981-10-8062-3

Butler, J. (2008). The compelling "hard case" for "green" hotel development. *Cornell Hospitality Quarterly, 49*(3), 234–244. DOI: 10.1177/1938965508322174

Chen, C. D., Su, C. H. J., & Chen, M. H. (2022). Are ESG-committed hotels financially resilient to the COVID-19 pandemic? An autoregressive jump intensity trend model. *Tourism Management, 93*, 104581. DOI: 10.1016/j.tourman.2022.104581 PMID: 35693760

Committee of Sponsoring Organizations of the Treadway Commission. (2013). *Internal control—Integrated framework*. COSO.

Elkington, J. (1994). Towards the sustainable corporation: Win-win-win business strategies for sustainable development. *California Management Review, 36*(2), 90–100. DOI: 10.2307/41165746

Filos, J. (2004). *Policies & procedures manual: Tool for organization and audit*. IQ Group Publishing. (In Greek)

Gaio, C., Gonçalves, T., & Sousa, M. V. (2022). Does corporate social responsibility mitigate earnings management? *Management Decision, 60*(11), 2972–2989. DOI: 10.1108/MD-05-2021-0719

Guilding, C., Kennedy, D. J., & McManus, L. (2005). Extending the boundaries of customer accounting: Applications in the hotel industry. *Journal of Hospitality & Tourism Research (Washington, D.C.), 29*(2), 173–194. DOI: 10.1177/1096348001025000205

Hayes, D. K., & Miller, A. A. (2022). *Revenue management for the hospitality industry* (3rd ed.). John Wiley & Sons.

Hendler, R., & Hendler, F. (2004). Revenue management in fabulous Las Vegas: Combining customer relationship management and revenue management to maximise profitability. *Journal of Revenue and Pricing Management, 3*(1), 73–79. DOI: 10.1057/palgrave.rpm.5170095

Heo, C. Y. (2013). Restaurant revenue management. In Legohérel, P., Poutier, E., & Fyall, A. (Eds.), *Revenue management for hospitality and tourism* (pp. 118–129). Goodfellow Publishers.

Hwang, J., & Wen, L. (2009). The effect of perceived fairness toward hotel overbooking and compensation practices on customer loyalty. *International Journal of Contemporary Hospitality Management, 21*(6), 659–675. DOI: 10.1108/09596110910975945

International Hospitality Institute. (n.d.). *Global hospitality code of conduct (HCODE) and pledge*. https://www.internationalhospitalityinstitute.com/code-of-conduct-pledge

Ivanov, S. (2014). *Hotel revenue management: From theory to practice*. Zangador.

Jackson, L. A. (2025). Hotel asset managers as catalysts for sustainable change. *International Hospitality Review*, 1–7.

Jagels, M. G., & Coltman, M. M. (2004). *Hospitality management accounting* (8th ed.). John Wiley & Sons.

Jamil, N. N., & Wahyuni, E. T. (2024). Unveiling greenwashing: Risks in sustainability and ESG reporting. *International Journal of Accounting. Finance and Business, 9*(57), 30–42.

Josephson Institute. (2013). *The six pillars of character*. Josephson Institute of Ethics.

Kasavana, M. L., & Brooks, R. M. (2020). *Managing front office operations* (10th ed.). American Hotel & Lodging Educational Institute.

Kimes, S. E. (1989). Yield management: A tool for capacity-constrained service firms. *Journal of Operations Management, 8*(4), 348–363. DOI: 10.1016/0272-6963(89)90035-1

Kimes, S. E., & Wirtz, J. (2003). Has revenue management become acceptable? Findings from an international study on the perceived fairness of rate fences. *Journal of Service Research, 6*(2), 125–135. DOI: 10.1177/1094670503257038

Koutoupis, A. G., & Pappa, E. (2018). Corporate governance and internal controls: A case study from Greece. *Journal of Governance and Regulation, 7*(2), 91–99. DOI: 10.22495/jgr_v7_i2_p8

Kyriakogkonas, P., Garefalakis, A., Pappa, E., & Kagias, P. (2022). Sustainable project management under the light of ESG criteria: A theoretical approach. *Theoretical Economics Letters, 12*(6), 1517–1538. DOI: 10.4236/tel.2022.126083

Lee, K. H., Cin, B. C., & Lee, E. Y. (2016). Environmental responsibility and firm performance: The application of an environmental, social and governance model. *Business Strategy and the Environment, 25*(1), 40–53. DOI: 10.1002/bse.1855

Lin, M. S., Zhang, H., Luo, Y., & Li, Y. (2024). Environmental, social, and governance (ESG) measurement in the tourism and hospitality industry: Views from a developing country. *Journal of Travel & Tourism Marketing, 41*(1), 154–168. DOI: 10.1080/10548408.2023.2293008

Lu, K., Onuk, C. B., Xia, Y., & Zhang, J. (2025). ESG ratings and financial performance in the global hospitality industry. *Journal of Risk and Financial Management, 18*(1), 24. DOI: 10.3390/jrfm18010024

Lu, W. M., Ting, I. W. K., & Huang, S. H. (2025). Environmental, social and governance (ESG) initiatives and firm efficiency in the global tourism and hospitality industry: The role of business strategy. *Asian Academy of Management Journal of Accounting and Finance, 21*(1), 275–312. DOI: 10.21315/aamjaf2025.21.1.10

Lunkes, R. J., Deggau, L. P., Codesso, M., Rosa, F. S., & Monteiro, J. (2025). The influence of online reviews and hotel digital responsibility on ESG practices and sustainability performance. *International Journal of Contemporary Hospitality Management, 37*(11), 3729–3747. DOI: 10.1108/IJCHM-12-2024-1972

Martin, K. (2019). Ethical implications and accountability of algorithms. *Journal of Business Ethics, 160*(4), 835–850. DOI: 10.1007/s10551-018-3921-3

Meng, X., & Shaikh, G. M. (2023). Evaluating environmental, social, and governance criteria and green finance investment strategies using fuzzy AHP and fuzzy WASPAS. *Sustainability (Basel), 15*(8), 6786. DOI: 10.3390/su15086786

Miller, P., & Smith, T. (2011). *Insight: Delivering value to stakeholders*. Institute of Internal Auditors Research Foundation.

Mitev, A. Z., Pintér-Szabó, L., & Irimiás, A. (2025). Overcoming energy barriers in hotels' green programs. *Annals of Tourism Research, 115*, 104061. DOI: 10.1016/j.annals.2025.104061

Modica, P., & Scanu, E. (2014). Day spa revenue management: Some examples from Italy. In Smith, M., & Puczkó, L. (Eds.), *Health, tourism and hospitality: Wellness, spas and medical travel* (2nd ed., pp. 269–273). Routledge.

Muhammad, N., Scrimgeour, F., Reddy, K., & Abidin, S. (2015). The impact of corporate environmental performance on market risk: The Australian industry case. *Journal of Business Ethics, 132*(2), 347–362. DOI: 10.1007/s10551-014-2324-3

Noone, B. M., & Mattila, A. S. (2009). Hotel revenue management and the Internet: The effect of price presentation strategies on customers' willingness to book. *International Journal of Hospitality Management, 28*(2), 272–279. DOI: 10.1016/j.ijhm.2008.09.004

OECD. (2023). *G20/OECD principles of corporate governance*. OECD Publishing.

Oh, H. J., Lee, B., Ma, H. H., Jang, D., & Park, S. (2024). A preliminary study for developing perceived ESG scale to measure public perception toward organizations' ESG performance. *Public Relations Review, 50*(1), 102398. DOI: 10.1016/j.pubrev.2023.102398

Oliver Yébenes, M. (2024). Climate change, ESG criteria and recent regulation: Challenges and opportunities. *Eurasian Economic Review, 14*(1), 87–120. DOI: 10.1007/s40822-023-00251-x

Orkin, E. (2003). The emerging role of function space optimization in hotel revenue management. *Journal of Revenue and Pricing Management, 2*(2), 172–174. DOI: 10.1057/palgrave.rpm.5170063

Papatheodorou, A., & Tsiotsou, R. H. (2020). Seasonality in tourism: Trends, impacts, and strategic approaches. *Annals of Tourism Research, 81*, 124–137.

Pappa, E., Filos, J., Garefalakis, A., & Kyriakogkonas, P. (2022). Implementing strategic management via code of ethics: A quantitative research on private sector in Greece. *Theoretical Economics Letters, 12*(4), 1126–1136. DOI: 10.4236/tel.2022.124061

Pappa, E., Georgitseas, P., Tantis, G., & Kyriakogkonas, P. (2024). Audit ESG reports through blockchain technology in business enterprises. In *Business, Management and Economics: Research Progress* (Vol. 5, pp. 90–107). DOI: 10.9734/bpi/bmerp/v5/2628

Passas, I. (2024). The evolution of ESG: From CSR to ESG 2.0. *Encyclopedia*, *4*(4), 1711–1720. DOI: 10.3390/encyclopedia4040112

Rasekh, L., & Li, Y. (2011). Golf course revenue management. *Journal of Revenue and Pricing Management*, *10*(2), 105–111. DOI: 10.1057/rpm.2009.44

Research Institute for Tourism. (2024). *ESG sustainability in the Greek hotel sector.*

Shaikh, I. (2022). Environmental, social, and governance (ESG) practice and firm performance: An international evidence. *Journal of Business Economics and Management*, *23*(1), 218–237. DOI: 10.3846/jbem.2022.16202

Szerb, L., & Gábor, I. (2022). Sustainable hospitality and tourism: Integrating corporate governance into strategic decision-making. *Sustainability*, *14*(5), 2207.

Vallen, G., & Cadado, M. (2000). Ethical principles for the hospitality curriculum. *The Cornell Hotel and Restaurant Administration Quarterly*, *41*(2), 44–51. DOI: 10.1177/001088040004100216

Vukotić, S., Mirčetić, V., Arsić, M., & Karabašević, D. (2026). Smart hospitality in the 6G era: The role of AI and terahertz communication in next-generation hotel infrastructure. *WORLD (Oakland, Calif.)*, *7*(1), 4. DOI: 10.3390/world7010004

Wang, X. L., Heo, C. Y., Schwartz, Z., Legohérel, P., & Specklin, F. (2015). Revenue management: Progress, challenges, and research prospects. *Journal of Travel & Tourism Marketing*, *32*(7), 797–811. DOI: 10.1080/10548408.2015.1063798

Wibawa, K. D., & Septianto, T. (2024). Unlocking sustainable development: ASEAN ESG and economic growth implication. *Advances in Environmental Innovation*, *1*(2), 176–188.

Yu, J., Chiriko, A. Y., Kim, S. S., Moon, H. G., Choi, H., & Han, H. (2025). ESG management of hotel brands: A management strategy for benefits and performance. *International Journal of Hospitality Management*, *125*, 103998. DOI: 10.1016/j.ijhm.2024.103998

Yu, J., Kim, S., Chiriko, A. Y., Moon, H. G., Choi, H., & Han, H. (2024). Environmental, social, and governance (ESG) in the hotel industry: A strategy for brand management, brand tribalism, and brand choice. *Journal of Travel & Tourism Marketing*, *41*(9), 1226–1243. DOI: 10.1080/10548408.2024.2406346

Zhang, B., & Jung, S. (2026). How environmental, social, and governance (ESG) activities relate to hotel booking intentions: Evidence from PLS-SEM and fsQCA. *Sustainability (Basel), 18*(1), 325. DOI: 10.3390/su18010325

Zhang, Y., & Kim, H. (2022). ESG and profitability: Evidence from the hospitality industry. *Sustainability*, *14*(1), 178.

Zientara, P., Adamska, J., & Bąk, M. (2025). *Social sustainability and the employee: Labor, employment relations, and the hospitality industry*. Routledge. DOI: 10.4324/9781003534266

Compilation of References

Aaker, D. A. (1996). *Building strong brands*. Free Press.

Abad, P., De la Fuente-Cabrero, C., González-Serrano, L., & Talón-Ballestero, P. (2019). Determinants of successful revenue management. *Tourism Review*, *74*(3), 666–678. DOI: 10.1108/TR-07-2018-0091

Abdou, A. H. (2025). Smarter technologies, innovation, and managerial capabilities driving hotel sustainability: The integration of resource-based view and dynamic capabilities perspective. *Tourism and Hospitality*, *6*(5), 252. DOI: 10.3390/tourhosp6050252

Abernethy, M. A., Li, W., Zhang, Y., & Shi, H. (2023). Firm culture and internal control system. [Object Identifier] [DOI]. *Accounting and Finance*, *63*(3), 3095–3123. DOI: 10.1111/acfi.13020

Abrate, G., & Viglia, G. (2016). Strategic and tactical price decisions in hotel revenue management. *Tourism Management*, *55*, 123–132. DOI: 10.1016/j.tourman.2016.02.006

Abu Afifa, M. M., & Saleh, I. (2021). Management accounting systems effectiveness, perceived environmental uncertainty and companies' performance: The case of Jordanian companies. *The International Journal of Organizational Analysis*, *30*(2), 259–288. DOI: 10.1108/IJOA-07-2020-2288

Adekunle, B. I., Chukwuma-Eke, E. C., Balogun, E. D., & Ogunsola, K. O. (2024). Optimizing internal control systems through blockchain-based financial reporting: Opportunities and risks. *International Journal of Management and Organizational Research*, *3*(1), 213–222. DOI: 10.54660/IJMOR.2024.3.1.213-222

Aguilera, R. V., & Crespi-Cladera, R. (2016). Global corporate governance: On the relevance of firms' ownership structure. *Journal of World Business*, *51*(1), 50–57. DOI: 10.1016/j.jwb.2015.10.003

Aguilera, R. V., Filatotchev, I., Gospel, H., & Jackson, G. (2008). An organizational approach to comparative corporate governance: Costs, contingencies, and complementarities. *Organization Science*, *19*(3), 475–492. DOI: 10.1287/orsc.1070.0322

Aguilera, R. V., & Jackson, G. (2010). Comparative and international corporate governance. *The Academy of Management Annals*, *4*(1), 485–556. DOI: 10.5465/19416520.2010.495525

Aguilera, R. V., Marano, V., & Haxhi, I. (2019). International corporate governance: A review and opportunities for future research. *Journal of International Business Studies*, *50*(4), 457–498. DOI: 10.1057/s41267-019-00232-w

Akmeşe, H., & Güderoğlu, M. (2017). Konaklama İşletmelerinde Bir Yönetim Muhasebesi Uygulamasi Olarak Gelir Yönetiminin Müşteri Algisi. [JSHSR]. *International Journal of Social and Humanities Sciences Research*, *4*(15), 1896–1909.

Aktepe, H. S., & Candemir, Z. (2024). Algılanan Değer Modeli (Perceived Value Model). *Tüketici Davranışlarında Kullanılan Modeller: Geçmişten Günümüze Tüketici Davranışlarını Belirlemede Kullanılan Modeller*, 137.

Al Mushattat, M. A. J., Al-Sulaiti, K., Al Halbusi, H., Alhitmi, H. K., & Al-Sulaiti, I. (2025). Investigating innovative tourism and hospitality sustainability: Modeling the moderating roles of mobile information technology and green human resource management. *Discover Sustainability*, *6*(1), 1064. DOI: 10.1007/s43621-025-01811-8

Alderighi, M., Nava, C. R., Calabrese, M., Christille, J. M., & Salvemini, C. B. (2022). Consumer perception of price fairness and dynamic pricing: Evidence from Booking.com. *Journal of Business Research*, *145*, 769–783. DOI: 10.1016/j.jbusres.2022.03.017

Alles, M. G. (2015). Drivers of the use and facilitators and obstacles of the evolution of big data by the audit profession. *Accounting Horizons*, *29*(2), 439–449. DOI: 10.2308/acch-51067

Al-Okaily, J., Dixon, R., & Salama, A. (2019). Corporate governance quality and premature revenue recognition: Evidence from the UK. Social Science Research Network. https://doi.org/DOI: 10.2139/ssrn

Alola, U. V., Avci, T., & Ozturen, A. (2018). Organizational sustainability through human resource capital: The impacts of supervisor incivility and self-efficacy. *Sustainability (Basel)*, *10*(8), 2610. DOI: 10.3390/su10082610

Alrawadieh, Z., Alrawadieh, Z., & Cetin, G. (2021). Digital transformation and revenue management: Evidence from the hotel industry. *Tourism Economics*, *27*(2), 328–345. DOI: 10.1177/1354816620901928

Altamuro, J., & Beatty, A. (2010). How does internal control regulation affect financial reporting? *Journal of Accounting and Economics*, *49*(1–2), 58–74. DOI: 10.1016/j.jacceco.2009.07.002

Altin, M. (2017). A taxonomy of hotel revenue management implementation strategies. *Journal of Revenue and Pricing Management*, *16*(3), 246–264. DOI: 10.1057/s41272-017-0077-1

Altin, M., Schwartz, Z., & Uysal, M. (2017). "Where you do it" matters: The impact of hotels' revenue-management implementation strategies on performance. *International Journal of Hospitality Management*, *67*, 46–52. DOI: 10.1016/j.ijhm.2017.08.001

Alzeban, A. (2020). The impact of audit committee, CEO, and external auditor quality on the quality of financial reporting. *Corporate Governance (Bradford)*, *20*(2), 263–279. DOI: 10.1108/CG-07-2019-0204

Alzeban, A., & Gwilliam, D. (2014). Factors affecting the internal audit effectiveness: A survey of the Saudi public sector. *Journal of International Accounting, Auditing & Taxation*, *23*(2), 74–86. DOI: 10.1016/j.intaccaudtax.2014.06.001

Amanamah, R. B., Anaman, P. D., Ahmed, I. A., Quayson, J. A., Akyen, B., & Donkor, C. (2025). Internal controls and financial reporting accuracy in hotels: The role of management commitment and employee training. *SEISENSE Business Review*, *5*(1), 29–49. DOI: 10.33215/65wnpf71

Ampountolas, A., & Bai, Y. (2026). Optimizing hotel demand forecasting through ensemble models: A Modern Portfolio Theory approach. *Tourism Management*, *113*, 105314. Advance online publication. DOI: 10.1016/j.tourman.2025.105314

Ampountolas, A., Shaw, G., & James, S. (2021). Examining the relationships between market indicators and hotel pricing approaches. *Tourism Economics*, *27*(8), 1591–1614. DOI: 10.1177/1354816620925225

Anderson, C. K. (2012). The impact of social media on lodging performance. *Cornell Hospitality Report*, *12*(15), 6–11.

Anderson, U. L., Head, M. J., Ramamoorti, S., Riddle, C., Salamasick, M., & Sobel, P. J. (2017). *Internal auditing: Assurance and advisory services*. Institute of Internal Auditors Research Foundation.

Angelaki, E., Garefalakis, S., & Samaras, I. (2026). Environmental impact assessment in coastal and island tourism as a tool for sustainable development. *Sustainability Research in the Mediterranean*, *2*(2), 107–118. DOI: 10.13052/srm2795-0514.008

Angelini, G., Costa, M., & Guizzardi, A. (2025). Complex data in tourism analysis: A stochastic approach to price competition. *Big Data Research, 40*, 100520. DOI: 10.1016/j.bdr.2025.100520

Anshori, M. Y., Herlambang, T., & Abu Yaziz, M. F. (2025). Optimizing occupancy of hospitality sector using Support Vector Regression and Genetic Algorithm. *Journal of Revenue and Pricing Management 2025 25:3, 25*(3), 243–249. DOI: 10.1057/s41272-025-00539-4

Anshori, M. Y., Katias, P., Herlambang, T., Meutia, N. S., Othman, Z. B., & Azmi, M. S. (2025). Predicting hotel revenue using gradient boosting regression and support vector regression: a comparative analysis. *Journal of Revenue and Pricing Management 2025 25:3, 25*(3), 274–283. DOI: 10.1057/s41272-025-00557-2

Appelbaum, D., Kogan, A., Vasarhelyi, M., & Yan, Z. (2017). Impact of business analytics and enterprise systems on managerial accounting. *International Journal of Accounting Information Systems, 25*, 29–44. DOI: 10.1016/j.accinf.2017.03.003

Appel, I. R., Gormley, T. A., & Keim, D. B. (2016). Passive investors, not passive owners. *Journal of Financial Economics, 121*(1), 111–141. DOI: 10.1016/j.jfineco.2016.03.003

Applying IFRS: Disclosure of accounting policy information | EY - Global. (n.d.). Retrieved September 3, 2026, from https://www.ey.com/en_gl/technical/ifrs-technical-resources/applying-ifrs-disclosure-of-accounting-policy-information

Arena, M., Arnaboldi, M., & Azzone, G. (2010). The organizational dynamics of enterprise risk management. *Accounting, Organizations and Society, 35*(7), 659–675. DOI: 10.1016/j.aos.2010.07.003

Arıkan, E., & Parlakkaya, R. (2020). Beş Yıldızlı Otel İşletmelerinde Gelir Yönetimi Uygulamalarina İlişkin Nitel Bir Araştirma. *Elektronik Sosyal Bilimler Dergisi, 19*(75), 1255–1274. DOI: 10.17755/esosder.552750

Arimany, N., Fitó, M. A., & Orgaz, N. (2015). *Economic consequences of accounting standards in the hotel industry: Lobbying arguments versus expected impact*. Social Science Research Network.

Arnejo, A., & Sarsale, M. (2025). Measuring hotel financial performance: A bibliometric review. *Hotel and Tourism Management, 13*(2), 117–135. DOI: 10.5937/menhottur2500017A

Ashbaugh-Skaife, H., Collins, D. W., Kinney, W. R.Jr, & LaFond, R. (2009). The effect of SOX internal control deficiencies on firm risk and cost of equity. *Journal of Accounting Research, 47*(1), 1–43. DOI: 10.1111/j.1475-679X.2008.00315.x

Atsız, O., Öğretmenoğlu, M., & Akova, O. (2022). A bibliometric analysis of length of stay studies in tourism. *European Journal of Tourism Research, 31*, 3101. Advance online publication. DOI: 10.54055/ejtr.v31i.2305

Avdylaj, A., & Asllanaj, R. (2023). The impact of accounting on business decision-making: A case study of the hotel industry in Kosovo. *Multidisciplinary Science Journal, 6*(6), 2024100. DOI: 10.31893/multiscience.2024100

Avi, M. S. (2022). Revenue managers in hotels: Is revenue focus enough? *International Journal of Tourism and Hotel Management, 4*(2), 55–74. DOI: 10.22271/27069583.2022.v4.i2a.58

Aydan, G., & Atılgan, K. Ö. (2023). Tüketicilerin kişiselleştirilmiş fiyatlandırma ile dinamik fiyatlandırma uygulamalarına yönelik tutumlarının incelenmesi. *Pamukkale Üniversitesi İşletme Araştırmaları Dergisi, 10*(1-Prof. Dr. Feyzullah EROĞLU Armağan Sayısı), 243-256.

Aydın, B., & Akyol, Ş. (2013). Otel işletmelerinin kriz dönemlerinde uyguladıkları pazarlama stratejileri: İstanbul'da faaliyet gösteren beş yıldızlı otel işletmelerinde nitel bir araştırma. *Seyahat ve Otel İşletmeciliği Dergisi, 10*(1), 23–35.

Aziz, H. A., El Gayar, N., Saleh, M., & El Shishiny, H. (2008). A randomized model for group reservations in a hotel's revenue management system. *Proceedings of the 6th International Conference on Informatics and Systems (INFOS 2008)*, Cairo, Egypt.

Aziz, H. A., Saleh, M., Rasmy, M. H., & ElShishiny, H. (2011). Dynamic room pricing model for hotel revenue management systems. *Egyptian Informatics Journal, 12*(3), 177–183. DOI: 10.1016/j.eij.2011.08.001

Bae, J. H. (2022). Developing ESG evaluation guidelines for the tourism sector: With a focus on the hotel industry. *Sustainability (Basel), 14*(24), 16474. DOI: 10.3390/su142416474

Bakker, C. C., Parawiyati, P., & Pangastuti, D. A. (2024). The effects of information systems and the utilization of information technology on the quality of financial reports with internal control as moderation. Journal of Economics. *Finance and Management Studies, 7*(1), 476–482.

Balińska, A., & Olejniczak, W. (2022). Aplikacje turystyczne w ocenie użytkowników. *Studia Periegetica, 39*(3), 23–38. DOI: 10.5604/01.3001.0016.0762

Balios, D., Kalantonis, P., & Zaroulea, T. (2022). Corporate governance mechanisms and earnings management. *Journal of International Business and Entrepreneurship Development, 14*(3), 304–328. DOI: 10.1504/JIBED.2022.126950

Balios, D., Katsikis, V. N., Naoum, V. C., & Zaroulea, T. (2024). The effect of industry level characteristics and cross-country differences on earnings management: A European comparative perspective. *Journal of Governance & Regulation*, *13*(2), 403–418. DOI: 10.22495/jgrv13i2siart16

Balli, F., Uddin, G. S., & Shahzad, S. J. H. (2019). Geopolitical risk and tourism demand in emerging economies. *Tourism Economics*, *25*(6), 997–1005. DOI: 10.1177/1354816619831824

Baltazar, M. B. (2008). Revenue marketing and its application within the hospitality industry: History and future development. In *Pricing Perspectives: Marketing and Management Implications of New Theories and Applications* (pp. 175–205). Palgrave Macmillan UK. DOI: 10.1057/9780230594890_8

Bandalouski, A. M., Egorova, N. G., Kovalyov, M. Y., Pesch, E., & Tarim, S. A. (2021). Dynamic pricing with demand disaggregation for hotel revenue management. *Journal of Heuristics 2021 27:5*, *27*(5), 869–885. DOI: 10.1007/s10732-021-09480-2

Barone, E., Mason, S., Mora, A., & Procházka, D. (2026). Changing the paradigm for revenue recognition: Literature review on intended and unintended effects of IFRS 15 and ASC 606. *Accounting in Europe*, *23*(2), 218–245. DOI: 10.1080/17449480.2025.2528899

Barreda, A. (2017). Financial marketing decisions in the hospitality industry. In *Routledge Handbook of Hospitality Marketing* (pp. 132–147). Routledge. DOI: 10.4324/9781315445526-11

Barten, M. (2024, June 04). *NRevPAR explained: Net revenue per available room*. Revfine. https://www.revfine.com/nrevpar

Bashir, B., Rashid, M., & Bashir, Z. (2024). Impact of ownership structure and corporate governance on earnings management. *SEISENSE Journal of Management*, *7*(1), 1–20. Advance online publication. DOI: 10.33215/c1qkdq06

Bastos, B. P. D. (2023). *Determinants of revenue management frameworks as enablers for cloud and e-commerce hospitality management*. Sustainability in Tourism., DOI: 10.54517/st.v4i2.2486

Baum, T. (2015). Human resources in tourism: Still waiting for change? – A 2015 reprise. *Tourism Management*, *50*, 204–212. DOI: 10.1016/j.tourman.2015.02.001

Beattrice, V. A. (2015). Corporate governance mechanisms and earnings management: A state-of-the-art review. *Annals of the Faculty of Economics*, *1*(1), 982–990.

Bebchuk, L. A., & Hirst, S. (2019). Index funds and the future of corporate governance: Theory, evidence, and policy. *Columbia Law Review, 119*(8), 2029–2146.

Becken, S., & Hay, J. (2022). Sustainable tourism and the role of water resources. *Environmental Science & Policy, 128*, 49–56.

Belesis, N. D., Kampouris, C. G., Fousteris, A. E., & Varouxis, D. (2025). Evaluating the effectiveness of internal control systems: Evidence from financial and audit performance data. Corporate Board: Role. *Duties and Composition, 21*(3), 76–86.

Belobaba, P. P. (1987). Air travel demand and airline seat inventory management. *PhD Dissertation*, Massachusetts Institute of Technology.

Bergen, M., Dutta, S., & Walker, O. C.Jr. (1992). Agency relationships in marketing: A review of the implications and applications. *Journal of Marketing, 56*(3), 1–24. DOI: 10.1177/002224299205600301

Berle, A. A., & Means, G. C. (1932). *The modern corporation and private property*. Macmillan.

Bhagat, S., & Black, B. (2001). The non-correlation between board independence and long-term firm performance. *The Journal of Corporation Law, 27*(2), 231–274.

Bhattacharya, A. (2025). A study on profitability analysis of different revenue streams in a hotel: Rooms, food and beverage (F&B), and events. *International Journal of Scientific Research in Engineering and Management, 9*(5), 1–9. DOI: 10.55041/IJSREM49057

Bian, J., & Çalıyurt, K. T. (Eds.). (2018). *Regulations and applications of ethics in business practice*. Springer. DOI: 10.1007/978-981-10-8062-3

Bilgihan, A., Okumus, F., Nusair, K., & Kwun, D. J. (2016). Information technology applications and competitive advantage in hotel companies. *Journal of Hospitality and Tourism Technology, 7*(1), 102–118.

Bimantari, P. M. K., Arnawa, I. P., & Wiryanata, I. G. N. A. (2025). Analisis Peranan Income Audit Pada Pengendalian Internal Di Hotel The Westin Resort & Spa Ubud Bali. Jurnal Ekonomi. *Manajemen Pariwisata Dan Perhotelan, 4*(3), 579–589.

Bodea, T., & Ferguson, M. (2014). *Segmentation, revenue management and pricing analytics*. Routledge. DOI: 10.4324/9780203802151

Bolton, L. E., Warlop, L., & Alba, J. W. (2003). Consumer perceptions of price fairness. *The Journal of Consumer Research, 29*(4), 474–491. DOI: 10.1086/346244

Boo, H. C., Remy, D., & Lee, K.-H. (2025). Drivers, barriers, and challenges in NREVPAR and REVPAC adoption – towards a revenue management adoption scale. *International Journal of Hospitality Management, 127,* 104116. Advance online publication. DOI: 10.1016/j.ijhm.2025.104116

Boyd, A. E. (2007). The future of pricing: How airline ticket pricing has inspired a revolution. In Yeoman, I., & McMahon-Beattie, U. (Eds.), *Revenue management and pricing: Case studies and applications* (pp. xx–xx). Thomson Learning.

Bozkurt, Ö., & Göral, M. (2013). Otel işletmelerinde yenilik stratejileri. İçinde M. Mesci & Ö. Bozkurt (Ed.), *Otel işletmelerinde yenilik yönetimi* (ss. 91–108). Sidas.

Brar, V., Jha, P., Jain, S., Mehrotra, S., Kumar, A., Jha, C. K., & Gupta, D. (2025, July). Deep reinforcement learning for dynamic pricing strategies in revenue management. In 2025 3rd World Conference on Communication & Computing (WCONF) (pp. 1-5). IEEE. DOI: 10.1109/WCONF64849.2025.11233694

Brickley, J. A., & Dark, F. H. (1987). The choice of organizational form: The case of franchising. *Journal of Financial Economics, 18*(2), 401–420. DOI: 10.1016/0304-405X(87)90046-8

Broccardo, L., Ballesio, E., Yaqub, M. Z., & Mohapatra, A. K. (2025). A bridge to success: The role of management accountants' intellectual capital in driving organizational decision-making through knowledge management. *Journal of Knowledge Management, 29*(5), 1365–1411. DOI: 10.1108/JKM-04-2024-0452

Brotherton, B., & Mooney, S. (1992). Yield management—Progress and prospects. *International Journal of Hospitality Management, 11*(1), 23–32. DOI: 10.1016/0278-4319(92)90033-R

Brown, J. R., Dev, C. S., & Zhou, Z. (2003). Broadening the foreign market entry mode decision: Separating ownership and control. *Journal of International Business Studies, 34*(5), 473–488. DOI: 10.1057/palgrave.jibs.8400050

Bruns-Smith, A., Choy, V., Chong, H., & Verma, R. (2015). Environmental sustainability in the hospitality industry: Best practices, guest participation, and customer satisfaction. *Cornell Hospitality Report, 15*(3), 6-16, https://hdl.handle.net/1813/71174

Buhalis, D., Harwood, T., Bogicevic, V., Viglia, G., Beldona, S., & Hofacker, C. (2019). Technological disruptions in services: Lessons from tourism and hospitality. *Journal of Service Management, 30*(4), 484–506. DOI: 10.1108/JOSM-12-2018-0398

Bulchand-Gidumal, J., William Secin, E., O'Connor, P., & Buhalis, D. (2024). Artificial intelligence's impact on hospitality and tourism marketing: Exploring key themes and addressing challenges. *Current Issues in Tourism, 27*(14), 2345–2362. DOI: 10.1080/13683500.2023.2229480

Bulgan, G., & Soybali, H. H. (2011). Antalya Belek Bölgesindeki Beş Yıldızlı Otel Işletmelerinde Düşük Sezonda Konaklayan Alman Müşterilerin Hizmet Beklentilerinin Ve Memnuniyet Düzeylerinin Değerlendirilmesi. *Journal of Yasar University, 21*(6), 3572–3597.

Bull, A. O. (2006). Industrial economics and pricing issues within tourism enterprises and markets. *International handbook on the economics of tourism*, 138.

Burnett, B. M., Martin, G. W., & Reppenhagen, D. A. (2021). Managerial discretion in revenue recognition amidst financial restatements and implications for GAAP compliance. *Journal of Business Finance & Accounting, 48*(7–8), 869–894. DOI: 10.1111/jbfa.12504

Butler, J. (2008). The compelling "hard case" for "green" hotel development. *Cornell Hospitality Quarterly, 49*(3), 234–244. DOI: 10.1177/1938965508322174

Button, K. (2010). *Transport economics* (3rd ed.). Edward Elgar.

Button, K., & Taylor, S. (2000). International air transportation and economic development. *Journal of Air Transport Management, 6*(4), 209–222. DOI: 10.1016/S0969-6997(00)00015-6

Buzacott, J. A. (2000). Service system structure. *International Journal of Production Economics, 68*(1), 15–27. DOI: 10.1016/S0925-5273(99)00133-4

Cadbury, A. (1992). *Report of the Committee on the Financial Aspects of Corporate Governance*. Gee and Co Ltd.

Caldentey, R. A., & Wein, L. M. (2002). Revenue management of a make-to-stock queue. *Manufacturing & Service Operations Management, 4*(1), 4–6. DOI: 10.1287/msom.4.1.4.288

Çalık, Ü. (2023). Otel İşletmelerinde Pazarlama Stratejileri Üzerine Bir Değerlendirme. *Selçuk Üniversitesi Akşehir Meslek Yüksekokulu Sosyal Bilimler Dergisi*, (16), 57–77.

Campos, F. C. D. A., Gomes, C., Cardoso, L., & Santos, L. L. (2022). Management accounting practices in the hospitality industry: The Portuguese background. *International Journal of Financial Studies, 10*(4), 88. DOI: 10.3390/ijfs10040088

Campos, F. C. D. A., Santos, L. L., Gomes, C., & Cardoso, L. (2022). Management accounting practices in the hospitality industry: A systematic review and critical approach. *Tourism and Hospitality, 3*(1), 243–264. DOI: 10.3390/tourhosp3010017

Canöz, F. (2022). *Üst düzey otel yöneticilerinin dönemsel krizleri değerlendirmesi...* (Doktora tezi). Necmettin Erbakan Üniversitesi.

Caylor, M. L. (2008). Strategic revenue recognition to achieve earnings benchmarks. Social Science Research Network. https://doi.org/DOI: 10.2139/ssrn.885368

Cengiz, E., Kaynakci, E., Nanu, L., & Cavusoglu, M. (2025). Optimizing hotel profitability: How cost system sophistication drives financial performance in the hotel industry. *Journal of Quality Assurance in Hospitality & Tourism*, •••, 1–15. DOI: 10.1080/1528008X.2025.2601706

Cesaret, B., & Katok, E. (2025). A behavioral study of capacity allocation in revenue management. *The Journal of the Operational Research Society, 76*(3), 514–527. DOI: 10.1080/01605682.2024.2370872

Çetiner, H., & Yaylı, A. (2020). Animasyon aktivitelerinde deneyim kalitesinin otel işletmelerinin imajı, konukların değer algısı ve tekrar satın alma niyetine etkisi. *İşletme Araştırmaları Dergisi, 12*(1), 749-768.

Chakraborty, P. P. (2025). Digital transformation in hospitality. In Thaichon, P., Dutta, P. K., Haghi, A. K., & Dutta, S. (Eds.), *Digital disruption in hospitality, AI, and emerging technologies: A roadmap to personalized experiences, enhanced operations, and revenue growth* (pp. 157–188). Emerald Publishing Limited., DOI: 10.1108/978-1-83608-796-020251009

Chatterjee, S., Chaudhuri, R., Gupta, S., Sivarajah, U., & Bag, S. (2023). Assessing the impact of big data analytics on decision-making processes, forecasting, and performance of a firm. *Technological Forecasting and Social Change, 196*, 122824. DOI: 10.1016/j.techfore.2023.122824

Chaudhuri, A., & Holbrook, M. B. (2001). The chain of effects from brand trust and brand affect to brand performance: The role of brand loyalty. *Journal of Marketing, 65*(2), 81–93. DOI: 10.1509/jmkg.65.2.81.18255

Chau, L., Anh, L., & Duc, V. (2025). Valuing ESG: How financial markets respond to corporate sustainability. *International Business Review, 34*(3), 102418. DOI: 10.1016/j.ibusrev.2025.102418

Cheliatsidou, A., Sariannidis, N., Garefalakis, A., Passas, I., & Spinthiropoulos, K. (2023). Exploring Attitudes towards Whistleblowing in Relation to Sustainable Municipalities. *Administrative Sciences, 13*(9), 199. DOI: 10.3390/admsci13090199

Chen, H., Wang, S., Yang, D., & Zhou, N. (2025). COSO-based internal control and comprehensive enterprise risk management: Institutional background and research evidence from China. Encyclopedia, 5(3), Article 106.

Chen, C. D., Su, C. H. J., & Chen, M. H. (2022). Are ESG-committed hotels financially resilient to the COVID-19 pandemic? An autoregressive jump intensity trend model. *Tourism Management, 93*, 104581. DOI: 10.1016/j.tourman.2022.104581 PMID: 35693760

Chen, C. F., & Rothschild, R. (2010). An application of revenue management in the hotel industry. *The Journal of Hospitality Financial Management, 18*(1), 45–60. DOI: 10.1080/10913211.2010.10653887

Cheng, M., Dhaliwal, D., & Zhang, Y. (2013). Does investment efficiency improve after the disclosure of material weaknesses in internal control over financial reporting? *Journal of Accounting and Economics, 56*(1), 1–18. DOI: 10.1016/j.jacceco.2013.03.001

Chenhall, R. H. (2003). Management control systems design within its organizational context: Findings from contingency-based research and directions for the future. *Accounting, Organizations and Society, 28*(2–3), 127–168. DOI: 10.1016/S0361-3682(01)00027-7

Chen, J., Xu, Y., Yu, P., & Zhang, J. (2023). A reinforcement learning approach for hotel revenue management with evidence from field experiments. *Journal of Operations Management, 69*(7), 1176–1201. DOI: 10.1002/joom.1246

Chen, M. M., Beaufort, C., & Earl-Erpelding, K. (2024). Should independent upmarket hotels work with daily deals platforms? An empirical case study from Switzerland. *Tourism and Hospitality Research*, •••, 14673584241311294. DOI: 10.1177/14673584241311294

Chen, N., & Hu, M. (2023). Frontiers in service science: Data-driven revenue management: The interplay of data, model, and decisions. *Service Science, 15*(2), 79–91. DOI: 10.1287/serv.2023.0322

Choi, S., & Mattila, A. S. (2004). Hotel revenue management and its impact on customers' perceptions of fairness. *Journal of Revenue and Pricing Management, 2*(4), 303–314. DOI: 10.1057/palgrave.rpm.5170079

Choi, S., Song, M., & Jing, L. (2023). Let your algorithm shine: The impact of algorithmic cues on consumer perceptions of price discrimination. *Tourism Management, 99*, 104792. Advance online publication. DOI: 10.1016/j.tourman.2023.104792

Çifçi, H., & Kızılırmak, İ. (2025). Vegan Restoranlarda Müşteri Deneyimi Bileşenlerinin Netnografi Analiziyle İncelenmesi: Tripadvisor Örneği. *Aydın Gastronomy, 9*(2), 353–373. DOI: 10.17932/IAU.GASTRONOMY.2017.016/gastronomy_v09i2007

Çilkara, S. U. (2024). *Müşteri segmentasyonu ve fiyatlandırma stratejileri. Tüketici davranışlarında kullanılan teoriler: Geçmişten günümüze tüketici davranışlarını belirlemede kullanılan teoriler içinde (ss.* Eğitim Yayınevi.

Claessens, S., & Yurtoglu, B. B. (2013). Corporate governance in emerging markets: A survey. *Emerging Markets Review, 15*, 1–33. DOI: 10.1016/j.ememar.2012.03.002

Coetsee, D., Mohammadali-Haji, A., & Van Wyk, M. (2022). Revenue recognition practices in South Africa: An analysis of the decision usefulness of IFRS 15 disclosures. *South African Journal of Accounting Research, 36*(1), 22–44. DOI: 10.1080/10291954.2020.1855886

Cohen, M. C., Miao, S., & Wang, Y. (2025). Dynamic Pricing with Fairness Constraints. *Operations Research, 73*(6), 3027–3043. DOI: 10.1287/opre.2023.0123

Çolak, O., & Koşan, L. (2018). Fiyat Farklilaştirma Araci Olarak Fiyat Duyarlilik Ölçümü: Bir Otel İşletmesinde Uygulama. *Çukurova Üniversitesi Sosyal Bilimler Enstitüsü Dergisi, 27*(2), 137-153.

Combs, J. G., Ketchen, D. J.Jr, & Short, J. C. (2011). Franchising research: Major milestones, new directions, and its future within entrepreneurship. *Entrepreneurship Theory and Practice, 35*(3), 413–425. DOI: 10.1111/j.1540-6520.2011.00443.x

Committee of Sponsoring Organizations of the Treadway Commission. (2013). *Internal control—Integrated framework*. COSO.

Contractor, F. J., & Kundu, S. K. (1998). Modal choice in a world of alliances: Analyzing organizational forms in the international hotel sector. *Journal of International Business Studies, 29*(2), 325–356. DOI: 10.1057/palgrave.jibs.8490039

Coulter, K. S. (2001). Decreasing price sensitivity involving physical product inventory: A yield management application. *Journal of Product and Brand Management, 10*(5), 301–317. DOI: 10.1108/EUM0000000005846

Cravens, D. W., Piercy, N. F., & Baldauf, A. (2009). Management framework guiding strategic thinking in rapidly changing markets. *Journal of Marketing Management, 25*(1-2), 31–49. DOI: 10.1362/026725709X410025

Crawford-Welch, S. (1990). Market segmentation in the hospitality industry. *Hospitality Research Journal, 14*(2), 295–308. DOI: 10.1177/109634809001400232

Cross, R. G. (1997). *Revenue management: Hard-core tactics for market domination*. Broadway Books.

Cross, R. G., Higbie, J. A., & Cross, D. Q. (2009). Revenue management's renaissance: A rebirth of the art and science of profitable revenue generation. *Cornell Hospitality Quarterly, 50*(1), 56–81. DOI: 10.1177/1938965508328716

Dalton, D. R., Daily, C. M., Ellstrand, A. E., & Johnson, J. L. (1998). Meta-analytic reviews of board composition, leadership structure, and financial performance. *Strategic Management Journal, 19*(3), 269–290. DOI: 10.1002/(SICI)1097-0266(199803)19:3<269::AID-SMJ950>3.0.CO;2-K

Davenport, T. H., & Harris, J. G. (2017). *Competing on analytics: The new science of winning*. Harvard Business Review Press.

de Bastos, B. P. (2023). Contribution of hotels' revenue management for supply chain sustainability. *Journal of Revenue and Pricing Management, 22*(4), 294–305. DOI: 10.1057/s41272-022-00380-z

De Larrea, G. L., & Gregory, A. M. (2020). Informing timeshare exchange services on the drivers of customer-driven co-production. *International Journal of Hospitality Management, 91*, 102645. DOI: 10.1016/j.ijhm.2020.102645

DeFond, M., & Zhang, J. (2014). A review of archival auditing research. *Journal of Accounting and Economics, 58*(2–3), 275–326. DOI: 10.1016/j.jacceco.2014.09.002

Demirtaş, N. (2010). *Otel işletmeciliği*. Ankara Üniversitesi Uzaktan Eğitim Merkezi.

Demydyuk, G. V., & Carlbäck, M. (2024). Balancing short-term gains and long-term success in lodging: The role of customer satisfaction and price in hotel profitability model. *Tourism Economics, 30*(4), 844–875. DOI: 10.1177/13548166231199156

Deng, F., & Zhou, C. (2022). Sustainable development of corporate governance in the hospitality and tourism industry: The evolution and the future. *Sustainability (Basel), 14*(7), 4286. DOI: 10.3390/su14074286

Denis, D. K., & McConnell, J. J. (2003). International corporate governance. *Journal of Financial and Quantitative Analysis, 38*(1), 1–36. DOI: 10.2307/4126762

Denizci Guillet, B. (2020). An evolutionary analysis of revenue management research in hospitality and tourism: Is there a paradigm shift? *International Journal of Contemporary Hospitality Management, 32*(2), 560–587. DOI: 10.1108/IJCHM-06-2019-0515

Denizci Guillet, B., & Chu, A. M. C. (2021). Managing hotel revenue amid the COVID-19 crisis. *International Journal of Contemporary Hospitality Management, 33*(2), 604–627. DOI: 10.1108/IJCHM-06-2020-0623

Denizer, D. (1991). Konaklama işletmelerinde fiyatın önemi ve fiyat farklılaştırması. *Anatolia: Turizm Araştırmaları Dergisi, 2*(5), 23–25.

Depken, C. A.II, & Stephenson, E. F. (2018). Hotel demand before, during, and after sports events: Evidence from Charlotte, North Carolina. *Economic Inquiry, 56*(3), 1764–1776. DOI: 10.1111/ecin.12572

Dewi, N. K. M., Wiryanata, I. G. N. A., & Lilasari, L. N. T. (2025). Analisis dampak digital payment pada pengendalian internal penerimaan di Hotel Grand Hyatt Bali. Riset Ilmu Manajemen Bisnis dan Akuntansi, 3(4), 102–114. **https://doi.org/**DOI: 10.61132/rimba.v3i4.2236

Diavastis, I. E., Chrysafis, K. A., & Papadopoulou, G. C. (2024). Determinants of accounting information systems success: The case of the Greek hotel industry. *International Journal of Financial Studies, 12*(2), 42. DOI: 10.3390/ijfs12020042

Didin, S., & Köroğlu, Ç. (2008). Konaklama işletmelerinin satışlar-maliyetler bakımından rekabet edebilme durumu ve gelecekten beklentileri. *Uluslararası Yönetim İktisat ve İşletme Dergisi, 4*(7), 109–118.

Dimitrova, T. (2025). Certain highlights on the major changes in the uniform system of accounts for the lodging industry 12th revised edition. *Economics and Computer Science, 11*(2), 13–18. https://eknigibg.net/ojs/index.php/ecs/article/view/28

Ding, Z. (2025). The Correlation between Data-driven Dynamic Pricing Strategies and Revenue Optimization for Technology Enterprises. *American Journal Of Big Data, 6*(05), 37–44. DOI: 10.71465/ajbd3430

Doğanlı, B. (2025). Dijital pazarlama kampanyalarında müşteri davranışlarının dönüşüm oranları üzerindeki etkisi: Veri analitiği ve random forest modeli yaklaşımı. *Politik Ekonomik Kuram, 9*(2), 596–610. DOI: 10.30586/pek.1605496

Doğan, S., & Eker, Ş. (2022). Geleneksel seyahat acentelerinin çevrim içi seyahat acentelerini tercihi üzerine bir araştırma. *Journal of Recreation and Tourism Research, 9*(1), 16–32.

Dornyoh, E., Moore, M. A., Yeboah, R., Ocloo, A. T., & Dacosta, F. D. (2026). The science and speculations driving revenue management decisions in hotels in Cape Coast. *International Journal of Hospitality & Tourism Management, 10*(1), 7–21. DOI: 10.11648/j.ijhtm.20261001.12

Doyle, J., Ge, W., & McVay, S. (2007). Determinants of weaknesses in internal control over financial reporting. *Journal of Accounting and Economics, 44*(1–2), 193–223. DOI: 10.1016/j.jacceco.2006.10.003

Drury, C. (2018). *Management and cost accounting* (10th ed.). Cengage Learning.

Duani, N., Barasch, A., & Morwitz, V. (2024). Demographic pricing in the digital age: Assessing fairness perceptions in algorithmic versus human-based price discrimination. *Journal of the Association for Consumer Research, 9*(3), 257–268. DOI: 10.1086/729440

Efthymiou, M., & Christidis, P. (2023). Low-cost carriers route network development. *Annals of Tourism Research, 101*, 103608. DOI: 10.1016/j.annals.2023.103608

Ege, M. S. (2015). Does internal audit function quality deter management misconduct? *The Accounting Review, 90*(2), 495–527. DOI: 10.2308/accr-50871

Ehima, E., & Amede, O. F. (2025). Effect of internal control components and revenue leakage: Evidence from financial institutions in Edo State, Nigeria. *Gusau Journal of Accounting and Finance, 6*(2), 94–109. DOI: 10.57233/gujaf.v6i2.07

Eisenhardt, K. M. (1989). Agency theory: An assessment and review. *Academy of Management Review, 14*(1), 57–74. DOI: 10.2307/258191

El Haddad, R., Hallak, R., & Assaker, G. (2015). Price fairness perceptions and hotel customers' behavioral intentions. *Journal of Vacation Marketing, 21*(3), 262–276. DOI: 10.1177/1356766715573651

Elbanna, S., Kamel, H., Fatima, T., & Eid, R. (2022). An investigation of the causality links in the balanced scorecard: The case of the Gulf Cooperation Council hospitality industry. *International Journal of Contemporary Hospitality Management, 34*(7), 2594–2615.

Elkington, J. (1994). Towards the sustainable corporation: Win-win-win business strategies for sustainable development. *California Management Review, 36*(2), 90–100. DOI: 10.2307/41165746

Emeksiz, M. (2001). *Beş yıldızlı otel işletmeleri için getiri yönetimi uygulama modeli* (Yayımlanmamış doktora tezi). Anadolu Üniversitesi.

Enes, K., & Koşan, L. (2024). Using time-driven activity-based costing in restaurant business: Levelled application of a case study. *Heliyon, 10*(4), e25157. DOI: 10.1016/j.heliyon.2024.e25157 PMID: 38370254

Enz, C. A., Canina, L., & Lomanno, M. (2004). Why discounting does not work: The dynamics of rising occupancy and falling revenue among competitors. *The Cornell Hotel and Restaurant Administration Quarterly, 45*(1), 59–71. DOI: 10.1177/0010880403260103

Enz, C. A., Canina, L., & Walsh, K. (2001). Hotel-industry averages: An inaccurate tool for measuring performance. *The Cornell Hotel and Restaurant Administration Quarterly, 42*(6), 22–32. DOI: 10.1177/0010880401426002

Erdem, B. (2010). Otel endüstrisinde yeni bir trend: Dizayn oteller. *Gazi Üniversitesi Ticaret ve Turizm Eğitim Fakültesi Dergisi*, (1), 115–132.

Eren, E. C., Zhang, Z., Rauch, J., Kumar, R., & Kallesen, R. (2024). Revenue management without demand forecasting: A data-driven approach for bid price generation. *Journal of Revenue and Pricing Management, 23*(6), 499–516. DOI: 10.1057/s41272-023-00465-3

Ergün, S., & Şahin, S. (2017). İşletme talep tahmini üzerine literatür araştırması. *Ulakbilge, 5*(10), 469–487. DOI: 10.7816/ulakbilge-05-10-11

Esteban, L. P., & Devesa, M. J. S. (2011). Determinants of earnings benchmarks in the Spanish hotel industry. *Tourism Economics, 17*(1), 53–72. DOI: 10.5367/te.2011.0024

Esteban, L. P., & Devesa, M. J. S. (2011). Earnings management in the Spanish hotel industry. *Cornell Hospitality Quarterly, 52*(4), 466–479. DOI: 10.1177/1938965511402930

European Commission. (2010, April 27). *Volcanic ash cloud crisis: Commission outlines response to tackle the impact on air transport*. MEMO/10/152.

Evans, M. E., Houston, R. W., Peters, M., & Pratt, J. H. (2012). The financial reporting environment, reporting discretion, and earnings management: US GAAP versus IFRS. *The Accounting Review*.

Evliyaoğlu, G., Keskin, E., & Sert, A. N. (2025). The role of orange flag application in preventing food waste in tourism enterprises. Journal of multidisciplinary academic tourism, 10(2), 241-249.

Eyster, J. J., & deRoos, J. A. (Eds.). (2011). *The Cornell School of Hotel Administration on hospitality: Cutting edge thinking and practice*. John Wiley & Sons.

Falk, M. T., & Vieru, M. (2021). Short-term hotel room price effects of sporting events. *Tourism Economics, 27*(3), 569–588. DOI: 10.1177/1354816620901953

Fama, E. F., & Jensen, M. C. (1983). Separation of ownership and control. *The Journal of Law & Economics, 26*(2), 301–325. DOI: 10.1086/467037

Farouk El Gayar, N., Saleh, M., Atiya, A., El-Shishiny, H., Alkes Youhanna Fayez Zakhary, A., & Abdel Aziz Mohammed Habib, H. (2011). An integrated framework for advanced hotel revenue management. *International Journal of Contemporary Hospitality Management, 23*(1), 84–98. DOI: 10.1108/09596111111101689

Fatemi, A., Glaum, M., & Kaiser, S. (2018). ESG performance and firm value: The moderating role of disclosure. *Global Finance Journal, 38*, 45–64. DOI: 10.1016/j.gfj.2017.03.001

Feng, M., Li, C., & McVay, S. (2009). Internal control and management guidance. *Journal of Accounting and Economics, 48*(2–3), 190–209. DOI: 10.1016/j.jacceco.2009.09.004

Fernandez, N. O., Gerrikagoitia, J. K., & Alzua-Sorzabal, A. (2014). Dynamic pricing patterns on an Internet distribution channel: The case study of Bilbao's hotels in 2013. In *Information and Communication Technologies in Tourism 2015* (pp. 735–747). Springer.

Filos, J. (2004). *Policies & procedures manual: Tool for organization and audit*. IQ Group Publishing. (In Greek)

Florido-Benítez, L. (2025). Air transport: A complex perspective for US Disney and Universal theme parks. *Journal of the Air Transport Research Society, 4*, 100051. DOI: 10.1016/j.jatrs.2024.100051

Forsyth, P. (2006). Martin Kunz Memorial Lecture. Tourism benefits and aviation policy. *Journal of Air Transport Management, 12*(1), 3–13. DOI: 10.1016/j.jairtraman.2005.09.001

Fresno-Aranda, R., Fernandez, P., Gamez-Diaz, A., Duran, A., & Ruiz-Cortes, A. (2025). Pricing4APIs: A rigorous model for RESTful API pricings. *Computer Standards & Interfaces, 91*, 103878. Advance online publication. DOI: 10.1016/j.csi.2024.103878

Frias-Aceituno, J. V., Rodríguez-Ariza, L., & García-Sánchez, I. M. (2013). The role of the board in the dissemination of integrated corporate social reporting. *Corporate Social Responsibility and Environmental Management, 20*(4), 219–233. DOI: 10.1002/csr.1294

Friede, G., Busch, T., & Bassen, A. (2015). ESG and financial performance: Aggregated evidence from more than 2000 empirical studies. *Journal of Sustainable Finance & Investment, 5*(4), 210–233. DOI: 10.1080/20430795.2015.1118917

Gaio, C., Gonçalves, T., & Sousa, M. V. (2022). Does corporate social responsibility mitigate earnings management? *Management Decision*, *60*(11), 2972–2989. DOI: 10.1108/MD-05-2021-0719

Gao, J. (2025). Optimizing hotel revenue management through dynamic pricing algorithms and data analysis. *Journal of Computational Methods in Sciences and Engineering*, *25*(2), 1200–1209. DOI: 10.1177/14727978241298467

Garefalakis, A., Stratidaki, F., Angelaki, E., Antonaki, D., & Papademetriou, C. (2026). Governance and financial outcomes of ESG implementation in tourism enterprises: A case study from Greece. *International Journal of Financial Studies*, *14*(3), 61. DOI: 10.3390/ijfs14030061

Garrigos-Simon, F. J., Narangajavana, Y., & Palacios-Marqués, D. (2017). The power of social media in the tourism industry. *Tourism Management Perspectives*, *21*, 65–73.

Gatera, A. (2024). Role of artificial intelligence in revenue management and pricing strategies in hotels. *Journal of Modern Hospitality*, *3*(2), 14–25. DOI: 10.47941/jmh.1957

Gazzoli, G., Kim, W. G., & Palakurthi, R. (2008). Online distribution strategies and competition: Are the global hotel companies getting it right? *International Journal of Contemporary Hospitality Management*, *20*(4), 375–387. DOI: 10.1108/09596110810873499

Giedt, J. Z. (2017). The roles of receivables and deferred revenues in revenue management. Social Science Research Network. https://doi.org/DOI: 10.2139/ssrn.2424848

Gillan, S. L., Koch, A., & Starks, L. T. (2021). Firms and social responsibility: A review of ESG and CSR research in corporate finance. *Journal of Corporate Finance*, *66*, 101889. DOI: 10.1016/j.jcorpfin.2021.101889

Gim, J., & Jang, S. (2023). Earnings management practices of the lodging industry: Diverging behaviors of lodging REITs and lodging C-corporations. *Tourism Economics*. Advance online publication. DOI: 10.1177/13548166231189142

Goh, B. W., & Li, D. (2011). Internal controls and conditional conservatism. *The Accounting Review*, *86*(3), 975–1005. DOI: 10.2308/accr.00000041

Gomes, C., Malheiros, C., Lima Santos, L., & Campos, F. (2025). Ascertaining restaurant financial sustainability by analyzing menu performance. *Tourism and Hospitality*, *6*(1), 47. DOI: 10.3390/tourhosp6010047

Gonçalves, B., Coelho, L. S., & Pinto, P. (2024). Earnings management in the hospitality industry: A systematic literature review. *Tourism & Management Studies, 20*(1), 65–77. Advance online publication. DOI: 10.18089/tms.20240105

González-Serrano, L., & Talón-Ballestero, P. (2022). Revenue management and e-tourism: The past, present, and future. In Xiang, Z., Fuchs, M., Gretzel, U., & Höpken, W. (Eds.), *Handbook of e-Tourism* (pp. 1261–1288). Springer., DOI: 10.1007/978-3-030-48652-5_76

Gordon, L. A., Loeb, M. P., & Tseng, C. Y. (2009). Enterprise risk management and firm performance: A contingency perspective. *Journal of Accounting and Public Policy, 28*(4), 301–327. DOI: 10.1016/j.jaccpubpol.2009.06.006

Granados, N., Gupta, A., & Kauffman, R. J. (2003). Online and offline demand and price elasticities: Evidence from the air travel industry. *Information Systems Research, 14*(4), 379–395. DOI: 10.1287/isre.14.4.379.24899

Grande, K., & Haynes, N. (2025). Campsite revenue management decision-making: A semi-systematic review. *Tourism and Hospitality Research, 25*(2), 387–405. DOI: 10.1177/14673584231218111

Granlund, M. (2011). Extending AIS research to management accounting and control issues. *International Journal of Accounting Information Systems, 12*(1), 3–19. DOI: 10.1016/j.accinf.2010.11.001

Grochowski, M. F., JABLONOWSKA, A. A., Lagioia, F., & Sartor, G. (2022). Algorithmic price discrimination and consumer protection: a digital arms race?. Technology and regulation, 2022, 36-47.

Guilding, C., Kennedy, D. J., & McManus, L. (2005). Extending the boundaries of customer accounting: Applications in the hotel industry. *Journal of Hospitality & Tourism Research (Washington, D.C.), 29*(2), 173–194. DOI: 10.1177/109634800102500205

Guillet, B. D., & Mohammed, I. (2015). Revenue management research in hospitality and tourism: A critical review of current literature and suggestions for future research. *International Journal of Contemporary Hospitality Management, 27*(4), 526–560. DOI: 10.1108/IJCHM-06-2014-0295

Guillet, B. D., Zhang, Y. R., Madanoglu, M., & Gao, L. (2026). Attribute-based pricing in hotels: Analyzing industry, customer, and behavioral insights. *International Journal of Hospitality Management, 133*, 104445. DOI: 10.1016/j.ijhm.2025.104445

Guizzardi, A., Ballestra, L. V., & D'Innocenzo, E. (2022). Hotel dynamic pricing, stochastic demand and covid-19. *Annals of Tourism Research, 97*, 103495. DOI: 10.1016/j.annals.2022.103495 PMID: 36311899

Guizzardi, A., Pons, F. M. E., Angelini, G., & Ranieri, E. (2021). Big data from dynamic pricing: A smart approach to tourism demand forecasting. *International Journal of Forecasting, 37*(3), 1049–1060. DOI: 10.1016/j.ijforecast.2020.11.006

Gunarathne, N., & Lee, K. H. (2021). Corporate cleaner production strategy development and environmental management accounting: A contingency theory perspective. *Journal of Cleaner Production, 297*, 126050. DOI: 10.1016/j.jclepro.2021.127402

Guo, Q., Cheng, S., & Zhao, P. (2024). How to introduce a livestreaming channel: A case of the hotel at a fixed capacity. *International Transactions in Operational Research, 31*(5), 3531–3552. DOI: 10.1111/itor.13259

Gupta, S., & Lehmann, D. R. (2003). Customers as assets. *Journal of Interactive Marketing, 17*(1), 9–24. DOI: 10.1002/dir.10045

Gür, Ç., & Yıldız, M. S. (2016). Gelir yönetimi uygulamaları: Ankara'daki otel işletmelerinde bir araştırma. *Düzce Üniversitesi Sosyal Bilimler Dergisi, 6*(2), 15–36.

Guttentag, D. (2015). Airbnb: Disruptive innovation and the rise of an informal tourism accommodation sector. *Current Issues in Tourism, 18*(12), 1192–1217. DOI: 10.1080/13683500.2013.827159

Güzel, S. Ö., Uzut, İ., Mengü, C., & Şahin, M. A. (Eds.). (2022). *Turizm işletmelerinde gelir yönetimi*. Yalın Yayıncılık.

Habětínek, J. (2020). Is revenue management to meet earnings benchmarks informative? *The Journal of Hospitality Financial Management.*

Ha, H. Y. (2026). When rewards buffer service failures: The role of residual value in loyalty programs. *Journal of Hospitality and Tourism Management, 68*, 101530. DOI: 10.1016/j.jhtm.2026.101530

Hajli, N., Tajvidi, M., Gbadamosi, A., & Nadeem, W. (2020). Understanding market agility for new product success with big data analytics. *Industrial Marketing Management, 86*, 135–143. DOI: 10.1016/j.indmarman.2019.09.010

Hallberg, N. L. (2008). *Pricing capability and its strategic dimensions* (Doctoral dissertation, Lund University).

Hallin, C. A., & Marnburg, E. (2008). Knowledge management in the hospitality industry: A review of empirical research. *Tourism Management, 29*(2), 366–381. DOI: 10.1016/j.tourman.2007.02.019

Han, H., Yu, J., & Kim, W. (2019). Environmental corporate social responsibility and customer responses. *International Journal of Hospitality Management, 76*, 16–26.

Han, X. (2025). Value Chain-Oriented Cost Control in Tourist Hotels: A Data-Driven Performance Evaluation Using DEA and AHP. [IJISSS]. *International Journal of Information Systems in the Service Sector, 16*(1), 1–15. DOI: 10.4018/IJISSS.397669

Harahap, A. J. S., Vonita, R. N. S., Nuraeni, P., & Khairi, F. R. (2025). The role of accounting information systems in strengthening revenue budget management and village expenditure in Indonesia. *West Science Interdisciplinary Studies, 3*(12), 2248–2256. DOI: 10.58812/wsis.v3i12.2295

Hardy, A. (2020). *Tracking tourists*. Goodfellow Publishers., DOI: 10.23912/9781911635383-4277

Harea, R., & Harea, R. (2025). Aspects regarding the accounting of tourism and hotel services. In Învă ământul superior contabil: Provocări i solu ii: Culegere de teze tiin ifice (pp. 105–107). Academia de Studii Economice din Moldova. DOI: 10.53486/isc2025.29

Hayes, D. K., & Miller, A. A. (2011). *Revenue management for the hospitality industry*. John Wiley & Sons.

Haynes, N., & Egan, D. (2023). Transient price setting in the era of automated systems: the 'hands-on' hotel general manager lives on! *Journal of Revenue and Pricing Management 2023 23:1, 23*(1), 28–38. DOI: 10.1057/s41272-023-00447-5

Haynes, N. (2016). The evolution of competitor data collection in the hotel industry and its application to revenue management and pricing. *Journal of Revenue and Pricing Management, 15*(3–4), 258–263. DOI: 10.1057/rpm.2016.7

Hendler, R., & Hendler, F. (2004). Revenue management in fabulous Las Vegas: Combining customer relationship management and revenue management to maximise profitability. *Journal of Revenue and Pricing Management, 3*(1), 73–79. DOI: 10.1057/palgrave.rpm.5170095

Henriques, H., & Pereira, L. N. (2024). Hotel demand forecasting models and methods using artificial intelligence: A systematic literature review. *Tourism & Management Studies, 20*(3), 39–51. DOI: 10.18089/tms.20240304

Heo, C. Y. (2013). Restaurant revenue management. In Legohérel, P., Poutier, E., & Fyall, A. (Eds.), *Revenue management for hospitality and tourism* (pp. 118–129). Goodfellow Publishers.

Heo, C. Y., & Lee, S. (2011). Influences of consumer characteristics on fairness perceptions of revenue management pricing in the hotel industry. *International Journal of Hospitality Management, 30*(2), 243–251. DOI: 10.1016/j.ijhm.2010.07.002

Heo, C. Y., Viverit, L., & Pereira, L. N. (2024). Does historical data still matter for demand forecasting in uncertain and turbulent times? An extension of the additive pickup time series method for SME hotels. *Journal of Revenue and Pricing Management, 23*(1), 39–43. DOI: 10.1057/s41272-023-00421-1

Herath, R., Tham, J., Khatibi, A., & Azam, S. M. F. (2023). Revenue management practices and financial performance in star-rated hotels in Sri Lanka. *Journal of Law and Sustainable Development, 11*(11), e1538. DOI: 10.55908/sdgs.v11i11.1538

Hermalin, B. E., & Weisbach, M. S. (2001). Boards of directors as an endogenously determined institution: A survey of the economic literature (NBER Working Paper No. 8161).

HFTP. (2014). *Uniform system of accounts for the lodging industry* (11th ed.). https://hftp.org/usali

Hidayati, S., Nata, J. H., Reindrawati, D. Y., & Huda, M. N. (2025). The influence of dynamic pricing in enhancing room occupancy and room revenue in Bintan Island Resort. [The International Journal of Applied Business]. *TIJAB, 9*(1), 38–50. DOI: 10.20473/tijab.v9.I1.2025.58812

Hidayat, S. J., & Suyasa, I. G. W. (2024). Menu engineering analysis: An industrial reference for tourism students. *Proceeding of The International Global Tourism Science and Vocational Education*, 1(1), 43–62.

Hinterhuber, A. (2004). Towards value-based pricing: An integrative framework for decision making. *Industrial Marketing Management, 33*(8), 765–778. DOI: 10.1016/j.indmarman.2003.10.006

Hinterhuber, A. (2008). Customer value-based pricing strategies: Why companies resist. *The Journal of Business Strategy, 29*(4), 41–50. DOI: 10.1108/02756660810887079

Hoai, T. T., & Nguyen, N. P. (2022). Internal control systems and performance of emerging market firms: The moderating roles of leadership consistency and quality. *SAGE Open, 12*(3), 21582440221123509. DOI: 10.1177/21582440221123509

Ho, D. H., & Kim, H. S. (2025). Examining the influence of customer satisfaction and occupancy rates on RevPAR: Insights from 5-star hotels in Da Nang. *Culinary Science & Hospitality Research, 31*(2), 42–55. DOI: 10.20878/cshr.2025.31.2.006

Hoitash, U., Hoitash, R., & Bedard, J. C. (2009). Corporate governance and internal control over financial reporting: A comparison of regulatory regimes. *The Accounting Review, 84*(3), 839–867. DOI: 10.2308/accr.2009.84.3.839

Horngren, C. T., Datar, S. M., & Rajan, M. (2014). *Cost accounting: A managerial emphasis* (15th ed.). Pearson.

Hosany, S., & Witham, M. (2010). Dimensions of cruisers' experiences, satisfaction, and intention to recommend. *Journal of Travel Research, 49*(3), 351–364. DOI: 10.1177/0047287509346859

Hospitality Financial and Technology Professionals. American Hotel & Lodging Association, & Global Finance Committee. (2024). *Uniform system of accounts for the lodging industry, available at* https://usali.hftp.org/

Hossain, M. Z., & Hasan, L. (2024). Sustainable cost management and green business: The role of managerial accounting innovations. *European Modern Studies Journal, 8*(4), 464–484. DOI: 10.59573/emsj.8(4).2024.24

How to optimize your loyalty program through data and technology: PwC. (n.d.). Retrieved September 2, 2026, from https://www.pwc.com/us/en/services/audit-assurance/risk-modeling-services/loyalty-programs.html

Hristov, S. B., Đorđević, A., Kovačević, I., & Zečević, B. (2023). Ethical dilemmas as a result of the impact of revenue management on hotel guest behavior. *Marketing, 54*(4), 258–263. DOI: 10.5937/mkng2304258H

Huang, M. H., & Rust, R. T. (2021). A strategic framework for artificial intelligence in marketing. *Journal of the Academy of Marketing Science, 49*(1), 30–50. DOI: 10.1007/s11747-020-00749-9

Hu, L. (2010). Corporate governance and earnings management: Evidence from Singapore. *Journal of International Accounting Research.*

HVS. (2025). *HVS global perspectives: Our 2025 outlook, https://www.hvs.com/article/10107-hvs-global-perspectives-our-2025-outlooks

Hwang, J., & Han, H. (2018). A study on the application of the experience economy to luxury cruise passengers. *Tourism and Hospitality Research, 18*(4), 478–491. DOI: 10.1177/1467358416682068

Hwang, J., & Wen, L. (2009). The effect of perceived fairness toward hotel overbooking and compensation practices on customer loyalty. *International Journal of Contemporary Hospitality Management, 21*(6), 659–675. DOI: 10.1108/09596110910975945

Hyera, D. W., Kadigi, M. L., & Ndyetabula, D. W. (2025). Internal control systems and the revenue collection performance among local government authorities (LGA) in Tanzania. *Journal of Policy and Development Studies (Editon), 4*(1), 1–15. DOI: 10.51317/jpds.v4i1.676

Ibrahim, Y., Abbas, T., & Kamal, M. (2021). The use of electronic customer relationship management (e-CRM) features through hotel websites to enhance customer loyalty and brand image. *Journal of Association of Arab Universities for Tourism and Hospitality, 21*(1), 103–125. DOI: 10.21608/jaauth.2021.79828.1190

IFRS - IFRS 15 Revenue from Contracts with Customers. (n.d.). Retrieved September 2, 2026, from https://www.ifrs.org/issued-standards/list-of-standards/ifrs-15-revenue-from-contracts-with-customers/

İmamoğlu, S. Z., Erat, S., & İnce, H. (2023). *Yönetim biliminde yapay zekâ*. Nobel Akademik Yayıncılık.

Indian Accounting Standard (Ind AS) 115 | Companies Act Integrated Ready Reckoner|Companies Act 2013|CAIRR. (n.d.). Retrieved September 2, 2026, from https://ca2013.com/indian-accounting-standard-ind-115-2/

International Hospitality Institute. (n.d.). *Global hospitality code of conduct (HCODE) and pledge*. https://www.internationalhospitalityinstitute.com/code-of-conduct-pledge

Islam, M. S., Ali, M., & Azizzadeh, F. (2024). Consumer decision-making processes in digital environments: A psychological perspective. *Applied Psychology Research, 3*(1), 1362. DOI: 10.59400/apr.v3i1.1362

Ivanenko, V. (2025). Menu engineering as an effective analytical tool for enhancing restaurant performance. Economics. Management. *Innovations*, *2*(37), 294–315.

Ivanov, S., & Zhechev, V. (2012). Hotel revenue management: A critical literature review. *Tourism: An International Interdisciplinary Journal, 60*(2), 175–197. https://hrcak.srce.hr/file/125946

Ivanov, S. (2014). *Hotel revenue management: From theory to practice*. Zangador.

Ivanov, S. (2014). *Hotel revenue management: From theory to practice*. Zangador. DOI: 10.13140/RG.2.1.2714.8960

Ivanov, S., & Webster, C. (2017). Adoption of robots, artificial intelligence and service automation by travel, tourism and hospitality companies. *International Journal of Contemporary Hospitality Management.*

Ivanov, S., & Zhechev, V. (2012). Hotel revenue management: A critical literature review. *Tourism and Hospitality Management, 18*(2), 175–197.

Ivanov, S., & Zhechev, V. (2012). Hotel revenue management: A critical literature review. *Tourism: An International Interdisciplinary Journal, 60*(2), 175–197. DOI: 10.2139/ssrn.1977467

Ivanov, S., & Zhechev, V. (2012). Hotel revenue management: From theory to practice. *Tourism Review, 67*(1), 45–56.

Jackson, L. A. (2025). Hotel asset managers as catalysts for sustainable change. *International Hospitality Review*, 1–7.

Jackson, L. A. (2025). Corporate governance and environmental citizenship in global hospitality: A cross-national empirical study. *Sustainability (Basel), 17*(9), 3918. DOI: 10.3390/su17093918

Jagels, M. G. (2010). *Hospitality management accounting* (9th ed.). John Wiley & Sons.

Jamil, N. N., & Wahyuni, E. T. (2024). Unveiling greenwashing: Risks in sustainability and ESG reporting. *International Journal of Accounting. Finance and Business, 9*(57), 30–42.

Jang, Y., Liu, C. H., Weinbaum, D., & Yehuda, N. (2023). Performing up to par? Hospitality firms after ASU 2016-02. Social Science Research Network. https://doi.org/DOI: 10.2139/ssrn.4549994

Jayanti, R. K. (2021). An institutional theory perspective on retailer loyalty. *Journal of Relationship Marketing, 20*(2), 156–176. DOI: 10.1080/15332667.2020.1756025

Jensen, M. C., & Meckling, W. H. (1976). Theory of the firm: Managerial behavior, agency costs and ownership structure. *Journal of Financial Economics, 3*(4), 305–360. DOI: 10.1016/0304-405X(76)90026-X

Jiang, Y., & Wen, J. (2020). Effects of COVID-19 on hotel marketing and management: A perspective article. *International Journal of Contemporary Hospitality Management, 32*(8), 2563–2573. DOI: 10.1108/IJCHM-03-2020-0237

Jiao, F., & Lu, L. W. (2019). Earnings management, benchmarks, and market valuation: Evidence from hospitality firms. *Journal of Accounting and Finance, 19*(3). Advance online publication. DOI: 10.33423/jaf.v19i3.2034

Jo, H., & Harjoto, M. A. (2012). The causal effect of corporate governance on corporate social responsibility. *Journal of Business Ethics, 106*(1), 53–72. DOI: 10.1007/s10551-011-1052-1

Johansson, M., & Andersson, L. (2012). Pricing practices and value creation logics. *Journal of Revenue and Pricing Management, 11*(1), 64–75. DOI: 10.1057/rpm.2011.43

Josephson Institute. (2013). *The six pillars of character*. Josephson Institute of Ethics.

Kafetzi, F.-C. (2025). *Evaluation of contemporary revenue management systems in the tourism industry* (Master's thesis, University of Macedonia).

Kagias, P., Kourgiantakis, M., Passas, I., Ragazou, K., & Bakeas, S. (2023). CG and Prosperous Investment Decisions — The Paradigm of Mergers and Acquisitions. In Governance and Financial Performance: Current Trends and Perspectives (pp. 275–300). World Scientific Publishing Co. https://doi.org/DOI: 10.1142/9789811260506_0011

Kagias, P., Garefalakis, A., Passas, I., Kyriakogkonas, P., & Sariannidis, N. (2024). Whistleblowing Based on the Three Lines Model. *Administrative Sciences, 14*(5), 83. DOI: 10.3390/admsci14050083

Kahneman, D., & Klein, G. (2009). Conditions for intuitive expertise: A failure to disagree. *The American Psychologist, 64*(6), 515–526. DOI: 10.1037/a0016755 PMID: 19739881

Kaman, G. S., & Bölükbaş, R. (2024). Konaklama işletmelerinde getiri yönetiminin uygulanması. *Üçüncü Sektör Sosyal Ekonomi Dergisi, 59*(3), 1248–1261.

Kamola, M., & Arabas, P. (2020). Improving time-series demand modeling in hospitality business by analytics of public event datasets. *IEEE Access : Practical Innovations, Open Solutions, 8*, 53666–53677. DOI: 10.1109/ACCESS.2020.2980501

Kaplan, R. S., & Cooper, R. (1998). *Cost and effect: Using integrated cost systems to drive profitability and performance*. Harvard Business School Press.

Karadeniz, E., Beyaz, F. S., Ünlübulduk, S. N., & Kayhan, E. (2020). COVID-19 salgınının turizm sektörüne etkilerinin ve uygulanan stratejilerin değerlendirilmesi: Otel yöneticileri üzerinde bir araştırma. *Türk Turizm Araştırmaları Dergisi, 4*(4), 3116–3136. DOI: 10.26677/TR1010.2020.554

Karaman, Ö. (2021). Yapay zeka destekli kişiselleştirme algoritmalarının tüketici zihninde filtre balonu yaratma etkisinin incelenmesi. *Süleyman Demirel Üniversitesi Vizyoner Dergisi, 12*(32), 1339–1351. DOI: 10.21076/vizyoner.896059

Kasapoğlu, V. (2007). *Maliyet temeline dayalı fiyatlandırma yöntemleri* (Yüksek lisans tezi). Sakarya Üniversitesi.

Kasavana, M. L., & Brooks, R. M. (2020). *Managing front office operations* (10th ed.). American Hotel & Lodging Educational Institute.

Khalil, N., Che Abdullah, S. N., Haron, S. N., & Hamid, M. Y. (2024). A review of green practices and initiatives from stakeholder's perspectives towards sustainable hotel operations and performance impact. *Journal of Facilities Management, 22*(4), 653–682. DOI: 10.1108/JFM-03-2022-0025

Kheirollah, A. (2014). Governance-adjusted earnings management and information asymmetry. Social Science Research Network. https://doi.org/DOI: 10.2139/ssrn.2578657

Kiani Mavi, R., Kiani Mavi, N., Olaru, D., Biermann, S., & Chi, S. (2022). Innovations in freight transport: A systematic literature evaluation and COVID implications. *International Journal of Logistics Management, 33*(4), 1157–1195. DOI: 10.1108/IJLM-07-2021-0360

Kiel, G. C., & Nicholson, G. J. (2003). Board composition and corporate performance: How the Australian experience informs contrasting theories of corporate governance. *Corporate Governance, 11*(3), 189–205. DOI: 10.1111/1467-8683.00318

Kılıç, B., & Uslu, T. (2019). Porter'in rekabet modelinin İstanbul'daki zincir otel işletmelerinde incelenmesi. *Uluslararası Global Turizm Araştırmaları Dergisi, 3*(2), 83–98.

Kim, D., Hong, S., Park, B. J., & Kim, I. (2020). Understanding heterogeneous preferences of hotel choice attributes: Do customer segments matter? *Journal of Hospitality and Tourism Management, 45*, 330–337. DOI: 10.1016/j.jhtm.2020.08.014

Kimes, S. E. (2017). *The future of hotel revenue management. Cornell Hospitality Report, 17*(1), 3–10. https://vtechworks.lib.vt.edu/items/c390bff0-cf5a-4a7c-bd68-ce7112de1c75?utm_source=chatgpt.com

Kimes, S. E. (1989). The basics of yield management. *The Cornell Hotel and Restaurant Administration Quarterly, 30*(3), 14–19. DOI: 10.1177/001088048903000309

Kimes, S. E. (1989). Yield management: A tool for capacity-considered service firms. *Journal of Operations Management, 8*(4), 348–363. DOI: 10.1016/0272-6963(89)90035-1

Kimes, S. E. (1999). Implementing restaurant revenue management: A five-step approach. *The Cornell Hotel and Restaurant Administration Quarterly, 40*(3), 16–21. DOI: 10.1177/001088049904000315

Kimes, S. E. (2000). Revenue management on the links: Applying yield management to the golf-course industry. *The Cornell Hotel and Restaurant Administration Quarterly, 41*(1), 120–127. DOI: 10.1177/001088040004100129

Kimes, S. E. (2011). The future of hotel revenue management. *Journal of Revenue and Pricing Management, 10*(1), 62–72. DOI: 10.1057/rpm.2010.47

Kimes, S. E. (2016). The evolution of hotel revenue management. *Journal of Revenue and Pricing Management, 15*(3–4), 247–251. DOI: 10.1057/rpm.2016.27

Kimes, S. E., Chase, R. B., Choi, S., Lee, P. Y., & Ngonzi, E. N. (1998). Restaurant revenue management: Applying yield management to the restaurant industry. *The Cornell Hotel and Restaurant Administration Quarterly, 39*(3), 32–39. DOI: 10.1177/001088049803900308

Kimes, S. E., & Singh, S. (2009). Spa revenue management. *Cornell Hospitality Quarterly, 50*(1), 82–95. DOI: 10.1177/1938965508324868

Kimes, S. E., & Wirtz, J. (2003). Has revenue management become acceptable? Findings from an international study on the perceived fairness of rate fences. *Journal of Service Research, 6*(2), 125–135. DOI: 10.1177/1094670503257038

Kim, M., Roehl, W., & Lee, S. K. (2019). Effect of hotels' price discounts on performance recovery after a crisis. *International Journal of Hospitality Management, 83*, 74–82. DOI: 10.1016/j.ijhm.2019.04.006

Kizildag, M., Weinland, J. T., & Demirer, I. (2023). Financial sensitivity analysis of small lodging establishments during COVID-19. *Journal of Hospitality and Tourism Insights, 6*(5), 2257–2272. DOI: 10.1108/JHTI-05-2022-0176

Kliestik, T., Hrosova, L., Valaskova, K., & Svabova, L. (2022). Do firms in the tourism sector manage earnings? Evidence from V4 countries. Journal of Tourism and Services. https://doi.org/DOI: 10.29036/jots.v13i25.376

Kloostra, J. (2022). Algorithmic pricing: A concern for platform workers? *European Labour Law Journal, 13*(1), 108–126. DOI: 10.1177/20319525211060360

Koçoğlu, C. M., & Yurt, B. Ç. (2020). Otel tercihleri kapsamında fiyat algısı bileşenlerinin ilişkisi üzerine bir araştırma. *Uluslararası İktisadi ve İdari İncelemeler Dergisi, 27*, 179–192.

Konstantopoulos, G., Giannarakis, G., Xenaki, M., Thanasas, G., & Garefalakis, A. (2026). Operational labor shortages and authentic hospitality: Evidence from Greek hotels. *Tourism and Hospitality, 7*(6), 180. DOI: 10.3390/tourhosp7060180

Koşan, L., & Türkseven, Y. Ç. (2022). Otel işletmelerinde gelir yönetimi süreci üzerine bir değerlendirme. *Turizm Ekonomi ve İşletme Araştırmaları Dergisi, 4*(1), 71–90.

Kotler, P., Bowen, J. T., Makens, J. C., & Baloglu, S. (2017). *Marketing for hospitality and tourism* (7th ed.). Pearson Education.

Kotler, P., & Keller, K. L. (2016). *A framework for marketing management* (6th ed.). Pearson.

Kotler, P., & Keller, K. L. (2016). *Marketing management* (15th ed.). Pearson.

Koutoupis, A. G., & Pappa, E. (2018). Corporate governance and internal controls: A case study from Greece. *Journal of Governance and Regulation, 7*(2), 91–99. DOI: 10.22495/jgr_v7_i2_p8

Krajewski, L. J., Ritzman, L. P., & Malhotra, M. K. (2013). *Operations management: Processes and supply chains* (10th ed., global ed.). Pearson.

Kruhlyanko, A., Peniuk, V., Ursakii, Y., & Verstiak, O. (2025). Mathematical modeling for enhancing business strategies in the hotel and restaurant industry: Implications for economic stability. *Advances in Nonlinear Variational Inequalities, 28*(3s, 3S), 386–400. DOI: 10.52783/anvi.v28.3066

Kumari, V. P., & Raj, S. A. (2025). Optimizing revenue and pricing for UPI transactions using AI-based dynamic pricing models. *Journal of Revenue and Pricing Management 2025 25:4, 25*(4), 395–408. DOI: 10.1057/s41272-025-00561-6

Kumar, V., & Reinartz, W. (2016). Creating enduring customer value. *Journal of Marketing, 80*(6), 36–68. DOI: 10.1509/jm.15.0414

Kyriakogkonas, P., Garefalakis, A., Pappa, E., & Kagias, P. (2022). Sustainable project management under the light of ESG criteria: A theoretical approach. *Theoretical Economics Letters, 12*(6), 1517–1538. DOI: 10.4236/tel.2022.126083

La Porta, R., Lopez-de-Silanes, F., Shleifer, A., & Vishny, R. (1999). Corporate ownership around the world. *The Journal of Finance, 54*(2), 471–517. DOI: 10.1111/0022-1082.00115

La Porta, R., Lopez-de-Silanes, F., Shleifer, A., & Vishny, R. W. (1998). Law and finance. *Journal of Political Economy, 106*(6), 1113–1155. DOI: 10.1086/250042

La Porta, R., Lopez-de-Silanes, F., Shleifer, A., & Vishny, R. W. (2000). Investor protection and corporate governance. *Journal of Financial Economics, 58*(1–2), 3–27. DOI: 10.1016/S0304-405X(00)00065-9

Labanowski, L., Fracz, P., Wotzka, D., & Dabrowski, I. (2024). Studying The Interrelations Between USALI Parameters And GOP Through Wavelet Coherence Analysis. In ECMS (pp. 70-76). DOI: 10.7148/2024-0070

Labanowski, L., Fracz, P., Wotzka, D., & Foltys, J. (2024). Application Of The Nonlinear Autoregressive Model With Exogenous Inputs For Predicting The Gross Operating Product Based On USALI Data. In ECMS (pp. 77-83). DOI: 10.7148/2024-0077

Lafontaine, F., & Blair, R. D. (2005). *The economics of franchising*. Cambridge University Press.

Lampropoulos, S. D., Thanasas, G. L., Garefalakis, A., & Passas, I. (2025). Harmonizing Sustainability and Resilience: The Integral Role of Internal Audit in ESG Implementation—A Review. *International Journal of Financial Studies, 13*(4), 194. DOI: 10.3390/ijfs13040194

Larcker, D. F., & Richardson, S. A. (2004). Fees paid to audit firms, accrual choices, and corporate governance. *Journal of Accounting Research, 42*(3), 625–658. DOI: 10.1111/j.1475-679X.2004.t01-1-00143.x

Law, R., Leung, D., & Chan, I. C. C. (2020). Progression and development of information and communication technology research in hospitality and tourism: A state-of-the-art review. *International Journal of Contemporary Hospitality Management, 32*(2), 511–534. DOI: 10.1108/IJCHM-07-2018-0586

Lee, K. H., Cin, B. C., & Lee, E. Y. (2016). Environmental responsibility and firm performance: The application of an environmental, social and governance model. *Business Strategy and the Environment, 25*(1), 40–53. DOI: 10.1002/bse.1855

Lee, S. H. (2014). Managerial process of discount decision-making in the lodging industry. *International Journal of Hospitality Management*.

Lee, S. H., Deale, C. S., & Lee, J. (2022). Does it pay to book direct? Customers' perceptions of online channel distributors, price, and loyalty membership on brand dimensions. [Sayfa aralığı doğrulanmalı]. *Journal of Revenue and Pricing Management, 21*(6), 657–670. DOI: 10.1057/s41272-022-00382-x

Lee, S., O'Neill, J. W., & McGinley, S. (2016). Effects of economic conditions and other factors on hotel sale prices. *International Journal of Contemporary Hospitality Management, 28*(10), 2267–2284. DOI: 10.1108/IJCHM-07-2014-0363

Lee, S., Pan, B., & Park, S. (2019). Revpar vs. Goppar: Property- and firm-level analysis. *Annals of Tourism Research, 76*, 180–190. DOI: 10.1016/j.annals.2019.04.006

Lentz, M., Berezan, O., & Raab, C. (2022). Uncovering the relationship between revenue management and hotel loyalty programs. *Journal of Revenue and Pricing Management, 21*(3), 306–320. DOI: 10.1057/s41272-021-00331-0

Leonandri, D. G., & Erpurini, W. (2025). The Qualitative Study on the Use of Managerial Accounting Information in Resource Allocation Decision-Making in Hotels. JASa (Jurnal Akuntansi, Audit Dan Sistem Informasi Akuntansi), 9(1), 12-20.

Li, M., & Ma, S. (2015). Hotel revenue management performance influencing mechanisms: A theoretical framework. *International Journal of Contemporary Hospitality Management.*

Lima Santos, L., Gomes, C., Malheiros, C., Crespo, C., & Bento, C. (2024). Factors influencing hotel revenue management in times of crisis: Towards financial sustainability. *International Journal of Financial Studies, 12*(4), 112. DOI: 10.3390/ijfs12040112

Ling, L., Guo, X., & Yang, C. (2014). Opening the online marketplace: An examination of hotel pricing and travel agency online distribution of rooms. *Tourism Management, 45*, 234–243. DOI: 10.1016/j.tourman.2014.05.003

Lin, M. S., Zhang, H., Luo, Y., & Li, Y. (2024). Environmental, social, and governance (ESG) measurement in the tourism and hospitality industry: Views from a developing country. *Journal of Travel & Tourism Marketing, 41*(1), 154–168. DOI: 10.1080/10548408.2023.2293008

Littlewood, K. (1972). *Forecasting and control of passenger bookings.* In *Proceedings of the 12th AGIFORS Symposium* (pp. 95–117). American Airlines.

Li, Y., & Singal, M. (2019). Capital structure in the hospitality industry: The role of the asset-light and fee-oriented strategy. *Tourism Management, 70*, 124–133. DOI: 10.1016/j.tourman.2018.08.004

Li, Y., & Singal, M. (2022). Corporate governance in the hospitality and tourism industry: Theoretical foundations and future research. *Journal of Hospitality & Tourism Research (Washington, D.C.), 46*(7), 1347–1383. DOI: 10.1177/10963480211011718

Lu, H., & Wang, S. (2018). Does lifting the objective-price constraint in revenue recognition increase value relevance? *Asian Review of Accounting, 26*(4), 545–570. DOI: 10.1108/ARA-08-2017-0126

Lu, K., Onuk, C. B., Xia, Y., & Zhang, J. (2025). ESG ratings and financial performance in the global hospitality industry. *Journal of Risk and Financial Management, 18*(1), 24. DOI: 10.3390/jrfm18010024

Lunkes, R. J., Deggau, L. P., Codesso, M., Rosa, F. S., & Monteiro, J. (2025). The influence of online reviews and hotel digital responsibility on ESG practices and sustainability performance. *International Journal of Contemporary Hospitality Management, 37*(11), 3729–3747. DOI: 10.1108/IJCHM-12-2024-1972

Lu, W. M., Ting, I. W. K., & Huang, S. H. (2025). Environmental, social and governance (ESG) initiatives and firm efficiency in the global tourism and hospitality industry: The role of business strategy. *Asian Academy of Management Journal of Accounting and Finance, 21*(1), 275–312. DOI: 10.21315/aamjaf2025.21.1.10

Magnini, V. P., Honeycutt, E. D.Jr, & Hodge, S. K. (2003). Data mining for hotel firms: Use and limitations. *The Cornell Hotel and Restaurant Administration Quarterly, 44*(2), 94–105. DOI: 10.1016/S0010-8804(03)90022-X

Ma, H., Zhang, H., Tian, D., Yue, D., & Hancke, G. P. (2024). Optimal demand response based dynamic pricing strategy via Multi-Agent Federated Twin Delayed Deep Deterministic policy gradient algorithm. *Engineering Applications of Artificial Intelligence, 133*, 108012. Advance online publication. DOI: 10.1016/j.engappai.2024.108012

Mao, Z., Liu, T., & Li, X. (2023). Pricing mechanism of variable opaque products for dual-channel online travel agencies. *Annals of Operations Research, 329*(1), 901–930. DOI: 10.1007/s10479-021-04163-4

Maravelaki, A., Zopounidis, C., Lemonakis, C., & Passas, I. (2021). Corporate Governance as a Tool for Fraud Mitigation. In Papadakis, S., Garefalakis, A., Lemonakis, C., & Zopounidis, C. (Eds.), *Machine Learning Applications for Accounting Disclosure and Fraud Detection* (pp. 1–15). IGI Global Scientific Publishing., DOI: 10.4018/978-1-7998-4805-9.ch001

Mariani, M. (2020). Big data and analytics in tourism and hospitality: A perspective article. *Tourism Review, 75*(1), 299–303. DOI: 10.1108/TR-06-2019-0259

Mariani, M. M., Baggio, R., Fuchs, M., & Höepken, W. (2023). Business intelligence and big data in hospitality and tourism: A systematic literature review. *International Journal of Contemporary Hospitality Management.*

Martin, I. W., Lopez, J. L., & Olsen, L. (2019). Policy design and the politics of city revenue: Evidence from California municipal ballot measures. *Urban Affairs Review, 55*(5), 1312–1338. DOI: 10.1177/1078087417752474

Martin, K. (2019). Ethical implications and accountability of algorithms. *Journal of Business Ethics, 160*(4), 835–850. DOI: 10.1007/s10551-018-3921-3

Mashige, R., Hewson, D., & Mabaso, C. (2025). The influence of cultural cuisine on restaurant revenue: Implications for financial sustainability. *African Journal of Hospitality, Tourism and Leisure, 5*(14), 989. DOI: 10.46222/ajhtl.19770720.685

Matviienko, M. (2019). *The financial aspect of revenue management in hospitality.* Economics and Management of Tourism. DOI: 10.31375/2226-1915-2019-4-119-130

Méatchi, S., & Camus, S. (2020). Revenue management pricing in the hotel sector: Reducing perceived unfairness to encourage willingness to pay. [English Edition]. *Recherche et Applications en Marketing*, *35*(3), 102–123. DOI: 10.1177/2051570720954760

Meatchi, S., Camus, S., & Lecointre-Erickson, D. (2021). Perceived unfairness of revenue management pricing: Developing a measurement scale in the context of hospitality. *International Journal of Contemporary Hospitality Management*, *33*(10), 3157–3176. DOI: 10.1108/IJCHM-11-2020-1344

Mei, Z. (2026). Dynamic pricing strategy driven by deep reinforcement learning with empirical analysis on the collaborative optimization of hotel revenue management and customer satisfaction. *International Journal of High Speed Electronics and Systems*, *35*(06), 2540865. DOI: 10.1142/S0129156425408654

Meng, X., & Shaikh, G. M. (2023). Evaluating environmental, social, and governance criteria and green finance investment strategies using fuzzy AHP and fuzzy WASPAS. *Sustainability (Basel)*, *15*(8), 6786. DOI: 10.3390/su15086786

Mensah, P. O., Mensah, H. K., Osei, B. A., & Iddris, F. (2026). Antecedents of Sustainable Performance in Hotels: The Mediating Role of Green Innovation Strategy. *International Journal of Hospitality & Tourism Administration*, *27*(3), 568–592. DOI: 10.1080/15256480.2025.2494591

Mercan, R., & Sandıkcı, M. (2024). Bleisure tourism: Business and leisure together. In *Future tourism trends volume 1: Tourism in the changing world* (pp. 3–15). Emerald Publishing Limited.

Mesa-Pérez, E. (2024). The rise of compliance systems? The evolution of internal control through the accounting literature. *Revista Española de Financiación y Contabilidad*, *53*(3), 302–322. DOI: 10.1080/02102412.2023.2255416

Metwalli, M. Z. (2025). The Impact of Accounting Principles on Managerial Decision-Making in Small and Medium Enterprises. *International Journal of Accounting and Management Sciences*, *4*(3).

Mia, L., & Patiar, A. (2001). The use of management accounting systems in hotels: An exploratory study. *International Journal of Hospitality Management*, *20*(2), 111–128. DOI: 10.1016/S0278-4319(00)00033-5

Michael, S. C. (1999). The elasticity of franchising. *Small Business Economics*, *12*(4), 313–320. DOI: 10.1023/A:1008019418231

Millauer, T., & Vellekoop, M. (2019). Artificial intelligence in today's hotel revenue management: Opportunities and risks. *Research in Hospitality Management*, *9*(2), 121–124. DOI: 10.1080/22243534.2019.1689702

Miller, P., & Smith, T. (2011). *Insight: Delivering value to stakeholders*. Institute of Internal Auditors Research Foundation.

Minich, I. (2025). Hotel revenues under economic instability: Adaptation strategies. *Ekonomichnyy Analiz*, *35*(1), 484–492. DOI: 10.35774/econa2025.01.484

Minor, K., Ivanov, S., & Bratec, M. (2025). Hotel daily deals: A revenue management perspective. *Tourism and Hospitality Management*, *31*(3), I–XII. DOI: 10.20867/thm.31.3.10

Mirkova, I., & Padrón-Fumero, N. (2025). From vulnerability to resilience: Empowering stakeholder-driven just transitions in island tourism economies. *Energy Research & Social Science*, *121*, 103966. DOI: 10.1016/j.erss.2025.103966

Mirzayeva, G., & Türkay, O. (2016). Rekabet stratejilerinin değerlendirilmesi: Bakü'deki otel işletmeleri üzerine bir araştırma. *Uluslararası Türk Dünyası Turizm Araştırmaları Dergisi*, *1*(1), 74–83.

Mishra, D., & Vijayvargy, L. (2025). Smart tourism supply chains: Integrating AI, advanced analytics, and robotics for enhanced customer experiences. In *Handbook of Business Analytics* (pp. 196–218). CRC Press. DOI: 10.1201/9781003514282-11

Mitev, A. Z., Pintér-Szabó, L., & Irimiás, A. (2025). Overcoming energy barriers in hotels' green programs. *Annals of Tourism Research*, *115*, 104061. DOI: 10.1016/j.annals.2025.104061

Mitra, S. K. (2020). An analysis of asymmetry in dynamic pricing of hospitality industry. *International Journal of Hospitality Management*, *89*, 102406. DOI: 10.1016/j.ijhm.2019.102406

Modica, P., & Scanu, E. (2014). Day spa revenue management: Some examples from Italy. In Smith, M., & Puczkó, L. (Eds.), *Health, tourism and hospitality: Wellness, spas and medical travel* (2nd ed., pp. 269–273). Routledge.

Mohammed, I., & Denizci Guillet, B. (2026). Stakeholder perspectives on integrating explainable artificial intelligence into hotel revenue management system. *Tourism Economics*, *32*(4), 804–824. DOI: 10.1177/13548166251382289

Moon, J., & Sharma, A. (2014). Franchising effects on the lodging industry: Optimal franchising proportion in terms of profitability and intangible value. *Tourism Economics*, *20*(5), 1027–1045. DOI: 10.5367/te.2013.0336

Morgan, M., Elbe, J., & de Esteban Curiel, J. (2009). Has the experience economy arrived? The views of destination managers in three visitor-dependent areas. *International Journal of Tourism Research, 11*(2), 201–216. DOI: 10.1002/jtr.719

Morritt, R., & Weinstein, A. (2012). *Segmentation strategies for hospitality managers: Target marketing for competitive advantage*. Routledge. DOI: 10.4324/9780203050095

Moula, H. S., Yaghoubyan, S. H., Malekhosseini, R., & Bagherifard, K. (2024). Customer type discovery in hotel revenue management: A data mining approach. *Journal of Revenue and Pricing Management, 23*(3), 238–248. DOI: 10.1057/s41272-024-00474-w

Muhammad, N., Scrimgeour, F., Reddy, K., & Abidin, S. (2015). The impact of corporate environmental performance on market risk: The Australian industry case. *Journal of Business Ethics, 132*(2), 347–362. DOI: 10.1007/s10551-014-2324-3

Musa, A., & Ibrahim, M. T. (2024). Does the effectiveness of risk management committee mitigate earnings management practices? Journal of International Business [JIBE]. *Economics and Entrepreneurship, 9*(1), 84–99.

Muslim, M. (2025). The failure of governance and internal controls in preventing fraud in the company. *Advances in Managerial Auditing Research, 3*(1), 15–29. DOI: 10.60079/amar.v3i1.418

Myers, L. A., Schmardebeck, R., Seidel, T. A., & Stuart, M. D. (2022). The impact of managerial discretion in revenue recognition: A reexamination. *Contemporary Accounting Research, 39*(3), 2130–2174. DOI: 10.1111/1911-3846.12775

Nababan, D. R., Situmorang, E., & Zelmiyanti, R. (2025). An analysis of the implementation of the job costing method in pricing determination at PT Banana Cake. *Journal Research of Social Science, Economics, and Management, 5*(4), 3954–3964. DOI: 10.59141/jrssem.v5i4.1180

Nagle, T. T., & Müller, G. (2018). *The strategy and tactics of pricing* (6th ed.). Routledge.

Narulita, F. D., Baderi, R., & Hidayati, C. (2025). The use of Big Data and business intelligence in management accounting decision making. *Journal of Advances in Accounting, Economics, and Management, 2*(4), 1–18. DOI: 10.47134/aaem.v2i4.706

Nazlan, N. H. (2024). The Effect of Price Transparency on Young Travellers' Choices: An Experimental Study of Resort Packages. *Information Management and Business Review, 16*(3), 1170–1179. DOI: 10.22610/imbr.v16i3S(I)a.4229

Nedzvedskyi, Y., Baneva, I., Kushniruk, V., Velychko, O., & Cherven, I. (2024). Financial planning and budget management in hospitality and dining establishments: Navigating the financial landscape of the hotel and restaurant sector.

Netemeyer, R. G., Krishnan, B., Pullig, C., Wang, G., Yagci, M., Dean, D., & Wirth, F. (2004). Developing and validating measures of facets of customer-based brand equity. *Journal of Business Research, 57*(2), 209–224. DOI: 10.1016/S0148-2963(01)00303-4

Noone, B. M., Enz, C. A., & Glassmire, J. (2017). Total hotel revenue management: A strategic profit perspective. *Cornell Hospitality Report, 17*(8), 3–14. https://hdl.handle.net/1813/70992

Noone, B. M., & Mattila, A. S. (2009). Hotel revenue management and the Internet: The effect of price presentation strategies on customers' willingness to book. *International Journal of Hospitality Management, 28*(2), 272–279. DOI: 10.1016/j.ijhm.2008.09.004

Noone, B. M., & McGuire, K. A. (2013). Pricing in a social world: The influence of non-price information on hotel choice. *Journal of Revenue and Pricing Management, 12*(5), 385–401. DOI: 10.1057/rpm.2013.13

Noone, B. M., McGuire, K. A., & Rohlfs, K. V. (2011). Social media meets hotel revenue management: Opportunities, issues and unanswered questions. *Journal of Revenue and Pricing Management, 10*(4), 293–305. DOI: 10.1057/rpm.2011.12

Novatiani, R. A., Kusumah, R. W. R., Yadiati, W., Rachmat, A. H., & Rachman, A. (2024). Internal auditor competence and internal control: Improving internal audit quality to prevent fraudulent financial statements. *Cogent Business & Management, 11*(1), 2409339. DOI: 10.1080/23311975.2024.2409339

Nowotny, S., Hirsch, B., & Nitzl, C. (2022). The influence of organizational structure on value-based management sophistication. *Management Accounting Research, 56*, 100797. DOI: 10.1016/j.mar.2022.100797

Nugraha, A. J. A., & Arifin, B. M. E. (2023). Financial and Cost-Volume-Profit Models in Developing a Hotel. Journal of Economics. *Management and Trade, 29*(12), 81–89.

Nunan, D., & Di Domenico, M. (2022). Value creation in an algorithmic world: Towards an ethics of dynamic pricing. *Journal of Business Research, 150*, 451–460. DOI: 10.1016/j.jbusres.2022.06.032

Nunes, C. R., & Machado, M. J. C. V. (2020). Benchmarking in the hotel industry: The use of USALI. *International Journal of Process Management and Benchmarking, 10*(3), 382–396. DOI: 10.1504/IJPMB.2020.107939

O'Connor, P. (2020). Online tourism and hospitality distribution: A perspective article. *Tourism Review, 75*(1), 290–293. DOI: 10.1108/TR-06-2019-0216

O'Connor, P., Assaker, G., & Haddad, R. E. (2025). Online travel agency participation: An empirical investigation of its financial contribution to US hotel profitability. *Cornell Hospitality Quarterly, 66*(4), 527–538. DOI: 10.1177/19389655251318185

OECD. (2015). *G20/OECD principles of corporate governance*. OECD Publishing.

Oh, H. J., Lee, B., Ma, H. H., Jang, D., & Park, S. (2024). A preliminary study for developing perceived ESG scale to measure public perception toward organizations' ESG performance. *Public Relations Review, 50*(1), 102398. DOI: 10.1016/j.pubrev.2023.102398

Oh, H., Fiore, A. M., & Jeoung, M. (2007). Measuring experience economy concepts: Tourism applications. *Journal of Travel Research, 46*(2), 119–132. DOI: 10.1177/0047287507304039

Oliver Yébenes, M. (2024). Climate change, ESG criteria and recent regulation: Challenges and opportunities. *Eurasian Economic Review, 14*(1), 87–120. DOI: 10.1007/s40822-023-00251-x

Orhan, B. K. (2025). SERVQUAL modeli çerçevesinde yüksek ve düşük fiyatlı otellerdeki olumsuz yorumların karşılaştırmalı analizi. *Ankara Hacı Bayram Veli Üniversitesi Turizm Fakültesi Dergisi, 28*(2), 99–130. DOI: 10.55931/ahbvtfd.1800722

Orkin, E. (2003). The emerging role of function space optimization in hotel revenue management. *Journal of Revenue and Pricing Management, 2*(2), 172–174. DOI: 10.1057/palgrave.rpm.5170063

Oses, N., Gerrikagoitia, J. K., & Alzua-Sorzabal, A. (2016). Modelling and prediction of a destination's monthly average daily rate and occupancy rate based on hotel room prices offered online. *Tourism Economics, 22*(6), 1380–1403. DOI: 10.5367/te.2015.0491

Osmanoğlu, Ş. (2019). *Konaklama işletmeleri rekabet ortamında getiri yönetimi uygulamaları* (Yüksek lisans tezi). İstanbul Üniversitesi, Sosyal Bilimler Enstitüsü.

Otley, D. (2016). The contingency theory of management accounting and control: 1980–2014. *Management Accounting Research, 31*, 45–62. DOI: 10.1016/j.mar.2016.02.001

Otoo, F. N. K., Kaur, M., & Rather, N. A. (2023). Evaluating the impact of internal control systems on organizational effectiveness. *LBS Journal of Management & Research, 21*(1), 135–154. DOI: 10.1108/LBSJMR-11-2022-0078

Özdemir, V., & Hekim, N. (2018). Birth of industry 5.0: Making sense of big data with artificial intelligence, the internet of things and next-generation technology policy. *Omics : A Journal of Integrative Biology, 22*(1), 65–76. DOI: 10.1089/omi.2017.0194 PMID: 29293405

Özsoy Erarslan, A. (2025). Getiri yönetimi. İçinde G. Deniz (Ed.), *İtibar ve getiri yönetimi: Büyük veri ve stratejik yaklaşımlarla teoriden uygulamaya* (ss. 16–23). Nevşehir Hacı Bektaş Veli Üniversitesi Yayınları.

Paiva, I., & Lourenço, I. (2016). Determinants of earnings management in the hotel industry: An international perspective. *Corporate Ownership and Control, 14*(1), 449–457. DOI: 10.22495/cocv14i1c3p5

Pajrok, A. (2022). Issue of allocation of overheads-the practice of the Hungarian hotel industry= Питання розподілу накладних витрат-практика готельної індустрії Угорщини= Általános költségek felosztásának kérdésköre-a magyar szállodaipar gyakorlata. *ACTA ACADEMIAE BEREGSASIENSIS-ECONOMICS*, (1), 297–311. DOI: 10.58423/2786-6742/2022-1-297-311

Palmer, A., & McMahon-Beattie, U. (2008). Variable pricing through revenue management: A critical evaluation of affective outcomes. *Management Research News, 31*(3), 189–199. DOI: 10.1108/01409170810851285

Papagianni, E., Evgenidis, A., Tsagkanos, A., & Megalooikonomou, V. (2024). Tourism demand in the face of geopolitical risk: Insights from a cross-country analysis. *Journal of Travel Research, 63*(8), 2094–2119. DOI: 10.1177/00472875231206539

Papatheodorou, A., & Tsiotsou, R. H. (2020). Seasonality in tourism: Trends, impacts, and strategic approaches. *Annals of Tourism Research, 81*, 124–137.

Pappa, E., Georgitseas, P., Tantis, G., & Kyriakogkonas, P. (2024). Audit ESG reports through blockchain technology in business enterprises. In *Business, Management and Economics: Research Progress* (Vol. 5, pp. 90–107). DOI: 10.9734/bpi/bmerp/v5/2628

Pappa, E., Filos, J., Garefalakis, A., & Kyriakogkonas, P. (2022). Implementing strategic management via code of ethics: A quantitative research on private sector in Greece. *Theoretical Economics Letters, 12*(4), 1126–1136. DOI: 10.4236/tel.2022.124061

Parmenter, D. (2015). *Key Performance Indicators: Developing, Implementing, and Using Winning KPIs* (3rd ed.). Wiley. DOI: 10.1002/9781119019855

Passas, I. (2023b). Accounting for integrity: ESG and financial disclosures: The challenge of internal fraud in management decision-making [Doctoral dissertation, Hellenic Mediterranean University]. DOI: 10.12681/eadd/55359

Passas, I., Ragazou, K., Giannopoulos, P., & Kagias, P. (2023a). CG and Viable Corporate Debt. In Governance and Financial Performance: Current Trends and Perspectives (pp. 155–170). World Scientific Publishing Co. DOI: 10.1142/9789811260506_0007

Passas, I. (2024). The Evolution of ESG: From CSR to ESG 2.0. *Encyclopedia, 4*(4), 1711–1720. DOI: 10.3390/encyclopedia4040112

Passas, I., & Garefalakis, A. (2025). The Impact of Fraud Perception and ESG-Washing on Investment Trust: Integrating Corporate Governance Theory and Empirical Evidence. *Accounting and Auditing, 1*(3), 9. DOI: 10.3390/accountaudit1030009

Pekdemir, T., & Küçükaltan, E. G. (2024). Organizational resilience and crisis management relationship on hospitality businesses. *İşletme Araştırmaları Dergisi, 16*(1), 206–222.

Pellinen, J. (2003). Making price decisions in tourism enterprises. *International Journal of Hospitality Management, 22*(2), 217–235. DOI: 10.1016/S0278-4319(03)00019-7

Pereira, L. N., & Cerqueira, V. (2022). Forecasting hotel demand for revenue management using machine learning regression methods. *Current Issues in Tourism, 25*(17), 2733–2750. DOI: 10.1080/13683500.2021.1999397

Petricek, M., Chalupa, S., & Melas, D. (2021). Model of price optimization as a part of hotel revenue management: Stochastic approach. *Mathematics, 9*(13), 1552. DOI: 10.3390/math9131552

Petrick, A., Steinhardt, C., Gönsch, J., & Klein, R. (2012). Using flexible products to cope with demand uncertainty in revenue management. *OR-Spektrum, 34*(1), 215–242. DOI: 10.1007/s00291-009-0188-1

Phillips, R. (2021). *Pricing and revenue optimization* (2nd ed.). Stanford University Press.

Pike, S., & Mason, R. (2011). Destination competitiveness through the lens of brand positioning: The case of Australia's Sunshine Coast. *Current Issues in Tourism, 14*(2), 169–182. DOI: 10.1080/13683501003797523

Pine, B. J., & Gilmore, J. H. (1998). The experience economy. *Harvard Business Review*, *76*(6), 18–23. PMID: 10181589

Pine, B. J., & Gilmore, J. H. (1999). *The experience economy*. Harvard Business School Press.

Ponte, E. B., Carvajal-Trujillo, E., & Escobar-Rodríguez, T. (2015). Influence of trust and perceived value on the intention to purchase travel online: Integrating the effects of assurance on trust antecedents. *Tourism Management*, *47*, 286–302. DOI: 10.1016/j.tourman.2014.10.009

Poretti, C., Jérôme, T., & Das, P. (2024). Plural form business strategy and financial reporting quality in hospitality firms. *Journal of Hospitality and Tourism Management*, *59*, 60–69. DOI: 10.1016/j.jhtm.2024.03.008

Post, C., & Byron, K. (2015). Women on boards and firm financial performance: A meta-analysis. *Academy of Management Journal*, *58*(5), 1546–1571. DOI: 10.5465/amj.2013.0319

Power, M. (1997). *The audit society: Rituals of verification*. Oxford University Press.

Prideaux, B. (2000). The role of the transport system in destination development. *Tourism Management*, *21*(1), 53–63. DOI: 10.1016/S0261-5177(99)00079-5

Putra, I. G. B. N. P., & Anggiriawan, I. P. B. (2025). Sustainable Hospitality in Bali: Synergy of Good Corporate Governance, Internal Control System, and Quadruple Bottom Line. *South Asian Journal of Social Studies and Economics*, *22*(11), 22–32. DOI: 10.9734/sajsse/2025/v22i111202

Qi, R., Jin, D., Chen, H., Mou, X., & Ali, F. (2024). Strategic-level perceived fairness of hotel dynamic pricing: the role of cues and the asymmetric moderating effect of inflation attribution. *Journal of Revenue and Pricing Management 2024 23:3*, *23*(3), 249–261. DOI: 10.1057/s41272-024-00479-5

Raab, C., Berezan, O., Christodoulidou, N., Jiang, L., & Shoemaker, S. (2018). Creating strategic relationships with online travel agents to drive hotel room revenue: An OTA perspective. *Journal of Hospitality and Tourism Technology*, *9*(1), 125–140. DOI: 10.1108/JHTT-10-2016-0069

Rafi, M. I. A., Aprelianingrum, A., Indraswari, S. A. D. T., Erong, E. A. E., Wicaksono, F., Putriani, A. A. Y., & Yovita, M. (2025). Hubungan Cost Estimation Reliability, Sales Volume Forecasting, Dan Cost Structure Flexibility Terhadap Keberhasilan Cost-Volume-Profit Analysis Sebagai Alat Perencanaan: The Relationship of Cost Estimation Reliability, Sales Volume Forecasting, and Cost Structure Flexibility to the Success of Cost-Volume-Profit Analysis as a Planning Tool. Citizen. *Jurnal Ilmiah Multidisiplin Indonesia*, *5*(6), 1680–1689.

Ragazou, K., Passas, I., Garefalakis, A., Galariotis, E., & Zopounidis, C. (2023). Big Data Analytics Applications in Information Management Driving Operational Efficiencies and Decision-Making: Mapping the Field of Knowledge with Bibliometric Analysis Using R. *Big Data and Cognitive Computing*, *7*(1), 13. DOI: 10.3390/bdcc7010013

Ramos, C. M. Q., Correia, M. B., Rodrigues, J. M. F., Martins, D., & Serra, F. (2015). Big data warehouse framework for smart revenue management. In *Advances in Environmental Science and Energy Planning* (pp. 13–22). *(Yayıncı bilgisi doğrulanmalı)*

Rao, A. R., & Monroe, K. B. (1989). The effect of price, brand name, and store name on buyers' perceptions of product quality. *JMR, Journal of Marketing Research*, *26*(3), 351–357.

Rasekh, L., & Li, Y. (2011). Golf course revenue management. *Journal of Revenue and Pricing Management*, *10*(2), 105–111. DOI: 10.1057/rpm.2009.44

Reem, M., Rasoolimanesh, S., & Wijesinghe, S. N. R. (2022). Sustainability indicators in hotels: A systematic literature review. *Asia-Pacific Journal of Innovation in Hospitality and Tourism*, *11*(1), 149–178.

Remy, D., Tan, S., Boo, H. C., & Tee, S. (2023). Revenue Management Metrics Study (Version 1). Singapore Institute of Technology. DOI: 10.25447/sit.24145212.v1

Remy, D., Boo, H. C., & Tee, S. W. W. (2023). From traditional to new hotel revenue management metrics. *Tourism and Hospitality Management*, *29*(2), 221–233. DOI: 10.20867/thm.29.2.6

Research Institute for Tourism. (2024). *ESG sustainability in the Greek hotel sector*.

Reuters. (2017, November 29). Indonesia reopens Bali airport as wind clears volcanic ash. *Reuters*.

Reuters. (2021, September 26). Airport closed as La Palma volcano eruption intensifies. *Reuters*.

Revenue Recognition. (n.d.). Retrieved September 2, 2026, from https://fasb.org/projects/recently-completed-projects/revenue-recognition-summary?utm_source=chatgpt.com

Risnawati, H., Sumarga, H. E., & Purwanto, S. (2019). The effect of service quality, prices, and location of companies on customer satisfaction and its implications for customer loyalty. [Sayfa aralığı doğrulanmalı]. *International Review of Management and Marketing*, *9*(6), 38–45. DOI: 10.32479/irmm.8736

Rohim, N. I., Rose, M., & Mayardit, F. K. (2024). Accounting information systems as a tool for effective petty cash control: Evidence from a hotel case study. *Journal of Islamic Economics Perspectives*, *6*(2), 117–127. DOI: 10.35719/11mxed32

Romney, M. B., & Steinbart, P. J. (2018). *Accounting information systems* (14th ed.). Pearson.

Roussy, M., & Brivot, M. (2016). Internal audit quality: A polysemous notion? *Accounting, Auditing & Accountability Journal*, *29*(5), 714–738. DOI: 10.1108/AAAJ-10-2014-1843

Sainaghi, R. (2010). Hotel performance: State of the art. *International Journal of Contemporary Hospitality Management*, *22*(7), 920–952. DOI: 10.1108/09596111011066617

Saitta, S., D'Amico, V., & Farinella, G. M. (2024). Dynamic Price Prediction for Revenue Management System in Hospitality Sector. In DATA (pp. 218-228). DOI: 10.5220/0012707700003756

Saleh, M. M. A., Jawabreh, O., & Abu-Eker, E. F. M. (2023). Factors of applying creative accounting and its impact on the quality of financial statements in Jordanian hotels. *Journal of Sustainable Finance & Investment*, *13*(1), 499–515. DOI: 10.1080/20430795.2021.1962662

Salsabila, D., & Islamudin, A. (2025). Analisis Sistem Pengendalian Internal pada Penerimaan Kas dan Verifikasi Invoice pada Hotel XYZ. *Jurnal Riset Rumpun Ilmu Ekonomi*, *4*(2), 507–516. DOI: 10.55606/jurrie.v4i2.6157

Santos, L. L., Silva, E., Gomes, C., & Malheiros, C. (2026). Rethinking revenue management in the tourism industry's new era. *International Journal of Marketing, Communication and New Media*. https://doi.org/DOI: 10.54663/2182-9306.2026.SpecialIssueCMTH.11-24

Santos, L., Malheiros, C., Gomes, C., & Guerra, T., 2020. TRevPAR as hotels performance evaluation indicator and influencing factors in Portugal. *EATSJ - Euro-Asia Tourism Studies Journal*, 1, 93–105. DOI: 10.58345/KQMJ7114

Sari, M. P., & Wibowo, W. A. (2025). Empirical analysis of hotel strategic management accounting practices. *Advances in Accounting Innovation, 1*(2), 167–177. DOI: 10.69725/aai.v1i2.192

Sarnıç, A. (2025). İşletme zekâsından yapay zekâya: Türkiye'nin hızlı büyüyen firmalarında yapay zekâ uygulamaları üzerine bir içerik analizi. *Nevşehir Hacı Bektaş Veli Üniversitesi SBE Dergisi*, (Sosyal Bilimlerde Yapay Zeka: Kuram, Uygulama ve Gelecek Perspektifleri), 300-319.

Sarvari, P. A., Ustundag, A., & Takci, H. (2016). Performance evaluation of different customer segmentation approaches based on RFM and demographics analysis. *Kybernetes, 45*(7), 1129–1157. DOI: 10.1108/K-07-2015-0180

Schwartz, Z., Altin, M., & Singal, M. (2017). Performance measures for strategic revenue management: Revpar versus goppar. *Journal of Revenue and Pricing Management, 16*(4), 357–375. DOI: 10.1057/rpm.2016.23

Şeker, A. (2025). Stratejik öneriler ve yol haritası. İçinde G. Deniz (Ed.), *İtibar ve getiri yönetimi* (ss. 67–78). Nevşehir Hacı Bektaş Veli Üniversitesi Yayınları.

Setiawan, F., & Saptutyningsih, E. (2022). Willingness to pay for destination quality improvement: Case study of Baru Beach, Yogyakarta. *Journal of Economics Research and Social Sciences, 6*(1), 31–43. DOI: 10.18196/jerss.v6i1.13363

Shah, M. S. M. (2025). A study on determinants of hotels' strategic choices: Collaboration or competition with OTAs in Srinagar. *The Quintessential*, 21–33. *(Dergi bilgisi doğrulanmalı)*

Shaikh, I. (2022). Environmental, social, and governance (ESG) practice and firm performance: An international evidence. *Journal of Business Economics and Management, 23*(1), 218–237. DOI: 10.3846/jbem.2022.16202

Shakya, J. (2025). Cost-volume-profit analysis for profit planning and control in hospitality industry: A study of Aloft, Kathmandu, Thamel. *MVIC Journal of Management and Information Technology, 1*(1), 63–76. DOI: 10.3126/mvicjmit.v1i1.77320

Sheng, J., Amankwah-Amoah, J., Khan, Z., & Wang, X. (2021). COVID-19 pandemic in the new era of big data analytics: Methodological innovations and future research directions. *British Journal of Management, 32*(4), 1164–1183. DOI: 10.1111/1467-8551.12441

Shleifer, A., & Vishny, R. W. (1997). A survey of corporate governance. *The Journal of Finance, 52*(2), 737–783. DOI: 10.1111/j.1540-6261.1997.tb04820.x

Shniekat, N., Jawabreh, O., & Saleh, M. M. A. (2021). Efficiency and effect on the competitive advantage of management information systems (MIS) in classified hotels in the city of Petra. Academy of Strategic Management Journal, 20(Special Issue 2), 1–12.

Shrestha, Y. R., Ben-Menahem, S. M., & von Krogh, G. (2019). Organizational decision-making structures in the age of artificial intelligence. *California Management Review*, *61*(4), 66–83. DOI: 10.1177/0008125619862257

Siddappa, S. (2006). *Statistical modeling approach to airline revenue management with overbooking* (Doctoral dissertation, The University of Texas at Arlington).

Sigala, M. (2020). Tourism and COVID-19: Impacts and implications for advancing and resetting industry and research. *Journal of Business Research*, *117*, 312–321. DOI: 10.1016/j.jbusres.2020.06.015 PMID: 32546875

Silveira, L., Santos, N., & Moreira, C. O. (2023). The liberalisation of air transport and the impacts on travel and tourism: The case of the Azores Archipelago. *Sustainability (Basel)*, *15*(5), 4488. DOI: 10.3390/su15054488

Silvestre, P., Antonio, N., & Carrasco, P. (2026). Navigating uncertainty: Enhancing hotel cancellation predictions with adaptive machine learning. *Information Technology & Tourism*, *28*(1), 9. DOI: 10.1007/s40558-025-00349-9

Singal, M. (2015). How is the hospitality and tourism industry different? An empirical test of some structural characteristics. *International Journal of Hospitality Management*, *47*, 116–119. DOI: 10.1016/j.ijhm.2015.03.006

Sitzimis, I. (2026). Air tourism as a driver of coastal and ferry transport demand in Greece: A quantitative assessment. *Case Studies on Transport Policy*, *23*, 101688. DOI: 10.1016/j.cstp.2025.101688

Sjäfjell, B., & Tsagas, G. (2022). Integrating sustainable value creation in corporate governance: Company law, corporate governance codes and the constitution of the company. In Sjäfjell, B., Tsagas, G., & Villiers, C. (Eds.), *Sustainable value creation in the EU: Towards pathways to a sustainable future through crises* (pp. 209–236). Cambridge University Press. DOI: 10.1017/9781009243841.014

Smith, B. C., Leimkuhler, J. F., & Darrow, R. M. (1992). Yield management at American Airlines. *Interfaces*, *22*(1), 8–31. DOI: 10.1287/inte.22.1.8

Smithson, S., Devece, C. A., & Lapiedra, R. (2011). Online visibility as a source of competitive advantage for small- and medium-sized tourism accommodation enterprises. *Service Industries Journal*, *31*(10), 1573–1587. DOI: 10.1080/02642069.2010.485640

Sohn, J., Tang, C., & Jang, S. (2011). Asset sales and earnings management in the U.S. hotel industry. *The Journal of Hospitality Financial Management.*

Song, H., & Li, G. (2008). Tourism demand modelling and forecasting: A review of recent research. *Tourism Management, 29*(2), 203–220. DOI: 10.1016/j.tourman.2007.07.016

Song, H., Witt, S. F., & Li, G. (2008). *The advanced econometrics of tourism demand.* Routledge. DOI: 10.4324/9780203891469

Sönmez Karapınar, E. (2024). Dijital pazarlama. İçinde Ş. Karaca (Ed.), *Turizm ve dijital pazarlama: Teori ve uygulamalar* (s. 35). Özgür Yayınları. https://doi.org/ DOI: 10.58830/ozgur.pub603.c2539

Spira, L. F., & Page, M. (2003). Risk management: The reinvention of internal control and the changing role of internal audit. *Accounting, Auditing & Accountability Journal, 16*(4), 640–661. DOI: 10.1108/09513570310492335

Srijuntrapun, P., Sukwong, P., & Marshall, A. (2022). The role of food waste hierarchy as Thai hotels seek to fulfill their corporate social responsibility. *Heliyon, 8*(10), e11201. DOI: 10.1016/j.heliyon.2022.e11201 PMID: 36303920

Srivastava, A. (2013). Selling-price estimates in revenue recognition and earnings informativeness. Social Science Research Network. https://doi.org/DOI: 10.2139/ssrn.1078584

Stavropoulou, E., Spinthiropoulos, K., Ragazou, K., Papademetriou, C., & Passas, I. (2023). Green Balanced Scorecard: A Tool of Sustainable Information Systems for an Energy Efficient Business. *Energies, 16*(18), 6432. DOI: 10.3390/en16186432

Strauss, A. K. (2009). *Optimisation in choice-based network revenue management.* Lancaster University.

Suhaemi, U., & Hidayah, N. (2025). Earnings management: The role of corporate governance, reputation, and financial distress. *Neraca Keuangan, 20*(2), 353–359. DOI: 10.32832/neraca.v20i2.19840

Suno Wu, J., Barbrook-Johnson, P., Font, X., & Torres-Delgado, A. (2024). Combining realist evaluation and appreciative inquiry: A participatory, learning-focused methodology for tourism interventions. *Annals of Tourism Research Empirical Insights, 5*(2), 100152. DOI: 10.1016/j.annale.2024.100152

Sun, X., Jiao, Y., & Tian, P. (2011). Marketing research and revenue optimization for the cruise industry: A concise review. *International Journal of Hospitality Management, 30*(3), 746–755. DOI: 10.1016/j.ijhm.2010.11.007

Susilowati, E. (2023). Cost management and strategic decision making: The role of managerial accounting. Atestasi. *Jurnal Ilmiah Akuntansi*, *6*(1), 457–473.

Suwandi, S., Manurung, R., & Ibrokhimov, N. (2024). The role of managerial accounting information in enhancing financial performance and decision-making of micro enterprises. Harmoni Economics. *International Journal of Economics and Accounting*, *1*(1), 1–10.

Suwitri, S. A. N., Gede, I. G. K., & Wajdi, M. (2025). Enhancing hospitality business visibility through strategic search engine optimization (SEO) implementation in digital marketing platforms. *Journal of Commerce, Management, and Tourism Studies*, *4*(2), 272–286. DOI: 10.58881/jcmts.v4i2.370

Swalih, M. M., Ram, R., & Tew, E. (2024). Environmental management accounting for strategic decision-making: A systematic literature review. *Business Strategy and the Environment*, *33*(7), 6335–6367. DOI: 10.1002/bse.3828

Syahputri, W. D., Midiastuty, P. P., Suranta, E., & Putra, D. A. (2023). Earnings management before, during, and after COVID-19 in the hospitality sector. *Ilomata International Journal of Tax and Accounting*, *5*(1), 60–76. DOI: 10.52728/ijtc.v5i1.1000

Szerb, L., & Gábor, I. (2022). Sustainable hospitality and tourism: Integrating corporate governance into strategic decision-making. *Sustainability*, *14*(5), 2207.

Talal, M., Garfan, S., Qays, R., Pamucar, D., Delen, D., Pedrycz, W., & Simic, V. (2025). A comprehensive systematic review on machine learning application in the 5G-RAN architecture: Issues, challenges, and future directions. *Journal of Network and Computer Applications*, *233*, 104041. DOI: 10.1016/j.jnca.2024.104041

Taliani, E. C. (2015). *Revenue management impact on management control systems.* Revista de la Facultad de Ciencias Económicas., DOI: 10.18359/rfce.1623

Talluri, K. T., & Van Ryzin, G. J. (2004). *The theory and practice of revenue management.* Springer., DOI: 10.1007/b139000

Talón-Ballestero, P., González-Serrano, L., Flecha-Barrio, M. D., & Orea-Giner, A. (2023). Revenue management strategies during the COVID-19 crisis. *International Marketing Review*. Advance online publication. DOI: 10.1108/IMR-12-2021-0387

Talón-Ballestero, P., González-Serrano, L., Soguero-Ruiz, C., Muñoz-Romero, S., & Rojo-Álvarez, J. L. (2018). Using big data from Customer Relationship Management Information Systems to determine the client profile in the hotel sector. *Tourism Management*, *68*, 187–197. DOI: 10.1016/j.tourman.2018.03.017

Talón-Ballestero, P., Nieto-García, M., & González-Serrano, L. (2022). The wheel of dynamic pricing: Towards open pricing and one to one pricing in hotel revenue management. *International Journal of Hospitality Management, 102*, 103184. DOI: 10.1016/j.ijhm.2022.103184

Tan, J., & Dwyer, L. (2014). Managing distribution channel conflict in the hotel industry. [Sayfa aralığı doğrulanmalı]. *International Journal of Marketing & Business Communication, 3*(1), 1–10.

Tarakçı, İ. E., & Göktaş, B. (2020). Turizm işletmelerinde hizmet hataları ve hizmet telafisi yöntemlerinin müşteri memnuniyeti üzerindeki etkisi: Bir uygulama. *Türk Turizm Araştırmaları Dergisi, 4*(1), 259–278. DOI: 10.26677/TR1010.2020.311

Tascón, M. T., Castro, P., & Valdunciel, L. (2024). Effects of financial restrictions on firms' financial resilience against the COVID-19 pandemic: Evidence from the European hospitality industry. *Applied Economics, 56*(58), 8226–8241. DOI: 10.1080/00036846.2023.2289951

Tehranian, H., Cornett, M. M., Marcus, A. J., & Saunders, A. (2006). Earnings management, corporate governance, and true financial performance. Social Science Research Network. https://doi.org/DOI: 10.2139/ssrn.886142

Tek, Ö. B. (1999). *Pazarlama ilkeleri*. Beta Yayınları.

Temel, E., & Anbarcı, M. (2025). Yoksa rasyonel tüketici eğilimleri de esasında hedonik mi? Tüketicilerin rasyonel satın alma eğilimleri ve haz üzerine fenomenolojik bir çözümleme. *Kapadokya Akademik Bakış, 9*(1), 38–70. DOI: 10.69851/car.1660721

Thanh, T. V., & Kirova, V. (2018). Wine tourism experience: A netnography study. *Journal of Business Research, 83*, 30–37. DOI: 10.1016/j.jbusres.2017.10.008

Tiwari, V. (2024). Role of data analytics in business decision making. *Knowledgeable Research A Multidisciplinary Journal, 3*(01), 18-27.

Tonidandel, S., King, E. B., & Cortina, J. M. (2018). Big data methods: Leveraging modern data analytic techniques to build organizational science. *Organizational Research Methods, 21*(3), 525–547. DOI: 10.1177/1094428116677299

Toukabri, M., & Chaouachi, M. (2025). Exploring the Influence of Corporate Social Responsibility, Blockchain Transparency, and Cultural Alignment on Consumer Trust and Premium Pricing Willingness for Local Food in Saudi Arabia. *Current Research in Nutrition and Food Science, 13*(1), 304–316. DOI: 10.12944/CRNFSJ.13.1.20

Trans Maldivian Airways. (n.d.). *Frequently asked questions.* Trans Maldivian Airways.

Tranter, K. A., Stuart-Hill, T., & Parker, J. (2009). *An introduction to revenue management for the hospitality industry: Principles and practice for the real world.* Pearson.

Tse, T. S., & Poon, Y. T. (2012). Revenue management: Resolving a revenue optimization paradox. *International Journal of Contemporary Hospitality Management, 24*(4), 507–521. DOI: 10.1108/09596111211226798

Tuomi, A., Ashton, M., & Ivanov, S. (2026). Dynamic price differentiation in restaurant revenue management. *International Journal of Revenue Management, 16*(5), 10080199. Advance online publication. DOI: 10.1504/IJRM.2026.10080199

Turner, M. J. (2013). Hotel management contracts: A particularly rich research context. Journal of Hotel and Business Management. https://doi.org/DOI: 10.4172/2169-0286.1000e107

Turner, M. J., & Guilding, C. J. (2011). Motivations of hotel owners and operators to engage in earnings management. *Qualitative Research in Accounting & Management, 8*(4), 358–381. DOI: 10.1108/11766091111189882

Uladi, A. İ., & Arı, E. S. (2023). Büyük veri, büyük veri analizi ve uygulama alanları. *Yönetim Bilişim Sistemleri Dergisi, 9*(1), 1–14.

Ulucan, E., & Kızılırmak, İ. (2018). Konaklama işletmelerinde talep tahmin yöntemleri: Yapay sinir ağları ile ilgili bir araştırma. *Seyahat ve Otel İşletmeciliği Dergisi, 15*(1), 89–101. DOI: 10.24010/soid.415343

Ünal, S., & Sezgin, A. A. (2021). Büyük veri (big data)'nin yapay zeka uygulamalarında toplumsal sınıflandırmaya yönelik kaygılar. *AJIT-e: Academic Journal of Information Technology, 12*(44), 47–70. DOI: 10.5824/ajite.2021.01.004.x

Uniform System of Accounts for the Lodging Industry | HFTP. (n.d.). Retrieved September 2, 2026, from https://usali.hftp.org/

UNWTO. (2021). *International tourism and COVID-19 impact report.* World Tourism Organization.

Ural, T. (2008). Değer temelli fiyatlama: Ürünün tüketici değer algısına göre fiyatlanması. *Anadolu Üniversitesi Sosyal Bilimler Dergisi, 8*(2), 1–16.

Uyar, A., Kilic, M., Koseoglu, M. A., Kuzey, C., & Karaman, A. S. (2020). The link among board characteristics, corporate social responsibility performance, and financial performance: Evidence from the hospitality and tourism industry. *Tourism Management Perspectives, 35*, 100714. DOI: 10.1016/j.tmp.2020.100714

Uyun, L. (2025). The role of big data in managerial accounting decision-making: A literature review. Count: Journal of Accounting. *Business and Management*, *3*(2), 78–88.

Vallen, G., & Cadado, M. (2000). Ethical principles for the hospitality curriculum. *The Cornell Hotel and Restaurant Administration Quarterly*, *41*(2), 44–51. DOI: 10.1177/001088040004100216

Van Ryzin, G. J., & Talluri, K. T. (2005). An introduction to revenue management. In *Emerging theory, methods, and applications* (pp. 142–194). Informs.

Vasarhelyi, M. A., Kogan, A., & Tuttle, B. M. (2015). Big data in accounting: An overview. *Accounting Horizons*, *29*(2), 381–396. DOI: 10.2308/acch-51071

Verhoef, P. C., Kannan, P. K., & Inman, J. J. (2015). From multi-channel retailing to omni-channel retailing. *Journal of Retailing*, *91*(2), 174–181. DOI: 10.1016/j.jretai.2015.02.005

Vinod, B. (2022). Introduction to hotel revenue management. *Management for Professionals*, 1–50. DOI: 10.1007/978-3-031-14302-1_1

Vives, A., Jacob, M., & Payeras, M. (2018). Revenue management and price optimization techniques in the hotel sector: A critical literature review. *Tourism Economics*, *24*(6), 720–752. DOI: 10.1177/1354816618777590

Vortelinos, D., Floros, C., Apostolakis, A., & Passas, I. (2025). Hotel Sales During COVID-19. In Dimotikalis, Y., & Skiadas, C. (Eds.), *Data Analysis and Related Applications 5: Models, Methods and Techniques* (Vol. 13, pp. 333–348). Wiley., DOI: 10.1002/9781394401604.ch21

Vortelinos, D., Passas, I., Floros, C., & Garefalakis, A. (2024). Corporate Social Responsibility and Country Governance: An International Comparative Study Amid the COVID-19 Pandemic. *International Journal of Financial Studies*, *12*(4), 110. DOI: 10.3390/ijfs12040110

Voss, G. B., Parasuraman, A., & Grewal, D. (1998). The roles of price, performance, and expectations in determining satisfaction in service exchanges. *Journal of Marketing*, *62*(4), 46–61. DOI: 10.1177/002224299806200404

Voukkali, I., Papamichael, I., Loizia, P., & Zorpas, A. A. (2023). The importance of KPIs to calibrate waste strategy in hospitality sector. *Energy Nexus*, *11*, 100211. Advance online publication. DOI: 10.1016/j.nexus.2023.100211

Vrionis, I. A., & Varelas, S. (2026). Implementing Sustainable Habits in Dynamic Pricing Through Revenue Management Strategies in the Hotel Industry—A Literature Review. *Springer Proceedings in Business and Economics*, 761–768. https://doi.org/DOI: 10.1007/978-3-032-12968-0_83/SAVE-RESEARCH

Vukolić, D., Gajić, T., Cabral, Ó., Veljović, S., & Knežević, S. (2025). Revolutionizing the hospitality industry: The impact of AI technologies on efficient food management and reduction of food waste. Journal of Tourism Futures, 1-29.

Vukotić, S., Mirčetić, V., Arsić, M., & Karabašević, D. (2026). Smart hospitality in the 6G era: The role of AI and terahertz communication in next-generation hotel infrastructure. *WORLD (Oakland, Calif.)*, *7*(1), 4. DOI: 10.3390/world7010004

Wamsler, J., Natter, M., & Algesheimer, R. (2022). Transitioning to dynamic prices: Should pricing authority remain with the company or be delegated to the service employees instead? *Journal of Business Research*, *139*, 1476–1488. DOI: 10.1016/j.jbusres.2021.10.067

Wang, X. L., Heo, C. Y., Schwartz, Z., Legohérel, P., & Specklin, F. (2015). Revenue management: Progress, challenges, and research prospects. *Journal of Travel & Tourism Marketing*, *32*(7), 797–811. DOI: 10.1080/10548408.2015.1063798

Wang, Z., Dong, X., & Yin, J. (2018). Antecedents of urban residents' separate collection intentions for household solid waste and their willingness to pay: Evidence from China. *Journal of Cleaner Production*, *173*, 256–264. DOI: 10.1016/j.jclepro.2016.09.223

Wardana, W. W., Haryanto, T., Jamil, I. R., Ismail, N. A., Heriqbaldi, U., Correa, E., Rohmah, W. N., & Ajija, S. R. (2025). Does improved accessibility translate into tourism growth? A difference-in-differences analysis of bridge infrastructure in Indonesia. *Annals of Tourism Research Empirical Insights*, *6*(2), 100189. DOI: 10.1016/j.annale.2025.100189

Weatherford, L. R., & Kimes, S. E. (2003). A comparison of forecasting methods for hotel revenue management. *International Journal of Forecasting*, *19*(3), 401–415. DOI: 10.1016/S0169-2070(02)00011-0

Webster, C., & Ivanov, S. (2020). Demographic change as a driver for tourism automation. *Journal of Tourism Futures*, *6*(3), 263–270. DOI: 10.1108/JTF-10-2019-0109

Wertenbroch, K., & Skiera, B. (2002). Measuring consumers' willingness to pay at the point of purchase. *JMR, Journal of Marketing Research*, *39*(2), 228–241. DOI: 10.1509/jmkr.39.2.228.19086

Weygandt, J. J., Kimmel, P. D., & Kieso, D. E. (2019). *Financial accounting* (10th ed.). Wiley.

Wibawa, K. D., & Septianto, T. (2024). Unlocking sustainable development: ASEAN ESG and economic growth implication. *Advances in Environmental Innovation, 1*(2), 176–188.

Xia, L., Monroe, K. B., & Cox, J. L. (2004). The price is unfair! A conceptual framework of price fairness perceptions. *Journal of Marketing, 68*(4), 1–15. DOI: 10.1509/jmkg.68.4.1.42733

Xiang, Z., Schwartz, Z., Gerdes, J., & Uysal, M. (2021). What can big data and text analytics tell us about hotel guest experience? *International Journal of Hospitality Management.*

Xiao, W., Zhang, S., Huang, Z., & Yu, Y. (2024, May). Multi-scenario pricing for hotel revenue management. In *Proceedings of the ACM Web Conference 2024* (pp. 3986-3994). DOI: 10.1145/3589334.3645350

Xiao, Z., Li, Y., Liu, X., & Gong, X. (2025). The impact of compensation information transparency on guest booking behavior in the home-sharing economy: An asymmetric information perspective. *International Journal of Contemporary Hospitality Management, 37*(12), 3897–3916. DOI: 10.1108/IJCHM-01-2025-0138

Yadav, S. J. (2025). Digital Platforms and Open Innovation: How Online Travel Agencies Shape the Future of Hospitality. In *Open Innovation and Technology in Tourism and Hospitality* (pp. 75-92). IGI Global Scientific Publishing.

Yang, Y., Nieto García, M., Viglia, G., & Nicolau, J. L. (2022). Competitors or complements: A meta-analysis of the effect of Airbnb on hotel performance. *Journal of Travel Research, 61*(7), 1508–1527. DOI: 10.1177/00472875211042670

Yao, D. Q., Wang, Z., Mukhopadhyay, S., & Cong, Y. (2012). Dynamic pricing strategy for subscription-based information goods. *Journal of Revenue and Pricing Management, 11*(2), 210–224. DOI: 10.1057/rpm.2010.48

Yarlagadda, K. C.KRISHNA CHAITANYA YARLAGADDA. (2025). AI-driven dynamic pricing: Optimizing revenue in digital marketplaces. *World Journal of Advanced Engineering Technology and Sciences, 15*(02), 2147–2157. DOI: 10.30574/wjaets.2025.15.2.0681

Yassin, M. M., Shaban, O. S., Al-Sraheen, D. A. O., & Daoud, K. A. A. (2022). Revenue standards and earnings management during COVID-19: IFRS versus GAAP. *Journal of Governance and Regulation, 11*(2), 80–93. DOI: 10.22495/jgrv11i2art7

Yeh, C. M. (2019). Ownership structure and firm performance of listed tourism firms. *International Journal of Tourism Research, 21*(2), 165–179. DOI: 10.1002/jtr.2250

Yelkur, R., & Nêveda DaCosta, M. M. (2001). Differential pricing and segmentation on the Internet: The case of hotels. *Management Decision, 39*(4), 252–262. DOI: 10.1108/00251740110391411

Yemer, M., & Chekol, F. (2017). The effect of internal controls systems on hotels revenue: A case of hotels in Bahir Dar and Gondar cities. [Oman Chapter]. *Arabian Journal of Business and Management Review, 6*(6), 19–37.

Yeoman, I. (2025). Expanding the frontiers of revenue and pricing management. *Journal of Revenue and Pricing Management, 24*(6), 503–505. DOI: 10.1057/s41272-025-00563-4

Yiğit, B. B. (2024). Fiyatlandırma stratejileri. İçinde Ö. S. Aykaç & A. Yılmaz (Ed.), *Pazarlama ve perakendecilik: Dijital çağın dönüşümleri* (ss. 103–130). Özgür Yayınları.

Yıldıztekin, İ. (2010). Konaklama hizmetlerinde maliyete dayalı fiyatlama ve fiyat değişiminin bölüm karlılığına etkileri. *Atatürk Üniversitesi İktisadi ve İdari Bilimler Dergisi, 23*(4), 215–240.

Young, M. N., Peng, M. W., Ahlstrom, D., Bruton, G. D., & Jiang, Y. (2008). Corporate governance in emerging economies: A review of the principal–principal perspective. *Journal of Management Studies, 45*(1), 196–220. DOI: 10.1111/j.1467-6486.2007.00752.x

Yu, J., Chiriko, A. Y., Kim, S. S., Moon, H. G., Choi, H., & Han, H. (2025). ESG management of hotel brands: A management strategy for benefits and performance. *International Journal of Hospitality Management, 125*, 103998. DOI: 10.1016/j.ijhm.2024.103998

Yu, J., Kim, S., Chiriko, A. Y., Moon, H. G., Choi, H., & Han, H. (2024). Environmental, social, and governance (ESG) in the hotel industry: A strategy for brand management, brand tribalism, and brand choice. *Journal of Travel & Tourism Marketing, 41*(9), 1226–1243. DOI: 10.1080/10548408.2024.2406346

Yulianti, R., Maryam, M., Hamdiah, C., Mahdi, M., & Khairuna, K. (2024). The role of internal control systems and good corporate governance in fraud prevention efforts: A literature review. *Frontiers in Business and Economics, 3*(1), 39–54. DOI: 10.56225/finbe.v3i1.325

Yurtlu, M., & Ateş, A. (2019). Online kanal yöneticisiyle otel oda fiyatlandırmada verim yönetimi. *Seyahat ve Otel İşletmeciliği Dergisi, 16*(2), 207–228. DOI: 10.24010/soid.471106

Zaki, K. (2022). Implementing dynamic revenue management in hotels during COVID-19: Value stream and wavelet coherence perspectives. *International Journal of Contemporary Hospitality Management, 34*(5), 1768–1795. DOI: 10.1108/IJCHM-08-2021-1043

Zaki, K. (2025). Revenue management reinvented: Leveraging technical know-how to unlock hotel efficiency. *Tourism and Hospitality Management, 32*(1). Advance online publication. DOI: 10.20867/thm.32.1.9

Zattoni, A., Dedoulis, E., Leventis, S., & Van Ees, H. (2020). Corporate governance and institutions: A review and research agenda. *Corporate Governance, 28*(6), 465–487. DOI: 10.1111/corg.12347

Zeithaml, V. A. (1988). Consumer perceptions of price, quality, and value: A means-end model and synthesis of evidence. *Journal of Marketing, 52*(3), 2–22. DOI: 10.1177/002224298805200302

Zhang, B., & Jung, S. (2026). How environmental, social, and governance (ESG) activities relate to hotel booking intentions: Evidence from PLS-SEM and fsQCA. *Sustainability (Basel), 18*(1), 325. DOI: 10.3390/su18010325

Zhang, Y., & Kim, H. (2022). ESG and profitability: Evidence from the hospitality industry. *Sustainability, 14*(1), 178.

Zhao, Q. (2024). Exploration on the protection of consumer rights and interests in big data price discrimination. *International Journal of Frontiers in Sociology, 6*(4), 15–20.

Zhyvko, Z., Rodchenko, S., & Holovach, T. (2023). EFFECTIVENESS OF INFORMATION SUPPORT FOR MANAGERIAL COLLABORATION AMONG HOSPITALITY INDUSTRY ENTERPRISES. Economics. *Finance and Management Review*, (4), 108–123.

Zientara, P., Adamska, J., & Bąk, M. (2025). *Social sustainability and the employee: Labor, employment relations, and the hospitality industry*. Routledge. DOI: 10.4324/9781003534266

About the Contributors

Ioannis Passas serves as an Assistant Professor in the Department of Business Administration and Tourism. He holds a PhD in Financial Accounting and Auditing from the same Department, where he teaches accounting courses at both undergraduate and postgraduate levels. In parallel, he teaches at Neapolis University Pafos in the postgraduate program entitled Forensic Accounting. He holds a range of internationally recognized professional certifications, including Certified Internal Control Auditor (CICA) and Certified Control Specialist (CCS) from the Institute for Internal Controls (IIC), the Certified Management Accountant (CMA) designation from the Institute of Chartered Accountants, as well as official certification as an Internal Auditor by the Hellenic State. In addition, he is certified by ACCA in accounting, finance, and sustainability-related subjects. His scholarly work has been presented at international conferences and published in numerous peer-reviewed academic journals, as well as in books and edited international volumes. He is the author of six academic books in his native language: five in the fields of Accounting and Managerial Accounting, and one in Research Methodology. His research interests focus on Financial Accounting, Auditing, CSR/ESG, financial integrity, and corporate governance. He also examines issues related to the quality of financial statements, disclosure mechanisms, and the functioning of accountability systems.

Markos Kourgiantakis is an Associate Professor at the Department of Business Administration and Tourism, Hellenic Mediterranean University, Crete, Greece. His research interests focus on e-business, marketing, consumer behaviour, revenue management and tourism marketing. He has publications on these topics in a range of scientific journals and has been involved in several related research projects. He has extensive experience as a business consultant.

Panagiotis Kyriakogkonas is an Associate Professor in Accounting and Finance at the University of Western Macedonia, with extensive academic and professional experience in internal auditing, corporate governance, and risk management. He is a

Certified Internal Auditor (CIA), CGAP, and CCSA, and has held senior internal audit and quality assurance roles in major Greek corporate groups. His research focuses on internal audit effectiveness, fraud and corruption prevention, ESG, and governance frameworks, with publications in internationally peer-reviewed journals and contributions to academic books.

Alexandros Garefalakis is a Certified Internal Controls Auditor (CICA), Certified Public Accountant (Fellow of CPA), Management Accountant (CMA), Certified Controls Specialist (CCS), and Business Consultant in numerous companies, organizations, and European programs since 2006. Additionally, he is an Associate Professor at the Dept. of Business Administration and Tourism at Hellenic Mediterranean University (HMU) in Greece. He holds a degree in Financial Applications, a Master degree in Accounting and Finance from University of Southampton and PhD in Accounting from Hellenic Open University. He has co-authored 11 books on Audit Accounting and Management Accounting issues. He has more than 100 publications in peer reviewed journals and participation in more than 40 national and international conferences. As well, he has been awarded first prize in innovation competition "Young Businessman" for the Intelligent Qualitative Analysis Database (AIQAD) and the Ma.Co.I index he has developed at 2003. He has eighteeeighteen (18) years of academic teaching experience (in undergraduate and postgraduate programs) and his areas of research interest include the Disclosure Narrative information, ESG, I.F.R.S, Management Commentary Index (Ma.Co.I), Auditing, Quality of Financial Statements, Weighting models in Accounting, Accounting and Operation Research, Multiple Criteria Decision-Making in Management Accounting.

***

Muhammad Azizurrohman is a lecturer at the Tourism Department of STP Mataram (Sekolah Tinggi Pariwisata Mataram), Indonesia. He is also a consultant for the Government of West Nusa Tenggara (NTB), contributing to tourism development and policy planning in the region. In addition to his academic and consulting roles, he serves as an editor and reviewer for several national and international academic journals. He obtained his Bachelor's degree in Development Economics from Universitas Muhammadiyah Yogyakarta, Indonesia. He later completed his Master's degree in Tourism and Management at National Chiayi University, Taiwan. He is currently pursuing his doctoral degree in Business and Management at Southern Taiwan University of Science and Technology, Taiwan. His research interests focus on tourism studies, particularly tourism policy, tourism management, sustainable tourism development, and community-based tourism. His work has been published in various national and international journals and contributes to the development of tourism strategies and policy frameworks, especially in Indonesia and the Southeast Asian region

Gaye Deniz is an Associate Professor at Nevşehir Hacı Bektaş Veli University. She completed her master's degree in Tourism and Hotel Management at Anadolu University and her Ph.D. in Business Administration at Gazi University. From 2004 to 2009, she gained experience in the private sector. Since 2009, she has served in the Faculty of Tourism, attaining her Associate Professor title in 2024. Her research interests focus on tourism management, hotel management, organizational behavior, and cultural heritage tourism.

Lokeshwari D. V. is an Assistant Professor in the Department of Commerce and Management at Dayananda Sagar College of Arts, Science, and Commerce, Bengaluru, India, with more than seven years of experience in teaching and academic administration. She has taught across undergraduate and postgraduate programmes and has held key institutional roles, including AICTE Coordinator, Placement Officer, BBA Programme Coordinator, IQAC Committee Member, and PG Department In-Charge (M.Com.). She is an active researcher with publications in reputed journals, conference proceedings, books, and book chapters, and holds two patents. Her research focuses on financial literacy, sustainable finance, artificial intelligence in financial inclusion, behavioural finance, and educational technology. She also contributes to the scholarly community as a reviewer and invited speaker at academic and professional forums.

Friday Edeh is an academic scholar and researcher with a strong focus on organizational behavior, management, leadership, human resource dynamics, and resilience in both corporate and hospitality sector contexts. He serves as a Senior Lecturer and Associate Dean of Research at the Department of Research and Innovations, College of Economics and Management, Kampala International University (Main Campus) in Uganda. He is also active as a post-doctoral researcher and engaged in international academic collaborations, including affiliations with universities such as INTI International University in Malaysia.

Reynal Fernandes Ph.D. in Commerce at CHRIST University. Her research areas are in Accounting and Finance with respect to the prediction of financial distress and the Restructuring of Companies. She has presented papers at several national and international conferences. Her area of interest is to find a solution for bankrupt companies through Machine learning techniques. Based on her research interest, she is currently working on a restructuring model for financially distressed companies in India through the application of Machine Learning Algorithms in her Ph.D.

Siriyama Herath is an Associate Professor of Accounting at Clark Atlanta University. Her academic distinction was highlighted in 2022 when she was named a Renwick Faculty Fellow at New York University's Stern School of Business. She holds impressive academic credentials, including a Ph.D. and MCOM Honors in Accounting from the University of Wollongong in Australia, and an MBA and BCOM (Hons) from the University of Colombo in Sri Lanka. Her extensive experience includes faculty roles at numerous institutions, such as the University of Lynchburg, Georgia State University, Georgia Institute of Technology, and several universities internationally. A prolific researcher, Dr. Herath has contributed over 70 publications, including 20 book chapters, with research focused on key areas like Accounting Education, Management Control, Data Analytics, and Sustainability Accounting. Her commitment to the field is further demonstrated by her current role as Editor-In-Chief for both the Asian Journal of Economics and Business and the Global Journal of Accounting and Economy Research, and her service on other editorial boards. She also holds a TESOL Professional Certificate from Arizona State University and the Professional Certificate in Google Data Analytics. Furthermore, she is a Distinguished Toastmaster (DTM) and has held leadership positions within Toastmasters International, serving as an Area Director and as President and Treasurer for the Georgia Institute of Technology club.

Husmaruddin Husmaruddin is an academic and currently serves as a lecturer concentrating in public sector financial management at the Faculty of Economics and Business at Muhammadiyah University of Palopo. He also actively provides assistance in local government financial management in South Sulawesi to create a pro-people regional budget (APBD). His academic qualifications are extensive, including a Bachelor of Economics, a Master of Management, and a Doctorate in Management from the Muslim University of Indonesia, Makassar. Husmaruddin is also a certified specialist in Artificial Intelligence (C.AIP) from the National Board of Directors (BNSP). Furthermore, he has authored several publications on management and made significant contributions to the academic community. His passion for reading, writing, and traveling reflects his commitment to lifelong learning and professional growth in his field.

Rizwan Khan is an Assistant Professor of Accounting and Finance with over nine years of academic and research experience. He holds a Ph.D. in Commerce from Aligarh Muslim University and is UGC-NET qualified. His research focuses on fintech, artificial intelligence in finance, Central Bank Digital Currencies (CBDC), and sustainable financial systems. He has published in Scopus-indexed journals and contributed to international academic volumes, including an edited book with IGI Global. He is currently serving as Co-Principal Investigator on an ICSSR-funded research project and is actively engaged in advancing research-driven teaching and innovation in financial studies.

Anastasios Konstantinidis is an assistant professor in the Department of Accounting and Finance at the University of Western Macedonia. He holds a master's degree in Business Informatics from the University of Macedonia. He holds a PhD in Production and Management Engineering from Democritus University in Behavioral Finance and Financial Investment Decisions. He has extensive professional experience in financial investments as an investment consultant and his scientific interests are in the field of Behavioral Finance and in finance in general with extensive research work in both journals and conferences.

James Meersman is part of the accounting faculty at Texas A&M University. He is a licensed CPA (TX) and has been teaching accounting for over a decade. His research interests include taxation, hospitality, CSR, education, and accounting history. Outside of academia, he also serves as a national instructor for both Big 4 accounting firms and industry leading CPA review companies.

Whedy Prasetyo is an academic pioneer in Fisheries and Blue Marine Accounting, a researcher, and a professional consultant with strong expertise in trandisipliner behavioral accounting, sustainability reporting, entrepreneurship, and taxation. He is currently a Lecturer in the Accounting Study Program, Faculty of Economics and Business, Universitas Jember, Indonesia, where he contributes strategically to the development and advancement of research ideas, particularly in fisheries and blue marine accounting and their behavioral dimensions. In addition to his academic role, Whedy Prasetyo is actively involved at the international level as a member of the International Forum of The Institute of Certified Management Accountants (ICMA), Australia and New Zealand, and serves as a Sustainability Reporting Assurer at the National Center for Sustainability Reporting (NCSR), Jakarta. At the national level, he holds the position of Vice Chairman of the East Java Regional Forum of Accounting, Management, and Economics, is an active member of the Indonesian Multiparadigm Accounting Society, and participates in professional activities within the Indonesian Institute of Accountants (IIA), East Java Region.

Rismawati Rismawati is a distinguished academic and consultant with a robust focus on sustainability reporting. She currently holds the position of lecturer and Head of the Quality Assurance Institute at Universitas Muhammadiyah

Palopo, where she has been pivotal in ensuring the quality of university processes and outputs since February 2020. Additionally, she serves as an Assurer for Sustainability Reporting at the National Center for Sustainability Reporting in Jakarta, specializing in the evaluation of sustainability reports for mining companies across Indonesia. Her academic qualifications are extensive, comprising a Bachelor's degree in Economics and Accounting, a Master's degree in Accounting Science, and a Doctorate in Accounting from Universitas Brawijaya, Malang. Rismawati is also a certified specialist in sustainability reporting, risk management, and tax planning, holding several prestigious certifications including Certified Sustainability Reporting Specialist (CSRS), Certified Risk Management Practitioner (CRMP), Certified Management Accountant (CMA) and Certified Enterprise Risk Analysis (CERA). In her professional capacity, she has provided consultancy services in financial management and tax compliance for companies such as PT. Reski Barito Timur and PT. Helay Raya. Furthermore, she has authored multiple publications on Social Accounting, Sustainability Accounting, Management Accounting and CSR, contributing significantly to the academic community. Her interests in reading, writing, and travel reflect her commitment to lifelong learning and professional growth in her field.

Manish Sharma is an academician, researcher, and hospitality professional with over 20 years of combined industry and teaching experience in the field of Tourism and Hospitality Management. He is currently serving as Assistant Professor at Amity University, Noida. His research interests include Hospitality 5.0, human-centric guest experiences, tourism communication, employee behavior, and service innovation. Dr. Sharma has published several research papers in Scopus, ABDC, Web of Science, and UGC-Care indexed journals and has presented papers at national and international conferences. He is also actively involved in academic research, curriculum development, and mentoring students in higher education.

Rajnish Shukla, Professor, at Amity School of Hospitality, is an alumnus of IHM – Hyderabad & XLRI- Jamshedpur. An Experienced chef with PhD in Hospitality. He has served Hospitality Industry & Academia for 31+ years and has published several edited books & research papers in International Journals of Repute. Dr Shukla has also done his MBA in HR from XLRI and has worked extensively in the field of Medical and Wellness tourism and has a good knowledge and understanding of it. His primary research areas are - Hospitality services in Hospitals, Service Quality Assessment, Patient's Satisfaction, Gastronomic Explorations in India, Consumer Behavior and Talent Management in Hospitality.

Ioannis Sitzimis is an Assistant Professor at the Department of Business Administration and Tourism of the Hellenic Mediterranean University. His research interests focus on transport economics and management, maritime and ferry transport, tourism mobility, pricing, and investment evaluation. His work examines the interaction between transport systems, regional accessibility, business performance, and sustainable development. He has published research in international peer-reviewed journals and participates in applied research and teaching in transport economics, financial management, and investment analysis.

Medha Tiwari is a Head of Sales & Marketing with 25 Years of Experience. Proven track record of delivering measurable revenue growth through strategic business development, exceptional client service, and high-impact stakeholder partnerships. Adept at driving new business acquisition while cultivating long-term relationships with key decision-makers, C-suite executives, and major account holders — consistently delivering client retention, loyalty, and channel revenue growth. Experienced in leading full-cycle pre-opening sales and marketing initiatives, ensuring properties capture their fair market share from day one. A natural leader known for transforming underperforming teams into high-achieving units through motivation, accountability, and a clear vision. Combines hands-on client engagement with strategic account management to identify opportunities, architect solutions, and close high-value deals that deliver exceptional outcomes for all stakeholders. Core Strengths: Integrity · Executive Presence · Strategic Thinking · High Energy · Team Leadership · Strong Work Ethic · Self-Motivation · Perseverance · Commitment to Excellence

Index

A

B

C

D

E

F

R

S

U

V

Y

www.ingramcontent.com/pod-product-compliance
Lightning Source LLC
LaVergne TN
LVHW062029101126
852251LV00005B/55